ESSENTIALS
OF RESEARCH METHODS
IN CRIMINAL JUSTICE
AND CRIMINOLOGY

ESSENTIALS OF RESEARCH METHODS IN CRIMINAL JUSTICE AND CRIMINOLOGY

THIRD EDITION

Frank E. Hagan
Mercyhurst College

Prentice Hall

Boston   Columbus   Indianapolis   New York   San Francisco   Upper Saddle River
Amsterdam   Cape Town   Dubai   London   Madrid   Milan   Munich   Paris   Montreal   Toronto
Delhi   Mexico City   Sao Paulo   Sydney   Hong Kong   Seoul   Singapore   Taipei   Tokyo

Vice President and Executive Publisher: Vernon Anthony
Senior Acquisitions Editor: Eric Krassow
Editorial Assistant: Lynda Cramer
Director of Marketing: David Gesell
Senior Marketing Manager: Adam Kloza
Senior Marketing Coordinator: Alicia Wozniak
Production Manager: Holly Shufeldt
Creative Director: Jayne Conte
Cover Designer: Suzanne Duda
Cover Photo: Fotolia
Full-Service Project Management/Composition: Integra
Printer/Binder: LSC Communications, Inc.

Library of Congress Cataloging-in-Publication Data
Hagan, Frank E.
   Essentials of research methods in criminal justice and criminology / Frank E. Hagan.—3rd ed.
      p. cm.
   Includes bibliographical references and index.
   ISBN-13: 978-0-13-512100-9
   ISBN-10: 0-13-512100-0
   1. Criminology—Research—Methodology.   2. Criminal justice, Administration of—Research—Methodology.   I. Title.
HV6024.5.H35 2012
364.072—dc22

                                                         2010032829

Prentice Hall
is an imprint of

www.pearsonhighered.com

ISBN 10:   0-13-512100-0
ISBN 13: 978-0-13-512100-9

Contents

3

6

7

10

11

Preface

New to This Edition

- Material previously found in Chapters 4 and 5 have been moved, and a new Chapter 4 has been created.
- Internet surveys are more prominently presented, as is person research.
- The Human Terrain System and Minerva Consortium are discussed.
- Interviewing active offenders and gaining entry to correctional facilities are discussed.
- Steffensmeier's *Confessions of a Dying Thief* has been added.
- In addition, the following have been newly included for this edition:
  - Zimbardo's "Lucifer Effect"
  - Sherman's "Scientific Method's Scale"
  - Visual criminology
  - The Scarlet M in corrections research
  - Resolution of the Iowa "Monster Study"
  - Telephone focus groups
  - The latest on shield laws

The first edition of *Research Methods in Criminal Justice and Criminology* was prepared in the early 1980s, when no comprehensive research text existed that directly addressed the areas of criminal justice and criminology. This third *Essentials* edition eliminates the last two chapters of the eighth edition.

The text remains a comprehensive one, emphasizing sources and resources of classic and contemporary research in the field. There continues to be an acceleration of publications employing increasingly more sophisticated and esoteric research designs and statistical analysis. The intent of this core edition remains the same as the previous ones, that is, to reduce the gap that exists between the types of materials appearing in professional journals and publications in the field and the ability of students and professionals to understand them. The approach is to use criminological and criminal justice studies to illustrate research methods, because it is as important to become familiar with examples of research in the field as it is to learn fundamental research skills.

This edition features major revisions throughout, while retaining a vital core of material from the previous version. The organization of the work will carry the student through the sequence of the research process. Instructors may wish to shuffle the order of the chapters, however, to suit their syllabus or research style.

The first chapter introduces the area of criminological and criminal justice research while attacking commonsense approaches to research. Chapter 1 also outlines the steps in research elaborated on in Chapters 3 through 11. Following the issue of problem formulation in the first chapter, Chapter 2 examines the important issue of research ethics. More information is provided on the Iowa "Monster study" and Zimbardo's "Lucifer effect." The Minerva Consortium and Human Terrain system are also debated. Research design is detailed in Chapter 3.

In Chapter 4, sampling strategies and the *Uniform Crime Reports* and its recent major revision are examined. Chapter 5 looks at survey research, particularly mail questionnaires, Internet surveys, and self-report studies. Chapter 6 concentrates on interviews and telephone surveys, particularly recent developments in victim surveys. Participant observation and case studies are the subject of Chapter 7. Such field studies represent some of the most fascinating literature in the field, and the intent of the chapter is also to familiarize the reader with many of such studies.

Chapter 8 explores the interesting world of nonreactive or unobtrusive techniques, which include criminal justice and criminological applications involving secondary and content analysis, physical trace analysis, the use of official data, and observational strategies—all of which are useful cost-effective means of gathering data. Alternative means of data gathering, such as surveys, field studies, and unobtrusive methods, often contain strengths missing in experimental research.

The important issues of validity and reliability are detailed in Chapter 9; triangulated strategies are proposed as the single most logical path by which to resolve these questions. In all of these chapters, examples of both classic and contemporary research in criminal justice and criminology are used as illustrations. In addition to providing an overview of research methods, this text also presents a review and analysis of research literature. Chapter 10 discusses scaling and index construction and features new and expanded coverage of crime severity scales, salient factor scores, and prediction scales. Chapter 11 features "Policy Analysis and Evaluation Research," the world of research applied to evaluating the question "what works?" It is hoped that the style of presentation will convert many readers who may begin the course with apprehension into relatively fluent users of "researchese," a valuable and useful international language.

In addition to updating tables, figures, references, and examples, some other changes have been made in this edition. A number of exhibits have been added to illustrate or provide more detail on research issues, and useful Web sites are presented in all chapters. A box featuring the American Psychological Association (APA) reference style has been included, as have updates on NIJ's research agenda. Greater discussion is also added on the ethical aspects of Internet research, competitive intelligence as a research skill, the evaluation of Web sites, and the validity of Internet data. The issue of plagiarism is explored in more depth. The new chapter on "Policy Analysis and Evaluation Research" reflects the growing importance of this subject. Discussion of the Campbell Collaboration and the Blueprints Program of Successful Program Implementation has also been added.

I would like to thank the many people who have assisted in various ways in writing the editions of this text. I would also like to thank the reviewers of this and previous editions. These have included Howard Abadinsky, St. John's University; John Hudzik, Michigan State University; and John Smykla, University of Alabama. Appreciation is also extended to James Adamitis, University of Dayton; Rosy Ekpenyong, Michigan State University; Randy Martin, Indiana University; Robert Mutchnick, University of Pennsylvania; Shirley Salem, Southern University; and Frank Schmalleger. Also serving as past reviewers have been Pamela Tontodonato, Kent State University; Laure Weber Brooks, University of Maryland; William E. Thornton, Loyola University; Malcolm D. Holmes, University of Texas at El Paso; Michael Blankenship, Boise State University; Sean Gabiddon, Penn State University—Harrisburg; Wanda Foglia, Rowan University; Obie Clayton, Morehouse Research Institute; Shirley Williams, Jersey City State College; Art Jipson, Miami University; Ray Newman, Polk Community College; John E. Eck, University of Cincinnati; Angela West, University of Louisville; Robert Costello, Nassau Community College; Allan Y. Jiao, Rowan University; Stephen D. Kaftan, Hawkeye Community College; Sudipto Roy, Indiana State University; Lisa L. Sample, University of Nebraska—Omaha; Minerva Sanchez, Sam Houston State University; Susan F. Brinkley, University of Tampa; Victor Ortloff, Troy State University; Amir B. Marvasti, Penn State University—Altoona; Debra E. Ross, Grand Valley State University; Bill Tafoya, University of New Haven; and Elizabeth Grossi, University of Louisville. Although much of what is good about this book is due to the many fine suggestions of the reviewers, the author is solely responsible for any shortcomings. I would like to thank my former professors Marie Haug, Marvin Sussman, and Dan Koenig, as well as my departmental colleagues Pete Benekos and Tina Fryling.

Finally, I would like to thank my wife, MaryAnn, whose continuing support, editing, data entry, and encouragement made completion of this new edition possible. I would like to encourage students as well as faculty to contact me with any questions, comments, or suggestions via e-mail: *fhagan@mercyhurst.edu*.

F.E.H.

ESSENTIALS OF RESEARCH METHODS IN CRIMINAL JUSTICE AND CRIMINOLOGY

1

Introduction to Criminal Justice Research Methods

THEORY AND METHOD

Most students of criminal justice or criminology approach a course in research methods with the enthusiasm of a recalcitrant patient in a dentist's office. Even if the experience is not going to be painful, it most certainly is not anticipated to be exciting or interesting. Being primarily people oriented or pragmatically oriented, the criminal justice student expects to mildly tolerate an experience that seems quite remote from the real world and practical, everyday problems in criminal justice.

Scientific Research in Criminal Justice

Critics of many applications of scientific research to the criminal justice system view such efforts as either elucidation of the irrelevant, obscure jargonizing, or academic intimidation—a detailed elaboration of what any person with common sense knows. To make matters worse, all of these efforts take place at a substantial cost, usually to the taxpayer, at a time when action-oriented programs that really count are being cut back.

Some recent research findings are illustrative:

1. Females and the elderly fear crime because they are the most heavily victimized of all groups.
2. Victims of crime seldom know or recognize their offenders.
3. Crime is rising by leaps and bounds and is at an all-time high.
4. The larger the city, the greater the likelihood that its residents will be victims of crime.
5. In general, residents of large cities believe that their police are doing a poor job.
6. African Americans and Hispanics are less likely than the population as a whole to report personal crimes to the police.
7. Most residents of large cities think that their neighborhoods are not safe.
8. African Americans are overrepresented on death rows across the nation; however, this overrepresentation is more pronounced in the South than in other regions.
9. Crime is an inevitable product of complex, populous, and industrialized societies.
10. White-collar crime is nonviolent.
11. Regulatory agencies prevent white-collar crime.
12. The insanity defense allows many dangerous offenders to escape conviction.

What could be more obvious than these findings? If anything, all that we have learned is that Uncle Sam continues to waste tax money on useless studies. The real purpose of presenting these findings was to make a point: *Sometimes common sense is nonsense.* Each of the preceding statements is incorrect and represents a myth about crime (Bohm and Walker, 2006; Pepinsky and Jesilow, 1992; U.S. Department of Justice, 1978; Walker, 2005; Wright, 1985). The actual findings were as follows:

1. Rates of victimization are higher for males than females and for younger rather than older people.
2. In a large percentage of violent crimes, particularly domestic violence, victims know and recognize their offenders.
3. Beginning in the early 1990s, crime has been declining in the United States.
4. The residents of smaller cities have higher rates than those of larges cities for certain crimes such as assault, personal or household larceny, and residential burglary.
5. The opinions of residents of numerous cities across the nation indicate that the vast majority is satisfied with the performance of their police; four out of five residents of the twenty-six cities surveyed gave ratings of good or average.
6. Crimes committed against African Americans and Hispanics are just about as apt to be reported as are crimes against victims in general.
7. Nine out of ten persons living in twenty-six large cities surveyed felt very or reasonably safe when out alone in their neighborhoods during daytime. A majority (54 percent) felt the same at night.
8. African American overrepresentation on death row is less pronounced in the South than in other major regions of the country.
9. Crime is not a major concern in some developed countries, and in Japan it has actually decreased in the post–World War II period (Adler, 1983; Clinard, 1978).
10. Unsafe work conditions and the marketing of unsafe products kill and maim more Americans each year than street muggers and assailants (Hills, 1987).
11. Regulatory agencies have been understaffed, underfinanced, and inadequate in controlling white-collar crime (Clinard and Yeager, 1979).
12. Despite media attention, insanity defense cases are rare; successful ones are even more rare (Morris, 1987).

Common Sense and Nonsense

A number of works attempt to tackle the *commonsense* issue head-on, such as *Sense and Nonsense about Crime and Drugs* (Walker, 2005), *Myths That Cause Crime* (Pepinsky and Jesilow, 1985), *The Great American Crime Myth* (Wright, 1985), and *The Mythology of Crime and Justice* (Kappeler, and Potter, 2005).

What was assumed to be obvious in our example appeared so after the results were presented. If people agreed with the findings, they considered them obvious, whereas if they disagreed, they viewed them as unscientific because common sense told them so. Hirschi and Stark (1969) in "Hellfire and Delinquency" found a very weak relationship between church attendance and nondelinquency. In speaking to a "damned if you do and damned if you don't" phenomenon, they indicate that had they found a strong relationship as common sense would have suggested, they would have been accused of wasting time on the obvious. Because their study countered common sense, it was attacked as false, stupid, or an illustration of inadequate methods.

Brown and Curtis (1987, p. 3) indicate that:

> Many practitioners within criminal justice have met with repeated failure over the years because they relied upon only their common sense. Thus, millions of dollars have been spent on police patrol efforts that do not reduce crime, judicial practices that are widely perceived as unfair, rehabilitation programs that do not rehabilitate offenders and countless other failures.

In *The Natural History of Nonsense* (1958), Evans outlines numerous examples of common sense–nonsense issues that have hindered human progress. The earlier beliefs that the Earth is flat and that it is the astrological center of the universe are but two of these examples. In testimony before Congress protesting threatened drastic cuts in funding for social science research and in response to attacks on the social sciences as employing obscure jargon and explicating the obvious or common sense, Herbert Simon counterattacked, asserting that the common sense of the social sciences is not a mirror of society but a result of research:

> The social sciences are often discounted because much of what they learn seems to be common sense. Well, it is common sense today to say that if you drop a feather and a rock together in a vacuum, they will fall at the same pace. It was not common sense before Galileo . . . [O]ne of the basic aims of the social sciences must be to take knowledge that comes out of the laboratory—knowledge that may be stated in language that is hard to understand—and make it part of the common sense of our society. (Prewitt and Sills, 1981, p. 6)

Many of the terms used in everyday conversation originated in social science research; however, little credit is given for these theoretical accomplishments because the discoveries, once labeled, were quickly absorbed into conventional wisdom.

In an essay celebrating twenty-five years of criminal justice research sponsored by the National Institute of Justice (NIJ) (the research arm of the U.S. Department of Justice), Blumstein and Petersilia (1994, p. 36) state:

When compared to the public debate about these issues, which is still often focused on ideological issues and simplistic solutions to complex problems, it is clear that the thinking resulting from research, backed up by strong evidence, is very sophisticated, but it still has a long way to go to become an important part of the public debate. Researchers must also remember that the revolution in thinking brought about by Galileo and Copernicus took far longer than twenty-five years to become widely diffused to European thinking.

The most interesting phenomenon about those who propose a commonsensical approach to criminal justice is that the debunker often simply substitutes his or her own subjective biases and experience for the more scientific approach found lacking. Wilkins addresses those who argue the antiscientific view (wherein each individual is unique and defies measurement and prediction):

> The objection states that prediction is useless (or dangerous?) because the individual is unique. Prediction is said to be either (or both) impossible or undesirable, and this argument rests on the complexity of human relationship . . . If the case is unique, what experience can the clinician use to guide him? . . . Statistical experience can be based on samples of the population which we know to be unbiased. A clinician has only his own sample to guide him with no guarantee of its lack of bias. . . . If these features are "intangible," how can we know that they exist? How in fact does the clinician take them into account? Can they not be described in words? If not, are they more than the prejudices of the observer? (Wilkins, 1978, pp. 233–236)

As we will see in Chapter 9, verbal descriptions of phenomena are not much different than numerical measures of some entity; the latter simply force the analyst to be more precise and rigorous, while thinking through the concept under study in a more disciplined manner. Thus, common sense and experience certainly serve important functions in sensitizing us to a subject. However, our separate experiences might better be viewed as limited case studies of a subject matter that may not be entirely generalizable to the universe of such subjects or as observations that may be limited by time, place, and the subjective biases of the observer.

In addition to common sense as a rival explanation to science, there are other competing sources of knowledge. Authorities or experts are sources, but sometimes they are simply wrong. Tradition (past authorities) may also mislead us. Currently the media represents a very powerful source of information on crime, but their portrayals may not reflect reality and often aim to entertain or gain revenue rather than to inform. Related to the commonsense approach to research, but of vital importance in criminal justice, are the questions "So what?" and "Of what practical use are these findings?"

These subjects will be discussed in detail in Chapter 11.

Why Study Research Methods in Criminal Justice?

Rather than viewing certain elementary research concepts and procedures in scientific methodology as foreign elements, the criminal justice professional may, once he or she has mastered them, discover very valuable tools for assessing current and future directions in the field.

Once familiar with these tools, much of the anxious sanctimony bestowed upon technical reports, academic concepts, and research findings can be dispensed with. Many readers of this text have a healthy cynicism or critical and suspicious approach to research findings and probably know and employ more about research methodology than they are aware. In most cases they simply lack conceptual frameworks, scientifically acceptable tags, or sufficient knowledge of the language of research methods to defend their views in an appropriate manner. Research methods provide the tools necessary to approach issues in criminal justice from a more rigorous standpoint and enable a venture beyond opinions based solely on nonscientific observations and experiences (see Black, 1993).

Although many readers may never undertake their own research, all will be consumers or recipients of findings and policies based upon research. It is not unusual to find students as well as professionals in criminal justice who are unable to fully understand reports and journal articles in their own field. Other fields may have this same problem; however, one might certainly be wary of a surgeon who is performing an operation without an understanding of the latest article on the procedure in the *Journal of the American Medical Association*. Similarly, in striving for professional status, it is imperative that criminologists and criminal justice professionals comprehend and critically evaluate new developments in their field (Hagan, 1975). Mastery of this material will assist in this endeavor. A very interesting outcome upon completion of the material is that many find themselves carefully reading and interpreting the tables presented in studies and skipping much of the prose. This procedure, which reverses the usual pattern at the beginning of the course, results in a great economy of time and effort.

An analogy can be drawn between learning research methods and studying to become a movie director or critic (Tontodonato and Hagan, 1998). A movie director or critic cannot simply view a film and report, "You just have to see it." They must be more concerned with technique. What is the plot? Who are the heroes/heroines/villains? From what point of view is the story told: first person or third person? What was the denouement? Research methodologists are also interested in ransacking studies and breaking them down into essentials. What are the research design and hypothesis? What data-gathering procedures were employed? What were the independent and dependent variables? What type of data analysis and conclusions were made regarding the null hypotheses? Upon completing this book, it is hoped that the student will become prolific in being an active consumer of research.

Much of what appears in this text as research methods in criminology and criminal justice is not unique to criminal justice but is borrowed from the other social sciences and applied to criminal justice topics and examples. The techniques are applicable to a wide variety of areas and in that sense are excellent broad-based skills.

The Emergence of Science and Criminal Justice

Humankind's long stride toward understanding and explaining the universe might be viewed as a marathon that has accelerated into a 100-yard dash in the past two centuries. In an attempt to provide a stage for our purposes and avoid philosophical discourses that could occupy far too much time for our purposes, this development can be described succinctly. Human beings, through the creation of symbols or abstractions such as language, are able to develop knowledge. *Knowledge* is what people create symbolically to represent reality.

Knowledge might also be viewed as our presently accepted level of ignorance. There is no guarantee that what one historical generation considers to be a wise policy or procedure will not be considered ignorant by the next generation. Less than 100 years ago, "feebleminded" persons were locked up permanently for the protection of society because "feeblemindedness causes crime" (McCaghy, 1999, p. 10). Not long before that, the physically ill were bled to "cure" their illness. At present, these methods are considered ignorant and even detrimental. It is important to recognize the changes in methods between present day and 100 years ago.

The early French sociologist Auguste Comte described the "progression of knowledge as being one from predominantly theological or supernatural explanations of reality to metaphysical or philosophical ones and finally to scientific approaches" (Comte, 1877). Rather than looking to otherworldly explanations, philosophy sought explanations in worldly events through a new spirit of inquiry—rationality and logical explanation. **Science** combined this spirit of rational explanation with method—empiricism, experimentation, or what has come to be called the scientific method. The scientific orientation emphasized observation, measurement, replication (repetition of observation), and verification (checking on the validity of observations). Science subjects ideas or theories to tests through observation, quantification, and empirical analysis. Unlike the philosopher's often sole reliance on logic and argumentative reasoning, all scientists can be said to be from Missouri, the "Show Me" state. **Replication** is the repetition of experiments or studies utilizing the same methodology. **Verification** is confirmation of the accuracy of findings or attainment of greater certitude in conclusions through additional observations.

Replication

Verification

Systematic application of the scientific method to research problems provided major breakthroughs in the development of knowledge. While the scientific era has enabled humankind to take giant strides in explaining and harnessing physical reality, more recently the social sciences, of which criminal justice is a progeny, have attempted to apply these same procedures to their subject matters—society, human behavior, politics, or, of concern in our enterprise, crime and criminal justice.

Because we have gained mastery over more simple and more controllable physical reality, why, as intelligent humans, is it not possible to gain the same explanation, prediction, and control over such recurring social phenomena as crime, violence, and their many ramifications?

Criminology and criminal justice as interdisciplinary disciplines draw upon many fields, both academic and applied, and, in terms of appropriate research methodology, have not only borrowed and adapted but have made many of their own contributions as will be presented throughout this book. Whether criminal justice is a science is argued even by practitioners within the field. Criminal justice researchers, unlike physical scientists, find their subject matter a topic of popular discussion in which the layperson's experience is viewed as just as good a guide to policy as that of the researcher. The same people who would not dream of arguing about molecules, atomic weights, or quasars feel quite qualified to address issues of crime and punishment. In this writer's view, the appropriate employment of scientific methodology and procedure qualifies a discipline to claim scientific status. Although this topic is certainly worthy of debate elsewhere, the approach throughout this text is a very pragmatic one—we are employing scientific procedures and therefore contributing to the development of a young science.

The Probabilistic Nature of Science

As social scientists, criminologists and criminal justice researchers assume that the subject matter they study is probabilistic—that is, they believe that effects will most often occur when certain causes are present, but not in every single case. In predicting general patterns, trends, and relationships among groups, social scientists do not expect these patterns to hold in each individual case or do not expect absolute determinism. If researchers show a relationship between rising unemployment rates and suicide rates, they are not assumed or considered to be wrong if the newly unemployed do not commit suicide. Researchers do attempt to estimate the probability of their predictions being accurate. For example, there is an 85 percent chance that a savings and loan thief such as Charles Keating will be white, upper-middle class, and a college graduate.

Proper Conduct of Critical Inquiry

Bayley (1978) offers three suggestions for improving criminal justice research:

1. Research requires interdisciplinary efforts as well as the tackling of field-oriented, practical problems.
2. Researchers should cease giving speeches to practitioners about the value of research and attack their practical concerns with a realistic appraisal of error proneness of any research endeavor.
3. It is time to be done with "methodological narcissism," methods for methods' sake.

The latter is aptly illustrated by the well-known Martinson Report, which was published in the early 1970s. Martinson (1974) raised quite a storm in the field of corrections when, based on his evaluation of rehabilitation programs throughout the United States, he concluded that none of these programs reduced recidivism or rehabilitated clients. Later, in retracting his own previously devastating "almost nothing works" critique of corrections research, Martinson (1978, p. 4) advised that it was time to avoid "methodological fanaticism" (what

Bayley called **methodological narcissism**), in which substance is overlooked   Methodological narcissism
in the name of method. Preferred rigor in research design is seldom realized in
criminal justice field studies. This does not justify throwing out "the baby with
the bath water." Instead, such problems represent challenges to the criminal
justice researcher, rather than a justification for self-defeating pessimism and
methodological capitulation.

Hirschi and Selvin give sound advice to those either doing research or criticizing the research of others. The proper conduct of critical inquiry requires
that "those concerned with good research should be objective and vigilant as well
as sympathetic" (Hirschi and Selvin, 1973, pp. 273–274). *Objectivity* entails value
neutrality or a dispassionate approach to the subject matter that holds constant
personal bias (Weber, 1949). *Vigilance* involves a concern for accuracy and
efforts to eliminate error. Error, however, is ever present in research. The only
perfect research is no research, which suggests the last point: empathy. In critiquing the research of others, *empathy* or a willingness to put oneself in the
role of the researcher is important. *If a student of research is afraid of making errors in research, then he or she probably should do none, because error
is omnipresent.* In criticizing other research, one often need not go far to find
some error. The question is not whether errors are present, but, rather, whether
reasonable attempts were made to acknowledge and/or eliminate the most obvious errors. Only when such errors so grossly compromise the accuracy of findings and conclusions thereof, should one scathingly attack other research.

Approaches to Theory and Method in Criminal Justice

Theory in criminal justice represents an attempt to develop plausible expla-   Theory
nations of reality, which in this case is crime and the criminal justice system.
Theory attempts to classify and organize events, explain the causes of events,
predict the direction of future events, and understand why and how these
events occur (Turner, 1997, p. 2). It represents a reasonable and informed guess
as to why things are as they appear and to explain their underlying nature and
meaning. Kraska (2006, pp. 167–168) explains:

> It [theory] defines the parameters for how we think about our objects
> of study, and provides us the lenses through which we filter our sub-
> ject matter in order to make sense of complex phenomena. It gives us
> our organizing concepts, frames our research questions, guides our
> scholarly interpretations, and is an unavoidable presence in crime con-
> trol policy, practice and decision making.

Much criminological theory possesses a global or sensitizing quality that
alerts us to critical issues, but often lacks the quality of formally testable, scientifically verifiable propositions (Hagan, 2008, p. 94). Without the generation of
useful theoretical explanations, a field is intellectually bankrupt; it becomes
merely a collection of war stories and carefully documented encyclopedic

accounts. It fails to explain, summarize, or capture the essential nature of its subject matter. Theory asks: What is the point of all of this? What does it mean? Why are things this way? Willis (1983), in a review of twenty-five criminal justice textbooks, noted almost a "trained incapacity" or unwillingness to deal with theoretical issues and a tendency to concentrate on what fictional character Joe Friday, in the old television series *Dragnet,* called "just the facts."

In *The Structure of Scientific Revolutions,* Thomas Kuhn (1970) describes how the evolution of new knowledge, rather than being slow and incremental, is often dependent upon new paradigms that may stand previous assumptions on their heads. A **paradigm** is "some implicit body of intertwined theoretical and methodological belief that permits selection, evaluation, and criticism" (1970, pp. 16–17). A new paradigm represents a new model or revolutionary schema with which to view reality. Paradigms organize reality by giving structure, framework, and perspective from which to investigate reality. Kuhn viewed scientific knowledge as achieving breakthroughs by revolutions fueled by the inability to explain anomalies by means of the existing scientific tradition. The old paradigm (normal science) is made obsolete by the new paradigm through this process of revolution. In a related phenomenon, sometimes new knowledge takes place or is discovered by a process of serendipity, a wholly unanticipated and surprising discovery. In the process of doing research on one topic, a discovery is made that addresses some different topic. Exhibit 1.1 describes the paradigm shift in policing. Copernicus and Galileo turned astronomy upside down with their discovery that the Earth was not the center of the universe. In Archeology, the pre-Clovis paradigm challenged the prevailing estimate of human habitation in the Americas.

Edwin Sutherland's concept of "white-collar crime" (1940) serves as an example of a paradigm revolution in criminology, a radical reorientation in theoretical views of the nature of criminality. After Sutherland, crime was no longer viewed solely as an activity of the underclass. Copernicus' astronomical theory of the universe made totally irrelevant the previous paradigm of astrology. Walker (2001, p. 74) indicates the following:

> Finally, Kuhn's perspective cautions adherents of the prevailing paradigm to recognize that there is nothing permanent or timeless about their viewpoint. This paradigm, which organizes their thinking, research, and policy proposals, was the product of a scientific revolution that replaced an earlier paradigm. Science, however, like time, marches on. We cannot predict what kind of scientific revolution lies in the future and will overthrow the assumptions shared by virtually everyone reading this article.

Methodology (methods), on the other hand, involves the collection of accurate facts and/or data regarding the nature of crime and criminal justice policy. *In short, while theory addresses the issue "why," methodology concerns itself with "what is."* There usually exists in any field a certain division between those who are primarily interested in generating theory and who view their efforts as classical scholarship akin to philosophy and those (methodologists)

Paradigm

Methodology

EXHIBIT 1.1 ▶

The Paradigm Shift in Policing

Blankenship and Brown (1993) claim that the criminological literature typically refers to competing theories as paradigms. A paradigm shift of sorts has occurred in American policing beginning with the "Kansas City Preventive Patrol" experiment (Kelling, 1998), which will be discussed in detail in Chapter 3. Conducted in the early 1970s, police administrators were at first astounded to find that neither increases nor decreases in police patrol seemed to affect the crime rate, public fear of crime, or public satisfaction with the police. Rapid response to calls for service and preventive patrol had been two inviolate doctrines until then. Rather than viewing such findings as negative, police executives discovered they had a lot more discretion than they had anticipated in deploying their forces. Under the "rapid response to service paradigm," police spent most of their time rushing to the scene of calls for service despite the fact that most people waited half an hour after an event was discovered to report the crime to the police. Preventive patrol seldom came upon crimes in progress. Being busy with patrol and answering calls, the police had little time to *investigate* trivial matters.

In a classic article entitled "**Broken Windows**," James Q. Wilson and George Kelling (1982) proposed a radically different paradigm. Kelling (1998) indicates the following:

Just as unrepaired broken windows can signal to people that nobody cares about a building and lead to more

serious vandalism, untended property, disorderly persons, drunks, obstreperous youth, etc.—both create fear in citizens and attract predators.

Neighborhood disregard, drunks, panhandlers, youth gangs, and other "trivial" incivilities unsettle a community and produce fear and disrupt the life of a neighborhood. The large decrease in crime in New York City in the 1990s was attributed in part to a new policing paradigm emphasizing community policing and zero tolerance for previously ignored aggressive panhandlers, subway turnstile hoppers, vagrants, and those involved in disorderly conduct. Enforcing the previously ignored small things gave police a better handle on crime (Kelling and Wilson, 1999).

Discussion of the "Crime Dip" later in Chapter 4 will examine other reasons for the decline in crime. Harcourt in *Illusions of Order: The False Promise of Broken Windows Policing* (2001) and Taylor in *Breaking Away from Broken Windows* (2001) question the "Broken Windows Paradigm." They point out that crime had already begun to decline in New York before Chief William Bratton introduced the broken windows policy and declined just as drastically in cities such as San Diego that never used the strategy. Similarly, Karmen in *New York Murder Mystery: The True Story Behind the Crime Crash of the 1990s* (2001) credited the end of crack dealer turf wars for much of the decline (see Miller, 2001).

Sources: Kuhn, Thomas. *The Structure of Scientific Revolutions.* 2nd ed. Chicago, IL: University of Chicago Press, 1970. Kelling, George A. "Police and Communities: The Quiet Revolution." *Perspectives in Policing.* National Institute of Justice, June 1998. Wilson, James Q., and George L. Kelling. "Broken Windows: The Police and Neighborhood Safety." *The Atlantic Monthly* (March, 1982): 27–28.

who are viewed as technical and scientific in their approach. In speaking to Criminology's fascination, if not obsession, with preferred statistical fads and methodological tools and techniques at the expense of theory, Sampson and Laub (2005, p. 911) indicate the following:

The bigger problem is that criminology seems obsessed with tools rather than keeping its eyes on the prize. Indeed we worry less about groups being reified than the methods themselves; when methods rule, we lose focus on the fundamental processes that explain crime and its persistence and cessation over the life course. For us, the bottom line of sound research design and basic scientific inquiry is that methods are inextricably linked to, and the servant of, theory.

Good criminal justice requires both.

Theory devoid of method—explanation without accurate supportive data—is just as much a ritualistic dead end as method devoid of theory. The former resembles armchair theorizing, while the latter resembles a fruitless bookkeeping operation. Both theory and method should be viewed as means to an end, the end being sound criminal justice knowledge.

Pure versus Applied Research

Pure research

Applied research

Pure (basic) research is concerned with the acquisition of new knowledge for the sake of science or the development of the field, whereas **applied research** is practical research concerned with solving immediate policy problems. Although we addressed the issue of common sense briefly by means of "myths of crime," there still exists the broader issue: Criminal justice has experienced conflict between two camps, *the applied practitioner* and *the nonapplied academic*. Although this division is in part stereotypical, as mutual exclusivity is not in fact the case with these groups, for heuristic purposes we consider these as "ideal types."[1] Being on the front lines of the criminal justice system, practitioners are most interested in *applied research*, studies, and findings that speak directly to policy issues. Academics, on the other hand, are more concerned with *pure research*, which may have no immediate applicability but contributes to the knowledge base and scientific development of the discipline. Although the practitioner may view the pure scientific researcher as off in a closeted ivory tower or a likely candidate for former senator Proxmire's Golden Fleece Award for irrelevant research,[2] the pure scientific researcher may view many of the policy recommendations of applied research as shamanism, or quackery, an attempt to give advice or guide policy without adequate theoretical or methodological support. In speaking to the issue of premature application, Friedman (1980) puts it succinctly: "If you eat the cookies before they are ready you can get sick."

In reality, neither pure nor applied research fits these neat stereotypical views (Rabow, 1964). Some of the most apparently obscure and abstract research projects may produce the critical discoveries that in the long run produce more applied payoffs than hundreds of premature applied projects. On the other hand, many existing projects require informed decisions, which, although not perfect or entirely supported by research findings, represent the best we have to offer at the time. A study of state correctional agency practitioners (Light and Newman, 1992) found that while such practitioners strongly supported social science research, they reported using it very little in comparison with other types of information and knowledge.

---

[1]Weber (1949) viewed "ideal types" as useful analytic devices that extract pure or overgeneralized elements of a reality, but seldom exist in pure form. Wilson's (1968) "Watchman," "Service," and "Legalistic" styles of policing are an illustration.

[2]In the late 1970s, the late senator William Proxmire attracted considerable publicity by presenting awards to government-sponsored research projects with esoteric titles that he viewed as irrelevant. Proxmire was the subject of an $8 million libel and slander suit by experimental psychologist Dr. Ronald R. Hutchinson as a result of his being identified as a recipient. See "Golden Fleece Suit Reaches Supreme Court," Footnotes, *American Sociological Association*, 7 (May 1979), 5.

Many of the major and important scientific discoveries of ancient and modern times were made not by the kings' wizards commissioned to immediately perform alchemy or other applied magic, but by abstract "tinkers"—Galileo, Copernicus, Einstein, and Pasteur. What is regarded as renegade, pure, and ivory-tower research of one epoch often finds itself the basis for important applied breakthroughs in the next. As mentioned previously, in the late 1970s, in an attempt to point out wasteful government funding of "irrelevant" research projects, Senator Proxmire periodically would publicize and give his infamous Golden Fleece Award. To the layperson, obscure sounding studies such as "The Sex Life and Mating Habits of Bees in the Upper Amazon Basin" appear to be projects deserving of derision and attack until at a later date scientists speculate that "killer bees" that are resistant to existing chemical insecticides may invade North America and result in human deaths.

An excellent example of a basic research project is the Project on Human Development in Chicago Neighborhoods (Visher, 1994) (see Exhibit 1.2).

EXHIBIT 1.2 ▶

The Project on Human Development: An Accelerated Longitudinal Design Using Nine Spaced-Age Cohorts

Being the largest longitudinal study ever undertaken in criminal justice/criminology, NIJ's Project of Human Development in Chicago Neighborhoods was unprecedented in scope. It examined a broad range of factors at the community, family, and individual level that were believed predictors of crime and deviance. A team of researchers headed by Albert Reiss Jr. (Yale) and Felton Earls (Harvard) conducted the study and examined everything from gestation, infancy, and childhood to adulthood to age thirty-two. Such a prospective design would usually have taken thirty-two years; but the unique feature of the research design, an accelerated longitudinal design depicted in Figure 1, sped up the timetable.

Between 1994 and 2002 the investigators gathered detailed data about 11,000 individuals and their communities. A preliminary five-year planning phase and the accelerated longitudinal design provided data much more quickly

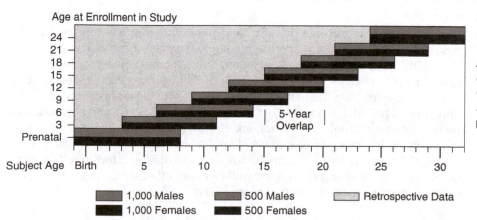

Figure 1
Project on Human Development, Accelerated Longitudinal Design 2002—Completion of Study. Source: Visher, 1994, p. 13.

than the standard longitudinal design. Overlapping age cohorts were studied, each with five-year overlap periods, thus mimicking a thirty-two-year longitudinal study. Figure 2 describes the key variables examined in the research.

Data collection began in Chicago in August 1994. For three years prior, exploratory studies of topics and methods took place and research protocols were pretested. Subjects and their families were interviewed across the nine age cohorts. Support from a variety of community organizations was solicited particularly in investigating mental health, child development, and substance abuse. It was hoped that the multidisciplinary approach integrating community, family, school, peer, and individual characteristics would do much to advance our understanding of crime causation and in developing future crime control policy.

The Community
  Social, economic, and
    demographic structure
  Organizational/political structure
  Community standards and norms
  Informal social control
  Crime, victimization, and arrests
  Social cohesion
  Residential turnover
  Level of involvement in drug and
    gang networks

The School
  Academic achievement
    expectations
  School policies regarding social
    control School conflict
  Teacher–student relationships

Strengths and weaknesses of the
  school environment

Peer Relationships
  Composition and size of social
    network
  Substance abuse and delinquency
    by peers
  Deviant and prosocial attitudes of
    peers
  Location of peer networks
    (school or community)
  Changes in peer relationships
    over time

The Family
  Family structure
  Parent–child relationships

Parent disciplinary practices
Parent characteristics
Family mental health
Family history of criminal
  behavior and substance abuse

The Individual
Physical and mental health status
Impulse control and sensation-
  seeking traits
Cognitive and language
  development
Ethnic identity and acculturation
Leisure-time activities
Self-perception, attitude, and
  values

Figure 2

Project on Human Development: The Contents and Factors to Be Studied.

Source: Visher, 1994, p. 14.

Sources: Visher, Christy A. "Understanding the Roots of Crime: The Project on Human Development in Chicago Neighborhoods." *National Institute of Justice Journal* (November 1994): 9–15; Interim reports can be obtained from: The Project on Human Development in Chicago Neighborhoods, Harvard School of Public Health, Department of Maternal and Child Health, 677 Huntington Avenue, Boston, MA 02115.

The project has its own updated Web site: http://phdcn.harvard.edu/

This study represents the efforts of over 100 scientists representing the fields of pediatrics, biology, psychology, sociology, and criminology (NIJ, 1997). Begun in 1989, the project involved an ongoing, overlapping, longitudinal (studies over time) analysis of 8,000 residents of 343 Chicago neighborhoods from birth to age thirty-two. The subjects were tracked for several years while examining their development in an effort to determine how family and neighborhood factors influence criminal behavior. Exhibit 1.3 provides an example of applied research—crime analysis. Examples of applied research will be featured in subsequent chapters in this book, including crime profiling, crime analysis, crime mapping, and statement analysis as well as many other studies that are specifically undertaken in order to address immediate policy needs.

EXHIBIT 1.3 ▶

Crime Analysis: Applied Criminal Justice Research

Steven Gottlieb, Sheldon Arenberg, and Raj Singh's *Crime Analysis* (1994) is the classic work in the burgeoning applied research field of crime analysis. They make the distinction between four types of law enforcement analysis (1994, pp. 11–12):

Crime analysis allows the analyst to determine who's doing what to whom by its focus on crimes against persons and property (homicide, rape, robbery, burglary, theft, etc.). **Crime analysis** can be defined as systematic, analytic processes aimed at providing practical information related to crime patterns. It often involves providing trend correlations to assist in management and in the solving and prevention of crime. The functions of crime analysis include (1994, pp. 15–16):

- Identification of crime patterns
- Crime forecasting
- Target profile analysis
- Provision of investigative leads
- Provision of support data to community policing and crime prevention programs

- Assistance in case clearance
- Support for departmental planning activities
- Analysis of operational data for departmental planning

The growing use of crime analysis by police departments and federal agencies will be featured in later exhibits in this book.

Intelligence analysis aids the determination of who's doing what with whom by its focus on the relationships between persons and organizations involved in illegal—and usually conspiratorial—activities (narcotics trafficking, prostitution rings, organized crime, gangs, terrorism, etc.).

Operations analysis enables the analyst to ascertain how the agency is using its internal resources by its focus on the examination of personnel deployment and workload distribution patterns.

Investigative analysis is an exceedingly specialized type of analysis that is frequently used in the investigation of unusual or serial homicide cases. This form of analysis uses crime scene evidence and information regarding the background of victims to develop physical, behavioral, and psychological profiles of the suspect(s) responsible for the crime(s).

Source: Gottlieb, Steven, Sheldon Arenberg, and Raj Singh. *Crime Analysis: From First Report to Final Arrest.* Montclair, CA: Alpha Publishing, 1994.

Evaluation research, which will be discussed in detail in Chapter 11, is a branch of applied research that examines public programs and policies. Do programs work? How well do they work? How can they be made to work better? These are some of the questions asked in evaluation research.

The 1967 report of the President's Commission on Law Enforcement and Administration of Justice called for creating a research program in criminal justice at the federal level. In 1968, the National Institute of Law Enforcement and Criminal Justice, now called National Institute of Justice, was created. Prior to this, the U.S. Department of Justice had no research and development program. Doris MacKenzie (1998, p. 3) explains the inadequacy of the effort:

When this nation wants to win wars, excel in the race to conquer space, or improve conditions for our rural populations, we put money into research. Perhaps one of the largest reasons criminal justice research has not reached the achievements of other fields is the limited funding given to research activities.

Despite the fact that crime is considered one of the major U.S. social problems, federal funding for criminal justice research has been meager. For example, a 1988 study by the National Science Foundation (NSF) found per capita expenditures for research in health ($432), energy ($11), space ($19), transportation ($4), environment ($4), agriculture ($3), education ($2), and commerce ($.53) greatly exceeded the criminal justice research funding of $.13 (NSF, 1988). Furthermore, the domestic research commitment of $21 million for NIJ in 1989 ($100.6 million in 1997) was substantially below the $229 million for the National Eye Institute, the $167 million for the National Endowment for the Arts, the $140 million for the National Endowment for the Humanities, and the $127 million for the National Institute for Dental Research (Petersiha, 1991). Despite the limited funding provided for criminological research, the potential of the research to aid in public policy decisions is clearly shown by the work that has been completed (Sherman et al., 1997).

Qualitative and Quantitative Research

Quantitative research

Qualitative research

In **quantitative research** concepts are assigned numerical value, whereas in **qualitative research** concepts are viewed as sensitizing ideas or terms that enhance our understanding. Research methods in the social sciences, of which criminal justice is heir, have followed two basic philosophical traditions. *The first legacy* reflects a historical, intuitive, or observational approach and suggests that the physical and social sciences are distinct entities.[3] It emphasizes a *qualitative approach* to understanding the reality under investigation. Classic

Verstehen

sociologist Weber described it as a **Verstehen** (in German, *understanding or empathy*), in which researchers hope to immerse themselves in the subject matter and develop "sensitizing concepts" that enhance their understanding and explanation of reality (Weber, 1949). Many field studies and participant observation studies, in which the researcher lives with and experiences a group's way of life from the group's perspective, serve as examples. Qualitative research offers the investigator the opportunity to alter and even add data collection processes during the study. This grounded theory approach enables a shifting of gears to focus upon issues that were not assumed to be of importance at the time of the beginning of the project.

Positivism, a natural science approach, is often used to describe the *second legacy*. This empirical orientation suggests that the same approach applicable to studying and explaining physical reality can be used in the social sciences. This second tradition is a *quantitative approach* and is concerned with measuring social or, in our case, criminal justice reality. While qualitative research emphasizes a verstehen approach in which researchers immerse themselves in the subject matter

[3]The qualitative approach is illustrated by such writers as Weber (1949), Garfinkel (1967), and Blumer (1969) and by groups that advocate "symbolic interactionism" or "ethnomethodology."

and develop empathetic understanding, the quantitative approach favors studying "phenomena that can be measured, observed, "objectified" and examined empirically." (Worrall, 2000, p. 359)

Although both legacies as pure ideal types may represent dead ends in criminal justice research, moderate expressions of either of these strategies have, as we will discover in Chapter 3, a role in enhancing our understanding of criminal justice. An extreme qualitative approach would provide **historicism**— *seeing all* social events as a distinct chronicle of unique happenings. This would involve a denial that any scientific generalities could be drawn from the world of human events. Such a stance is antiscientific. On the other polar extreme is **scientism**, or extreme positivism, in which the researcher takes the stance that "if you cannot measure it, it is not worth studying or commenting on." Although historicism may jade those from the traditional humanities in their view of criminal justice as a discipline, scientism is most often the orientation of physical scientists, who may view fields such as criminal justice as a pretender to the scientific throne or one of a score of "Johnny-come-lately" pseudosciences. Such physical scientists may feel that unless criminal justice or social science researchers can attain the same rigorous control over the conditions of study as in the physical sciences, they are somehow involved in an inferior enterprise, an amateur imitation of real science. Obviously, social phenomena cannot be put in a test tube or maze.

Criminal justice as an emergent, interdisciplinary, applied scientific field requires for its mature development a full array of qualitative and quantitative approaches, pure and applied research efforts, and theoretically incisive as well as methodologically sound studies and evaluations to gain the academic respectability it both aspires to and deserves.

[margin note: Historicism]

[margin note: Scientism]

Researchese: The Language of Research

Sprechen Sie Researchese? To the uninitiated, the language of research is almost like being exposed to a foreign language. How often have we heard a frustrated reader of a report say, in despair and disgust, "Why don't these people write in English?" This common reaction might even be described, to coin a phrase, as **research shock**—a sense of disorientation experienced by a person when suddenly confronted with an unfamiliar style of presentation and research language. What one is reacting to is not complexity or the unlearnable, but merely the unfamiliar. Those of you who are in-service, criminal justice professionals or who have taken only a few courses in criminology or criminal justice soon discover that you have accumulated much of the specialized language of the field. When you use this argot around others not in the field, you may be surprised that others are unaware of these terms. This, incidentally, explains why many occupational groups cling together socially because others cannot fully appreciate their jargon or ideology. It also explains why many spouses at parties request in despair, "Please stop talking shop!" So, even though at first much of the terminology seems clumsy, stick with it, and by the completion of this text you too will

[margin note: Research shock]

Researchese

be able to read, write, and think **researchese** (the language of research). Researchese is a valuable international language and a useful tool for negotiating and understanding the latest literature in your field.

The notion of causality, a complex subject in philosophy, is the very essence of scientific inquiry. Science assumes that elements of reality can be isolated, defined, explained, and predicted—that science holds the key to unlocking the mysteries of the ages. Scientific investigation assumes that causal principles and laws underlie reality and that by discovering these elements, science can predict and control reality (Wilkins, 1976). This process begins by naming things.

Concepts

Concepts

Concepts are abstract tags put on reality and are the beginning point in all scientific endeavors. Not to be confused with reality itself, concepts are symbolic human creations or constructs that attempt to capture the essence of reality. In deciding on a name for some phenomenon, we are attempting to describe, understand, classify, or become more sensitized to some element of reality. Examples of concepts that are used in criminological and criminal justice studies include crime, recidivism, cynicism, intelligence, risk on parole, defendant's appearance, and police patrol. Age, sex, race, religion, and social class are other concepts with which we are quite familiar. Concepts may be viewed as qualitative, sensitizing/global notions or can be converted into *variables* through *operationalization*.

Operationalization

Operationalization

Operationalization defines concepts by describing how they will be measured. *Working definition* or *operational definition* are other terms used to refer to this process. The notion of operationalization can be defined in response to the statement: "I measured it by _____." Completion of this sentence constitutes the operationalization of the concept. This process of operationalization has now quantified (assigned numerical values to) a concept and converted it from an abstract, verbal entity to a measurable quantity or variable.

Variables

Variables

Variables are concepts that have been operationalized or that can vary or take on different values of a quantitative nature. They are the mortar and brick of scientific investigation. Theoretically, variables can be of a qualitative nature. For example, qualitative distinctions could be made regarding a person's age (old or young), but the measurement of actual chronological age would be considered more exact. Crime may be operationalized in a study as having been measured by official police statistics, surveys of victims, or self-admission reports. Different measures may yield slightly different pictures and therefore should be defined. Similarly, recidivism may be defined by means of rearrest rates, reincarceration (imprisonment or jail) rates, or other measures that could produce quite different assessments of the success or failure of programs. Table 1.1 provides some illustrations of the conversion of various concepts into variables by means of operationalization.

Table 1.1
RESEARCHESE: BASIC TERMS

Concept	Operationalization	Variable
Cynicism	A Cynicism Scale consisting of 20 questions ranging from 1 (low cynicism) to 3 (high cynicism) for each	Cynicism Score 20 (low) to 60 (high)
Intelligence	Administration of an intelligence test that compares mental age (scores on a test) with chronological age	IQ (Intelligence Quotient), for example, range of below 55 to 145+
Risk on parole	A Parole Risk Prediction Scale called "Salient Factor Score"	Parole Risk Score ranging from 0 (poor risk) to 10 (very good risk)
Defendant's appearance	Raters used a scale and rated defendants from 0 (poor) to 10 (excellent)	Appearance Rating Score 0 (poor) to 10 (excellent)
Police patrol	Precincts were assigned to be either proactive (increased patrol), reactive (decreased patrol) or controlling (same as usual patrol)	Police Patrol Strategy: ■ proactive ■ reactive ■ control

Independent (Predictor)[a] Variable (X) (usually demographic variable or a treatment) e.g., Appearance, Police Patrol, Age, Sex, Race, Social Class

Dependent (Outcome)[a] Variable (Y) (usually behavior/attitudes) e.g., Crime, Recidivism, Cynicism, Intelligence, Risk on Patrol

[a] Identification of independent and dependent variables has been oversimplified for heuristic purposes.

Dependent and Independent Variables

The **dependent** (*outcome*) **variable** is the variable one is attempting to predict and by convention is denoted by the letter Y. Common outcome variables in criminal justice are concepts such as crime or recidivism. Table 1.1 illustrates that ordinarily the dependent variable is some behavior or attitude that is usually the subject of one's study.

Dependent variable

The **independent** (or *predictor*) **variable** is the variable that causes, determines, or precedes in time the dependent variable and is usually denoted by the letter X (or any letter other than Y). An independent variable in one study may become a dependent variable in another. For example, a study of the impact of poverty (X) upon crime (Y) finds poverty as a predictor (independent) variable, whereas a study that looks at race (X) as a predictor of

Independent variable

poverty (*Y*) finds poverty as an outcome (dependent) variable. The treatment variable is always an independent variable, as are demographic variables such as age, sex, and race.

Theories/Hypotheses

Theories

Hypotheses

Theories were described previously as *attempts to develop plausible explanations of reality*. They are usually general or broad statements regarding the relationship between variables. **Hypotheses** *are specific statements regarding the relationship between* (usually two) *variables* and are derived from more general theories. A *research hypothesis states an expected relationship between variables in positive terms*. For example, poverty causes crime. The *null hypothesis* is a *hypothesis* of *no difference* and is the one actually tested statistically. For example, poverty is not related to crime. One approach to research involves formulation of hypotheses, the operationalization or measurement of the variables, and the testing or bringing of evidence to bear upon these. Figure 1.1 outlines a model of the research process.

Examples of the Research Process

A brief description of this process is shown in Durkheim's (1951) classic study of suicide, which was originally conducted in 1897 and was one of the first empirical studies in deviant behavior. At the time Durkheim performed his study—in the late nineteenth century—little in the way of empirical analysis had been undertaken in the social sciences. Contrary to popular views of the time, Durkheim proposed that group membership affects suicide. From this he deduced the specific hypothesis that religious denomination, marital status, and the like would affect suicide rates. He operationalized his key variables or indicators of group membership by assuming that married people have greater group ties than singles, or that Judaism and Catholicism required greater group religious orientation than Protestantism, which was more individualistic. Through analyzing the available official suicide records in European countries at the time, he simply compared rates for each variable subcategory. Drawing the general conclusion that singles and Protestants had higher suicide rates than married people, Jews, and Catholics, he inferred from these findings a now modified theory: Group membership does affect suicide.

In examining Figure 1.1 as well as our example, note that reasoning may proceed by means of an a priori assumption (before-the-fact reasoning), wherein a theoretical idea precedes any attempt to collect facts or use as a posteriori assumption (after-the-fact reasoning).

The former is an example of a deductive process of reasoning, with reasoning based on hypothesis or theory, and the latter illustrates the inductive process, with reasoning based on inference of facts or particulars to general principles or theory. Thus, theory to fact is *deduction* and fact to theory is *induction*.

Deduction

Induction

Deduction involves moving from a level of theory to a specific hypothesis, whereas **induction** entails inferring about a whole group on the basis of knowing about a case or a few cases. Sherlock Holmes' famous compliment to Dr. Watson,

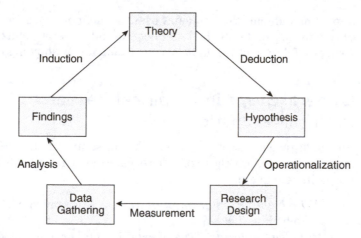

Figure 1.1
A Model of the Research Process.

"Brilliant deduction, my dear Watson," should probably have read "induction" because Watson, in helping Holmes solve a case, was proceeding a posteriori from specific facts or evidence to a conclusion or theory.

Recidivism among Juvenile Offenders

In order to further illustrate the research process, let us examine a hypothetical example. In an experimental correction program called Salvation House, half of those scheduled for incarceration are sent instead to this new community-based treatment program on the basis of a very general theory that offenders better adjust, or are more likely to become rehabilitated, in a community rather than in prison. A specific *hypothesis* derived from this theory (using, as we will describe in Chapter 3, an interrupted time-series design) is that the Salvation House experimental group will experience lower recidivism than the control group of incarcerateds. The *dependent variable* (Y) is recidivism, and the predictor or *independent variable* (X) is assignment to jail or Salvation House. The concept "recidivism" is defined as a reduction in both the quantity and quality (seriousness) of crime commission over a one-year period after release compared with a similar period prior to assignment to either correctional program.

Suffice it to say that each group was examined before and after treatment. *Data gathering* involved the simple examination of official statistics kept by police and probation/parole agents on violations, as well as the weighting of the seriousness of these offenses. Let us suppose the *analysis* demonstrated a "suppression effect"—a decline in both the quantity and seriousness of offenses of the Salvation House assignees. We might now draw the empirical generalization that less recidivism is demonstrated as a result of community-based corrections, at least in our limited case study. We thus lend support to our original theory that correction in the community appears to be more successful than isolated incarceration, at least in bringing about some decline in the seriousness and quantity of offenses. The theory is not set up for reanalysis and investigation.

An actual evaluation of juvenile intensive aftercare probation for serious offenders in Philadelphia (Sontheimer and Goodstein, 1993) found it had a major impact on reducing the frequency of subsequent offenses, but not the incidence of recidivism. Had only the latter been used to operationalize recidivism, then a successful project would have been evaluated as showing no difference.

General Steps in Empirical Research in Criminal Justice

Although research varies considerably in scope, style, and procedure, most studies—particularly those of a more quantitative nature—follow these general **steps in research:**

1. *Problem formulation.* Review, selection, and specification of the area to be investigated.
2. *Research design.* Type of experimental or nonexperimental approach, studies of a group (or groups) at one time or over a period of time, and use of control groups.
3. *Data collection methods.* Choice of a variety of methods such as observation, reanalysis of existing data, questionnaires, and interviews.
4. *Analysis and presentation of findings.* Summarizing, reporting, and statistically analyzing where appropriate and presenting findings.
5. *Conclusions, interpretations, and limitations.* What the researcher believes the study has to say.

Despite the neat, logical appearance of the research reported in journal articles, it is the rare project that follows these steps in a straightforward fashion. Some research, for instance, is exploratory and hypothesis generating rather than hypothesis testing in nature. The steps remain, however, a useful heuristic device for explaining the process at this stage in a simple manner. Although we will discuss problem formulation next, the organization of the text is designed to follow these steps. Chapter 2 examines ethics in research, Chapters 3–8 look at different data-gathering methods, and subsequent chapters discuss the presentation of findings and their interpretation. By combining these steps with the model of the research process described in Figure 1.1, we find that the investigator is often faced first with the issue of finding a research problem.

Problem Formulation: Selection of Research Problem

Problem formulation may be guided by many considerations including personal experiences. Take your gut feelings seriously and pursue them. Chances are that each of us has unique experiences or sensitivities that give us an edge in terms of interest or feel for a subject. This is an advantage that should be recognized and acted on. Practical concerns may govern one's decision—data are available on the job, our agency needs to have a similar study done, or the subject is manageable and likely to be completed in the time allotted. The latter is certainly an important consideration in academic theses and dissertations.

In selecting a research problem one should look for gaps in theory or the current state of the art, feasibility of doing the research, ambiguous and conflicting findings in the current literature, as well as the potential timeliness of policy implications. Additionally, the availability of funding and sponsorship is an important consideration, particularly in large-scale projects. The NIJ has an active research agenda and specified the following areas for funding for fiscal year 2007 (NIJ, 2006):

- Research on sex offenders
- Analysis of existing data
- Trafficking in human beings
- Retail drug markets
- Electronic monitoring for moderate to high risk offenders
- Abuse, neglect, and exploitation of elderly individuals
- Research on policing and public safety interventions
- Sexual violence
- Rape in correctional settings
- Intimate partner violence and stalking
- Transnational crime
- Terrorism

Other sources that may influence one's choice of a research problem include administrative decision-making needs, scientific or intellectual interests, and/or attempts to ameliorate crime or injustice. One should kick around topics and ideas with fellow students, advisors, and professors and search and browse the literature. Peruse the library stacks and consider replication studies of previous research. Minority and feminist scholars have charged that much research and scholarship in criminology and criminal justice has ignored minorities and females and has originated primarily from a white, androcentric (male-centered) bias (Chesney-Lind, 1989; Mann, 1993; Russell, 1992). Exhibit 1.4 examines some of these issues.

Problem Formulation: Specification of Research Problem

The mere selection of a subject for investigation is only the beginning. One must now formulate hypotheses, define key concepts, indicate appropriate operationalization, or decide upon a qualitative sensitizing approach, decide upon research strategies, and finally relate one's research problem to broader issues in criminal justice.

One key way to search for research problems is, of course, through a literature review. Such a search will more likely than now hone what may have begun as a simple, vague hunch. Many novice researchers, anxious to get on with the task, view the problem formulation and literature review stages of a research project as a waste of precious time or a painful process preceding the actual research. In reality, this is the most important period of a study; it refines

EXHIBIT 1.4 ▶

Feminist Perspectives and Research Methods

Feminist theory has emerged as a major force in criminology and criminal justice. While it has many expressions, it draws on Marxist, interactionist, and critical theory and advocates a methodology that differs from the dominant empirical positivism. Some feminist writers view the latter as failing to include gender as a central force and as being blind to its own ideological bias, an androcentrism that ignores females as a central part of crime and justice issues. "Observers are gendered beings, and the research act is a gendered production. Feminism lays positivism to rest in the human disciplines" (Denzin, 1984; Denzin, 1989, pp. 66–67). In calling for nonsexist research methods, Eichler (1988) speaks of "gender insensitivity" in social science research. This involves an ignoring of gender as an important social variable.

Others attack "malestream" approaches to empirical criminal justice and argue that feminist writings and voices should be incorporated into the mainstream of criminal justice education (McDermott, 1992; Renzetti, 1993). Such inclusion of feminist methods in social research (Reinharz, 1992) can be illustrated by a study by Elizabeth Stanko (1990), *Everyday Violence: How Women and Men Experience Sexual and Physical Dangers*, in which she used in-depth interviews to tap women's experiences that do not turn up in standard surveys.

Feeling that much nonfeminist research is sexist due to cultural beliefs and a preponderance of male researchers, feminists question perspectives that assume traditional gender roles. This bias particularly has expressed itself in the past in writings on topics such as rape and domestic violence.

In a content analysis of twenty-two introductory criminal justice texts in print in 1989, Dorworth and Henry (1992) found that women and blacks were underrepresented in photographs as authorities. While women were overrepresented as victims, blacks were overrepresented as offenders. Criminology has omitted black females by equating "woman" with white woman and "black" with black male. McDermott (1992, pp. 247–248) enjoins:

> The newer feminist perspectives suggest that reality isn't clean and tidy, and that experiences don't come in little boxes that are ready to be labeled and counted. . . . It is frightening but necessary to begin to understand knowledge as situated and as socially constructed, and to view our methods of obtaining knowledge as potentially biased. We should encourage our students to consider the potential contributions of newer perspectives and to acknowledge that the issues surrounding methodology and epistemology [how we come to know] exist and are real. There is no other way to move forward.

Sources: Denzin, Norman. *The Research Act*. Englewood Cliffs, NJ: Prentice-Hall, 1989; 66–67; Denzin, Norman. "An Interpretation of Recent Feminist Theory: A Review Essay." *Sociology and Social Research* 68 (1984): 712–718; McDermott, Joan M. "The Personal is Empirical; Feminism, Research Methods, and Criminal Justice Education." *Journal of Criminal Justice Education* 3 (Fall, 1992): 237–249; Eichler, Magrit. *Nonsexist Research Methods*, Boston: Allen and Unwin, 1988. Renzetti, Claire M. "On the Margins of the Malestream (Or They Still Don't Get It. Do They?)" *Journal of Criminal Justice Education* 4 (Fall, 1993): 219–234; Stanko, Elizabeth. *Everyday Violence*. London: Pandora, 1990; and Dorworth, Vicky, and Marie Henry. "Optical Illusions." *Journal of Criminal Justice Education* 3 (Fall, 1992): 251–260.

that which is to be examined and relates it to current and past inquiries, thus preventing the reinvention of the wheel or rediscovery of a dead end. Table 1.2 lists selected journals and abstracts that are useful in a literature review in criminal

Table 1.2
LITERATURE REVIEW SOURCES

Selected Journals Relevant to Criminal Justice and Criminology[a]	
American Criminal Law Review	Journal of Family Violence
American Journal of Criminal Justice	Journal of Justice Issues
American Journal of Police	Journal of Law and Society

(continued)

Table 1.2   Continued

Selected Journals Relevant to Criminal Justice and Criminology

American Journal of Sociology	Journal of Legal Studies
American Sociological Review	Journal of Police Science and Administration
British Journal of Criminology	Journal of Quantitative Criminology
British Journal of Sociology	Journal of Research in Crime and Delinquency
Canadian Journal of Criminology	Journal of Society Administration
Corrections Digest	Judicature
CJ International	Justice Quarterly
Crime and Delinquency	Law and Society Review
Crime and Social Justice	NIJ (National Institute of Justice) Reports
Criminal Justice and Behavior	Police Chief
Criminal Justice Ethics	Police Studies
Criminal Justice Newsletter	The Public Interest
Criminal Justice Policy Review	Public Opinion Quarterly
Criminal Justice Review	Social Forces
Criminology	Social Problems
Federal Probation	Social Science Quarterly
International Journal of Criminology and Penology	Sociological Inquiry
Journal of Contemporary Criminal Justice	Sociology and Social Research
Journal of Crime and Justice	Victimology
Journal of Criminal Justice	Violence and Victims
Journal of Criminal Law and Criminology	

Abstracts/Indexes[b]

Abstracts on Police Science	Police Science Abstracts
Crime and Delinquency Abstracts	Psychological Abstracts
Criminal Justice Abstracts	Reader's Guide to Periodical Literature (for popular sources only)
Criminal Justice Periodical Index	Social Science Index
Criminology and Penology Abstracts	Social Sciences Citation Index
Document Retrieval Index	Sociological Abstracts
Encyclopedia of Crime and Justice	
New York Times Index	

[a]This list is only a selection of journals and not an exhaustive list.

[b]These are among the many abstracts that are available in the reference section of the library. For more details on sources of information in criminal justice and criminology, see Chapter 8.

justice and criminology. Sources of existing data are treated in more detail in the section "Use of Available Data and Archives" in Chapter 8.

Students have available to them instant access to thousands of academic journals and periodicals from any computer with an Internet connection. In addition to abstracts many of these online data sources contain full documents that may be viewed or downloaded. Figure 1.2 shows another example of a

Figure 1.2
Online Research.

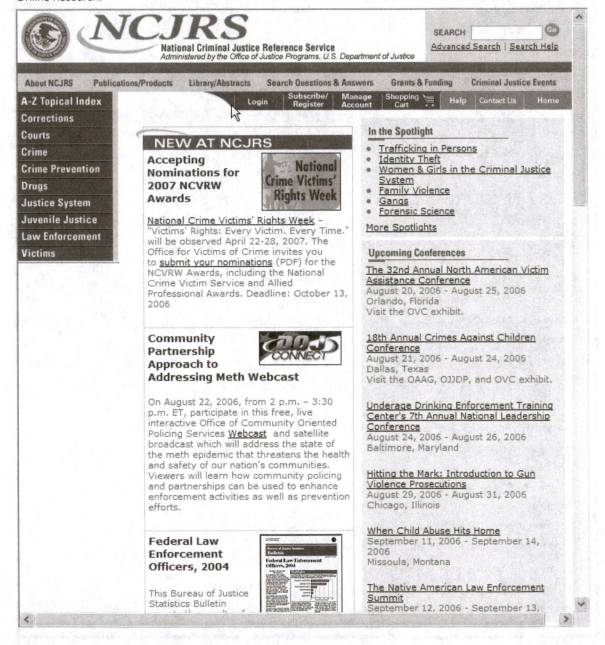

resource for online research, the searchable National Criminal Justice Reference Service site. In using Web browsers to search titles, researchers should use Boolean operators such as AND, OR, and NOT (using such capitalization) in order to linksearch words together. This will help narrow or broaden your search (Clarke and Schultze, 2005).

Exhibit 1.5 provides an illustration of the growing online services available on computer networks and the electronic highway. Conducting Internet searches using search engines such as Yahoo, Infoseek, or Excite is a useful means of becoming more familiar with one's topic while also conducting a literature review.

EXHIBIT 1.5 ▶

The World Wide Web (WWW)

The World Wide Web (WWW) is the fastest growing component of the Internet. Through the use of Web browsers such as Netscape and/or Internet Explorer scholars are able to access a variety of information. Search engines such as Yahoo, Lycos, Excite, and Infoseek will search by topic/author and provide listings of sites that can be found on the Web. Once the listing of sites is provided, the search engines will list several Web addresses that are called uniform resource locators (URLs). For example, Cecil Greek's homepage at the University of South Florida is http://www.criminology.fsu.edu/cjlinks/. Each of these sites contains clickable listings that will connect you with other Web fpages. *Some useful criminal justice sites on the World Wide Web include*:

Site	Address
Cecil Greek	www.criminology.fsu.edu/cjlinks/
National Institute of Justice	www.ojp.usdoj.gov/nij/
Bureau of Justice Statistics	www.ojp.usdoj.gov/bjs/
National Criminal Justice Reference Service	www.ncjrs.org
Financial Crimes Enforcement Network	http://www.fincen.gov/
Drug Enforcement Agency	www.usdoj.gov/dea/deahome.html
Federal Bureau of Investigation	www.fbi.gov/
Federal Bureau of Prisons	www.usdoj.gov/bop/bop.html
Library of Congress	www.loc.gov/
National Archives	www.nara.gov/
United Nations Criminal Justice and Crime Prevention	www.un.org/
United Nations Crime and Justice Information Network	www.ifs.univie.ac.at/~uncjin/uncjin.html

(continued)

EXHIBIT 1.5   Continued

Site	Address
National Archive of Criminal Justice Data (Interuniversity Consortium on Political and Social Research—University of Michigan)	www.icpsr.umich.edu/NACJD/home.html
U.S. Department of Justice	www.usdoj.gov/
U.S. Federal Judiciary	www.uscourts.gov/
The White House	www.whitehouse.gov/WH/Welcome.html
National Institute on Drug Abuse	www.nida.nih.gov/
Office of International Criminal Justice	www.oicj.org
Pavnet Online (Partnership Against Violence)	http://www.pavnet.org
Amnesty International	www.organic.com/Non.profits/Amnesty/index.html
U.S. Census	www.census.gov/
Central Intelligence Agency	http://www.cia.gov/
U.S. Secret Service	www.ustreas.gov/treasury/bureaus/usss/usss.html
Bureau of Alcohol, Tobacco, and Firearms	www.atf.treas.gov/
Drug Enforcement Agency	www.usdoj.gov/otj/otj.html
Office of Juvenile Justice and Delinquency Prevention	www.ncjrs.org
National Clearinghouse for Alcohol and Drug Information	www.health.org/
U.S. Government Printing Office	www.access.gpo.gov/
National Security Agency	http://www.NSA.org
Britannica Online	http://www.britannica.com/
Department of Justice Career Opportunities	www.usdoj.gov/careers.html
National Employment Listing Service (NELS Bulletin)	http://www.justice.gov/careers/careers.html
General Accounting Office	www.gao.gov/
National Institute of Justice	www.ojp.usdoj.gov/nij
Justinfo Online	www.ncjrs.org/justinfo/
New York Times Navigator	www.nytimes.com/library/cyber/reference/cynavi.html#pub

Table 1.3 presents an abbreviated version of the American Psychological Association (APA) style manual, which is the most widely used reference style in the social sciences.

Table 1.3
APA (AMERICAN PSYCHOLOGICAL ASSOCIATION) REFERENCE STYLE

The following is an abbreviated version of the most widely used style reference manual in the social sciences and criminal justice—the *Publication Manual of the American Psychological Association* (APA). Consult the APA Manual for more details (www.apastyle.org).

Reference citations are incorporated directly into the paper.

Hagan (2009) indicates that the APA style incorporates citations directly in the text.

Direct quotes should provide a page number and "p" or "pp" either after the year or at the end of the quote.

Hagan (2009, p. 10) indicates that "the APA style incorporates citations at the end of the quote."

For two or more authors, use "and" in the text and "&" in the citation.

Hagan and Rooney (2009) claim that the Steelers are the best team in the NFL. Writers have claimed **(Hagan & Rooney, 2009)** that the Steelers are the best team in the NFL.

Internet sources are cited in the same manner as print sources.

Provide the name of the author(s) followed by the year of publication: **(Hagan, 2009)**. If no author is given, use the name of the document: **(*NFL Yearbook*, 2009)**.

REFERENCES

Alphabetize all references at the end of your paper.

Hagan, F. E. (2009). *Research methods in criminal justice and criminology* (8th ed.). Upper Saddle River, NJ: Prentice-Hall.

Two or more authors

Hagan, F. E., & Tontodonato, P. (2004). Classical and sociological theories of delinquency. In P. Benekos & A. Merlo (Eds), *Corrections: dilemmas and directions.* Cincinnati: Anderson.

Journals

List author, year, and title of the article without quotation marks, with the first word and any proper nouns capitalized, name of the journal italicized, volume number italicized, and inclusive page numbers not preceded by "p" or "pp."

Hagan, F. E. (1986). Sub rosa criminals. *Clandestine Tactics and Technology, 11,* 298–320.

In addition to consulting the actual APA publication manual (www.apastyle.com), the reader might find it more convenient to consult books or periodicals that use the APA style for examples.

Source: Adapted by the author from the *Publication Manual of the American Psychological Association* (www.apastyle.org/elecre.html).

Summary

In this introductory chapter we discussed why those who attack criminological or criminal justice research as being common sense often deceive themselves with nonsense, substituting their own personal bias or ignorance for objective, scientific information. The study of research methods was described as an invaluable tool for understanding the latest developments in criminal justice as well as in society. *Knowledge* is what people create symbolically to represent reality and was described by Comte as "progressing through three stages": theological (supernatural), metaphysical (philosophical and rational), and scientific (rational plus scientific method or proof). Criminal justice strives for scientific status. Scientists rely upon probabilistic knowledge, that is, predicting general trends, not each case.

In conducting or critiquing studies, researchers are advised to avoid *methodological narcissism* (fanaticism for one method or method for method's sake). Those concerned with good research should be objective, vigilant (for error), and sympathetic (because all research is infested with error). *Theory* is an attempt to develop plausible explanations of reality, whereas *methodology* is an attempt to collect accurate facts or data. Both are indispensable in providing sound criminal justice knowledge. New knowledge often takes place due to paradigm shifts. A paradigm is a model or scheme with which reality is viewed. *Pure research* is directed at the acquisition of new knowledge for its own sake, whereas *applied research* is interested in knowledge for the practical resolution of an existing problem. *Quantitative research* (positivism) is concerned with measuring social reality by using the scientific method.

Researchese, the language of research, includes *concepts* (abstract tags put on reality), *operationalization* (defining concepts by describing how they will be measured), *variables* (operationalized concepts or concepts that vary), *theories* (general statements regarding relationships between variables), and *hypotheses* (specific statements regarding the relationship between variables). Variables may be *dependent* (*outcome*) (the variable one is attempting to predict, denoted by the letter Y) or *independent* (the predictor variable, denoted by the letter X or any letter other than Y).

The *research process* was illustrated as a circular process from theory to hypothesis to research design to data gathering to findings and then back to theory.

The *general steps in empirical research in criminal justice* are problem formulation, research design, data-collection methods, analysis/presentation of findings, and conclusions/interpretations/limitations. The first step—problem formulation—was discussed in this chapter; the remaining steps will be the subject of subsequent chapters.

The feminist perspective on research methods offers an alternative to androcentric bias in criminology.

KEY CONCEPTS

Replication	Crime analysis	Variables
Verification	Quantitative research	Dependent variable
Methodological	Qualitative research	Independent variable
narcissism	Verstehen	Theories
Theory	Historicism	Hypotheses
Paradigm	Scientism	Deduction
Methodology	Research shock	Induction
"Broken Windows"	Researchese	Steps in research
Pure research	Concepts	Problem formulation
Applied research	Operationalization	Feminist perspectives

REVIEW QUESTIONS

1. Name a myth or inaccurate commonsense view of crime or criminal justice other than one presented in this chapter. Indicate how research has clarified this misconception.

2. Are criminology and criminal justice sciences? Discuss some developments that support their claim to scientific status.

3. What is the role of theory in criminological/criminal justice research, and why has there been such a shortage of new theory since the 1960s?

4. Choose a recent journal article and identify: (a) the research problem, (b) research design, (c) data-gathering strategy, (d) dependent variable/s, (e) independent variable/s, and (f) operationalization of the key dependent and independent variables.

5. What is the feminist perspective on research methods? Why is there a need for such a perspective? How does it differ from the "malestream"?

USEFUL WEB SITES

Research Navigator *www.researchnavigator.com*

Allyn and Bacon Criminal Justice Online *www.ablongman.com/criminaljustice*

Academy of Criminal Justice Sciences *www.acjs.org*

United Nations Crime and Justice Information Network *www.uncjin.org*

Criminal Justice Megalinks *www.apsu.edu/oconnort/*

Cecil Greek's Criminal Justice Web Site *www.criminology.fsu.edu/cjlinks/*

NIJ International Center *www.ojp.usdoj.gov/nij/international*

Web Center for Social Research Methods *www.socialresearchmethods.net/*

National Criminal Justice Reference Service (NCJRS) *www.ncjrs.org/*

2

Ethics in Criminal Justice Research

Ethical Horror Stories

Biomedical Examples

Nazi doctors tortured, maimed, and murdered innocent captive subjects. Some scientists have purposely allowed subjects to suffer and even die of a disease while withholding a known cure. As part of other experiments, researchers have deceived people into believing that they were electrocuting people; they have created an artificial prison in which participants become hostile and aggressive; or they have spied on secret sexual activity and later showed up at the subjects' homes and invaded their privacy as part of a scientific survey. Intelligence agencies have employed social scientists to gather data on dissidents in third world countries and, along with the military, have employed researchers and scientists (including former Nazis) to conduct often bizarre and dangerous experiments on unknowing subjects. If all of these situations resemble plots for a Stephen King gothic novel, they are not. Each is an actual example of a project that has raised ethical controversies.

Major ethical concerns about the use of human subjects in research originally arose as a result of the outrageous examples of inhuman Nazi experiments during World War II. Dr. Josef Mengele, the "Angel of Death," performed horrifying human experiments in which captive subjects were tortured and killed in the name of scientific research. These experiments were coldblooded and inhumane. In the name of medical research, people were infected with diseases, used as guinea pigs to test new drugs, administered poisons, and exposed to extreme temperatures and decompression to test reactions to high altitudes (Katz, 1972). After the war, the Nuremberg trials defined such behavior as war crimes and crimes against humanity. The *Nuremberg Code* set forth principles governing the use of human subjects in research, including the requirement that such subjects "voluntarily consent" to participate in a study (Wexler, 1990, p. 81).

In the infamous *Tuskegee Syphilis Study* (Brandt, 1978), the U.S. Public Health Service withheld penicillin, a known cure for syphilis, from 425 uneducated black male sharecroppers who suffered from and eventually died of untreated syphilis. This study, which began in 1932 before a cure for syphilis was available, was completed in the 1970s, well after such medicine was developed. Such inhumane biomedical research on unsuspecting subjects did not end with the Tuskegee Study (Jones, 1982). In the 1960s, live cancer cells were injected into elderly patients at a Brooklyn hospital without their knowledge. The U.S. military services, during and after World War II, exposed their own soldiers to mustard gas and nuclear radiation, resulting in cases of chronic ailments and premature death. During the post–World War II Cold War era, American intelligence agencies, with the cooperation of the scientific community, performed bizarre and dangerous experiments on unknowing subjects. In the early years of the Cold War, American intelligence agencies had become convinced that the Communists had developed secret mind control and brainwashing techniques and that it was necessary in this battle for human minds and world domination to pull out all the stops (Hagan, 2006; Scheflin and Opton, 1978).

This explains, but does not condone, the following abuses:

- Government researchers slipped LSD into the drink of an unsuspecting government employee, who then committed suicide. Later, the government refused to tell his grief- and guilt-stricken family what really happened.

- In the 1950s, using code names like Bluebird, Artichoke, and MKUltra, the CIA, FBI, and U.S. military experimented with behavior-control devices and interrogation techniques, including ESP, drugs, polygraphs, hypnosis, shock therapy, surgery, and radiation. These experiments involved secret testing on unsuspecting citizens and, if death or injury occurred, a cover-up (Cousins, 1979; Simon and Eitzen, 1996).

- In 1988, the CIA agreed to pay damages to eight Canadian citizens who had been victims of experiments at a Montreal mental hospital (Witt, 1988, p. 2A). As an example, a Canadian teenager seeking medical treatment for an arthritic leg was first given LSD, and then he was subjected to electroshock therapy and forced to listen to taped messages saying, "You killed your mother." Such studies were conducted on more than 100 Canadians and were financed by the CIA and conducted by an American doctor who had been the former president of the American Psychiatric Association.

- In 1986, the House Energy and Commerce Subcommittee uncovered the fact that during a thirty-year period beginning in the mid-1940s, federal agencies had conducted exposure experiments on American citizens, including injecting them with plutonium, radium, and uranium. These studies included feeding radium or thorium to elderly patients during an experiment at the Massachusetts Institute of Technology, irradiating inmates' testes with x-rays, and exposing people to open-air fallout tests and feeding them real fallout from a Nevada test site (Lawrence, 1988). It was later revealed that the U.S. military even employed former Nazi doctors and scientists, using them to conduct chemical experiments on U.S. military personnel at Fort Dietrick (Aberdeen, Maryland).

- Situ and Emmons (1999) in *Environmental Crime* describe the often overlooked, massive governmental experiment of open-air nuclear testing in the post–World War II period. Between 1951 and 1963, the U.S. government detonated 126 nuclear bombs in the sky above Nevada. Each detonation sent a cloud of radiation aloft equal to that released during the Chernobyl nuclear disaster in the former Soviet Union. Such testing spoiled soil in Virginia, milk in New England, wheat in South Dakota, and fish in the Great Lakes. During the same period, U.S.

Army infantry were ordered to observe nuclear tests from unprotected trenches.

■ In an incredibly insensitive experiment, for four months during the Depression, researcher and graduate student Mary Tudor and her professor, Wendell Johnson, taught children at an Iowa orphanage a "lesson they would never forget"—how to stutter ("Lessons," 2001). While the experiment helped thousands of children overcome speech difficulties, this took place at the expense of some of the children unnecessarily being subject to lives as outcasts and misfits. Thirteen of her subjects who are still alive learned of the experiment in 2001 when reporters from the *San Jose Mercury News* contacted them. The now stuttering children had been divided into two groups of eleven, one labeled normal speakers and given positive speech therapy and the other group induced to stutter. Eight members of the treatment group became permanent stutterers. While Tudor had guilt feelings and returned to the orphanage a number of times to attempt to reverse the damage, Johnson did nothing and became very prominent in his field of speech pathology due to the findings. Tudor describes how during the experiment the trusting orphans greeted her, running to her car and helping to carry in materials for the experiment. In 2007, the state of Iowa agreed to pay $925,000 to six of the subjects of the study who had been harmed by the University of Iowa researchers. The 1939 experiment became known as the "Monster study" because of the methods used by the researchers. *The San Jose Mercury News broke the story in 2001 based on statements by Mary Tudor* (Associated Press, 2007: 8A).

Institutional Review boards

■ In 1998, a Department of Health and Human Services (HHS) report concluded that the federal system for protecting human research subjects was breaking down. The report claimed that **Institutional Review boards (IRBs)**, which judge the ethical merits of research, were overburdened, insufficiently staffed, and subject to conflict of interest (Weiss, 1998). Although the details of one study were more complicated than described, newspapers reported that physicians in New York offered to give Toys R Us gift certificates to thirty-six healthy black and Hispanic elementary school pupils if the children agreed to enroll in a medical study that required them to take a potentially life-threatening drug (actually low doses of fenfluramine). The drug was used to measure levels of brain hormone implicated in antisocial behavior. The older brothers of the young males were delinquent, and the study was designed to examine whether this increased the latter's delinquency potential.

■ In another controversial University of California study, schizophrenic youths were required to discontinue their medication. This caused some to be confused, violent, and lose their ability to concentrate. One committed suicide. Of particular concern in these studies was the cavalier manner in which vulnerable populations (young, mentally disturbed, and minorities) were put at risk.

In a blatant example of professionals selling out their research integrity to commercial interests, it was reported in 2008 that drug manufacturer **Merck** wrote research reports praising their drugs and then paid doctors to attach their names. The ghostwriting of medical research studies was published in professional journals. Merck had manipulated dozens of articles in order to promote Vioxx, a later recalled drug (Guterman, 2008; Saul, 2008).

Exhibit 2.1 considers a controversial experiment with an AIDS vaccine in third world countries.

Social Science Examples

Most of the foregoing examples have been *biomedical* in nature; but because social and behavioral research likewise puts subjects at risk, its activities have led to similar ethical concerns. Many social scientific studies related to crime and deviance have come under scrutiny. The three social scientific studies that seem to be cited in the literature most often are: Stanley Milgram's *Obedience to Authority* (1974), Philip Zimbardo's simulated prison experiment (1972, 1973, 1974), and Laud Humphreys' *Tearoom Trade* (1970).

In his classic *Obedience to Authority* study, Stanley Milgram had one very important objective: He wanted to discover the causes of the Holocaust. During the Nazi era in Germany, some people performed their gruesome duties as if it was "just another day at the office." How and why do average, "normal" people commit the most monstrous acts? In Milgram's study, which was

---

EXHIBIT 2.1 ▶

AIDS Research in Africa and Asia: Is It Ethical?

In September 1997, an international debate began when it was revealed that American-sponsored field experiments with azidothymidine (AZT) vaccine (a believed treatment for AIDS) was being conducted in Asia and Africa on pregnant women who had been diagnosed with the AIDS virus. While some of the women (the experimental group) were given AZT, others (the control group) were given placebos. Critics charged that, by not giving AZT to all, the newborns of the control group were knowingly being given AIDS. Defenders of the experiment pointed out that without the experiment there would have been no AZT treatment for anyone in such poor countries. They argued that such treatment was ethical since half of the women who had received some treatment would have otherwise received none. Such treatments are routine in wealthier countries such as the United States as soon as AIDS is diagnosed.

Critics also drew parallels with the Tuskegee Syphilis Experiment and questioned the morality of withholding a likely cure, while proponents noted that the findings promised to discover a shorter, cheaper course of AZT treatment that could protect newborns. Marjorie Speers is in charge of human subject protection at the Center for Disease Control and Prevention (CDC).

> Consent is another minefield, Speers said. U.S. regulations require individual informed consent. In other nations, husbands consent for wives and tribal leaders consent for villagers. To ask for more is insulting. Speers said the very notion of informed consent is alien in parts of the former Soviet Union after decades of totalitarianism. And the CDC was forced to cancel research in two Arab countries because the governments refused to allow women to serve on ethical review panels. (Long, 1998)

Source: Long, Karen. "AIDS Research Abroad Raises Ethical Concerns." *The Cleveland Plain Dealer* (May 20, 1998): A–1.

designed to answer this question, volunteer subjects were recruited and paid to act as "teachers" while "confederates" (fake subjects who were really in on the study) acted as "pupils." The subjects (teachers) were then deceived into believing that each time they threw a lever on a shock apparatus, they were administering gradually more painful electric shocks to pupils, whom they could hear but not see. When the pupils failed to answer a question correctly, the teachers were to administer shocks. Despite protests from the pupils, teachers were willing to administer levels of voltage that they believed to be dangerous, particularly when assured by lab assistants, who appeared as scientific authorities, that such behavior was necessary. Subjects experienced personal turmoil both during and immediately after the experiment, although debriefing (explaining the purpose of the study after-the-fact) seemed to have resulted in no long-term harm. Do experimenters have the ethical right to deceive and put subjects in a position of emotional stress in the name of science? Despite the fact the IRBs would not approve of such studies today, this has not stopped television programs such as *Dateline NBC* from conducting such programs in 2010.

In Philip Zimbardo's *simulated prison study*, male, undergraduate, paid volunteers assumed the roles of either guard or prisoner. A mock prison was constructed in the basement of a Stanford University building, and prisoners and guards assumed their respective roles, complete with uniforms, nightsticks, and mirrored sunglasses for the guards and numbers and prison garb for the prisoners. While the experiment was to have lasted at least two weeks, individuals became so carried away with the roles—passivity and hostility by prisoners and aggressive and dehumanizing behavior by guards—that Zimbardo cancelled the study after six days rather than risk harm to the participants. The

Lucifer effect

Lucifer effect (www.lucifereffect.org) is a concept coined by Zimbardo to refer to a transformation of human character that causes good people to engage in evil actions. This could include sexual degradation and torture such as at Abu Ghraib prison in Iraq. In *The Lucifer Effect: Understanding How Good People Turn Evil*, Zimbardo (2007a) describes one of the experiments in the Stanford study called the "humping experiment":

> After a brief consultation, our toughest guard (nicknamed "John Wayne" by the prisoners) and his sidekick devised a new sexual game. "OK, now pay attention. You three are going to be female camels. Get over there and bend over, touching your hands to the floor." When they did, their naked butts were exposed because they had no underwear beneath their smocks. John Wayne continued with obvious glee, "Now you two, you're male camels. Stand behind the female camels and *hump* them."

Although their bodies never touched, the zombie-like prisoners began to simulate sodomy. One of Zimbardo's associates, after observing similar exercises, berated him for contributing to the suffering of human beings. This snapped Zimbardo back to his senses and led to his cancelling the experiment (Zimbardo, 2007b).

In 2002, the British Broadcasting Corporation (BBC) cancelled plans to replicate for television the "notorious" Stanford experiment, featuring 15 participants, for fear for their emotional and physical well-being. The volunteers had been "incarcerated" in a simulated "prison" at Elstree studios in Hertfordshire. The BBC had advertised for volunteers, warning participants that those chosen would be exposed to "exercise, tasks, hardship, hunger, solitude and anger" (Wells, 2002). Overseen by two psychologists, Alex Haslam (Exeter University) and Stephen Reicher (St. Andrews University), as well as an independent "ethical committee," the experiment was terminated only a day or two short of the planned ten days. Zimbardo himself commented, "That kind of research is now considered to be unethical and should not be redone just for sensational TV and Survivor-type glamour. I am amazed a British university psychology department would be involved" (Wells, 2002).

The possibility of such potential harm is even worse if the subjects do not consent to participate in a study; in such experiments, observation usually takes place in private settings and the behavior involves activity that society may regard as immoral or illegal. All of these factors were present in Laud Humphreys' controversial study, *Tearoom Trade* (1970), one involving secret male homosexual behavior in public restrooms. Pretending to be a "watchqueen" (voyeur), Humphreys served as both a lookout and hidden observer of such behavior. He copied license numbers and traced them to the owners' homes. Changing his appearance, Humphreys showed up at their homes under the guise of a mental health researcher.

Although Humphreys' research was important to the criminal justice system, which gained important insights into the nature of such participants who engage in impersonal homosexual liaisons in public places, was the obtaining of such knowledge justified, given the risk for potential harm to subjects if their secret sexual behavior were to become known to legal authorities, family, or employers? Even though Humphreys claimed to have taken great precautions to protect the anonymity of the subjects, did he have the right to put them in harm's way without their permission? Is there any way of studying such behavior without using deceit and deception? Should criminological researchers study only volunteers?

An amusing example is provided by a disguised observational study of the "Church of Satan." The researcher (Alfred, 1976) felt guilty that he had deceived members of a satanic cult, until he revealed his misrepresentation and was applauded by the group, since lying is considered an appropriate satanic act.

What if the researchers are themselves the subject of deception? Through various fronts during the 1960s and 1970s, the CIA, apparently without the knowledge of the recipients, funded social psychological research by such names as Sherifs, Orne, Rogers, Osgood, and Goffman (Marks, 1979, p. 121), and it financed the publication of more than 1,000 books, pretending that they were the products of independent scholarship (Cook, 1984, p. 287).

In *Project Camelot* (Horowitz, 1965), for example, U.S. researchers studied student and peasant insurgency movements in Chile. Because this was an area of the world where government opponents routinely "disappeared," many subjects were justifiably suspicious of this effort, and they feared the data it would generate. Believing that the "Yanqui" researchers were gathering this information for intelligence purposes, they thought the study would have a chilling effect on dissent. Although the researchers denied such CIA involvement at the time, some of the researchers later discovered that their data were in fact being gathered for intelligence purposes. The government of Chile, which had been unaware of the project, expelled the researchers and brought to an end the infamous *Project Camelot*. Following questions are among the many raised by this study: Should researchers do the bidding of intelligence agencies, thus acting as spies? Whose side is social research on? Should researchers refuse certain sponsorship or specify the conditions under which sponsorship will be accepted?

In 1998, over 100 boys ages six to eleven were given fenfluramine, a diet drug, in order to see if it reduced aggression (Associated Press, 1998). Researchers claimed that the dosages were not harmful. The Food and Drug Administration (FDA) estimated that one-third of all adults who took the diet pill regularly may have experienced significant heart valve damage. Fexfluramine and a related drug, Redux, were recalled by the FDA in the summer of 1997.

There has been no shortage of ethical horror stories, including those involving correctional research on prisoner "volunteers". Mitford in *Kind and Unusual Punishment* (1973) documents abuse of inmates by medical researchers, as does Allen Hornblum in his book *Acres of Skin* (1998). Hornblum relates his first experience with such experiments on entering a Pennsylvania prison in 1971 and noticing bizarre patchworks of gauze on many prisoners and being told that the prisoners were testing perfumes. They were human guinea pigs not only for perfumes but also for soap, cosmetics, and even dioxin (radioactive isotopes and psychological warfare agents). Hornblum's research revealed that, by 1969, 85 percent of all new drugs were being tested on prisoners.

Hornblum used the Freedom of Information Act in order to obtain old records and found that most of the subjects were never checked for long-term effects. Claiming that one researcher, University of Pennsylvania professor Albert Kligman, ran a virtual human research factory using prisoners as guinea pigs, Hornblum documents:

- The Army tested an incapacitating agent, EA 3167, a chemical warfare agent which caused subjects to experience hallucinations and confusion for up to three weeks. The inmates referred to EA 3167 and other mind-altering drugs that they received as LSD.
- Kligman lied about his credentials in order to test radioactive isotopes on prisoners.
- He tested dioxin, a component of Agent Orange, for Dow chemical, but went beyond their instructions by subjecting several inmates to 7,500 micrograms or 468 times the required dosage. Two inmates later sued, settling for only a few thousand dollars (Kinney, 1998).

By the late 1970s a National Commission for the Protection of Subjects of Biomedical and Behavioral Research suggested banning such a practice. The

U.S. Food and Drug Administration agreed, and by the early 1980s most prison testing was outlawed. Former prisoners who had participated in such experiments related negative psychological and physiological harm long after the experiment. Most participants were poor and uneducated (Kinney, 1998).

In *Darkness in El Dorado: How Scientists and Journalists Devastated the Amazon*, Tierney (2001) alleges major ethical violations by anthropologists who violated the human rights of the Yanomami, a native people to Brazil and Venezuela. The Yanomami were injected with a measles vaccine known to be virulent in isolated populations. A subsequent epidemic ensued, and the research team supposedly was instructed not to assist the dying Yanomami. No informed consent was gained from the vulnerable tribe (Fleur-Lobban, 2000). These accusations threw the American Anthropological Association into turmoil, with a committee charging Tierney's accusations were largely false, but that many of his other points were well founded (Glenn, 2006).

To illustrate the seriousness with which federal agencies view the protection of human subjects, on July 19, 2001, the U.S. federal government cancelled all federal funding for research projects at Johns Hopkins University due to the death of a subject in a university-run experiment. In 2000, Hopkins had led the nation in federally funded research. The dead volunteer subject had participated in an asthma experiment in which the informed consent form failed to adequately advise her of the experimental nature of the drug that killed her when she inhaled it.

Julianne Basinger in an article entitled "Research at What Cost?" (2001) examines the case of Shawn Wight, a twenty-six-year-old graduate student from Ohio State, whose participation in research cost him his life. Accompanied by his professor, Shawn and other graduate students were on a high-altitude expedition in Western China to examine and drill ice cores from glaciers. He developed severe reactions to the altitude, which ultimately resulted in his death. While emergency measures for dealing with such problems appeared inadequate, the State of Ohio ruled in favor of the university in a $24 million liability suit brought by Wight's parents. The case represented a wake-up call to universities and research directors, and Ohio State has since improved its procedures and oversight functions. There is growing awareness of the risks involved in research for not only the subjects but also the researchers and their employees (Craig, Corden, and Thornton, 2000).

Researcher Fraud and Plagiarism

A fundamental expectation of any piece of scientific research is that it be accurate, honest, and properly referenced. This, incidentally, is the reason why professors harp upon these themes when correcting student papers; those who ignore these lessons may be haunted by them later in life.

Research fraud occurs when researchers purposely fabricate or misrepresent their findings. Despite the pressure on researchers to "publish or perish"— tenure and grants are often dependent on their success in getting published in research publications—the actual number of cases of research fraud are relatively rare. In 1989, however, the HHS started an Office of Scientific Integrity to address this issue (Neuman, 1991, p. 438; "Fraud in Research," 1994). Exhibit 2.2 describes

Research fraud

The Minerva Consortium and the Human Terrain System

Academia has a long history of aiding the military and intelligence agencies, going back to the Office of Strategic Services in World War II, Vietnam War, and the cold war and before. Franz Boas, the father of American Anthropology, once complained that his colleagues were spying on the German navy during World War I while pretending to do research. Critics of such activity argue that it violates the neutral-observer status of the discipline ("Embedded Anthropologists," 2007: B4). During World War II, the Manhattan Project enlisted the talents of scientists and academics to develop the atom bomb. Also, at this time, the Army Psychological Warfare unit recruited social scientists to develop wartime propaganda tools and means of promoting allied military morale and undermining enemy morale.

In 2006, the Pentagon launched the program entitled "the Human Terrain System" in which academics were recruited to conduct field research in Afghanistan and Iraq to assist the U.S. military in waging a smarter counterinsurgency war (Ephron and Spring, 2008). The specialists were charged to map the populations of the communities, identify clans and conflicts between them, and advise the military on obtaining local support. Some possible participants in the Human Terrain System program were discouraged when the American Anthropological Association indicated that such researchers would most likely be violating the ethics of their profession because

they would be contributing data that might be useful in military operations. **The Minerva Consortium** is named for the Roman goddess of wisdom. In 2008, it was introduced by Robert Gates, secretary of defense, in a speech before the Association of American Universities (Goldstein, 2008). During the address, Gates quoted historian Arthur M. Schlesinger Jr.'s 1957 speech after the Russians' Sputnik beat the United States into space, when Schlesinger said that the United States "must return to the acceptance of eggheads and ideas if it is to meet the Russian challenge" (Goldstein, 2008: B4). The Minerva Consortium established a project that finances social science research that was relevant to national security. Such a proposal had been met with mixed reactions. The project was variedly charged with the following: It is a justification of imperialism, is needed to counteract jihadist ideology, will be used to justify human rights abuses, will provide an opportunity to break new ground in the social sciences, and will contribute to a further militarization of the universities and produce a brain drain from other areas of research. At least two graduate students who had volunteered to serve in the Human Terrain System were killed in Afghanistan (Glenn, 2008). Partly in response to some of these criticisms, the military began to train their own personnel in conducting such field research.

the controversial Minerva Consortium and the Human Terrain System that recruits academics to assist in the war on terrorism.

Perhaps the most celebrated case of a researcher's dishonesty was that of Sir Cyril Burt, a famous British psychologist, whose studies on twins had demonstrated the inherited nature of intelligence. After his death, researchers discovered that he had faked his data and had even created nonexistent coauthors (Wade, 1976). It should be noted, however, that more recent investigations of the Burt affair have drawn differing conclusions (Hearnshaw, 1979), with some reviewers indicating that Burt was innocent of outright fraud and that some of his detractors may have been guilty of character assassination (Fletcher, 1991; Joynson, 1989). In 1995, Dr. Gerald L. Gerson, after examining Louis Pasteur's 102 laboratory notebooks, charged that Pasteur had misled, lied, secretly stolen a rival's techniques, and otherwise deceived the scientific world in order to receive grants, patents, and awards (Altman, 1995). Exhibit 2.3 depicts two legendary research scams.

Plagiarism

Plagiarism, as most college students know, is a type of fraud in which a writer presents the ideas or work of someone else as his or her own. Prominent

EXHIBIT 2.3 ▶

Legendary Research Scams

Most famous cases of research fraud have taken place in medicine and the physical sciences, but two cases in the social sciences have raised considerable controversy: the "Piltdown Hoax" and the "Tasaday Hoax." The Piltdown Hoax was perpetrated in England in 1911 with the claim that the fossil remains of the evolutionary "missing link" between apes and humans had been discovered. The unearthed bones had some features of humans and some features of apes. In the 1950s, researchers using carbon dating were able to document that the remains were of recent origin and that the human skull had simply been combined with portions of the jaw of an orangutan, and then the entire remains were treated to appear to be very old in origin (Broad and Wade, 1983; Spencer, 1990; Weiner, 1955).

A similar outright fraud took place in the 1970s in the Philippines. Large-scale media exposure, including television documentaries, was given to the discovery of a lost tribe, the Tasaday, a peaceful, "Stone Age" community that had no previous contact with the modern world. Later investigations revealed that no humans had probably ever lived on the supposed Tasaday Island and that the entire hoax had involved government officials encouraging local peasants to pretend to be primitives in order to attract tourists or other publicity (Marshall, 1989).

figures such as Senator Joseph Biden, Alex Haley, John Hersey, Martin Luther King, Jr., Doris Kearns Goodwin, and Stephen Ambrose have been accused of plagiarism. Researchers should be very careful to properly acknowledge—and therefore not take credit for or steal—the ideas of others (Broad and Wade, 1983; LaFollette, 1992). Figure 2.1 describes some of the issues related to plagiarism. Publishers of academic journals have begun using anti-plagiarism software such as iParadigms, Turnitin, and CrossCheck to detect plagiarism (Rampbell, 2008: A17).

Scientific misconduct may involve any number of other offenses including negligence, deception, cover-ups of misconduct, reprisals against whistleblowers, malicious allegations of misconduct in science, and even violations of due process in the handling of misconduct ("On Being a Scientist," 1998). Other categories of misbehavior may include sexual or other forms of harassment, misuse of funds, gross negligence in professional activity, and/or tampering with the experiments of others or with instrumentation and violations of government research regulations.

The Office of Research Integrity (ORI) is a federal agency supported by the U.S. Public Health Service that is concerned with detecting and preventing scientific misconduct. It evaluates all investigative records submitted by institutions and helps determine whether there has been misconduct at these institutions that receive support from the HHS. The U.S. federal definition of research misconduct includes fabrication, falsification, or plagiarism in proposing, performing, or reviewing research results (Titus, Wells, and Rhoades, 2008). In 2006, 2,212 research scientists, a response rate of 51 percent, responded to a survey regarding research misconduct. Of these, 192 scientists (8.7 percent) indicated having observed or had direct evidence of researchers in their own departments committing one or more incidents of misconduct over the past three academic years. They described a total of 265 incidents (Titus, Wells, and Rhoades, 2008).

Figure 2.1
Plagiarism.

Plagiarism involves the theft of another person's words or ideas and presenting them as your own. The advent of the Internet in particular raises problems in that some students mistakenly believe that, because they can easily copy such material with the click of a mouse, the information does not have to be referenced, cited, or acknowledged in any other way. Others mistakenly assume that their professors will be unable to track down the actual sources of information; this is no longer the case since professors now have access to Web sites that can search the Internet for plagiarized material.

The most blatant forms of plagiarism involve the use of another's work, the purchase of research papers, or knowingly copying whole sections of another work into a paper without acknowledgment. Simply changing sentence order or a few words in a passage is not enough—it is still plagiarism.

Avoiding Plagiarism

While you should credit sources for ideas or words that are not your own, it is not necessary to document the obvious or common knowledge. Paraphrasing involves restating "in your own words" materials written or spoken by another person; you reflect the original material in your own words. Merely changing a few words and the order of phrases is plagiarism, not paraphrasing. In taking notes and collecting sources for your paper, be sure to keep track of your sources so that you can later properly acknowledge them. Your professor may require different documentation styles, although most prefer the APA (American Psychological Association) style (see www.researchnavigator.com). It is crucial that sources be cited and acknowledged within the text itself. A paper featuring no cited sources followed by a list of works used is not acceptable. Directly quoted material should be identified by means of quotation marks.

Source: Melissa Payton. *Evaluating Online Resources with Research Navigator: Criminal Justice.* Upper Saddle River, NJ: Pearson/Prentice Hall, 2004, 23–27, www.researchnavigator.com.

The Researcher's Role

Ethical concerns in criminal justice research raise potential problems for the researcher with respect to the various roles she or he must often play. The role of researcher as scientist may intersect with, and sometimes conflict with, the roles of criminal justice practitioner, citizen, and humanitarian. Rabow (1980), for instance, sees the conflict of scientific and treatment roles in corrections as hindering the effort to improve and apply treatment successfully.

Role of researcher

The **role of researcher** requires that one be objective and "value free" in approaching and reporting on the subject matter. As was indicated, particularly in our previous treatment of participant observational studies of criminals, such a stance often impinges on one's concept of the proper role of a criminal justice practitioner. The practitioner is involved in programmatic efforts to prevent, rehabilitate, and otherwise process criminals and/or crime. Such a role obviously conflicts with the role of neutral observer and scientist. Similar conflicts may take place with one's role as citizen or humanitarian, wherein one is concerned with cooperating with public officials or expressing concern and supporting efforts for eliminating inequitable social conditions or human maladies. In a classic statement, Polsky directs himself to the moral issues of field studies of criminals:

> If one is effectively to study adult criminals in their natural settings, he must make the moral decision that in some ways he will break the law himself. He need not be a "participant" observer and commit the criminal acts under study, yet he has to witness such acts or be taken into confidence about them and not blow the whistle. . . . According to Yablonsky, nonmoralizing on the part of the researcher, when coupled with intense interest in the criminal's life, really constitutes a romantic encouragement of the criminal. . . . [Polsky feels] the burden of proof rests upon those who claim that abstention from moralizing by the field investigator has any significantly encouraging effect on criminal's lifestyles, and they have not supplied one bit of such proof. Finally, our society at present seems plentifully supplied with moral uplifters in any case, so one needn't worry if a few sociological students of crime fail to join the chorus. (Polsky, 1967, p. 139)

The National Advisory Committee on Criminal Justice Standards and Goals addresses the intersection of researcher as scientist, criminal justice practitioner, and citizen:

> Criminal justice researchers who are funded by, work closely with, or are employees of agencies whose functions include law enforcement can encounter ethical problems when they appear to assist in law enforcement activities. Although most researchers would support the objective of enhancing the effectiveness of the criminal justice system and recognize their duties as citizens to do so, the progress of research may nonetheless be undermined by failure to distinguish between their roles as researcher and the roles of other criminal justice personnel. The burden of maintaining this distinction falls on both researchers and agencies, but researchers who study any type of organization should guard against having to assume any nonresearch roles or even appearing to do so. (National Advisory Committee, 1976, p. 131)

In self-mediating the potential conflicting roles of the criminal justice researcher, it is incumbent upon the investigator to enter the setting with eyes wide open. A decision must be made beforehand on the level of commitment to the research endeavor and the analyst's ability to negotiate the likely role conflicts. Although there are no hard-and-fast rules and each research enterprise is in many ways a unique reality, the *researcher's primary role is that of scientist*. That is not to say that this role should in all cases take total precedence over other agenda; however, the researcher should determine limits, priorities, and subject accountability as soon as practicable in embarking on a study (Punch, 1986; Reynolds, 1982).

Research Targets in Criminal Justice

Criminal justice research focuses on a variety of *targets* or subject matter: the criminal, the victim, the criminal justice system, and practitioners, as well as the general public. Each of these topics raises unique ethical problems or concerns for the investigator. One group that has been a traditional source of research subjects and of increasing controversy has been the incarcerated.

A national prison research commission report questioned the legitimacy and ethicality of prison research in the United States. They doubted whether prisoners' voluntary decisions to participate in studies reflect volunteerism or fear that not to "volunteer" would bring reprisals. Instead of banning all such investigations the committee called for a review by outside boards that would be made up of various constituencies including prisoners, prisoner advocates, and representatives of racial and cultural minorities (Branson, 1977).

Ethics and Professionalism

Criminologists and criminal justice researchers as social scientists strive for acceptance as *professionals*. The regulation of ethically acceptable research conduct may take one of three forms:

- Codes of ethics and institutional review boards, which are adopted by professional associations or institutions doing research (such as universities).
- Procedures imposed by the federal government (primarily to regulate biomedical research, but with bearing on social research).
- Legal regulation in the courts. (Reynolds, 1982, p. 100).

Following what has been identified as the "classic professionalism model," occupations and occupational incumbents attempt to convince the public, lawmakers, and other professionals that they are deserving of high respect, prestige, autonomy, privilege, and remuneration on the basis of two key elements (Hagan, 1975). The first is that the occupation begins to generate its own esoteric and useful knowledge. Many of the methodological issues addressed in this text are illustrative of major steps that have been taken in this direction. Unless criminologists and criminal justice researchers view themselves as simply efficient, bureaucratic technocrats or social accountants, it is essential that its incumbents ascribe to a code of ethics, a dedication to service or science in which trust, integrity, and ethicality is assumed. *Thus, on the basis of the knowledge and service (ethics) dimensions, occupations may claim or be granted autonomy or high professional regard.* Public askance of claims by car sales personnel, insurance agents, morticians, florists, and the like basically questions the relevance or applicability of this model to all who aspire. Criminologists and criminal justice investigators, unless they wish to be regarded in the same league as used car salespeople with a gimmick, must encourage the highest of ethical ideals not only in dealing with clients but also in conducting research. Furthermore, such regulation of conduct must be mandated from within the profession, rather than solely being imposed by outside government funding agencies (Hagan, 1975).

Some take strong issue with this view and see **professional ethics** as "a deceit and a snare"; a means by which the establishment within an occupation can control and hide its activity from the public and thereby create a monopoly. Even if the occupation takes its self-policing seriously, it is used as a club to control deviance of the more creative nonestablishment members whose new ideas are vital, particularly for young professions (Douglas, 1979, p. 13). Douglas feels that ethical rules are created for outside public consumption, so that an occupation can gain a monopoly, and have little impact within the group. On the other hand, this view may be overly cynical because, if a group refuses to set its own standards, whether rigid or flexible, it is solely at the mercy of outside regulatory groups (such as government agencies) to set standards for it. Douglas seems to view codes of ethics as a pincer attack on field studies by quantitative researchers within and government bureaucrats without. Revisions of the HHS guidelines to be discussed shortly may, in part, have calmed these fears.

Professional ethics

Ethics in Criminal Justice Research

In 1998, the Academy of Criminal Justice Sciences (ACJS) began drafting a code of ethics that included a research code of ethics. The American Society of Criminology developed a similar draft that year. This presentation is given very much in the same spirit used by the National Advisory Committee on Criminal Justice Standards and Goals in describing its **Ethical Principles for Criminal Justice Research**.

Ethical Principles for Criminal Justice Research

> The intent . . . is not to propose a rigid set of guidelines for each researcher to follow. Rather, the principles and recommendations call attention to contemporary issues that neither policymakers nor researchers may have considered in a systematic manner. The application of these principles and recommendations must be tailored to the needs of each individual research project according to the unique conditions that surround it. (National Advisory Committee, 1976, p. 38)

The last statement cannot be emphasized enough. Much of the academic guerrilla warfare taking place regarding ethical codes is a reaction to the Orwellian "big brother" approach in which dictating and controlling the research enterprise is common. Rigid commandments will only invite subterfuge and hypocrisy. Reynolds (1982, p. 103) indicates that "the development of federal procedures for prior review of research with human participants is dramatic evidence of the failure of associations to convince the public that their members are to be trusted as individuals or that the associations are to be trusted to control them."

Historically, the most important source of guidance for ethical research in the United States was the Department of Health, Education, and Welfare's

HEW guidelines for protection of human subjects **(HEW) Institutional Guide to DHEW Policy on Protection of Human Subjects** (1971), which requires that any grant recipients abide by its stipulations. Since 1980 the most important source has been that of the HHS. Both the codes of ethics of professional associations (internal controls) and federal requirements (external controls) are constantly changing.

History of Federal Regulation of Research

Until revision of the HHS guidelines in 1981, bitter debate took place between the social science research community and federal officials with respect to the applicability of informed consent requirements (at that time, HEW guidelines) to much of social science research. Initiated in the 1960s and eventually extended to all federally funded research, the guidelines required the informed consent of research participants as well as prior review by IRBs weighing the costs to participants versus the benefits to science and society. Although each agency, including the Department of Justice, had its own separate requirements, the HEW (now HHS) procedures were the most developed and tended to be adopted by the other agencies (Reynolds, 1982, p. 104). IRBs are research screening committees set up in colleges and universities to oversee the ethical propriety of research.

In a sense, the original HEW guidelines were comparable to a researcher's "Miranda warning"—basic information that must be assured with respect to the consent of research subjects. The original 1971 HEW guidelines contained six elements for obtaining informed consent (Code of Federal Regulations, 1975, pp. 11854–11858):

1. A fair explanation of the procedures to be followed and their purposes, including identifications of any experimental procedures.
2. A description of any attendant discomforts and risks that can be expected.
3. A description of any benefits reasonably to be expected.
4. A disclosure of any appropriate alternative procedures that might be advantageous for the subject.
5. An offer to answer any inquiries concerning the procedures.
6. Instruction that the person is free to withdraw consent and discontinue participation at any time without prejudice to him or her.

Because HEW supported both physical (particularly biomedical) and social science research, these rules originally applied equally. Some critics suggested that this marriage produced unworkable requirements, particularly when applied to field research.

Informed consent The requirement that sponsored research include provisions for making the subjects aware of the intentions of the study and sign **informed consent** forms obviously represented problems in field research of deviants. Weppner saw two problems that this requirement raised for *Street Ethnography* (1977, p. 41). The first is the possible desire of subjects, if engaged in deviant or illegal activity, to remain anonymous, and second, the difficulty of gaining informed consent from others who turn up on the scene but are not the primary subjects of observation. He felt that a strict interpretation of HEW guidelines would make street ethnography impossible and the ability of subjects to withdraw might also destroy random samples in other types of research. O'Connor, in reviewing revised recommendations of HEW guidelines, also felt that, "If the recommendations of the Commission are accepted as they stand, the covert observation debate, long an issue of contention within social research, will have been settled" (O'Connor, 1979, p. 253). The settlement would be a ban against such research. Talarico (1980, p. 207) views the issue as a two-edged sword in that important concerns for privacy may protect influential system officials from needed investigation. Should criminal justice become a subject that studies solely volunteers?

Assuming that the specter of criminal justice researchers as mad Nazi scientists is misplaced, and that professional investigators do not go out of their way to harm or threaten the well-being of respondents, some privacy invasion is necessary. Sometimes investigative research strategies involve deceit and infiltration as necessary approaches to studying hidden behavior. This intrusion is tolerable if potential harm to respondents is avoided and if the researcher takes adequate steps to assure that the respondents' identity is protected in any publications (Douglas, 1978). Such protection may include, as Denzin suggests, the decision to delete or not report certain portions. Publication is delayed until the subjects have left the scene, and thus the information is no longer threatening to their status (Denzin, 1989, p. 336).

Informed consent was viewed as applicable in controlled biomedical and psychological experimentation where researchers have definite plans for their subjects, but in fieldwork the issue was seen as less straightforward. Wax (1980, pp. 275–276) identifies six paradoxes of consent as applied to the practice of fieldwork:

1. Many people studied may be semiliterate and not accustomed to the legal argot of forms.
2. Many will distrust a situation requiring their endorsement of a piece of paper.
3. Consent of subjects is a continual process dependent on mutual learning and evolution.
4. Knowing nothing of ethnography, they have no basis upon which to decide to give or not to give consent.
5. Ethnography involves observation and discussion and not a rationalistic a priori analysis.
6. Fieldwork is an evolving process; thus the subjects of investigation are likely to shift during the course of study.

A related question is "Are all subjects equally deserving of informed consent?" Public figures and institutions can be observed by anyone and are less vulnerable than private citizens in private places (Thorne, 1980). The right to privacy may not apply to Hitler, Stalin, the Ku Klux Klan (KKK), or Murder Incorporated, (Fichter and Kolb, 1953). Galliher very lucidly makes this point:

While all people may be worthy of the same respect as human beings, it does not necessarily follow that their activities merit the same degree of protection and respect. As indicated earlier, Lofland questioned possible prohibitions on the undercover study of fascist groups. It is questionable whether the files of the American Nazi Party are deserving of the same respect as any other data source; must one secure the active cooperation of the Ku Klux Klan, or for that matter of the Pentagon, before conducting research in their organizations or with their personnel? While doing research in South Africa, van den Berge concluded "From the outset, I decided that I should have no scruples in deceiving the government...." The question is, how much honor is proper for the sociologist in studying the membership and organization of what he considers an essentially dishonorable, morally outrageous, and destructive enterprise? Is not the failure of sociology to uncover corrupt, illegitimate, covert practices of government or industry because of the supposed prohibitions of professional ethics tantamount to supporting such practices. (Galliher, 1973, p. 96)

Application of the same rule intended to protect the powerless from powerful institutions is misdirected (Galliher, 1980, p. 305). Applications of HEW standards to Woodward and Bernstein's Watergate investigations would have changed the course of American history (O'Connor, 1979, p. 264).

The Belmont Report

Reaction to concerns regarding written informed consent led to the National Research Act of 1974, which created the National Commission for the Protection of Human Subjects (NCPHS). NCPHS reviewed the HEW guidelines and developed revised guidelines, ***The Belmont Report****: Ethical Principles and Guidelines for the Protection of Human Subjects of Research*, in which it proposed altering the role of IRBs so as not to interfere with the investigator's freedom of research and recommended alteration of the informed consent in the case of field research (HEW, 1978). Chambers (1980, p. 331) indicates that a distinction is also made between biomedical and social science research, with the latter viewed as having lower potential risk and thus potentially subject to fewer restrictions in the review process.

O'Connor (1979), in a review of the implications of The Belmont Report, claims that many of the same restrictions on medical research still bind IRBs overseeing social science research.

The Belmont Report (National Commission for the Protection of Human Subjects, 1978) called for the recognition of *three basic principles*:

The principle of respect for persons
The principle of beneficence
The principle of justice

According to the *principle of respect for persons*, individuals are to be treated as autonomous agents, and, if autonomy is diminished, they are entitled to protection. The principle of respect for persons is realized through informed consent. The *principle of beneficence* requires that research not harm subjects and that possible benefits be maximized and potential harm minimized. This is

The Belmont Report

implemented through *risk-benefit assessment*. Finally, the *principle of justice* asks that both the benefits and burdens of research be distributed equitably through the selection of subjects (O'Connor, 1979, p. 229).

Perhaps the final resolution of the application of HEW regulations to social and behavioral research took place in January, 1981, with the publication of new regulations by the HHS. Taking into account most of the criticisms by social scientists of the original regulations, it virtually excludes most social science research from the regulations. The types of research excluded from the review requirements are survey or interview procedures, observations of public behavior, and the use of existing data if these are not linked to identifiers ("Regulations on the Protection of Human Subjects," 1981).

Institutional Review Boards (IRBs)

Since The Belmont Report, most of the decisions regarding protection of human subjects in research are under the purview of IRBs. Any research conducted within the jurisdiction of the university, its faculty, administration, or students is subject to its oversight. These committees consist of professors as well as professionals from the community who check research proposals in order to assure that no harmful procedures are employed, participants are not in harm's way and have availed informed consent, and subjects' privacy and confidentiality are protected. Studies should not begin until they have been approved by the IRB. Even though much social science research is exempt, it must still be reviewed. In such circumstances the proposal is usually given an expedited review. Although distinctions were to be made between biomedical and social science research, the same restrictions in the Belmont Report on medical research were still being used in overseeing social science research.

In response to the Belmont Report as well as criticism by social scientists of strict federal regulations designed to regulate biomedical research, major changes in the *HHS guidelines* and federal regulation of research took place on January 26, 1981 (Federal Register 46, no. 16, 8366–8392). These changes reduced dramatically HHS review over most social science research and placed the actual decisions involving studies in the hands of IRBs—committees at the researcher's home institution. Principal changes included the following:

- The regulations apply only to research with human subjects conducted with HHS or supported fully or in part by HHS funds.
- Most areas of social science and criminal justice research, for example, most field studies, are exempt from the regulations.
- Many projects (particularly routine biomedical research) are now qualified for "expedited" review, usually approval by only one member of the IRB.

The new federal regulations were viewed as minimal standards, and local IRBs could require higher standards if they wished. The new guidelines acknowledge that HHS has no jurisdiction over research receiving no federal funding.

Figure 2.2 illustrates the procedures one must address in order to have one's research proposal approved by an IRB. The actual procedures will vary, of course, by institution. Most are posted on college or university Web sites.

PAGE 1

Date Submitted: Advisor's Name (if applicable):
Investigator(s):   Advisor's Signature of Approval:
                                                       ☐ Check here if advisor has approved research
Address: Title of Research Project:
E-mail: Date of Initial Data Collection:
Telephone Number:

Please describe the proposed research and its purpose, in narrative form:

Indicate the materials, techniques, and procedures to be used (**submit copies of materials**):

PAGE 2

1. Do you have **external funding** for this research (money coming from outside the College)?
   Yes ☐   No ☐

   Funding Source (if applicable):_____

2. Will the participants in your study come from a **population requiring special protection**; in other words are your subjects someone other than Mercyhurst College students (i.e., children 17 years old or younger, elderly, criminals, welfare recipients, persons with disabilities, NCAA athletes)?   Yes ☐   No ☐

   If your participants include a population requiring special protection, describe how you will obtain consent from their legal guardians and/or from them directly to insure their full and free consent to participate.

   Indicate the approximate number of participants, the source of the participant pool, and recruitment procedures for your research:

   Will participants receive any payment or compensation for their participation in your research (*this includes money, gifts, extra credit, etc.*)?   Yes ☐   No ☐

   If yes, please explain:

3. Will the participants in your study be at any physical or psychological **risk** (risk is defined as any procedure that is invasive to the body, such as injections or drawing blood; any procedure that may

Figure 2.2
Mercyhurst College, Institutional Review Board Research Proposal.

cause undue fatigue; any procedure that may be of a sensitive nature, such as asking questions about sexual behaviors or practices) such that participants could be emotionally or mentally upset? Yes ☐   No ☐

Describe any harmful effects and/or risks to the participants' health, safety, and emotional or social well-being, incurred as a result of participating in this research, and how you will insure that these risks will be mitigated:

4. Will the participants in your study be **deceived** in any way while participating in this research? Yes ☐   No ☐

If your research makes use of any deception of the respondents, state what other alternative (e.g., non-deceptive) procedures were considered and why they weren't chosen:

5. Will you have a written **informed consent** form for participants to sign, and will you have appropriate **debriefing** arrangements in place?   Yes ☐   No ☐

PAGE 3

Describe how participants will be clearly and completely informed of the true nature and purpose of the research, whether deception is involved or not **(submit informed consent form and debriefing statement)**:

Please include the following statement at the bottom of your informed consent form: "Research at Mercyhurst College which involves human participants is overseen by the Institutional Review Board. Questions or problems regarding your rights as a participant should be addressed to Dr. Terry F. Pettijohn; Institutional Review Board Chair; Mercyhurst College; 501 East 38th Street, Erie, Pennsylvania 16546–0001; Telephone (814) 824–2371."

6. Describe the nature of the data you will collect and your procedures for insuring that **confidentiality** is maintained, both in the record keeping and presentation of this data:

7. Identify the potential **benefits** of this research on research participants and humankind in general.

Please submit this file and accompanying materials to the IRB Chair, Terry Pettijohn, via electronic mail (tpettijohn@mercyhurst.edu) for review *(revised 8/2003 tfp)*.

Source: Reproduced with permission of the Mercyhurst College Institutional Review Board.

Figure 2.2
Continued

Research Activities Exempt from HHS Review

Research activities exempt from HHS review include research in educational settings related to normal educational practices, such as curriculum strategies and instructional techniques. Also exempt is research using educational tests, as long as confidentiality is maintained. Most important to social science researchers is the general exemption for research involving survey or interview procedures, except where all of the following conditions exist:

Responses are recorded in such a manner that the human subjects can be identified, directly or through identifiers linked to subjects.

The subject's responses, if they became known outside the research, could reasonably place the subject at risk of criminal or civil liability or be damaging to the subject's financial standing or employability.

The research deals with sensitive aspects of the subject's own behavior such as illegal conduct, drug use, sexual behavior, or use of alcohol. All research involving survey or interview procedures is exempt, without exception, when the respondents are elected or appointed public officials or candidates for public office.

Similarly, research involving the observation (including observation by participants) of public behavior is exempt, except where all of the following conditions exist:

Observations are recorded in such a manner that the human subjects can be identified, directly or through identifiers linked to the subjects.

The observations recorded about the individual, if they became known outside the research, could reasonably place the subject at risk of criminal or civil liability or be damaging to the subject's financial standing or employability.

The research deals with sensitive aspects of the subject's own behavior such as illegal conduct, drug use, sexual behavior, or use of alcohol.

Research involving the study of existing data, documents, records, pathological specimens, or diagnostic specimens is exempt, if these sources are publicly available or if the information is recorded by the investigator in such a manner that subjects cannot be identified, directly or through identifiers linked to the subjects (*Federal Register* [January 26, 1981], 386–388).

The specific areas identified for expedited review had relevance primarily to biochemical rather than social science research, for example, the use of medical and dental diagnostic equipment. The one area that had some relevance was studies of perception, cognition, game theory, or test development in which there is little stress placed on, or manipulation of, subjects (*Federal Register* [January 26, 1981], 8392).

Projects that are not exempt still require full review, in which case the IRB must weigh the cost and benefits of such studies.

> [T]he IRB is expected to consider the extent to which risks to the participants are minimized, the relationships between risks and anticipated benefits of research, and the importance of the knowledge to be developed. The IRB will also consider the equitable selection of subjects and the acquisition and documentation of informed consent, it will monitor participants when necessary to ensure their safety and make provisions for protecting their privacy. If participants are vulnerable to coercion (such as mental patients and children), additional safeguards should be considered. (Reynolds, 1982, p. 106)

The "Elements of Informed Consent" applicable to nonexempt programs detail specific guarantees to subjects required of all projects, additional requirements for more hazardous projects, exceptions for evaluations of existing public programs, and exceptions for "deceptive research" in which subjects are informed afterward so as not to destroy the scientific purposes of the project (*Federal Register* [January 26, 1981], 8389–8390). These are expanded requirements of the original HEW guidelines discussed previously. There are fewer objections by social researchers now, because most of their projects are exempt.

In reviewing federal regulation of research, the National Research Act of 1974 had created IRBs to monitor research, but ambiguous guidelines from the HEW and the utilization of biomedical guideposts created a storm of protests from social scientists. The revised regulations represented a victory of sorts for the social sciences.

Initially, the withdrawal of some government regulation over many areas of social research was a recognition that professional groups will regulate their own ethical conduct. However, giving much of the regulatory power to IRBs may have opened yet again a "Pandora's box." Ferrell and Hamm (1998, p. xiv) indicate:

> Beginning in the late 1970s, but not fully taking hold until the 1990s, Institutional Review Boards (IRBs) at most colleges and universities have made ethnographic work on criminal and deviant groups almost impossible to conduct. Even the new Code of Ethics of the American Sociological Association yields to the decisions of these boards, claiming that if projects are disapproved by these agencies, the research, in the association's eyes, is unethical. Potentially gone, then, is any ethnographic research involving a covert role for the investigator (thus removing hidden populations further from view), any ethnographic research on minors that does not obtain parental consent (obviously problematic for youth involved in deviance and crime or who are victims of parental abuse), and any ethnographic research on vulnerable

populations or sensitive (including criminal) issues without signed consent forms that explicitly indicate the researcher's inability to protect subjects' confidentiality.

Ferrell and Hamm (1998, p. xv) conclude that government forces do not believe that researchers can police themselves. Berg (2007, p. 65) points out some of the controversy related to IRB's expansion of their authority and potentially challenging academic freedom in research. Initially created to review consent agreements to protect human subjects in federally funded research, over time they expanded their mandate to include all research in institutions funded or unfunded. The gauntlet of obtaining IRB approval before undertaking a research project may have forced some to throw in the towel and not pursue some research projects. Perhaps the IRBs became too big for their britches.

National Institute of Justice's Human Subject Protection Requirements

NIJ's Regulations on Confidentiality

National Institute of Justice's **(NIJ's) Regulations on Confidentiality** protect individuals by forbidding the use of any research or statistical information that might identify them. In addition, the institute has adopted the HHS *Model Policy on Human Research Subjects*. This policy requires that each institution engaged in NIJ research provide written assurance that it will comply with these regulations as codified at 45 Code of Federal Regulations (CFR) paragraph 46. Pursuant to that policy, each research project falling within the guidelines established by HHS must be approved by the recipient's IRB prior to initiation of the project. Approval by the IRB need not precede the submission of a proposal to NIJ, but it must be obtained prior to the beginning of any research activity (NIJ, 1994). Applicants should file their plans to protect sensitive information as part of their proposal. Necessary safeguards are detailed in 28 CFR paragraph 22. A short "how-to" guideline for developing a privacy and confidentiality plan can be obtained from NIJ program managers.

In addition, the U.S. Department of Justice has adopted human subjects policies similar to those established by the U.S. Department of Health and Human Services. In general, these policies exempt most NIJ-supported research from IRB review. However, the institute may find in certain instances that subjects or subject matters may require IRB review. These exemptions will be decided on an individual basis during application review. Researchers are encouraged to review 28 CFR 46, paragraph 46.101, to determine their individual project requirements (NIJ, 1994, p. 30). While admitting that IRBs have done much to protect human subjects, some feel that we have unnecessarily handicapped researchers who pose little harm to subjects and that we should exempt such low-risk studies from federal regulation (Shamoo, 2007: B16). Current policies may accomplish this in part through "expedited review" in which a member of the IRB may give a quick approval of such low-risk research. The American Association of University Professors' Committee on Academic Freedom and Tenure issued a report in 2006 indicating that IRBs may have overextended their reach into areas such as oral history, cultural anthropology, and journalism, which involve little risk. Such regulation may violate the First Amendment by restraining a faculty member's speech (Shamoo, 2007: B16). Similar regulation of studies involving public data and undergraduate research projects should also be exempt.

The federal policy on human subjects that formerly applied to HHS research (45 CFR 46, A) has now been adopted by seventeen federal agencies including the Justice Department (28 CFR 46, 512, and 22). Subpart A, known as the *Common Rule*, may be found at http://ohrp.osophs.dhhs.gov/ under the category "policy guidance." It requires that informed consent include a statement about how the researcher will maintain confidentiality (Sieber, 2001, p. 2).

Confidentiality of Criminal Justice Research

Regulations on the confidentiality of research and statistical data were enacted as part of the 1973 amendment to the Omnibus Crime Control and Safe Streets Act. Section 524(a) reads:

> Except as provided by Federal law other than this title, no officer or employee of the Federal Government, nor any recipient of assistance under the provisions of this title, shall use or reveal any research or statistical information furnished under this title by any person and identifiable to any specific private person for any purpose other than the purpose for which it was obtained in accordance with the title. Copies of such information shall be immune from legal process, and shall not, without consent of the person furnishing such information, be admitted as evidence or used for any purpose in any action, suit, or other judicial or administrative proceedings. (LEAA, 1979, p. 1)

This law basically constitutes a "shield law" for researchers performing federally funded research. **Shield laws** constitute a governmental immunity from prosecution; a state-guaranteed right to confidentiality for researchers if they are subpoenaed. "All identifiable research or statistical information is with limited exceptions, immune from administrative or judicial process" (Dahmann and Sasfy, 1982, p. 13). Investigators may be encouraged to probe more sensitive topics because they are able to protect their data. This law also protects respondents by ensuring that the data they have provided will not be used to invade their privacy. Guidelines such as those of the HHS or NIJ are, of course, established, issued, and promulgated by federal agencies, that is, governmental bodies outside of the occupation. They are intended for data gathered under their auspices or sponsorship. Of primary concern is the fact that the Freedom of Information Act of 1976 makes it possible for individuals to obtain access to nonclassified information that is collected with public funds. This could include field data that could compromise confidentiality (Chambers, 1980, p. 332). Trend, for instance, describes a project in which he was involved where, after the fact, the General Accounting Office (GAO) requested "unrestricted access to certain records" he and others had gathered as part of a Housing and Urban Development project.

Shield laws

They wanted the case files so that an audit could check family sizes and incomes as part of an eligibility study (Trend, 1980, p. 344). Eventually, a compromise was worked out that allowed a GAO audit while maintaining confidentiality. Trend, as a result of his experience, offers the following advice:

> Telling people to read the contract they sign, to know how far they're willing to go if pressed, and to not make promises they cannot keep all seems pretentious and sappy. . . . In the end, the best advice I can give is to not be gulled into thinking that your notes are sacrosanct and nobody can get to them no matter what. If you're sure of your contract, your client, and your own resolve, then promising confidentiality in writing may increase the chances that you can maintain it. However, if none of those prerequisites obtain, then the time to stop and think is before you start the research. (Trend, 1980, p. 348)

In 1972, the U.S. Supreme Court ruled that journalists had no right to refuse to name their sources. Despite this, as of 2007, 33 states and the District of Columbia have enacted shield laws for journalists (Kiely, 2007: 5A). Without guarantees of confidentiality, there is less of a chance that whistleblowers and informants will provide important information. In many important cases, prosecutors have attempted to turn journalists into witnesses and to have them break their promises of confidentiality. Confidential information was instrumental in revealing abuses at Walter Reed Hospital, torture at Abu Ghraib prison, Watergate, Enron, and drug scandals in professional sports. In 2007, the U.S. House of Representatives passed legislation prohibiting courts and federal prosecutors from forcing journalists to violate confidentiality except in cases vital to national security or in prosecuting a crime that is not available by any other means (When Reporters Can't Shield, 2007: 12A). As of July, 2008, the House of Representatives had passed such federal shield law legislation. At the time, the U.S. Senate and President Bush opposed such legislation even though the House bill still required reporters to disclose sources in the case of national security.

EXHIBIT 2.4 ▶

Code of Research Ethics of the Academy of Criminal Justice Sciences (ACJS)

Objectivity and Integrity in the Conduct of Criminal Justice Research

1. Members of the Academy should adhere to the highest possible technical standards in their research.
2. Since individual members of the Academy vary in their research modes, skills, and experience, they should acknowledge the limitations that may affect the validity of their findings.
3. In presenting their work, members of the Academy are obliged to fully report their findings. They should not misrepresent the findings of their research or omit significant data. Details of their theories, methods, and research designs that might bear upon interpretations of research findings should be reported.
4. Members of the Academy should fully report all sources of financial support and other sponsorship of the research.

5. Members of the Academy should not make any commitments to respondents, individuals, groups, or organizations unless there is full intention and ability to honor them.

6. Consistent with the spirit of full disclosure of method and analysis, members of the Academy, after they have completed their own analyses, should cooperate in efforts to make raw data and pertinent documentation available to other social scientists, at reasonable costs, except in cases where confidentiality, the client's rights to propriety information and privacy, or the claims of a field worker to the privacy of personal notes necessarily would be violated.

7. Members of the Academy should provide adequate information, documentation, and citations concerning scales and other measures used in their research.

8. Members of the Academy should not accept grants, contracts, or research assignments that appear likely to violate the principles enunciated in this Code, and should disassociate themselves from research when they discover a violation and are unable to correct it.

9. When financial support for a project has been accepted, members of the Academy should make every reasonable effort to complete the proposed work on schedule.

10. When a member of the Academy is involved in a project with others, including students, there should be mutually accepted explicit agreements at the outset with respect to division of work, compensation, access to data, rights of authorship, and other rights and responsibilities.

11. Members of the Academy have the right to disseminate research findings, except those likely to cause harm to clients, collaborators, and participants, those which violate formal or implied promises of confidentiality, or those which are proprietary under a formal or informal agreement.

Disclosure and Respect of the Rights of Research Populations by Members of the Academy

12. Members of the Academy should not misuse their positions as professionals for fraudulent purposes or as a pretext for gathering intelligence for any individual, group, organization, or government.

13. Human subjects have the right to full disclosure of the purposes of the research as early as it is appropriate to the research process, and they have the right to an opportunity to have their questions answered about the purpose and usage of the research.

14. Subjects of research are entitled to rights of personal confidentiality unless they are waived.

15. Information about subjects obtained from records that are open to public scrutiny cannot be protected by guarantees of privacy or confidentiality.

16. The process of conducting criminal justice research should not expose respondents to more than minimal risk of personal harm, and members of the Academy should make every effort to ensure the safety and security of respondents and project staff. Informed consent should be obtained when the risks of research are greater than the risks of everyday life.

17. Members of the Academy should take culturally appropriate steps to secure informed consent and to avoid invasions of privacy. In addition, special actions will be necessary where the individuals studied are illiterate, under correctional supervision, minors, have low social status, are under judicial supervision, have diminished capacity, are unfamiliar with social research, or otherwise occupy a position of unequal power with the researcher.

18. Members of the Academy should seek to anticipate potential threats to confidentiality. Techniques such as the removal of direct identifiers, the use of randomized responses, and other statistical solutions to problems of privacy should be used where appropriate. Care should be taken to ensure secure storage, maintenance, and/or destruction of sensitive records.

19. Confidential information provided by research participants should be treated as such by members of the Academy, even when this information enjoys no legal protection or privilege and legal force is applied. The obligation to respect confidentiality also applies to members of research organizations (interviewers, coders, clerical staff, etc.) who have access to the information.

20. While generally adhering to the norm of acknowledging the contributions of all collaborators, members of the Academy should be sensitive to harm that may arise from disclosure and respect a collaborator's need for anonymity.

21. All research should meet the human subjects' requirements imposed by educational institutions and funding sources.

22. Members of the Academy should comply with appropriate federal and institutional requirements pertaining to the conduct of their research.

Source: The full code of ethics is available on the Associations' Web site: *www.ACJS.ORG*

In addition to governmental regulations, more fully developed professions attempt to police themselves and to establish their own guideposts for ethical conduct. In 1998, the ACJS adopted and in 2001 the American Society of Criminology was deliberating codes of ethics for research.

Ethical Issues in Criminology/Criminal Justice Research

From what has been thus far indicated, there is no limit to ethical issues confronting criminal justice researchers (Adamitis and Haghighi, 1989). Criminal justice researchers adhere to most of these principles as a matter of professionalism, although as we will see, rigid adherence to a checklist is simplistic and does a disservice to the complexity of the research experience. These guidelines are often difficult to interpret in individual cases. The codes of ethics include that the criminal justice researcher take personal responsibility to:

- Avoid procedures that may harm respondents.
- Honor commitments to respondents and respect reciprocity.
- Exercise objectivity and professional integrity in performing and reporting research.
- Protect confidentiality and privacy of respondents.

Avoid Research That May Harm Respondents

As a general rule, in the name of science, *researchers should not conduct studies that may be harmful to subjects*, particularly if the potential harm has not been explained to the subjects and their informed consent elicited. The National Advisory Committee on Criminal Justice Standards and Goals suggests that participants give their formal consent to serve as subjects, based on full knowledge of the experiment (National Advisory Committee, 1976, p. 38).

It is the researcher's duty to assume personal responsibility for all phases of the project as it may potentially impinge on the well-being of subjects. If, after considering the ethicality of research, problematic areas still exist, the investigator should seek out advice from university, professional, or governmental committees to ensure adequate safeguards. Failure of a researcher to obtain informed consent or give full disclosure of the study to respondents increases the need to safeguard confidentiality. Thus, when deception is necessary in a study, it becomes more incumbent on the people conducting the study to prevent harm and where appropriate debrief, reassure, and explain the project afterward to subjects (Lee, 1993).

The informed consent issue is a complex one, particularly in correctional research. As experimentation entails unequal or different treatment of experimental and control groups, is the unequal treatment justified for research or scientific purposes? There is a major issue of informed consent in prison research. Communication beforehand as to who is in the treatment and who is not creates "reactivity" or "Hawthorne effects." There are studies in which the aim is to hide the treatment in order not to arouse anxiety.

The protection of human subject guidelines is also viewed as proposing a **risk/benefit ratio**, wherein the potential benefits must outweigh the possible hazards to respondents. That is, some risks are justified as long as the scientific knowledge gained exceeds the potential harm. Douglas (1979, p. 30) perhaps correctly suggests that in the final analysis the attempt to rationalize a cost-benefit analysis of research borders on the simplistic in that the conclusion is almost always going to be ruled in favor of science. Such a decision-making process converts the researcher into a "moral administrator" who assumes the right to inflict harm on the subjects in the name of science—once again the mad scientist hangup (Reiman, 1979, p. 45). Although an interesting philosophical debate, the fact of the matter is that most criminal justice researchers simply have no interest in being Dr. Frankenstein. Obviously, any research that is likely to impose long-term harm on participants is anathema to ethical concepts of investigation. In the name of research one should not espouse behavior that would not be considered acceptable in normal interpersonal conduct. The exclusion of most social science research from review by HHS guidelines was a frank recognition that there has been little documented harm associated with such studies.

Risk/benefit ratio

Honor Commitments to Respondents and Respect Reciprocity

Researchers have an ethical responsibility to keep any promises or agreements made with subjects during and after the course of study. The notion of **reciprocity** involves a mutual trust and obligation between researcher and subject. The researcher would have been unable to obtain information without the cooperation of participants who were willing to share information of themselves in the belief that the investigator is obliged not to betray this trust by using the information in an inappropriate manner or one that may prove harmful or embarrassing to the subject. Klockars feels that simple researcher–subject models such as in biomedical research do not begin to capture the complexity of reciprocal obligations in field research.

Reciprocity

> Vincent was not only my subject but also my teacher, student, fence, friend and guide. Likewise to Vincent, I was not only researcher but biographer, confidant, customer, friend, and student. These roles, most of which involve multiple obligations and responsibilities and expectations, are potentially in conflict not only in the researcher-subject dimensions but in other dimensions as well. To speak of the working relationship between the life historian and his subject as a researcher-subject relationship simply misconstrues what happens in the context of life history work. The researcher who treats his friends as subjects will soon find that he has neither. (Klockars, 1977, p. 218)

Exercise Objectivity and Professional Integrity in Performing and Reporting Research

Honesty, integrity, and *objectivity* are essential expectations of ethical professional conduct. The researcher should attempt to maintain a value-free, politically indifferent approach to the subject matter. Personal, subjective feelings should be kept separate from a disinterested scientific study of things as they are. The researcher first and foremost is an investigator, not a hustler, huckster, salesperson, or politician. Researchers should bar themselves from studying subjects or subject matter for which they feel they cannot properly control potential subjectivity such as a strong aversion or affinity toward the object of investigation.

It is important that researchers be frank and honest in conducting their affairs. Researchers should not misrepresent their research abilities or generalize beyond their data. The researcher, in addition to having a concern for accuracy, should avoid any statistical misrepresentations of findings or purposely choose techniques that are most likely to produce positive results. Unethical practices or sponsors who attempt to control the outcome should be avoided. Finally, the researcher has a responsibility to communicate results to professional audiences that are in the best position to judge the findings. Of course, the investigator should always give proper acknowledgment to others who assisted in the research.

An example of a fake survey that clearly violated the rules of integrity was conducted by Francis Flynn of Columbia University's Business School (Foster, 2001). In 2001, Flynn wrote a letter on department stationery to 250 restaurant owners in New York City indicating that he had been stricken with food poisoning after eating at their establishments. Flynn claimed to be conducting a study of how owners respond to polite versus enraged-sounding customer complaints. When one owner contacted the Dean of the Business School, the project was canceled and letters of apology sent to the restaurant owners.

Protect Confidentiality and Privacy of Respondents

Erikson takes a very rigid stand in suggesting that the criminal justice researcher should avoid deliberate misrepresentations of his or her identity when entering the private realm of subjects' lives, which otherwise would be barred to the researcher. He feels that it is generally unethical to misrepresent the purpose of research (Erikson, 1978, p. 244). Although such an inflexible view is not always appropriate, its general applicability to much research is warranted. To give a personal example of naiveté regarding this matter, the author, while doing field research for a graduate thesis, ineptly handled this privacy matter and almost sabotaged a research project.

In researching life in the early development of the new town of Columbia, Maryland, the author began attending many community meetings to get a feel of the temper of the pioneers in the young community. Having spotted an announcement in the local paper of a meeting of the "Informal Discussion Group," whose topic was to be the "Economics of New Towns," the author, after consulting with his research mentor, attended the meeting. As perhaps should have been surmised by the group's name, the meeting was very "informal" with less than ten people in attendance and conversation never got around to the scheduled topic. The main point of discussion revolved around griping by the residents about feeling like they were living in a glass bowl. Sightseers on weekends created traffic jams outside their homes; national news magazines had interviewed, at one time or another, nearly everyone in the room or members of their family. Worse yet, one person complained that he heard that the developer was bringing in his behavioral scientists to see if "us rats are running the maze properly." At this point the author began to feel very uncomfortable as I had failed to announce my purposes beforehand or ask permission to attend the session. Finally, since everyone but the author had participated in the discussion, one person indicated that he had not heard anything from me. I then proceeded to explain that I was a graduate student doing research, and he (a local councilman) took down my name and affiliation. Not surprisingly, the meeting ended almost immediately afterwards even though I tried to explain that I was a harmless researcher and not a spy for the developer. Needless to say I regretted my naiveté in not making known my presence from the beginning, and the feeling of having invaded one of the last privileged sanctuaries of the harassed residents was very much impressed upon me. The very next day a representative of the developer (who had obviously heard from the councilman) requested and had a meeting with the author and his mentor, and to his credit offered to assist in my research on the community as long as the data gathering would avoid direct participant observation. A study of the planning process was viewed as far less obtrusive under the circumstances. (Hagan, 1968, p. 128)

The folly of naively approaching the research setting without making one's presence known is certainly illustrated by this example. But what about secret observation? Erikson's stance (1978) would exclude many subjects from inquiry. Roth (1962) suggests that in a sense most research design in the social sciences involves a level of deceit, because the exact nature of the study is often hidden. The revelation of the true purpose would either bias the outcome or eliminate the possibility of research (Henslin, 1972, p. 48). To answer a question we asked earlier in this chapter, criminal justice should not restrict its research targets to volunteers.

Confidentiality.
All social science researchers, including criminal justice investigators, have a special obligation to protect the **confidentiality** of such information.   Confidentiality

As indicated previously, confidentiality of government-sponsored research is guaranteed in Section 524(a) of the Omnibus Crime Control Act of 1973 as amended. In gaining access to confidential government data, the criminal justice researcher is generally interested in identification of subjects for sampling and follow-up purposes.

Researchers rarely require records containing the direct identification of individuals or organizations except during the initial stages of a project when possible personal identifiers should be deleted or destroyed or if needed for follow-up *link files* (which match coder identifiers to personal identifiers) should be stored in a remote and secure location. (National Advisory Committee, 1976, pp. 42–43)

Government-sponsored research appears to provide safeguards to ensure confidentiality of data. What of the private researcher?

Ethical Problems

Unlike priests, doctors, or other client-oriented practitioners, the independent criminal justice researcher has no legally recognized privilege of confidentiality. Such researchers are then potentially vulnerable to subpoena . In that sense, social science researchers find themselves in a situation akin to the journalist in which they must decide whether they would be willing to go to jail rather than violate confidentiality. Soloway and Walters (1977), in examining Pennsylvania Penal Code and decisions on this matter, clarify some of the issues regarding researcher complicity or culpability. In most instances the researcher would actually have had to assist, aid, or abet the actual commission of a specific criminal act to be liable under statutes in that state. Soloway and Walters proclaimed this warning:

> Let us not bask too very long in this unaccustomed legal comfort, for, while such laws seem to relieve us of responsibility prior to a governmental investigation, they pertain very little after such an investigation has begun. Once a criminal investigation and/or prosecution has commenced, we are still absolved of a legal responsibility to come forward, of our own accord, with our information. Once summoned to so testify, however, we have no legal recourse but to divulge our information and its source under the threat and consequence of a contempt citation. This was made amply clear in the U.S. Supreme Court's landmark decision in 1972 against Paul Branzburg, a journalist investigating junkies in Kentucky, and Earl Caldwell, a journalist investigating the Black Panthers and other militant black organizations. (Soloway and Walters, 1977, p. 175)

These decisions held basically that a journalist or investigator had no privilege to refuse appearance before a grand jury or to decline answering questions regarding sources or information received in confidence. James (1972, p. 139) is the only case Soloway and Walters could find that involved a scientific investigator being subpoenaed. In this case the subpoena was dropped when the investigator produced a previously signed agreement to safeguard the confidentiality of sources.

Wolfgang (1981, 1982) reports that in his cohort study (Wolfgang et al., 1972) four respondents admitted involvement in criminal homicide and seventy-five were involved in forcible rape for which none of them had been arrested. Members of the research staff could have theoretically been prosecuted for "misprision of a felony" (being accessories after the fact), which, although outdated in most states, is a federal offense.

Two anthologies explore this "no man's land" of field research. Ferrell and Hamm's (1998) *Ethnography at the Edge* and Miller and Tewksbury's *Extreme Methods* (2001) examine ethical dilemmas raised in studying active criminals in their natural settings. Other researchers who have faced hazards in conducting their research have included: James Inciardi (1993), who was arrested while conducting research in a crack house and also had a price put on his head by a crack dealer; Bourgois (1989) was heavily questioned by police during his research on the crack economy; while Armstrong (1993) was arrested and threatened during his field research on British soccer fans.

Longmire (1983) in a survey of a sample of members of the American Society of Criminology found that 63 percent indicated having experienced one or more ethical dilemmas. With respect to ethical problems impacting on participants, the biggest problem was confidentiality problems, with 9 percent so indicating. Professional ethical issues were more of a problem, with 27 percent indicating that they had experienced pressure to engage in undesired research. This involves primarily academic institutions "twisting the arm" of researchers to pursue research in areas for which there is grant money.

Although vulnerability to subpoena is an ever-present threat to social science researchers, Reynolds (1979) was able to find fewer than a dozen such cases, and most incidents seemed to involve newspersons.

In discussing the run-in with the law of Yablonsky (1968a), author of *The Hippie Trip*, Irwin states that:

> There has been some concern expressed over the danger of arrest while studying criminals, mainly because the researcher will have firsthand knowledge of felonies and misdemeanors. . . . To my knowledge the closest anybody ever came to having legal sanctions imposed on him because of his research was Lewis Yablonsky. . . . The judge asked him nine times if he had witnessed Gridley [one of his informants] smoking marijuana. Yablonsky refused to answer because of the rights guaranteed him in the Fifth Amendment of the United States Constitution. Although he did not actually receive any legal sanctioning, he stated that the incident was humiliating and suggested that researchers should have guarantees of immunity. Despite this case, I feel there is small risk of being prosecuted. If we keep our "heads straight" and avoid being sucked in or bowled over by the criminal world, and thereby do not slip or plunge into greater complicity than knowledge of crimes, we actually do have immunity. (Irwin, 1972, pp. 128–129; see also Yablonsky, 1968b)

In 1979, political scientist Samuel Popkin became the first American professor incarcerated for defending his right to maintain confidentiality regarding *The Pentagon Papers*. Popkin had refused to reveal his sources to a federal grand jury and subsequently spent one week in jail until the jury was dismissed (Wolfgang, 1982, p. 395).

The Brajuha Case (Weinstein Decision)

In April of 1984, Judge Jack B. Weinstein of the U.S. Eastern District Court of New York ruled that:

> Serious scholars [Mario Brajuha] cannot be required to turn over their fieldnotes in a grand jury investigation when the government fails to establish a "substantial need" for them to do so. Weinstein's ruling establishes a "qualified priv1ilege not to reveal documents or confidential sources" for social science researchers, akin to the privileges enjoyed by journalists. . . . According to Weinstein, "Serious scholars are entitled to no less protection than journalists." (Erikson, 1984)

The *Weinstein decision* cited as support the American Sociological Association's code of ethics, which indicates that "Confidential information provided by research participants must be treated as such by sociologists, even when this information enjoys no legal protection or privilege and legal force is applied" (Erikson, 1984).

The researcher in this case was Mario Brajuha, a sociology graduate student at SUNY–Stony Brook, who had been subpoenaed by a grand jury investigating a restaurant fire. He had been doing a participant observation study of the restaurant as a waiter for ten months prior to the fire and had collected data for his dissertation.

The Weinstein decision was appealed by the prosecutors and, in a directive issued by the court of appeals judge, a compromise of sorts was struck. Brajuha's defense attorney prepared an edited version of Brajuha's field notes, which was accepted as sufficient to satisfy the original subpoena and dismissed the case against him. As Brajuha's attorney explains:

> From the beginning, Mr. Brajuha was prepared to testify as to his observations and nonprivileged communications. . . . In the context of this case, a claim of privilege with respect to (his) observations was unnecessary. The issues in this litigation centered around the portions of the research journal which contained communications with privileged sources and matters of personal privacy, for example, opinions. (Thaler, 1985, p. 1)

A standard procedure for attempting to protect the identity of subjects, organizations, or communities is the use of **pseudonyms** (false names) in publications. "Doc," "Chic," "The Lupollo Family," "Deep Throat," "Wincanton,"

Pseudonyms

"Cornerville," "Slumtown," and "Middletown" are but a few of the many aliases given such subjects often to little avail. For instance, even the Trobriand islanders were aware of Malinowski's books, and one even indicated that he did not understand their system of clans and chiefs (Barnes, 1970). Gans in *The Urban Villagers* (1962) noted that during an election in the same West End Boston area Whyte had studied, one of the candidates had received negative voter reaction based in part on Whyte's description of the individual years ago in *Streetcorner Society* (1955).

Despite Klockars' efforts to protect his fence's identity, vanity won the day:

> I also told Vincent that I would not reveal his identity unless it meant that I was going to jail if I did not, and he told me that he really could not expect me to do more. These contingencies notwithstanding, Vincent just could not resist a little advance publicity.
>
> He told everybody—judges, lawyers, politicians, prosecutors, thieves, hustlers, and most of his good customers. He started this word-of-mouth publicity campaign a full year before the book appeared in the *New York Times Book Review*; anyone who did not know who Vincent Swaggi really was simply confessing that they were outsiders to the Philadelphia scene. (Klockars, 1977, p. 214)

Vincent even sold and gave away autographed copies in his store, although he turned down offers to appear on nationally televised talk shows. Threats to researchers may come from many sources. In the Ofshe case the threat was from an organization he studied, whereas in the Hutchinson case it was from a member of Congress.

The Ofshe Case

Organizations or individuals may file lawsuits against researchers. In the 1960s, Synanon (a drug rehabilitation program headquarters in California) had received widespread, positive, national publicity. In the early 1970s, Richard Ofshe, professor of sociology at the University of California at Berkeley, began an investigation of the organization and, along with journalist colleagues, began to uncover and expose patterns of extreme violence and intimidation employed by Synanon. In addition to scholarly works and an investigative newspaper series, Ofshe and colleagues published a book which was later the basis of a CBS television movie (Maldonado, 1987).

Since 1979, the Synanon foundation has filed three lawsuits charging Ofshe with libel and slander. Although the cases were eventually dismissed or charges were dropped by the Synanon litigants, Ofshe was fortunately assisted by the University of California at Berkeley with legal costs, since the basis of the suits rested on his academic research. In 1987, Ofshe was awarded over $500,000 for costs of litigation by a Marin County judge in connection with his fight against the Synanon suits. "Based on a preliminary review, the amount is believed to be one of the most substantial costs of litigation ever granted to an academic in a case involving pursuit of research and academic freedom" (Maldonado,

1987, p. 3). Ofshe is continuing to press his legal case, charging Synanon with malicious prosecution and hoping for a ruling that the suits were a form of harassment and attack on academic freedom.

The Hutchinson Case

During the 1950s, the United States went through a period of "anti-Communist" hysteria led by Senator Joseph McCarthy of Wisconsin. Many people had their careers and lives ruined by innuendos that they were, or had been, associated with Communists. During this period, intellectual debate was intimidated or closed as researchers and others retreated from controversial topics and the onslaught of political demagoguery. Beginning in the 1970s, a new brand of McCarthyism presented itself, although this time the device was public ridicule and the charge against its targets was that federally funded researchers were "ripping off" the taxpayers' money on useless studies of "ridiculous" topics.

Ironically, one of the chief engineers of the new McCarthyism was the very man who took the senatorial seat of the late Joseph McCarthy, the late senator William Proxmire. Through his infamous "Golden Fleece of the Month Awards," Proxmire intended to call public attention to the waste of public tax money on research works whose titles sounded absurd. This ridicule of specific research impugned the integrity and motivation of the researchers themselves, in particular, Ronald Hutchinson. According to the Fund to Protect Scholars from Defamation (1980):

> Possibly because of Proxmire's bias against social scientists, Ron's work was selected for an "award" and, although he has admitted the statement to be inaccurate, Proxmire issued a press release charging that Ron had personally received a half million dollars in research funds. Proxmire also charged that Ron had "made a fortune from his monkeys." Focusing ridicule on the fact that some of Ron's work involved jaw clenching as a measure of aggression, Proxmire accused him of taking a "bite out of the taxpayers" and characterized seven years of scientific research as "monkey business," "transparently worthless," and "nonsense which had 'made a monkey out of the American taxpayer.'" Representatives of agencies which funded the research, however, described it as "of particular importance," "well designed," "well executed," "valid," "sound," and a "moderate expenditure." ONR [Office of Naval Research] described the research as the first objective testing system for measuring and examining aggressive behavior. In addition to his written statements, Proxmire also ridiculed Ron's work in radio and television shows and either directed or permitted his aides to pressure agencies funding Ron's research to terminate funding.
>
> The "Golden Fleece" was a disaster in Ron's life and those associated with him, as it has been in the lives of other recipients. In order to continue his work, Ron set up a laboratory at his own expense. In 1976–1977 his salary was only 33 percent of what it had been in

1974–1975. The scholarly work of a productive scientist was seriously disrupted. The effect was not limited to his professional life. As a result of the sarcastic and demeaning publicity, his children were embarrassed at school. Each press release brought with it still other invasions of his privacy in the form of phone calls and "hate" mail. Those of us who were close to him at the time know that he was subjected to extreme physical and emotional stress.

In a law suit finally brought before the Supreme Court, Hutchinson and Proxmire agreed to settle out of court. Besides a public apology on the floor of the Senate by Proxmire, payment was made to Hutchinson of $10,000 from Proxmire's own personal funds. While Hutchinson encumbered huge legal fees, the U.S. Senate paid Proxmire's legal bills of around $130,000. (Fund to Protect Scholars from Defamation, 1980)

Important in the Supreme Court's willingness to hear this case was its decision that research scientists could sue for defamation of character even if they were receiving federal research funds and that senatorial privilege did not extend to remarks made outside the Senate chamber.

Although the Hutchinson case represents the most glaring example of what has been characterized as the new McCarthyism, more subtle attacks certainly continue. A related concern is the possibility that criminal justice and other social science researchers will concentrate inquiry into fundable, safe, societally directed areas and thus avoid controversy or studies that may uncomfortably focus on "crime in the suites."

Section B(7) of the American Sociological Association (ASA) Code of Ethics states: "Confidential information provided by research participants must be treated as such by sociologists, even when this information enjoys no legal protection or privilege and legal force is applied" (American Sociological Association, 1984, p. 3).

The Scarce Case

In 1990, Rik Scarce was a Ph.D. sociology student at Washington State University and published a book entitled *Eco-Warriors: Understanding the Radical Environmental Movement* (Scarce, 1990). Using various sources the book also utilized interviews with members of Earth First!, the Sea Shepherd Conservation Society, and the Animal Liberation Front (ALF). These groups had been extensively involved in direct action campaigns and civil disobedience. He had begun a dissertation on the Radical Environmental Movement. Scarce had been unaware that, as a student, his research had to be preapproved by the University's IRB. When an ALF raid in protest of animal experimentation took place on the campus, Scarce was subpoenaed to appear before a grand jury.

Scarce was interrogated by FBI agents and subsequently jailed for 157 days for contempt of court after refusing to violate the ASA code of ethics, which forbade him from sharing confidential information with law enforcement authorities. Scarce warns that, if researchers make absolute assurances of confidentiality, they should be fully aware of what those assurances portend—"a conscious decision to go to jail rather than relent in the face of legal pressure to violate confidentiality agreements" (Scarce, 2001, p. 271).

When an anthropologist involved in a medical lawsuit refused to turn over her field notes, the American Anthropological Association issued a statement that said researchers have "primary ethical obligations to the people, species, and materials they study …" but these "may be affected by the requirements of other codes, laws and ethics of the country" (Wilson, 2003). Instead of arguing in the courts for greater protection of confidentiality, some social scientists have backed away from promising confidentiality. Rik Scarce states that this view says, "I'll try as hard as I can [to protect confidentiality], but if worse comes to worse I may have to give you up" (Wilson, 2003). *New York Times* reporter Judith Miller was jailed on July 6, 2005, for contempt of court for not revealing who in the White House leaked the identity of a CIA agent. She was later released when the informant, Scooter Libby (an aide to Vice President Cheney), came forward. Scarce maintains that proposed Congressional legislation for shield law protection for such journalists should include social scientists (Scarce, 2005a, 2005b).

Perhaps as a footnote to the Scarce case is another related to environmental issues. In September 1998 the University of Denver "withdrew" an article that they had already agreed to publish. The article, "The Critical Need for Law Reform to Regulate the Abusive Practices of Transnational Corporations: The Illustrative Case of Boise Cascade Corporation in Mexico's Costa Grande and Elsewhere," had been published in the *Denver Journal of International Law and Policy*, September 1998 edition. The Summer, 1999 edition printed an "errata" notice that "this article has been retracted for its lack of scholarship and false content" (Monaghan, 2000, p. A14). The authors, Professors Mark Buchanon, William Wines, and Donald Smith, received the letter from the Boise Cascade Corporation, the target of criticism in the article. Despite vigorous denials by the university, the authors claim that the university caved in to the intimidation and did not even contact the authors before retracting their article. University officials denied that threats of a lawsuit were instrumental in their highly unusual decision. In August 2000, the authors filed a lawsuit in federal court in Idaho, arguing that their reputations have been damaged and that university was guilty of breach of contract and destroyed two years' worth of scholarship.

In yet another twist related to censorship (in this case sponsorship) of research, it was reported in 1999 that Wyeth-Ayers Laboratories (producers of fenphen, a diet drug that was later found to be dangerous) hired ghostwriters for articles promoting the drug. It then used unknowing prominent researchers to publish works under their names. Only two of the ten articles paid for by Wyeth were published in medical journals before the drug was pulled from the market. Plans to publish the others were canceled. The company claimed, "This is common practice in the industry. It's not particular to us" ("Diet drug," 1999).

Emphasis in large universities on obtaining research funding may force scholars to abandon basic research and scholarship in favor of applied research and entrepreneurship, the "corporatization" of higher education. The concern is with knowledge being viewed as a private commodity rather than a public good and overemphasizing scholars as entrepreneurs rather than scholars (Desruisseaux, 1999).

The issue of ethics in criminal justice research draws greater attention now than in the past. Ethical concerns in research gain complexity with revisions in federal laws regulating privacy, confidentiality, and freedom of information; debates continue in the various professional disciplines involved in studying criminology and criminal justice. The desire to address these issues is reflected in the establishment of a specialized journal, *Criminal Justice Ethics*.[1]

Additional Ethical Concerns

The parent disciplines to criminology/criminal justice, such as sociology, psychology, political science, and anthropology have both unique and common ethical concerns, as reflected in their codes of ethics. Because professionals pride themselves on autonomy and self-regulation, these requirements are usually beyond any minimal standards set by government agencies. Some specific ethical considerations are incorporated by these codes. Although every effort may be made to preserve their anonymity, subjects should be made aware that they may unintentionally be compromised. A researcher's pseudonyms should not be indiscriminately revealed. Anthropologists indicate that, if secretive research is performed for a sponsor, such reports should also be released to the public and subjects. Researchers should be honest with sponsors regarding qualifications, capabilities, and harm, and open concerning the acknowledgment of sponsorship of research. Any government-supported research should be unclassified, and researchers should not use their research as a cover for government intelligence work.

If research has potential policy implications, it is even more imperative that investigators state the limitations of their findings. Relationships that may compromise objectivity or create a conflict of interest should be avoided. Psychologists insist on a high standard of competence, including use of the latest rules regarding validity and reliability of tests and measurements employed in research or practice. Political scientists have specific guidelines on involvement in the political arena, often a necessary part of the discipline. Sociologists mirror most of these same themes, but add that, regardless of work setting, they are obligated to report findings fully and without omission of significant data. Also as an ethical matter, researchers are obligated to make their data available to other qualified social scientists at reasonable cost once they have completed their study.

Avoiding Ethical Problems

Because of the nature of the subject matter, ethical problems are likely to present themselves in many criminal justice research projects. One way of avoiding ethical problems is to *carefully consider alternate means of data gathering*

---

[1]Published by Institute for Criminal Justice Ethics, John Jay College of Criminal Justice, 444 West 56th Street, New York, NY 10102.

that may not entail ethical problems. Some study designs pose less hazard than others. For example, perhaps existing data or some other unobtrusive method would make it unnecessary to collect new data. Rather than set up an experimental group and a control group in a prison, one could locate two similar prisons that already constitute natural experimental and control groups. Simulations, either human or computer, may enable one to address the same issue without as much of an ethics problem. One could seek conditions under which negative effects have already occurred (Bailey, 1987, p. 407–410). Similarly, the use of samples or only low levels of the treatment may reduce the potential harm.

The reporting of aggregative rather than individual data with proper prior destruction of identifiers may ensure protection. Such simulations as "mock jury studies" may also avoid ethical problems with real populations.

In an earlier discussion of sample surveys it was pointed out that there is a potential growing "respondent revolt" against the increased requests to participate in studies. All research is to some extent an imposition on the lives or time of subjects. By the same token, research also poses, as we have seen in this chapter, potential unethical impacts on those involved in a study. Although the points set forth in this section can alert the investigator to broad guideposts, the actual research path is in the last analysis the sole responsibility of the researcher.

Summary

Ethical horror stories were reviewed in order to document some examples of unethical behavior in research. Accounts of biomedical research by Nazis, the Tuskegee Syphilis Study, experiments on prisoners, as well as secretive research sponsored by intelligence agencies preceded discussion of social science examples. The latter included Milgram's "obedience to authority" study, Zimbardo's "simulated prison study," and Humphreys' *Tearoom Trade*. Plagiarism and researcher fraud such as the Piltdown and Tasaday hoaxes were also discussed as examples of scams and researcher misconduct.

As one of the social sciences, criminal justice must be concerned with many of the same issues of ethical behavior in conducting research on human activity. Potential role conflict exists for the investigator who has to balance the roles of researcher, criminal justice practitioner, citizen, and humanitarian. In mediating these roles it is essential that the researcher anticipate many of the possible points of friction beforehand, keeping in mind that *the researcher's primary role is that of scientist.*

Research targets in criminology and criminal justice include the criminal, the victim, the criminal justice system, practitioners, and the general public. Each research situation presents its own unique set of ethical problems, just as ethics itself is relative to the setting. Although science itself is ethically neutral, individual scientists cannot entirely avoid moral concerns in studying human groups or individuals. In aspiring for acceptance as professionals, criminal justice researchers attempt to demonstrate that on the basis of knowledge and ethical conduct they should be granted autonomy and high professional regard. Although this striving and establishment of ethical codes may be viewed as a smokescreen to gain monopolistic power, if a field fails to set its own standards, the government will set the standards for them. A code of ethical conduct in research that exists in criminal justice was still in draft stage in late 1998. The purpose of this chapter has been to call attention to key features. Rather than a rigid set of requirements, they might best be viewed as general principles that must be tailored to the unique features of individual research projects.

The most influential guidelines governing funded research in the United States are those of the HHS, *Model Policy on Human Research Subjects*. Researchers involved in ethnography or field studies were critical of the attempted application of these informed consent guidelines to participant observation studies and felt that they would make such studies impossible. Fieldwork was viewed as different in kind than biomedical and experimental studies of controlled subjects. The NCPHS (1978) in the Belmont Report partially revised these guidelines, putting their interpretation in the hands of review boards and suggesting an alteration of informed consent in the case of field research. Revision of HHS guidelines in 1981 virtually excluded most social science and criminal justice/criminological research from required review.

In addition to government agency regulations regarding funded research, professional associations, for example, the American Sociological and Psychological associations, have their own codes of ethics governing research. Taking both governmental and other professions' codes of ethics, some *Ethical Principles in Criminal Justice Research* are presented as suggestive elements of consideration in investigations: (1) researchers should avoid procedures that may harm respondents; (2) one should honor commitments to respondents and respect reciprocity; (3) investigators should maintain objectivity and exercise professional integrity in performing and reporting research; and (4) investigators should protect the confidentiality and privacy of respondents. In addition, discussion was presented that criminal justice researchers should be alert to the fact that they enjoy no legally recognized privilege of confidentiality (except, of course, in some cases of funded research that are restrictive in coverage).

Some ethical problems experienced by researchers such as Brajuha, Ofshe, and Hutchinson were discussed. Finally, some means of avoiding ethical problems are the use of alternate methods that possess fewer ethical problems, study groups that possess characteristics or natural treatments, the use of samples instead of larger populations, the reporting of only aggregative data, the use of simulations, as well as exposure of groups to only low levels of treatment. In the last analysis, researchers must assume personal responsibility for the morality of their research.

KEY CONCEPTS

Institutional Review
  Boards (IRBs)
The Lucifer effect
Research fraud

The Minerva
  consortium
Plagiarism
Role of researcher

Research targets
  in criminal
  justice
Professional ethics

Ethical principles for criminal justice research

HEW guidelines for protection of human subjects

Informed consent

The Belmont Report

NIJ's regulations on confidentiality

Shield laws

Risk/benefit ratio in research

Reciprocity

Confidentiality

Pseudonyms

REVIEW QUESTIONS

1. Research in criminal justice and criminology faces many ethical hazards. How concerned should researchers be with ethical conduct in research? What is the researcher's role, and what constitutes appropriate conduct?

2. The regulation of ethically acceptable research conduct may take one of three forms. Discuss these, and include your opinion as to which of these is most effective.

3. How did the new HHS guidelines resolve the principal objections of field researchers to the informed consent issue?

4. What are some elements of a code of ethics for criminology/criminal justice research?

5. Discuss some examples of researcher misconduct. Why does this occur, and how can it be prevented?

USEFUL WEB SITES

Journal of Criminal Justice Ethics *www.lib.jjay.cuny.edu/cje/*

Ethics and Justice *www.ethics-justice.org/*

Internet Research Ethics *www.nyu.edu/projects/nissenbaum/projects_ethics.html*

Office of Research Integrity *http://ori.dhhs.gov/*

Association of Internet Researchers (Ethics Working Committee) *http://aoir.org/reports/ethics.html*

Evaluating Web Sites: Criteria and Tools *www.library.cornell.edu/olinuris/ref/research/webeval.html*

Office of Human Research Protections (IRB Guidelines) *www.hhs.gov/ohrp*

National Academy of Sciences (Responsible Conduct in Research) *www.nap.edu/html/obas/*

Institute for Criminal Justice Ethics (John Jay College) *www.lib.jjay.cuny.edu/cje/html/*

Ethics in Academics

3

Research Design: The Experimental Model and Its Variations

Research design is the plan or blueprint for a study and includes the who, what, where, when, why, and how of an investigation. The research design should flow from the problem formulation and critical issues that were identified for observation. Who is to be investigated—an individual, one group, many groups, organizations, or communities? What is to be investigated—attitudes, behavior, or records? Where is the study to be conducted? Do we wish to look at the past (after-the-fact, post hoc, or a posteriori studies) or the present or to predict the future? Do we want to look at a group once or over time? Why do we wish to do the investigation—to describe, explain, or predict? Finally, how do we design the study so that upon completion we are able to address the hypotheses and present findings that resolve in some manner the research problem?

The Experimental Model

Some people view experiments as involving white-coated scientists with an impressive assortment of equipment tediously studying obscure phenomena in some isolated laboratory. Although such a picture may indeed be accurate in some instances, the experimental model contains many variations and should not be restricted to this stereotypical view. The experimental model will be treated in this chapter as the benchmark for comparison of all other research designs and methods. Most studies of an empirical nature in criminology and criminal justice can be viewed as variations of the experimental model (Campbell, 1977; Cook and Campbell, 1979; Weubben, Straits, and Shulman, 1974). The research design notation (Xs and Os) used in this chapter may at first appear intimidating, but if you give it a chance, you will find it excellent shorthand for dissecting any research study. This chapter contains more "researchese" than any other chapter, but if you bear with it, you will be rewarded by becoming fluent in the language of research.

Research Design in a Nutshell

In learning something new such as swimming or driving, the initial lessons seem the most difficult; once the foreignness of a new experience is overcome, the rest is relatively easy. Unfortunately, learning research methods is similar. The language of research design in this chapter by its very nature has this same foreignness at first. One philosophy is to teach something by simply doing it, such as throwing the student in the deep end of the pool or the fast lane on the Capitol Beltway (which, incidentally, is where this writer learned to drive). Rather than following this practice and throwing you in the deep end, let us begin with a short lesson. Read Figure 3.1, even if you do not fully understand it. It provides the "guts" of the entire chapter. As you are reading or after completing the chapter, you may wish to reread it because, if you understand Figure 3.1, you have the underlying logic of research design.

Causality

The ultimate purpose of all scientific investigation is to isolate, define, and explain the relationship between key variables in order to predict and understand the underlying nature of reality. The problem of *causality* has been a subject of continuing philosophical discussion, but scientific investigation is based on the a priori assumption that the fundamental nature of reality can be known—that causation lies at the basis of reality.

Resolution of the Causality Problem

To approach this matter, scientific investigation entails basically *three essential* **steps for resolving the causality problem.** *The first step* involves the demonstration of a relationship or covariance between variables. That is, one variable is related, it increases or decreases in value, in some predictable manner along with increases or decreases in the value of another variable. *The second step* consists of specifying or indicating the time sequence of the relationship. Which variable is the independent or predictor variable X, and which is the outcome or dependent variable Y? Generally, logic or knowledge of which variable comes first gives one the direction of causation. For instance, it would make more sense to assume that criminality of parents (X) would precede in time and

Steps for resolving the causality problem

X = treatment (independent variable), e.g., Foot Patrol
Y = outcome (dependent variable), e.g., Crime Rate
Z = any rival causal factor (other variables besides X that could really be causing a change in Y), e.g., history, selection bias, testing, etc.
O = observation (some measurement or assessment of dependent variable)
E = equivalence (randomization or matching)
$1, 2$ = time

Design 1: O_1XO_2 (One Group Before–After Design)

- A precinct with a crime rate of 1,000 (O_1) is exposed to foot patrol (X) for one year and then has a crime rate of 500 (O_2).
- Problem: Other variables (Z) could actually have caused the decline in crime rate (Y) rather than foot patrol (X), e.g., History, Selection Bias, Testing Effects.
- Solution: A better research design (such as Design 2) to control or exclude these rival causal factors (or other variables).

Design 2: EO_1XO_2
$\quad\quad\quad EO_1\ \ O_2$ (Classic Experimental Design)

- Two precincts as similar as possible (E, matching) on relevant characteristics are studied.
  Both are observed (O_1) and have a crime rate of 1,000.
  One precinct receives foot patrol (X) and is the experimental group.
  The other precinct receives no treatment (control group).
  After one year, the experimental precinct has a crime rate of 500 while the control group has a crime rate of 1,000 (or no change). The decrease is attributed to foot patrol.
- Rival causal factors (Z) were controlled for (excluded) by the classic experimental design, for example,
  The change could not have been due to some historical event if we assume that both groups were similar and exposed to the same history.
  The change could not be due to selection bias because we purposely chose two similar or matched precincts (E) and their crime rates were the same from the beginning (O_1)
  If there were testing effects (citizens were not surveyed; we used police reports), both groups should have reacted the same to an awareness of being studied.
  Thus, the relationship between X and Y is not due to Z [we have gained internal validity (accuracy)].
- Problem: Can we generalize this finding (foot patrol reduces crime) to all police departments in the country? This is the problem of external validity.
- One Solution: Replications (repeat studies) in other settings with other police departments.

Figure 3.1
Research Design in a Nutshell.

possibly predict criminality in offspring (Y), rather than vice versa. In most instances one has little difficulty in identifying the outcome (Y) one is interested in predicting. It is usually the subject of the study. Although this process of causality resolution in research has been greatly oversimplified for presentation purposes, most studies of an empirical and predictive nature in criminal justice can be found to undergo essentially the first two steps that have been outlined. *The third step* is the stage where many studies bog down and where research findings are subject to interminable debate. It involves the exclusion of **rival causal factors**, or the elimination of other variables that could conceivably explain away the original relationships the researcher had claimed. Other variables or rival causal factors may be responsible for the variations discovered (Denzin, 1989; Hirschi and Selvin, 1966; Steffensmeier and Terry, 1975).

Rival causal factors

In excluding rival causal factors, researchers are attempting to demonstrate that the relationship between X and Y is nonspurious. A **spurious relationship** is a false relationship, that is, one that is not caused by the believed variables, but can be explained by other variables. The presumed relationship between foot size (X) and intelligence (Y) may disappear (be demonstrated to be spurious) when controlled for age (Z). That is, among thirty-year-olds there is no relationship between foot size and intelligence.

Spurious relationship

To summarize and clarify this process, once again, the *three essential steps in resolving the causality problem* are as follows:

1. Demonstrate that a relationship exists between the key variables.
2. Specify the time order of the relationship.
3. Eliminate rival causal factors.

Suppose a researcher wanted to prove that a relationship exists between the increase in foot patrols in a precinct and a decline in crime. Assuming that foot patrols have been increased in the target precinct, the researcher looks at some measurement, such as precinct records of reported crime. If no relationship between increased foot patrols and crime is discovered, the entire process stops with step 1. There is little need to proceed if no relationship at all exists. If a decrease or for some reason an increase in crime is discovered, however, the researcher goes on to the next step. For our purposes we will assume that an increase in foot patrols is the predictor variable, X, and a decrease in reported crime is the outcome, Y. We assume that foot patrols affect crime rates, rather than vice versa. One could see, however, where a researcher might be interested in studying the latter; that is, high crime areas may more likely precipitate the deployment of foot patrols.

Finally, suppose a relationship was discovered and specified; namely, there was an increase in foot patrols and a decline in reported crime within the precinct. Does this then prove that increases in foot patrols will cause a decrease in crime as measured by crime reported to police? The answer to this question is no. The most obvious reason is that *correlation or relationship by no means implies or demonstrates causation.* Such a finding merely brings us to stage 1 or 2 of our steps in resolving the causality problem. If the prudent investigator has not already guessed, one's critics will very quickly point out that other variables could have accounted for this relationship.

Rival Causal Factors

Rival causal factors are any variables other than X (the treatment) that may be responsible for the relationship. It is traditional in the social sciences, following the lead of Campbell and Stanley (1963), to discuss these other variables, or rival causal factors, as being of two general types: *internal factors* or other variables within the study itself that may tend to invalidate one's findings and conclusions, and *external factors* or elements outside of one's immediate study that may imperil the researcher's attempts to draw generalizations from the study and infer one's findings to be true of larger populations.

Validity

Validity refers to accuracy or correctness in research. Internal factors question the internal validity of research, whereas external factors impugn the external validity of findings. The former asks whether the observational process itself produced the findings; the latter is concerned with whether the results were unique and applicable only to the group or target studied. In checking **internal validity**, one is concerned with whether a variable other than X (the treatment) may have produced a change in Y (the dependent variable). With **external validity** one asks what other variables may limit one's ability to generalize the findings in a study to larger populations or settings.

Internal validity

External validity

Internal Factors: Variables Related to Internal Validity

Campbell and Stanley's classic monograph, *Experimental and Quasi-Experimental Designs for Research* (1963), points to the following internal factors as possibly threatening the internal validity of a study:

History	Statistical regression
Maturation`	Selection bias
Testing	Experimental mortality
Instrumentation	Selection—maturation interaction

All of these are rival causal factors that could have been responsible for producing the results rather than the treatment assumed to be responsible. That is, although X and Y are related, the real reason for this relationship is Z, some other variable or rival causal factor.

History

History

History refers to other specific events that may have taken place during the course of the study and may have produced the results. For example, what events other than increased foot patrols may have occurred in the hypothetical precinct and accounted for the decrease in crimes reported? Perhaps the area was the target of a "Crime Watch" program that encouraged citizen vigilance and reporting; or a new employment program was initiated to hire unemployed youths; or urban renewal changed the nature of the population inhabiting the precinct. Social, seasonal, and other events may be responsible for changes in a study target. Garwood (1978) gives an example of a burglary reduction program using "operation identification" in which belongings are engraved to discourage burglars and fences. A northeastern experimental city received the treatment, operation identification, and, especially during January 1978, showed a dramatic decrease in reported burglaries. Can we assume that the X, operation identification, was responsible for bringing this about? No. On further investigation it was discovered that other cities without such a program, notably, Buffalo, Detroit, and Boston, demonstrated equally impressive declines in burglary. What may have occurred in January 1978 to account for this? It was the winter of incredibly deep, record-breaking, crippling snows in the Northeast, and thus bad weather, a historical hidden variable, was most likely responsible for the decline in burglary statistics. Similarly, a tough 1880 anti–horse theft law in New York City is not responsible for the virtual disappearance of such thieves 100 years later; rather, it is the historical change in transportation.

In reviewing shortcomings of sentencing research, Farrington (1978) points out that because of the lack of premeasures and control groups, it is difficult to assume that any decrease in crime after a change in legal penalties or sentencing is due to these changes or other unmeasured social changes that may have taken place at the same time.

Maturation

Maturation refers to biological or psychological changes in the respondents during the course of study that are not due to the experimental variable. "Time heals all wounds," according to the old medical dictum, refers to the phenomenon in medical research wherein a given number of patients can be expected to reveal improved conditions with or without treatment. Perhaps the precinct under investigation in our foot patrol example was in the process of change, either deterioration or upgrading, that brought about the change in crime reporting irrespective of foot patrol.

A hypothetical example may serve to illustrate maturation as a rival causal factor. An interesting controversy of the 1960s was fluoridation of water in the United States. Opponents claimed that the addition of such chemicals was potentially harmful. Suppose an avid supporter of such a view were to state, "In 1850 Erie, Pennsylvania, was the first city to fluoridate its water and not a single citizen from that time is alive today." Quite obviously the demise of this population was due primarily to natural causes, maturation, rather than the assumed cause, fluoridation.

In a more serious vein, claims as to the long-term effectiveness of rehabilitation programs must certainly control for the fact that as a given age cohort matures, its crime commission in general tends to decrease; that is, there are very few eighty-year-old cat burglars. As a more detailed example will illustrate later in this chapter, all other things being equal, older delinquents can be expected to show lower crime commission over time than younger delinquents.

Maturation

Testing

Testing

Testing (pretest bias) refers to the bias and foreknowledge introduced to respondents as a result of having been pretested. On a second testing the respondents are no longer naive regarding the subject matter and can make use of sensitivities, information, and attitudes garnered from the first testing. If one wanted to test a bank's reaction to a simulated robbery, the reaction of a bank that had been held up the previous day would probably not yield valid or typical results.

Instrumentation

Instrumentation

Instrumentation involves changes in the measuring instrument from the beginning or first period of evaluation to the second, later, or final evaluation. The measuring instrument may refer to observers, questionnaires, interviews, analyses of existing records, or any standard method of data gathering. Suppose, for instance, that in our foot patrol experiment, the method of recording citizen complaints was dramatically improved from what it had been at the beginning of the project. An increase in crimes reported to police at the end of the study could very well have resulted from instrumentation, a rival causal factor, rather than the assumed predictor variable—foot patrol. A major limitation of comparing crime rates of today with those of yesteryear relates to the continual improvement in record keeping so that an indeterminate proportion of the increase may simply be evidence of improved instrumentation. We will discuss this subject in detail in Chapter 4 in the section "The Uniform Crime Reports." The crime rate of a city may show an increase of 100 percent over the previous year, not necessarily because of increased crime commission, but because of installation of a computer, a change in the manner in which crime is measured or recorded.

Statistical Regression

Statistical regression

Statistical regression is the tendency of groups that have been selected for study on the basis of extreme high or low scores to regress or move toward the mean or average on second testing. As in our example, if a precinct was selected for study on the basis of an extremely high or low volume of citizen complaints, it is expected, irrespective of the treatment variable, that the second reading will be closer to the average for all precincts or certainly less at the extreme.

It should not be surprising that extremely high or low scores would move toward more normal scores upon retest. Extremely tall people as a group are likely to have children shorter than themselves, just as extremely short people are likely to have children taller than themselves. Imagine taking the first examination in a class that you detest; after having had a bad night the night before (illness, an all-nighter), you flunk the test. As a member of the lowest group, you are then chosen for study. But before the second test you have a normal night's sleep, so we might expect your performance to improve. The point is that the improvement may not be due to any increase in intelligence, but that your first test performance was atypical.

In critiquing reported positive claims of a program involving diversion alternatives for youths who would otherwise have been incarcerated, Gordon and associates point out that regression effects had been overlooked. The juveniles studied were chosen on the basis of extremely high crime commission that could be expected to decrease upon second observation even without intervention. Not surprisingly, it was claimed that the most extreme delinquents demonstrated the greatest drop in recidivism as a result of a wilderness program. The most likely explanation, however, was an expected regression toward the mean on the basis of the initial choice of extreme cases (Gordon et al., 1978).

Selection Bias

Selection bias occurs when the researcher chooses nonequivalent groups for comparison. Studies that compare the attitudes or behavior of volunteers and nonvolunteers are often subject to selection bias. If in our foot patrol study the precinct chosen for the experiment was characterized by high levels of citizen involvement and reportage of crime, and these data were compared with those for another nonfoot patrol precinct with historically low levels of reported crime, the rival causal factor, selection bias, rather than foot patrol, might explain the differences in findings.

Selection bias

Similarly, comparison of an experimental group consisting of all model prisoners and a control group of incorrigible prisoners would hardly be fair. Many demonstration projects have been accused of "creaming clients"—taking the cream of the crop—or stacking the deck by assigning the best clients to the treatment and the dregs to the control group.

Experimental Mortality

In studying the same group over a period of time, an expected loss of subjects can be anticipated. This loss is referred to as **experimental mortality.** In our foot patrol experiment a decline in residential population as a result of urban renewal would certainly impinge on the number of crimes reported. In correctional research, long-term recidivism studies have been handicapped by the inability to follow all or most of the original respondents. Perhaps those who cannot be found are more likely to be successes or failures than those on which data are available.

Experimental mortality

One method of assessing possible bias as a result of the loss of respondents is to compare known characteristics of respondents with those of nonrespondents. Similarity in such demographic characteristics as sex, age, race, and income may lead one to suspect that nonrespondents do not differ much from respondents and therefore introduce little bias.

Selection–Maturation Interaction

Obviously, factors within the experiment other than the assumed predictor variable may be responsible for the findings. Interaction or combination impacts of any or all of these variables may bring about the obtained results, for instance, interaction of selection bias and differential maturation of groups. **Selection–maturation interaction** was illustrated by Gordon et al. (1978) in their critique of a diversion program in which the researchers failed to control for age—selection bias—or to spot a potential maturation effect when older

Selection–maturation interaction

delinquents were placed in the wilderness programs that showed the greatest decline in recidivism. The latter can be viewed as a maturation effect in that as a group ages, its overall crime commission declines.

External Factors: Variables Related to External Validity

External factors refer to rival causal factors that negatively affect external validity or the representativeness or generalizability of study findings to larger populations beyond the group studied (Campbell and Stanley, 1963). The following are examples of external factors:

- Testing effects
- Selection bias
- Reactivity or awareness of being studied
- Multiple-treatment interference

Although a clever researcher may do much to control for the effects of rival causal factors within a study, this may not enhance the ability to generalize beyond the group studied. The testing effects and selection bias previously discussed as affecting internal validity also affect external validity (reactive or interaction effects of pretesting).

Testing Effects

Testing effects

Testing effects point to the tendency of pretests to destroy the naiveté of respondents with respect to the variable(s) being studied and decrease or, more predictably, increase the subjects' awareness or sensitivity, thus complicating the ability to generalize their responses to a larger population that has not been pretested. For illustrative purposes let us alter the foot patrol example by adding a different dimension. Assume that the purpose of introducing walking beats was to enhance community relations and public attitudes toward the police. At the beginning of the study, residents of the precinct were questioned regarding these matters; then foot patrols were introduced, and the residents were questioned again. A more favorable attitude toward police would be assumed to have been produced by walking patrols; however, perhaps it was induced in part, or primarily, by the group having been pretested and thus having had time to reflect and consider their views. Furthermore, attitudes in this precinct could not be generalized to other even similar precincts, without some hazard, unless a similar pretest–posttest had occurred there also.

Selection Bias

Selection bias can have negative impacts on the ability to infer findings beyond the group studied. Nonrepresentative selection of a study group obviously invalidates any attempt to generalize to larger populations. For instance, the purposive selection of a precinct with high citizen vigilance in responding to crime as the setting for an experiment in police deployment would not be a fair test of how this same program would operate in more typical settings.

Reactivity or Awareness of Being Studied

Reactivity or respondent awareness of being studied tends to produce atypical or unnatural behavior on the part of subjects. Most people have had experience with previously announced inspections, visiting or guest teachers, and the like to realize that behavior observed during that day tends to be at times quite different from what normally occurs. Similarly, if the sample foot patrol precinct were announced and continually covered in the media during the course of the experiment, the residents' behavior, as well as the behavior of the police, would be different than usual.

> Reactivity

This phenomenon is variously described as the "Hawthorne effect," "placebo effect," or "stooge effect," and will be discussed shortly. Thus, an awareness of being studied, rather than the experimental treatment, may become the major factor bringing about a particular outcome.

Multiple-Treatment Interferences

Multiple-treatment interference occurs when more than one treatment or predictor variable is used on the same subjects. The outcome may be brought about by a specific sequence or combination of independent variables that can be uncovered only by more complicated research designs, as will be examined later in this chapter. If the foot patrol officers also wore blazers and did not carry guns and gave out free tickets to sports events, a more positive attitude may have been produced by any one or combination of variables, in addition to or irrespective of foot patrols.

> Multiple-treatment interference

Related Rival Causal Factors

Hawthorne Effect

Although not distinct from those already discussed, a number of other Hawthorne-related terms for sources of invalidity can be identified. The **Hawthorne effect** serves as an example of reactivity resulting in atypical behavior or attitudes on the part of research subjects as a result of their awareness of being studied. This factor gets its name from a pioneering industrial study of a group of workers in the Hawthorne plant of the Western Electric Company in Chicago (Roethlisberger and Dixon, 1939). To the bemusement of the researchers, alterations in treatment designed to either increase or decrease worker efficiency consistently increased efficiency. Rather than reacting to the treatment variable, X, workers were reacting to a rival causal factor—the fact that they had been singled out for an important study. The workers reacted as they suspected the researchers wanted them to act, rather than as they would under normal circumstances. These acquiescent, "guinea pig," or "stooge," effects are likely in situations where the group being studied is aware that they are being studied.

> Hawthorne effect

Halo Effect

The **halo effect** was coined by Thorndike (1920, p. 25), who noticed that when supervisors rated subordinates, the ratings were all "higher than reality." It refers to observer bias in which observers, perhaps unconsciously, follow an initial tendency to rate certain objects or persons in a particular manner; this initial orientation carries over into all subsequent ratings. The less specified and discretionary the variable to be rated, the greater the danger of the halo effect (see Cooper, 1981).

Related in part, but more subtle than the halo effect, is the carryover into research of a phenomenon first noted by sociologist W. I. Thomas. His basic maxim of "the definition of the situation," or what others refer to as **self-fulfilling prophecy,** has a major bearing upon the bias of the researcher. "If groups or individuals define a situation as real, it is real in its consequences" (Thomas and Swaine, 1928, pp. 571–572). A researcher's own hidden biases and expectations may influence his or her perception of events so as to bring about that which had been assumed. Selective perception may lead to one ignoring anything that does not fit one's preset cognitive map and thus presents us with an experimenter effect (Rosenthal, 1966).

Post Hoc Error

Post hoc error comes from the Latin phrase *post hoc; ergo, propter hoc,* literally, "after this; therefore because of it." It is a fallacy to argue that one variable is the cause of an outcome because it precedes that outcome in time. What is considered an effect is often only a subsequent event. An example would be to argue that because every morning when the rooster crows the sun rises, the crowing causes the sunrise. Another example can be the common claims made by police chiefs that crime (reported crime) declined in their city in the 1980s because of new and effective policies. More likely than not, what one was observing was the predicted "crime dip" of the 1980s, resulting in part from demographic shifts in what has been described as the post–World War II "baby boom."

Gelles (1977) gives an example of such fallacious reasoning in research on child abusers. Sometimes psychological conditions that are identified as being present after the abuse incident are viewed as the cause of the incident, for example, abusers may be found to be paranoid and depressed, conditions that may be results of the incident, rather than its cause.

Placebo Effect

Complete enumeration of related tags or descriptions of rival causal factors would be endless and beyond our needs at this point. One final factor that often appears in literature is the **placebo effect**. This involves, similar to the Hawthorne effect, the tendency of subjects to react to a known stimulus in the predicted manner (Loranger, Prout, and White, 1961). Commonly used in medical research, the "sugar pill" or a placebo (fake treatment) with no known effects is administered to the study group to hide the real treatment group and also to control for the placebo effect. The actual effects of the true experimental pill can then be compared with effects induced in the control group by the sugar pill. Other terms used to refer to this same reactivity phenomenon are *evaluation apprehension* or *demand characteristics*. In the former, Rosenberg (1969) notes that subjects are apprehensive about participating in experiments, and this very anxiety may produce atypical behavior. "Was I a good subject?" is often the question asked by respondents who are willing to, in an acquiescent manner, elicit on demand characteristics they believe are sought by the researcher (Orne, 1969).

Researchers have found that subjects on placebos who experience pain relief actually have their own brains releasing pain-relieving chemicals called endorphins (Kaptchuk, Eisenberg, and Komaroff, 2002). The brain's amazing triumph over reality can be illustrated by studies in which hair growth was maintained or improved in 42 percent of balding men taking a placebo; smelling a placebo helped asthmatic children in Venezuela increase their lung function by 33 percent; and in a Japanese study, people exposed to fake poison ivy developed real rashes (Blakeslee, 1998).

To control for the "placebo," "Hawthorne," and "experimenter" effects, medical researchers have developed the gold standard for experimental research, the **double-blind experiment**, a design in which neither subjects nor people administering the experiment are aware of which group is the experimental group (the one receiving "real" treatment) and which group is the control group (the one receiving "phony" treatment) (Glaser, 1976, p. 773).

Double-blind experiment

Experimental Designs

Research designs are a major way of controlling for invalidity in research or, as in step 3, resolving the causality problem, a means of excluding rival causal factors (Cresswell, 1994). Previously in this chapter we indicated that experiments may be viewed as the benchmark for comparison of all other research methods. The language of research design is heavily couched in that of experimental designs, and a mastery of this specialized jargon is helpful in developing a standard taxonomy by which to classify various forms of research.

Research designs

Three general types of experimental designs are discussed in this section:

1. *Experimental designs* (sometimes called true experimental designs) are characterized by random assignment to treatment and control groups and include the classical, posttest-only control group, and Solomon four-group designs.
2. *Quasi-experimental designs* do not use random assignment of groups and instead employ matching or other means of obtaining equivalence of groups. Quasi-experimental designs include time-series and counterbalanced designs.
3. *Preexperimental designs* lack any equivalence of groups and include one- and two-group ex post facto and one-group before–after designs.

What we will describe as the classic experimental design is one of the most effective methods of controlling for internal rival causal variables before the fact. In that sense, the experiment becomes the point of departure for a comparison of all other research designs.

The Classic Experimental Design

Classic experimental design

The **classic experimental design,** which serves as a prototype for our discussion of all other research designs, *contains three key elements*:

- Equivalence
- Pretests and posttests
- Experimental and control groups

Equivalence

Equivalence refers to the attempt on the part of the researcher to select and assign subjects to comparison groups in such a manner that they can be assumed to be alike in all major respects. The two methods by which equivalence of groups to be compared is gained are randomization and matching. **Randomization** is the random assignment of subjects from a similar population to one or the other group(s) to be compared in such a way that each individual has an equal probability of being chosen and an equal probability of being assigned to any of the groups to be compared. We discuss the process of randomization more thoroughly in Chapter 4, but at this point it will suffice to indicate that one of the principal means of accomplishing randomization is by use of simple random samples or some means of selection in which each case in the population has an equal probability of appearing.

Randomization

Matching

Matching deals with assuring equivalence by selecting subjects for the second or other comparison groups on the basis of matching certain key characteristics such as age, sex, and race, so that the groups are similar or equivalent with respect to these characteristics. Matching and randomization can be combined. In the Cambridge-Somerville study (McCord and McCord, 1959), 325 pairs of boys were matched on delinquency potential and one member of each pair was randomly assigned to treatment (Farrington, 1983, p. 261).

pretest/posttest

Assuming that the groups are similar, both are exposed to a **pretest** or observation prior to exposure to treatment and a **posttest** or measurement after exposure to treatment. Finally, the group exposed to treatment is called the **experimental group**; the group that is not exposed to the stimulus or predictor variable is the **control group**. The original meaning of the term "control" is "check"—the term comes from "counter-roll," a duplicate register or account made to verify an account (Oakley, 1998).

Experimental group

Control group

For heuristic purposes, we adapt the notation developed by Campbell and Stanley (1963) for schematically depicting the various research designs: X equals treatment, O symbolizes observations (some researchers use T instead of O). Subscripts for O, such as O_1 and O_2, represent the first and second observations, respectively, and E stands for the equivalence of comparison groups. Please note that purists would be more conservative and insist that randomization (R) and not matching is necessary for a classic experimental design.

CLASSIC EXPERIMENTAL DESIGN

$E \qquad O_1 \qquad X \qquad O_2$

$E \qquad O_1 \qquad\qquad\quad O_2$

$E \ = \ $ equivalence

$O \ = \ $ observation

$X \ = \ $ treatment

$1,2 \ = \ $ time

Following our previous presentation of this design with our newly introduced notation, we find that the classic experimental design involves an equivalent assignment to experimental and control groups, which are observed both before and after the experimental group receives treatment.

Using some of the rival causal factors affecting internal validity, we can now examine the point that experimental designs are effective in controlling for many of these sources of error before the fact. Suppose a classic experimental design had been employed for the foot patrol experiment discussed earlier. Two precincts alike in all possible respects would have been chosen for study (equivalence). The experimental precinct would have been pretested prior to the treatment (foot patrol), whereas the control precinct would have received no treatment (retained usual patrol practices). At the end of the study both groups would once again have been observed and any differences between them would be assumed to have been produced by the deployment of foot patrols. History and maturation would not be likely rival explanations for these differences, because both groups were similar and thus exposed to the same historical and maturation conditions. Both groups were exposed to a pretest; thus, the differences could not result from the pretest, or at least the extent to which the pretest influences results can be assessed because it will show up in both groups. If it is assumed that both groups received the same instrument, changes in the instrument would not account for differences as long as these changes were the same for both groups. Statistical regression should be the same for both groups. Equivalence assures no selection bias, and experimental mortality should be the same.

This hypothetical foot patrol study is an example of a *field experiment*, a type of experiment that is conducted in a natural (field) setting; a *laboratory experiment* is a type of experiment that takes place in contrived or researcher-created conditions. Our next examples illustrate field experiments. Because most of these studies employ matching rather than randomization as the means of assuring equivalence, purists might argue that they are not true experimental designs but rather quasi-experimental designs.

Some Criminal Justice Examples of the Classic Experimental Design

Candid Camera

While the use of videotape for security purposes is routine today, at one time the usefulness of such electronic devices (in this case, photographs) was not commonly understood. In 1975, the Seattle Police Department installed hidden cameras in stereo speaker boxes in seventy-five commercial establishments identified as high-risk potential robbery victims. These businesses constituted the experimental group; a group of similar businesses received no treatment. The pretest for both groups consisted of gathering statistics on the percentage of robberies cleared by arrest and conviction rates prior to the study. If held up, a clerk triggered the camera by pulling a "trip" bill from the cash drawer. A special project director would make prints of the photograph of the robber available. A posttest comparing the two groups found that 55 percent of the robberies of experimental companies were cleared by arrest versus 25 percent of the control firms. Similarly, 48 percent of robbers at hidden camera sights were convicted, compared with 19 percent of the control group robbers ("Hidden Cameras Project," 1978).

Scared Straight

In the late 1970s, claims of reduced recidivism among juveniles in trouble with the law in response to visits with prisoners were illustrated by the Rahway prison project portrayed in the film *Scared Straight*. The assumption was that much of the "glamor" attached to criminal life by juveniles on the road to more trouble could be nipped in the bud by blunt, heart-to-heart dialogue with specially selected prisoners. Many jurisdictions began to set up what appeared to be a new gimmick in corrections. Later evaluations, however, suggested that the benefits claimed were premature.

Yarborough conducted an evaluation of the JOLT (Juvenile Offenders Learn Truth) program at the State Prison of Southern Michigan at Jackson. Unlike some earlier programs, verbal attacks and obscenities were de-emphasized. In 1978, subjects were randomly assigned to experimental and control groups and then measured at three- and six-month follow-up periods. All subjects were male and arrested or petitioned for an offense that, had they been adults, would have been criminal. No significant differences were found between those who had attended the JOLT session and those who had not. There were no differences in the proportion having petitions filed nor in the types of offenses committed (*Scared Straight*, 1979).

In 1987, WOR TV (Secaucus, New Jersey, June 21, 9:00 P.M. EST) aired a documentary entitled "*Scared Straight: Ten Years Later*." This program presented a very positive picture of the experiment, relying primarily on interviews with people who had attended. Finckenauer (1982), in *Scared Straight! and the Panacea Phenomenon*, felt that the original documentary (1977) had misled the American public into thinking this was a miracle cure for juvenile crime. Despite many problems and lack of cooperation in attempting to evaluate the "Juvenile Awareness Program" or "Lifer's Program" (*Scared Straight* program) at Rahway, Finckenauer found that his randomly assigned *Scared Straight* experimentals actually had higher seriousness delinquency scores afterward than the controls who did not attend the program. Similarly, many of the juveniles put through the program were not the hardened "junior criminals" the public had been led to believe.

A review of nine *Scared Straight* experiments over its thirty-three-year history indicated that, despite good intentions, the program not only did not deter future criminal behavior but actually led to more crime by program participants. The researchers concluded: "Given the possibility of harmful effects of interventions, government has an ethical responsibility to rigorously evaluate, on a continuing basis, the policies, practices, and programs it implements" (Petrosino, TurpinPetrosino, and Finckenauer, 2000).

Community Policing

Community policing has become a subject of much interest in law enforcement since the 1980s. The term broadly refers to a variety of strategies that attempt to get the police away from rapid response to service and closer to the community on a day-to-day basis. Order-maintenance, community crime prevention, problem solving, neighborhood safety, foot patrol, and a host of police–community relations strategies are all included under community policing (Mastrofski, 1992).

A variety of field experiments regarding the impact of neighborhood safety programs such as "neighborhood or block watch," "police storefronts," and "foot patrol" experiments have been undertaken. The Police Foundation's analysis of a neighborhood watch experiment in Houston found no noticeable reduction in crime compared with a similar area that had not received the program. Another Houston program established a police department storefront (a combination precinct station, social center, and community outreach center). Houston also experimented with personal-contact patrol in which officers attempted to stop and talk to as many citizens as possible. Despite problems in maintaining experimental conditions, some positive findings were obtained. The neighborhood watch and storefront programs had no noticeable impact upon crime reduction but an enormous impact upon reduction of citizen's fear of crime. In addition to reducing fear, the personal-contact patrol reduced household victimizations by one-half and resulted in improving the attitudes of residents on community issues (Sherman, 1985; Wycoff et al., 1985a, 1985b). Exhibit 3.1 describes a field experiment in Kansas City that met with success.

A continuing subject of debate has been public dissatisfaction with anonymous, routine policing in automobiles and requests for foot patrols, even though most police managers until recently viewed such assignments as inefficient deployment of limited police personnel. During the late 1970s, experiments with foot patrols were conducted in Newark, New Jersey, and Flint, Michigan (Police Foundation, 1981; Trojanowicz and Banas, 1985; Wilson and Kelling, 1982). The same findings were obtained in both studies (Kelling, 1985, p. 2): decreased fear of crime, greater citizen satisfaction, and greater appreciation of neighborhood values by the police. There also appeared to be greater job satisfaction, less fear, and higher morale for officers who patrol on foot than for officers who patrol in automobiles. The Flint study showed a decrease in service calls via telephone of 40 percent and a modest reduction in crime, whereas the Newark program showed no crime reduction. More replications (repeats of the experiments) are under way. Foot patrols are obviously no panacea but have been found popular, particularly when selectively implemented in densely populated urban areas.

In the 1990s, the National Institute of Justice had contracted a large number of studies of community policing ("Community Policing," 1992). For example, an evaluation of the Madison, Wisconsin, Police Department's "quality" policing program examined a community-oriented policing program with a new organizational design based on the work of management expert Edwards Deming. In comparing the experimental with the comparison police district it was found that in the experimental district the managers viewed themselves more as problem solvers, and employee attitudes regarding their work and organization improved. In addition, citizen interaction improved and their perception of crime as a problem was reduced. Citizens also expressed a more positive attitude toward the police (Wycoff and Skogan, 1994).

EXHIBIT 3.1 ▶

The Kansas City Gun Experiment

The United States has both the highest violent crime and homicide rate of any developed country as well as the largest armed civilian population in the world. National attempts to significantly control firearms are effectively blocked by the powerful National Rifle Association. Given these contingencies, what can police do to try to control growing youth homicide rates? One possibility tested in the Kansas City gun experiment by Sherman, Shaw, and Rogan (1995) was that greater enforcement of existing laws against carrying concealed weapons could reduce gun crime. With a Bureau of Justice Assistance "Weed and Seed" program grant, the Kansas City Police Department selected a target patrol beat and a control beat. The target beat had a 1991 homicide rate of 177 per 100,000 persons, about twenty times the national average. The control beat had a similar violent crime rate. The research design involved a matched groups before–after design. The "hot spot" target area received increased proactive patrols.

The actual technique the officers used to find guns varied, from frisks and searches incident to arrest on other charges to safety frisks associated with car stops for traffic violations. Every arrest for carrying concealed weapons had to be approved for adequate articulable suspicion with a supervisory detective's signature. (1995, p. 6)

Figure 1 illustrates the differences between the target beat and the comparison beat during the one-year experiment.

Gun crimes in the target beat decreased from 37 per 1,000 persons to 18.9, and guns seized increased from 9.9 to 16.8. The comparison beat showed little change in gun crime (22.6 to 23.6 per 1,000) and an actual decrease in guns seized (10.4 to 8.8 per 1,000). There was no displacement of gun crimes to surrounding areas. Drive-by shootings dropped from 7 to 1 in the target area, but doubled from 6 to 12 in the comparison area, again with no displacement effect. Figure 2 compares offenses by firearms.

Other positive findings were a decline in homicides in the target area, but not in the comparison area. Citizens in the target area were less fearful, but there was no change in fear in the comparison area. Two-thirds of those arrested for gun carrying in the target area were from outside the area.

Finally, only gun crimes were reduced by the directed patrols, which had no effect on calls for service or reduction of other crimes. Further replications were undertaken. Lawrence Sherman, the principal author of the report, was at the time on leave from the University of Maryland and serving as Criminologist to the Indianapolis Police Department in order to further test the program.

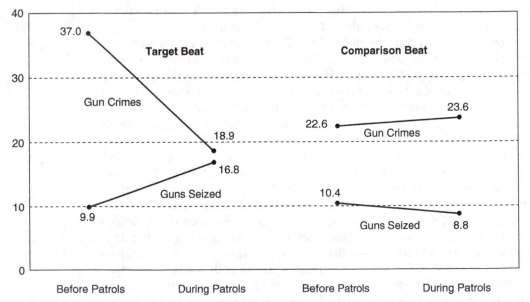

Figure 1

Kansas City Gun Experiment—Guns Seized per 1,000 Persons.

Source: Sherman, Shaw, and Rogan, 1995, p. 1.

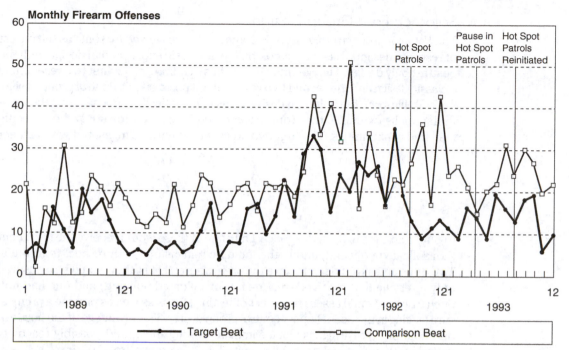

Figure 2
Total Offenses with Firearms by Month in Target and Comparison Beats.
Source: Sherman, Shaw, and Rogan, 1995, p. 7.

Source: Sherman, Lawrence W., James W. Shaw, and Dennis P. Rogan. "The Kansas City Gun Experiment." *National Institute of Justice Research in Brief,* January 1995. Document available from National Criminal Justice Reference Service, Box 6000, Rockville, MD 20849-6000; call 1-800-851-3420 or Internet lookncjrs@aspensys.com.

Other Experimental Designs

Other experimental designs include the *posttest-only control group design* and the *Solomon four-group design.*

Posttest-Only Control Group Design

To assess the impact of consolidated police departments on public satisfaction with policing in their area, Ostrom, Parks, and Whitaker conducted a *posttest-only control group design* (1973).

$$E \quad X \quad O$$
$$E \qquad O$$

Three Indianapolis neighborhoods with a consolidated police department were matched with three communities with independent police departments. The researchers discovered higher public satisfaction in the communities with independent departments. Without a pretest it is unclear, however, whether this difference could not in fact have been caused by other rival factors; for example, perhaps even before police department consolidation, the Indianapolis neighborhoods had lower degrees of satisfaction with their policing.

Solomon Four-Group Design

The *Solomon four-group design* (Solomon, 1949) is viewed by some as the purest of research designs. Basically it combines the classic experimental design with the posttest-only design. The Solomon design has four groups, the first two resembling a classic design and the second two resembling a posttest-only control group design.

To illustrate the Solomon design let us hypothetically suppose, using the same Indianapolis example, that four areas could be chosen for study from evenly matched communities. The first two areas would both be measured with respect

$$
\begin{array}{lllll}
E & O_1 & X & O_2 \\
E & O_1 & & O_2 \\
E & & X & O_2 \\
E & & & O_2
\end{array}
$$

to public attitude toward the police. Only one of these would receive the treatment (consolidated policing), and both would be remeasured with respect to attitude. Two other areas would not receive the premeasure; that is, they would be measured only after one had received treatment (consolidated policing) and one had not. Such a design would assess the effect of testing effects as well as provide a premeasure lacking in the posttest-only control group design. The advantage of the posttest-only control group design is that it eliminates testing effects and, possibly, reactivity entirely, although it lacks a measure of where the groups stood prior to the treatment. The Solomon four-group design obviously has the advantage of having the premeasure and, by adding the second two groups, has the same advantage as the posttest-only control group design. It is, however, expensive and difficult to implement and, therefore, not practical in many research situations.

The classic Solomon and posttest-only control group designs are examples of experimental designs. Randomization, in which equivalence is obtained by random assignment of subjects to experimental and control groups, is the key distinguishing characteristic of experimental designs. Preexperimental designs lack equivalence of groups, and quasi-experimental designs rely on matching of subjects to achieve equivalence. In many field experiments such as the Indianapolis example randomization may be inappropriate or impossible; as long as equivalence is assured, it can be argued that these are true experiments.

Preexperimental Designs

Research designs that lack one or two of the three major elements of experimental designs—equivalence or experimental and control groups—are designated as preexperimental designs.

ONE-GROUP EX POST FACTO DESIGN

$$X \quad O$$

ONE-GROUP BEFORE–AFTER DESIGN

$$O \quad X \quad O$$

TWO-GROUP EX POST FACTO DESIGN

$$
\begin{array}{ll}
X & O \\
& O
\end{array}
$$

One-Group Ex Post Facto Design

All of these preexperimental designs fail to provide equivalence or any assurance that the group(s) being studied is representative in any way of some larger population(s). The *one-group ex post facto design*, or one-shot case study, is quite typical of many early criminal justice demonstration projects. Our original example of the precinct foot patrol experiment, if it contained no preobservation, would serve as an illustration. Unlike true experimental designs, one-group ex post facto (after the fact) studies are subject to many internal invalidity factors or errors. One simply has chosen for study a group that has already been exposed to a particular treatment. Obviously, things other than the treatment could explain the outcome. If one finds a precinct that had experimental foot patrols or an agency with low recidivism rates, without premeasures, equivalence, and control groups, one is on shaky ground in concluding that lower crime rates or lower recidivism are due to these factors. Many studies, particularly field studies in criminology and criminal justice, are of the one-shot case study variety. Cressey's (1957) study of incarcerated embezzlers, for instance, may have major problems with respect to selection bias and reactivity but, on the other hand, may be the only way of obtaining exploratory information on a little-known topic. What one-group ex post facto studies lose in terms of internal control of error may be gained in terms of studying groups in natural field conditions.

Early research on the XYY or "supermale syndrome" assumed, on the basis of studies of incarcerated violent offenders, that an extra male chromosome may have been responsible for violent crime (Witkin et al., 1978). Only later examination of the general population suggested that it may be as prevalent among the "noncriminal" male population. As mentioned previously, in lamenting the shortcomings of studies of sentencing behavior, Farrington (1978) points out that few studies use both before and after measures, or compare a sentenced group with an unsentenced group, thus making it difficult to know whether changes in behavior are due to sentences, penalties, or other concurrent social changes.

In another example of a one-group ex post facto study, Heussenstamm (1971) reports on a field experiment in which subjects, none of whom had received traffic violations the previous twelve months, attached Black Panther bumper stickers to their automobiles. They attracted so many traffic citations that the experiment had to be canceled. That Heussenstamm had knowledge of the fact that the subjects had not received citations before the treatment may qualify the study as being an example of the next type, the one-group before–after design.

One-Group Before–After Design

The *one-group before–after design*, or one-group pretest–posttest design, is an example of a longitudinal design. A group, which is not necessarily chosen on the basis of representativeness, is observed, exposed to treatment, and again observed. The primary advantage of this design over the one-group ex post facto design is, of course, the presence of a premeasure. This adds, however, to the problem of testing effects and has the same problem as the one-group ex post facto design in that one's findings cannot be compared with those for a similar control group not exposed to treatment.

An example of a one-group before–after design is Pierce and Bowers' (1979) analysis of the impact of the Massachusetts Bartley–Fox gun law, which carried a one-year minimum prison sentence for the unlicensed carrying of firearms. With the use of recorded crime statistics and observations both before and after passage of the law, the earliest part of a longitudinal design suggested a decrease in gun-related assaults, robberies, and homicides; however, this was offset by increases in nongun assaults and robberies using other weapons. Without a control group the same problem exists as in our previous burglary reduction program (Garwood, 1978)—other variables may be responsible for these findings.

Two-Group Ex Post Facto Design

The *two-group ex post facto design* eliminates possible pretest reactivity by studying both an experimental and a control group after the experimental group has been exposed to some treatment. The primary problem with this design is that there is no way of being sure that the two groups were initially equivalent. Skillful selection of groups for comparison may be the only option a researcher has in some instances. Brown et al. (1970) surveyed two groups of parolees: those who had succeeded and those who had failed at parole. After the fact, they were asked to identify factors in the institution and community that assisted or impeded their adjustment. Such two-group ex post facto designs were heavily utilized in early biological and psychological theories. These theories in criminology that claimed genetic or personality differences between criminals and noncriminals suffered from what Reid (2005, p. 90) describes as the **dualistic fallacy**, the assumption that prisoners (who are supposed to represent criminals) and groups from the general population (all of whom are assumed to be noncriminals) represent mutually exclusive groups (or are nonoverlapping).

Dualistic fallacy

Cross-Sectional and Longitudinal Designs

Before going further, it is crucial to briefly introduce a general distinction used to describe research designs. *Cross-sectional designs* involve studies of one group at one time and usually refer to a representative sample of this group. *Longitudinal studies* are studies of the same group over a period of time and generally are studies of change (Menard, 1991).

Time-series designs involve variations of multiple observations of the same group at various times. Variations may include dividing the original group into equivalent groups and observing these portions longitudinally. In Chapters 5 and 6, we discuss the usefulness of panel designs in such surveys as the National Crime Victimization Survey in providing an in-depth view over time of the same study population. In a now classic criminological study, Wolfgang et al. (1972) used existing records to longitudinally trace the criminal or noncriminal careers of 9,945 boys born in Philadelphia in 1945.

In a replication that included females, Tracy, Wolfgang, and Figlio (1985) tracked the criminal history of males and females born in Philadelphia in 1958 who continued to live there from the age of ten until adulthood. Both studies were instrumental in identifying the concept of serious career criminals, finding that approximately 6 percent of the 1945 group had been responsible for 53 percent of arrests for violent crime and 71 percent for robbery, whereas 7 percent of the 1958 group had committed 75 percent of all serious crime by this group. Farrington (1979) conducted a similar study in London, begun in 1961, of boys eight to nine years old in state primary schools.

One of the earliest series of cohort analysis was done by the Gluecks, who studied 500 reformatory inmates over ten years and 1,000 juvenile delinquents for more than fifteen years (Glueck and Glueck, 1937, 1940). Such longitudinal designs are useful in giving us the long- and short-term variations over time. Another example of an ambitious longitudinal study was the Cambridge–Somerville Youth Study begun in 1937 and continuing with some interruption through 1945. Extensive data were gathered on each of the 650 boys who began the project including delinquency, neighborhood, family conditions, school behavior, intelligence, and personality. In 1955, the McCords (1959) reexamined the data and compared official and unofficial delinquents. Exhibit 3.2 examines a longitudinal study of child abuse and neglect victims. The Denver Youth Survey (Browning and Huizinga, 1999) is another example of a longitudinal study. It has been following 1,527 boys and girls from high-risk neighborhoods in Denver who were 7, 9, 11, 13, and 15 years old in 1987 in order to discover correlates of crime.

EXHIBIT 3.2 ▶

The Cycle of Violence and Victims of Child Abuse

In previous research, Cathy Spatz Widom (1992) found that childhood abuse or neglect increased the odds of future delinquency and adult criminality by an overall 40 percent. The research consisted of a longitudinal study of 1,575 cases from childhood through young adulthood. A group of 908 cases of child abuse or neglect processed by the courts between 1967 and 1971 were tracked using official records for fifteen to twenty years. A comparison group of 667 was matched by age, sex, race, and family social class. The study concluded that:

> While most members of both groups had no juvenile or adult criminal record, being abused or neglected as a child increased the likelihood of arrest as a juvenile by 53 percent, as an adult by 38 percent, and for violent crime by 38 percent. (1992, p. 1)

Using these same cases, Widom (1995) also examined the relationship between childhood sexual abuse and later criminal behavior, particularly sexual offenses. The key finding was that:

> People who were sexually victimized during childhood are at higher risk of arrest for committing crimes as

adults, including sex crimes, than are people who did not suffer sexual or physical abuse or neglect during childhood. However, the risk of arrest for childhood sexual abuse victims as adults is no higher than for victims of other types of childhood abuse and neglect. (1995, p. 2)

Compared with victims of physical abuse, child abuse victims are more likely to be arrested for prostitution. Victims of physical abuse were more likely to commit rape and sodomy than were sexual abuse victims or the nonvictimized. The long-assumed relationship between childhood sexual abuse, running away, and prostitution was not borne out by the research.

All of these findings relied on official statistics for measuring the dependent variable of crime commission. Continuing research in this series is examining other sources. An attempt is being made to reinterview all 1,575 subjects in order to discover other consequences of child abuse including social, emotional, cognitive, psychiatric, and health outcomes. Also to be examined are factors that protect child abuse victims from later negative consequences.

Sources: Widom, Cathy Spatz, "The Cycle of Violence." *National Institute of Justice Research in Brief*, October 1992; Widom, Cathy Spatz. "Victims of Childhood Sexual Abuse—Later Criminal Consequences." *National Institute of Justice Research in Brief*, March 1995. Documents can be obtained from the National Criminal Justice Reference Service, Box 6000, Rockville, MD 20849-6000; call 1-800-851-3420 or Internet lookncjrs@aspensys.com.

Time-series designs and *panel designs* are other terms used to refer to types of longitudinal studies, as are cohort and trend studies that are also variations of longitudinal designs. **Time-series designs** involve measuring a single variable at successive points in time. In an *interrupted time-series design*, measurements are taken at time points prior to treatment and for an equivalent period after intervention. The rate of crime committed one year prior to treatment could be compared with the rate for the first year after treatment (Schneider and Wilson, 1978). *Trend studies* analyze different samples of the same general population longitudinally, whereas *cohort studies* analyze subgroups over time, although each time may consist of a sample of the cohort. *Panel studies* examine the same select group or sample over time, as we will see in the National Crime Surveys. The most ambitious longitudinal study ever conducted in the social sciences is the previously discussed "Project of Human Development" of Chicago neighborhoods.

Although there has been some debate in the field of criminology regarding the overapplication of scarce federal research funds to expensive longitudinal studies, it is often the only way of sorting out many trends and causal relationships (Esbensen and Menard, 1990, p. 5).

Quasi-Experimental Designs

There are many variations of the experimental design. In fact, as mentioned previously, almost all research in criminal justice can be described using the notation with which we have been working. Because quasi-experimental designs rely on matching—the use of "comparison groups" or means other than randomization to obtain equivalence—the value of using comparison groups depends upon how similar the groups are on key variables to the treatment group. Some quasi- or semiexperimental designs include single time-series, multiple time-series, and counterbalanced designs.

Time-Series Designs

Time-series designs refer to the analysis of a single variable (for example, crime rate) at many successive time periods with some measures taken prior to treatment and other observations taken after the intervention. It is sometimes called an interrupted time series because the series of observations is interrupted by a treatment (*X*).

INTERRUPTED TIME-SERIES DESIGNS

$$O \quad O \quad O \quad O \quad X \quad O \quad O \quad O \quad O$$

It is desirable to have at least ten preobservations and a bare minimum of two, but probably more, postobservations (Schneider et al., 1978, pp. 2–13). Such designs are widely used in criminal justice research in examining the impact of a new law or treatment upon trends in crime.

Interrupted time-series designs then can be defined as an analysis of a single variable measured at many successive time points, with some measures taken prior to a treatment (interruption) and others taken after the treatment. Preproject observations are used as a basis for estimating the trend and differences between this projected trend, and the trend observed after treatment can be assessed to determine whether the treatment had an impact.

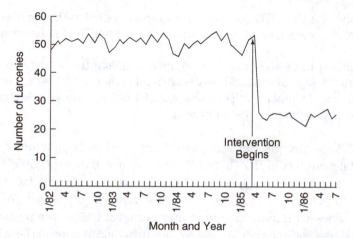

Figure 3.2
Time-Series Data for Larcenies from Automobiles in Newport News, Virginia. The Intervention (Treatment) Was a Problem-Oriented Policing Approach That Consisted of Special Tracking and Investigation of Crime Incidents.

Source: Spelman, William, and John E. Beck. "Problem-Oriented Policing." *Research in Brief.* National Institute of Justice (January 1987): 7.

Figure 3.2 depicts time-series data for a problem-oriented policing program (the treatment) designed to reduce larcenies from automobiles. The overall reduction in trend lines can be noted from before to after the intervention.

Figure 3.3 demonstrates the advantage of time-series designs over simple pretest–posttest designs. In both instances simple analysis of the last point before

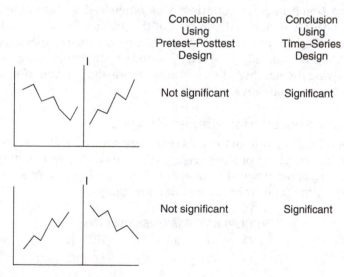

Figure 3.3
A Comparison of Pretest–Posttest Designs and Time-Series Designs.

Source: Schneider, Anne L., et al. *Handbook of Resources for Criminal Justice Evaluators.* Washington, D.C.: National Institute of Law Enforcement and Criminal Justice (1978): 2–47.

and the first point after the intervention would have led to the conclusion of no significant change where, in fact, examination of trend lines showed significant change.

Monahan and Walker (1990, p. 66) give an illustration of the superiority of a time-series design over a before–after design in their analysis of the impact of the Community Mental Health Centers Act of 1963. This program's goal was the reduction of state mental hospitalization.

In 1963, the year the act was passed, the resident population of state mental hospitals in the United States was approximately 500,000. In 1990, it was less than 150,000. These before–after figures have been used to persuade Congress of the effectiveness of the act. When a time-series with more than one measurement before the passage is used, however, the results seem quite different. A time-series shows the population of state mental hospitals to have increased each year from early in the century until 1955, and decreased each year thereafter, with no noticeable acceleration in the rate of decrease in 1963, the year the act was passed. In this light, the most plausible hypothesis is that the factor causing the population decrease began in the mid-1950's, and not in the mid-1960's. Many now view the introduction of psychotropic medication as the principal method of treating mental patients, which indeed began in 1955, as the most plausible hypothesis to account for the "deinstitutionalization" of mental hospitals.

In yet other variations of interrupted time-series designs, the impact of new prisons (experimental counties) was compared with matched/control counties in order to examine the impact of the prisons. Twenty variables were followed for two years before and two years after the prison openings (Smykla et al., 1984). The relationship between "War and Capital Punishment" was examined by studying the number of executions before, during, and after three war periods (Schneider and Smykla, 1990).

Multiple Interrupted Time-Series Designs

A distinction is also made between *single interrupted time-series designs*, which examine one group or site's preprogram and postprogram outcomes over time, and *multiple interrupted time-series designs*, which contrast one group's performance with that of relevant comparison groups.

MULTIPLE TIME-SERIES DESIGNS

O	O	O	O	X	O	O	O	O
O	O	O	O		O	O	O	O

Although a single interrupted time-series design might examine the impact of the 55-mph speed limit upon vehicular deaths, a multiple interrupted time-series design would compare a state with the new speed limit with one without it during the same period. For example, Connecticut's 1955 crackdown on speeding reduced traffic fatalities, whereas neighboring states without this program experienced no decrease (Campbell and Ross, 1980). In the 1960s, Boston and New York City had very restrictive handgun licensing laws but complained that their laws were defeated by guns brought in from nonrestrictive states. Zimring (1975) studied the impact of the Federal Gun Control Act of 1968 on interstate traffic in guns on homicide rates and found that handgun homicide rates actually grew faster in New York City and Boston (the restrictive cities) than the average trend for fifty-seven control cities. Such time-series designs are indispensable and widely used in criminological and criminal justice research because the subjects often require analysis of trends or long-range effects rather than short-term outcomes.

Counterbalanced Designs

Counterbalanced designs are intended to manage or control the problem of multiple-treatment inference in which X_1 refers to one treatment, X_2 a second, X_3 a third, and X_4 a fourth. By using four groups that are equivalent and exposing each group to all four treatments and observing after each combination of treatments, it becomes possible to isolate the treatment(s), combination of treatments, or sequence of treatments that produces the outcome. For example, in four precincts where the treatments were X_1—foot patrol, X_2—media campaign, X_3—police blazers, and X_4—unarmed police, perhaps the desired outcome is obtained only by X_3—police blazers and X_1—foot patrol in that sequence of introduction only. Such a design, although complex, is the only way to uncover such a relationship.

E	X_1O	X_2O	X_3O	X_4O
E	X_2O	X_3O	X_4O	X_1O
E	X_3O	X_4O	X_1O	X_2O
E	X_4O	X_1O	X_2O	X_3O

There are many other variations of the experimental model. Familiarity with the notation and basic designs we have discussed enables one to conceptualize these other designs as offshoots of the basic ones.

Some Other Criminal Justice Examples of Variations of the Experimental Model

The Provo and Silverlake Experiments

Empey and Erickson (1972) and Empey and Lubeck (1971) employed the classic experimental design to assess the effect of experimental community-based treatment programs in Provo, Utah, and Silverlake, Los Angeles. The subjects were all juveniles who were either serious and/or repeat offenders. All were ordinarily candidates for reformatories who were sentenced by a judge to probation or incarceration. All were male. None were seriously retarded, addicted to drugs, or had a history of serious assaultive violence.

Although both the Provo and Silverlake experiments are relatively complex in theoretical design and methodological execution, a brief review of two elements of the analysis will serve our purposes. One element in community resistance to community-based treatment programs has been the fear of crime perpetrated by those undergoing treatment. The Provo researchers, and later the Silverlake study, compared randomly assigned experimental and control groups from two disposition conditions. Our discussion is concerned primarily with the Provo Study, although the Silverlake experience is also briefly discussed.

PROVO RESEARCH DESIGN

Probation experimental group	E	O	X	O
Probation control group	E	O		O
Incarceration experimental group	E	O	X	O
Incarceration control group	E	O		O

Equivalence of groups was obtained by randomly assigning those given probation to the Provo program or regular probation and similarly assigning those scheduled for incarceration to either the Provo treatment or actual incarceration. With the incarceration group, randomization broke down because the population was too small, and the matched control group was selected using a state training school.

In evaluating arrest rates as an indicator of crime committed, the probation controls had a rate twice as high as the probation experimentals. Surprisingly, the arrest rate for "incarcerated" experimentals was almost as low as that for incarcerated controls. The latter were either on furloughs or escapees who, in addition, tended to commit more serious crimes. Similar findings were obtained in the Silverlake experiment, which added the variables of urban setting and race (20 percent Hispanic or African American, versus 100 percent Caucasian in the Provo study).

In analysis of yet another dependent variable, postprogram arrest rates, by means of a longitudinal follow-up four years after release, the experimental probation types were not greatly superior to regular probation control types (a 71 percent reduction in crime compared with the rate four years prior to the experiment, versus 66 percent for the regular probation group). The "incarcerated" experimental group showed a 49 percent reduction, whereas the incarcerated control group exhibited only a 25 percent reduction. Maturation or age did not affect these differences when controlled statistically; that is, these differences operated independently of age. Among some methodological problems introduced in the Provo experiment was a breakdown in equivalence, because the judge sentenced too few to the reformatory. Additionally, a possible Hawthorne effect was present, as suggested by the fact that the success rate for the control group given regular probation was higher than that for the same group before the experiment began. The probation officers' knowledge of the study may have had this impact (Hood and Sparks, 1971, p. 209).

Despite some problems, given the higher costs of incarceration, the Provo and Silverlake findings were a major demonstration of the utility of the community-based corrections movement. Exhibit 3.3 reports on evaluations of shock incarceration.

EXHIBIT 3.3 ▶

Evaluations of Shock Incarceration

With a burgeoning prison population in the 1980s, intermediate sanctions such as electronic monitoring, intensive probation, and shock incarceration became popular, cost-effective alternatives to overcrowding prisons. They turned out not to fit the role of a popular panacea. Often increased recidivism took place due to an increased "net of control" (Morris and Tonry, 1990) or increased technical violations due to greater surveillance during community supervision (Petersilia and Turner, 1990). While boot camp programs (shock incarceration) vary in content, most involve offenders participating in military-type training and variations of physical exercise, hard physical labor, ventilation therapy, substance abuse, and prerelease education. Doris Mackenzie and associates have examined a number of boot camp programs.

Examining a Louisiana boot camp (shock incarceration) program, Mackenzie and Shaw (1993) looked at shock incarceration releasees after two years of community supervision and compared these with similar offenders who had been given probation or parole. Four groups of offenders were compared: shock releases, probationers, parolees, and shock dropouts. These were contrasted with respect to technical violations (terms of supervision offenses), new crime arrests, and new crime convictions. The shock graduates had higher rates of technical violations and revocations than the probationers and parolees, lower rates of new convictions, and, in some analyses, lower rates of arrests and revocations for new crimes. There were no differences between shock alumnae and shock dropouts in the Louisiana study (1993). This study was an example of the utilization of a quasi-experimental design with comparison groups in which there was no random assignment of subjects. The shock experimentals were compared with offenders who had been eligible for shock incarceration but had received other treatments instead. Possible invalidities in such a design include selection bias (in that offenders were not randomly assigned) and the fact that shock offenders were more carefully scrutinized on release, which most likely accounted for the greater number of technical violations (1993, p. 483).

Between 1982 and 1992, the number of shock programs had increased to forty-one programs. In an evaluation of eight shock incarceration programs in Florida, Georgia, Illinois, Louisiana, New York, Oklahoma, South Carolina, and Texas, Mackenzie and Souryal (1994) found recidivism rates similar to comparable offenders who did not go through boot camps. Where shock offenders had lower rates, this may have been due to selection bias (specially selected offenders for the program). It appears that boot camp experience itself does not reduce recidivism (Travis, 1994). Successful programs were followed by six-month intensive supervision in the community. Participants in boot camps gave higher ratings to their experience and felt safer.

Sources: Mackenzie, Doris L., and James W. Shaw. "The Impact of Shock Incarceration on Technical Violations and New Criminal Activities." *Justice Quarterly* 10 (September 1993): 462–488; Mackenzie, Doris L., and Claire Souryal. *Multisite Evaluation of Shock Incarceration.* Rockville, MD: National Criminal Justice Reference Service, NCJ #150062, 1994; Travis, Jeremy. "Researchers Evaluate Eight Shock Incarceration Programs." *National Institute of Justice Update*, October 1994.

The Kansas City Preventive Patrol Experiment

Yet another variation of the classic experimental design was employed in the *Kansas City preventive patrol study* (Kelling et al., 1974).

Experimental Group I (Reactive Patrols)	E	O_1	X_1	O_2
Experimental Group II (Proactive Patrols)	E	O_1	X_2	O_2
Control Group (Usual Patrols)	E	O_1		O_2

A fifteen-beat area of the city was divided into three matched five-beat groups. The first group was reactive in patrol procedure; that is, officers responded only to calls for service and did not deploy preventive patrols. The second group was proactive and increased preventive patrols up to three times the normal levels. Usual deployment, or preventive patrols at their normal levels, was assigned to the control group.

Outcome variables analyzed prior to the treatments, O_1, included reported crime and victimization surveys of citizens and businesses. Posttreatment outcomes in citizen and business victimization and perception of security and reported and unreported crime showed no statistically significant differences among the three types of patrol areas studied. Despite methodological criticisms such as the location of cars withdrawn from reactive patrol, small size of beats, and small numbers used in the survey, the study suggested that police administrators have greater leeway than they supposed in patrol deployment (Chaiken, 1976; Davis and Knowles, 1975; Kelling and Pate, 1975; Larson, 1975; Pate et al., 1975). Similar replications of the Kansas City experiment essentially confirmed the same findings ("Albuquerque," 1979).

In a review of the Kansas City data, critics concluded that it was not likely that randomization had been used in beat assignments (Feinberg, Singer, and Tanur, 1985). Kelling, the principal director of the project, admitted that the police selected the beats on the basis of the department's needs (Fagan, 1990, p. 110). Research by Sykes (1984) further illustrates the need to measure different outcomes of increased enforcement efforts. In examining saturation patrol as a deterrent to drunk driving, he found that it did deter some types of deviant behavior but was not a "panacea."

The Minneapolis Domestic Violence Experiment

A 1977 Police Foundation (1977, p. iv) study in Kansas City found that in the two years preceding a case of domestic assault or domestic homicide, the police had been at the address of the incident five or more times in half of the cases. This suggested that the police had an opportunity to attempt to head off domestic violence. Beginning in the late 1960s the police had been encouraged to train their officers and utilize counseling and family crisis intervention strategies in domestic dispute cases. By the 1980s concern for the rights of female victims, possible lawsuits against police for failure to make arrests where subsequent violence occurred, and a more conservative punitive-policy orientation led to a questioning of this policy.

In 1983, the *Minneapolis Domestic Violence Experiment* (Sherman, 1985; Sherman and Berk, 1984a, 1984b) was undertaken to attempt to provide evidence as to the most effective strategy. The research design is similar to the Kansas City Preventive Patrol Experiment—that is, it contains three groups (two with different treatments and one control). In Minneapolis, police officers volunteered to give up their discretion in handling simple (misdemeanor) domestic assaults and take whatever action was dictated by a random system: instructions written on a card and drawn from an envelope at the scene. Three different instructions were given: (1) *arrest* the suspect; (2) *separate* or remove the suspect from the scene for 8 hours; or (3) *advise* and mediate.

MINNEAPOLIS DOMESTIC VIOLENCE EXPERIMENT

Arrest	E	O_1	X_1	O_2
Separate	E	O_1	X_2	O_2
Mediate[*]	E	O_1		O_2

[*]Mediation could be considered a third treatmark of X_3

After the police intervened, researchers attempted to interview the victims every two weeks for the next six months as well as monitor police records to check if there were any subsequent assaults. The results appeared to be dramatic: 37 percent of the "advised" subjects and 33 percent of the "separated" subjects had recidivated (committed new assaults within six months); however, only 19 percent of the "arrested" subjects were repeaters. This reduction was accomplished even though arrest usually entailed only a night in jail.

The Minneapolis experiment has been both the most widely accepted and the most influential policy experiment of recent years; no other policy experiment has had quite the same impact on criminal justice policy. It's effect may be explained in part by the conservative tenor of the times, which emphasizes a law enforcement orientation for solving social problems; it may also be explained by the very aggressive dissemination of the study's findings (Binder and Meeker, 1991). Buzawa and Buzawa (1991) note that even though the research project was a modest pilot study with acknowledged limitations, extraordinary efforts to publicize the results in the national media resulted in premature police policy changes. In the first published replication of the study in Omaha, Nebraska, the researchers Dunford, Hiuzinga, and Elliott (1989, 1990) found that arrest alone did not have any greater impact than mediation or separation.

Binder and Meeker (1991) have provided the most thorough critique of the Minneapolis study. They cited several objections:

- The areas chosen for study were two Minneapolis precincts with the worst domestic violence rates.
- Officer participation in the study was not only voluntary, but poor. By study's end, about 28 percent of the cases were being processed by only three officers.
- Approximately 60 percent of the Minneapolis sample of victims and suspects were unemployed, whereas a similar study by Ray (1982) in the New York City area found that most were employed.
- Nearly 60 percent of the Minneapolis sample had previously been arrested, and only one-third had had husband–wife relationships. By comparison, in Ray's study (1982) only 10 percent had previous records, with two-thirds being married couples.
- The comparison treatments of separation or mediation by police officers without special training were not realistic comparison points.
- Other problems with the statistical analysis (Binder and Meeker, 1988) of prison crowding and of internal factors such as "officer interest in victim's story" raised further questions regarding the study's broad conclusions.

Further replications will tell us if we have too quickly embraced an "arrest panacea" for handling domestic disputes. Results from six replications seem to suggest that arrest does not work more effectively in deterring domestic assault.

The point of all of this is to suggest that research is an ongoing process and one in which replication is essential; panaceas or simple solutions based on one study are suspect.

If you refused to be intimidated by the researchese in this chapter and learned your *X*s and *O*s and how research design is a powerful tool for controlling rival causal factors, you are now conversant in the language and actually have gotten through the worst part. In the following chapters we attempt to make you fluent in this language.

The Experiment as a Data-Gathering Strategy

We have thus far viewed experiments primarily from the standpoint of research design; however, the experiment is also a data-gathering strategy. Through its three key features of assuring equivalence of groups, pre- and posttests, and experimental and control groups, the experiment is a powerful strategy for research.

As a research design strategy, the experiment consists of blueprints outlining the conduct of the study. Saying that the experiment is the benchmark of comparison for other designs suggests that by using the X and O notation scheme, we can depict a basic model of a research study and also the potential strengths and weaknesses of such a design or research plan. The experiment is also a tool for data gathering, a strategy for obtaining and analyzing data. As a data-gathering strategy, the experiment has many variations that are defined by the setting. These variations range from laboratory experiments to field experiments, the former having greatest control over experimental conditions (thus high internal validity); but because of the very controlled atmosphere, problems may exist in terms of artificiality or external validity. Field experiments have fewer internal controls but greater external validity. In discussing relative advantages and disadvantages of the experiment, it is difficult to distinguish whether critics are talking about a design or data-gathering strategy or whether they are critiquing laboratory and/or field experiments or both.

Advantages of Experiments

Advantages of experiments

The **advantages of experiments** are many. They offer the best control for factors that tend to affect the internal validity of studies. The researcher is able before the fact, by the very design of the study, to control for many of the rival causal factors that tend to invalidate findings. The experimenter can control for the effects of many variables by including or excluding them from the study design.

A second advantage of experiments is that they are *relatively quick* and *inexpensive*. In contrast to many of the other data-gathering strategies that we will examine in Chapters 4–8, an experiment generally produces the required data necessary for analysis rather quickly. Depending on the scope of the study and required staff, facilities, and equipment, the experiment may represent a bargain compared with the expense of surveys or field strategies.

Another advantage of the experiment is its *manageability*, because the researcher is able to call the shots by controlling the stimulus, the environment, the treatment time, and even the degree of subject exposure. The conditions and conduct of experiments are often so rigorously defined that they lend themselves to replication by which the design and methodology can be repeated by other investigators. This is a major advantage over some field studies and surveys where it may be more difficult to repeat all of the ingredients.

Experimental strategies can be applied to natural settings in which the researcher has the best of both worlds, rigorous control and a more natural setting. If conditions can be viewed as realistic by subjects, *experiments may be the only way of studying certain complex behaviors.* Additionally, "natural experiments," which "occur as part of a natural process, where neither the setting nor the randomization process are controlled" (Fagan, 1990, p. 13), may present themselves without any intervention by the researcher. For example, a new treatment program might be implemented, but it might be applied to only half of the subjects due to funding shortages.

Disadvantages of Experiments

Despite the many advantages of experiments as a data-gathering strategy, there are potential disadvantages a researcher should take into account in whether experiments are the preferred strategy. The major **disadvantage of experiments** is their *artificiality.* In essence, the very controls imposed by the researcher to control for rival causal factors internal to an experiment may create artificial conditions that impede the ability to extrapolate to larger populations that are subject to natural conditions. In controlling for extraneous conditions, one may literally be creating a mere shadow of the former entity. This problem is more severe with laboratory experiments than field experiments.

Disadvantage of experiments

In a typical critique of the contrived nature of some experiments, Field showed how many laboratory simulations of jury decision making using college students as jurors may be in error. Using randomly selected students and nonstudents in juror roles, Field (1978) found students to be significantly more lenient in their sentencing. Thus, experimental results have no assumed built-in validity. Some of the scorn with which some experimental researchers view data obtained by other social science and criminal justice researchers using field research methods is misplaced.

Other major problems relate to the general difficulty of doing experimental research in terms of obtaining human subjects or situations/conditions in which one can properly manipulate the variables to be investigated. Major ethical issues can be raised by using experimental research. Luskin points out the difficulty of implementing experimental designs in court research. Court personnel may decline to experiment with new procedures or be unable to manipulate key variables (Luskin, 1978). Hackler suggests that in evaluations of delinquency prevention programs, traditional experimental–control group procedures are nearly impossible, create unnecessary stress for program staff, and may produce hostility toward the researcher. After-the-fact statistical analysis is in this instance viewed as far less obtrusive and more useful than precontrolled studies (Hackler, 1978). Most judges are unwilling to permit treatment decisions to be governed by pure random selection. In fact, one professor of criminal law indicated that such assignment could constitute a violation of the right to due process (Glaser, 1976, p. 775), although others point out that most randomized experiments are ethical and legal (Erez, 1986). *Experimenter effects* may also occur in experiments in which those conducting the research actually selectively observe that they wish to see or unconsciously give cues to the subjects as to the desired behavior or attitudes expected. Experiments provide an excellent method for controlling for factors regarding internal validity, but they are often weak with respect to external validity.

Summary

Assumptions of causality rest at the basis of scientific investigation. Three essential steps are necessary to attempt to resolve the causality question: demonstration of relationship, specification of time order, and control for, or exclusion of, rival causal variables. The experimental model is one of the most powerful means of controlling for rival causal factors before the fact through the design of research. Rival causal factors may be treated as factors affecting internal validity and those affecting external validity. Although the former are errors introduced because of flaws within the study, the latter are factors that impinge on the generalizability of the study to larger populations. Factors affecting internal validity include history, maturation, testing, instrumentation, statistical regression, experimental mortality, and interaction effects such as selection–maturation interaction. Those impacting on external validity include testing effects, selection bias, reactivity, and multiple-treatment interference. Related invalidating factors include the Hawthorne effect, the placebo effect, the halo effect, and post hoc error.

The classic experimental design is the benchmark or point of departure for all other research designs. That is, in a sense, all forms of research can be viewed as a variation of the experimental model. The three basic components of the classic experiment are pretest and posttest, experimental and control groups, and equivalence. In addition, familiarization with the notation of experimental designs is a useful heuristic device for breaking down the essentials of a research design. Classic experimental designs provide for the most rigorous before-the-fact control over factors of internal validity, and different variations enable control for rival causal factors. Illustration of the various designs with examples from criminal justice research provides the reader some familiarity with applications of these designs from the criminology and criminal justice literature.

After this review and examination of examples of the experimental model and its variations, Chapter 4 will explore the relative advantages and disadvantages of alternatives to the experimental model in criminal justice and criminology.

Experimental methods of gathering data have distinct *advantages* such as rigid control over rival factors within the experiment, the relative quick and inexpensive manner in which readily quantifiable data can be gathered, and overall manageability from the standpoint of the researcher. The *disadvantages* of experiments often outweigh their advantages, particularly in dealing with criminal justice subject matter. Major shortcomings of the experimental method include artificiality, which may hinder its generalizability to wider populations, and difficulty in applying the approach to human subjects and situations in criminal justice.

Examples of the Kansas City Gun Experiment, Child Abuse Victims, and Violence and Shock Incarceration illustrated various research designs in this chapter.

KEY CONCEPTS

Steps for resolving the causality problem
Rival causal factors
Spurious relationship
Internal validity
External validity
History
Maturation
Testing
Instrumentation
Statistical regression
Selection bias
Experimental mortality

Selection–maturation interaction
Testing effects
Reactivity
Multiple-treatment interference
Hawthorne effect
Halo effect
Self-fulfilling prophecy
Post hoc error
Placebo effect
Double-blind experiment
Research designs

Classic experimental design
Equivalence
Randomization
Matching
Pretest/posttest
Experimental group
Control group
Dualistic fallacy
Time-series designs
Advantages/disadvantages of experiments

REVIEW QUESTIONS

1. How does research design control for rival causal factors? Describe, for example, how the classic experimental design controls for history and maturation.

2. Find a recent journal article that employs an experimental, preexperimental, or quasi-experimental design. Name, describe, and illustrate the design, and discuss any rival causal factors controlled for in this design.

3. Why are time-series designs particularly useful in criminal justice studies?

4. Design a hypothetical study, and discuss how your design controls for many rival causal factors.

5. Discuss the Kansas City Gun Experiment. What type of research design was employeand what were the major findings of the project?

USEFUL WEB SITES

Uniform Crime Reports *www.fbi.gov/ucr/ucr.htm*

Sourcebook of Criminal Justice Statistics *www.albany.edu/sourcebook/*

National Incident-Based Reporting System (NIBRS) *www.ojp.usdoj.gov/bjs/nibrs.htm*

Bureau of Justice Statistics *www.ojp.usdoj.gov/bjs/*

CJ Ed (Researching Criminal Justice) *www.cjed.com/rschers.htm*

Justnet (Justice Technology Information Network) *http://www.justnet.org/*

4

The Uniform Crime Reports and Sampling

This chapter, in part, serves as an introduction to the next four chapters, which deal in detail with alternatives to the experiment as a data-gathering strategy. These alternatives include surveys, participant observation, case studies, and unobtrusive measures. The chapter begins with an examination of the FBI Uniform Crime Reports (UCR). The UCR serves as a data source, and, for a time, it was about the only source of information consulted by researchers in examining crime and criminal behavior. Because most of our later discussion of sources, such as victim and self-report surveys, are contrasted with the UCR, it receives early and separate coverage in this chapter.

Alternative Data-Gathering Strategies

As has been indicated, the classic experimental design rests as a reference point with which to compare all other research strategies; however, this by no means suggests that the experiment as a method of data gathering is better or a more desirable strategy. This debate among social scientists, who disagree about which means of data gathering is best, illustrates the notion of *methodological narcissism* (discussed in Chapter 1), which causes individuals to become so committed to a particular research strategy that they consider all other approaches inferior. The final resolution of this issue will be discussed in Chapter 9 under triangulation, where we will argue that the best resolution of many of these issues is simply to employ multiple methodologies or a wide array of instruments. Arguments that suggest its superiority are misplaced in that the experiment, despite its obvious strengths with respect to internal controls, tends to have primary weaknesses that other techniques do not have with respect to external validity. Outside of captive prisoner research, many topics in criminal justice require "real world" strategies, or approaches that bring the researcher into the actual environment of naturally occurring events (Filstead, 1971). Researchers may wish to examine the controlled experiment as the ideal in this field and consider whether or not alternatives are more acceptable, if not more powerful.

Experiments are, therefore, by no means the most effective data-gathering strategy. Depending on one's subject matter a variety of techniques may be more appropriate or perhaps necessary, because not all subjects lend themselves to experimentation. Figure 4.1 is an attempt to illustrate the relative strengths and weaknesses of major data-gathering strategies. As has been indicated, experiments are an outstanding method by which the researcher can exercise great control over factors that may impair internal validity, as well as yield relatively quick and inexpensive quantitative data; however, such an approach trades such control for its chief limitation of artificiality.

As we proceed down the vertical arrows in our illustration, we discover that the subsequent techniques become in general less quantitative, and the research exercises less control over rival causal factors impacting on internal validity. On the other hand, as we move away from experimentation, the researcher gains external validity and moves closer to the natural environment in which behavior occurs (Bouchard, 1976). This scheme is intended as an

Figure 4.1
Alternative Data-Gathering Strategies in Criminal Justice: A Heuristic Model.

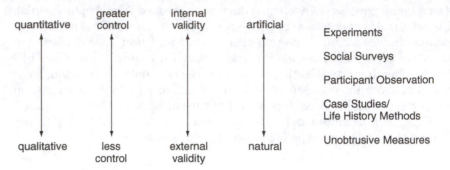

"ideal type" that overgeneralizes to simplify presentation. The model is not entirely true in all cases; for example, some unobtrusive methods can be very quantitative. In fact, our division of methods of data gathering is also somewhat arbitrary but hopefully it organizes these methods in a manner that clarifies their presentation.

The Uniform Crime Reports

The UCR has traditionally been the most widely cited on crime in the United States. It is also used as a point of comparison for other data-gathering procedures, particularly victim surveys and self-reports.

Beginning in 1930, the U.S. Department of Justice instituted the compilation and publication of national crime statistics (UCR). Although participation in the program by police departments and reports to the Federal Bureau of Investigation (FBI), which assumed responsibility as a clearinghouse, was voluntary in nature, the number of departments and comprehensiveness of reports have continually improved over the years. Large metropolitan areas were the best participants.

Most newspaper and other media accounts are based on summaries presented in the UCR. In most instances, these are data presented in an uncritical and alarmist manner without supplying many of the qualifying problems with the official crime statistics reported. Being the major source of crime statistics in the United States until 1974, the UCR basically comprises crimes known to, and recorded by, local police departments. Figure 4.2 illustrates the relationship between crime committed and other sources of crime statistics including the UCR (crimes recorded).

Although in Chapter 6 we will explore the usefulness of victimization surveys in estimating the number of crimes committed, it is unclear whether it is possible to obtain an accurate estimate of the volume of annual crime in American society. For various reasons, not all crimes committed are discovered; for instance, some crimes involve situations in which the victim is not aware of having been victimized or there is no identifiable victim. Not all crimes discovered are reported to the police and not all crimes reported to the police are recorded by the police. Although some may be concealed, a number of crimes reported are unfounded or defined by investigating officers as not

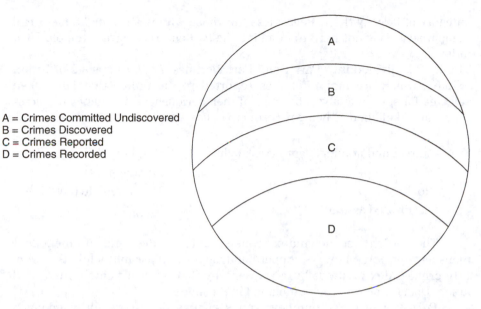

Figure 4.2
*Theoretical
Relationship between
Crimes Committed
and Official Statistics.*

A = Crimes Committed Undiscovered
B = Crimes Discovered
C = Crimes Reported
D = Crimes Recorded

constituting a criminal matter. Thus, even though crimes recorded by the police have an uncertain relationship to actual crimes committed, the UCR represented until 1974 the available statistics on crime in American society. The further removed statistics are from the crime committed, the weaker the figures are as estimates of the true crime level. For instance, number of arrests, indictments, convictions, incarcerations, and other dispositions such as probation or parole are all inadequate in estimating the amount of crime in a society. They have much more to do with police efficiency or allocation to correctional systems or other societal policies toward crime. The researcher who chooses to utilize official statistics must become familiar with any shortcomings or sources of bias they may contain.

The FBI receives these data from local police departments. In the majority of states there are operational state UCR programs in which the states require local departments to report their data to the state and then share such data with the federal government. In the 1980s, 98 percent of the police agencies operating in metropolitan statistical areas (MSAs),[1] about 94 percent of "other" cities, and 90 percent in rural areas reported. The Census Bureau estimates that about 97 percent of the total national population was covered by the report.

The Violent and Property Crime Indexes

In 2004, the FBI decided to stop reporting the crime index and report instead two indexes: the violent crime index and the property crime index. An advisory board felt that the original crime index had been distorted by including the

[1]MSA includes central cities (over 50,000) and contiguous counties that are functionally integrated economically and socially with the core cities.

category of larceny-theft. Regardless, for those who wish to make historical comparisons, it is not hard to combine the two and reconstruct the old UCR index.

The UCR is divided into Part 1 and Part 2 crimes. *Part 1* consists of **index crimes**, which are major felonies reported to the police that have been selected for special analysis because of their seriousness, frequency of occurrence, and likelihood of being reported to police. The *index offenses* are:

Index crimes

Murder and nonnegligent manslaughter	Burglary
Forcible rape	Larceny-theft
Robbery	Motor vehicle theft
Aggravated assault	Arson[2]

The violent crime index consists of murder and nonnegligent manslaughter, forcible rape, robbery and aggravated assault, while the property crime index includes burglary, larceny theft, motor vehicle theft, and arson. Data for arson are not included in the index.

Part 2 crimes are nonindex crimes such as simple assault, vandalism, gambling, and drunkenness. In all, twenty-two other crimes (twenty-one, excluding arson) are accounted for under Part 2 offenses. Although the FBI indicates that it cannot vouch for the validity of data received from individual police agencies, it attempts to examine all reports for accuracy, question any unusual changes in trends, undertake special inquiries if necessary, and eliminate, estimate, and otherwise control for at least the most crass errors.

Table 4.1 contains the UCR Index.

Crime Rate

Crime rate

The **crime rate** is expressed as the number of crimes per unit of population, in this case per 100,000. Such a statistic enables control of population size and thus permits a fair comparison of different size units. The growth in crime one reads about in the paper is usually based on the crime rate for the index offenses (excluding arson). Although the notion of scales and indexes will be treated in Chapter 10, for the purposes of this chapter it is important to realize that the crime index is unweighted; that is, each offense is merely summed and in a sense given the same importance as all other offenses. The crime rate is the total number of 7 original index crimes per 100,000 population.

$$\text{crime rate} = \frac{\text{number of index crimes}}{\text{population}} \times 100{,}000$$

[2]In October of 1978, the U.S. Congress passed a law that required that arson be included as a Part 1 or index crime.

Table 4.1
THE UCR VIOLENT AND PROPERTY CRIME INDEXES, 2008

Crime Index Offense	Number	Rate per 100,000
Murder and nonnegligent manslaughter	16,272	5.4
Forcible rape	89,000	29.3
Robbery	441,855	145.3
Aggravated assault	834,885	274.6
Burglary	2,222,196	730.8
Larceny-theft	6,588,873	2,167
Motor vehicle theft	956,846	314.7
Arson[1]	—	—
Violent crime[2]	1,382,012	454.5
Property crime	9,767,915	3,212.5

[1]Although arson data are included, sufficient data are not available to estimate totals for this offense.
[2]Violent crimes are offenses of murder, forcible rape, robbery, and aggravated assault. Property crimes are offenses of burglary, larceny-theft, and motor vehicle theft. Data are not included for the property crime of arson.
Source: Modified from U.S. Department of Justice, *FBI Uniform Crime Reports: Crime in the United States, 2008*. Washington, D.C.: U.S. Government Printing Office, September, 2009.

Cautions in the Use of UCR Data

The following statement serves as a caution in using any official government statistics:

> The government is very keen on amassing statistics. They collect them, add them, raise them to nth power, take the cube root and prepare wonderful diagrams. But what you must never forget is that every one of these figures comes in the first instance from the *chowty dar* (village watchman), who puts down what he damn pleases. (Stamp, 1929, pp. 258–259; cited in Webb et al., 1981, p. 89)

Although the UCR has been steadily improved and refined in its more than half a century of existence and can serve useful purposes, a researcher using these data for the analysis of crime must exercise caution and be aware of the limitations of these statistics. An impressive body of literature on the UCR has accumulated that point out these deficiencies.

Factors Affecting the UCR

Although no attempt will be made here to summarize the many fine critiques of the UCR and many of the points to be elaborated overlap, some of the primary shortcomings of this source of crime data can be detailed:

- As previously suggested in Figure 4.2, recorded statistics represent only a portion of the true crime rate of a community. Although we will examine victim surveys in detail later, the Bureau of the Census victim surveys suggest that there is possibly twice as much crime committed as appears in the official statistics.

- The big increase in the crime rate beginning in the mid-1960s and extending through the 1970s was in part explained by better communication, more professional police departments, and better recording and reporting of crimes. Surprisingly, for instance, there appears to be a positive relationship between a larger, improved, and professionalized police establishment and rising crime rates. Higher urban crime rates are related in part to the fact that there is a higher proportion of formal policing and professional law enforcement in such areas. Increased urbanization itself also has its own impact.

- Increased citizen awareness of crime and a general change in public morality may have resulted in a larger proportion of crimes committed being reported to the police. The usual and expected Saturday night barroom brawl of fifty years ago is now regarded as a serious assault warranting police attention. In light of the success of the civil rights movement, many more ghetto residents report crimes to the police, expressing confidence in the greater willingness of the police to respond to ghetto crime.

- Generally, most federal cases, "victimless" crimes, and white-collar crimes are not contained in the UCR. Many of the analyses of age, sexual, and racial characteristics of those arrested, then, describe the inept and poor criminal or concentrate on "crime in the streets" rather than "crime in the suites."

- Changes in police administration, politics in the statistical tabulating process, and simply more attention to better record keeping have had a major impact on crimes recorded. Obvious inadequacies in statistics from a jurisdiction are checked out by the FBI. In 1949, for instance, the FBI refused to publish New York City Police Department statistics. With improved recording, the robbery rate jumped 800 percent. Other changes in police practices showed jumps of 61 percent in Chicago in 1961 because of a change in chief, 202 percent in Kansas City in 1959 because of reforms, and 95 percent in Buffalo in the early 1960s (President's Commission, 1967, p. 25). In 1998, the Philadelphia Police Department was accused of routine downgrading of crime reports in which stabbings and beatings were recorded as hospital cases and burglaries became lost property ("Thousands of Rape Claims," 1999). In 2004, it was charged that the city of Atlanta had understated its crime rate shortly before being approved for hosting the Olympics by 22,000 crimes. In 1999, Philadelphia's Sex Crimes Unit dismissed as noncrimes several thousand reports of rape (Associated Press, 2004). In a humorous example of questionable statistics, the St. Paul, Minnesota, police department reported having solved 215 rape cases in 1999, but reported that only 200 rapes had been committed. It had also reported solving eleven more than took place in 1997. The department claimed a bookkeeping error. It turns out that the department had been too generous in labeling cases as "cleared" beyond the guidelines provided by the FBI. The national clearance rate for rape is about 50 percent.

Crime rates have a mysterious way of dropping if required for political purposes. Nixon's identification of the District of Columbia as a target of a crime-busting program resulted in a dramatic drop in the crime rate that was more likely a matter of classifying crimes out of the index. Until 1973, grand larceny of $50 or more could simply be classified as under $50 and thus out of the index (Glaser, 1978, p. 58). An interesting example of statistical shenanigans occurred in the mid-1970s during police negotiations in Cleveland under the administration of Mayor Ralph Perk. The police were told that if they expected a 5 percent salary increase, they would have to demonstrate greater efficiency by dropping the crime rate by a similar amount. Predictably, the crime rate recorded a drop in index crimes. Such manipulation of crime statistics is not limited to the United States. In 2008, charges were levied by criminologists that the British Home Office was manipulating research on crime by deliberately withholding or disrupting it. The office was accused of suppressing statistics and studies that might reflect poorly on government policies (BBC, 2008).

Sherman (1998) has argued that the more crime data are used to evaluate the police, the greater the temptation is to cheat. He proposed creating separate, independent crime audits as a solution.

- In addition to those factors already indicated, Savitz (1978) notes some **limitations of the crime index**. He summarizes a large number of elements that at the very least must be considered in using the index. *In interpreting UCR statistics one must keep in mind what arrest statistics do and do not include.* Arrests do not equal crimes solved or suspects found guilty. Many potential crimes are also unfounded by police. These are complaints that, on investigation by police, are determined not to be criminal matters.

  Limitations of the crime index

- In cases of a multiple offense, only the most serious crime is recorded for statistical purposes. Most crimes that are committed are not index offenses. Questions have been raised that auto theft, a less serious crime with high reportability and clearance, artificially inflates the crime index and might best be dropped from the Part 1 designation (Savitz, 1978).

- Rhodes points out that inflation caused incidents like bicycle theft to become larceny, an index crime. In 1973, all larcenies were included as index offenses, thus sharply increasing the crime rate (Rhodes, 1977, p. 168). At the same time, greater insurance coverage of property crimes encourages their reporting.

■ To be explored later in Chapter 10 is the problem that the crime index is an *unweighted index*; that is, a murder counts the same or has the same weight as a bicycle theft. Imagine two cities each with a crime rate of 100 per 100,000 population. In City A, 100 murders were recorded, whereas in City B 100 joyrides were recorded. Somehow, these crime rates should not be regarded as the same. Most bodily injury crimes are "nonindex" or Part 2 crimes (Savitz, 1978).

■ The existence of the "crime index" may cause police agencies to concentrate on these crimes at the expense of other crimes.

■ Although in 1978 Congress required that arson be included as an index offense, it has never been included in the crime index because of the unreliability of arson offense information. Jackson (1988) compared UCR arson data with a national survey of 683 fire departments and found significant underreporting in the UCR. He explains that arson is unlike other index offenses since determining whether a fire was purposefully set or attempted requires a specific investigation.

■ Raising yet another limitation, Wilbanks (1986) points out that despite the fact that the media are fond of ranking cities with respect to index crimes, the UCR itself correctly cautions against comparing statistical data of individual reporting units from cities, counties, and states solely on the basis of their population coverage. Such features as population density, size of locality, age structure, population mobility, economic and cultural conditions, climate, strength of law enforcement agencies and their policies, politics, citizen attitudes, and reporting practices are all factors that complicate such comparisons.

Related UCR Issues

Crime dip

Although it does not speak to any inaccuracy in the UCR itself, demographic shifts may provide some explanation for rapidly rising or falling crime rates. Some criminologists had forecast the **crime dip** in the 1980s, a general stabilization or decline in the crime rate. Although other factors offset the decline, this prophecy was based on changes in population distribution. For UCR crime rates, the maximal age range of criminality is fifteen to nineteen or twenty to twenty-four if an adult cohort is considered. After World War II, the United States experienced an unprecedented "baby boom," a much larger than usual proportion of births beginning in 1946 and extending through the 1950s. This group at first overwhelmed the capacity of hospital nursery wards; later, elementary schools and high schools were hard pressed to meet the demands for space. In the late 1960s, colleges could not expand fast enough to accommodate demand. Today most of these sectors have either stabilized or declined in demand as the economy struggles to supply jobs and housing for the now mature "baby boom" group. Similarly, the criminal justice system was struggling to deal with the larger-than-normal group in the maximum crime-committing ages. As this group moves into middle age and a smaller proportion of the population will be found in the high-crime ages, the criminal justice system will hopefully find itself with a far more manageable situation. A counterbalance to this demographic shift is the relationship between arrest rates and race. If the birthrates and crime rates of minorities remain higher than the general population, we may not see much of a drop in the crime rate.

Other variables that may also explain this decline include a greater reliance on longer sentences, incarceration and incapacitation of serious offenders, a decline in the number of state UCR programs, and an almost unnoticed decline in the per capita number of police in the United States since the 1980s. The researcher who decides to make use of official statistics such as the UCR must become familiar with their inadequacies to avoid drawing inappropriate conclusions. Despite the shortcomings that have been identified, the UCR remains an excellent source of information on police operations. Exhibit 4.1 presents attempts to explain the crime dip of the 1990s and the early twenty-first century.

EXHIBIT 4.1 ▶

The Crime Dip

From the earliest compilation of national crime statistics in the 1930s by the FBI in its UCR until the early 1960s, the crime rate in the United States had been declining; so much so that some prognosticators had unwisely predicted that, given existing trends, growing affluence in America might make crime a rarity by the twenty-first century. By the mid-1960s recorded crime did an abrupt about-face and rose at unprecedented levels producing yet new forecasts of unrepentant explosions in the crime rate. A slight leveling off in the early 1980s was interrupted by an epidemic of youth violence beginning in the mid-1980s with the advent of crack cocaine and the ready willingness to use weapons to defend warring turf. By the 1990s, just at the time that an assumed inevitability of such high crime rates was setting in, an unexpected decline took place, particularly in large cities. Between 1993 and 1997 index crimes dropped over 20 percent.

The cause(s) of this decline remains a subject of dispute. Some factors associated with the decline in the crime rate in the 1990s include (Witkin, 1998, pp. 28–37)

- a healthy economy
- crime prevention programs
- decline in domestic violence
- an incarceration binge
- compstat and community policing

- decline in the crack epidemic
- abortion

The healthiest U.S. economy in over thirty years characterized by low unemployment and low inflation has been viewed as primarily responsible for falling crime rates. The relationship is not entirely clear, however. In the 1960s, crime rates rose sharply during periods of low unemployment. Sunbelt cities with low unemployment had higher crime rates than older cities with high unemployment. In the 1990s, murder in New York City fell over 66 percent despite high unemployment (Witkin, 1998, p. 30).

Crime prevention, which holds much promise with early intervention programs with high risk youth, has thus far demonstrated only modest influence on crime rates.

Domestic murders, those among intimates, showed a 40 percent decrease between 1976 and 1996. This is explained in part by a decline in marriages among twenty- to twenty-four-year-olds as well as improved opportunities for women to escape abusive relationships.

The imprisonment binge in the United States has been phenomenal from about 744,000 in 1985 to 1,726,000 individuals in 1997 incarcerated in federal, state, and local prisons and jails. This represents the largest incarcerated population in the world including Russia. Locking up an additional million prisoners must have an impact; however, "New York

City has displayed some of the most dramatic drops in crime, but the state prison population—70 percent of which is from the city—has increased only about 8 percent since 1993. Conversely, the law-and-order state of Utah raised its incarceration rate by 19 percent from 1993 to 1996—but its violent-crime rate went up" (Witkin, 1998, p. 31).

Better policing has also been credited with the decline. New York City, which showed sharp decreases, utilized "compstats" (computer or compare statistics) to computer map and identify **hot spots** (high crime areas) where they would concentrate their policing efforts. A focus on small, nuisance crimes as suggested by Wilson and Kelling's "Broken Windows" (1982) theory was pointed to. This postulates that small crimes left unpunished breed more serious crimes. Nationwide, however, some cities that employed no new strategies also experienced plunging crime rates as others who innovated saw rising ones.

The end of the crack cocaine epidemic, which began rising in 1986, is a promising explanatory factor. This epidemic had been combined with the carrying of guns in order to secure operations. These same guns were then used to settle disputes previously resolved by fistfights. By the early 1990s the crack crisis waned, as did the violent crime rate. In some cases territories stabilized, and in others the ravages of the drugs on family members as well as incarceration took its toll.

A final, controversial explanation is posed by Levitt and Donohue (1999), who propose that the advent of legalized abortion with the 1973 *Roe* v. *Wade* decisions explains half the drop in crime since 1991. Unwanted, potential criminals were not born, and crime declined beginning in 1992, just when they would have reached their peak crime years (eighteen to twenty-four).

Source: Witkin, Gordon. "The Crime Bust: What's behind the Dramatic Drug Bust?" *U.S. News and World Report,* May 25, 1998, pp. 28–37.

UCR Redesign

Redesign of the UCR system

Beginning in 1977, the International Association of Chiefs of Police, as well as the National Sheriffs Association, called for a major **redesign of the UCR system** and, after more than ten years of effort by committees, task forces, and project staffs, the first major revision in the sixty-year history of the program was accomplished (Poggio et al., 1985; Rovetch, Poggio, and Rossman, 1984). The lengthy process of the redesign study enabled redesign teams to take advantage of the decade's revolution in computer technology.

National Incident-Based Reporting System

The National Incident-Based Reporting System (NIBRS)

The major change in the new UCR program was its conversion to a **National Incident-Based Reporting System (NIBRS)**, which involves a unit-record reporting system in which each local law enforcement agency reports on each individual crime incident and on each individual arrest. The original UCR only reported summary counts. The NIBRS uses fifty-two data elements to describe victims, offenders, arrestees, and circumstances of crimes. While the UCR focuses on eight index crimes, NIBRS has twenty-two Group A offenses, including bribery, counterfeiting/forgery, drug and narcotic offenses, extortion/blackmail, fraud, kidnapping, pornography, nonforcible sex offenses, and firearms violations.

Participation by law enforcement agencies in the program depends upon a department's data-processing resources. If an agency cannot meet full participation requirements, it may limit itself to reporting details of incidents involving the UCR's eight index crimes rather than the NIBRS's expanded list of twenty-two crimes (Dodenhoff, 1990, p. 10). NIBRS divides data collection into two levels. *Level I* covers all law enforcement agencies and requires basic

Group A incident-based data on the twenty-two categories of offenses. *Level II* participation includes an additional eleven-category Group B list of lesser offenses, as well as more detail in submissions. Agencies serving populations in excess of 100,000 plus a sampling of 300 smaller agencies will participate in Level II. Exhibit 4.2 reports on features of the NIBRS.

EXHIBIT 4.2 ▶

The National Incident-Based Reporting System (NIBRS)

With 1991 data, the UCR program of the FBI began moving from summary counts to a more comprehensive and detailed reporting system known as the NIBRS. By 1982 the Bureau of Justice Statistics (BJS) had already provided over $11 million to the states to establish centralized state-level UCR programs. In a 1985 report, an FBI-BJS task force that BJS underwrote recommended an incident-based system. When the Attorney General approved NIBRS, BJS allocated an additional $13 million to the states to implement the system.

NIBRS versus the Traditional UCR System

The traditional, summary-based UCR system counts incidents and arrests, with some expanded data on incidents of murder and nonnegligent manslaughter. NIBRS, which will eventually replace the traditional UCR as the source of official FBI counts of crimes reported to law enforcement agencies, is designed to go far beyond the summary-based UCR in terms of information about crime.

One important difference between the two systems is number of crime categories. The traditional UCR counts incidents and arrests for the eight offenses of the FBI Crime Index and counts arrests for other offenses; NIBRS provides detailed incident information on forty-six *Group A* offenses representing twenty-two categories of crimes (table A). NIBRS, unlike the traditional UCR, also makes a distinction between attempted and completed crimes.

In September 1982, a BJS-FBI task force undertook a study of improvements to the Uniform Crime Reporting Program, which was created in 1930. Law enforcement organizations, state UCR program managers, and the research community strongly supported this effort. In January 1984, a conference considered various recommendations, and in 1985, BJS and the FBI released Blueprint for the Future of the Uniform Crime Reporting Program.

The resulting program, the NIBRS, collected its first data in 1991. An estimated 40 percent of the nation will report to NIBRS by the end of 1994. NIBRS represents a new way of thinking about crime, providing details about victims, offenders, and the environments in which they interact. This report on the first NIBRS data is a beginning step toward using the data for planning and evaluating law enforcement responses to crime. It also illustrates the close partnership among BJS, the FBI, and the more than 17,000 state and local law enforcement agencies.

NIBRS collects arrestee information on the 46 *Group A* offenses and an additional 11 *Group B* offenses (table B). Unlike the traditional UCR, NIBRS requires arrests as well as exceptional clearances to be linked to specific incidents.

In addition to expanded crime categories, NIBRS definitions of certain offenses are more inclusive than the traditional UCR definitions. For example, the NIBRS definition of rape has been expanded to include male victims.

In incidents where more than one offense occurs, the traditional UCR counts only the most serious of the offenses. NIBRS includes information about each of the different offenses (up to a maximum of ten) that may occur within a single incident. As a result, the NIBRS data can be used to study how often and under what circumstances certain offenses, such as burglary and rape, occur together.

The ability to link information about many aspects of a crime to the crime incident marks the most important difference between NIBRS and the traditional UCR. These various aspects of the crime incident are represented in NIBRS by a series of more than fifty data elements (table C). The NIBRS data elements are categorized in six segments: administrative, offense, property, victim, offender, and arrestee. NIBRS enables analysts to study how these data elements relate to each other for each type of offense.

Administrative segment includes the originating agency identifier (ORI) and incident numbers that uniquely identify each incident. These tie together all the records of a single incident. The administrative segment also includes the date and hour of the incident and, if relevant, exceptional clearance information.

Offense segment includes the type of offense(s) reported, whether the offense was attempted or completed, whether the offender was suspected of using drugs or alcohol, the type of location where the offense occurred (such as a store or residence), the type of weapon or force used, and whether the offender was motivated by bias against the victim's race, religion, ethnicity, or sexual orientation. For certain offenses, the type of criminal activity (such as possessing, selling, or transporting) is indicated. For burglary incidents, the method of entry and the number of premises entered are included.

Property segment includes (for all property offenses, extortion, kidnapping, and a few other specified offenses) the type of property loss (burned, counterfeited, destroyed, seized, or stolen), the type of property involved (such as cash or jewelry), the value of the property, and, if recovered, the recovery date. For incidents of motor vehicle theft, special indicators for the number of stolen and recovered vehicles are included. For drug offenses, the type and quantity of illegal drug(s) seized are included.

Victim segment includes a victim identification number, the UCR code for offense(s) committed against the victim, and the victim's sex, age, race, ethnicity, and resident status. In cases where the victim is not an individual, codes are used to distinguish among businesses, financial institutions, governments, religious organizations, and society at large. For incidents of homicide or aggravated assault, codes describing the circumstances of the incident (such as an argument or drug deal) are provided. In incidents where the victim is injured, information describing the injury (such as fractures or lacerations) is included. Each victim is linked by an offender number to the offender(s) who committed an offense against him or her, and the nature of the victim's relationship (such as family member, acquaintance, or stranger) to each offender is reported.

Offender segment includes information on the age, sex, and race of the offender.

Arrestee segment includes information on persons arrested in connection with the incident, including the date of arrest, and the age, sex, race, ethnicity, and resident status of the arrestee.

An example of how those interested in the study of crime can tap the potentially rich source of new information represented by NIBRS is seen in the Supplementary Homicide Reports data published annually by the FBI in its *Crime in the United States* series. Cross tabulations of various incident-based data elements are presented, including the age, sex, and race of victims and offenders, the types of weapon(s) used, the relationship of the victim to the offender, and the circumstances surrounding the incident (for example, whether the murder resulted from a robbery, rape, or argument). These data were provided to the FBI for about 87 percent of the 24,703 murders reported nationwide in 1991.

For other violent crimes such as rape and robbery, UCR data beyond the summary counts have generally been limited to a univariate distribution by month. With the advent of NIBRS, the supplemental data elements that were previously available only for murder incidents can now be used in the analysis of other violent crimes.

Of course, NIBRS also provides some data elements that were not previously available for any violent crimes, including murder. These new data elements include whether the offender was suspected of using alcohol or drugs shortly before or during the incident, the type of location of the crime, the resident status of the victim, and the nature of any injuries sustained by the victim.

For robbery incidents, NIBRS also provides previously unavailable data describing the property that was lost and its value. Using NIBRS, a researcher could study carjackings, for example, by selecting robbery incidents that included a vehicle as the property description.

Source: Reaves, Brian A. "Using NIBRS Data to Analyze Violent Crime." Bureau of Justice Statistics Technical Report, October, 1993.

NIBRS Versus UCR

Some key differences between the NIBRS and the UCR program include (Rantala, 2000) the following:

- *Incident-Based Versus Summary Reporting.* The UCR reports Part I (index) offenses and Parts I and II arrest data in aggregate (summary) form. NIBRS, which requires detailed data on individual crime incidents and arrests, receives separate reports for each incident/arrest. These reports include fifty-two data elements describing the victims, offenders, arrestees, and circumstances of the crime.

- *Expanded Offense Reporting.* The UCR is a summary-based system and collects totals on criminal incidents in eight offense classifications within the Part I type. NIBRS receives detailed reports on twenty-two categories and forty-six offenses in the Group A list. It adds the following list to the original UCR Part I crimes: bribery, counterfeiting and forgery, vandalism, drug offenses, embezzlement, extortion and blackmail, fraud, gambling offenses, kidnapping, pornography, prostitution, nonforcible sexual offenses, weapons law violations, and stolen property offenses. In addition many of the Part I offenses have been expanded. For example, the forcible rape category now includes all forcible sexual offenses, such as forcible sodomy, sexual assault with an object, and forcible fondling.

- *New Offense Definitions.* In addition to expanding the original list of UCR offense categories, NIBRS revised the existing definitions of crime. Rape, for example, is defined as "the carnal knowledge of a person, forcibly and/or against that person's will; or, not forcibly or against a person's will where the victim is incapable of giving consent because of his/her temporary or permanent mental or physical incapacity" (Rantala, 2000).

- *Elimination of the Hierarchy Rule.* Under the UCR **hierarchy rule**, if multiple crimes took place within the same event, only the single most serious crime was reported. NIBRS eliminates the hierarchy rule and cites all crimes reported as offenses within the same incident.

  Hierarchy rule

- *Greater Specificity of Data.* Because it collects more specific information regarding criminal incidents, NIBRS data will eventually lead to more detailed crime analysis, criminal profiling, and crime reporting. NIBRS will also have the capability of providing breakdowns regarding victims, cost, involvement of weapons, injuries, and the like, innovations that had not been possible in the past.

- *Crimes Against Society.* Whereas the UCR distinguishes between "crimes against person" and "crimes against property," the addition of many new offense categories in NIBRS necessitated the creation of a new category—"crimes against society." This category includes crimes such as drug offenses, gambling violations, pornography, and prostitution.

- *Attempted versus Completed Crimes.* The UCR system reports many attempted crimes as completed ones. The NIBRS system will include a designation of each crime as either attempted or completed.

- *Designation of Computer Crime.* With NIBRS data of the future, it will be possible to determine whether a traditional crime, for example larceny, was committed by computer. But this specificity will not eliminate the traditional classifications that are important for historical trend analysis.

- *Better Statistical Analysis.* NIBRS will permit a greater opportunity for examining interrelationships between many variables such as offenses, property, victims, offenders, and arrestees.

These features represent the first major overhaul of the UCR system in more than fifty years.

On a final note, mention should be made of the growing international effort with respect to crime statistics. Organizations such as Interpol, the United Nations, and the World Health Organization all have programs of collection. Some of the problems in analyzing these data are the same as those affecting the UCR. Difficulties in analyzing crime data across countries include varying definitions of crime, differences in recording practices, differences in the law, the stage of the system when crime is recorded, factual inequalities among countries in age and urban/rural structure, and specific problems associated with recording crime (statistics may be related to politics or measures of system workload) (van Dijk and Kangaspunta, 2000).

Sampling

Some research involves a complete enumeration of the total population, households, or the target of study. Ever since 1790, the U.S. Census has attempted to survey every household unit—man, woman, and child—every ten years. Similarly, city directories attempt to count and obtain information on all persons eighteen years of age or older who reside within their urban target areas.

Sampling

Rather than attempting to enumerate an entire population, most studies make use of sampling. **Sampling** is a procedure used in research by which a select subunit of a population is studied in order to analyze the entire population. Sampling enables an inexpensive, relatively quick assessment, by even small groups of researchers, of a population that is often so large that complete enumeration is prohibitive. The logic of sampling enables one to make inferences to a larger population (Kish, 1965).

Sampling frame

The initial step in selecting a sample is to develop a **sampling frame**, a complete list of the population (or universe) that one is interested in studying. For example, if one is interested in generalizing to all judges in California, a complete list of such judges would constitute the sampling frame.

Types of Sampling

The major types of sampling procedures are as follows:

Probability	**Nonprobability**
Simple random	Quota
Stratified random	Accidental
Cluster	Purposive
Systematic (multistage)	Snowball

Probability Samples

Probability samples refer to samples that permit estimation of the likelihood   Probability samples
of each element of the population being selected in the sample.

Simple random samples (SRSs).

SRSs are samples in which each element of the population (or universe) has an equal probability of being selected. Sometimes the mnemonic device EPSEM samples is used to denote the key features of an SRS (Babbie, 1992, p. 197).

EPSEM, a means of sample selection, is an acronym that stands for Equal Probability of SElection Method. This method provides a way for selecting a sample in which each and every unit or person in the population has the same or equal chance of appearing in the sample. EPSEM or probability samples are very important in the field of statistics because the various calculations and estimations of statistics assume that the sample was chosen by some probability method. In describing samples that use an equal probability of selection method, we will use the shorthand acronym EPSEM.

If probability methods have been utilized in selection of the sample, the concept of sampling error enables researchers to assess confidence limits so that with a given degree of error they can assume that what is true of the sample is true of the population and that the sample mean approximates that of the population.

Procedure.

To select an SRS, it is necessary to acquire a clear and complete list of all elements of the population because all elements must be independently and randomly chosen. Suppose there were thirty people in a room and a simple random sample of five were to be drawn. One could give each person a number, drop these numbers into a hat, scramble them, and then draw five, one at a time. State lottery daily numbers usually make use of an honest gambling device procedure that is essentially an SRS. What if, as in a large survey of the public, one wished to draw a simple random sample of adults from a city of a million. Obviously, one would not put numbers in a hat. To sample such large populations, researchers make use of a table of random numbers. Figure 4.3 illustrates a theoretical population and a hypothetical typical table of random numbers.

To select a sample of ten inmates, one would first number the list of inmates, and then choose a random start, for example, the top left of table of random numbers. As the entire population consists of fifty cases, numbers from 00 to 99, or two-digit numbers, would enable each name to have an equal probability of selection. Numbers from 51 to 99 are, of course, unusable; if these numbers are chosen, they should be skipped and the selection process continued until the next two-digit number between 01 and 50. According to Figure 4.3, the first number is 07—Albert Bruno, the second is 00—no case, the third is 16—Mike Federici, and so forth, until ten cases are chosen. If the same number is chosen twice, it is skipped because each respondent should appear only once in the sampling frame. For complex sampling, various computer programs are available that provide an SRS of a specified size.

Angelo, Gerald	Clemons, Randy	Kozak, Dave	Parks, Zeke	Thiel, Myrtle
Bell, Earl	Dammer, Harry	Lewis, Ed	Penn, Wally	Thompson, Mary
Bender, Harry	Dutkowdky, Andrew	Mack, Bob	Quick, Bob	Tierney, Estelle
Benekos, Peter	Edsel, Earl	McGill, Bill	Rapp, Sean	Unterwagner, Jim
Bethune, David	Erisman, Mike	Morris, Tom	Rasp, Doug	Vance, Lance
Bozo, Boris	Frederici, Mike	Mucha, Fred	Ross, Joe	Vega, Terence
Bruno, Albert	Goblick, Al	Norris, Herb	Runt, Juan	Wahlen, John
Burns, Rich	Hairbreath, Harry	Numa, Tod	Saxon, Sid	Wayne, Mike
Buxton, Bob	Harlow, Joe	Obernan, Stan	Simmons, Mary	Weeks, Bary
Buzawa, Eve	Johnson, Leroy	Parker, Omar	Simpson, Ted	Zeno, Mike

TABLE OF RANDOM NUMBERS*

07001	61569	08812	07344	92880	71728
43102	29751	87806	12031	56214	41387
61622	71481	20091	37658	99612	28143
50126	51296	07509	61483	25143	61974

Figure 4.3
Sampling Frame of Inmates of San Rocco Correctional Institution.
*This table of random numbers is provided for illustration purposes only.

Advantages/Disadvantages.
The chief advantage of the SRS is that it enables the use of statistical probabilities that are necessary in many statistical procedures. The primary disadvantages of the SRS, however, are that it *requires a complete list of the population to be sampled* and, if large numbers are involved, it *can become a rather tedious and cumbersome procedure*, although this can be offset by computer. The SRS *by no means guarantees a representative sample*. On the last point, by chance it is possible in our San Rocco sample to obtain a sample that is 50 percent female, even though females represent only 10 percent of the population. As we will see in our discussion, the probability of this occurring is small, but it certainly is possible. Such a nonrepresentative sample certainly raises problems for a researcher attempting to infer to the larger population. Primarily for this reason, much survey research involving sampling utilizes stratified random samples.

Some examples of research employing SRSs include a study of New York City drug laws by Japha (1978) in which he randomly selected cases from the Criminal Court of Manhattan of persons convicted for a nondrug felony who had been given a nonincarceration sentence. In addition, he drew random samples of cases entering court for arraignment, cases reduced or dismissed at first arraignment, clients in drug treatment programs, and males held on felony charges in Manhattan. Sparks (1982), in a study of Massachusetts statewide sentencing guidelines, constructed a random sample of 1,440 convicted criminals who had been sentenced in Massachusetts Superior Court during a one-year period.

Stratified Random Samples.

These rely on knowledge of the distribution or proportion of population characteristics to choose a sample that assures representativeness of these characteristics. Such characteristics are generally demographic in nature, such as age, sex, race, social class, or of pertinence to the study, such as area of residence, nature and type of criminal record, region, or some quality of importance in the analysis.

The general procedure involves dividing the population into strata or groups based on the variable(s) of stratification and then selecting the sample either proportionately or disproportionately, depending on the decision made in this regard. For **proportionate stratified samples**, sample subjects are chosen in roughly the same ratio as exists in the population. For instance, suppose that in our San Rocco study of fifty inmates, we wanted to choose a proportionate stratified sample by sex of ten inmates. Because one of ten subjects is female in the population, we must be certain that only one of the ten subjects in the sample is female. Such a procedure assures representativeness by sex, unlike the SRS in which half of the sample were females.

Proportionate stratified samples

Disproportionate stratified sampling involves oversampling—taking a larger than proportionate number of certain groups to assure the appearance of a sufficient number of cases for comparative purposes of a group that is small in the population. Again, returning to our example in Figure 4.3, suppose that we wished to investigate differences between male and female inmates at San Rocco. An SRS could result in a sample of all males, which would certainly destroy our ability to even conduct the study. A proportionate stratified sample would yield one female and nine males, a situation that would be quite hazardous because, on every variable of analysis, the 100 percent response of females would be referring to only one respondent. A disproportionate stratified sample might take all five female subjects and compare them with a sample of male respondents, for example, five males. There is generally no problem in comparing males with females using a disproportionate stratified sample; however, if inferences were to be attempted from a sample that is overrepresentative of females to all inmates, the sample is obviously nonrepresentative. *Weighting* of sample responses is a recommended procedure to adjust sample data to enable inference to the general population. Basically, weighting involves the differential assignment of adjustment factors to data to take into account the relative importance of that data.

Disproportionate stratified sampling

Table 4.2 illustrates this process. The responses of the males in the sample would in actuality carry nine times more weight than those of females.

Table 4.2

SAN ROCCO CORRECTIONAL INSTITUTION: WEIGHTING OF DISPROPORTIONATE SAMPLE

	Population	Disproportionate Stratified Sample	Weight
Male	45	5	9 ×
Female	5	5	1 × or none

That is, each response of males in the sample actually represents the response of nine males—the respondent and eight others—whereas the female respondent represents only herself. Thus, disproportionate stratified sampling permits comparisons between subgroups where at least one of the subgroups might otherwise be too small. In the early victimization surveys of select U.S. cities conducted by the U.S. Census Bureau on behalf of the Department of Justice, the sampling frame was the complete housing inventory for the city as determined by the *1970 Census of Population and Housing*. To select a stratified sample, the city's housing units were categorized into 105 strata, for example, own or rent, occupied or unoccupied, and single-family or multiple-dwelling unit (*Criminal Victimization Surveys in Milwaukee*, 1977). Garofalo describes the sampling procedure utilized in the initial study of eight cities involved in LEAA's High Impact Crime Reduction Program:

> Supplemental samples were drawn from new construction permits issued in each city. Census Bureau interviewers visited the housing units selected and interviewed residents about personal and household victimizations suffered during the preceding twelve months. About 10,000 households or 22,000 individuals were interviewed in each city. . . . The samples were sufficiently large to make reliable estimates of what the attitude responses would have been if everyone in the city had been interviewed. (Garofalo, 1977, p. 14)

The numbers in the victimization survey report are weighted estimates as if the entire population were surveyed. The history of the operation of Bureau of Justice Statistics–sponsored victimization surveys—will be covered in depth in Chapter 6.

In an analysis of characteristics of high- and low-crime neighborhoods in Atlanta, Greenberg, Williams, and Rohe (1982) utilized a stratified random sample from three matched pairs of neighborhoods selected on the basis of crime, racial, and income characteristics. A study of the relationship between narcotics addiction and criminal activity in Baltimore by Nurco et al. (1985) involved a sample of 354 male narcotic addicts who were selected using a stratified random sample of a population of 6,149 known narcotics abusers who had been arrested or identified by the Baltimore Police Department between 1952 and 1976. The sample was selected not on the basis of criminality but by race and year of police contact.

Cluster Sampling.

This is generally used in surveys that involve field interviews and is most useful in studies that involve widely dispersed subjects. The population to be surveyed is divided into clusters, for example, census tracts, blocks, and sections, and then a probability sample of clusters is selected for study. Such a sampling procedure is less time consuming and costly, particularly in terms of field staff. Once the clusters are chosen, other sampling procedures, such as a systematic sample of every nth house, may be employed. Cluster sampling is particularly useful as a means of reducing travel costs in field interviewing.

An example of the use of cluster sampling is provided by Schuerman and Kobrin's (1986) study of neighborhood change and criminal activity in Los Angeles. They drew a sample from census tract clusters in Los Angeles County that were defined as high-crime areas in 1970. They then used a statistical procedure to assemble contiguous census tracts into 192 clusters or neighborhoods and studied the impact of socioeconomic and demographic trends in these areas on crime rates. Sigler and Johnson (1986; see also Sigler and Haygood, 1988), in a study of public perceptions of sexual harassment in Tuscaloosa, Alabama, employed a multistage, stratified cluster sample in which grids on city maps, blocks, and residences were the sampling units.

Systematic Samples.

In *systematic samples* every nth item in a list is included in the sample. (In the language of statistics, n represents every second, third, fourth, or nth case.) Purists insist that such a sample is a nonprobability sample, because various patterns, for example, ethnic surnames, may exist in a list that would destroy its representativeness. If offenders or arrestees were listed in order of offense seriousness, the final sample may be biased. This writer has chosen to place systematic sampling in the probability group because the majority of researchers feel that it satisfies the EPSEM requirement and belongs in the probability group. To illustrate systematic sampling, let us return to Figure 4.3, the San Rocco example. Suppose we wished to select a sample often from a population of fifty. Assuming the names are already numbered, we would select first the proper sampling interval, in this case every fifth name. Sampling intervals are selected by the ratio of sample size to population size—in our example, ten of fifty or one of five. By choosing every fifth, theoretically every name in the population list has an equal probability of being chosen so long as one uses a *random start*. **Random start** involves randomly choosing where the interval will begin within the first interval—in this case, 1 to 5. For example, if the number 3 were chosen from a table of random numbers, the sample selected with the every fifth sampling interval would be 3, 8, 13, 18, 23, 28, 33, 38, 43, and 48. As long as one both suspects that there is no pattern in the population list and uses the proper sampling interval and random start, such that each individual or unit has an equal probability of being chosen, then a probability sample exists. The obvious advantage of systematic samples is their relative ease of selection, although it may become burdensome with large populations. In choosing a systematic sample from a uniformly spaced list of names, a simple procedure, once the random start is selected, is to mark off with a ruler or other measuring rod and proceed down the list until all cases are selected.

Random start

Multistage Sampling.

This involves combinations of stratified, cluster, simple random samples, and/or other sampling procedures. For example, a national survey of neighborhood crime might stratify first on the basis of region—north, east, south, and west. Within regions, clusters are randomly selected, and within the selected regions, blocks are randomly selected for door-to-door household interviews. Multistage sampling can become quite complex, as illustrated by the study of media crime prevention campaigns by O'Keefe et al. (1984).

The population examined included a national sample of the noninstitutionalized civilian population of the United States age eighteen and over. A one-call quasi-probability sample design was employed, based upon the Roper Organization's master national probability sample of interviewing areas. First, 100 counties were chosen at random proportionate to population after all counties in the nation had been stratified by population size within geographic region. Second, cities and towns were randomly selected from the sample counties according to their population. Third, four blocks or segments were then drawn within each location. Quotas for sex and age, as well as for employed women, were set in order to assure proper representation of each group in the sample (O'Keefe et al., 1984, in Loftin, 1987, p. 100).

Nonprobability Samples

Any sampling procedure that violates the EPSEM is viewed as a nonprobability sample.

Quota Samples.

These are nonprobability stratified samples. The researcher attempts to ensure that the sample proportions, for example age, sex, and race, resemble those of the population, but does not fill these proportions or quotas on the basis of an EPSEM. Rather than attempting to ensure that each element of each quota has an equal chance of appearing in the sample, the researcher uses skilled judgment to select adequate numbers to fill each quota. The data are collected and analyzed on an ongoing basis until an adequate decision or prediction of outcome becomes possible. Quota sampling is the favorite technique of many private marketing and consumer survey organizations. Often at shopping malls, interviewers eyeball shoppers until someone appearing to fit the requirements of one of their quotas is identified—for example, a black male in his forties. At times the interviews are aborted when, on the basis of demographic information, it turns out that the interviewer guessed wrong on a characteristic and the individual is not needed in the quota.

An illustration of a quota sample is provided in a Philadelphia bail experiment conducted by Goldkamp and Gottfredson (1984). First, a sample of judges was selected from Philadelphia Municipal Court, and then cases from court files were selected according to a stratified quota sampling design by which cases were chosen on the basis of both seriousness of charge and judge.

A quota sample was also used in a study of criminal victimization among the homeless in Birmingham, Alabama (Fitzpatrick, LaGory, and Ritchey, 1993). The researchers used a previous Birmingham Homeless Enumeration and Survey Project to construct sampling parameters and stratified on geographic site, gender, and race. They then conducted a quota sample survey of 150 homeless adults by randomly selecting persons from each homeless shelter or public site to match the proportions found in the previous enumeration. After determining the number of respondents required from the site, interviewers selected subjects on the basis of sex and race. The demographic characteristics of the sample matched those of previous studies conducted in Texas and Tennessee.

Accidental Samples.

These are the favorite "person on the street" interviews where the "researcher" makes little attempt to ensure representativeness of the sample. This is well illustrated by many television commercials, for example, "Nine out of ten doctors recommend _____." Which nine of ten? An interview of the easiest and most accessible generally will not yield data from which one could infer to larger populations.

Purposive Samples.

Purposive (judgmental) **samples**, on the other hand, represent the selection of an appropriate sample based on the researcher's skill, judgment, and needs. This type of sampling is well used on election nights when the major networks, based on sample precincts, are able to quite accurately predict the likely outcome, often with a small margin of error with only 2 percent of the votes cast. Marketing studies often use test areas that possess characteristics quite similar to those of the nation. Both political campaign planners and market analysts have made use of **focus groups**. Organizers of these focus groups bring together purposively selected volunteers in order to measure reactions to or attitudes about products, candidate speeches, and the like (Krueger, 1994, 1997; Morgan, 1993; Stewart and Shamdasani, 1990).

Purposive

Focus groups

The use of focus groups and mock trials as courtroom tools are burgeoning areas of applied research. *Focus groups* involve bringing together a group of purposely selected volunteers in order to measure reactions to or attitudes concerning products, candidates, defendants, and the like. They are a means of gathering in-depth, qualitative data. In measuring business products, a focus group of eight to twelve people may be brought together for a roundtable discussion of one to two hours. Such participants are often recruited by telephone, matched on key demographic characteristics, and offered an incentive to participate. Topics to be discussed are planned in conjunction with the client or research issue. In addition to videotaping the discussion and observation, often through two-way mirrors, subjects are also requested to fill out a questionnaire. Developed during the early years of World War II by social scientists working for a predecessor to the Voice of America, Sociologists Robert Merton and associates (Merton, Fiske and Kendall, 1956) and Paul Lazarsfeld had used focus groups to measure radio morale-boosting programs. Until its reemergence in the 1980s, the technique was primarily used in the area of marketing research.

The dynamics of focus group interviews lies in the group process in which participants influence each other, opinions change, and new views emerge. The participants learn from each other (Krueger, 1997, p. 20). In the final analysis, the true test of focus group results is whether they work in predicting product sales, future behavior, court outcomes, or whatever the topic under investigation. Researchers can ask a small group of six to twelve people questions that will stimulate lively discussion. The focus group members are the experts giving their opinion to the researcher.

Wanting to find out about kids who frequent crack houses, Bowser hung out in an inner city neighborhood and, once accepted, invited kids to join a focus group at a local pizza place and asked them how to go about surveying the subject (Bowser and Sieber, 1993). Such groups can operate very inexpensively and simply. Most researchers employ a discussion leader plus two assistants (note takers). Some essential elements of conducting focus groups include (Bowser and Sieber, 1993, pp. 81–82) the following:

- Organize questions and probes beginning with general to concluding questions.
- Reduce these to five to seven general questions.
- Define your target population.
- Select homogeneous groups of six to twelve people. Do not mix genders, socioeconomic status, or people who might be guarded around each other.
- Select good gatekeepers to aid in recruitment.
- Effectively invite them and provide incentives.
- Find a comfortable and private setting.
- Conduct the focus group, serve food, and summarize.
- Organize responses around major themes.
- Prepare and disseminate the report.

The purpose of focus groups of mock jurists is to identify and apply information on characteristics of potential jurists in order to effect positive trial strategy. What are some themes and tactics that might best communicate the case to the jury (Moore, 1998)?

Mock trials are more elaborate in simulating a trial in all respects. This involves attorneys (or actors) presenting both sides of their cases in a simulated courtroom setting that includes the voir dire (jury selection), preliminary instructions, opening statements, direct and cross examination of witnesses, presentation of evidence, and closing arguments. Deliberations are videotaped and post-verdict discussions take place in order to monitor the decision-making process and discover which documents, evidence, or arguments were most persuasive. Such activities can assist in predicting panel reaction to charges, defenses, and possible awards in civil cases. Juror profiles for particular cases can also be developed, enabling the targeting of certain demographic, personality, and attitudinal characteristics. In order to explore this topic further, visit jury simulation consulting firms on the Internet by entering "jury simulations" as the search item on a Web browser such as Excite, Yahoo, or Infoseek.

Figure 4.4 describes the use of focus groups to successfully guide jury selection in the notorious Birmingham Church Bombing Trial, which in 2001 won convictions of a former Ku Klux Klansman responsible for the attack.

Criminal profiling refers to attempts to construct typical characteristics of certain types of criminals. Holmes (1989) used a purposive sample and talked to offenders, asking them questions about their crimes, motivations, and crime scenes. This technique is used by researchers—for example, by those in the FBI's Behavioral Research Unit—for forecasting purposes and to aid in the investigation of certain types of criminals such as serial murderers. In a

Mock trials

Criminal profiling

In 2001, a Birmingham jury took only two hours to convict a former Klansman in the 1963 church bombing. Thomas Blanton, Jr., was sentenced to life in prison for the murder of four black girls who died in the September 15, 1963, explosion at the 16th Street Baptist Church. Using jury consultants, prosecutors organized two focus groups and polled 500 residents of the Birmingham area. With defense lawyers and judges, they devised a 100-question survey that potential jurors completed at the beginning of the trial. Questions related to attitudes toward interracial dating and the King holiday were used.

Much of the evidence against Blanton was circumstantial. The prosecution claimed that it entered the evidentiary phase of the trial confident that they had selected a receptive jury. The prosecution purported that it struck potential jurists due to their attitudes rather than race and sex per se. The defense argued that the real intent of the prosecution had been to remove white men or was based on racial lines. The judge ruled that the prosecution had provided race-neutral reasons for its selection.

Source: Kevin Sack, 2001. "Research Guided Jury Selection in Bombing Trial." *New York Times*, May 3: A12.

Figure 4.4
Research Guided Jury Selection in the Birmingham Church Bombing Trial

criminal profiling of forty-one convicted serial rapists, 76 percent were found to have been sexually abused as children. This same profile found that the majority of serial rapes had not been reported to authorities (Hazlewood and Warren, 1989). Exhibit 4.3 describes the crime profiling process.

EXHIBIT 4.3 ▶

Crime Profiling

Crime profiling (also called crime investigative analysis) has been practiced on various levels in the social sciences for years. Classic fictional detectives such as Sherlock Holmes and Charlie Chan tried their hand, as did a host of profilers of figures such as Hitler, the Boston Strangler, and the Mad Bomber. In *Profiling Violent Crimes* (1996, p. 8), Ronald and Stephen Holmes indicate that the profiler should have three goals:

A complete profile provides the criminal justice system with (a) a social and psychological assessment of the offender, (b) a psychological evaluation of the suspected offender's belongings, and (c) suggestions for the most efficient and effective way for police to go about interviewing the suspect once he or she is apprehended.

Douglas, et al. (1992, p. 310) define crime profiling as involving seven steps:

1. Evaluation of the criminal act itself
2. Comprehensive evaluation of the specifics of the crime scene(s)
3. Comprehensive analysis of the victim
4. Evaluation of preliminary police reports
5. Evaluation of the medical examiner's autopsy protocol
6. Development of the profile with critical offender characteristics
7. Investigative suggestions predicated on construction of the profile

Components of the offender profile include (Federal Bureau of Investigation, 1991) the following:

age, sex, and race
marital status/adjustment
level of intelligence
sexual adjustment and perversions
social adjustment
appearance and grooming
employment history/adjustment

emotional adjustment

work habits

location or residence in relation to crime scene

personality characteristics

evaluation and analysis of the criminal act

motive for the offense

lifestyle

prior criminal arrest history

sequence of events during the offense

mood of the offender before, during, and after the offense

The crime-profiling approach has been found particularly useful in investigating arsons, bombings, kidnaps, murders, child molestations, and serial murders/rapes. In the profiling process, data are collected and assessed, the situation reconstructed, hypotheses formulated, profile developed and tested, and results reported (Douglas and Burgess, 1986, p. 9). Beginning in the late 1970s, the FBI's profiling program, housed in its Behavioral Sciences Investigative Unit, has enjoyed a high media profile since its success in predictions related to the Wayne Williams serial murder case in Atlanta in the early 1980s. Based on interviews with over thirty serial murderers in prison, the profilers predicted he would be a black male, early- to mid-twenties, and a police buff (he impersonated a police officer).

Profiling may not be entirely accepted by old-line investigators, as illustrated in the case of criminologist Bill Tafoya. In 1993, then FBI agent Tafoya was assigned to the Unabomber investigation in San Francisco. His profile, which was not accepted, was uncanny and would most likely have led to an earlier bust of Ted Kaczynski. Contrary to the prevailing profile, Tafoya indicated the bomber was probably in his early fifties (Kaczynski was fifty-three when apprehended). He predicted the bomber would have a graduate degree, maybe a Ph.D.; a background in the "hard" sciences, perhaps engineering or math; and was an antitechnology Luddite (Witkin, 1997).

Sources: Holmes, Ronald, and Stephen Holmes. *Profiling Violent Crimes.* 2nd edition. Thousand Oaks, CA: Sage Publications, 1996; Douglas, John, et al. *Crime Classification Manual.* New York: Lexington Books, 1992; and Miethe, Terance D., and Richard McCorkle. *Crime Profiles: The Anatomy of Dangerous Persons, Places, and Situations.* Los Angeles, CA: Roxbury, 1998.

Although purposive samples are not probability samples, their usefulness is judged on the basis of whether they work in predicting future behavior or attitudes of the target population, for example, voting patterns and consumer behavior.

The following caveat was issued by Sheley and Wright (1993, p. 3) in their study of juvenile possession of firearms by selecting purposive samples of 835 male serious offenders incarcerated in six juvenile facilities in four states and 785 male students in ten inner-city high schools near these facilities:

It should be stressed that these findings are technically not generalizable to other settings and populations. The four states serving as research sites for this study were not a probability sample of States. Moreover, to maximize percentages of respondents involved in the behavior of interest, the study purposely focused on serious juvenile offenders and on students from especially problematic inner-city schools. Therefore, the six correctional facilities and ten high schools (and by virtue of the voluntary nature of participation in the study, the respondents in those institutions) serving as research sites were not probability samples of their respective universes.

Nonetheless, comparison of inmate respondents' profiles with those known through studies of youth in similar institutions indicates that the present sample was not dissimilar to samples of State maximum-security wards serving as subjects of other studies. Moreover, a 1984 study of inner-city high school students' criminal activity employed data collected from randomly selected high school students from inner-city, high-crime neighborhoods in four cities and indicated age and race breakdowns very similar to those found among the student respondents.

A large number of evaluation studies in criminal justice employ purposive sampling as illustrated by the following. To assess the impact of determinate sentencing on institutional climate and prison administration, Goodstein et al. (1984) studied three states that had recently implemented determinate sentencing and purposely chose states that differed in the types of determinate sentencing enacted. In an age cohort analysis of arrest rates, Greenberg and Larkin (1985) chose twenty-five large cities for study on the basis of geographic representativeness. The detailed planning in choosing a purposive sample can be illustrated in Jacob's (1984) study of ten city governments' responses to crime from 1948 to 1978. The cities were chosen on the basis of fiscal strength, type of city government, region, quality of urban life, possession of sufficient research capabilities, accessibility (cooperativeness in the past) to research, availability of prior research, and program initiativeness (had received federal grants in the past). Pate et al. (1986) studied fear of crime in Houston and Newark, the former representing a new, growing city with low population density and the latter a mature, high-population density city with declining economic resources. Toborg's (1981) choice of sites in her study of pretrial release practices in nine jurisdictions was based on very practical reasons, which probably exist in most purposive samples: geographic diversity, wide range of (release) types, accurate and accessible records, and a willingness of agencies to cooperate with the study. Agency contacts and cooperation are essential in such studies because, without such "hospitality," suspicion will very likely undermine the project.

Snowball Sampling.

This is a type of strategy employed particularly in exploratory studies of little-known or hard-to-obtain subjects (Goodman, 1969; Biernacki and Waldorf, 1981). It basically entails obtaining a first subject and, on the basis of this subject, gaining an entrée and introduction to a second subject, then a third, and so forth. Gradually, as many subjects as practicable are accumulated. Polsky (1967) employed this strategy in studying uncaught criminals, as did Solomey (1979) in his study of undercover police. Alex (1969) also employed this strategy in order to study black police officers in New York City. Such a sampling procedure may be the only means of obtaining data on little-known or secretive subject matter. In order to study "The Social Organization of Drug Use and Drug Dealing Among Urban Gangs," Fagan (1989) used a snowball sample of gang member respondents. Initial subjects were recruited through neighborhood agencies, and gang members who were recruited later were nominated by these first respondents. All participants received payment for their cooperation in the form of caps, T-shirts, or coupons to music stores.

In contrasting a history of Asian gangs in San Francisco, Toy (1992) interviewed sixty-four active gang members as well as nine respondents for historical purposes. Utilizing a snowball sampling technique, subjects were initially recruited through neighborhood social service agencies and then asked to refer other gang members. Respondents were paid $50 and another $40 for each successful referral.

In an Australian study, Dance (1991) utilized a snowball sample to study recreational intravenous drug users. The author asked everyone she knew if they were familiar with any intravenous drug users. After asking about fifty people she met Roger, an intravenous drug user with whom she developed a rapport. After he told his friends that she was trustworthy, she was ultimately able to interview others.

The selection of the sample and instrument to be used for data collection is always governed by time, cost, and staff available to collect and analyze the data. Unless selection probabilities can be estimated, statistical inference to larger populations is hazardous. In the hands of skillful researchers, however, and for specific research problems, nonprobability samples may be preferred.

Sample Size

There is no simple answer to the question: "What is an appropriate size sample to choose?" It depends on a number of considerations, and there is no predetermined appropriate sample size for all conditions. The choice of sample size can depend on the degree of accuracy required, the funds available, the expected frequency (or rarity) of the characteristic to be observed, and the anticipated subclassification of the variables. It's important to note that without a representative sample, sample size becomes irrelevant. A small representative sample would yield a better estimate of the population than a much larger sample.

The size of the sample is statistically determined by the size of the sampling error to be tolerated rather than the total size of the population (Kish, 1965). The larger the sample size, the smaller the sampling error or extent to which the sampling values can be expected to differ from population values. Depending on available funds, researchers should attempt to obtain as large a sample as is practical. Statistical tables for determination of sample sizes are available in standard statistical texts. For instance, for the 95 percent probability that a sample will have less than a plus or minus 5 percent error in estimating the population, a population of 500 would require a sample of 217, a population of 1,000 needs a sample of 286, a population of 10,000 requires 370, and a population over 100,000 must have a sample of roughly 400. SPSS has sample power software to determine appropriate sample size (available at www.spss.com/software/spower).

The sample size also depends on the expected frequency (or rarity) of the characteristic to be observed in the population. For example, in the discussion of victim surveys in Chapter 6, it will be indicated that a sample of 60,000 households is used for the National Crime Survey of the entire U.S. population. A similar number was required for each city surveyed as part of the original central city surveys. Why are such large samples required in victim surveys when similar public opinion surveys are sometimes conducted with only a few hundred in the sample? Because nearly everyone has an opinion, whereas victimization for a specific crime may be rare, thus requiring a large sample in order to obtain a few cases.

Related to the last point is the fact that too small samples may provide too few cases for analysis once the sample is subclassified. For example, if the study entailed comparison of three race categories by ten different crime victimizations, some of the subclassifications (e.g., Asians who have been burglarized) may yield too few cases for statistical analysis. In such cases larger samples are required than minimums expressed in statistical tables.

The reader is advised to examine statistical texts on sampling for more technical detail on this subject (Bachman and Paternoster, 1997; Kish, 1965), as well as to consult journal articles and examine sample sizes employed in similar studies.

Summary

Criminal justice data gathering frequently requires real-world strategies as well as the use of alternative approaches, such as social surveys, participant observation, case study/life history methods, and unobtrusive measures. None of these methods is inherently superior to the others, although their relative strengths and weaknesses can be broken down with respect to quantitative/qualitative strength, greater or less control over rival factors, control over factors of internal/external validity, and artificiality/naturalness (see Figure 4.1).

The UCR is given special treatment in this chapter so that it will not be lost in our discussion of other studies using available data or official statistics. Until recently, criminology and criminal justice in the United States have heavily relied on the UCR for research purposes. Most popular presentations on crime rates in the United States are usually taken uncritically from the UCR without a full appreciation of the limitations of these data. The UCR is published annually by the FBI and represents not crimes committed, but crimes reported to, and recorded by, the police. In general, the further from the actual offense commission, the poorer the official statistics are in providing an accurate picture of crime. The participation of local police departments in the uniform crime reporting system has improved over the years, with about 98 percent of the national population covered by 1978. The original *Crime Index* consisted of a simple summated index of seven (arson, added in 1978, equals eight) crimes considered more serious, most likely reported, and most frequently occurring. The violent index offenses are murder and nonnegligent manslaughter, forcible rape, robbery, and aggravated assault, while the property index offenses are burglary, larceny-theft, auto theft, and arson. The *crime rate* is the number of crimes per unit of population. Investigators using the UCR for research purposes should become familiar with its major limitations, which make it a particularly hazardous statistic for comparing crime over time or measuring actual crime commission.

In 1985, a blueprint for a redesigned UCR program was developed, and by the early 1990s it had begun to be implemented. This program featured a NIBRS, which will eventually replace the traditional UCR. This comprehensive system provides far more detail than the previous summary-based one.

Sampling involves scientifically selecting a microcosm of a larger population to which one wishes to infer, usually at great savings in time and cost. There are two major types of sampling: probability samples and nonprobability samples. In probability samples, which consist of simple random, stratified, cluster, and systematic samples, an EPSEM is employed. Each type has relative advantages or disadvantages over the others that must be considered prior to the decision to employ one. Nonprobability samples do not make use of an EPSEM procedure and thus make hazardous the employment of statistical techniques that assume this. They also make problematic any generalization to the larger population from which the sample was drawn. The major types of nonprobability samples are quota, accidental, purposive, and snowball. Even though these do not employ EPSEM procedures, careful use of nonprobability samples can be an effective tool in gaining information regarding larger populations.

Focus groups are purposively selected groups brought together to measure reactions to some stimuli. *Criminal profiling* is an attempt to construct typical characteristics of certain types of criminals.

KEY CONCEPTS

Alternative data-gathering strategies

Uniform crime report (UCR)

Index crimes

Crime rate

Factors affecting UCR

Hot spots

Limitations of the crime index

Crime dip

Redesign of the UCR system

The National Incident-Based Reporting System (NIBRS)

Administrative segment

Offense segment

Property segment

Offender segment

Arrestee segment

Hierarchy rule

Sampling

Sampling frame

Probability samples

Simple random sample

EPSEM

Stratified random sample

Proportionate stratified sample

Disproportionate stratified sample

Cluster sample

Systematic sample

Random start

Multistage sample

Quota sample

Accidental sample

Purposive sample

Focus groups

Mock trials

Criminal profiling

Snowball sample

REVIEW QUESTIONS

1. What is the UCR? What are its major components? What are the major components of the crime index? What is the calculation of crime rate? What have been some major identified shortcomings of the UCR?

2. Given the identified shortcomings of the UCR, read and then discuss how features of the redesigned UCR may eliminate some of these shortcomings.

3. Discuss the National Incident-Based Reporting System (NIBRS). What are some of its principal features as well as advantages over the traditional UCR?

4. What are some possible explanations for the crime dip of the 1990s?

5. Discuss the various types of sampling and when it would be most appropriate to use each one.

6. For what is weighting used in disproportionate stratified sampling, and why would samples be disproportionately drawn in the first place?

USEFUL WEB SITES

The Welcome Gateways (Research Design) *http://omni.ac.uk/browse/mesh/C0035171L0035171.html*

Preventing Crime: What Works, What Doesn't, What's Promising *www.ncjrs.org/works/wholedoc.htm*

Campbell Collaboration *www.campbellcollaboration.org/*

A Social, Psychological, Educational, and Criminological Trials Register ED: change to:*http://www.geb9101.gse.upenn.edu*

Cybrary: The World's Criminal Justice Directory *http://talkjustice.com/cybrary.asp*

Methods Reading List *http://web.crim.ufl.edu/grad/methods_readings.pdf*

Randomized Experiments (A Tutorial) *www.socialresearchmethods.net/tutorial/Belue/rand.html*

Research Designs (North Carolina State University) *www2.chass.ncsu.edu/garson/pa765/design.htm*

Scientifically Based Research (ERIC Digest) *www.ericfacility.net/databasesERIC_Digests/ed474304.html*

5
Survey Research: Questionnaires

Survey Research

Survey research, an area that is emerging as a strength in criminal justice research, is an excellent tool for primary data gathering.

In Indiana, legislative hearings dealing with the death penalty for juveniles ended with the following statement (Hamm, 1989, p. 224):

> We have debated capital punishment for juveniles today and have come to various conclusions. Yet one thing we know for sure. Never fill out a questionnaire from a criminologist again.

Criminologist Mark Hamm was told this by both the press and other persons associated with the legislature. He was also told that his research "struck too close to the bone." Beginning in the fall of 1986, he received survey responses from eighty-five legislators (85 percent of the General Assembly). He was relatively certain that many of the legislators had filled out the survey themselves rather than relegating it to their staffs because, he said (Hamm, 1989, p. 223):

> [I]n my testimony on the juvenile death penalty before the Indiana General Assembly, a number of legislators indicated a familiarity with the substantive content of the survey. Indeed the survey became a heated topic of debate during these proceedings. My testimony—one among some thirty given before the General Assembly—was the only one terminated by the Legislature. It was cut short on the grounds that it was inappropriate to discuss statistical reasons why some legislators might favor the execution of juveniles and why others might not.

The fact that, as in this example, participants in a legislative hearing were threatened by the results of a survey certainly illustrates the power and potential usefulness of such an instrument.

In this chapter we examine mail questionnaire and self-report studies whose features successfully illustrate many of the opportunities and pitfalls of survey methods. Other major data-gathering approaches, such as interviews, victim surveys, and telephone surveys, will be the subject of Chapter 6.

Surveys have often been misunderstood by some researchers who have been socialized in the experimental tradition. Many times hostility appears between some theoreticians and practitioners with respect to the strong emphasis placed on the experimental tradition as an ideal in social science research. Part of this methodological argument may result from a lack of full appreciation of the nature of survey research methods and their potential as tools in investigating many important questions facing the criminal justice system. The notion of a survey connotes images of a poll or simple tally (count of opinion), but survey research has many purposes and can address many scientific problems beyond a simple count of opinion. *Descriptive survey research* may use statistical probability theory to assess sampling error. (Is what is true of the sample true of the population?) *Analytic survey research* attempts to explore questions of cause and effect similar to traditional experimental research. The experimenter utilizes research design *before* the fact to remove the effects of rival causal factors, whereas the survey researcher tries to remove these rival factors *after* the fact (after the data have been collected) through the use of statistical analysis.

A basic quality of survey research that is at times forgotten and is responsible for much potential error in interpretation of findings is that in most instances *surveys record either expressed attitude or claimed behavior and seldom the behavior itself.* In Chapter 7, we will detail potential errors in surveys in which the full importance of this statement will be explained, but at this stage, acceptance of this point as an article of faith will suffice. Previously we indicated that surveys are not just useful for political and consumer polls but are also effective means of addressing scientific questions and the causality problem. Rather than control for rival causal factors prior to the fact by means of research design, surveys generally employ quantitative methods and statistical procedures post hoc to control for extraneous variables and sources of invalidity, because natural field settings make the control of sources of invalidity more problematic.

Survey research may employ a variety of data-gathering methods ranging from the administration of structured questionnaires to captive audiences (such as all sections of Introduction to American Criminal Justice at a college or university), to mail questionnaires, field interviews, telephone surveys, and their variations. In this chapter we concentrate on the mail questionnaire. It is widely used and offers the possibility to discuss many issues that occur in the other types of survey approaches. We will first examine some guidelines for questionnaire construction.

Some Guidelines for Questionnaire Construction

Although it would be foolish for anyone to claim that there is only one way of constructing an effective questionnaire, a number of procedures have been established by practitioners through trial and error and custom.

The most crucial and most underestimated step in questionnaire construction involves clearly formulating the research problem and the data

Age

		Under 20	20s	30s	40s	50s	60s	Over 69
Victim of Serious Crime (1980)	Yes							
	No							

Figure 5.1
A Dummy Table for the Relationship between Victimization and Age.

required to speak directly to the research problem. A common method of specifying the relationship between research issues and data is creation of a variables list that is keyed to questionnaire items and dummy tables.

A **variables list** is constructed after the initial rough draft of the questionnaire. The concepts or variables to be measured are listed along with the numbers of the questions that purport to measure them. By rigorously reviewing a questionnaire in this manner, duplicative items, unmeasured concepts, or an emphasis that is undesirable may be discovered.

Variables list

Dummy tables are preliminary blank tables constructed prior to data gathering that suggest the type of data needed, as well as the type of data analysis. Figure 5.1 illustrates the use of a dummy table to call attention to data that will be needed for a two-variable cross-tabulation.

Dummy tables

Assuming that such a tabular analysis is planned, the researcher is now alerted to the need to check the data-gathering instrument to see if the questions for these two variables have been asked in a manner that would render itself to the type of categorization in the dummy table. The real utility of a dummy table is realized when the researcher discovers that he or she has failed to ask a question necessary to the study. Although variables lists and dummy tables may strike those anxious to get on with a study as ritualism, they act to ensure that the data needed are obtained before the fact, rather than after the fact when it may be too late. A basic maxim of research is no more data should be gathered than needed; however, blind application of this dictum is myopic. A study should be viewed as a research opportunity, one in which the basic needs of the present research enterprise as well as "riders" (related research questions that may be analyzed once the main project is completed) are present. For instance, in the course of a federally funded project on attrition among rehabilitation counselors, data gathered on professionalism can later be analyzed to address the issue of professional developments in the field (Hagan, Haug, and Sussman, 1975).

Questionnaire Wording

Sudman and Bradburn's *Asking Questions* (1982) is a gold mine of suggestions on questionnaire wording and construction. They caution you to resist writing questions until you have carefully thought through the research questions or problems. It is also quite useful to collect and borrow successful questions from other researchers. This may even enable the comparison of questions across studies (1982, p. 14).

The language used in questionnaires must be geared to the target population. If the study group is a specialized one, for example, forensic pathologists, then the use of occupational argot and technical language would be preferred. In fact, pretests of the instrument with members of this occupation may suggest appropriate terminology. On the other hand, if the general population is to be surveyed, a more common language should be used. Sometimes the questions may be structured in a too complex way that will not be understood by some respondents. For example, one might ask the question: "Do you think Congress should pass legislation to facilitate single-payer cost reimbursement plans for indigent clients?" (AAPOR, 2009). If the target group includes significant non–English-speaking populations, it may be necessary to employ bilingual strategies such as dual-language instruments. Faculty of foreign language departments at local colleges often prove to be invaluable consultants in this regard. Similarity of respondent understanding of language is particularly problematic in cross-cultural research. Anyone with exposure to foreign languages realizes that certain ideas, idioms, and jargon are not readily translated into another language. The same holds true across cultures with similar languages. Asking if a person has ever been mugged may puzzle others who may confuse the term with kissing or being served a drink.

Care must also be taken to identify clearly who should answer the questions, for example, head of the household or any adult member of the household. This writer was once the subject of a shopping mall marketing survey and, as part of an apparent quota sample, was asked his opinions regarding some sample cereal box covers. The covers featured pictures of sports figures and, after the completion of a fairly long interview, my wife asked me when I last purchased cereal. One could just imagine supermarkets loaded with cereal boxes picturing hockey players while consumers purchase those featuring smiling children.

Some of the following *suggestions on questionnaire wording and construction* are not intended to be either exhaustive or mutually exclusive:

- *Avoid biased or leading questions.* The classic example is, "Do you still beat your spouse?" No matter how respondents answer that question, they are admitting spousal abuse.

- *Avoid double-barreled questions.* Such questions ask two questions in one. Do not ask something like, "Do you walk to work or carry your lunch?" "Did you vote in the 2004 and 2008 elections?"

- *Avoid asking questions in an objectionable manner.* "Did you exercise your duty as a citizen and report this incident to the police?" Respondents would feel unpatriotic if they answered no.

- *Avoid assuming prior information on the part of the respondent.* One might ask, "Do you support the *Miranda* decision?"—only to discover too late that half of the respondents thought Miranda was a shortstop with the Pittsburgh Pirates.

- *Avoid vague wording.* Use language with as much common meaning as possible. One of the best examples of vague wording was a 1993 Roper poll that incredibly found that 22 percent of Americans apparently believed that the Holocaust may never have happened and

12 percent were unsure. These responses were caused by an awkwardly worded double-negative constructed sentence. "Does it seem possible or does it seem impossible to you that the Nazi extermination of the Jews never happened?" When resurveyed using properly worded questions, less than one percent expressed doubt regarding the Holocaust (Radwin, 2009).

■ *Avoid asking more than you need to know.* This merely adds unnecessary length to the instrument.

■ *Avoid "response set" patterns by using reversal questions.* Do not word all questions so that a positive or negative answer is the most desirable; otherwise, respondents may answer the first few and then check off the remainder in a similar fashion without even reading them.

Barton (1958, p. 67) provides humorous examples of many of the techniques that have been used as a means of asking threatening questions (cited in Sudman and Bradburn, 1982, pp. 54–55). In this case we want to ask, "Did you kill your wife?"

■ *The Casual Approach*: "Do you happen to have murdered your wife?"

■ *The Numbered Card*: "Would you please read off the number on this card which corresponds to what became of your wife?" (Hand card to respondent.)

1. Natural death
2. I killed her.
3. Other (What?) (Get the card back from respondent before proceeding.)

■ *The Everybody Approach*: "As you know, many people have been killing their wives these days. Do you happen to have killed yours?"

■ *The "Other People" Approach*:

(a) "Do you know any people who have murdered their wives?"

(b) "How about yourself?"

■ *The Sealed Ballot Technique*: In this version you explain that the survey respects people's rights to anonymity in respect to their marital relations and that they themselves are to fill out the answer to the question, seal it in an envelope, and drop it in a box conspicuously labeled, "Sealed Ballot Box," which is carried by the interviewer.

■ *The Kinsey Technique*: Stare firmly into respondent's eyes and ask in simple, clear-cut language, such as that to which the respondent is accustomed, and with an air of assuming everyone has done everything, "Did you ever kill your wife?" Put the question at the end of the interview. This "everybody does it approach" developed by Kinsey is called counterbiasing, which means asking the question in such a way that the behavior appears relatively frequent and normal.

Although Barton's wife-killing example involves a preposterous topic, the techniques used to ask threatening questions are quite common and useful in survey research.

Researchers must also decide whether open-ended (unstructured) or closed-ended (structured) questions will yield the necessary information:

> *Open*: Some people feel that certain parts of the criminal justice system do not work. Do you agree? If so, what parts?
>
> *Closed*: Some people feel that certain parts of the criminal justice system do not work. Is this belief _____ True, _____ False, _____ Don't Know. If true, what parts? _____ Police, Courts, _____ Corrections, _____ Other Specify _____

Although open-ended questions may provide greater detail and permit respondents to express their attitudes in-depth, such responses pose difficulty. Closed-ended (structured) questions, although they ease the coding process and are easier for respondents, may not give respondents an opportunity to explain fully their views.

To illustrate some question ambiguity in professionally designed surveys, the following illustrations were drawn from the presentation on analytical issues in victim surveys by the Crime Statistics Analysis Staff to the Panel for the Evaluation of Crime Surveys (Panel for the Evaluation of Crime Surveys, 1976, pp. 167–176):

> *Question*: Were the police informed of this incident in any way?
>
> 1. ❏ No
> 2. ❏ Don't Know—Skip to Check Item G.
>   Yes—Who told them?
> 3. ❏ Household member
> 4. ❏ Someone else
> 5. ❏ Police on scene
>
> *Some Problems*: The use of the term "informed" is a potentially suggestive one. The possibility may be ruled out that the police were on the scene or happened on the scene or may have been called without the respondent being aware.
>
> *Question*: **8a.** What were the injuries you suffered, if any?
>
> 1. ❏ None—Skip to 10a.
> 2. ❏ Raped
> 3. ❏ Attempted rape
> 4. ❏ Knife or gunshot wounds
> 5. ❏ Broken bones or teeth knocked out
> 6. ❏ Internal injuries, knocked unconscious
> 7. ❏ Bruises, black eye, cuts, scratches, swelling
> 8. ❏ Other—Specify _____

b. Were you injured to the extent that you needed medical attention after the attack?

    1. ❏ No—Skip to 10a.

    2. ❏ Yes.

c. Did you receive any treatment at a hospital?

    1. ❏ No

    2. ❏ Emergency room treatment only

    3. ❏ Stayed overnight or longer

       How many days?

Problems: Question 8b may be subject to varying interpretations. The interviewer training manual defines "need" as actually securing aid from a trained medical professional. However, to a respondent, "need" could be based on a conception of the seriousness of the injury. Because the interviewer may not always provide the official interpretation of "need," responses may reflect different interpretations of the meaning of the question. Question 8a responses 2 ("Raped") and 3 ("Attempted rape") were to be interpreted as determinants of physical injury, but attempted rape may involve only verbal threats. That is, the inclusion of attempted physical injury may cause distortions in data on physical injury.

Question 8c, in obtaining data on hospital care only, fails to identify other types of medical care, professional or nonprofessional or institutional or otherwise.

Question: **2.** About what time did this (most recent) incident happen?

    1. ❏ Don't know

    2. ❏ During the day (6:00 A.M. to 6:00 P.M.)

    3. ❏ 6:00 P.M. to midnight

    4. ❏ Midnight to 6:00 A.M.

Problem: Noncomparable categories of time provide too broad a category for daytime, which could be subdivided to 6:00 A.M. to noon and noon to 6:00 P.M.

Question: **11b.** How old would you say the person (offender) was?

    1. ❏ Under 12

    2. ❏ 12–14

    3. ❏ 15–17

    4. ❏ 18–20

    5. ❏ 21 or over

    6. ❏ Don't know

Problem: Category 5, "21 or over," is too broad and should be subdivided.

In asking opinion questions, *do not assume that the respondents have all the information necessary to make a meaningful or informed decision.* For instance, a researcher could ask, "Do you support the current interpretation of the *Miranda* decision?" Perhaps 60 percent of the respondents may say "yes"; however, not having asked the respondents if they had any idea what the *Miranda* decision was, it may turn out that 90 percent of the subjects did not know what it was and were too embarrassed to say so.

Some additional pointers include that the first several questions should be easy to understand, important to the study's purpose, and engage the respondent's interest. Questions should be grouped into logical order, and new sections should feature an introduction so that participants can switch mental gears (Narins, 1995, p. 8). Avoid too many skip questions; for example, "If the answer is 'yes,' skip to 5; and if 'none of the above,' skip to 6." This may be confusing to the respondent. If the survey has multiple pages, a booklet format is recommended. Attempt to make self-administered surveys easy to complete, with check boxes and lines easy to see and numbers to be circled far enough apart. Begin the instrument with a short introduction explaining its purpose, topics to be covered, how the results will be used, and any incentives for participation. Leave plenty of room for open-ended questions but do not supply lines, as these may constrain any comments (Narins, p. 9).

Pretest

Although formulation of dummy tables and a variables list and adherence to general points discussed so far will assist the researcher in the development of a potentially useful instrument, prior to using the questionnaire with target respondents a pretest of the instrument is a must. A **pretest** is a reconnaissance operation or exploratory testing of the instrument using subjects who are similar to the group to be studied. The pretest subjects are asked to critique the instrument, pointing out confusions or misunderstandings and perhaps suggesting more proper wording or issues to be explored.

Organization of the Questionnaire

The order of questions may influence the willingness of subjects to respond to the survey. A common error in surveys is to begin with the demographic items such as age, sex, and race. Although these questions are an important part of any survey, they are also routine and boring for most respondents. Such questions are better asked later or even last in the instrument (see Schuman and Presser, 1981). A good rule of thumb is "first impressions last." *A questionnaire is best begun with items that arouse interest and gain the respondent's attention.* The beginning of the survey is also not the appropriate place for sensitive items; one would not ask a person he or she had just met extremely personal questions. The following questionnaire illustrates what not to ask in the beginning:

A GUARANTEED LOW-RESPONSE QUESTIONNAIRE

What is your name?

How old are you?

What is your sex?

How much money do you earn?

Do you cheat on your income tax?

How is your sex life?

When was the last time you committed a crime?

Perhaps for good measure one could throw in, "Do you still beat your spouse?" and "Do you walk to work or carry your lunch?"

The questions should be arranged in a logical sequence that is readable, interesting, and easy to respond to. In mail surveys, open-ended questions should be kept to a minimum (see Schuman and Presser, 1996).

Coding

Coding is the assignment of numerical values to responses (information) gathered by a research instrument. As soon as or even before the data are gathered, the researcher can begin to construct a code for each item to be measured. Such codes are compiled into a *codebook*, which guides the numerical classification of questions to be coded. Figure 5.2 lists some typical questionnaire items. Figure 5.3 is a sample codebook for these same questions. The responses of a hypothetical respondent have been added for illustrative purposes.

The general purpose of the conversion of questionnaire information into numerical data is that, once this process is completed, the researcher can basically store the questionnaires and work from the summarized information— numbers. This can be particularly appreciated when a large number of cases and a large number of questions are asked. It becomes unmanageable to attempt to work directly from the original instrument.

To summarize, coding is development of a code for each question in the questionnaire. The combination of each code is called a **codebook**. All relevant questions are coded using the codebook as a guide, and these numbers are assigned to appropriate cells or columns on a codesheet or spreadsheet (Figure 5.4).

Throughout this process the code or codebook is used as a guide in reading the numerical information. The codebook may require revision during the course of the coding procedure, particularly for open-ended items that may call for considerable judgment on the part of the coder.

Each column in our codebook (Figure 5.3) represents a box or cell on the **codesheet** (or transfer sheet) (Figure 5.4). Coding may be handled in a variety of ways, depending on the nature of the data-gathering instrument and the resources available. In addition to use of a separate codesheet, researchers may employ self-coding (similar to the pencil-in answer sheets used in machine-scored tests) or edge coding (in which the margins of the questionnaire itself are used for coding, thus eliminating the need for separate coding sheets). Self-coding instruments can be entered automatically by an optical scanning sensor device, whereas edge-coded questionnaires can be designed so that they are precoded and can be directly keyboard entered. Such instruments are usually limited to closed or structured response questions. Figure 5.5A illustrates this same data input into an SPSS spreadsheet, while Figure 5.5B shows ten cases on an SPSS spreadsheet from a file called "employee."

Let us illustrate the coding procedure by means of the hypothetical responses in the sample survey instrument (Figure 5.2) and our sample code-book (Figure 5.3).

According to the codebook, we must first assign a "study number" to this project. This item does not refer to any question number in the instrument and is assigned by the researcher. Because this is our first hypothetical study, we will call it study 1. Code 1 is assigned to cell 1 on the codesheet (Figure 5.4).

If only one study is being analyzed, creation of a computer file name may eliminate the necessity for a study number for each case. The next item in the codebook is the "case number" that is assigned to the respondent. Assume that the top of the questionnaire indicated that this was case 16. Because cells 2, 3, and 4 have been reserved to record respondent case numbers, it appears that more than 100 and fewer than 999 subjects were expected to participate in the study. Recording case number 16 in cells 2 and 3 would result in its being read as $16X$ (X being 0 to 9). Instead, 016 should be coded in cells 2, 3, and 4, respectively. The next item in the code is the "coder identification." In larger studies, each coder is given a coder number beforehand. Our hypothetical coder is number 14; therefore, we enter 14 in columns 5 and 6.

Finally, we begin coding actual substantive items in the sample survey instrument with question 1—sex. The respondent indicated that she was female, which, using our code, is a 2. This is entered in column 7 on the codesheet. Question 2—race—finds the response is "white," which is also a 2 in the code

Figure 5.2
Sample Survey Instrument.

Background Information

Please circle or fill in the correct information about yourself.

1. Sex: (circle one)   Male   (Female)
2. Race: (circle one)   Black   (White)   Other _____
                                                                      (specify)
3. Religious background in your home: (circle one)

   (Catholic)   Jewish   Protestant   Other _____
                                                                      (specify)
4. Present marital status: (circle one)

   Married   Single, never married   (Separated or divorced)   Widowed
5. When were you born? ___6___   ___42___
                              (month)   (year)

QUESTION	ITEM	COLUMN	CODE
-	Study Number	1	As assigned
-	Case Number	2–4	As assigned
-	Coder Identification	5–6	As assigned
1.	Sex	7	1. Male
			2. Female
			9. Not ascertained
2.	Race	8	1. Black
			2. White
			3. Other
			9. Not ascertained
3.	Religious Background	9	0. None
			1. Catholic
			2. Jewish
			3. Protestant
			4. Other
			9. Not ascertained
4.	Present Marital Status	10	1. Married
			2. Single, never married
			3. Separated or divorced
			4. Widowed
			5. Not ascertained
5.	Age	11–12	Code last two digits of year respondent was born. Not ascertained

Figure 5.3
Sample Codebook.

and is entered in column 8. Proceeding in similar fashion, 1—"Catholic"—is entered in column 9, and 3 for "separated or divorced" is marked in column 10. Finally, a two-digit code was necessary to accommodate the last two digits in year of birth. In this case the numbers 4 and 2 were coded in columns 11

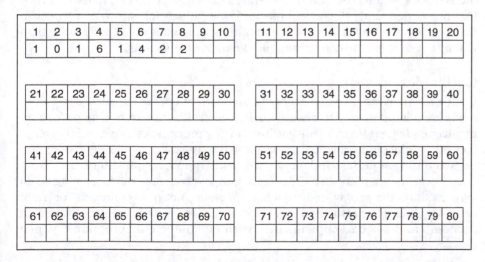

Figure 5.4
Sample Codesheet. Codes Assigned to Cells 1–8 Refer to the Coding of the Survey Instrument (Figure 5.2) Using the Codebook.

	STUDY	CASE	CODER	SEX	RACE	RELIGION
1	1	16	14	2	2	1

Figure 5.5A
Example of Data Entry Using a Spreadsheet.

				C:\SPSSSV\EMPLOYEE.SAV					
	ID	GENDER	RACE	GENRACE	AGE	EDUC	JOBCAT	SALARY	SALBEGIN
1	1	0	0	1	41	15	5	57000	27000
2	2	0	0	1	36	16	1	40200	18750
3	3	1	0	3	65	12	1	21450	12000
4	4	1	0	3	46	8	1	21900	13200
5	5	0	0	1	39	15	1	45000	21000
6	6	0	0	1	35	15	1	36000	13500
7	7	0	0	1	37	15	1	36000	18750
8	8	1	0	3	27	12	1	21900	9750
9	9	1	0	3	48	15	1	27900	12750
10	10	1	0	3	47	12	1	24000	13500

Figure 5.5B
Examples of a Spreadsheet Data File.

and 12, respectively. Although our sample codebook was a simple one for illustrative purposes, the same basic procedure is followed for all relevant items in longer instruments.

Figure 5.6 illustrates the process involved in downloading a study from the National Archive of Criminal Justice Data (NACJD). Care must be taken that one understands the codebooks and other idiosyncrasies with respect to the data. Research staff at NACJD and other similar sites are usually more than willing to assist in clarifying issues and answering questions.

Coder Monitoring

Coder monitoring

Coder monitoring involves checking the work of coders for accuracy. Coder monitoring is necessary to ensure quality control in research. One procedure involves coder *verification and reconciliation* procedures as essential quality-control checks on mechanical error. Each questionnaire is double coded; that is, two different coders independently code the same questionnaire. Next, disagreements are identified. Reconciliation involves the coders coming to an agreement on the proper code. Such a procedure not only eliminates outright errors in coding but also results in greater uniformity and consistency. Such a process can also be supplemented with computer edit programs, which

NATIONAL ARCHIVE of CRIMINAL JUSTICE DATA

THE SOURCE FOR CRIME AND JUSTICE DATA

Download Data

Search/Browse Holdings
Restricted Data
Advanced Search

Online Data Analysis

Archiving Data

Reports & Publications

About NACJD

Mission/Programs
Educational Resources
Archiving Activities
Sponsors
Conferences

Need Help?

Help Documentation
Contact NACJD
Video Tours
Other Criminal Justice Sites
Funding for Data Analysis

Data Resource Guides

Capital Punishment in the United States

Chicago Women's Health Risk Study

Expenditure and Employment for the Criminal Justice System

Federal Justice Statistics Program

Geographical Information Systems

Homicide

Homicides in Chicago

Law Enforcement Management and Administrative Statistics

National Corrections Reporting Program

National Crime Victimization Survey

National Incident-Based Reporting System

National Juvenile Corrections Data

Project on Human Development in Chicago Neighborhoods (PHDCN)

Survey of Inmates in State and Federal Correctional Facilities

Uniform Crime Reporting Program

Violence Against Women

Search

Data Holdings   Related Literature   Web Site

Enter search term(s):

anywhere

⦿ words
◯ exact phrase   [Search]

MyData

What is MyData?
Login/Account Info
Download Saved Files
Logout

Announcements

NCRP Data - Restricted Access...
NIJ FY2010 Forthcoming Solicitation: Data Resources Program...
Notice to National Corrections Reporting Program Users...
Recently Released Publications...
Recent updates...

Figure 5.6
Download—National Archive of Criminal Justice Data.
Source: www.icpsr.umich.edu/cgi-bin/archive.prl?path=NACJD;format=tb;study=6542&emai...

identify by column the incorrect values (those not defined by the codebook as proper values). Unfortunately, unchecked mechanical errors may be the true rival causal factor in many pieces of reported research. Thus, the results of a survey may not be due to accurate measurement; rather, they may simply be due to miscoding, data entry, and other human and mechanical mistakes. In some instances, precision and care in earlier stages of a project are disregarded once the "boring" routine of "number crunching" is begun.

Keyboard Entry

The **keyboard entry** technique is the most widely used means of inputting data. The data typed on the keyboard are displayed on a video terminal. The terminal displays case 1, variable name 1, and prompts (asks for information) for case 1. Once these data are input, the screen prompts for the data for case 2; eventually, all of the data are entered. The computer can save the data (as a file in its memory) or output it onto some medium, for example, paper (printout), magnetic tape, or diskettes, for later use. The printout is produced by a printer. Data stored in memory or on tape or a disk are referred to as a completed *data file*.

Keyboard entry

Mail Surveys

Most readers of this book are probably already familiar with the properties of mail questionnaires because participation in such surveys is becoming a common cultural phenomenon in North America and other developed countries. The most common type of **mail survey** is the self-administered, mailback variety in which a stamped, addressed return envelope is enclosed.

Mail survey

The mail survey is a popular instrument for research because it promises, at a minimum of time and expense, to deliver fairly wide coverage for a study. Perhaps this asset of the mail questionnaire has made it the favorite instrument of a variety of organizations selling products, soliciting opinions, collecting charitable donations, and attempting to conduct social, scientific, or criminal justice research. In the 1970s, a special conference of the American Statistical Association addressed itself to the growing concern of nonresponse in such surveys. It appeared as if the potential respondents were becoming overburdened. In the mid-1960s, large private research organizations could expect roughly a 75 percent response rate in mail surveys; by the mid-1970s this figure had dropped to 60–65 percent. This is assuming even a number of follow-up inquiries to solicit participation (American Statistical Association, 1974).

In *The Phantom Respondent*, John Brehm (1993) notes some alarming trends about the growing nonresponse problem in polls and surveys such as the National Election Studies (NES) based at the University of Michigan and the General Social Survey (GSS) at the University of Chicago. The former is done every federal election year since 1954 and the latter every year since 1972 (Morin, 1993). While the NES averaged nonresponse of less than 10 percent in the 1950s, by the 1990s it had the same 20–30 percent nonresponse as the GSS. The major media polls have 30–50 percent nonresponse (Morin, 1993). A study of 141 articles from leading managerial and behavioral science journals in 1975, 1985, and 1995 discovered that the average response rate in academic surveys was 55.6 percent, actually 48.4 percent in 1995 (Baruch, 1999). The key question is whether the nonrespondents differ significantly from respondents, and the answer is yes. Overrepresented in surveys are the elderly, blacks, women, the poor, and the less educated. Men, young people, whites, and the wealthy are underrepresented.

Those considering using mail surveys as their means of data collection should consider the fact that they are competitors for the time of respondents who are becoming increasingly more difficult to interest in participating. A prudent researcher should, prior to deciding to employ mail surveys, carefully consider the relative advantages and disadvantages as well as alternative data-gathering strategies that might make it unnecessary to collect new data. The definitive source on mail survey and related survey research is the journal *Public Opinion Quarterly*, a publication of the American Public Opinion Association, an organization that sets standards in the field and to which most reputable private research organizations belong. One practice of such organizations, for instance, is a 5 percent verification check on surveyed subjects to assure accuracy of data; that is, 5 percent of those already questioned are questioned again to certify their responses.

Although the problems and prospects raised by a particular survey vary from study to study, a presentation on general disadvantages and advantages of mail surveys may help one decide whether it is the appropriate data-gathering method for a study.

Advantages of Mail Surveys

As previously suggested, one important attractive feature of mail surveys is that they *afford wide geographical and perhaps more representative samples at a reasonable cost, effort, and time.* Compared with the personal interview (discussed in Chapter 6), the mail survey *requires no field staff*, thus eliminating transportation and other costs. By the same token, it *eliminates interviewer bias effects*, because there are no interviewers. Mail surveys may tend to *afford the respondents greater privacy* as well as an opportunity to think out their responses, leading to *more considered answers*. This is particularly the case for a survey attempting to obtain detailed information that may require checking records, files, historical documents, and the like. For example, in a survey of presidents of professions related to rehabilitation, this author asked questions such as the following:

Advantages of Mail Surveys

Question: What was the average budget of your organization from 2000 through 2003? (If it would be easier, you may wish to supply the information yearly.)

Average Income _____

Average Expenditures _____

Total Assets _____

Net Assets _____

Optional: 2000 2001 2002 2003

Question: On the next page are a series of events that are believed relevant by some writers in the field to the history of the development of occupations and their professional associations. Please supply estimates and answers.

Event	Estimated Date	Comments (For instance, where, if applicable?)
1. At what time did work in your field emerge as a full-time occupation?	_____	_____
2. When was the first training school established?	_____	_____
3. When was the first state licensing law in your field established (if any)?	_____	_____
4. When was the first formal professional "code of ethics" adopted?	_____	_____

Obviously, such questions are most appropriately asked in a mail survey, which enables the respondent to devote adequate time to look things up, rather than in an on-the-spot interview.

Disadvantages of Mail Surveys

Disadvantages of Mail Surveys

The chief problem with many mail surveys is *nonresponse*. Inexperienced researchers without sponsorship may be fortunate to obtain a 20 percent rate in first-wave mailings, that is, a one-time-only survey without follow-up (Miller, 1991, p. 77). Even with fairly high rates of return, the researcher is still faced with the problem of *possible differences between respondents and nonrespondents* with respect to the issue being investigated. Other potential problems may exist with respect to *a lack of uniformity in response, slowness of response to follow-up attempts, the possibility that a number of respondents may misinterpret the questions,* and *escalating costs if several follow-ups are required.* Although these and other problems create difficulties, they are by no means insurmountable, as demonstrated later in this chapter. Still, these disadvantages must be seriously considered by the researcher and addressed in some fashion by means of planning, prior to the first canvass.

Ways of Eliminating Disadvantages in Mail Surveys

An entire arsenal of techniques is at the disposal of the clever researcher to attempt to outmaneuver many of the problematic elements of the mail survey. The nonresponse problem can be broken down into two groups: those who have yet to respond and those who refuse to cooperate in the survey. It is standard practice in research, unlike encyclopedia sales, to honor a potential subject's right to refuse to participate in a study. So long as this rate is small, less than 1 percent, for instance, it is an expected loss in surveys. Further pleas to the respondent to participate, such as "We do hope you will reconsider," stretch a delicate boundary and may be conceived as harassment on the part of the respondent. If high refusal rates are expected, a far better strategy is oversampling to create a replacement pool. Although this introduces some potential error in that the replacement subjects may not match the subjects they replace, at least the study can continue with a filled sampling frame. The researcher must acknowledge this potential source of error.

Ways of increasing responses in mail surveys

Some **ways of increasing responses in mail surveys** include, but are not limited to, the following:

- Follow-up
- Offering remuneration
- Altruistic appeals
- Use of attractive format
- Sponsorship

- Endorsements
- Personalization
- Shortened format
- Good timing

Follow-up

The use of techniques to increase response in surveys is limited only by the imagination and perhaps the time and finances of the researcher. Of major importance in most surveys is the *follow-up* with respondents. Continued efforts to solicit response may include renewed mailing(s) of the original questionnaire, mailings of shortened versions of the instrument, postcards, telephone calls, interviews, telegrams, mailgrams, and their combinations (Heberlein and Baumgartner, 1978). Some researchers mail a "reminder/thank you" postcard three days after the initial mailing to encourage response. An interesting procedure sometimes followed is enclosure of an identifying postcard with an anonymous survey form so that the respondents can, at the time they return the form, register that they have responded and should not receive further reminders (Dillman, 1972, 1976). In general, special delivery and certified delivery are superior to first-class mail which, in return, is superior to second- and third-class mail. Certified mail can yield a return receipt verifying delivery. If first-class letters are marked "address correction requested," postal authorities will notify the sender of the filed forwarding address to which the letter has been redirected.

A common practice for determining proper timing for the follow-up is illustrated by a hypothetical study (Figure 5.7).

Beginning on June 1, 1,000 residents of Millvale were mailed questionnaires. Returns began to arrive on June 4. The daily number of returns peaked on June 16. By June 23, the replies, encouraged by the second mailing (or first follow-up), began to arrive and peaked around July 15. At that time a second follow-up was undertaken, the results of which tailed off in late August, when a third request was mailed to respondents. The third follow-up had little impact on encouraging

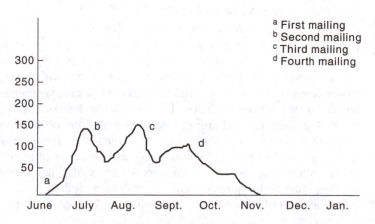

a First mailing
b Second mailing
c Third mailing
d Fourth mailing

Figure 5.7
Millvale Victimization Survey.

more responses and, because the end of the targeted period for data gathering was nearing, no further follow-up probes were assumed necessary.

Offering Remuneration

Offering remuneration involves offering rewards or incentives to survey participants. It may, depending on subject and type of respondents, increase response. Some researchers actually enclose, rather than just promise, payment on the assumption that people will feel guilty about keeping the money and not answering the survey. A variation of inducement is the offer to share a summary or copy of the report with interested respondents. A word of caution—financial offerings may be out of order with some subjects; for example, a one-dollar offer might insult wealthy or influential subjects, or an offer of coupons for free chocolate bars would be in poor taste in a survey dealing with hunger and starvation. In the latter instance, *altruistic appeals* to the respondents' concern for science and humanity would be more effective.

Church (1993) analyzed thirty-eight studies on the impact of incentives in mail surveys and found prepaid incentives were more effective than promised ones. Other findings were that prepaid monetary incentives were better than gifts offered with the initial mailing, response rates increase with larger amounts of money, and that promises of money or gifts do not significantly increase response rates. Singer et al. (1999), in a replication of Church, found that the effects of incentives were only modest.

Attractive Format

An *attractive format* for the instrument may impress on the respondent the important nature of the study. Although cost limitations may determine the ultimate *appearance of a questionnaire*, a ditto reproduction is less desirable than a mimeograph, which again is inferior to a lithograph or a good print job. Other possibilities include colored paper and print, photographs, illustrations, and booklets. Anything that can attract interest in the survey may enhance response.

Sponsorship and Endorsements

Sponsorship and *endorsements* are excellent means of enhancing the potential prestige and legitimacy of the survey in the eyes of respondents. Generally, *the greater the public visibility and reputation of the organization sponsoring or conducting the survey, the greater the potential response.* Unattached researchers or students generally can expect poorer response than known persons or organizations in the field. For students, letters from professors bearing the college insignia and urging response would be more effective than the student's own cover letter. *Endorsement cover letters from prominent individuals*, for example, presidents of national organizations of which the respondents are members, may increase response. A survey of police officers may yield better response if the questionnaire is accompanied by letters urging response from the chief of police and the president of the local Fraternal Order of Police.

In a mail survey of the 100 largest police departments in the United States regarding police undercover practices, Hamilton and Smykla (1994) were able to achieve an 87 percent response rate. This high response may have been achieved in part due to the fact that the cover letter came from the New York Attorney General's Office and one of the authors was a known practitioner in the law enforcement community.

Personalization

Personalization of survey instruments is the attempt to make less impersonal the appearance of the survey package or follow-up probes. Because all good mail surveys should contain stamped, addressed return envelopes, some feel the attachment of colorful commemorative stamps to the envelopes adds more personalization than bureaucratic and impersonal postage meters. Better yet, commemorative stamps that deal with topics related to the subject matter of the survey may call additional attention to the survey. A criminal justice survey featuring a stamp with Justitia, the blind goddess of justice, would certainly be eye-catching. More research needs to be undertaken in this regard, however, for Heberlein and Baumgartner (1978) found the highest response rates for government-sponsored studies in which a franked or metered postage was used. This was believed to lend an "official" air to the project.

A handwritten "P.S." on the cover letter urging response has been claimed to increase response, as does personalization of the cover letter by use of the respondent's name (Dillman and Frey, 1974). In one survey of presidents of national professional associations, this writer stumbled upon a gimmick that, although prohibitive in larger surveys, ensured a last-resort response from a few remaining important respondents. After four unsuccessful follow-up probes that included requesting professionals from these fields to look them up at national conventions and urge response, a personal touch worked. A visit to a local museum of art yielded some occasional cards that featured a colorful reproduction of a famous masterpiece. Through sheer luck the campus post office was selling commemorative stamps with famous paintings, one of which matched the cards. The combined visual impact, along with a handwritten final request for participation on the card, elicited cooperation (Hagan, 1975).

Shortened Format

Shortened format of follow-up instruments may encourage response from those who were previously hesitant because of the length of the original instrument. Although a "reminder/thank you" postcard sent a few days after an initial mailing is likely to result in a higher response rate, a last-resort postcard featuring the minimum essential questions will at least salvage information on key items, as well as give some reading of how a group that would have been nonrespondents differs from respondents. In a review of the literature on methods of improving response rates in mail surveys, Heberlein and Baumgartner (1978) claim that longer survey forms were perceived as more important than shorter forms, and, all, other things being equal, were associated with greater response.

Good Timing

Good timing for survey mailing includes avoiding competitive seasons or other historical events that may impede response. Vacation periods should be avoided. Household questionnaires should arrive near the end of the week, whereas business surveys are likely to fare better at the beginning of the week. Other gimmicks have been developed by imaginative researchers. Again, *The Public Opinion Quarterly* is an excellent source of such "trade secrets."

Despite valiant efforts, because of time, cost, and other factors most surveys do not expect 100 percent response rates. One way to assess the impact of nonresponse bias on results is to compare characteristics of the survey respondents with known characteristics of the general population. For instance, even though we may have a 60 percent response rate and no way of knowing for sure how the 40 percent nonrespondents differ from those cooperating in the survey, knowledge that the respondents were representative of the population with respect to age, sex, race, income, and other key characteristics may give us greater confidence in these findings.

In a survey of victims in which only 125 of 450 questionnaires were returned and the prosecutor's office prohibited follow-up mailings to victims, the researchers (Erez and Tontodonato, 1992) assessed the representativeness of the sample by comparing respondents with nonrespondents, finding that the former were more serious cases but were similar on other relevant variables.

In an imaginative combination of research strategies, Sigler and Johnson (1986), studying a sample of the general population of Tuscaloosa, Alabama, first sent a postcard to households indicating that they had been selected for study. Then three days later, Johnson personally delivered the self-administered questionnaire by hand to each adult in residence and arranged a time for retrieval. Of the 300 delivered to 170 households, 174 were retrieved with 30 refusals, netting 144 usable questionnaires.

How do researchers know which of these approaches works in increasing response rates? The answer is to conduct experiments. If 1,000 surveys were mailed and half were on white and half on blue paper, and twice as many were returned if the paper was blue, we could conclude that using blue paper might increase response rates.

The Tailored Design Method

Ziegler (2006, p.30) indicates that surveys now exist in a "surveyed out" population that is less likely to respond. Utilizing what Dillman (2000) calls the "tailored design method" (TDM), he uses multiple contacts seeking response and endorsements to increase response rates. This involves tailoring the survey to the group being studied in order to foster trust, increase rewards, and decrease the cost of participation. Particularly problematic is obtaining the participation of reluctant, busy professionals or elite policy makers.

The TDM was originated by Dillman (1978; 2000). Particularly in his *Mail and Internet Surveys: The Tailored Design Method*, Dillman (2000) uses an approach that relies heavily on social exchange theory as a framework. This consists of the three elements of rewards, costs, and trust. Using TDM in a survey of prosecutors in four states, Ziegler (2006) was able to obtain a response rate of 90 percent in one state and 76 percent overall. Some of the procedures and assumptions of the TDM involved (Ziegler, 2006) the following:

- The most effective means of increasing response rates in mail surveys use multiple contacts. These may include prenotice letters, telephone calls, introductory letters enclosed with the questionnaire, thank you cards, follow-up reminders, follow-ups with certified mail, and overnight delivery.
- Endorsements from credible external parties combined with multiple contacts are particularly effective.
- If more than one endorsement is required, researchers should start with the one most likely to prove successful and then use "snowball endorsing"—use the first organization's endorsement in order to obtain others.
- Offer to present one's findings at meetings of the organizations involved.
- Use the less authoritative term "encourage" to participate rather than endorse.

Self-Reported Measures of Crime

Self-report surveys are data-gathering methods that involve asking respondents to admit to various behaviors. In an attempt to overcome some of the inadequacies of official measurements of crime, such as the Uniform Crime Reports (UCR) discussed in Chapter 4, criminologists have developed surveys in which subjects are asked to admit to the commission of various crimes and deviant acts, particularly delinquent ones. Nettler (1978, pp. 97–113) provides an excellent review of such studies, which he breaks down into the following types:

Self-report surveys

- Anonymous questionnaires
- Anonymous questionnaires in which respondent is identifiable and response can be validated by later interviews or police records
- Signed questionnaires validated against police records
- Anonymous questionnaires identified by number and validated by follow-up interviews and threat of polygraph (lie-detector test)
- Interviews
- Interviews validated against official records

In addition to those indicated by Nettler, other researchers have employed peers (Gold, 1966) and detached workers (Short and Strodtbeck, 1965) as informants.

Most self-report surveys have been conducted in the United States with the primary subjects being schoolchildren, high school students, or college students (Glaser, 1978, p. 72; Hood and Sparks, 1971, p. 19). Such studies have not been limited, however, to youths and young adults. In an early study by Wallerstein and Wyle (1947) of adults from all walks of life using a mailed self-report method, 99 percent of the respondents admitted that they had committed at least one offense. In another early study, Porterfield (1946) found a similar rate of admitted delinquency among Texas college students as existed among officially processed delinquents.

In a unique study, Greenwood and Abrahamse (1982) studied 2,000 inmates' self-reports of past conduct and utilized these data to construct a parole prediction scale. Previous parole prediction scales had been based entirely on objective records and other criteria. Studies of crime admissions by incarcerated ex-addicts (Inciardi, 1979) and career offense admissions (Petersilia, Greenwood, and Lavin, 1977) have been useful in complementing official statistics. Adult populations have been studied, through self-reports, by Tittle and Villemez (1977), who sampled adults in three states, and by O'Donnell et al. (1976), who conducted a nationwide survey of drug use.

Major self-report surveys using national probability samples include work by Gold (Gold and Reimer, 1974); the "Youth in Transition" studies of Bachman and associates (Bachman, O'Malley, and Johnston, 1978); and the "Monitoring the Future" surveys, which involve an annual survey of high school seniors (Bachman, 1978; Osgood et al., 1989). The best known of these recent self-report surveys is the *National Youth Survey* (NYS). The NYS included a multicohort design, a national probability sample of youth born in the period from 1959 to 1965. The survey began with eleven- to seventeen-year-olds in 1976 and followed up with four consecutive surveys of the same group (Jackson, 1990, pp. 39–40).

The NYS was found to yield valid and reliable data, indicating delinquency/crime levels much higher than in the National Crime Survey (victim surveys) or in UCR (Huizinga and Elliot, 1984).

A particularly innovative research program sponsored by the National Institute of Justice (NIJ) was the Arrestee Drug Abuse Monitoring (ADAM) program. This program will be described in detail in Chapter 9 as an illustration of validation of self-reports. Basically, arrestees were asked questions regarding their drug use behavior and then to provide urine specimens, which could be tested for drug use. Such a program provided an ingenious way for estimating drug usage among criminal populations; it also provided a barometer on the impact various policies have on drug use. Unfortunately, the program was discontinued in 2004 by the George W. Bush administration due to budget cuts. The National Crime Victimization Survey, to be discussed in Chapter 6, is also a self-report survey (Cantor and Lynch, 2000).

Some Problems with Self-Report Surveys

Nettler (1978, p. 107) states the matter succinctly by pointing out that "asking people questions about their behavior is a poor way of observing it." In specifying difficulties in the accuracy of self-reports on other types of behavior such as voting and medical treatment (Deutscher, 1966; LaPiere, 1934; Levine,

1976), critics wonder why we should expect respondents to be accurate and honest in admitting deviant behavior. The major **problems with self-report surveys** relate to inaccurate reporting, use of poor or inconsistent instruments, deficient research designs, and poor choice of settings or subjects (Nettler, 1978, p. 107).

American studies of self-reported crime include many items that may not be regarded as delinquent.

The often small and nonrepresentative nature of some of the samples used may limit their generalizability. Many samples, for example, had poor representation of blacks. In addition to possible difficulties presented by the lack of complete anonymity in some surveys, self-report studies may be subject to lying, poor memory, and telescoping, or the moving of past incidents into the time frame being studied. Many studies fail to provide a time reference during which the claimed offenses were to have taken place.

Until recently, self-report surveys have been plagued by lack of replication and overreliance on one-shot case studies often of atypical populations. They had not been conducted in a standardized fashion; often as many different instruments as studies were employed with little comparability of settings or populations. Bersoff and Bersoff (2000) claim that the risks to respondents in self-report surveys of having far more personal information unprotected is greater than in observational or experimental studies. Such anonymous surveys requiring neither Institutional Review Board review nor informed consent may invade privacy and cause emotional upset by probing into painful experiences.

Strengths of Self-Report Surveys

Despite the preceding criticisms, an impressive body of research has accumulated that highlights the **strengths of self-report surveys.** Both the validity and the reliability of this method and utilization of the method have steadily improved. Junger-Tas and Marshall (1999) indicate that the self-report method has improved greatly over the years, and many of its problems and limitations have been addressed.

Reliability

In examining the reliability in self-report surveys, Hirschi (1969, p. 56) found only moderate correlations in admissions of the six kinds of crimes he measured. Clark and Tifft (1966) found about an 82 percent reliability for subjects who were retested regarding self-admissions when they were threatened with a lie detector the second time. Dentler and Monroe (1961) found a 96 percent concordance between first and second self-reporters, and Kulik et al. (1968) found a 98 percent agreement with little difference if the questionnaire is anonymous or signed.

Contrary evidence is provided by Farrington (1973). He had English boys respond to thirty-eight crimes listed on separate cards and place them into piles as to whether they did or did not commit these acts. On retest two years later, only 75 percent of the original crimes were readmitted and half of these were more serious crimes. Gertz and Talarico (1980) point out important and often overlooked sources of unreliability—clerical carelessness and coding error.

Validity

The validity of self-report surveys rests on whether people tell the truth or can accurately recollect past crimes or incidents of deviant behavior. Following are some means of attempting to get at the *validity of such studies*:

- Validity checks using official or other data
- Checks using other observers (peers)
- Use or threat of polygraph
- "Known-group" approach
- "Lie scales"
- Measures of internal consistency
- Recheck reports using interviews

Use of Other Data

Self-report data can sometimes be checked against official police records, school records, and other sources or criteria. There is a paradox of the critics of official statistics using these same statistics to validate what is claimed to be a superior self-report instrument. Given our previous discussion of problems with official statistics, it is unclear what type of overall relationship would be desired.

A significant number of studies have been conducted employing *checks against official statistics*. Some of these have been discussed in part in our previous analysis of self-report surveys. In interviews with boys in Utah, Erickson and Empey (1963) found that a check of court records indicated that none of the boys lied about having been in court or failed to describe the offense. Voss (1963) found a strong relationship between admissions and official police records in his Hawaiian sample. Farrington (1973) also found agreement, concluding that self-reported delinquents were quite similar to official delinquents. Hirschi (1969) had mixed feelings, with general underreporting among his sample. McCandless et al. (1972) found even a poorer matchup between admissions and police records. On the other hand, Hardt and Hardt (1977) found a strong correspondence between self-reported violations and police statistics; based on this correspondence as well as other checks they made on their data, they concluded that many of the conflicting reports in previous surveys may have resulted from the use of inadequate instruments. Hirschi (1969) also checked other records such as truancy reports and admitted school suspensions.

Use of Other Observers

Checks using other informants, peers, or people who might be able to speak to the respondents' behavior constitute yet another way of obtaining some validation. Gold (1966) interviewed associates of the respondent to check whether the person was either told about or observed the acts claimed by the respondent. Short and Strodtbeck (1965) used confirming reports of detached workers.

Use of Polygraph

The use of, or threat of, polygraph validation was employed by Clark and Tifft (1966). They found less than 20 percent changed their initial responses when threatened with a "lie detector" test.

Known-Group Validation

In **known-group validation** (Nye and Short, 1957; Voss, 1963) groups whose official transgressions are already a matter of record are studied, and their self-admissions are compared to this same behavior. Hardt and Hardt (1977) used, as part of their sample, those who had been previously identified through official arrest statistics. They concluded that such groups yielded valid responses. Nye and Short, as well as Voss, found significant differences between "known delinquents" and others. Nettler points out that there is an essential problem in attempting to validate an instrument with a criterion, in this case official statistics, which itself is of questionable validity. As a possible explanation, Hardt and Hardt (1977) found that the majority of boys ranking high on the self-report scale did not have an official police record. Comparing initial with later responses, however, they found that most respondents changed something, and most of these changes were in the direction of admitting more deviance. Although minor offenses like truancy and stealing tended to be underreported, major offenses like violence and sex offenses were overreported.

Known-group validation

Use of Lie Scales

Another useful tool for checking the validity of responses is the employment of **lie scales** or "truth scales," a series of questions that measure truthfulness of respondents in answering a survey. Previously, we discussed the tendency of respondents in experiments and surveys to be agreeable or to give the researcher what they think is desired. "Lie scales" attempt to assess this, usually by asking the respondents to admit to a type of behavior that—it is assumed—no one person would have performed or by trying to cross up the respondents by having them give inconsistent responses. Some other procedures involve having the respondent deny behavior that—it is reasonably assumed—everyone would perform. Such questions are usually weaved among other attitudinal questions in the survey. Figure 5.8 gives typical "lie scales."

Lie scales

In scoring "lie scales," researchers set a limit for the number of "incorrect" answers to questions they are willing to tolerate before questioning the truthfulness of the respondent and thus calling into question all other responses of that individual. These cases would be dropped from the analysis. Such procedures are quite commonly used in standard personality inventories such as the Minnesota Multiphasic Inventory.

Figure 5.8
*Examples of a Lie
Scale.*

1. I always tell the truth.
2. Sometimes I tell lies.
3. Once in a while I get angry.
4. I never feel sad.
5. Sometimes I do things I am not supposed to do.
6. I have never taken anything that did not belong to me.
7. I have never kept anyone waiting for an appointment.

Measures of Internal Consistency

Internal consistency

Related to "lie scales" is the measurement of the **internal consistency** of an individual's response by using interlocking items. This involves the repetition of similar items, sometimes expressing them first in a positive and then a negative manner. For example, one might say, "I always tell the truth," and then later in the survey say, "I never tell a lie." Hardt and Hardt (1977) in their self-report survey asked first whether the respondent had ever been warned or questioned by police, and later whether the subject had ever been arrested or ticketed by the police. It was assumed that a positive response to the latter would require a positive answer to the former question; if not, the subject's responses were considered inconsistent. In combination with the "lie scale," this measure of inconsistency was used as the means of discarding questionable respondents. The use of reversals, stating some of the questions in a negative manner, is a means of checking response sets. The latter refers to the tendency of subjects to answer all of the items, often without reading many of them, on the basis of their answers to the initial questions. That is, if the respondents strongly agreed with the first few items, then they might simply check off this same response for the remainder. This is also a partial check on socially desirable response patterns.

Use of Interviews

Subsequent interviewing of subjects permits probing regarding the details and context of the acts. For example, claims of the respondent can be questioned and the criminal intent of the acts can be established (Hood and Sparks, 1971, p. 68). Primary disadvantages of this approach are that anonymity of subjects is lost (Gold, 1966), and there may be a tendency for concealment of offenses depending on the characteristics of the interviewer (Coleman, 1961, pp. 16–17).

Although self-report surveys have their limitations, they do provide another measure of criminality in addition to official statistics. Particularly when combined with victim surveys, they offer another means of assessing unreported crime. Chilton (1993, pp. 6–7) even suggests that it might be time for criminologists to propose the creation of a National Self-Report Survey. Such a representative survey would most likely face serious political and methodological problems, but would certainly give us a broader picture of crime. Requests for such serious data are almost certain to be "inconvenient for someone's party position on crime and its causes" (1993, p. 8).

Internet Surveys

The use of the Internet to conduct surveys is a relatively new and quickly evolving approach. Changes are taking place so rapidly that what is presented here is only a brief introduction. Internet surveys take two different forms: e-mail surveys and Web-based surveys; but the potential is enormous for camera-based, face-to-face interviews, chat groups, and inexpensive telephone surveys using the Internet.

Advantages of Internet Surveys

The potential advantages of Internet surveys are compelling. If research is limited to specialized populations (for example, employees or association members), theoretical access of 100 percent is possible. Internet surveys can be done faster and cheaper than even telephone surveys. In fact they are free and have the advantage over the latter, particularly with large samples, which are ordinarily limited by the number of telephones and interviewers (Schaefer and Dillman, 1998, p. 379). A mixed-mode strategy of using e-mail when possible and other methods when not possible has been found to be effective. Web surveys are much cheaper and more accurate than paper-and-pencil surveys, and data processing is much faster and cheaper (Schaefer and Dillman, 1998, p. 379). Results can be published online instantly for viewing by the respondent as a reward for participating. While Internet surveys may incur little coding or data entry costs because the data are captured electronically, labor costs for design and programming may be high (Schonlai, Fricker, and Elliott, 2002).

Disadvantages of Internet Surveys

The disadvantages of Internet surveys include that e-mail has generally failed to produce comparable results to mail techniques. Such surveys have sampling problems and are limited to those with e-mail accounts. Although more than half of all households in the United States have computers, only 42 percent had Internet access in 2000. The risk of coverage error has limited most e-mail surveys to specialized populations. In one study, e-mail surveys with only one contact achieved a 28.5 percent response; but two follow-ups raised this to 57 percent (Schonlai, Fricker, and Elliott, 2002, p. 380). The sampling bias in Internet surveys of the population would most predictably undercount females, minorities, the elderly, and the undereducated. Internet surveys, just as mail surveys, are self-administered questions and suffer from the problem of misinterpretation of questions. E-mail respondents may lack anonymity in their responses, and employers have the potential to monitor employee messages.

Research using the Internet may raise special ethical problems (Hamilton, 1999). The rapid growth in such studies may have outpaced the ability of those concerned with ethical standards to monitor them. Most online research sites do not use safeguards, such as signed consent forms, to protect respondents. Online researchers seldom design Web sites to send participants to a debriefing page on completion of the study. The confidentiality of online responses is also a problem. While the Internet is characterized by confidentiality, the researcher might use a "cookie" to identify the computer from which the response was submitted (Hamilton, 1999). Hackers could intercept responses to sensitive items. IRBs have been seldom consulted on such studies and are ill-prepared to deal with them if they were consulted. Standardized guidelines for this purpose are necessary.

Procedures in Internet Surveys

Market research has found Web-based research particularly useful and is fueling Web site design and better means of utilizing this strategy (Krauss, 1998). Web surveys can use color photography, video clips, and other dramatic enhancements. Some helpful hints in Internet surveys include the following (McCullough, 1998, p. 32):

- KISS (Keep It Simple, Stupid). Be as simple and straightforward as possible with questions.
- Do not ask what they can't answer. For example: "Did your toilet training as a child affect your sex life as an adult?"
- Don't sell. This is another way of saying avoid leading questions.

The next step is to put it on the Web. One might respond, "Sorry, I don't do windows" (McCullough, 1998, p. 32). It is probably easiest to have someone with Web design experience produce the site. Try your younger sibling or relative.

Ways of increasing response rates on Web surveys (McCullough, 1998, p. 33) include the following:

- Banner ads on Web sites
- E-mail invitations
- Telephone invitations
- E-mail panels

Banner ads on sites frequently visited by one's target audience have been found to be quite effective. The use of purchased lists for e-mail risks having one's message mistaken for "spam" (unsolicited junk e-mail). One approach is to identify up front where you obtained their name. Calling people on the telephone and asking if they have Web access and then inviting them to participate can also work. In fact, multiple methodologies can be employed at any time. Some marketing companies are now using e-mail panels to do longitudinal research.

E-mail-based surveys are done by means of an attachment that the respondent can answer and return via e-mail or download and mail. Web-based surveys utilize a Web site to attract usually invited respondents to answer questions online. McCullough (1998, p. 30) outlines the steps in a survey utilizing a Web site:

- Understand clearly what questions you want answered.
- Know with whom you want to talk.
- Write a questionnaire and put it on the Web.
- Build traffic to that questionnaire.
- Analyze the data.

The writing of specific, measurable, and useful questions involves the same procedure that we discussed under questionnaire construction. Specialized populations such as orchid growers can be found by visiting Web sites relevant to their interest. Web surveys are very similar to traditional surveys but may actually contain more flexibility and control. They can be programmed to check that answers fall within a specified range and utilize amazing research aids (1998, p. 30).

E-mail can be personalized by eliminating the names of multiple recipients from the top of the screen. Avoid using the carbon-copy function or sending a group message. This also prevents the respondent from accidentally sending their reply message to each of the other recipients. As Internet access becomes more universal, the potential of Internet surveys will become more common. It is important that we as criminological and criminal justice researchers not be left behind.

Hybrid techniques have been developed to enhance the representativeness of Internet surveys. For example, random samples of the national population are contacted by phone and then hooked up to the Internet. Theoretically, this yields a representative sample to whom questionnaires can be sent over the Internet and be completed in the privacy of their homes (Morin, 2000, p. 34). With response rates below 50 percent, there is reason to question whether random samples are truly random. Imaginative use of quota samples and volunteer samples has been successfully used in online voter polling. The popularity of Internet surveys has led to the creation of for profit Internet survey firms who will design surveys for you. One such firm, Surveymonkey.com (www.surveymonkey.com), advertises that it will do the following:

- Permit you to choose from over twenty question types such as multiple choice, rating scales, and open-ended questions.
- Support a variety of languages.
- Validate survey responses.
- Use over fifty survey templates.
- Change the color, size, or style of the survey.
- Add logos.
- Collect responses through a link to your survey e-mail or posting the survey on a Web site.
- Send follow-up reminders to nonrespondents.
- View results as soon as they are collected.
- Protect and keep private all collected data.

Online interviewing also presents many new opportunities as well as challenges for researchers (Kivitis, 2005). The popularity and relative newness of Internet surveys have raised significant ethical and legal questions with respect to human subjects on the Internet. Some recent concerns about ethical issues and Internet research have arisen as a result of online researchers not consistently following guidelines with respect to informed consent of subjects, possible multiple submission of response, and the danger of computer hackers intercepting messages (Hamilton, 1999). The American Association for the

Advancement of Science (AAAS) also identified some emergent issues (Frankel and Siang, 1999). They raised the question: What is private information in cyberspace? AAAS saw a particular need for better instruction of independent review boards regarding online research.

For those interested in doing their own Web survey, Dale Nesbary's *Survey Research and the World Wide Web* (2000) is a very useful primer.

Summary

It is most important to remember that surveys, for the most part, measure respondent attitude and not behavior.

Characteristics and qualities of mail surveys have been described in detail because many of their features are similar to those of other data-gathering strategies in criminal justice survey research. The chief disadvantages of the mail survey include nonresponse, unpredictable uniformity in response, slow replies, possible misinterpretation of questions, and costly follow-up. To be weighed against these are the many advantages of mail surveys, including wide geographical coverage with a minimum of time, minimal cost and effort, no field staff required, no interviewer bias, greater privacy, and the opportunity for more considered replies.

Some possible ways of reducing nonresponse in mail surveys are follow-up, payment or altruistic appeals, attractive format, sponsorship, endorsements, personalization, shortened format, and good timing.

Some guidelines exist for questionnaire construction. First, there should be a clear notion of what is to be measured and a certainty that the instrument can address this. The uses of variables lists and dummy tables are intermediary steps. Among the suggestions discussed were the uses of language appropriate to respondents; clear specification of respondents; avoidance of biased, leading, or objectionable questions; and the types of questions to use. A pretest, or trial run, of the instrument is an absolute necessity. The questionnaire should begin with the most interesting questions; biographical items should appear later or last.

Coding is the assignment of numerical values to questionnaire items. A code is developed for each question and entered into a codebook. Each question is coded in the appropriate column or cell. The codebook information is keyboard entered into a data file on the computer with each column corresponding to a variable identified in the codebook. These data are then edited and checked for errors and analysis begins. Coder monitoring involves checking the work of coders for accuracy.

Self-report surveys involve asking, usually anonymous respondents, to admit to a variety of offenses they had committed in the past. Keeping in mind our early injunction that reported behavior does not necessarily equal actual behavior, these surveys have been criticized for inaccurate reporting, poor use of instruments and research designs, and inadequate settings or study subjects. Despite these shortcomings, defenders of the technique have demonstrated accuracy and reliability by employing known-group comparisons and record checks, as well as "lie scales" and other methodological devices. Certainly, self-report surveys present the criminal justice researcher with another tool with which to measure crime.

KEY CONCEPTS

Variables list	Ways of increasing	Strengths of self-report
Dummy tables	response in	surveys
Coder monitoring	mail surveys	Known-group
Keyboard entry	Self-report surveys	validation
Mail surveys	Problems with	Lie scales
Advantages/	self-report	Internal consistency
disadvantages of	surveys	
mail surveys		

REVIEW QUESTIONS

1. What are some disadvantages of mail surveys? Discuss ways of eliminating them.

2. Suppose a student group planning on conducting a questionnaire survey discovered that you had taken a research course and asked you for some specific suggestions. What are some general recommendations that you would give?

3. What are some problems as well as benefits of self-report surveys as a data-gathering strategy?

4. What are some techniques for improving response rates in surveys?

5. What are some considerations one must take into account in doing Internet surveys?

USEFUL WEB SITES

Online Surveys (Tutorial) *www.socialresearchmethods.net/tutorial/ Abrahams/sbk16.htm*

The Gallup Organization *www.gallup.com*

U.S. Census Bureau (Criminal Justice Surveys) *www.census.gov/govs/ www/cj.html*

Social Surveys Online (United Kingdom) *http://qb.soc.surrey.ac.uk/ docs/home.htm*

General Social Survey (Retrievable Data Bases) *www.gss.norc.org*

National Opinion Research Center (NORC): University of Chicago *www.norc.uchicago.edu/*

United Nations Surveys on Crime *www.unodc.org/unodc/en/data-and-analysis/index.html*

The Survey System (Creative Research Systems) (includes sample size calculator) *www.surveysystem.com/sdesign.htm#top*

6

Survey Research

Interviews and Telephone Surveys

Interviewing can refer to a variety of face-to-face situations in which the researcher orally solicits responses. Berg (2001, p. 89) defines interviews as conversations with a purpose; the purpose being to gather information. These range from in-depth, lengthy interviews of one or a few subjects to fairly structured surveys of large groups. As with the other techniques of data gathering discussed, the advantages and disadvantages of interviewing as a means of obtaining information should be carefully considered along with other techniques before the decision is made to proceed.

Types of Interviews

Researchers use different terms to denote interviews. There are three basic forms:

Structured interviews
Unstructured interviews
Depth interviews

Although other types of interviews exist, such as the investigative interview used in journalism (Douglas, 1976) or the preliminary interview employed prior to a larger study, elements of these are contained in these three principal types.

Structured interviews, sometimes called closed interview schedules, usually consist of check-off responses to questions that are either factual or to which most responses easily fit an expectable pattern.

Structured interviews

> *Question*: Compared with last year, what type of job do you feel the local police are performing in preventing crime in your neighborhood?
> _____ Much better
> _____ Somewhat better
> _____ About the same
> _____ Somewhat worse
> _____ Much worse

> *Question*: In which of the following income ranges did your combined family income fall this past year?
> _____ Less than $10,000
> _____ $10,000–$20,000
> _____ $20,001–$30,000
> _____ $30,001–$40,000
> _____ $40,001–$50,000
> _____ More than $50,000

In structured interviews the interviewer should avoid soliciting additional comments but, when they occur, record them verbatim. The principal disadvantage of closed-ended questions is that they generally elicit only limited response patterns; their advantages are easy administration and data processing as will be seen later.

Unstructured interviews

Unstructured interviews have many variations depending on the purpose. Sometimes referred to as focused, clinical, or nondirective interviews, they generally provide for open-ended responses to questions. That is, unlike the closed interviews, no predetermined response categories are provided. To use an example with which all of us have had experience, the structured interview is comparable to an objective educational test consisting of multiple-choice and true-and-false items, whereas the unstructured interview is similar to essay tests or tests in which a person is asked to define or explain the topics being tested. Examples of open-ended response questions are as follows:

> *Question*: Do you think the police are better or worse in preventing crime in your local neighborhood than last year? _____
> *Question*: Why do you feel this way? _____
> *Question*: If you were personally the victim of a crime since January 1 of this year, could you explain the circumstances surrounding this incident? _____

In comparing the relative advantages and disadvantages of the unstructured questionnaire vis-à-vis the structured, the previous test question example is a useful touchstone for analogy purposes. The closed-ended items (for example, the analogy to true and false) are excellent for recording simple items in which likely categories of response can be predetermined. Such questions make codification and tabulation easy, but may not provide the depth and quality of response needed. Open-ended items may present a tabulation nightmare, but provide the qualitative detail and complexity of response that may be required, particularly if the subject of study is little known.

The **depth interview** is a more intensive and detailed interview, usually of fewer subjects than is the case in a standard survey, and is particularly useful in life histories or case studies. In a depth interview, the researcher has a general list of topics to be explored, but exercises great discretion and flexibility in the manner, timing, and direction of questioning. Such interviews are excellent for hypothesis-generating or exploratory research (Merton, Fiske, and Kendall, 1956).

Depth interview

Smykla (1987), with the approval of a state Department of Corrections, wrote to death row inmates and later, through further correspondence and visitation, requested from them names, addresses, and telephone numbers of family members. He was able to arrange interviews with forty family members and describe what he called their "distorted grief reactions." Classic examples of the use of depth interviews can be found in many case studies and oral histories such as Sutherland's *The Professional Thief* (1937), the result of in-depth interviews with a professional thief, or Laub's *Criminology in the Making* (1983), an oral history of American criminology based on interviews with leading criminologists. Cressey's *Other People's Money* (1953), which involved extensive interviews with 133 incarcerated embezzlers, also serves as an example. Other examples will be discussed in Chapter 7.

Advantages of Interviews

One chief attraction of the interview is the opportunity it provides for personal *contact between the researcher and the subject*. Such a situation presents many possibilities. Because of the face-to-face relationship, interviews generally bring about a *higher response rate* than mail surveys. Being on the scene, the interviewer can *clear up any misunderstandings or confusions* the respondent may have in interpreting questions. Additionally, the interviewer can also *act as an observer*, and not only record verbal responses, but also make note of his or her own impressions regarding the respondents and their environment.

Interviewers can also read questions to those with literacy problems and thus obtain a more representative sample.

Interviews provide an opportunity for the interviewer to make use of cards, charts, and other *audiovisual aids*. In asking individuals about their income, for instance, the researcher can hand the respondents a card with a list of income ranges and ask them to identify the range within which household income falls. Having greater flexibility, the interviewer can make return visits if necessary and pitch the language to the level of the respondent. Perhaps less deliberated responses reflect the respondents' true attitudes, and the nature of the interviewing process taps this. Unlike researchers who mail questionnaires, interviewers can determine the actual individual who is responding and can use *their discretion* as to the appropriate time at which to ask the more sensitive questions. With guarded or suspicious respondents, questions regarding income and the like can be saved for last, so as not to prematurely abort answers to the other questions; or such questions can be asked at a point in the interview when the subject appears most cooperative. Interviews are more flexible, may elicit more spontaneous responses, and can utilize more complex lines of questioning than is often possible in mail surveys.

Feminist researchers challenge what they call "malestream" (mainstream male) approaches to empirical criminal justice research (McDermott, 1992) for not incorporating feminist views. One researcher used in-depth interviews as a way of getting at women's experiences that are obscured in standard surveys (Stanko, 1990).

Disadvantages of Interviews

Despite the many advantages of interviews, they possess obvious problems. Some principal **disadvantages of field interviews** are that they may be very time consuming and costly. Although these problems can be offset in part by cluster sampling, covering widely dispersed households in person can be a problem. **Interviewer effect** or *bias* may be responsible for distorted results. Similarly, the *interviewer may make mistakes* in asking questions or recording information. Because of these problems the use of even a few interviewers requires supervision, training, and monitoring. In assigning and coordinating *field interviews*, the supervisor should be aware of the need for weekend and evening interviews to obtain representative responses. Interviewing becomes a particularly difficult strategy when attempting to obtain information from hard-to-reach populations, although by way of trade-offs respondents who do not own telephones can be reached.

Interviews may be problematic for respondents if factual data that must be looked up are requested. They are sometimes less convenient to the respondent and afford less anonymity than mail surveys. Perhaps the chief potential problems rest in the quality, integrity, and skill of the interviewers, factors that may be uneven in interview surveys.

Question wording in interviews can alter response. Exhibit 6.1 gives some examples from public opinion polls.

One must weigh the advantages and disadvantages of interviewing and compare them with those of other data-gathering strategies before deciding on the means of data collection.

Interviewing Aids and Variations

Although most standard interviews are recorded more or less on the spot by the interviewer, using either an interview schedule, a structured interview protocol, or, in the case of depth interviews, notes that can be reconstructed into finished form immediately after the interview, a variety of mechanical aids exist that lend even greater versatility and accuracy. In a small number of important interviews, *videotapes* may be used. The ASC/ACJS oral history project conducted videotape interviews of famous criminologists.

Interviewer effect

EXHIBIT 6.1 ▶

Public Opinion Polls

Survey research organizations such as Gallup, Roper, and Yankelovich play a critical role in taking the pulse of the American public's opinion regarding public policy. In 1994, 27 percent of the American public named crime as the most important problem. Surprisingly, only 3 percent had done so the previous year. Even though the official crime rate had actually declined from the previous year, 58 percent of those surveyed said crime in their community had gotten worse in the past year and 73 percent said crime in the country had worsened (Morin, 1994c).

Often the very wording of survey questions can produce differing results. In 1992, the American Jewish Committee was shocked when a poll they had commissioned by the Roper organization discovered that about one-third of those polled felt it was possible that the Holocaust either never happened or they were not sure. The actual question asked was (Morin, 1994a):

As you know, the term "Holocaust" usually refers to the killing of millions of Jews in Nazi death camps during World War II. Does it seem possible or does it seem impossible to you that the Nazi extermination of the Jews never happened?

In April 1994 Roper simplified the question to read:

Does it seem possible to you that the Nazi extermination of the Jews never happened?

Only 1 percent said it was possible that it never happened, and only 8 percent were unsure. In thirteen different polls, the Holocaust doubters varied from 1 to 46 percent.

Why? Question wording. The high group had questions that were ambiguous or even contained double negatives, as in our first example. When questioned specifically as to whether the Holocaust happened, 98 percent of the "doubters" changed their position and said it did happen (Morin, 1994a).

In one final example, Richard Morin (1994b), chief of polling for *The Washington Post*, points out how the wording of presidential approval questions produce skewed results. Most of the media polls such as *The Washington Post* and ABC News ask:

Do you approve or disapprove of the job that Bill Clinton is doing as President? Is that strongly or somewhat approve or disapprove?

The Washington Post tested whether a simpler response scale might produce a different response. They did a split-ballot test in which half of the respondents were asked the old questions (above) and half were asked the following:

Do you strongly approve, somewhat approve, somewhat disapprove, or strongly disapprove of the job Bill Clinton is doing as President?

While the first version produced 58 percent favorable, 38 percent unfavorable, and 4 percent no opinion, the second version yielded 62 percent approving, 32 percent disapproving, and 6 percent undecided. These illustrations clearly describe the critical importance of questionnaire construction and wording in not just measuring attitudes, but in some cases creating them.

Sources: Morin, Richard. "From Confusing Questions, Confusing Answers." *Washington Post National Weekly Edition* 18–24 (July 1994a): 37; Morin, Richard. "Ask and You Might Deceive." *Washington Post National Weekly Edition* 6–12 (December 1994b): 37; and Morin, Richard. "When the Method Becomes the Message." *Washington Post National Weekly Edition* 19–25 (December 1994c): 33.

The *recording of interviews by means of tape recorders* releases interviewers from the task of taking on-the-spot notes and enables them to concentrate on conducting the interview. Dictaphone transcription enables verbatim reconstruction of interviews and, although it produces an enormous amount of material, presents the researcher with the raw material to digest after the fact, rather than at the time of the interview. To illustrate that data gathering is limited only by imagination, Albini (1971), in *The American Mafia: Genesis of a Legend*, reported great success with mail interviews using cassettes. To cut expenses, time, and travel in interviewing police officials, organized criminals, and experts on organized crime, he mailed his interview protocol—list of questions—along with blank cassettes and was able to secure interviews with individuals who otherwise would not have been interviewed.

Although we will discuss the brief, structured telephone interview survey, the telephone interview can be expanded under special circumstances by tape recording interviews. An inexpensive electronic patch can be purchased at any electronics store and easily attached to a telephone to permit verbatim cassette recording of interviews. Unless one is involved in secretive measurement, an issue to be discussed in detail in Chapter 7, it is standard procedure to ask, prior to beginning an interview, the respondent's permission to record. Obviously, problems are raised with respect to the assurance of anonymity and respondent candor. These problems can sometimes be circumvented by agreeing beforehand to shut off the recorder for more sensitive items that may be identified as "off-the-record."

Pictorials, photographs, and motion pictures have all been successfully utilized to enhance studies involving interviews. For such sensitive items as income, respondents can be handed a card that contains income ranges and asked to specify the general range. Individuals can be asked to rank their preferences for various items listed on a card.

Another method for coping with resistance to sensitive questions is the **randomized response technique (RRT)** (Liu and Chow, 1976; Tracy and Fox, 1981). The technique, originally developed by Warner (1965), basically uses indeterminate questions; that is, the actual question answered is known only to the respondent and is unknown by the researcher. The interviewer is blind or unaware of the actual question a respondent is answering. The RRT is rather complicated to explain, but basically it uses known probabilities in order to estimate unknown proportions. Neuman (1993, p. 231) provides an example of one variation:

> Here is how RRT works. An interviewer gives the respondent two questions. One is threatening (e.g., "Do you use heroin?"), the other not threatening (e.g., "Were you born in September?"). A random method (e.g., toss of coin) is used to select the question to answer. The interviewer does not see which question was chosen but records the respondent's answer. The researcher uses knowledge about the probability of the random outcome and the frequency of the nonthreatening behavior to estimate the frequency of the sensitive behavior.

In Tracy and Fox's (1981) example, 100 married men are brought together in a room and asked to flip a coin. Next, they are asked to raise their hand if they either get a head on the coin or if they have abused their wives. If sixty hands are raised, we can assume ten wife abusers among those with heads on the coin, because fifty heads would be expected by chance. Additionally, ten of the fifty with tails would also be assumed to be abusers for a total of twenty estimated abusers. In an actual interview situation, a single respondent would be asked to respond to "anonymous" sensitive questions in the same manner. Despite some possible shortcomings, randomized response procedures have

Randomized response technique (RRT)

been found to yield more accurate results than direct questioning methods on sensitive items (Fox and Tracy, 1986). A variety of randomization procedures are employed. For example, Guerts, Andrus, and Reinmuth (1976) posed questions to subjects in pairs, one sensitive and one innocuous. The question answered is determined by a coin flip. They used the technique to analyze shoplifting, destruction, price altering, and other consumer violations. This technique has also been utilized to study abortion and fertility control, drug use, child abuse, drunk driving, sexual behavior, illegal gambling, and shoplifting (Klockars, 1982, p. 454).

General Procedures in Interviews

Much of this discussion on procedures in interviewing is applicable primarily to large, standardized field surveys; however, most of the specific suggestions have been derived from the experience of both survey research organizations and individual researchers and is appropriate advice even for individual projects.

Training and Orientation Session

For interview surveys, an adequate amount of time must be spent on training interviewers. These training sessions, which may last anywhere from a day to a week depending on the complexity of the study, should familiarize the interviewers with the organization carrying out the survey as well as the study's purposes. Details of the project should be provided to make the interviewers feel that they are an important part of the study and to prepare them to answer any questions regarding the intent of the survey. Hoinville, Jowell, et al. (1978, p. 117) indicate that an effective manner of impressing the importance of confidentiality of responses on interviewers is to ask them to sign a declaration of confidentiality promising not to disclose any information in their possession. Depending on the sampling plan, either a preliminary letter is mailed or a telephone call is made to schedule an appointment for the interview.

Arranging the Interview

Interviewers conducting household surveys should not arrive too early or too late, generally no earlier than 10:00 A.M. and no later than 8:00 P.M. Surveyors should be furnished with, possess at all times, and present identification to avoid being taken for door-to-door salespersons. A prominently displayed name tag featuring the official project name and a picture of the interviewer is frequently useful. On arrival, be sure that the proper person to be interviewed within the household is located. At this point the interviewer should not ask if the respondent wishes to be interviewed now, but rather matter-of-factly indicate that the respondent had received a letter about the survey and that the interviewer is there to conduct it.

If the interviewer is unsuccessful in scheduling a meeting with the respondent, he or she should keep written track of callbacks and avoid recalls on the same days or same times.

Demeanor of Interviewer

Advice to interviewers can be as simple as beware of dogs, carry a charged cell phone in case of emergency, and dress appropriately for audience and weather (Sanders, 1976, p. 273). Where possible, the field surveyors should match, as closely as possible, the subjects with respect to age, sex, race, social class, and dress. Attire should be comfortable, but the interviewer should be neither overdressed nor underdressed for the occasion. Interviewers should have experienced a few practice interviews beforehand so that they become familiar with the flow of the instrument to be employed. The interviewer's language style should also be adapted to the group being studied.

In addition to assuring the respondents that their responses will be held in strictest confidence, the interviewer should attempt to build up rapport with the subjects by being friendly and diplomatic, as well as convincing, regarding the importance of the study. The interviewer should attempt to give the impression that the interview will be a pleasant, interesting, and rewarding experience. Casual conversation can be effective in building rapport with clients. The weather, children, appearance of the home or grounds, sports, and the like are useful topics. Interviewers should try to communicate an air of acceptance of respondents' statements but must maintain their neutrality (Survey Research Center, 1969). In addition to being a sympathetic *diplomat*, the interviewer must be prepared to be a persistent *boor*, a person willing to ask the types of sensitive questions that generally are considered "nosey" in nature (Converse and Schuman, 1974).

Administration of the Structured Interview

In structured interviews, it is important for interviewers to become familiar with the flow of the questionnaire. The instrument should contain good transition statements that in a conversational style help the respondent to anticipate what comes next. It should be administered in an easy, informal, and friendly manner to avoid the appearance of an inquisition. For this reason, at no time should the study be referred to as an investigation. The purpose of a structured questionnaire is to standardize the manner in which responses are obtained (Survey Research Center, 1969). Therefore, interviewers should be instructed not to reword or change the questions in any way.

Although procedures may vary depending on the nature and type of interview survey, in general, questions should be asked in the order listed on the questionnaire. If clarification is necessary, the interviewer should mark down and list such necessary comments on the questionnaire itself.

If the person being interviewed resists answering sensitive questions, explain that the study is interested in a group picture of people of different incomes, ages, and backgrounds, and this information is important to the purposes of the study. In addition, the interviewer must assure the respondent that the information will be held in strictest confidence and no individuals will be identified in the final report.

Probing

Often the answer to a question does not provide enough information for the purposes of the study, and it therefore becomes necessary for the interviewer to probe. **Probing** involves asking follow-up question(s) to focus, expand, clarify, or further explain the response given. The interviewer should be familiar with what response is needed to each question to know when a probe is necessary. Given the following hypothetical example, it is obvious that a probe is necessary:

> *Question*: Do you think the police in this community are doing an adequate job in protecting the community?
> *Answer*: Yeah, I guess so.
> *Probe*: What do you mean by that? In what way?

Of possible assistance in the probe is the interviewer's informal mood and responsiveness to the answers provided by the respondent. The probe should not appear to be a cross-examination, but a natural extension of the interview. Conversation can be stimulated by frequent "uh-huh's" and "I see's" and by repetition of the respondent's answer while recording it. Occasional silence, although uncomfortable at times, may encourage more thoughtful and considered responses. Silence may also indicate, similar to police interrogations, that the interviewer is not going to accept that response. It is almost like saying "You are going to have to come up with something better or provide an improved explanation" (Sanders, 1976).

Most beginning interviewers have cold feet and fear hostile respondents. Such respondents are few; however, a problem can also be raised by the overly friendly respondent. Because the interviewer has imposed on the respondent's time and goodwill, a reasonably friendly socializing is usually required at the end of the session. What, however, of respondents who, during or after the interview, account in detail their life history, stories of the big war, or the perils of lumbago? If this occurs during the interview, some tolerance may be in order to permit the respondent a break from the demands of the interview schedule (Converse and Schuman, 1974). The digression can be reoriented by a polite interruption indicating that there is a question directly relating to that later. Demonstrating inattention such as putting down one's pencil or closing the interview schedule may also work. If the digression takes place after the interview, a polite excuse such as another appointment will usually work.

The Exit

As indicated, once the interview is completed the interviewer should carry on light conversation and be alert for any additional comments that the respondent may then offer. Such relevant remarks should be added to the interview notes as soon as possible after leaving the premises. Finally, the interviewer should thank the subject(s) for their time and hospitality and should clear up any concerns or doubts the respondent may have regarding the survey before leaving. Informal discussions after the interview can often lead to important "off-the-record" information. The interviewer can elicit such information by asking in an easy manner, "What do you think?" or "Is there anything else?" or similar open-ended questions.

Berg (2001, pp. 130–131) describes the ten commandments of interviewing:

1. "Never begin an interview cold." Make small talk and set the stage.
2. "Remember your purpose." Keep the subject on track.
3. "Present a natural front." Be relaxed and natural and not wooden.
4. "Demonstrate aware hearing." Be a real listener, and provide appropriate nonverbal response, such as smiling if the subject makes a joke.
5. "Think about appearance." Dress appropriately for the setting.
6. "Interview in a comfortable place." One where the respondent will be afforded both privacy and safety.
7. "Don't be satisfied with monosyllabic answers." Simple yes or no answers usually call for further probing questions.
8. "Be respectful." Assure them that you are really interested in what they have to say.
9. "Practice, practice, and practice some more."
10. "Be cordial and appreciative." Do not close the door for future researchers by inappropriate actions.

If you think about it, this constitutes pretty sound advice for a date, job interview, or life in general.

Recording the Interview

Interviewers should be instructed to write legibly, in pencil, as much of the relevant substance of the interview as possible. An inexpensive clipboard provides the necessary hard writing surface. The interviewer should distinguish personal observations from the actual interview by using parentheses. **Editing** entails reviewing the interview schedule after completion of the interview and cleaning it up and preparing it for analysis. The completed interview schedule should be self-explanatory.

Editing

The interviewer should have covered each item in the schedule. Unanswered questions should be marked NA for not applicable or simply X to indicate inappropriate. Where personal observations are included, it may help the coder (the person charged with assigning numerical values to the responses) if the interviewer cross-referenced any relevant items. For example, if an observation has an impact on the understanding of another question, some notation such as (see Q. 10 for further explanation) would be in order.

The interviewer should attempt to record as much as possible during the interview. Because it is often impossible to record such information verbatim, the jotting down of key passages for later expansion is helpful. Interviewers should avoid summarizing or paraphrasing responses but rather try to use the respondent's own words. Paraphrasing requires interpretation and may change the color and gusto of the real remarks. The interviewer need not ask obvious questions such as the sex of the respondent. Personal observations can be added at any point they appear pertinent to an understanding of the response, for example: (the respondent appeared very fearful and shaken when relating this incident). Finally, the end-of-the-interview protocol should include an opportunity for the interviewer to discuss any other observations that may lead to a fuller understanding of the context of the interview.

Field interview designers should make use of the face-to-face nature of such encounters to employ audiovisual and other materials that make the interview more interesting, as well as aid in the data-gathering process, particularly for overcoming reluctance to answer sensitive questions.

If the research project can afford the luxury of two interviewers per respondent, then much of the difficulty of recording and conducting an interview can be split, with one interviewer asking the questions and the other concentrating solely on recording responses.

Vignettes and Scenarios

Finch (1987, p.105) describes **vignettes** as "short stories about hypothetical characteristics in specified circumstances, to whose situation the interviewee is invited to respond." These vignettes are often short or typical **scenarios** (short descriptions of future possibilities) or stories about individuals, situations, and structures. These can be used with individuals, situations, and structures. Target respondents can include individuals or focus groups. In the case of the latter, vignettes may act as warm-up exercises or icebreakers to get people to interact. The stories are varied with respect to age, gender, ethnicity, and the like and are useful in exploring sensitive topics.

Vignettes

Scenarios

Offender Interviews

Decker (2005) points out that interviews with active offenders provide a picture of a different pattern of offending and different perceptions than those of incarcerated offenders. Such studies have particularly focused on drug dealers and users, residential burglars, armed robbers, gang members, and gun offenders. The now defunct Arrestee Drug Abuse Monitoring System used interviews with offenders to discern their drug use behavior.

Studies of active residential burglars in Odessa, Texas (Cromwell, Olson and Avery, 1991), Delaware (Rengert and Wasilchick, 2000), and St. Louis (Wright and Decker, 1994) documented the variety of motivations of burglars centered around a lifestyle of partying and keeping up appearances. Studies of armed robbers documented their versatility in offending patterns, high levels of victimization of the robbers themselves, and the pressures of maintaining their lifestyle (Wright and Decker, 1997). Interviews with gang members and gun offenders along with the previous types were able to note the beginning and end of their careers as well as their responses to various sanctions. The detailed examination of types of criminals overcomes some of the problems exhibited by developmental criminological studies that use data on property criminals and infer them to all types of criminals (Hagan, 2008, 2009). Decker (2005, p.17) identifies eleven specific procedures or items of concrete advice on conducting offender interviews:

1. Establish the goals of the interview.
2. Choose offenders to interview.
3. Determine who should conduct the interviews.
4. Find appropriate subjects.
5. Convince the subjects to participate.
6. Maintain field relations.
7. Conduct interviews.
8. Sort out the truth.
9. Analyze the interview results.
10. Present the findings.
11. Apply the interview results to tactical and strategic problem solving.

Most of the projects interviewing active offenders have relied on offers of incentives to participate. This may be in the form of cash (which works best) or vouchers. Maintaining contacts with subjects may pay future dividends in providing other subjects as well as contacts for future studies. Most researchers tape-record their interviews and transcribe them at a later date. Locations for the interview should be a place where offenders are not at undue risk. Validation of interviews is a paramount concern. This may be achieved by repeat interviews, interviews with peers, and comparisons with other sources of data. Many problem-oriented policing projects have utilized interviews with active offenders (www.cops.usdoj.gov). These have included interviews with prostitutes in Lancashire, England (Lancashire Constabulary, 2003), johns and prostitutes in Buffalo (Buffalo Police Department, 2001), and burglars in Chula Vista, California (Chula Vista Police Department, 2001).

Telephone Surveys

Although the interview ensures a high response rate and possesses many distinct advantages, the cost, size of staff, and time required often make it prohibitive for many surveys. If use is made of the widespread ownership of telephones, however, certain advantages of interviews can be gained without the need for a large field staff and at a fraction of the cost.

Advantages and Prospects of Telephone Surveys

The advantages of telephone surveys include not only the *elimination of a field staff* but also *simpler monitoring of interviewer bias*, because the supervisor can be present at the time interviews are conducted by listening to the interviewers or listening in on calls. Thus, potential bias or patterns can be caught early and corrected. Although even lengthy interviews can be obtained through inexpensive electronic patches between telephone and tape recorder, the primary intent of telephone surveys is to obtain wide and representative samples. Such surveys are *inexpensive and quick, generally yield a low nonresponse rate, and provide easy and inexpensive follow-up*. The growing tendency of organizations to obtain WATS lines—flat rate charges that permit fairly unlimited long-distance calls—has made national telephone surveys more of an economic possibility.

Sudman suggests that phone surveys are more effective in obtaining hard-to-locate respondents than person-to-person interviews. The potential for high refusals can be circumvented, particularly if short "yes" or "no" answers are used (Glasser and Metzger, 1972; Sudman, 1980). It should be mentioned that the Federal Trade Commission exempts survey and opinion research from the Do Not Call Registry, which was primarily targeting telemarketers.

Disadvantages of Telephone Surveys

Telephone interviews may have *difficulty in obtaining in-depth responses* or considered answers over the telephone. There may be some loss of the qualitative detail provided by face-to-face interviews. In the past, a major objection to telephone surveys has been that they tended to *exclude* those who do not own telephones or who have unlisted or new telephone numbers. In some large metropolitan areas a considerable proportion of the numbers are unlisted. Also, high mobility in developed societies may add a large portion of new numbers, and the poor and transient may not own phones. Although household telephone ownership overall is estimated by the Census Bureau at approximately 92 percent, it is less than this for African American and minority groups. Ownership for Hispanics in areas of the Southwest is as low as 65 percent. While telephone surveys can be quick and inexpensive, if the survey is global in nature, the cost could be prohibitive.

Additional, but not insurmountable, difficulties with telephone surveys include possible *high refusal rates*. This is related in part to problems in employing sensitive **screening questions.** These are initial queries made by the interviewer to determine whether the person who has answered the telephone fits the target population, for example, income and occupation. Telephone surveys must compete with unethical telemarketing such as "push polls," political negative campaigning disguised as legitimate polls. These are advocacy calls made under the guise of research.

Screening questions

The following describes screening procedures used in a national survey of stalking (Tjaden and Thoennes, 1998, p. 17):

Because much confusion exists about what it means to be stalked, the National Violence Against Women Survey did not use the word "stalking" in its screening questions. Including the word would have assumed that victimized persons knew how to define stalking and perceived what happened to them as stalking. Instead, the survey used the following behaviorally specific questions to screen respondents for stalking victimization.

Not including bill collectors, telephone solicitors, or other salespeople, has anyone, male or female, ever . . .

- Followed or spied on you?
- Sent you unsolicited letters or written correspondence?
- Made unsolicited phone calls to you?
- Stood outside your home, school, or workplace?
- Showed up at places you were even though he or she had no business being there?
- Left unwanted items for you to find?
- Tried to communicate in other ways against your will?
- Vandalized your property or destroyed something you loved?

Respondents who answered yes to one or more of these questions were asked whether anyone had ever done any of these things to them on more than one occasion. Because stalking involves repeated behaviors, only respondents who said yes were considered possible stalking victims. Respondents who reported being victimized on more than one occasion were subsequently asked how frightened their assailant's behavior made them feel and whether they feared their assailant would seriously harm them or someone close to them. Only respondents who were very frightened or feared bodily harm were regarded as stalking victims.

Telephone focus groups are a useful technique to tap participants from large or remote geographic areas (Hurworth, 2004). Such organized telephone groups can be conducted at a fraction of the cost of plane fares and hotel costs that would be incurred in bringing people to a centralized place. These can be conducted using a simple conference call using ordinary telephones, cordless phones, or speaker phones. Once recruits are sent confirmation letters containing informed consent forms, the studies are underway. A reminder call the day before the session is a must. At the time of the interview, the telephone company links in the interviewees and calls the interviewer. It is explained that there is a note taker online. Smaller groups (four to six persons) work better than larger face-to-face groups (Krueger, 2002, p.2). It is best for participants to use landlines as mobile phones can be problematic. While nonverbal cues cannot be seen, this seems to have little effect on outcome.

Computers in Survey Research

The first wave of computer usage in the social sciences involved data management and statistical analysis. The second wave has involved the development of software that has enhanced data collection. A variety of possibilities exist. In a variation of the standard questionnaire, respondents can be asked to use a computer terminal and input their responses to items on the computer screen. In **CAPI (Computer-Assisted Programmed Interviewing)** the researcher uses a laptop computer instead of a clipboard. The interview protocol appears on the screen, and the interviewer enters the responses. Inexpensive computers can be placed in respondent homes for longitudinal research. In one project, on completion of the study the respondents were given the computers as an incentive for having participated (Vasu and Garson, 1990). Computerized interviews may even have advantages over standard interviews in eliminating interviewer bias, obtaining more standardized responses, assuring anonymity, and reducing coding error (Monette, Sullivan, and DeJong, 1994, p. 114).

CAPI

Focus group research is particularly suitable for **CART (Continuous Audience Response Technology).** Such purposely selected groups are brought together to measure some stimuli. Respondents observe various video presentations and give their reactions on a continuous basis by means of a handheld keypad (similar to a remote control device) by pressing appropriate buttons. For example, the buttons might represent 0 (negative reaction) to 5 (neutral reaction) to 10 (positive reaction). Group and individual responses can be instantaneously recorded, calculated, plotted, displayed on the video screen, and played back and reanalyzed; all of this is on videotape for future analysis.

CART

Phone surveys can be done quickly, and they can make maximum use of computerization through **CATI (Computer-Assisted Telephone Interviews).** Software packages exist to promote CATI systems. The computer flashes the question to be asked on the monitor, the interviewer keys in the answer, and the program chooses the next question to be asked. This is particularly useful for contingency questions, ones in which the interviewer is instructed to skip to different sequences of questions contingent upon the answer to others. The computer immediately stores the response, can track inconsistencies in response, and can even track interviewer performance.

CATI

Respondent reluctance to admit sensitive information to an interviewer can be overcome in part by self-administration of the survey via computer. Tourangeau and Smith (1996) reviewed many studies of the effect of a computer as a tool for self-administered surveys and found no superiority. **ACASI (Audio Computer-Assisted Self-Administered Interviewing)** involves having the information on the screen simultaneously being played in earphones. They found much greater reporting of illegal drug use and multiple sex partners with ACASI than with CASI. **CASI (Computer-Assisted Self-Administered Interviewing)** involves the respondent interacting directly with the computer (but without audio).

ACASI

CASI

SPSS (Statistical Package for the Social Sciences) has software for analyzing open-ended survey responses. "TextSmart" (www.spss.com/software/textsmart) creates a list of keywords that capture the meaning of open-ended responses. Similarly the "Ethnograph v 5.0" produced by Sage Publications is a text-based, qualitative data analysis software which searches and notes segments of interest within the data, marks code words, and runs analyses.

Random Digit Dialing

Random digit dialing (RDD) is a sampling procedure that enables the researcher to overcome a major shortcoming of telephone surveys—new or unlisted telephone numbers. The basic procedure can be summarized:

1. Find the universe of exchanges for the area to be surveyed. Some telephone books conveniently list these in the first few pages of the directory. The complete list of such numbers constitutes the universe (population) to be surveyed.
2. Use some randomized scheme to select the numbers. For example, take every nth name on a page selected by means of a table of random numbers and use that telephone number. (Suppose 864-0681 is chosen.)
3. Retain the first four digits (in this instance, 8640) and, using a table of random numbers to complete the number, be careful not to go beyond the range of the universe as determined earlier. By this procedure, persons with unlisted and new numbers are included in the sample, although those who do not own telephones are not (Sudman, 1976, p. 65). Such random numbers can also be generated one at a time by a CATI system.

The following description of a random-digit-dialing (RDD) procedure is from a joint project by the National Institute of Justice and Centers for Disease Control and Prevention entitled, "Stalking in America: Findings from the National Violence Against Women Survey" (Tjaden and Thoennes, 1998, p. 15):

> The sample was drawn as a national, random-digit-dialing (RDD) sample of telephone households in the United States. The sample was stratified by U.S. Census region to control for differential response rates by region. Within regional strata, a simple random sample of working, residential, "*hundreds bank*" [emphasis mine] phone numbers was drawn. A hundreds bank is the first eight digits of any ten-digit telephone number (e.g., 301-608-38xx). A randomly generated two-digit number was appended to each randomly sampled hundreds bank to produce the full ten-digit, random-digit number. The random-digit numbers were called by SRBI [Schulman, Ronca, Bucuvalas, Inc.] interviewers from their central telephone interviewing facility. Nonworking and nonresidential numbers were screened out. Once a

residential household was reached, eligible adults in each household were identified. In households with multiple eligibles, the most-recent-birthday method was used to systematically select the designated respondent.

In a study commissioned by the Police Foundation, Tuchfarber and Klecka indicate that for only a quarter of the cost of personal interview survey techniques, police departments can obtain equally effective victimization and public opinion survey data in their communities. Data regarding crime trends, neighborhood safety, and police performance showed no difference between face-to-face and telephone surveys, whereas victimization rates for households were higher in the telephone surveys (Tuchfarber and Klecka, 1976; Tuchfarber et al., 1976). The differences that appear between face-to-face interviews and telephone surveys may be more of a result of the actual interviewers involved than differences in the methods. The skills required in a telephone interview may be quite different from those involved in direct personal interviews (Groves and Kahn, 1979).

The utilization of RDD procedures is illustrated in a study of citizen participation and community crime prevention in the Chicago area (Lavrakis, 1984; Skogan and Maxfield, 1981) and described in the following manner:

> A modified random-digit-dialing procedure was used to generate a total of 5,346 prospective sample numbers. A total of 1,803 interviews were completed. Within households respondents were adults (age nineteen or older) stratified by sex and age. For analytic purposes, the sample of 1,803 completed interviews was weighted by the inverse of the number of different telephone numbers in each household, in order to correct for the probability of reaching a household with multiple phones (in Loftin, 1987, p. 84).

Note the concern for accuracy in taking into account multiple telephone ownership, which certainly would not have been an issue only a few years ago (Lavrakis, 1993). RDD may include the computer generating telephone numbers from known area codes and prefixes.

Techniques Employed in Telephone Surveys

A number of procedures used in telephone surveys enable, in part, the overcoming of some of the limitations of this technique. Sensitive items such as income can be handled by a line of questioning employing a **branching procedure** in which income is narrowed down to broad estimates as in Figure 6.1. Such a procedure has been found to take no more time than the method of handing the respondent a card with income ranges used in face-to-face surveys (Sudman, 1980).

Branching procedure

The likelihood of refusals is greatest during the first minute of the telephone conversation. The interviewer should avoid screening respondents with

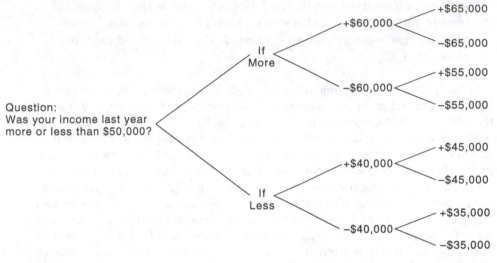

Figure 6.1
Branching Procedure Employed to Estimate Income in a Telephone Survey.

threatening or sensitive questions or questions that easily permit the subject to refuse. For example, the question "Is there anyone there who earns under $20,000 a year?" makes it easy for the respondent to say no, even if it is not true, realizing that such a response will abort the interview. It would be similar to a door-to-door encyclopedia salesperson beginning with the question "Do you own any encyclopedias?" (Sudman, 1980).

Even questions requiring scaled responses rather than simply "yes" or "no" answers can be answered over the telephone. For example, respondents can be asked about their attitudes or ratings of a subject by being requested to respond by picturing a thermometer ranging from very cold, cold, mild, warm, and very hot. Telephone dials or buttons themselves can be utilized to measure degrees of response ranging, for instance, from zero (the lowest rating) to nine (the highest rating) (Sudman, 1980).

More in-depth questions can be undertaken through the randomization of questions so that fewer but more detailed questions can be asked of each respondent. In this procedure, more of the respondents are asked the entire set of questions. The order of questions can also be randomized. For additional information on telephone surveys, consult Frey (1989), Groves et al. (1988), and Lavrakis (1993).

A new wrinkle in considering telephone surveys is "Do Cell Phones Affect Survey Research?" (2009). The growing ownership of cell phones by Americans and the growing number of those who rely solely on cell phones for telephone service are a real challenge to telephone surveys that rely upon landlines only. In 2006, 12.8 percent of U.S. households and 11.8 percent of adults were cell phone–only (Do Cell Phones Affect, 2009). Cell-only adults are different than landline-only owners. They are younger, less affluent, single, renters, urban, and more liberal. Among young people with 25–30 percent cell-only, the potential for bias is great. It is also a growing practice to offer respondents on cell phones a small amount of money to reimburse them for the cost of incoming calls (Do Cell Phones Affect, 2009).

Victim Surveys in Criminal Justice

In Chapter 4, we discussed major limitations of the use of official statistics such as the Uniform Crime Report (UCR) as an indicator of the overall crime problem of a society. Unrecorded crime, or the ***dark figure of crime***, as it was referred to by early European criminologists, has always escaped such official statistics. **Victim surveys** involve questioning a representative sample of the population to obtain an estimate of victimization, a portion of which is not reported to the police.

Dark figure of crime

Victim surveys

Even though Clinard (1978, p. 22) traces victim surveys as early as 1720 Denmark, surprisingly, it was not until the late 1960s that victim surveys were conducted on a large-scale basis to measure crime. On the basis of the results of these pilot surveys, a major victim survey effort was begun not only in the United States but also in Belgium, Canada, Denmark, England, Holland, Norway, Sweden, Switzerland, and West Germany (Nettler, 1978, pp. 94–95; Sparks, Genn, and Dodd, 1977, p. 3). Among both private and government-sponsored surveys, by far the most ambitious and sustained effort has been conducted in the United States by the Department of Justice's Bureau of Justice Statistics (BJS), which utilizes the U.S. Census Bureau as the data-gathering agent. The BJS was created by an act of Congress to coordinate the crime data generated by separate local, state, and federal agencies.

Other pilot surveys conducted by the Law Enforcement Assistance Administration (LEAA) in the early 1970s were invaluable in identifying major methodological issues to be addressed in later, larger BJS surveys. Such issues as recall periods, reverse validity checks (police records compared with survey reports), problems of under- and overreporting, credibility of respondents, and sampling questions were noted and had the benefit of a trial run (Panel for the Evaluation of Crime Surveys, 1976, pp. 33–48).

National Crime Victimization Survey

On the basis of the success of these studies, the National Crime Surveys were initiated in July 1972. Originally, the National Crime Surveys comprised the National Crime Panel Surveys and the Central City Surveys. Now, only the National Crime Panel studies are conducted, and these are referred to as the **National Crime Victimization Surveys (NCVSs).** According to the National Academy of Sciences panel responsible for evaluating these surveys, the survey design, sampling, and estimating schemes were among the most complex

NCVS

ever employed on such a large scale in the social sciences (Panel for the Evaluation of Crime Surveys, 1976, p. 8).

These surveys began as a collaboration between the U.S. Department of Justice (DOJ) and the U.S. Census Bureau. In 1969, LEAA, which had been created as a branch of DOJ in 1968, evolved a subbranch, the National Criminal Justice Information and Statistics Service (NCJISS) that became involved in the early surveys. Since 1980, NCJISS has become BJS.

Sampling

The surviving set of surveys of the NCVS (the national crime panel) consists of national surveys of housing units. Since 1991 the National Crime Survey has been known as the NCVS. Ongoing since 1973, data are obtained each year for a nationally representative sample of 77,200 households or nearly 134,000 people (Bureau of Justice Statistics, 2007). A housing unit remains in the sample for three years. The subsamples are designed so that every six months one group is rotated out of the sample and replaced by a new group. Rotation (reinterviews and replacement of panel subunits) enables the crime panel to remain fresh and representative. Without it the panel would eventually grow old and unrepresentative. The first and fifth interviews are conducted in person, while the others are via telephone.

The NCVS is conducted using a complex *stratified multistage cluster sample* (Panel for the Evaluation of Crime Surveys, 1976, pp. 10–11) and is described in the original language so that the reader may appreciate the sampling design:

1. A national sampling frame is developed in which about 2,000 Primary Sampling Units (PSUs) are defined as either a Standard Metropolitan Statistical Area (SMSA), a county, or a small group of contiguous counties.
2. These clusters are then stratified on the basis of size, density, population mobility, and other relevant socioeconomic criteria into 376 strata.
3. In the first stage, one PSU is chosen from each stratum with a proportionate probability with respect to population size.
4. In the next stages within each sample, PSU clusters of roughly four adjacent neighboring housing units are selected systematically so that each housing unit in the country has an equal probability of being selected.

Panel Design

Crime panel

Bounding

The NCVS consists of a crime panel. The **crime panel** repeats interviews every six months to bound or provide a benchmark for crime reports. **Bounding** involves using a pretest or initial interview to set a reference point for the survey reporting period. The initial interview sets a boundary or time period with which to compare future victimizations. In addition to general demographic information, these interviews probe such variables as victim–offender relationships, injury or loss suffered, the time and place of the incident(s), the time the crime is reported to the police, and other criminal justice matters.

Each subgroup of the crime panel is interviewed every six months for three years and then is rotated out of the panel and replaced by a new bounded subgroup.

The NCVS is conducted for the BJS by the Census Bureau. Initially, face-to-face interviews are attempted with a household informant (any competent adult eighteen years of age or older). The core survey averages approximately thirty minutes per household; previous pilot studies suggest that longer interview times increase refusal rates. The survey has two parts: screening questions and incident reports. Questions regarding personal victimizations are asked of each household member twelve years of age or older (if the person victimized is hospitalized, incompetent, or temporarily absent, proxy respondents are accepted). If victimization is claimed in the screening instrument, then the "incident reports" instrument is used to follow up on such details as clarification of the incident, determination of whether the incident was a crime, and information on offenders, offense, victim actions, economic loss, and the like. Subsequent interviews are obtained through a combination of personal and telephone interviews.

A Comparison of UCR, NCVS, and Self-Report Data

Menard (1987) examined five- to ten-year trends in crime and juvenile delinquency using UCR (official police data), the NCVS (victimization data), and the National Youth Survey (NYS) (self-reported delinquency). While the UCR showed steadily increasing rates of crime, the NCVS and NYS indicated stable or decreasing rates. Although the increase in the official statistics in the face of relatively stable crime commission rates might be taken as a positive sign of increased reporting and police effectiveness, it may also reflect an increased reliance upon formal legal controls and police professionalization. Table 6.1 compares the NCVS with the UCR.

Some Problems in Victim Surveys

From the initial pilot surveys of the late 1960s to the more recent ones, the Census Bureau and BJS researchers have been aware of a variety of shortcomings in surveys of victims and have tried to deal with them in various ways. Following are some potential **problems in victim surveys**:

Some problems in victim surveys

- Cost of large samples
- False reporting
- Mistaken interpretation of incidents
- Sampling bias
- Overreporting and/or underreporting
- Memory failure, decay, and telescoping

Table 6.1
THE NCVS VERSUS THE UCR

The Nation's Two Crime Measures

The National Crime Victimization Survey (NCVS) and the FBI's Uniform Crime Reports (UCR) measure various aspects of crime at the national level. These complementary series each contribute to providing a complete picture about the extent and nature of crime in the United States. Together the NCVS and UCR provide a more comprehensive assessment of crime in the United States than could be obtained from either statistical series alone.

THE NATIONALCRIME VICTIMIZATION SURVEY

Using stable data collection methods since 1973, the NCVS has the following strengths:

- It measures both reported and unreported crimes.
- It is not affected by changes in the extent to which people report crime to police or improvements in police record-keeping technology.
- It collects information that is not available when the initial police report is made including contacts the victim has with the criminal justice system after the crime, extent and costs of medical treatment, and recovery of property.
- It collects detailed information about victims and characteristics of the victimization including who the victims are, what their relationship is to the offender, whether the crime was part of a series of crimes occuring over a six-month period, what self-protective measures were used, and how the victims assess their effectiveness, and what the victim was doing when victimized.
- On occasion, it includes special supplements about particular topics such as school crime and the severity of crime.

THE UNIFORM CRIME REPORTS

The UCR program measures police workload and activity. Local police departments voluntarily report information to the Federal Bureau of Investigation (FBI) including the numbers of crimes reported to police, arrests made by police and other administrative information. The UCR program has the following strengths:

- It can provide local data about States, counties, cities and towns.
- It measures crimes affecting children under age twelve, a segment of the population that experts agree cannot be reliably interviewed in the NCVS.
- It includes crimes against commercial establishments.
- It collects information about the number of arrests and who was arrested.
- It counts the number of homicides (murders and nonnegligent manslaughters), crimes that cannot be counted in a survey that interviews victims. UCR also collects detailed information about the circumstances surrounding homicides and the characteristics of homicide victims.

Source: Bureau of Justice Statistics, 1993, p. 6; Federal Bureau of Investigation, "Appendix IV—The Nation's Two Crime Measures," *Crime in the United States, 2004*, Washington, D.C.: Government Printing Office, 2005.

- Interviewer effects
- Coding and mechanical error
- Problems measuring certain crimes

Although this list by no means covers all the difficulties encountered in conducting and interpreting victim surveys, it does enumerate the major ones.

Cost of Large Samples

In the discussion of sampling in Chapter 4, it was indicated that most large-scale public opinion surveys in the United States are conducted with sample sizes of less than a thousand or two. Victim surveys require such large samples because of the need to ensure the appearance of rare events. For example, in that the vast majority of respondents are not likely to have been victimized in the past year or six months, it becomes necessary to interview large numbers to obtain only a few victims. Glaser explains that by using official statistics one must survey ten respondents to obtain one victim. For more rare victimizations such as rape, even larger numbers are needed to obtain a few cases. Also, because sampling error is proportionate to the size of the sample instead of the size of the population being sampled, one often needs as large a sample to estimate victimizations in small or large cities as would be necessary for the entire nation (Glaser, 1978, p. 63).

False Reports

False reports on the part of respondents may produce erroneous victim data. Some falsity in victim reports should be expected according to Levine (1976, p. 98), who found that respondents were inaccurate in disclosing behavior with respect to voting, finances, business practices, sexual behavior, academic performance, and other activities. Certainly, one would be overoptimistic in assuming greater accuracy in recall of criminal victimization.

Mistaken Reporting

Mistaken reporting is another source of error in victim surveys. Thomas' "definition of the situation" holds that, if individuals inaccurately feel that a situation is real, it is nevertheless real in its consequences (Thomas and Swaine, 1928, pp. 571–572). A person who has lost something may inaccurately, but honestly, believe it was stolen. Perhaps the neighborhood paranoids do in fact believe people have been attempting to break into their house, when no such incidents ever took place. In addition, many respondents are ignorant of the complexities of legal definitions of criminal events and may report incidents that are not really crimes. Such incidents often tend to be regarded, even by respondents, as trivial, hardly worth the effort, or not really a police matter. Many of these events would most likely have been labeled "unfounded" by police, had a request been made for police investigation.

Poor Memory

Poor memory on the part of those surveyed is another potential difficulty in surveying possible victims of crime. Memory failure, or *recall decay*, refers to the phenomenon of progressive memory loss as the distance increases between the time of the event and the time of the interview concerning the event. For example, a crime that took place last week is more likely to be recalled as well as reported than a crime that occurred last month or last year.

Telescoping

A principal type of memory fading in victim surveys is **telescoping**—the tendency of respondents to move forward and report as having occurred events that actually took place before the reference period. That is, a crime that happened two years ago is mistakenly reported as having taken place within the last six months. In a pretest in the District of Columbia, the U.S. Bureau of Census (1970, p. 9) performed a *reverse record check* in which known crime victims were interviewed after the fact. About 20 percent of the victimizations in police records documented as having occurred before the reference period were reported by the survey sample as having taken place within the reference period. Similarly, the Dayton–San Jose surveys showing greater victimization reported in the first half of the year are a likely case of forward telescoping. Biderman (1970) suggests that some subjects may unconsciously telescope events to please inter-

viewers; thus, **demand characteristics** or overagreeableness on the part of those surveyed is a related problem in surveys of public victimization.

Sampling Biass

Sampling bias is a thorny problem in much survey research including victim surveys. Even the decennial U.S. Census of Population underenumerates the young, males, and members of minority groups. As Skogan (1978, p. 17) aptly points out, "Males, African Americans, and youths are much more likely than others to fall victim to most crimes, but they are less likely to be found and questioned." Although the Census Bureau estimates and attempts to correct for such nonresponse bias, it still remains a problem.

Overreporting and Underreporting

Overreporting in victimization surveys may be accounted for by the fact that when asked, respondents will report to interviewers acts that they ordinarily would regard as too trivial or unimportant to warrant police attention. Much of the deep, dark figure of crime consists of minor property crime, a good proportion of which would most likely have been "unfounded" by police (Black, 1970). While many critics of victim surveys have assailed their tendency to overreport certain categories of crime (Levine, 1976; Singer, 1978), these surveys also contain some of the same shortcomings of the UCR and other official police statistics in underreporting certain crimes. Victim surveys tend to *underreport* crimes, and because certain crimes are not reported or queried, victims do not tend to report crimes in which the perpetrator was a friend, relative, or family member. As with the UCR, victim surveys do not concern themselves particularly with corporate, occupational, organized, professional, political, and public order crime.

An additional concern in contrasting official police statistics with surveys of victims relates to different bases of comparison. Police statistics are based on the number of incidents, whereas victim surveys are based on individual victims. Glaser (1978, p. 64) gives the following example: Ten people from ten households were robbed in one holdup, and only one person was robbed in another. This was recorded as only two robberies in police statistics; however, potential victimizations are tallied in a survey of victims. Most victim surveys exclude nonresidents and foreign visitors, a serious underestimate of crime particularly in tourist cities and/or cities with large commuter populations.

Interviewer Effects

Any survey involving interviewers contains the potential for interviewer bias. Although outright deception and exaggeration are possibilities, more likely to occur are subjective bias on the part of the interviewer and the artificiality introduced by the interview situation. Levine (1976) suggests that interviewer self-interest may impact on the results in that the enumeration of many crimes may be thought to ensure more surveys and thus continued employment. Additionally, potential reactivity of respondents who are continually reinterviewed as part of the national panel may impact on their attitudes or reported victimizations (National Advisory Committee, 1976, p. 147). Panel fatigue or other response effects have been demonstrated to occur in the National Crime Panels.

Coding Unreliability and Mechanical Error

In addition to all of the previously mentioned sources of possible error, *human mistakes in coding*, data entry, and analyzing may account for significant inaccuracy. Sussman and Haug (1967) have pointed out the serious degree of unchecked *mechanical errors* in coding and data entry in general large-scale surveys.

Because of the concern over potential errors in the NCVS, its suspension was seriously considered in the late 1970s. Fortunately, this did not take place, and the NCVS has become institutionalized. Once viewed as a novel adjunct crime count, it is now perceived as an important social indicator, as noted more recently by adoption of its design principles by the United Nations.

Problems Measuring Certain Crimes

The NCVS obviously does not interview victims of murder, but Helen Eigenberg (1990) points out that the data on rape have been inadequate because NCVS never asked respondents directly whether they had been raped. Although she feels the new screening questions are an improvement over the old ones because they ask whether the subject has ever been assaulted, she thinks that "researchers must note that the NCVS has traditionally operationalized rape poorly" (1990, p. 655).

The NCVS rate does, however, appear to be a better measure of the true rate of rape over time than the UCR. The latter reflects trends in organization and management of rape victimizations (Jensen and Karpos, 1993). Improved operationalization of rape and domestic violence in the redesigned NCVS was implemented in 100 percent of the samples beginning July 1993 (Bachman and Taylor, 1994). In August 1995, the NCVS released the first report on rape data from the newly designed survey and doubled their estimate of the number of rapes. The new estimates asked specifically whether respondents were raped or sexually assaulted, whereas the previous protocol asked only about attacks of any kind without mentioning rape or sexual assault.

Benefits of Victim Surveys

Despite some methodological problems, many of which can be controlled as will be elaborated, victim surveys hold much promise:

1. They have become a model spurring international imitation.
2. Such studies present an opportunity to obtain a picture of victims and their characteristics.
3. Because of nonreporting in official statistics, victim surveys may be a more accurate estimate for commission of such crimes as rape and assault (National Advisory Committee, 1976, p. 145).
4. The potential exists, using telephone surveys (as discussed in this chapter), for local jurisdictions to conduct their own victim surveys to gauge, plan, and evaluate elements of police services.
5. Victim surveys are additionally useful for measuring crime costs with respect to injuries, insurance, and crime prevention programs (Skogan, 1978, p. 2).
6. They also assist in obtaining better descriptions of criminals and their methods of operation.
7. Such surveys also assess such issues as fear of crime, satisfaction with police services, attitude toward the police, and reasons for not reporting crimes to the police.

A Defense of Victim Surveys

Despite the shortcomings of victim surveys that have been elaborated, it should once again be pointed out that no method of data gathering is perfect. Many of these sources of error are not the sole province of victim surveys, but may apply equally to some of the other techniques of data gathering. Victim surveys are a relatively young endeavor in criminal justice. Much has already been learned. And much has yet to be learned in future methodological analyses.

The Department of Justice's BJS is constantly monitoring and attempting to update the methodological accuracy of the NCVS. In 1985, a panel of experts in criminology—The National Crime Consortium—was charged with the task of devising better screening questions to obtain better control over forgotten as well as sensitive items. Redesign of the NCVS reflects this effort.

Controlling for Error in Victim Surveys

Some common means of controlling for error in victim surveys, some of which have already been mentioned, are as follows:

- Use of panels
- Bounding of target groups

- Evaluations of coding
- Reverse record check surveys of known groups
- Reinterviews of the same group
- Interviews with significant others

Bounding

The use of panels in the NCVS permits the researcher to achieve bounding. The first interview with residents results in a panel that can then be followed up five times every six months before being dropped out of the sample. At each six-month interview, respondents are asked about events since the last interview. Bounding is made possible beginning with the initial interview during which the *boundary*, or *time period during which events were recalled as having taken place*, can be established. Any events recalled later can be tracked since the previous interview, thus eliminating telescoping of reports.

Simple coding procedures—the assignment of responses to categories—have high degrees of measurement error and intercoder discrepancies (Crittenden and Hill, 1971; Sussman and Haug, 1967). The utilization of different coders to classify the same data enables assessment of coding error.

Reverse Record Checks

Reverse record checks involve validation of reported behavior on the basis of studying a group whose behavior is already known. Pilot studies of known victims who had reported their incidents to police were conducted in Washington, D.C., Baltimore, and San Jose (Panel for the Evaluation of Crime Surveys, 1976, p. 33). The surveys found that recall deteriorates more quickly after six months, and particularly forgotten are crimes committed by close acquaintances. In the San Jose survey, 52 percent of assaults known to police were not reported in victim surveys (National Advisory Committee, 1976, p. 146). Reiss interviewed a sample of respondents who had reported crimes to the police the month before and discovered that one out of five failed to report to interviewers crimes they had reported to police the previous month (Reiss, 1967).

Reinterview of the same group enables an assessment of potential bias and interviewer bias. Results obtained by the initial interviewer can be compared with those obtained by the second interviewer. Such information can then be reconciled or resolved through agreement (Panel for the Evaluation of Crime Surveys, 1976, p. 63).

Interviews with significant others, peers, teachers, and the like provide a cross-check on claimed behavior.

Reverse record checks

Victim Surveys: A Balanced View

In 1974, when LEAA released the findings from its thirteen central city surveys, Donald Santarelli, then head of the organization, was quoted as having remarked "For the first time in history, we now have an accurate measure of crime in America—at least in these 13 cities" (Burnham, 1974, pp. 1, 51). Other popular reviews pointed to how victim surveys, in covering the dark figure of crime, showed that there was actually twice as much crime as appears in official police statistics. After review of the advantages and disadvantages of victim surveys it seems fair to conclude that:

1. For the types of personal and household crimes, both victim surveys and the UCR measure, the true rate is most likely somewhere between victim surveys, which overestimate crime, and the UCR, which underestimates crime.
2. For other types of crimes such as occupational, corporate, and public order crime, both measures underestimate crime.
3. Despite shortcomings, victim surveys present a needed separate and independent assessment of crime and other criminal justice matters of importance.

The problems encountered with most methods of data gathering are not inherent to the nature of the method; rather, the problems arise because the method is used as the sole means of assessment. Of particular concern is the fact that cost-cutting measures due to budgetary restrictions (instrumentation) threaten the viability of the NCVS.

Community Crime Victimization Survey Software

The BJS has produced Crime Victimization Survey (CVS) software that can be used by local government agency researchers to conduct their own victimization surveys. It uses the same question asked in the NCVS. In addition, it contains questions that can measure citizen attitudes toward crime, their neighborhood, and local policing services. The latest version, Justice Survey Software (JSS), is a free Web-based software for justice agencies to conduct their own surveys using standardized questions available from various sources (www.bjsjss.org).

Redesign of the National Crime Victimization Survey

In 1974, in response to an evaluation by the National Academy of Sciences and an internal review by a predecessor of the BJS, a project was begun to evaluate and redesign the NCVS. The evaluation was put together by a consortium of universities and private research firms and the staff from BJS and the Census Bureau. Implementation of some of these redesign plans was begun in 1986; others were phased in later (Taylor, 1989, p. 1).

The first changes, those which would have minimal impact on NCVS victimization rates, were introduced in July 1986. Most of these items related to the expanded list of questions, those that were added to the questionnaire that had remained fundamentally unchanged since 1972. These new questions related to drug and alcohol use by offenders, self-protective measures taken by victims, police actions, victim contact with the justice system, location of crime, victim's activity, and expansion of several existing questions (Whitaker, 1989, p. 2). Among other changes was the decision to use *CATI technology*. With this technology, questionnaire items can be flashed on a video monitor, and then interviewers can immediately enter responses on the keyboard. The redesigned NCVS program is also considering but has not implemented *CAPI technology*, which makes possible the use of portable laptop computers in field interviews. Although the proposed changes involve too many details for our presentation, it is worth noting some other modifications. These modifications include altering the scope of crimes measured or adding new topical supplements to the NCVS on a regular basis. Special questions will be periodically added to deal with timely topics, such as school crime or victim risk (Bureau of Justice Statistics, 1989).

Efforts were made in redesigning the NCVS to avoid disrupting the integrity of its longitudinal design. The new survey instrument was phased into the NCVS so as not to compromise trend data (Bachman and Taylor, 1994, p. 502). Exhibit 6.2 details the redesigned NCVS.

EXHIBIT 6.2 ▶

The Redesigned National Crime Victimization Survey

Additional Details About the Redesign of the National Crime Victimization Survey

The redesign of the NCVS.   In the mid-1970s, the National Academy of Sciences evaluated the NCVS for accuracy and usefulness. While the survey was found to be an effective instrument for measuring crime, reviewers identified aspects of the methodology and scope of the NCVS that could be improved. They proposed research to investigate the following:

- an enhanced screening section that would better stimulate respondents' recall of victimizations
- screening questions that would sharpen the concepts of criminal victimization and diminish the effects of subjective interpretations of the survey questions
- additional questions on the nature and consequences of victimizations that would yield useful data for analysis
- enhanced questions and inquiries about domestic violence, rape, and sexual attack to get better estimates of these hard-to-measure victimizations.

The Redesign Has Improved the Measurement of Domestic Violence

Respondents may be reluctant to report acts of domestic violence as crimes, particularly if the offender is present during the interview. In addition, victims may not perceive domestic violence as discrete criminal acts but as a pattern of abuse. Though these issues still pose measurement problems, the redesigned screening section includes explicit questions about incidents involving family members, friends, and acquaintances. Screening questions also include multiple references to acts of domestic violence to encourage respondents to report such incidents even if they do not define these acts as crimes. The survey staff review these reported incidents using standardized definitions of crimes. Thus, within the categories of violent crime measured by the NCVS, the redesign will produce fuller reporting of those incidents that involved intimates or other family members.

A Comparison of the Old and New Questionnaires Illustrates the Expanded Cues That Help a Respondent Recall an Incident

New

1. People often don't think of incidents committed by someone they know. Did you have something stolen from you OR were you attacked or threatened by—
   a. Someone at work or school—
   b. A neighbor or friend—
   c. A relative or family member—
   d. Any other person you've met or known?

(continued)

EXHIBIT 6.2 Continued

2. Did you call the police to report something that happened to YOU, which you thought was a crime?

3. Did anything happen to you, which you thought was a crime, but did NOT report to the police?

Old

1. Did you call the police to report something that happened to YOU, which you thought was a crime?

2. Did anything happen to YOU, which you thought was a crime, but did NOT report to the police?

The new NCVS has resulted in more victimizations being reported than when the old instrument was used. The survey now includes improved questions and cues that help victims to remember victimizations. Interviewers now ask more explicit questions about sexual victimizations. Victim advocates have also been instrumental in encouraging victims to talk more openly about these experiences ("National Crime Victimization . . .," 1994).

Reasons for Differences in Violent Crime Rates Because of the New and Old Screener Questions

The new screener questions provide more specific cues regarding kinds of items used as weapons and kinds of offender actions that better define the in-scope crimes of violence for the NCVS. In particular, the explicit cuing of rape and other sexual assaults has been added to the new screener. A side-by-side comparison of the new and old screener questions is provided.

Furthermore, two frames of reference have been added or more explicitly defined in the new screener. The first relates to crimes being committed by someone the respondent knows. The second relates to the possible location of a crime or activities the respondent may have been involved in. This screener question takes the few sporadically mentioned cues of location/activity in the old screener questions and creates another specific frame of reference with a greatly expanded list of location/activity cues.

Violent Crime Screener Questions

New

1. Has anyone attacked or threatened you in any of these ways—
   a. With any weapon, for instance, a gun or knife—
   b. With anything like a baseball bat, frying pan, scissors, or stick—
   c. By something thrown, such as a rock or bottle—
   d. Include any grabbing, punching, or choking,
   e. Any rape, attempted rape, or other type of sexual attack—
   f. Any face to face threats—

OR
   g. Any attack or threat or use of force by anyone at all? Please mention it even if you are not certain it was a crime.

2. Incidents involving forced or unwanted sexual acts are often difficult to talk about. Have you been forced or coerced to engage in unwanted sexual activity by—
   a. someone you didn't know before
   b. a casual acquaintance OR
   c. someone you know well?

Old

1. Did anyone take something directly from you by using force, such as by a stickup, mugging, or threat?

2. Did anyone TRY to rob you by using force or threatening to harm you?

3. Did anyone beat you up, attack you, or hit you with something, such as a rock or bottle?

4. Were you knifed, shot at, or attacked with some other weapon by anyone at all?

5. Did anyone THREATEN to beat you up or THREATEN you with a knife, gun, or some other weapon, NOT including telephone threats?

6. Did anyone TRY to attack you in some other way?

All Types of Crimes Screener Questions

New

1. Were you attacked or threatened OR did you have something stolen from you—
   a. At home including the porch or yard—
   b. At or near a friend's, relative's, or neighbor's home—
   c. At work or school—
   d. In places such as a storage shed or laundry room, a shopping mall, restaurant, bank, or airport—
   e. While riding in any vehicle—
   f. On the street or in a parking lot—
   g. At such places as a party, theater, gym, picnic area, bowling lanes, or while fishing or hunting—

OR
   h. Did anyone ATTEMPT to attack or attempt to steal anything belonging to you from any of these places?

2. People often don't think of incidents committed by someone they know. Did you have something stolen from you OR were you attacked or threatened by—
   a. Someone at work or school—
   b. A neighbor or friend—
   c. A relative or family member—

3. Did you call the police to report something that happened to YOU, which you thought was a crime?

4. Did anything happen to you, which you thought was a crime, but did NOT report to the police?

Old

1. Was anything stolen from you while you were away from home, for instance, at work, in a theater or restaurant, or while traveling?

2. Did you call the police to report something that happened to YOU, which you thought was a crime?

3. Did anything happen to YOU, which you thought was a crime, but did NOT report to the police?

Reasons for Differences in Burglary Rates Because of the New and Old Screener Questions

In general, the same frame of reference is established for burglary in the new and old screener. However, the new screener has several more specific cues. These additional cues relate to how the offender might have gotten into or attempted to get into the respondent's home and/or other types of buildings that may be on the respondent's property.

Burglary Screener Questions

New

1. Has somebody—
   a. Broken in or ATTEMPTED to break into your home by forcing a door or window, pushing past someone, jimmying a lock, cutting a screen, or entering through an open door or window?
   b. Has anyone illegally gotten in or tried to get into a garage, shed, or storage room?

   OR

   c. Illegally gotten in or tried to get into a hotel or motel room or vacation home where you were staying?

Old

1. Did anyone break into or somehow illegally get into your home, garage, or another building on your property?

2. Did you find a door jimmied, a lock forced, or any other signs of an ATTEMPTED break in?

3. Did anyone take something belonging to you or any member of this household, from a friend's or relative's home, a hotel or motel, or vacation home?

Motor Vehicle Theft Rates

There is no significant difference in motor vehicle theft rates between the new and old methods. One reason is that the new and old screener questions are very similar. Another reason is that motor vehicle thefts are highly salient events (demonstrated by the fact that they have the highest percent reported to police), suggesting little room for improvement in their measurement. Similar results were observed in the CATI research. While CATI increased ratios for most types of crime, it had no significant effect on motor vehicle theft rates.

Motor Vehicle Theft Screener Questions

New

1. Was it—
   a. Stolen or used without permission?
   b. Did anyone ATTEMPT to steal any vehicles?

Old

1. Did anyone steal, TRY to steal, or use it without permission?

Redesign of Type of Crime Classification Scheme

A major reclassification scheme has shifted most of what were previously categorized as personal crimes of theft into property crimes of theft. Under the old scheme, theft was characterized as a personal or household crime based on location of the incident. If an item were stolen from the grounds of a home, it was considered a household theft; if the same item were stolen from someplace away from the home, it was considered a personal theft. This distinction was rather arbitrary and unwieldy, since many items are jointly owned by members of a household. The redesigned NCVS classifies all thefts as household thefts unless there was contact between victim and offender. Personal thefts with contact (purse snatching and pocket picking) are now the only types of theft that are categorized as personal theft. Table 1 compares the old and new types of crime classification scheme.

Overlap Between the Old and New NCVS Methods

As discussed previously, an integral part of the planned transition from the old methods to the new methods of conducting the NCVS was to include a substantial overlap period in which both methods were implemented concurrently. Besides being used for comparing crime estimates, the overlap data can be used to extend earlier time trends data. Statistical models will be developed to adjust for the effects of the new methods on victimization reporting. Adjustment factors will be estimated at least for the major crime categories and possibly for other important variables if reliable differences are found.

(continued)

EXHIBIT 1.5   Continued

Table 1

**CHANGES IN TOTALS REFLECT THE HEADINGS UNDER
WHICH OFFENSES ARE COUNTED**

Type of Crime (New Classification)	1992 Crime Rate
Personal crimes	126.8
Crimes of violence	49.3
Rape/other sexual assault	2.9
Robbery	6.2
Completed	4.1
Attempted	2.1
Assault	40.2
Aggravated	11.1
Simple	29.1
Crimes of theft	77.5
Household crimes	180.8
Burglary	58.7
Household larceny	103.5
Motor vehicle theft	18.6
Personal crimes	51.1
Crimes of violence	49.3
Rape/other sexual assault	2.9
Robbery	6.2
Completed	4.1
Attempted	2.1
Assault	40.2
Aggravated	11.1
Simple	29.1
Purse snatching/pocket picking	1.8
Property crimes	325.3
Burglary	58.7
Motor vehicle theft	18.6
Theft*	248.0

*The theft category is a new crime category. It includes those crimes that were
previously classified in two other crime categories: *household larceny* and *personal
larceny without contact* (a subcategory of *crimes of theft*).

Source: Bureau of Justice Statistics, 1994a, p. 10.

Summary

Although many of the issues regarding survey research discussed in Chapter 5 are also applicable to this chapter, the purpose of this chapter has been to explore major elements of the interview, particularly as it is used in criminal justice research. Interviewing, which basically involves face-to-face interaction between the interviewer and the respondent, has many variations depending on the purpose of the interview. Principal among these variations are structured (closed response), unstructured (open-end response), and depth (focus) interviews.

Some general advantages of the interview method are personal contact, which affords observation, clarification of misunderstandings and control over respondents, and the opportunity to employ visual aids, make return visits, and gear language to the level of the respondent. Interviews are also more flexible than mail questionnaires. Disadvantages of interviews include their sometimes time-consuming and costly nature, potential interviewer bias and mistakes, need for field supervision, and difficulty in reaching certain respondents. Also, question wording in public opinion polls has been shown to radically alter response.

Some interview situations may lend themselves to the use of various electronic recording equipment or other aids that can be a considerable bonus. The randomized response technique, in which the interviewer is blind to the specific item (either a sensitive one or probability one) being answered, may assist in overcoming respondent reactivity to sensitive questions.

Some appropriate procedures in conducting interviews have been detailed. The interviewer should receive an orientation-and-training session to be made aware of the organization and the survey and to practice interviewing and become familiar with the instrument to be employed. Arrangement of the interview, proper protocol, demeanor of interviewers, and administration of the questionnaire, including probing and exiting, were detailed. Interviewers should follow established procedures in recording and editing their survey schedules.

The use of the telephone survey to assess victimization holds promise as a means of reducing the cost of victim surveys. Phone surveys have such limitations as reduced scope, less in-depth responses, high refusal rates, and exclusion of disproportions of certain populations, particularly the poor and minorities. On the other hand, they have the advantages of no field staff, simple checks on interview bias, inexpensiveness, quickness, and easy follow-up.

Computer software such as CART has greatly expanded the versatility of the interview. RDD enables the coverage of unlisted numbers, a previous shortcoming of phone surveys of victims. The use of more careful screening questions and branching procedures for sensitive items may reduce nonresponse. Clever procedures have been developed to ask even attitudinal scale questions by telephone.

Victim surveys have been surprisingly ignored as a means of measuring crime until relatively recently. As the result of pilot studies in the late 1960s, LEAA, in cooperation with the Census Bureau, began two major types of surveys that involved direct questioning of persons as to whether they had been victims of crime. The first type, the NCVSs, collected information from both central city households and commercial establishments. The second type, called the National Crime Panels, consisted of a national stratified multistage cluster sample of households and a two-stage probability sample of businesses. The unique characteristics of the crime panels were bounding of panels and reinterviews of respondents every six months until they were rotated out of the sample and replaced by a new unit.

Victim surveys are not without their problems. Principal among these problems are high cost, false reports, mistaken interpretation of incidents as crimes, memory failure and decay, sampling bias, over- and/or underreporting, telescoping, interviewer effects, and coding and mechanical error. In defense of surveys of victims, many of their shortcomings are also present in other techniques, and many of the problems identified are in part controllable through the use of panels, bounding, quality control, overcoding, reverse record checks, studies of known victim groups, reinterviews, and interviews of persons who know the victim. As was the case with self-report surveys, victim surveys provide a valuable additional assessment of crime.

Beginning in 1986, redesign of the NCVS began to be implemented. This redesign included plans to use CATI and, in the future, possibly CAPI. The redesigned NCVS improved particularly the measurement of domestic violence.

KEY CONCEPTS

Structured interviews	Telephone surveys	Dark figure of crime
Unstructured interviews	Advantages/	Victim surveys
Depth interviews	disadvantages of	NCVS
Advantages/	telephone surveys	Crime panels
disadvantages	Screening questions	Bounding
of interviews	CAPI	Some problems in
Interviewer effect	CART	victim surveys
Randomized response	CATI	Telescoping
technique (RRT)	ASCASI	Demand characteristics
Probing	CASI	Benefits of victim
Editing	SPSS	surveys
Vignettes	Random digit dialing	Reverse record check
Scenarios	Branching procedure	

REVIEW QUESTIONS

1. What are some distinct advantages of interviewing as a data-gathering strategy? Discuss some interviewing aids that further enhance this technique.

2. Suppose you were the director of a research project and assigned the task of running a short training program for the interviewers. What are some specific points you would present?

3. Compare the NCVS with the UCR as measures of crime in the United States.

4. What are some methodological problems in victim surveys as well as some means of controlling for them?

5. What are some techniques employed in telephone surveys, particularly in those that are designed to overcome identified shortcomings of telephone surveys?

6. What impact does the wording of questions have on response in surveys, public opinion polls, and victim surveys?

7. Discuss some redesign features of the NCVS particularly as it relates to the measurement of domestic violence.

USEFUL WEB SITES

National Crime Victimization Survey *www.ojp.usdoj.gov/bjs/cvict.htm*

The Survey System (Creative Research Systems) *www.surveysystem. com/sdesign.htm#top*

Crime Victimization Survey Software (Version 1.3) *www.ojp.usdoj. gov/bjs/pub/pdf/questions.pdf*

Telephone Interview Methodology (Washington State University) *http://survey.sesrc.wsu.edu/methodologies/telephone_surveys.htm*

Electronic Journals in Qualitative Research *www.qualitativeresearch. uga.edu*

Research Navigator *www.researchnavigator.com/articles/research.asp? p=171027seqnum=2*

Office of Juvenile Justice and Delinquency Prevention (OJJDP) *www. ojp.usdoj.gov*

Guide to BJS Web Site *www.ojp.usdoj.gov/bjs*

7

Participant Observation and Case Studies

Who are Chic Conwell, Doc, Long John, Vince Swaggi, Harry King, and Stanley the "Jack-Roller"? They are pseudonyms of legendary subjects of social science field studies and "native guides" to the criminal "turf" as well as to some of the most fascinating literature in criminology. In this chapter you will meet Chic Conwell, Sutherland's *The Professional Thief* (1937); Doc and Long John, members of Whyte's *Street Corner Society* (1943); Vince Swaggi, Klockars' *The Professional Fence* (1974); Harry King, Chambliss' safecracker in *The Box Man* (1975); and Stanley, a mugger in Shaw's *The Jack-Roller* (1930), and Snodgrass' *The Jack-Roller at Seventy* (1982).

A Critique of Experiments and Surveys

Some researchers feel that social science and criminal justice research have been overdependent on the artificial elements of questionnaires, interviews, and experimental settings. Such data-gathering approaches are viewed as creating, as well as measuring, attitudes and bringing about atypical roles and responses (Webb et al., 1966). Such strategies intrude into a setting as foreign elements, are limited to cooperative and obtainable populations, and tend to elicit stooge effects or response sets, particularly with much of the early corrections research.

Whyte (1981) laments the recent ascendancy of quantitative methods and decline of qualitative fieldwork and says that if a history of the current period of sociology were to be written, one of the chapters would have to be "Captured by Computer."

Verbal Reports Versus Behavior

Critics of such quantitative research suggest that little relationship exists between attitude and behavior and that more "sensitizing" strategies involving field studies contain greater accuracy (Deutscher, 1966; Phillips, 1971). Such writers typically cite a classic study to illustrate their point of nonconvergence of attitude and behavior—LaPiere's "Restaurant Study" (LaPiere, 1934). LaPiere traveled with a Chinese couple to a large number of restaurants on the West Coast and observed the treatment they received. Only 1 of 251 establishments refused them service. Later, he sent the same establishments a questionnaire; more than 90 percent replied that they would deny service. The disparity between what people say (attitudes) and what people do (deeds) illustrates the hazards of attitudinal measurement of behavioral items.

Although Chapter 9 will discuss in detail the validity of verbal reports, Levine cites a number of studies in which respondents misreported known behavior that could have been checked. People were inaccurate in reporting voting behavior, time of vaccination of children, money in savings accounts, level of loan debt, sexual activity, class attendance, and school grades. Studies of known crime victims found that a significant number failed to report to interviewers victimizations that they had already reported to the police (Levine, 1976).

In Chapter 3, it was suggested that error is ever present, even in the best research. Critics of more quantitative and artificial means of measurement indicate that instead of speaking of error in measurement, it would be more accurate to speak of the *error of measurement* (Deming, 1944; Phillips, 1971). These errors in surveys and experimental studies include variability in response as a result of the noncomparability of studies and differences caused by the methodologies employed. For example, telephone surveys may turn up greater victimization than face-to-face interviews. The degree and kind of canvass will impact on results. Interviewer bias, if unchecked, may produce error. In doing a study of rural elderly using five interviewing teams, this writer was startled to discover in a preliminary analysis the high level of fear of crime in what was assumed to be a pastoral setting. A quick check, however, revealed that one interview team produced the majority of cases in which crime was a perceived problem. During our weekly staff meeting it came to light that one of the interviewers, an elderly woman, had recently been victimized and unconsciously led her respondents into seeing crime as a primary problem. Fortunately, this was caught and corrected before it did major harm to the study results (Hagan, 1972).

Bias of auspices or sponsorship may compromise the results of many studies. For this very reason many criminal justice programs bring in outside, objective evaluators to analyze program outcomes. Certainly, a study of the benefits of a product would be more suspect if conducted by the manufacturer of a product, rather than by an independent laboratory.

Design imperfections, in either the instrument or the analysis, can produce inaccurate results. Failure to account for nonrespondents may compromise the results of surveys. Nonrespondents may differ considerably from those who cooperate in a survey. Much survey research, although planned and designed by professionals, is conducted by "hired hands": individuals who may have little interest in the accuracy or are unaware of idiosyncrasies and subtleties in data. Sussman and Haug (1967) point out that unchecked mechanical errors in coding and data entry may be more serious in survey data than many assume. Sampling errors and nonrepresentative samples may lead to error, as might errors in interpretation of findings on the part of the researchers.

Orne found that subjects in his experiments were willing to put up with boring, uncomfortable, painful, and ridiculous tasks if asked to do so by the experimenter. In fact, he was unsuccessful in finding experimental tasks that the subjects would refuse to perform. Most would yield to any request because "it's an experiment" (Orne, 1974). In one attempt to assign an obnoxious task, respondents were asked to perform serial additions of rows of digits and then tear up their answers and start all over again. The subjects so eagerly continued this dull and senseless task without refusal that the experimenter finally gave up (Orne, 1974, p. 142).

For these and other reasons, some critics feel that findings based on surveys and experiments are questionable, that much "artificial" research is really measurement error ("error of measurement"); therefore, more natural methods of data gathering should be employed.

A Defense of Quantitative Research

In defense of quantitative methods, it should be reiterated from Chapter 3 that error is ever present in all research. Many of these errors are not the exclusive problem of surveys and experiments alone but can be found in the very methods advocated by the critics. *The only perfect research is no research.* Also, many errors are not additive in their effect and may cancel each other, just as many of these potential errors are not inevitable but can be controlled before the fact, through research design, or after the fact, through statistical analysis.

Chapter 9 will illustrate that no data-gathering methodology alone has any guaranteed inherent superiority over another. So, although the problems with surveys and experiments may have been overstated, these criticisms remain the major reasons why some prefer more natural field methods, ethnographic or qualitative measures, such as participant observation.

Participant Observation

Participant observation has long been the favorite tool of anthropologists in studying preliterate tribes (Bernard, 1994). This is so much the case that it has been suggested in jest that the typical Navajo family consists of a grandparent, mother, father, three children, and an anthropologist.

Participant observation refers to a variety of strategies in which the researcher studies a group in its natural setting by observing its activities and, to varying degrees, participating in its activities.

Participant observation

A very moving call for field studies in an unpublished statement by Robert Park in the 1920s was recorded by Howard Becker, one of Park's students at the time:

You have been told to go grubbing in the library, thereby accumulating a mass of notes and a liberal coating of grime. You have been told to choose problems wherever you can find musty stacks of routine records based on trivial schedules prepared by tired bureaucrats and filled out by reluctant applicants for aid or fussy do-gooders or indifferent clerks. This is called "getting your hands dirty in real research." Those who thus counsel you are wise and honorable; the reasons they offer are of great value. But one thing more is needful: first hand observation. Go and sit in the lounges of the luxury hotels and on the doorsteps of the flophouses; sit on the Gold Coast settees and on the slum shakedowns; sit in Orchestra Hall and in the Star and Garter Burlesk. In short, gentlemen, go get the seat of your pants dirty in real research. (McKinney, 1966, p. 71)

The Chicago School of Sociology in the 1920s not only got the seat of their pants dirty, but positively wore them out, along with shoes and pens. Much of the early ethnographic work in criminology was pioneered by the students of this school. Perhaps with the demise of the funded "golden age of criminal justice research" (the 1970s), researchers may return to the qualitative methods and people-oriented Chicago School style research (Reichel, 1985).

The target populations of criminal justice research—the public, victims, criminals, and criminal justice functionaries—have been subject to a variety of methodological analyses. Although some fine examples of the use of participant observation exist in the field, it has been viewed as a neglected and underused technique in criminal justice. Despite this belief and police suspicion, clandestineness, and resistance to researchers, a disproportionate number of police studies have utilized participant observation as the major means of data gathering (Manning, 1972; Manning and Van Maanen, 1979; Sanders, 1977).

Contrary to advice offered by writers of leading criminology textbooks such as Sutherland and Cressey (1978), Polsky suggests that it is not unwise or impossible to study criminals in their natural environment. In his book *Hustlers, Beats, and Others*, Polsky (1967) describes how he successfully employed participant observation in studying uncaught organized criminals, pool hustlers, drug dealers, and con artists. Advocates of participant observation such as Polsky feel that we have been too dependent on studies of imprisoned criminals in an unnatural environment or on unquestioned use of official statistics, and that this has led to an inaccurate view of criminals and criminal behavior.

Previously, the point was made that all research may be viewed as a variation of the experimental model; Douglas (1972, 1976) suggests that, similarly, *participant observation may be viewed as the beginning point of all other research*. Before one can design a survey or experiment, one must observe the subject of the investigation sufficiently to know the proper areas to probe. As we have indicated, participant observation has been most heavily used in anthropology where it was often the only way of studying preindustrial groups without a written language, by employing methods other than questionnaires or other standard methods. It represents a commitment to a more inductive or sensitizing strategy. Weber (1949) referred to such strategies as illustrative of a **Verstehen approach**, one in which the researcher purposefully attempts to understand phenomena from the standpoint of the actors or to gain critical insight through an understanding of the entire context and frame of reference of the subjects under study.

Those of you who have had internship or service learning experiences have a sense of verstehen. It is difficult to describe the changes that take place and perspectives gained, but those exposed to the experience gain critical

Verstehen approach

insights that enable a greater appreciation for others and the setting in which they live or work.

Ethnography, ethnomethodology, and field studies are other labels for techniques similar to, if not the same as, participant observation (Denzin and Lincoln, 1993; Garfinkel, 1967).

Glaser and Strauss (1967) call for a *grounded theory approach,* by which a theory is developed during the data gathering, thus grounding it in the real world, rather than artificially predetermining which hypotheses will be looked at.

Types of Participant Observation

Previously, participant observation was defined in terms of the degree to which participation and observation may vary. Figure 7.1 suggests how each of the following items may vary (Gold, 1958): complete participation, participant as observer, observer as participant, and complete observation.

Complete participation takes place when the researcher not only joins in but actually begins to manipulate the direction of group activity. Such a strategy is rare and tends to violate an essential element of good participant observation—that the researcher attempt to avoid influencing the attitudes or behavior of the subjects under study. Another way of viewing complete participation is to label it "disguised observation," a subject to be treated in detail in Chapter 8.

The most frequently cited example of complete participation in the social science literature is the case of a group of researchers who joined a small doomsday cult called *When Prophecy Fails* (Festinger, Riecken, and Schachter, 1956). Because the group was small, questions were raised as to the extent to which the researchers brought about the behavior they wished to investigate.

Describing his research strategy as "complete participation," Marquart (1986) worked as a prison guard for nineteen months while collecting data on prison life. He was able to enter into more sensitive aspects of guard work, particularly after he established his credibility by successfully defending himself against an attack by an inmate. The *participant as observer* is the type that most people identify as constituting participant observation. The researcher usually makes his presence known and, although attempting not to influence situations, tries to objectively observe the activities of the group.

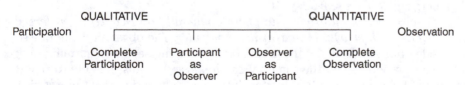

Figure 7.1
Types of Participant Observation.

Most of our discussion in this chapter will relate to this type. The *observer as participant* describes the one-visit interview. Even though the interviewers may not think so, they are also short-term participant observers. Holzman and Pines (1979) employed in-depth interviews of thirty primarily white, middle-class "johns" and were unable to find support for the "pathology-ridden depictions of the clients of prostitutes." Other examples involving in-depth interviews include Cressey's (1953) *Other People's Money*, which involved interviews with 133 incarcerated embezzlers; Klein and Montague's (1977) interviews with imprisoned, retired, and uncaught check forgers; and Letkemann's (1973) study of forty-five bank robbers and burglars. The last study provided much of what criminologists know regarding "casing" (looking over) of banks and the bank robber's dependence on uniformity of bank design, as well as handy parking. Experimental and unobtrusive measures may be viewed as a type of participant observation that stresses *complete observation*. Stein (1974), employing one-way mirrors, was able to secretly observe and record hundreds of sessions between prostitutes and their clients. In reality, specific studies seldom fall into any one of these categories, or "ideal types," and might better be viewed as falling along a continuum, as in Figure 7.1.

Henceforth, our discussion of participant observation will focus on the participant-as-observer type. It should be noted at this point that descriptions of and distinctions between types of participant observation, field interviews, and unobtrusive measures become somewhat arbitrary at times and that what one writer might call participant observation another might view as a type of interview or unobtrusive measure. Some studies are examples of more than one method; for example, an experimental design may be employed to conduct a simulation that involves disguised observation in which subjects are interviewed.

Characteristics of Participant Observation

Perhaps the most distinctive qualities of participant observation are its *demands on time and personal cost*. Cost here refers not to financial obligations but to personal involvement. As a general rule, the researcher is committed to studying a group for a considerable period, ranging from several weeks or months to several years. Participant observers hope to understand the frame of reference of the group they are studying. This is done by joining the group in their normal activities to experience things as they do. In doing so, the researcher may temporarily become a "different person" (Weinberg and Williams, 1972, p. 165).

The observer must attempt to operate mentally on two different levels: becoming an insider while remaining an outsider. The observer cannot be so far "inside," or socialized into the group, that everything seems so normal as not to be worth reporting. By the same token, the observer must be able to report patterns of behavior and interrelationships objectively and without moral bias. The role of "outsider" can be very valuable in that subjects may be willing to share important information because she or he is an outsider. Informants may be more willing to open up to neutral, reliable outsiders (Plate, 1975; Trice, 1970).

The researcher must avoid *oversocialization*, or *going native*. Some become so enamored by the new lifestyle of the group they are studying that they pass into a new identity and become too much a part of the group. Polsky, for instance, describes how some of the "uncaught criminals" he was studying told him that he would make a fine "wheelman" (driver of a getaway car) or "steer-horse" (accomplice who fingers the score in a con game) (Polsky, 1967). In doing his participant observation study of vice squads, Skolnick was asked to play a "john" (prostitute's customer), drive a stakeout van, surveil a bar for suspects, and offer advice on the legality of an arrest (Skolnick, 1966; National Advisory Committee, 1976, p. 131).

Objectivity in Research

The researcher must avoid not only overidentification with the study group but also aversion to it. The ability of social scientists to remain objective despite personal subjective bias is illustrated by the work of anthropologists. They occasionally find some of the attitudes, beliefs, and behaviors of the societies they study repugnant and immoral; however, they are trained not to judge but rather to record the meaning of these behavior patterns to the people who practice them. Famous anthropologist Malinowski, author of *Crime and Custom in Savage Society* (1926), *Argonauts of the Western Pacific* (1922), and other fine early studies of the Trobriand islanders, has been pointed to as a model of objectivity. Social scientists and others were shocked in the late 1960s when Malinowski's personal posthumous memoirs, *A Diary in the Strict Sense of the Word* (1967), were released. Although personally he found the group revolting, this bias was controlled and cannot be detected in his scholarly writings. This reflects an interesting debate in criminal justice research wherein Yablonsky, author of such field studies as *Synanon* (1965a) and *The Violent Gang* (1962), criticizes Polsky's view that the field researcher in criminal justice should avoid moralistic stances. Yablonsky (1965b) feels that such a posture is going too far, whereas Polsky claims that such a position is necessary to gain a full picture of group activity:

> Until the criminologist learns to suspend his personal distaste for the values and lifestyles of the untamed savages, until he goes out in the field to the cannibals and headhunters and observes them without trying either to civilize them or turn them over to colonial officials, he will be only a veranda anthropologist. That is, he will be only a jailhouse or courthouse sociologist, unable to produce anything like a genuinely scientific picture of crime. (Polsky, 1967, p. 147)

Manning looks at this same issue from the other side of the fence, in "Observing the Police":

> Does the observation, if it occurs, of brutality, harassment, incompetence, or malfeasance *obligate* the researcher to reveal immediately to the policeman's superiors, or should he overlook them and pussyfoot

in the interest of completing the study? Will a complete study have an even greater cumulative impact on the organization than revelation of instances of wrongdoing? (Manning, 1972, p. 258)

On this same general issue, some researchers take the stance that participant observation is obnoxious manipulation and immoral (Shils, 1961), or "psychological espionage," or necessary deception in order to obtain needed data (Gans, 1968). Becker perhaps best stated the argument supportive of Polsky's view of a nonmoralistic stance:

> In spite of the romantic yearnings of researchers and the earnest ideological assurance of some deviants, scientific requirements do not force us to join in deviant actions. But our scientific purposes often require us to hear about and on occasion to observe activities we may personally disapprove of. I think it equally indisputable that one cannot study deviants without foregoing a simple-minded moralism that requires us to denounce openly any such activity on every occasion. Indeed the researcher should cultivate a deliberately tolerant attitude, attempting to understand the point of view from which his subjects undertake the activities he finds distasteful. Amoralism that forecloses empirical investigation by deciding questions of fact *a priori* is scientifically immoral. (Becker, 1978a, p. 99)

"Going Native"

Soloway and Walters, in discussing ethnographic fieldwork, state the point succinctly: "Approaches must be found to avoid the dilemmas and pitfalls of a facile and unconstructive 'hipness' on the one hand and stagnating righteousness on the other" (Soloway and Walters, 1977, p. 176).

Perhaps an even more common outlook resulting from close contact with a new group over a sustained period is the *tendency of observers to overidentify with groups*. There are examples in the literature of an anthropologist who married a cannibal chief and of other individuals who, without being aware of it, have taken on the mannerisms of the groups they have studied. **Going native** is a situation in which the researcher identifies with and becomes a member of the study group and, in the process, abandons his or her role as an objective researcher. Toby (1986, p. 2) attacked criminologist John Irwin for a speech he gave before the American Society of Criminology, accusing him of romanticizing criminals:

Going native

> Irwin talks about prisoners as though all of them are victims of an oppressive society. And, in an aside to emphasize his point, he alluded to his personal history. (As is well known in the profession, Irwin served a prison term before becoming a criminologist.)
> Of course, John Irwin is not alone among criminologists in romanticizing criminals, in seeing virtue rather than moral flaws

in offenders. And I can well understand that a person who has himself served time in prison is aware of decent people, who, through adverse circumstances, committed crimes, were convicted and were sentenced to incarceration. I can even understand criminologists, who, like Edwin Sutherland, get to know and become quite attached to professional criminals. However, loving the man and hating the fault is quite different from denying the existence of the fault because criminals are human beings. . . .

I think of criminology as a discipline. By "discipline" I mean more than subject matter. I mean that we ought to restrain impulses, including benign impulses, that prevent us from seeing the world realistically. Just as anthropologists cannot be trusted (intellectually) when they go native to the extent that they glorify rather than study their preliterate societies, so a criminologist who has gone native cannot be trusted to tell us what criminals are like.

In 1999, a researcher at John Jay College of Criminal Justice was removed from a Health and Human Services–sponsored research project and accused of using, as well as buying, heroin for his research subjects. Allegedly he gave some junkies heroin as an incentive for granting interviews (Schneider, 1999).

General Procedures in Participant Observation

There is no one and only method of participant observation. There exists continual debate among field researchers themselves regarding specific operations; however, a core of customary procedures has accumulated with which researchers would not radically disagree, although they may on specific points.

McLuhan (1989, p. 167) whimsically stated that "the last person to ask how the water is is a fish." This is his way of suggesting that *it is generally not a good idea to attempt to study a group in which one has been a lifelong member*. First, the researcher is too far immersed in the culture to maintain objectivity. Second, the members of the group get to know the researcher too well and may often be unwilling to treat him or her as a researcher. The old speaker's rule of thumb holds that one must travel at least 100 miles from home grounds to be regarded as an expert.

Field Notes

One important practice that is essential in field studies is the *keeping of extensive and detailed* field notes *or diaries*. Webb et al. (1966, p. 196) state that "the palest ink is clearer than the best memory." Initial participant observation is often exploratory, and presumably the researcher does not fully understand the culture of the group. Thus, it is necessary to take complete notes on as many details as possible, even those that appear trivial, because it may be these very "unimportant details" that later provide the key to some important facet of the study. A good investigator records observations as often as possible and does not rely upon memory. As much importance and time should be allotted to recording observations as to participating, observing, and gathering such information. The participant observer, unlike the vacationer, cannot tell the reader that "you just had to be there to appreciate what I am telling you."

Berg claims that there is a 4:1 ratio of field-note writing to time in the field (Berg, 2007, p. 145). Novice field researchers in particular may wish to limit their initial time spent in actual fieldwork in order to assure that they will have the time and energy to put together quality field notes.

"Word crunching" (Dennis, 1984), the use of computers in qualitative analysis, has increased tremendously. Software programs such as Ethnograph (Tesch, 1990, 1991) are quite popular as is the adaptation of standard software packages such as Lotus 1-2-3, Gofer, HyperCard, WordStar, and WordPerfect (Berg, 2007, pp. 245–248). Word searches in WordPerfect, for example, can be utilized for content analysis purposes (Fielding and Lee, 1991).

Mnemonics

Often it is unwise or impossible to record notes on the spot. It may, however, be crucial that one be able to reconstruct in exacting detail much of what has taken place. Skilled researchers train themselves in an ancient art used by preliterate tribes to pass down word for word their traditions. Most are familiar with the closing chapter of Alex Haley's *Roots* (1976) in which Haley, after asking the tribal elder whether a Kunta Kinte ever lived in this village, received no direct answer. Instead he had to listen hour upon hour to an oral recitation of the chronological history of the tribe until the wise one mentioned the sought-for information. Using **mnemonics**, a system of memorizing, the elder was merely using his mind as a vast computer memory bank and effortlessly providing an extensive oral printout of information. We have all used *mnemonic devices*. In elementary school, "ROYGBIV" for the color spectrum, "*every good boy does fine*," and "FACE" for the musical scale, and poems to remember spelling or calendars, all provide useful tools for remembering. Anagrams (words or names), first letters of important lists, caricatures, and mental associations all permit later recall, reconstruction, and recording of important information.

Mnemonics

The recording of detailed notes on a dictaphone and their later transcription can be effective, although this method may prevent the researcher from thinking through the material and may yield huge transcripts that must be boiled down.

Other Recording Methods

Sanders (1977), in a participant observation study of detectives, quickly realized that taking notes made his subjects nervous. He cut down on this practice and began to leave the notebook open in the detectives' offices when he left each evening to show he had nothing to hide. Later he ceased taking notes on the spot altogether and used the time for relaxed observation to improve rapport. Sanders also took *photographs* to improve recall. These acted as a second type of field notes (Sanders, 1977, p. 200). Certainly, in the proper circumstances, tape recorders, videotapes, films, and other mechanical aids can greatly improve recall. Nevertheless, such devices must be used with caution or perhaps not at all if the subject matter is criminal activity, although they have successfully been employed with this group also (Klockars, 1977, p. 210; Sherizen, 1976).

Visual Criminology

The use of photographs in field studies has a long tradition particularly in anthropology (Emmison and Smith, 2000; Hurworth, 2003). Classic anthropologist Franz Boas used the technique in his study of the Trobriand Islanders. He used "photo-elicitation" in which photographs were shown to the subjects in order to get them to talk about specific rituals. There are a variety of other techniques that can be used. In "autodriving", the respondents themselves are asked to take photographs and to comment on them. "Reflexive photography" involves giving respondents cameras and asking them to take pictures that are then explored in subsequent interviews. "Photo novella" (picture stories) are another form of photo interviewing in which taking photos gives people a photo voice by later discussing particular needs or problems illustrated by these photos. Such techniques encourage more detailed interviews (Hurworth, 2003; Rose, 2001). Cecil Greek (2005) describes **visual criminology** as using photography as an ethnographic research method in criminal justice settings. Photographs can also be used for news media (crime photojournalism and war crimes photography) and the collection of evidentiary forensics and other legal material. He views visual criminology as a useful supplement and alternative to the dominant research paradigm of combining mathematics and text in academic criminology.

> Visual criminology

Whether the researcher is aware of it or not, a newcomer to a group is assigned a role by the old members. He or she is viewed as a potential, if not actual, disturbance. *Generally, it takes some time before the newcomer is accepted to the degree that the group becomes less suspicious and begins to act more naturally.* Usually, the smaller the group, the greater the potential disturbance introduced by the researcher; however, the longer the participant is present, the less the disturbance over time because he or she is eventually accepted by the respondents.

Tips on Participant Observation

In a classic statement on participant observation in criminology, Polsky (1967) offers some tips on studying criminals in their natural environment. He suggests that one should keep in mind that the *subject is in greater jeopardy as a result of being studied in the field* than is someone in jail. The researcher is more of an intruder, and the subjects are certainly freer not to cooperate. In studying criminals on their "turf," researchers should *avoid taking notes on the spot* and using standard data-gathering tools such as questionnaires or tape recorders. *Initially they should spend their time observing and listening, and avoid asking a lot of questions* (Spradley, 1970). The researcher's middle-class language styles and probing may prove irritating to subjects. William Foote Whyte, in *Streetcorner Society*, was never able to do an entirely success-ful analysis of the rackets in Cornerville because he blew an opportunity with a racketeer to whom he had been introduced (Whyte, 1943):

> One has to learn when to question and when not to question as well as what questions to ask.
>
> I learned this lesson one night in the early months when I was with Doc in Chichi's gambling joint. A man from another part of the city was regaling us with a tale of the organization of gambling activity I had been told that he had once been a very big gambling operator, and he talked knowingly about many interesting matters. He did most of the talking, but the others asked questions and threw in comments, so at length I began to feel that I must say something in order to be part of the group. I said: "I suppose the cops were all paid off?"
>
> The gambler's jaw dropped. He glared at me. Then he denied vehemently that any policemen had been paid off and immediately switched the conversation to another subject. For the rest of the evening I felt very uncomfortable.
>
> The next day Doc explained the lesson of the previous evening. "Go easy on that 'who,' 'what,' 'why,' 'when,' 'where' stuff, Bill. You ask those questions, and people will clam up on you. If people accept you, you can just hang around and you'll learn the answers in the long run without even having to ask the questions." (Whyte, 1943, p. 303)

These suggestions need not be limited to studying deviants, but apply to much field research in general. As an American Fulbright scholar in Uruguay, Smykla (1989, p. 29) described how his initial involvement entailed "inoffen-sive social interaction." This wins the subjects' confidence, identifies impor-tant contacts and who has the most prestige and insight, and permits the researcher to learn the words and symbols that will elicit response without forcing the researcher's own agenda and preconceptions.

Gaining Access

Polsky advises that one *learn the "argot"* (specialized jargon) of the group being studied, but avoid overusing it or trying too hard to be an insider. Initial introductions to criminals in the field may be gained by frequenting their haunts or sharing other common recreational interests. Becker (1963) recom-mends cabdrivers, reporters, bartenders, and cops as good sources of informa-tion on deviant hangouts, although his avenue to studying drug users was his performance in a jazz band. Polsky (1967) was very adept at playing pool, whereas Bryan (1965) was a counselor and gained access to other prostitutes through one of his clients who was in the trade. Some criminals spend a lot of time in court. Talese was successful in establishing contact with Bill Bonanno during a trial recess. Initially, he simply indicated that "Someday, months or years from now, I would like to sit down with him and discuss the possibility of writing a book about his boyhood" (Talese, 1971, p. 13). After many months Talese began to establish contact with young Bill and his family, although at first the family was suspicious and skeptical:

> Nor did I question them: I was sensitive to the situation and at this juncture I was more interested in the domestic atmosphere and the style of the people than in specific information. I was content to observe, pleased to be accepted. At night, after I returned home I recorded. (Talese, 1971, p. 501)

Becker (1978a) suggests various strategies for studying deviants. If previous status provides access to deviant groups, it should be taken advantage of. Ianni and Ianni were able to gain cooperation on the basis of mutual ethnic identity (Ianni and Ianni, 1972). Tewksbury and Gagne (2006, p.56) suggest the following roles to gain entry: knowledgeable insider, potential participant, marginal member, emphatic outsider, and knowledgeable outsider working with a knowledgeable insider.

If access is totally lacking, begin with incarcerated individuals. If the type of deviance being studied is prevalent, subjects may be obtained from larger samples of the population. Steffensmeier (1986, p. 1) describes how he first decided to undertake his study of The Fence, "Sam Goodman":

> I first met Sam Goodman, a white male, nearly sixty years of age, through the recommendation of several burglars I had been interviewing as part of a research project on the topic of female criminality. "Talk to Sam," they advised, "He's an 'old head,' knows his way around if anybody does." I did interview Sam—in January of 1980 in the Midstate Penitentiary where he was serving a three year term for stolen property. During this interview, in questioning Sam about the types of crimes women commit and the criminal roles they play, I found my interest shifting to questions about Sam himself, his life and his colorful criminal career. Since then, I have regularly interviewed and studied Sam, even after his release from prison in the summer of 1981 and on into the present time. (In 1994, Sam passed away, but not before contacting Steffensmeier and having him visit.)

Advertising for subjects in periodicals geared to their interests has been successfully employed (Lee, 1969). Finally, the offering of services that deviants need or cannot readily obtain elsewhere may induce them to reveal themselves. Bryan, for instance, offered counseling services to prostitutes (Becker, 1978a; Bryan, 1965; Johnson, 1990). Cromwell, Olson, and Avary (1991) gave a stipend of fifty dollars for each active burglar referred to their study of thirty active (uncaught) burglars. In addition, confidentiality and anonymity were promised in encouraging respondents to reconstruct their past burglaries as accurately as possible. Such insider accounts are very useful in acquainting researchers with the perspectives of the subjects (Cromwell, 1996). Exhibit 7.1 describes gaining access in a study of skinheads.

In 2008, the Pew Center on the States reported that more than one in hundred American adults was incarcerated, the largest per capita rate in the world. This fact makes research on what is taking place in such settings even more imperative. Scholars who undertake ethnographic research in prisons complain of growing hurdles to doing such investigations. These include

EXHIBIT 7.1 ▶

American Skinheads: The Criminology and Control of Hate Crime

Entering the world of violence, hate, and racial paranoia of skinhead subculture, "idiots with ideology," contains more than the usual challenge to field researchers. Similar to other field investigators (Thompson, 1967; Yablonsky, 1962), Mark Hamm's attempts were on one occasion greeted with violence. He was attacked by members of the American Front at the corner of Haight and Ashbury in San Francisco. Kicked in the shins with a pair of steel-toed Doc Martens was his punishment for having been seen conversing with an Indonesian prostitute.

Hamm (1993, pp. 100–101) describes his method:

I began to systematically collect data on the American skinheads in the fall of 1989. Drawing from the native field study approach, I started the investigation by visiting various U.S. cities where I tracked down skinheads in their natural habitat (street corners, bars, coffee shops, record stores, survivalist outlets, rock concerts, and motorcycle shops). These subjects were not hard to identify. They had shaved heads and wore white power and/or Nazi regalia. Two skinheads, for example, were tattooed in the middle of their foreheads with the mark of the swastika. To gain a broader context for the research, I used the same methods to interview skinheads on the streets of Montreal, Vancouver, London, Amsterdam and Berlin.

He simply approached these youths and asked if they would consent to an interview in a research project that was attempting to "set the record straight on skinheads." No electronic devices were used. Hamm offered ten dollars for a completed interview. Another technique involved getting membership lists from the underground teen press and Tom Metzger's publication WAR (White Aryan Resistance).

After sending letters to twenty-six skinhead leaders promising twenty-five dollars for a collect call telephone interview, Hamm obtained nine interviews plus an unexpected dividend. Three additional unsolicited leaders heard about the research, called, and were interviewed. Nonrespondents were sent five copies of a questionnaire and asked to fill one out and pass the others to four other members, and they would be paid ten dollars. This produced eight additional usable questionnaires. Using the Internet, Hamm next logged onto the WAR board. He identified himself as a sociologist with no axe to grind and offered ten dollars to any skinhead who came online and conversed. This yielded two responses. Finally, Hamm used the prison field methods approach and, with the cooperation of authorities, was able to interview incarcerated skinheads in four states. Hamm (1993, pp. 102–103) concludes:

In summary, then, I conducted thirty-six original skinhead interviews using native field methods, clandestine community agency techniques, and prison field study strategies. I controlled for paranoia by primarily focusing on subcultural leaders—or core members who are likely to display the highest rates and severity of hate crime violence—and by presenting myself as a sociologist operating independent of law enforcement and community service agencies. The early Haight street assault notwithstanding, I experienced no life-threatening violence.

Source: Hamm, Mark S. *American Skinheads: The Criminology and Control of Hate Crime*. Westport, CT: Praeger, 1993.

suspicious wardens, state approval boards, and institutional review boards that can greatly slow down the process (Glenn, 2008a). Britton (2003), author of *At Work in the Iron Cage: The Prison as Gendered Organization*, suggests that scholarly research be proposed that can help wardens with practical problems in their prisons. Trulson, Marquart, and Mullings (2004) provide guidelines for those attempting to gain entry to hard-to-access places such as prisons. This includes not just gaining access but also maintaining access. Before the late 1970s, researchers gained entry to prison settings on the basis of employment (Carroll, 1974; Clemmer, 1940; Goffman, 1961; Irwin, 1985; Marquart, 1986) or a relationship with a connected person (Jacobs, 1977; Sykes, 1958). Since that time, gaining entry to correctional environments has become more complicated.

Human subject consent, institutional research boards, and issues such as researcher liability and institutional litigation made entry more difficult. Tulson, Marquart, and Mullings (2004, pp. 477–479) provide ten tips for "breaking into prisons" and other criminal justice organizations:

1. Get a contact.
2. Establish yourself and your research.
3. Little things count, such as being on time and showing up when it is convenient for them, not you.
4. Make sense of agency data by keeping in contact.
5. Deliver competent, readable reports on time.
6. Request to brief the agency, and give a formal presentation of your findings.
7. Write a personal thank-you note to everyone involved.
8. Deal with adversity by planning ahead.
9. Inform the agency of data use including providing copies of the publication.
10. Maintain trust by staying in for the long haul and keep in contact.

Gatekeepers

Of major assistance in gaining access to a new social world is an *introduction to a gatekeeper, leader, or person who is willing to accept the purpose of the study and vouch for the researcher's presence.* A community worker's introduction of Whyte to Doc, leader of the Norton Street Gang, made access to Cornerville possible because Doc told everyone that Whyte was his friend (Whyte, 1943). Agar (1977, p. 145) indicates that transfer to the street with a trusted "native" has several advantages:

1. You have a guide to the territory. You quickly learn the social spaces in the neighborhood and the kinds of persons and activities that occupy each.
2. You have an introduction into at least some groups on the scene. The importance of this cannot be overemphasized. A straight outsider is often a "mark" just waiting for a disaster to occur. An introduction from a trusted insider immediately establishes an openness together with certain rights and obligations as so-and-so's friend.

Walker and Lidz (1977) suggest the employment of "indigenous observers," paid researchers from the ranks of those to be studied. Such remuneration is viewed as tangible reciprocity, or evidence of respect; such employment helps some to improve their circumstances; however, researchers must be certain that they are not eliciting demand characteristics or the creation of work as a result of the pay offer.

Adler in "Researching Dealers and Smugglers" (2000) gained access to drug dealers and smugglers by befriending a neighbor who was a member of one of the drug smuggling crew. Patricia Adler observed the neighbor at work and got to know other members of the crew and their women. The crew advanced the author's research by serving as key informants and giving taped interviews.

Announcement of Intentions

Polsky (1967) suggests that if researchers gain access on the basis of some common interest, for instance, gambling or drinking, they should very early on *indicate their true purpose*: "do not pretend to be one of them." Most subjects will accept the simple explanation that the researcher is writing a book on the subject, although Orenstein and Phillips (1978, p. 312) correctly recommend that a far more detailed explanation be given to the leaders, sponsors, or contact who must answer for the investigator's presence.

Sampling

Because of the very nature of most participant observational studies in criminal justice, particularly of sensitive subjects, the use of standard sampling procedures is inappropriate. Chapter 4 discussed *snowball sampling* as a much-used technique in field studies, in which the investigator builds subjects on the basis of faith and the introductions of former subjects. This further reinforces the necessity of being "up front" with key contacts.

Reciprocity and Protection of Identity

Reciprocity involves a system of mutual obligations. The research subjects help the investigator; now what is owed them?

Reciprocity would entail that the researcher permit the subjects to study him or her by answering questions they may ask. Of great importance in participant observation, particularly of criminals in the field, is *protection of the identity of informants*. Most researchers use *pseudonyms (aliases)* to shroud the actual names of the subjects. Some of these pseudonyms have now become legendary in criminology and criminal justice: Sutherland's professional thief "Chic" Conwell (Sutherland, 1937), the Iannis' Lupollo organized crime family (1972), and Klockars' professional fence Vincent Swaggi (1974). Related to this issue is the need for researchers to *decide beforehand the degree to which they wish to be privy to criminal activity*. Klockars (1977, p. 214) struck a deal with Vincent: "I also told Vincent that I would not reveal his identity unless it meant that I was going to jail if I did not, and he told me that he really could not expect me to do more."

Polsky (1967) tells us that although a researcher should not pretend to be "one of them," he or she should also not stick out like a sore thumb. For instance, Polsky wore short-sleeved shirts and an expensive watch in studying heroin use and trafficking. This signaled that he was not a user since an addict would have track marks from "shooting up" heroin and would have sold any items of value such as a watch in order to support his or her habit.

Finally, as we will discuss later in this chapter, not everyone should attempt to gather data by means of this technique. First, long hours of boredom may make huge demands on time before the few things the researcher wishes to observe occur. Second, there is *danger*; for instance, organized crime member Bill Bonanno was concerned with Talese's welfare during the "Banana Wars" in New York (Talese, 1971). Polsky (1967, p. 141) tells us that "most of the danger for the field worker comes not from the cannibals or headhunters, but from colonial 'officials.'"

Concern for Accuracy

Participant observers should, where possible, employ other methods to further validate findings (Irwin, 1972). The Iannis developed a pecking order or scale that they used to assign validity to the data they gathered (from highest to lowest):

1. Data gathered by direct observation where we were participants.
2. Data gathered by direct observation where we were not direct participants.
3. Interviews that can be checked out against documented sources, for example, records of arrest or business ownership.
4. Data corroborated by more than one informant.
5. Lowest priority is assigned to data gathered from only one source. In addition, informants were graded from "always reliable" to "unreliable" (Ianni and Ianni, 1972, pp. 188–189).

Similarly, Steffensmeier, in *The Fence: In the Shadow of Two Worlds* (1986, pp. 4–6), indicates the following validity checks:

1. The interview format provided a cross-check: Did the second, third, and fourth interviews all say the same thing? Some interviews were also tape recorded, and some were checked by Sam Goodman (the subject) himself.
2. Documents such as newspapers, personal documents, court records, letters, sales receipts, advertising, and the like were examined.
3. Observations of Sam at work were supplemented with interviews and meetings with customers, friends, and dealers.
4. Consultation took place with police and legal officials.
5. The data were consistent with biographies and autobiographies of thieves.

Another way of verifying the accuracy of observations is to use "member checking." This involves having participants check your report to see if you are misinterpreting or misunderstanding anything.

Examples of Participant Observation

This writer's personal interest in participant observation may be related to the fact that I was an unknowing subject in a journalistic field study by James Gittings (1966) entitled *Life Without Living: People of the Inner City*, a series of studies he conducted in the Pittsburgh and New York City areas. Part of his study of Millvale (near Pittsburgh) was a description of a corner gang—"the bridge boys"—with whom I occasionally had contact. From my youth, I recall a man (who, in retrospect, I now assume was working under the cover of a care-taker at a local private girls' high school) who would strike up conversations with us. In his book, Gittings described quite accurately local political corrup-tion, gambling operations, and a gang war that occurred while I was away at college. The competing sides in the battle ironically consisted of boys this writer had grown up with in his old neighborhood (in Pittsburgh) versus "the bridge boys" and others in his new neighborhood.

Although we have discussed a number of participant observation studies, some further examples demonstrate the versatility of such studies. Having previously conducted a participant observation study of a chapter of the Guardian Angels in Detroit, Albini (1986) conducted a field study from 1983 to 1984 of all Guardian Angels chapters in the United States and Canada. He underwent training, became a member of the organization, and patrolled with every chapter, concluding that they were not vigilantes as some had charged. Taylor (1984) in *In the Underworld* performed a two-year field study of uncaught professional criminals in the London underworld, whereas the Adlers in *Wheeling and Dealing* (1985) interviewed and observed for six years upper-level cocaine and marijuana dealers and smugglers. Sullivan (1989) spent more than four years studying youth gangs and crime on the streets of Brooklyn, while Sanchez Jankowski (1991) spent over ten years studying gangs in three cities (see Exhibit 7.2). Eleanor Miller (1986) did field research inter-viewing sixty-four prostitutes in Milwaukee, Marquart (1986) worked as a prison guard, and Hopper (1991) studied outlaw motorcycle gangs. Wright and Decker in *Armed Robbers in Action* (1997) and *Burglars on the Job* (1994) conducted field interviews with uncaught, active burglars and armed robbers. Caputo (2008) in *Out in the Storm: Drug Addicted Women Living as Shoplifters and Sex Workers* conducted three years of ethnographic research with 38 women with drug addictions primarily in the Philadelphia area. In order to support themselves they were involved in shoplifting and sex work.

In addition to participant observation studies of criminals and the public by Polsky (1967), Whyte (1943), Thrasher (1927), and Humphreys (1970), a variety of such studies have been done with the police as subjects. Kirkham (1976) in *Signal Zero* was a professor who became a police officer. Reiss (1971) and Skolnick (1966) did field studies of police operations. Numerous other examples exist in the literature, including case studies that concentrate on fewer subjects. The sometimes humorous subjects of participant observa-tion are represented in such titles as "The Milkman and His Customer: A Cultivated Relationship" (Bigus, 1978) or "The Cabdriver and His Fare: Facets of a Fleeting Relationship" (Davis, 1959).

EXHIBIT 7.2 ▶

Islands in the Streets

From 1978 to 1989 Martin Sanchez Jankowski conducted a participant observation study of about thirty-seven gangs in Boston, New York, and Los Angeles. The gangs were African American, Jamaican, Puerto Rican, Dominican, Chicano, Central American, and Irish as well as those of mixed ethnic origins. Jankowski's entree required two steps. First, he contacted community individuals or agencies that worked with these gangs and arranged introductions and subsequent meetings with gang leaders. He simply explained to the leaders that he was a professor and wanted to write a book, the idea of which many found interesting. Despite a Polish last name from his adopted father, Jankowski's Latino ancestry eased his cooperation from Latino and African American gangs.

Next, the gangs presented Jankowski with two tests. To test whether he was an informant, they committed illegal acts to see if he would turn them in to authorities. He was on one occasion falsely accused and physically attacked. The second test (for all gangs but the Irish) involved what other gang observers call a "beat down" or initiation rite. Jankowski would have to demonstrate how tough he was when other members would start a fight with him. Despite his training in Karate, this test created much anxiety. In the ten years of research he was only seriously injured twice.

After the initial period of suspicion, the gangs tended to forget or no longer care that he was conducting research. He was often with them during some risky situations and apparently handled himself up to their expectations. Perhaps the ultimate compliment was, "You don't look like a professor," and/or, "You don't act like one" (p. 13). Jankowski explains:

> In sum, I participated in nearly all the things they did. I ate where they ate, I slept where they slept, I stayed with their families, I traveled where they went, and in certain situations where I could not remain neutral, I fought with them. The only things I did not participate in were those activities that were illegal. As part of our mutual understanding, it was agreed that I did not have to participate in any activity (including taking drugs) that was illegal. (p. 13)

Jankowski carried two notebooks, a small pad and a larger $8\frac{1}{2}$ by 11 inch pad. He would record notes on both of these as well as use two tape recorders, one regular size and the other pocket size. The latter was used to record notes during the day. All of this was done, of course, with the gangs' permission.

Source: Jankowski, Martin Sanchez. *Islands in the Streets*. Berkeley, CA: University of California Press, 1991.

Hate groups have also been studied. Quarles (1991, 1997) studied members of the Ku Klux Klan (KKK), while Aho (1994) did a participant observational study of Christian Patriots in Idaho (see Exhibit 7.3). Goldstein et al. (1990) have conducted participant observation studies of drug users utilizing "ethnographic field stations," outposts established in the community (such as store fronts) for the purpose of collecting data and as a setting for interaction between researchers and subjects (Goldstein et al., 1990). Such sites facilitate the collection of longitudinal data from fairly large samples and enhance the researcher's legitimacy in the neighborhood. Indigenous observers (people from the neighborhood) were employed by Hagedorn (1994) to study gang members. They characterized four types of gang members: legits, homeboys, dope fiends, and new jacks. While "legits" were those who had matured out of the gang, "homeboys" represented the majority of African American and Latino adult gang members who alternated between legitimate jobs and drug sales; "dope fiends" sold drugs to feed their own habits, while "new jacks" pursued such sales as a career.

EXHIBIT 7.3 ▶

This Thing of Darkness: A Participant Observation Study of Idaho Christian Patriots

In two works, *This Thing of Darkness: The Sociology of the Enemy* and *The Politics of Righteousness: Idaho Christian Patriotism*, sociologist Jim Aho (1994, 1990) does a participant observation study of right-wing hate groups in order to investigate what kind of people join such groups and how people get into and out of such affiliations. Aho's goal was to understand these people from their point of view by mingling with them, attending their church services, reading their literature, as well as viewing videotapes and listening to cassettes. He points out that his "library of infamy" forced his wife to encourage him to keep his collection at the office rather than at home because his children were having nightmares. He also used snowball sampling to interview over 350 members of the radical right.

Beginning as a self-described naive researcher, Aho indicates that reality compelled him to alter his tone and entire direction of research. He had assumed most of the people would be different from him. They were not. They were not uneducated, transient, from unstable marriages,

working in isolated occupations or victims of status insecurity. Most did not progress into becoming more extremist and, in fact, many eventually left the movement. For most, their involvement was based on primary group networks (e.g., family, neighbors, and fellow workers). He expresses the view that people in the conventional community must not cut off ties with those who have joined hate groups. It is possible that they can still change.

Aho's research was conducted in the 1980s; he indicates that he could not do this research now (Aho, 1996). He claims that he was naive at the time and one must be careful when associating with research subjects. Most of the people were likeable, even inviting him to dinner or to stay at their homes. Indicating that he has grown impatient with their strange ideas (particularly since the Oklahoma City bombing), he clearly states that these people are serious when they say they are going to kill someone and naiveté can be dangerous.

Sources: Aho, Jim. "Hate Groups." Presentation at Social Science Division Speakers Series, Mercyhurst College, Erie, PA, April, 1996; Aho, Jim. *This Thing of Darkness: The Sociology of the Enemy*. Seattle, WA: University of Washington Press, 1994; and Aho, Jim. *The Politics of Righteousness: Idaho Christian Patriotism*. Seattle, WA: University of Washington Press, 1990.

Other unusual subjects of participant observation have been Skipper's "Stripteasers" (1979), Weinberg's "Sexual Modesty: Social Meanings and the Nudist Camp" (1968), and Cavan's *Liquor License* (1966), a study of mating behavior in singles bars. It is incumbent on the researcher using participant observation to consider some of the relative advantages and disadvantages of the technique over other means available for gathering data. Mimicking the style of the Chicago school, Grazian's (2008) *On the Make: the Hustle of Urban Nightlife* combines his own participant observation of singles bars in Philadelphia with 811 student narratives of lies and deceit in such nightclubs. "One of the themes of *On the Make* is the intense emotional labor of workers in such settings involved in maintaining jovial, flirtatious faux relationships with hundreds of customers each week (Glenn, 2008, p. 316).

Two recent works examine the extremes or edge of participant observation. Miller and Tewksbury in *Extreme Methods: Innovative Approaches to Social Science Research* (2001) and Ferrell and Hamm in *Ethnography at the Edge: Crime, Deviance, and Field Research* (1998) describe "edge or radical ethnography" or "edgework" involving researchers going to extremes if necessary to pursue their subject matter. Such methods may be viewed by some as unethical, dangerous, and innovative. Some examples include Lozano and Foltz (2001), who studied a coven of witches, while Ronai and Ellis's (2001) study of strippers involved the senior author as a full participant. Myers (2001) studied body modification including genital piercing, branding, burning, and cutting. Ferrell (1998) was an active participant in a hip-hop graffiti underground that he described as "illegal field research." Mattley (1998) did fieldwork with phone fantasy workers.

Advantages of Participant Observation

Participant observation represents a commitment to a sensitizing or "verstehen" strategy in which the researcher attempts to actually experience the life conditions of the study group. Such an approach generally produces *less prejudgments*, is *less disturbing* to respondents than experiments, and is *more flexible* and natural than more artificial means of data gathering. Contradictions between attitude and behavior become apparent. Being on the scene, the researcher can double-check assumptions regarding the meaning of observations. It is an excellent means of gathering detailed *qualitative data*, particularly on subjects about which little information may exist. All of this takes place in *more natural settings* in which the subjects normally carry out their activities. Participant observation has produced some of the most fascinating, informative, and readable literature in criminology and criminal justice. In addition, a full picture of criminal behavior should incorporate the offender's perspective (Wright and Bennett, 1990, p. 149).

Disadvantages of Participant Observation

A principal disadvantage of participant observation is its *very time-consuming nature*. Commitments of several months or even years are not uncommon. This may take precedence over one's previous lifestyle. It certainly is not the easiest way of performing a study, nor is it the preferred method for most. Carey describes such problems in studying "speed freaks" (those who inject massive quantities of amphetamines):

> The peculiar round of life . . . posed enormous practical difficulties. . . . Our conventional commitments . . . had to be put aside. . . . We were continually reassured by our medical collaborators that the possibility of contracting hepatitis was extremely remote. . . . It caused constant concern while in the field, however, for every vague malaise was interpreted as the onset of hepatitis. . . . Our middleclass notions of hygiene led to feelings of revulsion at the physical conditions in one flash house where most of our observations were conducted. (Carey, 1972, p. 82)

The observer is often not in a position to control the action and must often wait for the activities of interest to occur. In studying criminal groups, for instance, researchers may have to spend hours or days participating in what some may regard as boring activities, for example, marathon card games or drinking bouts before something noteworthy happens. As discussed previously, *overidentification or dislike of the group being studied can be problematic.*

Participant observation poses the *problem of gaining entry into and acceptance by a group*. It is perhaps the *most personally demanding technique.* Whyte voted numerous times in the same local election, Humphreys broke the law, Becker performed in a jazz band, and others have faked symptoms of mental illness (Caudill, 1958; Goffman, 1961; Rosenhan, 1973).

Ethical dilemmas are sometimes raised by this technique, particularly if uncaught criminals are the subject of study. Reciprocity indicates that because the subjects have given of themselves, they are owed something. On the other hand, where does one draw the line between the role as researcher and the role as responsible citizen? Those studying "deviant groups" may have to decide between participating in immoral or illegal conduct and blowing months of work.

There is a difference, however, between knowing about something illegal and actually doing it. This is the "it takes one to know one fallacy": the false belief that to understand a phenomenon one must have actively participated in it. Whyte (1943), having illegally voted numerous times, later expressed regret for having done so, finding it to be a foolish risk that did not increase insight. Certainly one would not have argued that Jonas Salk have polio to discover a cure or that Durkheim commit suicide to fully appreciate it. Although a researcher should avoid deceiving respondents, he or she must also avoid being deceived by the study group. The level of mutual cooperation is described by Sanders: "Instead of doing research 'on' detectives, the activity would be more accurately characterized as doing research 'with' detectives. In a way, the relationship was something like a master and an apprentice, with the researcher as the apprentice" (1977, p. 202).

Some researchers view deception as a necessary ploy to obtain information that cannot be gained in any other manner (Gans, 1968). Deception will be examined in greater detail in Chapter 8.

Participant observers must make major attempts to control their biases, which may heavily influence what they observe, record, and interpret. Liebow (1967), a white anthropologist studying lower-class black streetcorner men in the early 1960s, apparently had fewer problems than a middle-class black researcher doing a similar study as part of the same project. Fujisaka and Grayzel (1978), in an ethnographic prison study report on *observer bias* or "subjectivity," obtained different results in the same setting because of differences in their own social backgrounds.

A major challenge to participant observation is the fact that it generally *yields nonquantitative data* and thus may require greater literary and analytic skill at the write-up stage.

Case Studies

Case study methods are in-depth, qualitative studies of one or a few illustrative cases (Becker, 1978b). The types of studies included as examples of the case study approach vary greatly, from general field studies to studies of one individual. Because no consensus exists, we take the more general approach to case studies in this discussion.

Travis (1983, p. 46) has noted a decline in coverage of the case study approach in criminology and criminal justice texts and attributes this to its eclipse by quantitative methods and the unfortunate labeling of any case study as an example of a "one-shot case study" by Campbell and Stanley (1963).

Life History/Oral History

Life histories and oral histories are some methodologies employed in case studies. *Oral and life histories* are "recounts of events by participants" (Laub, 1983, p. 226). Journalists use the term *autobiography*, whereas historians and social scientists use *documentary expression* or *oral history*. Laub (1983), in *Criminology in the Making: An Oral History*, examines the history of criminology by means of in-depth interviews with major criminologists. In the 1990s, Frank Taylor has been instrumental in organizing and conducting the "Oral History Project," a joint undertaking of the Academy of Criminal Justice Sciences and the American Society of Criminology, to conduct videotape interviews with pioneers in criminal justice and criminology. Such research can be used to test theories and generate hypotheses for future research, as well as sensitize researchers to important questions (Laub, 1984). In addition, many subjects are not susceptible to more quantitative treatment, and case studies can provide insight into the subjective elements of institutional processes (Bennett, 1981; Bertaux, 1981; Kobrin, 1982).

Some Examples of Case Studies

Concentrating on single individuals, groups, or communities and employing life history documents, oral histories, in-depth interviews, as well as participant observation (Yin, 1994), the case study is quite versatile and has generated some fascinating literature. The classic example of a landmark case study in criminology was Sutherland's (1937) *The Professional Thief*, in which his informant, Chic Conwell, described the world of the professional thief. Some other examples from the academic literature are the Iannis' (1972) study of the Lupollo family in *A Family Business: Kinship and Social Control in Organized Crime* and Shaw's *The Jack-Roller* (1930), *Brothers in Crime* (1938), and *The Natural History of a Delinquent Career* (1931). Shaw's "Jack-Roller" (mugger), "Stanley," was followed up by Snodgrass (1982) in *The Jack-Roller at Seventy: A Fifty-Year Follow-up*. Klockars' *The Professional Fence* (1974) (a dealer in stolen property), given the pseudonym "Vince Swaggi," has his counterpart in Steffensmeier's *The Fence* (1986) and "Sam Goodman." Chambliss' *Box Man* (1975), a case study of a professional safecracker, has since been updated and entitled *Harry King: A Professional Thief's Journal* (King and Chambliss, 1984).

Darrell Steffensmeier and Jeffrey Ulmer updated Steffensmeier's classic with *Confessions of a Dying Thief* (Steffensmeier and Ulmer, 2006). They presented three decades in the life history of Sam Goodman, a professional fence. Steffensmeier's close relationship with a dying Sam Goodman illustrates the fact that research subjects and researchers can become more than just observers and subjects.

Many other case studies too numerous to detail have been employed in criminology and criminal justice and include studies of chronic alcoholics (Spradley, 1970), an armed robber (Allen, 1977), vice lords (Keiser, 1969), heroin addicts (Agar, 1973; Rettig, Torres, and Garrett, 1977), a jewel thief (Abadinsky, 1983), a "wise guy" (organized crime member) (Abadinsky, 1983), and an organized crime family (Anderson, 1979). Case studies of communities are illustrated by the President's Crime Commission study of "Wincanton" (Reading, Pa.) (Gardiner and Olson, 1968) and Blok's (1975) study of the Mafia

EXHIBIT 7.4 ▶

Confessions of a Dying Thief

Confessions of a Dying Thief : Understanding Criminal Careers and Illegal Enterprises by Darrell Steffensmeier and Jeffrey Ulmer (2006) is in part a twenty-year follow-up to Steffensmeier's *The Fence: In the Shadow of Two Worlds* (1986), but it is more than this. It uses "Sam Goodman's" ethnography to address important methodological and theoretical notions. Goodman was the pseudonym given to the professional thief that was the subject of these two case studies. Steffensmeier and Ulmer attempt to use Sam Goodman's life as a way of addressing major issues in Criminology. His life gives voice to a subculture that is not known by most criminologists and sociologists. His confessions tell us that deviants, even persistent criminals, are not deviant in all aspects of their lives. His life and accounts do not support life course/developmental theory, but do demonstrate the rewards and motives for criminal entrepreneurship. They challenge our simplistic views of criminal opportunity. *Confessions* provides an in-depth life history and picture of the criminal underworld as well as a look at criminal entrepreneurship more generally.

The book is not simply a case study, but a theory and methods book illustrated by a longitudinal case study. Sam's narrative is constantly checked against theories and methods. It is reminiscent of earlier, longitudinal studies such as Snodgrass' *The Jack-roller at Seventy* (1982), a follow-up of Shaw's (1930) study of Stanley. *The Jack-roller* and Gans' *The Urban Villagers* (1962), a follow-up of Whyte's *Street-corner Society* (1943). Steffensmeier and Ullmer attempt to correct for the fact that the prison samples used in most existing studies fail to represent successful offenders for whom crime is very remunerative. They feel that the field of criminology has become dominated by theories on petty criminals and that the "life course" perspective is not only not a new perspective but one that ignores a large portion of chronic serious offending. They criticize writers such as Moffit (1999) who they claim inaccurately sees the cause of persistent criminality as biological inferiority and inherited differences. The relationship between Steffensmeier and Goodman obviously was far more than one of researcher and subject and provides a vivid picture of the world of professional crime.

Sources: Much of this exhibit is drawn from Frank Hagan's remarks at "The Author Meets The Critics" session at the Academy of Criminal Justice Sciences Meetings in Los Angeles, California, March, 2006 on the occasion of the book receiving the Hindelang Award for Best New Book of the Year. Steffensmeier, Darrell. *The Fence: In the Shadow of Two Worlds*. Totowa NJ: Rowman and Littlefield, 1986; Steffensmeier, Darrell and Ulmer, Jeffery. *Confessions of a Dying Thief*. Totowa NJ: Rowman and Littlefield, 2007; Snodgrass, Jon. *The Jack-roller at Seventy*. Lexington, MA: D.C. Heath, 1982; Shaw, Clifford. *The Jack-roller*. Chicago, IL: University of Chicago Press, 1930; Gans, Herbert. *The Urban Villagers*. New York: The Free Press, 1962; Whyte, Jr., and William F. *Streetcorner Society*. Chicago, IL: University of Chicago Press, 1943; Moffit, Terry. "Adolescence limited and life course persistent antisocial behavior: A developmental theory," in Frank Scarpitti and Anne Nielsen, editors. *Crime and Criminality*. Los Angeles CA: Roxbury, 1999, pp. 206–231.

in a Sicilian village. Travis (1983) cites many one-time studies of such agencies as the police, corrections officers, and courts as representative of the numerous case studies in the field.

Journalistic Field Studies

A discussion of case studies would not be complete without mention of the many fine works by investigative journalists. A foremost sociological field researcher, William Foote Whyte (Fox, 1980, p. 2) acknowledges his debt to the writings of turn-of-the-century journalist Lincoln Steffens, author of *The Shame of the Cities* (1904), for having inspired him to undertake participant observation. Investigative journalists (similar to their television counterparts on "60 Minutes," "20/20," and "48 Hours") are interested in documenting and exposing social conditions and are generally less interested in theoretically incorporating their findings into the social science literature.

In *Paper Lion*, George Plimpton (1965) participated in the training camp of the Detroit Lions football team. In later investigations, he performed with a philharmonic orchestra and in a circus as a trapeze artist; played professional tennis; entered the entertainment industry; and was a photographer for *Playboy*, a professional hockey player, and a stand-up comic at Caesar's Palace (Plimpton, 1985). Thompson (1967) rode with the Hell's Angels motorcycle gang, whereas Talese (1971) studied the Bonanno organized crime family and also visited and worked in massage parlors (Talese, 1979). Terkel (1970, 1974, 1980, 1984) has made excellent use of first-person oral histories in describing historical events, such as the Depression and World War II, from the viewpoint of average people. Mills (1986) in *The Underground Empire* conducted a five-year field study of international drug trafficking organizations and concluded that the United States was fighting a two-faced war on drugs, one with phony rhetoric on the six o'clock news and the other with secret deals and tolerance of politically connected conspirators and countries in the name of foreign policy. Other collections of personal accounts and investigations (Denfield, 1974; Jackson, 1972; Plate, 1975) enable us to view the illegal world in the words of, and from the perspective of, the deviant. Firestone (1993) reviewed the extensive number of memoirs written by members of organized crime and notes how these accounts describe the erosion of mob ties, codes, and structures and the demise of the Mafia as we have known it.

The major advantage of the case study is its in-depth, qualitative view of a few subjects; the major problems associated with such methods are possible researcher bias and a typicality of the cases chosen for analysis.

The use of case study and life history material will be explored in further detail in our discussion of unobtrusive measures in Chapter 8, particularly in the discussion of biographies and autobiographies.

Single-Subject Designs

Not all case studies are qualitative. **Single-subject designs** are quantitative case studies that involve the longitudinal measurement of a dependent variable on a single subject or case. While time-series designs measure

Single-subject designs

groups, single-subject designs measure populations in which $N = 1$. In such designs the time interval is usually divided into a baseline period *(A)*, an intervention period *(B)*, and any number of additional variations.

Figure 7.2 depicts three types of single-subject designs (see Kazdin, 1982; or Tawney and Gast, 1984, for more detail).

AB is the *basic design*, while *ABA* or *ABAB* are examples of reversal designs. In the first such reversal design *(ABA)*, treatment is withdrawn *(A)* after a baseline period *(A)* and a treatment period *(B)*; in the last such design *(ABAB)*, after the treatment is withdrawn *(A)*, it is once again reintroduced *(B)*. *ABACA* is an example of a multiple-treatment design, where *C* represents a new treatment or one different from treatment *B* (Hagan, 1989).

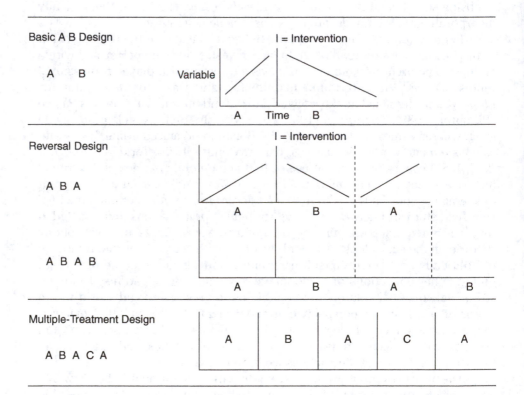

Legend

A = Baseline Phase or Period of Treatment Withdrawal

B = Treatment Phase

C, D = Additional Treatment Phase or Phases

Figure 7.2
Single-Subject Designs.
Source: Hagan, Frank E. "Single Subject Designs: A Strategy for Quantitative Case Studies." Paper presented at Academy of Criminal Justice Sciences Meeting, Washington, D.C., March 31, 1989.

By way of example, using the basic *AB* design, suppose that for the base-line period *A* we had plotted line *A*, measuring monthly levels of psychological depression of an inmate. The intervention *(I)* would entail starting the inmate in a counseling program, and line *B* would represent the measurement of monthly decreases in depression.

Traditional social science research utilizing group designs (*X*s and *O*s) is often inapplicable to case studies and practitioner needs. Hurwitz (1984, p. 41) contributed one of the few articles devoted to single-subject designs in criminal justice literature. In it he noted that relying on group designs (nomothetic) to measure the success of crime control programs blurs the individual cases of success or failure by using average achievement scores. As a result of this weakness in group designs, process evaluation models using time-series designs have become more popular; so too has the single-subject (idiographic) model, which assesses the intervention process with individual clients. The treatment may work for most individuals, but not all: "The treatment goals and desired direction of change for one individual may be counter to those of the overall group" (Robinson, Bronson, and Blythe, 1988, p. 38).

The single-subject technique is viewed as promoting research by practitioners simply because clinical service providers find it to be more practical than group designs. Such research provides hard evidence of a client's progress (Monette, Sullivan, and DeJong, 1994 p. 330). As with any case studies, single-subject designs do face the problem of generalizability—that is, can we generalize from this single case study to all such cases? However, replication is one means of addressing this concern. In the final analysis, single-subject designs appear to provide yet another useful methodological tool, which is particularly applicable to practice settings where group designs may not always be feasible.

Summary

Field study methods such as participant observation and case studies are viewed by their proponents as an *important alternative to more quantitative methods of data gathering* such as experiments and surveys. *Critics* of experiments and surveys point to a myriad of shortcomings, including artificiality, assumption of a connection between attitude and behavior, and the tendency of the findings to be a result of the method used rather than real findings. Type of canvass, instrument used, interviewer effects, biased sponsorship, nonresponse bias, mechanical errors, and demand characteristics of respondents are a few of the many rival causal factors that the critics feel invalidate many of the results of such studies. None of these problems is unique to more quantitative methods or is uncontrollable; thus, these criticisms do not inherently destroy the utility of such methods.

Participant observation is a strategy by which the researcher studies a group by, to varying degrees, participating in and observing their activities. Participant observation is a very useful technique in criminal justice and criminology and can be successfully employed to study uncaught, "successful" criminals, a much-needed approach in the field. In the past, criminal justice has been overreliant on studies using official statistics and incarcerated populations. Utilization of participant observation represents a commitment to a "verstehen," qualitative or sensitizing orientation, and renders in-depth descriptions of selected subjects.

Some *general characteristics* of these studies are their demanding nature (time and personal cost), simultaneous existence as an insider and an outsider, avoidance of overidentification as well as aversion, and maintenance of objectivity. Ethical issues related to such techniques are possible knowledge of illegal activities, confidentiality, privacy, and reciprocity.

General procedures in participant observation relate to the choice of study population, the need to keep a field diary, and mnemonic or other techniques for recalling events. *Suggestions for conducting field studies of criminals* are offered by those who have conducted such studies. Such topics as gaining access, acceptance, gatekeepers, proper conduct, gathering subjects, reciprocity, confidentiality, danger, and accuracy are discussed. *Single-subject designs* are described as quantitative case studies that involve longitudinal measurement of a variable dependent on a single subject or case.

Investigators considering the use of participant observation, in addition to considering the utilization of other techniques, should weigh the relative advantages and disadvantages of participant observation carefully before deciding to use it as the principal data-gathering device. *Major advantages* are fewer prejudgments, less disturbance, greater flexibility, more natural settings, and the sensitizing, qualitative nature of such studies. *Leading short-comings* are the very demanding nature of such research as well as such problems as gaining acceptance, maintaining objectivity, facing ethical dilemmas, avoiding oversocialization or aversion, and the nonquantitative nature of such information. Finally, *case studies* are briefly discussed as a form of participant observation that concentrates on one or a few illustrative examples. Examples of Hamm's skinheads study and Jankowski's *Islands in the Streets* were used to illustrate participant observation/field studies.

KEY CONCEPTS

Critique of experiments
  and surveys
Verbal reports versus
  behavior
Defense of quantitative
  research
Participant observation
Verstehen approach
Types of participant
  observation

Characteristics of
  participant observation
Objectivity in research
Going Native
General procedures
  in participant
  observation
Field notes
Mnemonics
Visual criminology

Participant observation
  of criminals
Advantages/
  disadvantages
  of participant
  observation
Single-subject design

REVIEW QUESTIONS

1. Mention some distinctive advantages of a qualitative strategy for data gathering, such as participant observation, over more quantitative approaches.

2. Mention some specific procedures followed by those conducting participant observation studies.

3. Discuss some of the special considerations participant observers must be aware of when studying criminals in field settings.

4. Of what importance have case studies been in criminological/criminal justice research? Provide examples that have used this approach.

5. Using Hamm's Skinheads and Jankowski's gang studies discuss some of the potential dangers as well as prospects of studying deviant groups on their turf.

USEFUL WEB SITES

Qualitative Research Methods (a Tutorial) *www.socialresearchmethods. net/tutorial/Mensah/default.htm*

The Qualitative Report (an Online Journal) *www.nova.edu/ssss/QR/ web.html*

Ethnographic Studies (Library of Congress) *http://lcweb.loc.gov/folklife/ other.html*

QualPage: Resources for Qualitative Research *www.qualitativeresearch. uga.edu/QualPage/*

Qualitative Social Research *www.qualitative-research.net/fqs/ fqs-eng.htm*

Introduction to Qualitative Research *www.uea.ac.uk/care/elu/issues/ research/res1cont.html*

How to Do Ethnographic Research *www.sas.upenn.edu/anthro/anthro/ cpiamethods*

8

Unobtrusive Measures, Secondary Analysis, and the Uses of Official Statistics

Unobtrusive measures are nonreactive methods of gathering data; that is, means of obtaining information in which subjects are not aware of being studied (Bouchard, 1976; Sechrest, 1980; Webb et al., 1966). The subject's lack of awareness of being studied eliminates reactivity or stooge effects. Sanders, in *The Sociologist as Detective* (1976), gives an excellent example of the use of unobtrusive measures by means of Conan Doyle's fictional master detective, Sherlock Holmes. Holmes, much like the social scientist, attempts to gather information to answer the research problem "Who killed the lord of the manor?" Through careful observation, questioning of respondents (suspects and witnesses), and collection and evaluation of evidence, he is able to speak of the plausibility of several rival hypotheses. Did the butler or rejected brother do it? Did the victim commit suicide? If the family dog did not bark the evening of the murder, perhaps the culprit was a friend or family member. Does one of the suspects develop a nervous tic when questioned? Other evidence is gathered through crime scene investigation or the analysis of physical evidence. Did the murderer leave any clues? By combining various methods of data gathering, including unobtrusive measures, Holmes is able to make a reasonable guess regarding which of the hypotheses to reject or not reject (Truzzi, 1976).

Webb and associates in *Unobtrusive Measures: Nonreactive Research in the Social Sciences* (1966) and in their revised edition entitled *Nonreactive Measures in the Social Sciences* (1981) describe these techniques as nonreactive methods in which undisturbed subjects are observed in natural or manipulated settings. Nonreactive methods usually involve clandestine, novel, and often "oddball" observations of existing situations. The observer is removed from the actual events, and the subject is not aware of being observed; therefore, the act of being studied tends not to elicit artificial behavior or "stooge effects."

An analogy can be drawn between unobtrusive methods and surveillance by security personnel in a commercial setting. Security people do not simply ask people, "Have you stolen anything?" and expect to be effective. Although uniformed personnel can discourage pilferage, clandestine methods (disguised shoppers, mirrors, and cameras) are far more effective in secretly observing the actual behavior.

Major Types of Unobtrusive Methods

The major types of unobtrusive methods are as follows:

- Physical trace analysis
- Archival, existing data, and autobiographies
- Simple observation
- Disguised observation
- Simulation

Physical trace analysis

Archival records

Content analysis

Secondary analysis

Observation

Simulation

Physical trace analysis is the study of deposits, accretion of matter, and other indirect substances produced by previous human interaction. Much like the archeologist or crime scene detective, the criminal justice researcher attempts to reconstruct, after the fact, the substance of the phenomenon. **Archival records**, memoirs, diaries, and historical documents contain much information that can provide a historical overview of criminological issues. The *analyses of available data* comprise not only the analysis of official statistics and records but also procedures such as content analysis and secondary analysis. **Content analysis** is the systematic classification and study of the content of mass media, for example, newspapers and magazines (Holsti, 1969). **Secondary analysis** entails the reanalysis of data that were previously gathered for other purposes (Hyman, 1972). **Observation** (similar to our discussion of complete observation in Chapter 7) involves strategies in which the researcher's participation with the subjects is kept at a minimum and the investigator carefully records activities of the subjects. In disguised observation the analyst covertly studies groups or individuals by temporarily misrepresenting his or her role. **Simulation** entails a variety of gaming strategies that attempt to imitate a more complex social reality.

Given many of the shortcomings of data-gathering methods discussed previously, such as increasing nonresponse and respondent hostility, it is imperative that the wise researcher ask "Do these data already exist, or is there some way of gathering this information without bothering respondents?"

As mentioned previously, the pure classification of research as unobtrusive measures or case studies or interviews is not mutually exclusive, and there is much overlap. Some examples could fit into a number of categories. To provide a picture of the diversity and flavor of unobtrusive measurement, a large number of examples from the general social science literature are presented, along with criminal justice examples, as the imaginative researcher could certainly employ many of these same techniques and apply them to criminal justice subjects. As a student reading all of them, it should be sufficient for you to know a couple of examples of each type of unobtrusive measurement.

Physical Trace Analysis

The popularity of media portrayals of crime scene investigation (CSI) impresses on the viewer the detail that can be surmised by modern investigative skills. While the actual ability of CSI to solve crimes is a bit exaggerated in the media, such research is not limited to crime scenes and murder investigations, but can be skillfully applied to social science research.

Physical trace analysis is well illustrated in the fields of criminalistics and crime scene investigation. The detective's search for clues and circumstantial evidence is analogous to the indirect research indicators attempted by the social researcher using physical trace analysis as the means of unobtrusive measurement. An example may be found in the method police patrols use to spot stolen cars—they look for dirty license plates on clean cars, or clean plates on dirty cars, assuming that the thieves switch plates. Borrowing from a technique used by "snoopy" superintendents for years, an investigator wishing to discover the level of whiskey consumption in a town that is officially dry did so by counting empty bottles in trash cans (Sawyer, 1961). In 1979, after a police raid on mobster Joseph Bonanno's "Joe Bananas" home, from which the manuscript for his memoirs was confiscated for intelligence purposes, the FBI revealed that for years they had been collecting Bonanno's garbage. As is common practice in many American communities, on the evening for trash pickup, the Bonannos would deposit their trash bags at curbside for pickup. Prior to the actual pickup, federal agents would swap lookalike trash bags and sift through Bonanno's trash. Information garnered was enough to precipitate the raid to get the actual manuscript ("Not So Quietly Flows the Don," 1979), which was later published as *A Man of Honor* (Bonanno, 1983).

A classic example in the social sciences is the case of "the hatching chick exhibit" at Chicago's Museum of Science and Industry. In an attempt to determine the popularity of various exhibits, the curators discovered that the selective erosion of floor tiles—their replacement rate—could serve as a rough index of visitor interest. Although the tiles in some parts of the museum had not been replaced for years, those surrounding the hatching chick exhibit required replacement every six weeks (Webb et al., 1966, p. 2). Care must be taken, however, in generalizing from indirect evidence. A similar museum that used to pride itself on having one of the largest volumes of public usage in the United States discovered that its attendance dropped dramatically when a building with large public restrooms was constructed next door (Wallis and Roberts, 1966, p. 160). Apparently, the large attendance figures were, in reality, a result of people using the restrooms. The level of vandalism in a community may serve as a measure not only of lawbreaking but also of affluence, as vandalism is primarily the product of affluent societies; in poorer societies, what little exists of value is carefully guarded (Clinard and Quinney, 1973, p. 59). In the early days of television, monitors at the Dayton, Ohio, Water Department were amused to discover that water pressure dropped considerably during commercials as people used bathrooms and sinks. This indirect index of program and commercial popularity has come to be referred to as the "Dayton Water Survey" (Simon, 1989, p. 60). In an interesting variation, a radio reporter, in what was called the "Royal Flush" experiment, conducted a political poll of sorts by broadcasting from atop the community water tower and asking listeners to register their preference for various political candidates by flushing their toilets as each name was announced. The drop in water level was used as a barometer and produced results closely matching the later vote (Webb et al., 1981, p. 2).

One researcher estimated the readership level of a printed advertisement by counting the number of different fingerprints on the page (Webb et al., 1981, p. 12). The size of attendance at a social event can be estimated by the amount of trash left behind (Webb et al., 1981, p. 19). Studies of graffiti (scrawlings or messages written on the walls of public facilities) have been done by Mockridge in *The Scrawl of the Wild* (1968). Others have found variation by sex, age, and education in which female graffiti had romantic themes, whereas male scribblings were erotic. Sales of burglar alarms or firearms in a community might be taken as an indirect index of fear of crime (Sechrest and Olson, 1971).

Graffiti can also be studied as an indicator of social environmental atmosphere and subcultures. Klofas and Cutshall (1985), for instance, studied graffiti from the walls of an abandoned juvenile correctional facility.

Use of Available Data and Archives

The National Institute of Justice (NIJ) was the pioneer among federal agencies in requiring that data sets from funded research be given to the agency upon completion of the project. In 1985, the National Academy of Sciences described this policy as "remarkable and a model for other research funding agencies," and in 1986, the National Science Foundation adopted a data resource policy similar to the NIJ policy that had been in existence since 1979.

Secondary Analysis

Secondary analysis, or the reanalysis of data that were originally gathered or compiled for other purposes, is an excellent economizer of researcher time in data gathering, nonreactive, and a resourceful use of the mountains of data generated in modern society (see Hyman, 1972; D. Stewart, 1984). Reanalysis of historical records, precinct and court records, and such documents as the Uniform Crime Reports (UCR), given certain recognized limitations, can make excellent use of data that, although gathered for other purposes, can be used to address research concerns in criminology and criminal justice.

Many second-hand stores have names like "Trash 'n Treasures," referring to the phenomenon that one person's trash is another's treasure. Our industrial society has generated so much material to be discarded that our trash sites are nearly filled to capacity. Similarly, our current postindustrial society generates information and data at considerable expense that, once they serve agency or organizational purposes, are often confined to the equivalent of a trash dump site. Some of these data consist of both **primary data sources**, which refer to raw data unaccompanied by any analysis or interpretation, and **secondary data sources**, which consist of analyses, syntheses, and evaluations of the information (Lutzker and Ferrall, 1986). Thus, the UCR itself would constitute a primary data source, whereas an existing research study that used the UCR and other sources to predict crime trends would be a secondary source. Such available data, consisting of both primary and secondary sources, represent a "gold mine" of information waiting to be exploited. *Primary records such as letters, diaries, and memoirs may provide insight into events or research issues long after they have occurred* (Gottschalk, Kluckhohn, and Angell, 1945).

Primary data sources
Secondary data sources

Personal Documents and Biographies

The use of personal documents in social research was pioneered by Thomas and Znaniecki in their classic sociological work *The Polish Peasant in Europe and America* (Thomas and Znaniecki, 1918). They made particularly good use of diaries and personal letters to provide in-depth, personal views of their subjects.

Diaries kept by subjects have also been used as a source of information on drug subcultures (Zimmerman and Wieder, 1974). In the latter, individuals may keep intimate journals, memoirs, and logs (Denzin, 1989). Popular with economists, marketing researchers and, more recently, sociologists, such self-completion diaries can be used to collect detailed information about behavior, events, or other aspects of an individual's daily life (Corti, 1993; Plummer, 1983).

The diary method involves investigators commissioning individuals to maintain a record of activities for a specified period of time (Courtright, 1995). In addition to combating memory decay, respondents are better able to reflect on their performances and have greater flexibility in recording events and their meaning than in a standard retrospective interview. This technique has been used to measure behavior such as television viewing, lifestyles, alcohol consumption, sexual behavior, and anxiety in children. Some variations of the method have included using the diary method in conjunction with follow-up interviews as well as questionnaires and "experience sampling methods," in which systematic self-reports are provided at random occasions. The latter may involve respondents carrying "beepers" (electronic pagers), which signal times for diary entries (Courtright, 1995). A computer-based anonymous group diary called the "electronic group diary" was used as a feminist research method to record incidents of sexism within an academic department (Reinharz, 1992). Pocket computers have been used to have respondents record answers at specific times (Taylor, Fried, and Kenardy, 1990). The provision of payment for training as well as recording devices such as tape recorders have all enhanced the diary method (Courtright, 1995).

Within many autobiographies and biographies of criminals exist useful insights that, when viewed with scrutiny and caution by a researcher, can be highly useful in analyzing crime, criminals, and criminal justice. Sanyika Shakur (Kody Scott), in *Monster: The Autobiography of an L.A. Gang Member* (1993), provides an autobiographical account of his violent life as a Crip gang member in south central Los Angeles.

The first criminal autobiographical life history in America appeared in 1807 with the publication of Henry Tufts' *The Autobiography of a Criminal* (Pearson, 1930). Tufts' description of his career as a thief, imposter, swindler, Indian doctor, and Revolutionary soldier began a long tradition of such works, many of questionable validity. The widespread interest on the part of criminals in such activities is illustrated by New York State's passage of the "Son of Sam" law to prevent serial murderer David Berkowitz and other criminals from profiting from any books, and by statements by Watergate conspirator John Dean— "I wish I could write a book and not have to make a living"—and Arthur Bremer (who attempted to assassinate George Wallace)—"How much do you think I'll get for my autobiography?" (Hagan, 1990, p. 110).

In the case of Maas' *The Valachi Papers* (1968), Joseph Valachi, former Mafia member and federal informant, was asked by federal authorities to set down on paper his recollections. It was hoped these remembrances would help fill in the holes in his testimony before the McClellan Commission, as well as provide some information that may not have turned up in earlier questioning. In editing and making more intelligible Valachi's story, Maas interviewed Valachi directly, interviewed past associates, and analyzed interrogation transcripts as well as other official sources and documents (Maas, 1968).

Another federal informer, Vincent Teresa (*My Life in the Mafia*, 1973), had his autobiography at first recorded on tape by Thomas Renner. Renner conducted these sessions in secret meeting locations while Teresa was under federal guard. Former associates of crime figures have been instrumental in biographies. Wolf, one of the authors of *Frank Costello: Prime Minister of the Underworld*, had been Costello's personal lawyer for thirty years (Wolf and DiMona, 1975). The behind-the-scenes quality of such literature can be illustrated by some of the incidents described in Pileggi's *Wiseguy: Life in a Mafia Family* (1985), which is the life story of Henry Hill, a career criminal who literally grew up in the mob. Hill gives his account of the Paul Vario organized crime family, the Lufthansa robbery at Kennedy Airport (until 1983 the most successful cash robbery in U.S. history, scoring $5 million in cash), the Sindona scandal, which nearly collapsed the Vatican bank, and the Boston College basketball point-shaving scandal.

In their study of *A Family Business*, discussed in Chapter 7, Francis and Elizabeth Ianni developed organized crime family charts on the basis of files of the U.S. Justice Department (Ianni and Ianni, 1972, p. 185). The potential usefulness of such official data is illustrated by the case of the DeCavalcante tapes. In the late 1960s, as a result of a trial of New Jersey organized crime figure Sam "The Plumber" DeCavalcante, more than 2,300 pages of tape logs were made available to the public by the U.S. Justice Department. The FBI had bugged DeCavalcante's plumbing and heating company office for almost four years, providing us with a rare glimpse of the inside day-to-day operations of the mob (Volz and Bridge, 1969).

In a revealing pseudo-autobiography Charles "Lucky" Luciano reveals the "true" story behind the mob's believed cooperation with the Allied effort during World War II (Gosch and Hammer, 1974). To create an incident that would require their assistance in waterfront vigilance against sabotage and hopefully secure Luciano's freedom from prison, the mob firebombed the soon-to-be-converted troopship, the French luxury liner *Normandie*. Although much credit was given to him for smoothing the Allied invasion of Sicily through Mafia underground contacts, Luciano claims that he never denied the acclaim, but had absolutely no contacts on the island with which to provide assistance. Luciano was given credit for securing the docks and assisting the invasion until he finally denied both in his autobiography. The hazards of using such information are pointed out by Abadinsky (1993), who claims that the Gosch and Hammer work on Luciano has been discredited and might best be cited as a possible example of fraud.

The hazards of using existing data and so-called "insider books" are illustrated by the numerous autobiographical accounts by major figures involved in the Watergate event. So much self-serving and contradictory information was presented by this group that the works might better be put in the fiction rather than nonfiction category. Taking a related illustration, publication of *The Brethren: Inside the Supreme Court* provided one of the first inside looks at a previously secretive and sacrosanct institution (Woodward and Armstrong, 1979). The authors, relying much on information supplied by 170 present and former clerks and staffers of the high bench, claim to have validated their data by checking at least three or four confirming sources. They made use of interviews, internal memorandums, letters, and conference notes, as well as diaries. Despite these efforts, legal experts and other well-informed court observers have been highly critical of its accuracy ("Sharp Blows at the High Bench," 1980).

Other illustrations of the use of existing data are in the areas of competitive intelligence and industrial espionage. Most of the "trade secrets" and operating regimen of companies are available through open sources. Images of "cloaks and daggers" and seductive, sable-coated countesses on the Orient Express stealing secrets have long been superceded by technological spying. The computer revolution and Internet have made "open sources," publicly available information, the most fertile ground for corporate intelligence. Online government and private information is openly available. The trick is to organize and analyze such information in a meaningful manner.

Examples of Secondary Analysis

Criminologists have made quite imaginative use of official statistics and other existing public documents to generate some very useful studies. The following examples represent only a fraction of many such studies, but they should help the reader appreciate the gold mine of data awaiting imaginative research prospectors eager to stake a claim. Glaser and Zeigler (1974) used official statistics to examine the relationship between homicide rates, death penalty, and sentencing policy in various states. Similarly, Erickson and Gibbs (1976) used official statistics such as the UCR and Bureau of Prisons statistics to discover an inverse relationship between crime rate and certainty of imprisonment, but not with length of imprisonment.

In "Danger to Police During Domestic Encounters: Assaults on Baltimore County Police," Uchida, Brooks, and Koper (1987) questioned recent research and police academy practice, both of which tend to underestimate the potential dangers to police who are mediating domestic (household) encounters. Using five sources of existing information—Baltimore County Police Department records on police assaults, police personnel records, calls for service data, Census Bureau demographic data, and the FBI's count of the number of law enforcement officers killed or assaulted—they found that domestic disturbances put police at great risk. In another example using two sources of existing data—Interpol and World Health Organization homicide data—Messner (1989) was able to support the hypothesis that economic discrimination was highly related to high homicide rates.

In order to study women who kill in domestic encounters, Mann (1988) drew a randomly selected sample of 296 cleared homicide cases in Chicago, Houston, Atlanta, Los Angeles, New York City, and Baltimore for the 1979–1983 period; in each case the perpetrator was a female. Mann traveled to each city to examine these cases and explains (Mann, 1988, p. 35):

> The completed homicide files of the sample cases for 1979–1983, some of which included photographs and autopsy reports and any other police record sources such as arrest and fingerprint files and FBI reports were examined minutely. I recorded information from these documents on previously designed research schedules after I had assigned each case a code number to insure confidentiality.

Sampson and Laub (1992) discovered sixty cartons of data that had been stored in the Harvard Law School basement. They recoded and computerized the data. In this secondary analysis of an existing longitudinal data set, they reanalyzed a classic study by Sheldon and Eleanor Glueck (1968), which had been conducted from 1940 to 1965. The study followed 500 delinquents and 500 matched nondelinquents for over a twenty-five-year period (Laub, Sampson, and Kiger, 1990). In an example of the longest longitudinal study in the history of criminology, the Gluecks (1968) followed the 500 delinquent men to age 32, while Sampson and Laub (1992) followed them through their young adult lives and again (2003) up to age 70.

Lieber and Sherin (1972) studied the influence of lunar cycles on homicides by analyzing both UCR data and meteorological data during a fifteen-year period in Dade County, Florida, and a thirteen-year period in Cuyahoga County, Ohio. Wolfgang, Figlio, and Sellin (1972) analyzed the delinquent records of a birth cohort—every boy born in 1945 who lived in Philadelphia between his tenth and eighteenth birthdays. This retrospective longitudinal study analyzed nearly 10,000 boys. In a replication of this study, Tracy, Wolfgang, and Figlio (1985) followed the criminal histories of boys born in Philadelphia in 1958 who lived there from the age of ten until adulthood.

Sutherland's *White Collar Crime* (1949) used the records of regulatory agencies, courts, and commissions to study the seventy largest American industrial and mercantile corporations and their violations over a forty-year period of laws regulating such things as false advertising, patent abuse, wartime trade violations, price-fixing, fraud, and intended manufacturing and sale of faulty goods.

Imaginative use of the official files of U.S. federal regulatory agencies has been made by Nader's Raiders. As part of this group's Center for the Study of Responsive Law, investigatory groups have published reports on air pollution (Esposito and Silverman, 1970), the Federal Trade Commission (Cox, Fellmeth, and Schulz, 1969), food and drug regulatory activities (Turner, 1970), antitrust activity (Green et al., 1973), and occupational safety violations (Page and O'Brien, 1973).

Clinard and Yeager's *Illegal Corporate Behavior* (1979) and *Corporate Crime* (1980) represent landmarks in the investigation of white-collar crime, superseding Sutherland's pioneering and more modest effort. In the first large-scale, comprehensive investigation of corporate crime, they conducted an analysis of administrative, civil, and criminal actions by twenty-five federal agencies against 477 of the largest American manufacturing corporations during 1975 and 1976. They also employed regulatory agency records to examine 105 of the largest wholesale, retail, and service corporations.

The analysis of documents, statistical and nonstatistical records of agencies, is fertile ground for research. Clinard's study, *The Black Market: A Study of White-Collar Crime* (1952), dealt with wartime pricing and rationing violations using the official records of federal agencies.

The records of store detectives were used by Mary Owen Cameron in her key study of shoplifting, *The Booster and the Snitch: Department Store Shoplifting* (1964). Certainly Durkheim's (1951) analysis of suicide statistics in different European countries provides an excellent example of one of the earliest uses of existing data in social science research.

Miller, as part of a twelve-city survey of gang violence, analyzed newspaper reports as one source to validate his findings that since the end of World War II there has been an increase in gang victimization of nongang members and more killings as a result of increased availability of firearms (Miller, 1975).

In an attempt to measure the concept of "professionalization" in different occupations, this writer (Hagan, 1975, 1976) examined a variety of existing sources in addition to gathering primary data. Included in the author's analysis were an obtrusive method (a survey of presidents of national professional associations) and unobtrusive methods, including a reanalysis of data previously gathered in a national survey of practitioners, literature supplied by national officers of the professional associations, data obtained in a literature review, and data from sourcebooks and from the *Encyclopedia of Associations*.

In an imaginative use of mass media, Phillips (1977, 1978) examined the impact of news media reports of suicides of famous people like Marilyn Monroe or fictional suicides in television soap operas on suicide rates and found that suicides increased after both. He also studied and discovered that homicides increase after professional boxing matches and decrease after executions. Using FBI and other police intelligence files, Anderson (1979) studied the "Benguerra" organized crime family (believed to be a pseudonym for the Angelo Bruno family in Philadelphia). Using New York City Police Department "rap sheets" (records of past offenses) of narcotics violators and their associates, Lupscha (1982) analyzed the "New Purple Gang" in New York.

In other examples, Exhibit 8.1 illustrates the use of Geographic Information Systems (GIS) to construct automated pin maps. Exhibit 8.2 illustrates a clever use of available data.

Limitations of Official Data

In addition to the problems in using UCR data for research purposes detailed in Chapter 4, official data may contain any or most of the same shortcomings. The investigator must remember that the data have been gathered for agency

EXHIBIT 8.1 ▶

Automated Pin Mapping: Applied Criminal Justice Research Using GIS for Crime Analysis

POLICE   *CHARLOTTE-MECKLENBURG POLICE DEPARTMENT*

Strategic Planning and Analysis

⊙ About SP&A   ⊙ SP&A Projects   ⊙ Summary Reports   ⊙ District Crime Stats   ⊙ Crime Maps   ⊙ GIS   ⊙ Research

Automated Pin Mapping

- *Display spatial patterns of events*

⊙ The locations of crime events, arrests, drug complaints, etc. are routinely displayed on maps. Usually, a particular type of offense or arrest is shown. This provides an easy method of viewing activities in an area rather than searching through a listing of events.

⊙ Maps can also be used to convey more than one type of information at a time. Crime locations can be symbolized according to the type of crime, the day of week, or M/O characteristics. M/O refers to a particular suspect's "modus operandi", or "method of operation", when committing a crime.

⊙ Maps are the quickest means of visualizing the environment (not just criminal). Typically, law enforcement agencies have limited their focus to offense and arrest information. By broadening the scope of analysis to include the total environment, the social, cultural, and physical conditions of a community can be taken into account. This creates the opportunity for agencies to identify the root cause(s) of a particular problem rather than addressing the symptoms of the problem.

- *Integrate community characteristics into the analysis of crime patterns*

⊙ To support Community Problem-Oriented Policing, community characteristics are routinely displayed on maps when analyzing crime patterns.

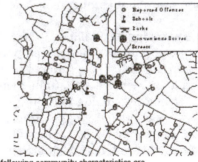

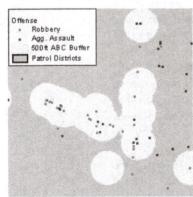

Offense
- Robbery
- Agg. Assault
  500ft ABC Buffer
  Patrol Districts

The following community characteristics are frequently depicted on maps:
- Schools   - Convenience Stores
- Parks   - ABC Permit Locations

⊙ For example, one might display the locations of aggravated assaults, robberies, and establishments with ABC permits to see if crime is clustering around locations that sell alcohol.

⊙ Officer defined drug markets are also an example of information that can be displayed on a map. Other mapping data such as convenience store locations, bus routes, and public housing can be displayed at the same time to analyze relationships between neighborhood characteristics, drug markets, and crime.

Source: Charlotte Mecklenburg Police homepage: www.charmeck.nc.us/cipolice/spab/gis/pinmaps.htm.

purposes and therefore may not contain the degree of accuracy or operationalization the researcher desires. Data may be deliberately "fudged" to give a favorable impression of the organization. Studies over time are hazardous because of instrumentation or changes in the record-keeping procedures of the agency. Of great dismay to the researcher is the realization that the variables have not been measured in the manner that the investigator had hoped. These are all obstacles but not always insurmountable ones. They might better be viewed as challenges to the imagination and cleverness of the researcher to see what she or he can tease out of official data.

EXHIBIT 8.2 ▶

Street Gang Crime in Chicago

Researchers examined Chicago gang homicide data over a twenty-six-year period, from 1965 through 1990, and detailed information on other gang-related crime from 1987 to 1990. Two methods of analysis were used to determine the extent to which neighborhoods differed in the type and concentration of street gang activity and to examine the neighborhood characteristics that were associated with high levels of lethal and nonlethal street gang activity. The information analyzed was primarily from Chicago Police Department (CPD) records, which were organized into three sets of data on Chicago homicides, street gang-motivated offenses, and street gang territories. Neighborhood characteristics and population data for rate calculation were obtained from the U.S. Bureau of the Census. This information was gathered by tract and aggregated into the seventy-seven Chicago community areas.

Researchers geocoded the address of each homicide and street gang-motivated incident. Boundaries of the community areas were mapped, geocoded offenses were aggregated by community area, and offenses were analyzed in relation to population and other community characteristics. Finally, the densest concentrations (hot spot areas) of individual addresses of street gang-related incidents were identified regardless of arbitrary boundaries and related to gang turfs, gang activity, and community characteristics.

Data on homicides. One of the largest and most detailed data sets on violence ever collected in the United States, the Chicago homicide data set contains information on every homicide in police records from 1965 to 1990. More than 200 variables were collected for the 19,323 homicides in this data set. The crime analysis unit of the CPD has maintained a summary—Murder Analysis Report (MAR)—of each homicide over the twenty-six-year period. On the basis of these reports, 1,311 homicides were classified as street gang motivated.

Data on street gang-motivated offenses. This data set included information on 17,085 criminal offenses that occurred from 1987 to 1990 that were classified by the police as street gang related. These offenses were categorized as follows:

- 288 homicides.
- 8,828 nonlethal violent offenses (aggravated and simple assault and battery).
- 5,888 drug offenses (violations related to possession or sale of hard or soft drugs).
- 2,081 other offenses (includes more than 100 specific crimes ranging from liquor law violations to intimidation, mob action, vandalism, robbery, and weapons law violations).

Data on street gang territory boundaries. This data set included the location of street gang territory boundaries in early 1991. These boundaries were based on maps drawn by street gang officers in Chicago's twenty-six districts, who identified the territories of forty-five street gangs—both major and minor—and noted areas that were in dispute between one or more street gangs.

Defining gang affiliation. These three data sets included several possible aspects of street gang affiliation for each incident—for example, the street gang affiliation of the offender or offenders, the affiliation of the victim or victims (if any), and the location of the incident within the boundaries of a gang's turf. In this study, researchers classified street gang–motivated criminal incidents according to the affiliation of the offender(s).

(continued)

EXHIBIT 8.2 Continued

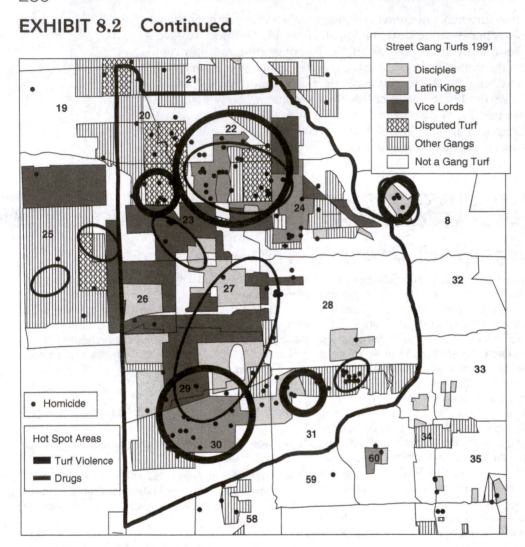

Figure 1

Street Gang-Motivated Homicide, Other Violence, and Drug Crime, 1987–1990.

Source: Chicago Police Department.

Source: Block, Carolyn Rebecca, and Richard Block. *Street Gang Crime in Chicago.* National Institute of Justice Research in Brief, December 1993, NCJ 144782.

Cross-national research in criminal justice and criminology is particularly hazardous. Carol Kalish (1989), former Director of International Programs, Bureau of Justice Statistics, points out:

Often the statistics are out of date; usually the statistics are incomplete; and occasionally the statistics are incomprehensible. Many countries do not report consistently from one year to the next; many countries do not report for every year; many countries do not report at all.

She also notes that, despite these problems, recent efforts by the United Nations (UN) and Interpol to gather more accurate data should persist. The UCR's experience can serve as an example of what can be accomplished. Because the statistics compiled by the fifty states have steadily improved, the UCR has been able to gather more accurate data. Bennett and Lynch (1990), for their part, compared four international sources of crime statistics (Interpol, World Health Organization, UN, and the Comparative Crime Data File) and found that similar problems existed in all the sources but that the homicide and theft statistics were comparable (see also Huang and Wellford, 1989).

Measuring Hidden Populations

In questioning often uncritically cited figures on how many heroin addicts there are and the amount they steal in New York City, Singer (1971) demonstrated that by taking numbers seriously, and checking them against other sources and available demographic information, the likely figure is much less than usually stated. Singer shows how a skillful researcher using available data can avoid accepting the same erroneous data that are picked up and passed on as fact, even by responsible research organizations.

Ecologists, among others, have a keen interest in estimating wildlife populations in given areas. Using such techniques as *mark–recapture* or removal, they are able to obtain a fairly accurate count of inhabitants. Utilizing capture statistics, for example, arrest rates, adaptations of such techniques are viewed as having potential in criminal justice (Burnham, 1980). Procedures have been proposed for estimating juvenile recidivism from aggregated official data (Wanat and Burke, 1980), the size of drug user populations (Demaree, 1980), and income unreported on individual income tax returns (Kenadjian, 1980).

Webb et al. (1981, p. 23) describe a case in which the Internal Revenue Service (IRS) attempted to estimate whether a barber, who kept few records, was paying sufficient taxes. They attempted to estimate his income on the basis of the number of towels he used. The tax court, while accepting the IRS estimate, disallowed IRS claims that the barber sometimes used the same towels twice and also indicated that the IRS estimate of three towels per haircut did not account for the fact that the barber occasionally gave free trims.

Historical and Archival Data

A potentially hazardous and relatively neglected area of criminal justice research has been the primary use of historical and archival data. Much of this omission of historical data has been due to the tendency of sociologists and social scientists to view history as a mere chronicle of unique events, part myth, allegory, and fiction (Inciardi, Block, and Hallowell, 1977, p. 9).

In an analysis of crime and punishment in the nineteenth century, Graff (1977) indicated that a great number of records on criminals, particularly jail registers, held promise for the history of criminals. Monkkonen (1979), in an article critical of Graff's position, indicates that great care must be taken in using such data, and he argues that consideration must be given to the original methodology and rationale under which such data were collected. With this warning in mind, neglected sources include annual reports of city, county, and state criminal justice agencies, as well as U.S. Bureau of Census data on state and local agencies (Monkkonen, 1979). At a minimum, such records complement aggregate data in providing more personal examples of criminal activity of the past (Graff, 1979). One must, of course, attempt to carefully weigh, double-check, and verify with other sources any information obtained through this method (Davies, 1956; Wheeler, 1970). In 1990, Monkkonen (1990) served as editor of a sixteen-volume series on *Crime and Justice in American History*, which represents an encyclopedic tour de force in historical criminology.

Many examples of the use of historical data exist. Kai Erickson (1966), for example, used official statistics to analyze deviance and immorality in *Wayward Puritans*, an analysis of Puritan New England. In tracing the genesis of the legend of the Mafia in Sicily, Albini (1971) consulted records, maps, and other government reports of the Italian Military Archives, to refute certain myths regarding the Mafia's origin. Chappell and Walsh use a historical case study of infamous London fence Jonathan Wild to shed light on professional fences (Chappell and Walsh, 1974; Howson, 1970). In order to examine the impact of death penalty–execution publicity on homicide rates, Bailey (1990) used Vanderbilt University's television news archives, which abstracts ABC, CBS, and NBC news programs. He looked at television publicity devoted to executions and monthly homicide rates from 1976 to 1987. His findings neither supported deterrence theory (since executions did not decrease homicides) nor brutalization theory (since executions did not increase killings).

In *American Assassins: The Darker Side of Politics*, Clarke (1982) attempted to address the "pathological myth" about assassins, the belief that most had suffered from and were motivated by some mental sickness, insanity, or derangement. He felt that most analyses of assassins' pathology committed post hoc error, the false assumption that because one variable or outcome follows another in time, it is the cause of that outcome. For example, assassins may act mentally abnormal after the fact because they have been caught and processed, not because they have a long-term condition that caused them to become assassins. Clarke compiled a list of different types including sane and politically motivated assassins by examining materials from the National Archives, Library of Congress, FBI, Secret Service, government agencies, court hearings and investigations, trial transcripts, diaries, autobiographies, medical records, newspaper clippings, tapes, and other biographical and historical documents.

Using the private archives of an American-Jewish self-defense organization in *East Side–West Side*, Block (1979) conducted a historiographical analysis of the cocaine trade in New York City from 1910 to 1918. Historiography involves the application of empirical social scientific methods to the analysis of history. The user of historical data should carefully weigh the validity of the sources used, asking questions such as "How reliable is the author?" "Do other sources agree?" or "Does it make logical sense?" (Inciardi, Block, and Hallowell, 1977, p. 25). The potential uses of available data in criminal justice and criminology have only begun to be tapped.

Exhibit 8.3 describes the use of GIS in criminal justice research.

EXHIBIT 8.3 ▶

Applied Research: Geographic Information Systems (GIS)

A very popular form of applied justice research has been borrowed from the field of geography—Geographic Information Systems (GIS). The NIJ has even established a "Crime Mapping Research Center" to advance applied and basic research involving analytic mapping of crime.* The Charlotte Mecklenburg Police homepage provides some illustrations. Examples of GIS analysis include the following:

Automated Pin Mapping The locations of crime events, arrests, drug complaints, etc., are routinely displayed on maps. Many times a particular street intersection, convenience store, bar, or some other location will be identified as a problem. GIS allows us to state the

extent and type of a problem within a defined distance of the source.

Hot Spot Analysis Analysts use computer software along with GIS to identify clusters or "hot spots" of crime.

Grid Analysis A grid composed of cells divides the police jurisdiction into smaller areas for detailed analysis.

Investigative Tool GIS can be used to help identify potential suspects to increase investigators' suspect base when no leads are evident.

Research GIS can be utilized to test criminological theories such as Crime Prevention Through Environmental Design (CPTED) and environmental criminology.

*Crime Mapping Research Center, National Institute of Justice, 633 Indiana Avenue, Room 302, Washington, DC, 20531

Content Analysis

Another important method of analyzing existing data is through *content analysis*, the systematic analysis and selective classification of the contents of mass communication. This technique is excellent for comparative and historical studies or for discerning trends in existing phenomena. It is often used by intelligence agencies to uncover potential changes in international diplomacy. Olson describes the process of content analysis in one study:

These categories and subcategories were devised in discussions among those who eventually coded the material. After initially reading many of the books, trial runs with various alternative categories were made. Following progressive refinement, the scheme was "frozen" for the complete study. This initial period of discussion provided not only a more refined scheme but also developed intimate knowledge of the scheme's meaning among those recording their observations. (Olson, 1976, p. 161)

The basic procedure in content analysis involves:

- The selection of categories and subjects to be analyzed
- The rigorous establishment of criteria for inclusion, a feature that ensures that the study can be replicated by others
- Carefully following the preestablished classification scheme
- Statistically analyzing the results (Berelson, 1952)

The best test of the usefulness of a content analysis scheme is its replicability—that is, a different group, using the scoring system and instructions assigned, should be able to come up with the same categorizations.

A number of imaginative subjects have been examined using content analysis. Davis (1952) studied the amount of space devoted to crime in select newspapers and related this to the local crime rates. Many forms of mass media such as newspapers, magazines, television, and movies contain subject matter that can be used for an analysis of popular stereotypes of deviants or shifts in public propaganda about crime. As part of a larger study of the fear of crime in four American cities, Bielby and Berk (1980) did a content analysis of accounts of crime and column inches devoted to the subject in large city newspapers. In a study of government response to crime, Jacob, Lineberry, and Heinz (Jacob et al., 1980) examined and reanalyzed a wide variety of available data, such as changes in local ordinances and state criminal codes, changes in amount and distribution of police workforce, court decisions, inmate populations, court and correctional expenditures, type and shifts of city government, and mayorality election year and their relationship to UCR data. They also examined newspapers. The sample comprised nine city newspapers over a thirty-one-year period, using randomly selected proportions of weeks. Page one articles (or articles on the first three pages of tabloids) and letters to the editor were examined and classified.

In another study of how the news production process, both print and electronic, affected the presentation of crime in the media, Chermak (1994) did a content analysis of nine newspapers and three evening television newscasts. He coded nine newspapers for content every fifth day for the first six months in 1990 and an additional eighteen days for a three-month period in 1991 of the *Cleveland Plain Dealer*. Also coded were local evening broadcasts in Albany, Cleveland, and Dallas for seven nights a week for an eight-week period in 1991. He followed this up with ethnographic observations of newsrooms as well as with forty interviews of people in the news trade.

Researchers have done content analysis of the following:

- Newspaper reports of gang activity (Miller, 1975)
- Popular articles about marijuana using them to measure the effectiveness of propaganda campaigns designed to assist in the passage of stricter drug laws (Becker, 1970)
- Jokes, comic strips, and popular culture regarding mental illness and insanity (Scheff, 1966)
- The history of the stereotype of assassins and hashish usage (Mandel, 1966)

Wolfgang, Figlio, and Thornberry (1978) used content analysis as well as other techniques to examine the scientific status of the field of criminology. Part of the analysis involved reading, classifying, coding, and rating 4,417 works. The raters used a scale from seven for the highest to one for the lowest for evaluation of scientific merit.

Welch, Fenwick, and Roberts (1997) did an analysis of definitions of crime and moral panic by examining experts' quotes in feature newspaper articles on crime.

As part of an attempt to develop a model of professionalization, this author did a content analysis of thirty-seven major writers on the subject and identified twenty-nine different criteria (Hagan, 1975). Similarly, Table 8.1 shows a content analysis by this writer (Hagan, 1983) of major dimensions of selected writers' definitions of the concept "organized crime."

Although many of these writers discussed the issue, a large number never bothered to define the concept; among those that did, there was no consensus

Table 8.1

A CONTENT ANALYSIS OF DIMENSIONS OF SELECTED WRITERS' DEFINITIONS OF ORGANIZED CRIME*

DIMENSION	ABADINSKY (1981)	ALBINI (1971)	BARLOW (1981)	CLINARD AND QUINNEY (1973)	CONKIN (1981)	CRESSEY (1969)	HASKELL AND YABLONSKI (1974)	INCIARDI (1975)	MACK (1975)	MALTZ (1976)	ORGANIZED CRIME TASK FORCE (1967)	SUTHERLAND AND CRESSEY (1974)	VETTER AND SILVERMAN (1978)
Nonideological	X										X		
Organized hierarchy continuing	X	X	X	X	X	X	X	X	X	X	X	X	X
Violence (force or threat of force)	X	X		X	X		X	X	X	X	X		X
Restricted membership	X				X						X		
Rational profit through illegal activities	X	X	X	X	X	X		X	X		X	X	X
Public demand		X	X	X			X	X				X	
Corruption (immunity)		X	X	X	X	X	X	X		X		X	X
Monopoly				X		X		X	X			X	
Specialization				X				X					
Code of secrecy			X		X								
Extensive planning							X				X		

*Many writers, including those of textbooks, fail to supply explicit definitions of organized crime.

Source: Hagan, Frank E. "The Organized Crime Continuum: A Further Specification of a New Conceptual Model." *Criminal Justice Review* 8 (Fall 1983):53. Reprinted with permission.

on all elements, although the majority seemed to agree on certain elements of organizations—use of force or threats of force, profit from provision of illicit services that are in public demand, and assurance of immunity of operation.

Berg (2007, p. 308) makes the distinction between "manifest content analysis" (looking at those elements that are physically present and countable) and "latent content analysis" (where one examines the underlying themes of the physically presented data). Seven major elements can be counted in content analysis: words, themes, characters (persons), paragraphs, items (e.g., book, letter, and speech), concepts, and semantics (how strong or weak are words that are used) (2007, pp. 313–314). Payne and Gainey (2000) content analyzed comments of thirty electronic-monitoring program supervisors surveyed by the Virginia State Crime Commission. They used both thematic and semantic content analyses.

In many larger content analysis studies, more than one person is involved in the coding of information; therefore, high inter-rater reliability is essential for the integrity of a content analysis. Computer software such as NUD*IST has been developed to aid in the content analysis of interview data.

There has been a large growth in computer software that supports the analysis of qualitative data (Miles and Huberman, 1994).

Content Analysis by Computer

Inexpensive optical scanners make it possible to create text files from raw printed material. Such text files can then be searched, classified, and categorized using computer software designed for such purposes. Hypersearch, which is designed for Macintosh computers, is one such example. Word search capabilities of standard computer software such as WordPerfect or Word for Windows can also be utilized to perform some of the classification and identification functions.

A variety of software now exists for analyzing qualitative data. These include DataEase, Ethnograph, Filemaker Pro, HyperQual, HyperRESEARCH, NUD*IST, and QualPro. They store and organize notes and assist in finding patterns in these notes.

Meta-Analysis

Meta-analysis

The term **meta-analysis** was coined by Gene Glass (1976) and refers to quantitative analysis that reviews, combines, and summarizes the results of many different studies dealing with the same research question. It could be described as a transcending "analysis of analysis." Whereas a literature review qualitatively summarizes and analyzes, meta-analysis could be viewed as "quantitative reviewing" (Green and Hall, 1984). Furthermore, while secondary analysis reanalyzes an original data set, meta-analysis involves summarizing and comparing the statistical results of multiple data sets.

Wells (1991, p. 1) indicates:

Most studies end with a call for more research and more elaborate analysis. But perhaps the task is to make better use of the data and studies we already have, adopting analytic procedures that are more deliberately cumulative and integrative. . . . [T]he technique of *meta-analysis* provides an explicit strategy for summing and synthesizing results across multiple separate studies to produce cumulative conclusions.

Smith and Glass (1977, p. 760) suggest that

[s]cholars and clinicians are in the embarrassing position of knowing less than has been proven, because knowledge, atomized and sprayed across a vast landscape of journals, books and reports, has not been accessible. Extracting knowledge from accumulated studies is a complex and important methodological problem which deserves further attention.

Traditional qualitative literature reviews may be turning into an inappropriate means of summarizing empirical literature (Wells, 1991, p. 2). While the basic steps involved in meta-analysis are little different from a good research review, its emphasis on quantification maximizes precision and replicability. There is even computer software available to assist with this task (Wells, 1991, p. 10).

Wells (1991, p. 4) tells us that the *steps in meta-analysis* are slightly different from those of any good research review. These steps involve the following:

- Conceptualizing and specifying clearly the content of the research problem and its basic terms
- Searching the literature and selecting a representative set of studies relevant to the review
- Building a base of relevant data for the review by summarizing, describing, and coding the features of separate studies and translating them into comparable categories and terms
- Analyzing the database of studies for patterns of significant effects and for theoretically meaningful correlations
- Providing a summary description of the results and some evaluation

In one example, Smith and Glass (1977) analyzed 375 studies of psychotherapy and counseling and concluded that there were only negligible differences in the effects produced by different therapy types; they also determined that the typical therapy client was better off than 75 percent of the untreated subjects. Rosenthal (1976, 1978) used meta-analysis to examine the frequency of recording errors in observational studies and found that, although only one percent of all observations were in error, about two-thirds of the errors favored the hypothesis of the observer.

Although meta-analysis has been employed in hundreds of studies in the field of psychology, it is used relatively infrequently in criminal justice. In his own search of the literature, Wells (1991, p. 11) found only sixteen examples in criminal justice since 1980; in the vast majority of these cases, meta-analysis was used to evaluate the effectiveness of treatment rather than to analyze theoretical propositions. Tittle, Villemez, and Smith (1978) performed a meta-analysis on empirical studies examining the relationship between social class and criminality. Loeber and Stouthamer-Loeber (1986) did a meta-analysis of family factors and delinquency, while Whitehead and Lab (1989) meta-analyzed correctional treatments. Wells and Rankin (1991) did a meta-analysis of the literature on broken homes and delinquency. Finally, Pratt and Cullen (2000) did a meta-analysis of studies examining Gottfredson and Hirschi's "general theory of crime" and found support for their proposition that low self-control increases involvement in crime. Exhibit 8.4 illustrates two other examples of unobtrusive measurement—the identification and analysis of hot spots.

EXHIBIT 8.4 ▶

Applied Criminal Justice Research: Hot spot Analysis

POLICE   CHARLOTTE-MECKLENBURG POLICE DEPARTMENT

Strategic Planning and Analysis

About SP&A   SP&A Projects   Summary Reports   District Crime Stats   Crime Maps   GIS   Research

Hotspot Analysis

- *Identify concentrations of particular types of offenses, arrests, etc.*

"Where is the densest concentration of incidents on the map?" has been one of the most common spatial questions asked in law enforcement. Two approaches have commonly been used to attempt to answer this question:

1. Areal analysis - analysis of density within predetermined boundaries,
2. Graduated symbol analysis - analysis of relative frequency of occurrences at specific places or addresses.

While either of these techniques may be useful answering certain questions, both suffer from serious limitations as methods for identifying and managing hotspot area. If clusters are to be compared over time, a consistent method for determine clustering is needed.

The Illinois Criminal Justice Information Authority developed a computer program called STAC (Spatial and Temporal Analysis of Crime) for performing cluster analysis. The purpose of this process is to identify areas that contain especially dense clusters of events—typically referred to as "hotspots". These high concentration areas are areas that usually demand police attention.

For example, STAC allows an analyst to identify all of the areas in a patrol district where at least 5 robberies occurred within a 1000 feet radius. These areas are then outlined on the map. Using STAC to identify hotspots provides analyst a consistent method to measure concentrations of criminal events over time.

Each month, violent crime, robbery, residential burglary, commercial burglary, larceny from auto, and auto theft hotspots are calculated for each patrol district. Reports summarizing the time of day, day of week, victim race, etc. are provided along with each hotspot map.

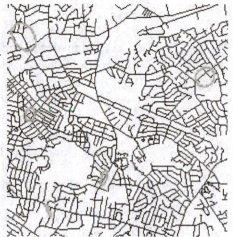

- *Compare the locations of hotspots across time or compare hotspots or different crime types*

Crime hotspots that have been identified over several months can be displayed at the same time. This allows for the identification of areas with chronic problems and indicates the direction in which a crime problem may be shifting. These types of maps can also be used to solicit resources for an area from other public and/or private agencies in order to work towards solving a community's problems.

Hotspots of different offense types can be displayed to identify where they intersect. For instance, residential burglary hotspots can be displayed along with robbery hotspots to discover where they overlap. A more detailed analysis of these intersecting areas can then be performed.

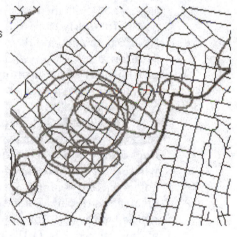

Source: Charlotte Mecklenburg Police homepage: www.charmeck.nc.us/cipolice/spab/gis/pinmaps.htm.

Sources of Existing Data

Also classified under unobtrusive methods is the usefulness of literature reviews or review of the results of studies by others to assess and develop one's own research problem. Services such as those provided by the National Criminal Justice Reference Service (NCJRS) in this regard replace hours of tedious library searches with computer searches and the provision of annotated bibliographies.

A thorough literature review of existing books, articles, journals, and other publications is, in reality, as important a part of data gathering as the primary collection of data. The National Advisory Committee on Criminal

Justice Standards and Goals (NACCJSG) encourages researchers to utilize available data:

> Criminal justice agencies have been overwhelmed with data collection efforts, and much of the information already collected remains unused by researchers. The difficulty of knowing what data exist, the geographical dispersion of resources, problems of access, and questions of validity and suitability for research all lead to a continued preference by researchers to collect new data for each project. (National Advisory Committee, 1976, p. 55)

Some sources of criminal justice statistics are the UCR, the *National Crime Survey*, and *National Prisoner Statistics* (formerly *Prisoners in State and Federal Prisons and Reformatories*) published by the U.S. Department of Justice, and *Federal Prisons* released by the Federal Bureau of Prisons. Various federal agencies, for example, the Treasury Department and the Drug Enforcement Agency (DEA), publish annual reports of the trends and numbers of violations under their jurisdiction.

The Department of Justice, through its Bureau of Justice Statistics (BJS) and particularly the NCJRS, provides indispensable services to users. The NCJRS compiles and disseminates information through Selective Notification of Information (SNI), which is e-mailed to users and provides updated annotated listings of publications, computer search services titles and abstract for books and journal articles. BJS publishes the *Sourcebook of Criminal Justice Statistics* annually.

Offender-Based Transaction Statistics (OBTS) collect felony arrest records from those participating states that detail such cases from booking to final disposition. Such processing begins with fingerprinting and ends either when the case is dismissed or when the arrested person is acquitted or convicted and sentenced. Local criminal justice agencies record arrest data on disposition documents and fingerprint cards, and these records are then forwarded to the state's criminal information repository, which updates appropriate master records. OBTS receives data from these repositories. BJS regularly solicits states to extract and submit such data following OBTS guidelines (Bureau of Justice Statistics, 1989).

Researchers can also obtain original data from agencies or other researchers and reanalyze the data for their own purposes. Problems in using such data relate to their location, permission or access, validity and reliability, possible misinterpretation of codes, and other nuances in the data that may not have been of concern to the original researcher. Incomplete data and, in some cases, inadequate form of the data may also be problematic.

Researchers interested in classified government information can file under the federal Freedom of Information Act (see Sherick, 1980) and, unless the data are viewed as essential to national security, they should be made available for legitimate scholarly or investigative research. The National Archives and Federal Records Administration and Library of Congress have mountains of such historical and declassified documents. As an example, in

1987, a researcher discovered a handwritten draft of the Bill of Rights in the National Archives that no one knew existed. Some declassified FBI files that are available are investigative case files of the Bureau of Investigation (the FBI's predecessor), 1908–1922; the file on the Black Panther Party, North Carolina, 1968–1976; "Communist Infiltration of the Southern Christian Leadership Conference" investigative files; the Martin Luther King, Jr., assassination file; Malcolm X FBI surveillance file; Cointelpro: Counterintelligence Program file; the firebomb and shooting at Kent State file; Watergate investigation file; HUAC—House Un-American Activities Committee file; and the Albert Einstein file.

Exhibit 8.5 features an example of an item from declassified FBI files that can be downloaded from the FBI homepage (www.fbi.gov/foipa/foipa.htm). Due to enormous "Freedom of Information Act" requests for information on serious matters as well as requests for the whereabouts of Elvis, UFOs, and Hitler, the FBI has made 16,000 pages from thirty-seven investigations available on the Net. Ultimately it intends to post all 1.3 million pages of files already opened to the public and available at FBI headquarters. It is more economical for the bureau to post such information rather than undergo the expense of answering many individual requests for the same information.

Imagine that in doing research you would be able to do all of the following:

- Have a computer search done of as many as hundred different data banks on your topic and identify and supply short (roughly, 500-word) summaries (annotated bibliographies) of what each article, book, or source contains.

- Have any of the items that you are interested in that are not available at your library made available either in full document or microfiche form within a couple of weeks.

- Be able, if you have any questions, to call toll-free experts on your topic for further advice on sources.

- Be able to obtain (at a fraction of the cost of the original study) the raw data files with codebooks (guides to what the data mean) for your own reanalysis.

- Be able to use sophisticated prewritten (canned) computer programs to analyze these data.

All of these services are currently available and used by criminological and criminal justice researchers.

Data Archives (or *data libraries*) are institutes or organizations that store data resources (raw data) from previous studies. The world's largest repository of computer-readable social science data is the Inter-University Consortium for Political and Social Research (ICPSR) at the Institute for Social Research in Ann Arbor, Michigan. Since 1978, within the ICPSR, the BJS has funded the creation of the National Archive of Criminal Justice Data (NACJD; formerly, CJAIN, the *Criminal Justice Archive and Information Network*) to encourage the sharing of data resources. Data (from original studies) are available free of charge (see Exhibit 8.6).

EXHIBIT 8.5 ▶

X-Files at the Federal Bureau of Investigation

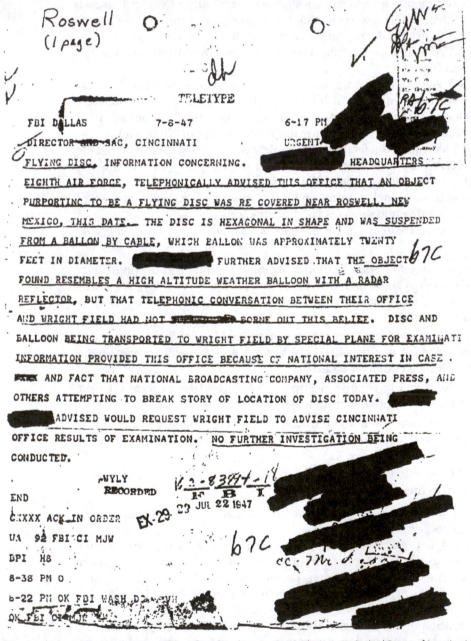

Source: Federal Bureau of Investigation homepage: www.fbi.gov/foipa/foipa.htm; see also Theoharis, A. FBI (Federal Bureau of Investigation): An Annotated Bibliography and Research Guide. New York: Garland Publishing, 1994.

EXHIBIT 8.6 ▶

National Archive of Criminal Justice Data

The NACJD is sponsored by the BJS and housed at the ICPSR at the University of Michigan. In 1996, it was announced that its 525-plus collection of computerized crime and justice data were now available over the Internet free of charge through the NACJD Web site (www.icpsr.umich.edu/NACJD/archive.html). The archive homepage appears below along with some examples of studies available. If you are unaware of a specific study number, you can "browse" choosing any subject area, a beginning letter of a title or of a principal investigator's last name or ICPSR study number. Both codebooks and data sets can be accessed online as well as downloaded.

 Download Data

NACJD Home | ICPSR | Bureau of Justice Statistics | NIJ
What's New | Analysis | Download Data | Site Guide | Search | Contact NACJD

Use this page to search, browse, and access crime and justice data at the ICPSR. All data accessed from this menu are publicly available for browsing and downloading.

Note : All of the search and browse utilities on this page now access the most up-to-date information available. Please report studies which appear to be mistakenly omitted to webmaster.

SEARCH (Help)	SUBJECT	TITLE	P.I.	BROWSE
		A B C D E F G H I J K L M N O P Q R S T U V W X Y Z	A B C D E F G H I J K L M N O P Q R S T U V W X Y Z	Recent Additions
Enter ICPSR Study Number if Known: [____] enter	I. Attitude Surveys			Recent Updates
	II. Community Studies			
	III. Corrections			Forthcoming
	IV. Court Case Processing			
Search Holdings:	V. Courts			Serial Data
[____]	VI. Criminal Justice System			
Titles ▼	VII. Crime and Delinquency			BJS Collections and Activities at NACJD
[search] [reset]	VIII. Official Statistics			NIJ Collections and Activities at NACJD
Search Notes:	IX. Police			
	X. Victimization			Most Popular Data
Searching is **not** case sensitive. Multiple, space-delimited terms are interpreted as AND queries. **Quoted** queries are interpreted as a single search term.	XI. Drugs, Alcohol, and Crime			NIJ Data Resources Catalog, 1998 (11th Edition) 📄
				NACJD Catalog, 1998 edition. (4.1 MB Download) 📄
				Data on Desktop Media

Go to the top of this page | Return to the NACJD home page

Send technical questions to: web-support@icpsr.umich.edu
Send data questions to: nacjd@icpsr.umich.edu
NACJD: http://www.icpsr.umich.edu/nacjd

(continued)

EXHIBIT 8.6   Continued

Below are some examples of studies to be found:

James Alan Fox: *Uniform Crime Reports: Supplemental Homicide Reports 1976–1992*

Marvin Wolfgang, Robert Figlio, and Thorsten Sellin: *Delinquency in a Birth Cohort in Philadelphia, Pennsylvania, 1945–1963*

Murray Straus and Richard Gelles: *Physical Violence in American Families, 1985*

Alfred Blumstein and Jacqueline Cohen: *Adult Criminal Careers, Michigan, 1974–1977*

James Wright and Peter Rossi: *Armed Criminals in America: A Survey of Incarcerated Felons, 1983*

Malcolm Klein, Cheryl Maxson, and Margaret Gordon: *Police Response to Street Gang Violence in California, 1985*

Delbert Elliott: *National Youth Survey: Wave V, 1983*

Robert Figlio, Paul Tracy, and Marvin Wolfgang: *Delinquency in a Birth Cohort II: Philadelphia, Pennsylvania, 1958–1988*

Cathy Spatz Widom: *Child Abuse, Neglect, and Violent Criminal Behavior in a Midwest Metropolitan Area of the United States, 1967–1988*

Richard Berk and Lawrence Sherman: *Specific Deterrent Effects of Arrest for Domestic Assault: Minneapolis, Minnesota, 1981–1982*

Dane Archer and Rosemary Gartner: *Violence and Crime in Cross-National Perspective, 1900–1974*

John H. Laub and Robert J. Sampson: *Criminal Careers and Crime Control in Massachusetts (The Glueck Study): A Matched-Sample Longitudinal Research Design, Phase 1, 1939–1963*

A burgeoning area of employment where students can apply their research methods skills is competitive intelligence research. Not to be confused with cloak-and-dagger economic espionage, which uses illegal means of gathering data, in this type of research, mouse and keyboard are employed, using "open source" (publicly available) documents on the World Wide Web. Company home pages provide organization charts, customer lists, executive biographies, corporate plans, mergers, documents, and research-and-development information. Job postings may signal a company's new directions.

This information can be gathered to measure one's rivals and to note trends and pricing. Company annual reports may provide too much information for rivals. In a *New York Times* article, "Corporate Intelligence: A Cloakhold on the Web," Sreenath Sreenivasan (1998) suggests visiting the following Web sites if you want to take a competitive intelligence cruise.

Fuld and Company   *www.fuld.com*
This intelligence index features links to 300 sites related to intelligence gathering by industry, as well as a guide to questions to be asked, such as information technology and employee defections.

Montague Institute   *www.montague.com*
This site offers a Web journal that features using the Internet for competitive intelligence.

Society of Competitive Intelligence Professionals   *www.scip.org*
This organization provides a database of experts available to discuss their specialties.

Michigan State University School of Criminal Justice on Intelligence Espionage
www.ssc.msu.edu/~cj/scip.html
The School of Criminal Justice at Michigan State, working jointly with the Society of Competitive Intelligence Professionals, has produced a site dedicated to intelligence and espionage laws worldwide.

Figure 8.1

Applied Criminal Justice Research: Competitive Intelligence.

Source: Sreenath Sreenivasan. 1998. "Corporate Intelligence: A Cloakhold on the Web." *New York Times*, March 2: C4. See also Anne Covey. 2001. "Hands-On Corporate Research Guide." *Corpwatch.* www.corpwatch. org/research/prd.jsp?articleid=945.

A very practical application of the research skills that you have been learning in this course is in the growing demand for research analysts in the area of competitive intelligence, which utilizes "open source" materials to investigate economic enterprises. Figure 8.1 examines competitive intelligence.

Observation

Observation is a strategy of data collection in which the investigator attempts to examine the activity of subjects while keeping her or his presence either secret or to a minimum, so as not to interfere. This may take the form of laboratory observations or more "naturalistic" field observations. Our sleuth Holmes not only questioned suspects, but carefully observed exterior body and physical signs, expressive movements or "body language," the "silent language" of the eye, and facial movements.

Cavoir and Howard (1973) had raters assign attractiveness ratings to pictures of juvenile offenders and to members of a control group of nondelinquent high school graduates. The delinquents received poor ratings. Applying an observational strategy in an actual setting, Stewart examined the "Defendant's Attractiveness as a Factor in the Outcome of Criminal Trials" (1979). All other things being equal, he found that less attractive defendants were more likely to receive heavier sentences than more attractive defendants. Both of these examples involved observation as an unobtrusive means of data gathering.

An important study that well illustrates the controversy surrounding observational studies in the field is the "Chicago jury study." A group of researchers had received permission to "bug" actual jury deliberations. Despite the fact that great pains were taken to ensure that any names or other identifying elements would be eliminated and screened by the overseeing judicial officials, legislators felt that the potential scientific merit of such a study was outweighed by the need to secure the sanctity of the jury room. Finally, federal legislation was passed to prohibit the study, as well as any future similar studies, making it a federal crime to record such deliberations (Vaughn, 1967). Similar controversy was raised by other studies. Stewart and Cannon's (1977) study of bystander reactions to "simulated theft," using stooges or accomplices as thieves to speed up the action, raised controversy that abbreviated the study. They describe how their "simulated thefts" were abruptly brought to a halt:

> The investigators took pains to make sure that the study was safe and sought the advice of local security firms, a professor of law enforcement who was also a former FBI agent, and a local businessmen's association. All of these individuals and groups gave the authors their support and advice.
>
> However, a local newspaper, without consulting the senior author, printed distorted accounts of the investigator's intention to

stage robberies to study people. Because of the external pressures resulting from this biased and largely misleading publicity, experiments
II and III, which were to be sequels of the present one, were cancelled.
No reporters at any stage attempted to contact either of the investigators, nor was any mention made of the fact that the so-called "robberies" did not involve violence in any way, nor that a local merchants'
organization had advocated a need for such research. In addition, a local security firm gave the authors its full support and backing.
(Stewart and Cannon, 1977, p. 322)

A very innovative example of an observational study is a component of
the previously discussed "Project on Human Development in Chicago
Neighborhoods" (Earls and Visher, 1997). Systematic social observation was
used to record and measure each neighborhood's social organization and
changes over time in year 1, 4, and 8 of the study. Teams of six observers videotaped each "face block" (one side of a block) in the eighty selected Chicago
neighborhoods. In all, 27,000 face blocks were studied with video cameras
affixed to a van. Beginning in the summer of 1995, both life and behavior were
recorded seven days a week from 7 A.M. to 7 P.M. In addition, the teams kept
observer logs relating to neighborhood activities and general appearance of the
community. The presence of garbage on the streets, abandoned cars, and
parking violations were dutifully recorded. Initial systematic observation
identified over 200 variables including features of the face block, presence of
people, land use, and people's reaction to the van (Earls and Visher, 1997).

Manning (1976), in an excellent review of methodologies used in studies
of police, identified a number of studies that employed observational strategies. He distinguishes between "active role" observers, where participation
was emphasized, and "passive role" observers, where the primary emphasis
was placed on observation. In all of the passive role observations of police
work he described, the observer's presence was made known to the subjects
(see, for instance, Banton, 1964; Black, 1968; Buckner, 1967; Reiss, 1968).
Because the observer's presence is known, such studies are not fully unobtrusive in nature, although the true purpose of the observation may be hidden
from the subjects. Black (1970), in a systematic observation of police–citizen
transactions in Boston, told the officers that his research was concerned with
citizen behavior rather than police behavior, whereas it involved both.

In the 1990s, the NIJ sponsored police observational studies in
Indianapolis, Indiana, and St. Petersburg, Florida, in order to replicate landmark
police observational studies of the 1960s and 1970s with the specific intent of
examining how police operate in the era of community policing. Officers were
accompanied on their beats in order to observe their interaction with suspects
and citizens. In Indianapolis, researchers observed police in twelve neighborhoods about three years after the city began community policing. In addition to
systematic observation of officers on patrol, other methods included observations of supervisors, private interviews with patrol officers and their supervisors,
and telephone interviews with residents (Mastrofski, Parks and Worden, 1998).

In what is described as "systematic social observation," Mastrofski and his associates (1998) observed the police in their "natural" setting (in the field) and recorded their observations according to procedures that could be duplicated by other observers. Strict rules were constructed so that researchers could make scientific inferences, and the method of observation did not rely on that which was being observed. Such observation is independent and does not rely on the accuracy, candor, or recall of those being observed. The cost, time, and dependence on police cooperation limit the techniques used in routine studies.

Using observations as well as tape recordings, Zimmerman and West (1975) studied conversations in public and in lab settings and observed that men were responsible for 96 percent of interruptions in conversations. In a lab setting, men made 75 percent of the interruptions in opposite-sex stranger conversation. Incorrect eyewitness identifications cause more convictions of innocent persons than any other reason. Wells and Bradfield (1998) in "Good, You Identified the Suspect" had 352 people watch a surveillance camera videotape of a fictional robbery in which a security guard was killed. They next asked the viewers to identify the killer from a photo spread of five faces (none of which were the actual robber). After the subjects made their choices, they were randomly told: "Good. You identified the actual suspect in the case," or "Oh. You identified number X. The suspect is number Y," or they received no feedback. Then, each person answered a questionnaire regarding their confidence in their observations. Those who had received positive feedback were extremely confident of the accuracy of their observation including their view of the culprit, having paid greater attention and being able to make out details of the robber's face. "Positive feedback distorted the witnesses' reports of almost every aspect of the identification process" (1998).

In a subsequent study, most eyewitnesses denied that positive feedback influenced their views. Wells and Bradfield concluded that lineups and photo spreads should be supervised by someone unrelated to the case.

Purists would insist that if a person's presence is known, the method is no longer unobtrusive; however, if the true purpose of one's presence is unknown, such as in disguised observation, the mere act of being on the scene may not elicit reactivity.

An indirect measure of sexual or occupational bias could be measured by having groups rate written or videotaped presentations or speeches in which only the name or occupation assigned is changed. In a study of the impact of the stigma of ex-convict status on subsequent employment, Schwartz and Skolnick (1962) sent prospective employers resumés in which only the criminal record varied. They discovered that as the criminal record condition changed—from no record or acquitted (with a letter from the judge) to acquitted (with no letter) to convicted—there was a steady decline in job offers.

To measure the popularity of various organizations, Milgram (1969) cleverly introduced the *lost letter technique*, in which letters addressed and stamped, but unposted, were "lost" in specified areas. The addresses varied; for example, "The American Nazi Party," "Ku Klux Klan," and the like. On the basis of the percentage returned, some indication of the relative unacceptability of these organizations was gained. The technique obviously yields only an indirect measure, but it certainly represents an imaginative means of assessment. The hazards of such research are illustrated by the case of a criminologist who was arrested while attempting to conduct such a study at a shopping mall. Variations of the lost letter technique include a study in which wallets containing cash in an envelope (Tucker et al., 1977) or lost letters containing cash (Farrington and Knight, 1979; and Knox and McTiernan, 1973) were left on the street.

Reader's Digest "lost" more than 1,100 wallets over five years in 117 cities in the United States, Europe, Asia, Canada, Australia, New Zealand, and Latin America. Each contained $50 in local currency as well as a name and phone number. Forty-four percent of the wallets were not returned, while every wallet was returned in Denmark and Norway. Seven of ten were returned in the United States, where Seattle residents were most honest and Atlanta residents the least (Joseph and Mullins, 2001).

Disguised Observation

Another dimension is added to observation when the investigator assumes a clandestine role. In Chapter 7, we mentioned Stein's (1974) study of prostitute—customer relations by employing one-way mirrors and secretly observing and recording hundreds of sessions. Humphreys's (1970) study of male homosexual behavior in public restrooms raised considerable debate regarding the issue of disguised observation versus invasion of privacy. He pretended to be a "peeper" (voyeur) or lookout for males participating in homosexual activity in public restrooms. He secretly recorded license numbers of participants. Later, after tracing their licenses, and under a different guise and disguise, he interviewed these men in their homes. Although he claimed to take great pains to protect the privacy and identity of respondents, without their permission, Humphreys certainly placed the subjects in a situation of potential harm and possible blackmail if the data were to fall into the wrong hands.

Disguised observation

Disguised observation involves any type of research in which the researcher hides his or her presence or purpose for interacting with a group (Roth, 1962). As in our discussion of participant observation, researchers who conduct such investigations do so without the subject's prior approval. Some view such behavior as privacy invasion, voyeurism, or snooping (Von Hoffman, 1970); others view such deception as necessary to conduct social scientific studies of many forms of behavior that could not be observed appropriately in any other manner (Stricker, 1967). To study difficult subjects in the field, researchers have posed as "thieves and victims" (Stewart and Cannon, 1977), a "watch queen" (Humphreys, 1970), a "mental patient" (Caudill et al., 1952), "Black Panther supporters" (Heussenstamm, 1971), "naive international tourists" (Feldman, 1968), and a "caretaker" (Sherif and Sherif, 1966), to mention a few.

Steffensmeier and Terry (1973) and Steffensmeier and Steffensmeier (1976) found that shoplifters (role-playing students) dressed as hippies were more likely to be reported than those dressed conventionally.

Feldman (1968) used disguised observation to study the honesty of the French, Greeks, and Americans given the opportunity to cheat in transactions in which either a fluent stranger or foreigner asked directions, overpaid cashiers and taxicab drivers, or the like. On this same subject of dishonesty, one of the earliest series of consumer investigations of this sort was conducted by the *Reader's Digest* in the 1940s. They brought previously checked-out products to establishments for repair. On the basis of their investigations, they concluded that 63 percent of the garages, 64 percent of the radio repair shops, and 49 percent of the sample watch repair shops were dishonest (Riis, 1941a, 1941b, 1941c). A rival causal factor, of course, would be incompetence. In a more recent study of insurance fraud in the auto-body repair business, Tracy and Fox (1989) borrowed damaged cars from a rental car company and then approached a sampling of Massachusetts repair shops for estimates for repair work. If the estimators were told that the car was covered by insurance, the estimates were nearly one-third higher.

In defense of covert research, Douglas describes how early doctors were accused of ghoulish crimes in their attempts to study the human body scientifically:

> As doctors, lawyers, and other professionals have done over the centuries, sociologists must work purposefully to carve out a special *moral niche*. . . . Exceptions to important social rules, such as those concerning privacy and intimacy, must be made only when the research need is clear and the potential contributions of the findings to general human welfare are believed to be great enough to counterbalance the risks. If we can agree that these factors are present . . . then we should have the courage to try to change the morals of our society and to do the research with as little invasion of privacy as possible. (Douglas, 1972, pp. 8–9)

One major problem with observational studies is the potentially long period of waiting for results or expected behavior to occur. Allen Funt, director of the popular television program *Candid Camera*, discovered that large amounts of time had to be expended while waiting for something to happen (Webb et al., 1966, pp. 156–158). Finally, in later programming formats, Funt relied on **confederates** (persons planted to facilitate that which is to be observed) to speed up the action. One could imagine, for instance, attempting to observe the willingness of bystanders to come to the aid of a victim by means of a hidden camera. Years may pass before even one observational case would present itself. To illustrate how the use of confederates speeds up the observational process, let us examine Stewart and Cannon's "simulated theft" study once again:

Confederates

> Each subject was selected by the criterion that he or she be seated at a bench and engaged in no activities other than relaxing. . . . After a subject was selected, the victim (confederate) walked to within three meters of the subject, clearly in his or her line of sight. The victim would then produce a cigarette, and would begin his search for a

match. Upon finding no match, the victim would make sure that the subject was observing him before any other manipulation took place. (Stewart and Cannon, 1977, pp. 318–319)

Next, the authors varied the stimulus by having the confederate ask the subject to watch his bag while he ran into a store or by simply, in a preoccupied manner, leaving the bag and also going into the store. About two minutes later, another confederate dressed as a working person, a business executive, or a priest would steal the bag. As soon as the subject reacted by any movement or utterance, he or she was immediately approached by an assistant to the researchers and the debriefing process was begun (Stewart and Cannon, 1977).

Perhaps the classic example of disguised observation using confederates is Asch's (1951) study of group pressure. Experimental confederates were instructed to choose the wrong answer in a series of perceptual processes in which the correct answer was obvious, for example, "Which of these lines is the shortest?" The naive subject responded after the others had done so incorrectly, and the willingness of the subject to comply with the group, or exercise correct independent judgment, was assessed.

Rosenhan (1973), in "On Being Sane in Insane Places," had himself and several associates placed into a mental hospital as fake patients. They pretended to have symptoms of schizophrenia, and from the vantage point of patients, and unbeknownst to the staff, they were able to record the real world of the mental institution. Once diagnosed as mentally ill, the patients had a difficult time escaping this definition of the situation and in convincing the doctors that they were not disturbed. With the average stay of nineteen days, each was eventually released with the diagnosis of being schizophrenics in remission.

As part of the ASC/ACJS "Oral History Project" (American Society of Criminology and Academy of Criminal Justice Sciences, 2004), William Chambliss describes a disguised observational study of political corruption by suggesting that "good research should scratch where it itches." Having read various studies of police–citizen contact involving researcher ride-alongs with police, he wanted to study the issue from the citizen side. Shaving off his beard and dressing as a truck driver, a former occupation he had practiced, he hung around areas where most of the vice arrests were made. One day a police officer entered a back room, and, when he left, a worker in the establishment matter-of-factly mentioned that he was the bag man (picking up bribes). Gaining permission to enter the back room, he observed a local gambling operation. He discovered a huge industry in gambling, prostitution, and other illegal activity. Finally deciding to come clean, he called one of his main informants and invited him to the university and explained his deception. The informant was not disturbed by the deception and said he could tell Chambliss many things, as did others. Chambliss explained to others that he was a professor at a university studying organized crime and that they could trust him not to reveal information in any way that would bring harm to them. He explained that he already had such information for six months and that nothing had happened.

Formby and Smykla (1981, 1984) assigned students in a criminal justice simulation class to perform disguised observations to examine whether passersby would assist drunks (role-playing students) in unlocking their car doors to drive home and, in a separate study, whether passersby would intervene to prevent burglars (role-playing students) from attempting to break into automobiles. For the burglary study each group consisted of a car, a driver, a thief, and two observers; the "crime" was committed in a variety of high–pedestrian traffic locations. Of sixteen incidents of auto burglary, only two instances of overt citizen awareness took place, neither of which produced sufficient intervention to end the burglary or call the police. The latter, of course, had already been alerted to the study's existence. In the drunk-driving study (Formby and Smykla, 1984), students were assigned the roles of drunk, observer, safety person, and police officer (the latter were actual police officers who were students in the class). "Students assigned the role of drunks were splashed with whiskey and vigorously applied it to their hands, neck and face. Drunks practiced their roles and benefited from the critique of instructor and students in modeling the drunk behavior." Sixty-two percent of the eighty-five pedestrians helped the drunk open the car door. In 2007, Smykla and colleagues (Crow, Hough, Mosley, Smykla and Tatum, 2008) replicated the drunk-driver students. About one-third of the subjects who believed the student was drunk helped him or her to unlock the car door, compared with 62 percent in 1984.

In an Urban Institute study of racial bias against black job seekers, selected pairs of black and white men applied for 476 entry-level jobs. Even though each pair was equally qualified, blacks were three times as likely as whites to face discrimination.

> Ten pairs of men between nineteen and twenty-four years old were dispatched to respond to randomly chosen help-wanted ads published last summer [1990] in the Washington Post and Chicago Tribune. The men were paired to be similar in appearance and manner. One team, for instance, consisted of a 6-foot-4 inch bearded white and a 6-foot-2 inch bearded black. Each team memorized similar biographies and practiced interviews to minimize differences. Nearly all the help-wanted ads were for retail, hotel, restaurant or other service jobs. (Wessel, 1991, p. A9)

Blacks fared worse than whites far more often in Washington, DC, than in Chicago. In Washington, DC, 60 percent of blacks versus 16 percent of whites were treated less favorably than their counterparts. This less favorable treatment entailed waiting longer or having a shorter interview or receiving discouraging comments from interviewers.

Inspired by this and similar research, federal agencies have increasingly embraced the use of undercover investigators to examine discrimination in the marketplace. The Equal Employment Opportunity Commission (EEOC) uses "matched-pair testers": investigators with different skin colors who pose as consumers or prospective employees. Evidence from such direct testing is perceived as quite compelling to juries in discrimination lawsuits. Such testers have also been used to test fair-housing practices as well as the treatment of minority shoppers in department stores (Wynter, 1998, p. B1).

As a final example, in order to examine questionable sales practices of "junk bond" mutual funds, Donald Anspach posed as a "pseudo-client" (pretend client) and let the salespeople make their sales pitches while he carefully recorded the deceptive and misleading proposals (Anspach, 1990).

Observational studies can be considerably enhanced through voice telegraphy validation, polygraph validation, videotaping, motion pictures, photography (including infrared photography), and other mechanical aids to data gathering.

Simulations

One way of avoiding problems of unobtrusive measurement in the field is through the use of simulations. A *simulation* is a *situation or game that attempts to mimic, or imitate, key features of reality*. Simulations may range from very simple, relatively nonserious play activities or games to highly complex computer simulations of the world economy or international diplomacy (Guetzkow, 1962; Haney, 1976). As was the case in the "Chicago jury study" discussed earlier, it is often impossible to study the actual subjects in real-life situations. Even though the subjects studied in a simulation may differ from real subjects, it may be the only choice in some circumstances. Simulated jury studies, although they have been criticized for artificiality, overreliance on volunteers or college undergraduates, and the like, have been predictive of actual jury deliberations (discussed in part in Chapter 3) (Colasanto and Sanders, 1978; Landy and Aronson, 1969).

Two well-known and controversial studies that illuminate some key issues of research through simulation are Haney, Banks, and Zimbardo's "Simulated Prison Study" (1973) and Milgram's *Obedience to Authority* experiment (1974). Haney, Banks, and Zimbardo created a "mock prison" and used undergraduates to play the roles of prisoner and guard. The overzealous undergraduates, particularly the guards, got carried away with their roles, became more aggressive and even violent; at the same time, the prisoners became increasingly more hostile and passive. In the end, the experiment had to be prematurely brought to a halt for fear of danger to the participants.

Milgram's simulations with *Obedience to Authority: An Experimental View* attempt to address conditions under which people will "follow orders" when told to do so by what appear to be competent authorities, even if these activities appear immoral or harmful to others. Using volunteers from a variety of backgrounds and without explaining the true purpose of the exercise, Milgram and researchers told the subjects that they were involved in a study regarding learning. The subjects were introduced to other subjects (actually confederates in the experiment) who were identified as pupils in the experiment. The subject-teachers were shown a shock-generating machine with which it was explained they were to deliver jolts to pupils who would be behind a screen attempting to answer questions. If the answer was wrong, the subject-teachers were instructed to flick a succession of switches marked with various labels from small voltage up to "XXX." None of the subjects refused to flick at least one switch, and a large proportion administered even the highest voltage when reassured to do so by the researcher, despite screams and cries of protest from the confederates. Although the simulation could certainly be criticized for artificiality and "demand characteristics," Milgram claims the experiment was real to the participants, many of whom claimed to have suffered some psychological problems after the experiment, after reflecting on what they had done. Fortunately, follow-up inquiries found no lasting impacts.

Not all simulations contain the potential ethical problems of the Milgram studies. Most do not involve hidden or manipulative processes, and most elicit the informed consent of subjects, but all simulations or disguised experimentation should involve the **debriefing** of subjects to reassure them and explain the full purposes of the study.

Debriefing

Simulations such as "mock trials," in which participants play the roles of principal actors in a courtroom, may be used for research as well as teaching or training purposes. Such training can be quite realistic, serious, and hopefully preparative to actual situations. As part of a larger study of plea bargaining, Miller, McDonald, and Cramer (1980) administered a simulation to 136 prosecutors and 104 defense attorneys. McDonald and Cramer (1980), in a quasi-experimental design, manipulated such variables as prior record of defendant and strength of case. Computer simulations of complex social processes can be utilized to trace alterations in systems introduced as a result of changes in specific variables. Assuming that the simulation model is accurate, such theoretically introduced changes can be assessed before they are attempted in the real world, at great savings in cost and potential error.

A relatively novel approach to research is the use of virtual reality computer simulations in the courtroom. Computerized images are increasingly being used as evidence in the courtroom. The distinction can be made between "animation" and "simulation." *Animations* are similar to photographs that recreate a scene or process. *Simulations* involve computer models that analyze and imitate an activity. Between animation and simulation is reconstruction; for example, evidence, witness statements, and the like may be used to recreate an accident scene.

Virtual reality computer simulations may be admitted as evidence at a trial if they are accurate in depicting the underlying testimony that they are intended to illustrate. "Desktop" virtual reality presents 3-D images on high-resolution computer screens and is controlled by keyboard, mouse, or joystick. In the far more dramatic and revolutionary "immersion" virtual reality, the user enters a computer-generated "landscape" by wearing special equipment (gloves, suits, goggles, and headsets) which enable interaction with a computer-generated virtual world. The user's movements can be used to modify the module's graphics. Virtual reality allows the juror to "experience" the scene and "see") things actually happening.

Virtual reality as an evidentiary tool is revolutionary, but at this point not in wide use in the courtroom. Its dramatic ability to influence jurists may also be its weakness in influencing them beyond the evidence. Some current obstacles to its implementation include the following:

- Does its probative value (ability to prove a fact in issue) exceed its danger of misleading or prejudicing a jury?
- Will it evoke emotions that will cause a jury to decide a matter on an improper basis?
- Does its prohibitive cost exceed the benefits?
- Is its accuracy still dependent on the information programmed into it (e.g., evidence, witness statements, and the like)?
- How authentic is the demonstration?
- How qualified are the experts who authored it?
- How valid and reliable is the software?

Advantages of Unobtrusive Measures

Nonreactivity

The chief advantage of unobtrusive methods of data gathering is their **nonreactivity**. If the subjects are unaware that they are being studied, then it might be assumed that the behavior or attitudes observed are *more natural*, unhampered by reactive effects to testing or artificial experimental arrangements. Nonreactive measures are also a means of *avoiding the over-reliance on attitudinal data*, or verbal descriptions by respondents, about their behavior.

Mechanical aids, both audio and visual, greatly enhance the data-gathering process in unobtrusive measurement. The use of *recording hardware can increase accuracy*, is often better than a human observer, and provides a permanent record for later analysis. Such gadgets as voice-activated tapes require little monitoring and relieve the boredom of observing nonactivity.

The collection of physical evidence is *inconspicuous and grants anonymity*. Archival records enable the *study of phenomena over time*. Observational studies have the advantages of *gaining information firsthand* and taking into account nuance and context of the behavior. If it is behavior that is the object of interest, its actual observation is *superior to survey claims*. A major consideration is the fact that *nonreactive measures may be the only means of studying some research problems*.

To overcome the often time-consuming nature of this technique, *researchers can employ accomplices* to precipitate the type of behavior they wish to investigate. By making use of data already gathered by others, the researcher can conduct large-scale and even international analysis *quickly and inexpensively*. Such data exist in large quantity and await clever investigators to tease out appropriate and useful analyses. No claim is made for the superiority of unobtrusive measures over other means of gathering data, but they are highly useful, particularly when combined with other methods.

Disadvantages of Unobtrusive Measures

The leading disadvantages in employing secretive means of gathering data are ethical questions, particularly that of *privacy invasion*. Because the permission of respondents to participate or be observed has not been requested, the researcher is in a sense an uninvited snooper; and because the subjects are not on guard, the behavior or attitudes they display may relate to private or intimate behavior that may prove embarrassing, or even dangerous to the subjects, were the information to fall into the wrong hands.

Criminal justice researchers, unlike some practitioners, have no state-granted **right to confidentiality** or recognized entitlement to privileged communication. They can be subpoenaed for information and be jailed for obstruction of justice. Possessing confidential information with the consent of subjects would be hazardous enough in such circumstances, but without their prior approval, such information would certainly put the subjects potentially in harm's way.

Right to confidentiality

Some other possible difficulties with clandestine methods relate to the representativeness of the subject(s). They *may be atypical and therefore not generalizable* to larger similar groups. In most instances, the purpose of the investigation is to infer to this larger group. For instance, the NIJ may sponsor a study in Cleveland, Ohio, not because they are interested in Cleveland per se, but because they hope to generalize to other similar cities.

Unobtrusive measurement can also be a *very time-consuming enterprise*, although accomplices can be employed to speed up the action. Such approaches are also subject to *possible observer bias*, unless carefully monitored by the research field director. Unlike participant observation, in which the researcher can test out interpretations of attitude as it intersects with behavior, unobtrusive studies concentrate primarily on behavior and thus may be removed from the subjective meanings attached to this behavior by the actors involved.

The use of available data or public observations may, of course, overcome some of the disadvantages we have elaborated. Existing records and archival data may have been previously contaminated by reactive biases or subject to selective deposit (what remains is not typical) or selective survival (what survives is not typical). The major problem with nonreactive methods is their accuracy when they are used as the only measure of some phenomenon.

Summary

Unobtrusive measures are secretive, or nonreactive, means of gathering data. They refer to a variety of methods in which the subjects are not aware they are being studied and thus are less likely to act artificially. The *major types of unobtrusive measures* are physical trace analysis; archives, existing data, and autobiographies; simple and disguised observation; and simulation. *Physical trace analysis* is analysis of deposits, accretions, or other indirect signs of human activity. Some principal methods of analyzing available data are content analysis and secondary analysis. *Content analysis* is systematic classification and analysis of the subject matter of human communication, such as publications and mass media. *Secondary analysis* is the reanalysis of data that had been previously gathered by someone else. Personal documents, biographies, autobiographies, and existing official data represent fertile sources for the analysis of available data. The use of sources of existing data in criminal justice has been considerably augmented by organizations such as the NCJRS.

Observation makes use of a strategy in which the analyst minimizes interaction with the subjects to carefully record and examine their behavior. In *disguised observation*, the researcher covertly enters the research scene without the knowledge or permission of the subjects. This technique often makes use of *confederates* or accomplices who facilitate the desired activity to be observed, as well as *debriefing sessions* in which the true purposes of the deception are explained to the subjects and any anxiety introduced is hopefully allayed. *Simulation strategies* involve attempts to imitate more complex realities by means of games or controlled experiments or computer models.

Numerous examples of criminal justice and criminological research attempting to utilize elements of these approaches are presented. The relative advantages and disadvantages of unobtrusive measure are detailed. Chief advantages of *unobtrusive methods* are that they are more natural, are nonreactive, depend less on verbal reports, and make excellent use of available data. Among some of the disadvantages are ethical and privacy invasion issues, lack of license to confidentiality, nonrepresentativeness of groups studied, possible time-consuming nature of the procedure, and observer bias.

The use of unobtrusive measurement in criminal justice research presents an opportunity to observe groups naturally and is limited only by ethics and the imagination and creativity of the investigator.

KEY CONCEPTS

Unobtrusive measures	Primary data sources	Advantages of
Physical trace analysis	Secondary data sources	unobtrusive measures
Archival records	Meta-analysis	Nonreactivity
Content analysis	Sources of existing data	Disadvantages of
Secondary analysis	Disguised observation	unobtrusive
Observation	Confederates	measures
Simulation	Debriefing	Right to confidentiality

REVIEW QUESTIONS

1. What are the major types of unobtrusive methods? Give an example of each from studies in criminology and criminal justice.

2. What are some advantages and examples of the use of secondary analysis in criminology and criminal justice?

3. What are data archives, and of what use are they in research?

4. What are the relative advantages and disadvantages of unobtrusive measures as a strategy of research?

5. Discuss how the blocks in Exhibit 8.2 utilized existing data in order to investigate gangs in Chicago.

USEFUL WEB SITES

National Archive of Criminal Justice Data *www.icpsr.umich.edu/nacjd/*

Bureau of Justice Statistics *www.ojp.usdoj.gov/bjs*

Sourcebook of Criminal Justice Statistics *www.albany.edu/sourcebook*

Consortium for Qualitative Research Methods (Division of the American Political Science Association) *www.asu.edu/clas/polisci/cqrm/index.htm*

Infomine: Scholarly Internet Resource Collections (Government Sources) *http://infomine.ucr.edu/cgi-bin/search?govpub*

CIA Library and References *www.cia.gov*

Federal Bureau of Investigation *www.fbi.gov/*

World Factbook of Criminal Justice Systems *http://bjs.ojp.usdoj.gov/content/pub/htm/wfcj.cfm*

9

Validity, Reliability, and Triangulated Strategies

Much of the preceding text has concentrated on the weaknesses of individual data-gathering strategies. This chapter explores the issue of measurement and specifies operational procedures for attacking problems of validity and reliability in research, with emphases on multimethod strategies.

Error in Research

Error is another term for invalidity, and sources of potential error or invalidity are ever present, even in some of the best research. In fact, as we have reiterated throughout this book, the only perfect research is no research. By way of example of this truism, Walters and White in "Heredity and Crime: Bad Genes or Bad Research" (1989) point to many methodological flaws in such genetic studies. Particularly problematic in such studies has been the question of operationalizing zygosity, that is, of determining whether twins were monozygotic (identical) or dizygotic (fraternal). Walters and White note that contrary to popular belief monozygotic twins are not always identical looking, nor are all identical-looking twins monozygotic. Advances such as blood and serum typing provide for more valid measurement.

In lamenting the lack of validity in much of the research on physical child abuse, Mash and Wolfe (1991, p. 10) note:

> Research into [child] abuse has been plagued by such interrelated methodological problems as a lack of a priori predictions; a narrow research focus on physical injuries; an insensitivity to important child development parameters; poorly defined independent and dependent variables; confounded variables; inadequate and/or biased sampling; lack of adequate demographic descriptions; no or poorly matched comparison groups; the use of inappropriate measures of unknown or inadequate reliability and validity; the use of nonblind experimenters and coders; inappropriate analysis and illegitimate inferences and interpretations.

The question of validity, as we will see, logically precedes that of reliability. **Validity** asks "Does my measuring instrument in fact measure what it claims to measure?" Is it an accurate or true measure of the phenomenon under study? **Reliability**, on the other hand, concerns the stability and consistency of measurement. If the study were repeated, would the instrument yield stable and uniform measures? Before consideration of the consistency of measurement, accuracy should be assumed. A consistent inaccurate measurement of a phenomenon is one that is predictably wrong and therefore not very useful. Criminological and criminal justice research have made major strides since the 1970s when major critics were not very impressed with the work that had been done.

Validity

Reliability

Figure 9.1 presents some ways of spotting bogus (invalid) claims in scientific research.

In Chapters 3–8 we reviewed the many sources of error and critiques of the validity and reliability of much of the quantitative research conducted in the social sciences and, specifically, criminal justice. Bailey (1971), for instance, in a review of a sample of hundred correctional outcome reports, concluded that much of the research was invalid, unreliable, and based on poor research design. Generally, the more rigorous the design, the less the likelihood that significant outcomes in treatment will be claimed. In their review of criminological research, Hood and Sparks (1971, p. 9) were led to the following conclusion: "Yet the unhappy fact is that much criminological research—even in recent years—is so defective methodologically as to be virtually worthless; and many other studies are so limited in this respect that very little weight can be put on their conclusions." Although later modifying his views and admitting that perhaps he had been too methodologically narcissistic, Martinson (1974) blasted correctional research in his now famous "nothing works" criticism. He felt that there was little evidence of significant programs in corrections that had any important impact on reducing recidivism.

Robert Park has identified seven warning signs that a scientific claim is outside the bounds of rational scientific discourse or is bogus.

1. *The discoverer pitches the claim directly to the media.* Good science is exposed to the scrutiny of other scientists (peer-reviewed) first, before it is disseminated to the general public, who are not in a professional position to judge. If the discoverer's findings cannot stand up to the scrutiny of fellow scientists, then perhaps they are bogus.
2. *The discoverer says that a powerful establishment is trying to suppress his or her work.* The discoverer claims that mainstream science is part of a conspiracy of government and business.
3. *The scientific effect involved is always at the very limit of detection.* There is a lack of clear, scientific evidence.
4. *Evidence for a discovery is anecdotal.* "Data" is not the plural of "anecdote." Modern science distrusts anecdotal evidence.
5. *The discoverer claims that a belief is credible because it has existed for centuries.* Ancient folk wisdom, however repackaged, does not match the output of modern scientific research.
6. *The discoverer has worked in isolation.* The myth of the lone genius inventor stands in sharp contrast to modern scientific breakthroughs, which are almost always a synthesis of the work of many scientists.
7. *The discoverer must propose new laws of nature to explain an observation.* If we must change existing laws of nature or propose new ones, the discovery is almost certainly wrong.

Figure 9.1
Warning Signs of Voodoo or Bogus Science
Source: Robert L. Park. 2003. "The Seven Warning Signs of Bogus Science," *Chronicle of Higher Education*, January 31: B20; see also Robert L. Park. 2002. *Voodoo Science: The Road from Foolishness to Fraud.* New York: Oxford University Press.

Reasons for Lack of Validation Studies in Criminal Justice

As part of its recommendations regarding research designs, the National Advisory Committee on Criminal Justice Standards and Goals (1976, p. 53) indicated that "Descriptions of proposed research designs should include in at least rudimentary form, a comparison of the selected design with possible alternatives and, where applicable, an indication of the methods to be used to overcome the inherent weaknesses of the selected design." In this same assessment of *Criminal Justice Research and Development*, the advisory committee noted that despite the great need for validation and replication of studies in criminal justice, few have been conducted. *Some reasons for the lack of validation studies in criminal justice are as follows*:

- Little professional esteem in replication
- Lack of complexity in technique
- Design faults in original study
- Unfavorable climate
- Interjurisdictional disputes
- Tradition

It is unfortunate that *less professional prestige* is assigned to replication studies. Often, professional journals are not interested in publishing such results, considering it old news. Unlike laboratory experiments in the physical sciences, which are easily replicable, much criminal justice research may be of a nontechnical quality, making exact replication more difficult. *Design faults* in original studies, often called attention to by the researcher to bring about improvements in future studies, make exact replication of studies unlikely. Any change makes the validation study different than the original; thus, any differences found may be the result of instrumentation rather than flaws in the initial study.

The *unfavorable climate* for validation research is due to the human nature of organizational findings. Most organizations simply have little interest in objective findings that may shed negative light on the agency, particularly at budget time. If the initial study had positive results, then the point of view might be why restudy the obvious, particularly when funding for existing programs is needed. If the results were negative, there would not likely to be a warm reception for yet another study.

Interjurisdictional and agency differences are so large that even several studies of agencies in different jurisdictions may still be viewed by officials in criminal justice agencies in other states or domains as inapplicable to the differing conditions in their province.

Finally, the *lack of a research tradition* that would support validation studies in criminal justice research may create a self-fulfilling prophecy in that researchers tend not to view the need to carefully outline their methodology so as to permit replication and possible future validation. To encourage such a tradition, the National Advisory Committee called for expeditious federal funding of small-scale unsolicited proposals that involve inexpensive validation studies. In this same mode, comparative international research was viewed as an additional and important source of assessing the validity and reliability of criminal justice research.

In concluding the section on validation, the National Advisory Committee on Criminal Justice Standards and Goals recommended that:

> Research projects intended to validate previous research play an important role in the advancement of knowledge. Validation studies should be encouraged as initial steps of larger studies and should be funded as separate projects in greater numbers than in the past. Validations should be carefully designed and reviewed, however, to determine whether there are serious obstacles to successful completion. When few obstacles are present, as in small-scale validations, procedures should be available for funding and publishing such studies expeditiously.

> 1. In order to facilitate validation studies, R&D [Research and Development] funding agencies could require that R&D projects be documented in a form that permits validation.
> 2. Data used in a research project could be made available to other researchers, within existing confidentiality constraints (National Advisory Committee, 1976, p. 54).

Ways of Determining Validity

Let us examine appropriate procedures with which to determine the reliability and validity of measuring instruments. Table 9.1 provides a summary of the types of validity and reliability.

Following are the *types of validity*:

- Face validity
- Content validity
- Construct validity
- Pragmatic validity
- Convergent–discriminant validity

Face Validity

Face validity, the simplest measurement, asks, "Does the measuring instrument appear, at face value, to be measuring what I am attempting to measure?" Such an approach to establishing validity is very judgmental and does not rest particularly on any empirical grounds. It simply looks good, or strikes informed judges as a reasonable attempt to measure the point in question. Hardt and Hardt (1977) were satisfied with the face validity of a self-report scale they administered to a group of high school students. They noted that the prosocial behavior item, "helping parents," received the

Face validity

Table 9.1
TYPES OF VALIDITY AND RELIABILITY

Types of Validity

Face	Does the measuring instrument appear "at face value" to be measuring what I am attempting to measure?
Content	Does each item or the content of the instruction measure the concept in question?
Construct	Does the instrument in fact measure the concept in question?
Pragmatic	Does the instrument in fact measure the concept in question? current status (concurrent validity) or future outcomes (predictive validity) of the concept being measured?
Convergent–discriminant	Does use of different methods or measures (triangulation) of the concept yield similar results, while use of the same method to measure different concepts produces different (discriminate) results?

Types of Reliability

Test–retest	When the same instrument is administered at least twice to the same group, are the results or scores the same (or stable)?
Multiple forms	Does the administration of a disguised or alternate version of the same instrument to the same group result in the same (stable) scores?
Split-hald techinque	In the administration of the instrument to one group at one time, are separate halves of the instrument similar in response (are they consistent?)

highest endorsement as expected, as did two more trivial antisocial items, "fist fighting" and "smoking." Again, as anticipated, the least frequently reported items were more serious ones such as "joyriding" and "drug experimenting."

To explain all of the types of validity, we use an example to which most students should relate very well: a midterm examination in research methods. The concept that the instrument (the exam) is supposed to be measuring is "student knowledge of research methods." Suppose your class, which I am sure is very bright, took the examination, and most of you flunked despite the fact that all of you have given the class reasonable effort and are Dean's List students in other classes. Arguments with the professor are going nowhere, until one student questions the face validity of the examination. The instructor checks and, sure enough, realizes that he or she had asked the department secretary to make copies of a four-year-old test based on different books and entitled "Research Methods in Psychology."

Content Validity

Content validity entails examining each item—the content of an instrument— to judge whether each element measures the concept in question. Similar to face validity, content validity is also judgmental and usually nonempirical in nature; however, an item analysis may be employed to eliminate nondiscriminatory items. Using our midterm examination once again, although students may have been relatively satisfied with their general performance, all of them missed questions 40 and 56 and all of them had questions 1 and 2 correct. All of these questions tap a constant; the concept being measured does not vary because everyone gets them correct or incorrect. Although no student will argue about the easy questions, one student indicates that questions 40 and 56 deal with subject matter that is covered later in the text and is not part of the assigned material. Such items should be eliminated from the scoring.

Construct Validity

Construct validity (sometimes called concept validity) is perhaps the most theoretical and philosophically basic question. It asks whether the instrument in question does, in fact, measure what it has been designated to measure (Cronbach and Meehl, 1955). The problem may be with the label given to the scale rather than the instrument itself. Perhaps an excellent measurement is obtained of something other than what the instrument was claimed to measure. Construct validation involves skillful reasoning rather than measurement per se, because there seldom exists any criterion against which the measure may be compared. Selltiz and associates (1959, p. 160) indicate that if the predictions are not borne out, it may not be clear whether the problem lies with the measuring instrument itself or in the concept it is believed to represent. One more rigorous manner of approaching the issue of construct validity, "convergent–discriminant validation," will be discussed shortly. Construct validity, then, refers to the fit between theoretical and operational definitions of terms (Maltz and McCleary, 1977). In discussing methodological inadequacies of psychological research on prisoners, Reppucci and Clingempeel (1978) identified poor construct validity as a chief limitation. Those engaged in personality research with prisoners should use multiple measures, including natural treatments, behaviors, and settings, together with unobtrusive measures.

Returning to our midterm test example, suppose it is an objective test in which the questions are phrased in very sophisticated, esoteric language. The score on the test may be highly related to possession of an English major or high verbal SAT scores rather than a knowledge of research methods. This midterm test in research methods tended to be a better measure of knowledge of the English language. One of the major criticisms of some IQ tests is that they measure middle-class background more than intelligence.

Pragmatic Validity

The types of validation discussed so far entail theoretical or judgmental procedures, whereas **pragmatic validity** asks, "Does it work?" There are *two types of pragmatic validity*: concurrent validity and predictive validity. **Concurrent validity** concerns itself with whether the measure enhances the ability to gauge present characteristics of the item in question. The ability to accurately forecast future events or conditions defines **predictive validity**. Both concurrent validity and predictive validity are sometimes referred to as examples of criterion validation because both seek outside criteria as means to assess the accuracy of measurement. Use is made of some outside checks that could in no way be influenced by the measure under question. Sources of primary validation include files of juvenile and criminal courts, clinic records, data on income, education, marital status, school records, and the like.

Pragmatic validity

Concurrent validity

Predictive validity

In concurrent validation of a recidivism scale, crime commission of those who score as high or low risk on parole would be examined for differences.

A predictive validation of a recidivism scale would entail checking, for example, five years later, to see whether the index worked as predicted.

One problem in the attempt to demonstrate pragmatic validity is that for many abstract concepts employed in the social sciences and criminal justice, appropriate indicators may not be readily available or may be of questionable validity. For instance, concurrent or predictive validation of fear, cynicism, witness perception, or police morale might be quite difficult compared with checking reported age or education.

Schlesinger (1978), in assessing predictions of the dangerousness of 122 juveniles one year after release from a clinic, discovered that the variables used for diagnosis of juveniles undergoing treatment had very poor predictive ability. Some problems in performing predictive validation studies with such subjects are the uncertain reliability of many of the variables, the bias of a sample based on juvenile offenders, and inaccurate offender records. The latter entails the frequent problem of finding adequate criteria with which to assess the validity of measures.

Concurrent validation of our midterm exam might ask whether scores of the midterm agree with the performance of students on other assignments and quizzes that had been given so far. For example, if everyone had been doing above-average work until then, why did everyone flunk the midterm? Something is wrong, and that something could be the validity or appropriateness of the test. Predictive validity might ask whether performance on this midterm exam predicts a student's final grade in the course.

In a final example, in "A Longitudinal Validation Study of Correctional Officer Job Performance as Predicted by the IPI and MMPI," Shusman and Inwald (1991) explored the predictive validity of two personality tests, the Minnesota Multiphasic Inventory (MMPI) and the Inwald Personality Inventory (IPI). Could these two tests forecast correctional officer job performance an average of three and one-half years into the future? Using data on absences, tardiness, disciplinary actions, and supervisors' reports, they found that the IPI was a better predictor.

Convergent–Discriminant Validation/Triangulation

Convergent–discriminant validation involves the use of multiple methods to measure multiple traits (Campbell and Fiske, 1959). The logic of convergent–discriminant validation holds that by "using different methods (interview, questionnaire, experiment, observation) of measuring a construct, the results should be similar, whereas the same method measuring different things should yield dissimilar results" (Campbell and Fiske, 1959, p. 81). Thus, the use of different techniques to measure the same concept should yield the same findings (*convergence*), whereas the use of one technique to measure different things should yield different results (*discrimination*) (see Figure 9.2).

The use of multiple methods to measure the same phenomenon is also referred to as **triangulation** (Campbell and Fiske, 1959; Webb et al., 1966).

Triangulation methods assume that it is relatively hopeless to attempt to demonstrate the validity or reliability of one measurement using only one method. The use of multiple methods enables the introduction of "methods used" as a variable or rival causal factor. If there is no difference in findings despite the use of different methods, then any one method, for example, experimenter or interviewer effects, could not be responsible for producing the findings.

Although measurements of a concept (alienation) using different methods should yield the same results, measurements of different concepts with the same method should yield different results. If a student's midterm, final, and term paper scores are all Fs, there is convergence; however, if every time Professor Jones gives an objective midterm in any course everyone receives an F, the problem is the method. The problem is not the inadequacy of a particular method, it is that the method is used alone. It is fruitless to be concerned with the validity or reliability of the measurement of one concept, at one time, using only one measure.

In order to study decision making in jury trials, Reed observed actual jury trials, recording jury selection proceedings, the length and nature of the testimony, legal objections and rulings, and other measures. Next, interviews were conducted with attorneys and jurors in cases where a verdict was returned. Finally, an experimental jury simulation study was conducted to analyze many of these same issues. Reed claims that among the advantages of combining research methodologies were gaining access into the legal milieu, obtaining active cooperation of the presiding judge, and gaining

Figure 9.2
Convergent–Discrimination Validation: X, Similar Findings; –, Dissimilar Findings.

Trait	Experiments	Surveys	Unobtrusive Measures
Alienation	X	X	X
Anomie	—	—	—
Authoritarianism	—	—	—

100 percent cooperation from attorneys and 74 percent cooperation from jurors. In addition, the simulation was able to contain variables with applied value (Reed, 1976).

In our previous discussion of participant observation (Chapter 7), we described how Clarke (1982) utilized multiple sources to construct his typology of assassins. Similarly, we saw how journalists, such as Maas (1968) in *The Valachi Papers*, do not rely only on the testimony of an informant, but carefully use other independent sources to verify this information. Lupscha (1982) identifies the following sources of information that may be triangulated to obtain valid, convergent data on organized crime: informers, congressional hearings and investigations, court trial transcripts and depositions, articles in newspapers and popular periodicals, investigative reporting, wire surveillance transcripts, memoirs/biographies/autobiographies, government reports and releases, National Institute of Justice-assisted research, archival/historical documents, and in-depth interviews. Field studies could also be added to this list. The point is that the larger the number of independent sources that say the same thing, the greater the confidence attached to the findings. An analogy can be drawn to a criminal trial in the United States, where the prosecution is responsible for convincing a judge and jury of the guilt of a defendant who has pleaded innocence. The prosecution may present evidence, witnesses, and expert testimony, question and cross-examine, and bring to bear as many independent sources of information as possible to make the case. The state, however, must "prove" its case "beyond a reasonable doubt"; that is, it may never be able to make the case absolutely that the individual is guilty. Similarly, researchers seldom absolutely "prove" the validity of their findings; rather, they eliminate rival causal factors and errors to the point at which a sufficient number of independent, objective sources have been brought to bear that there is a high probability (but not absolute certainty) that the conclusions are valid.

The Project on Human Development in Chicago Neighborhoods utilized a triangulated strategy that featured a community survey, an observational survey, a survey of neighborhood experts, police incident files, public health and other official records, as well as census data regarding poverty concentrations and ethnic residential patterns (Earls and Visher, 1997).

By introducing, as a variable, different observers, interviewers, or methods of data collection, the researcher is able to control for invalidity of the method. The greater the number of diverse, converging measures on a phenomenon, the greater the confidence in the validity of the measure (Brewer and Hunter, 1983).

To validate scales measuring police probity, personal integrity, departmental anticorruption policy, and peer support for corrupt practices, Fishman (1978) compared the survey results with prior knowledge of the departments by an advisory board of an anticorruption management project. In addition, other sources of validation included the evaluation of the corruption level of the departments by a panel of experts, an examination of departmental records, a study of newspaper articles in each city covering a two-year period, as well as in-depth interviews with departmental brass and officers. On the basis of these pieces of corroborating evidence, Fishman found that responses to the instrument significantly differentiated corrupt from noncorrupt organizations and claims that the questionnaire is useful in aiding police administrators in evaluating the moral climate of their departments.

Some additional examples of triangulation methodology are the use of court records, in-court observations, and a simulation game in a study of plea bargaining (Miller, McDonald, and Cramer, 1980) and the use of court records, observations of conferences, and interviews of participants in a study of pretrial settlement conferences (Kerstetter and Heinz, 1979).

Researchers should use *pretests* to measure the validity and reliability of instruments prior to their use in a study. *Pretests* or *pilot studies* are preliminary studies conducted with a few subjects to test the instrument and uncover any obvious problems before administering it to the study population. This is similar to a firedrill or test run of a racing car. A piece of computer slang to remember in this regard is "GIGO" (garbage in—garbage out), which indicates that inadequately measured concepts that have been assigned numbers and often have been subjected to sophisticated analysis are no better than the initial operationalization decision.

In the long run, validity is never entirely demonstrated or proven; rather, invalidity is lessened, or researchers are able to express greater degrees of confidence in their data. (For further detail on validity, see House [1980] and Thorndike and Hagen [1977].)

Reliability

Reliability is demonstrated through stable and consistent replication of findings on repeated measurement. Thus, there are two types of reliability: stability and consistency.

Stability of measurement is determined by whether, assuming that conditions (rival causal factors) have not changed, a respondent will give the same answer to the same question on second testing. A different score on second testing may not be caused by the unreliability of the measurement, but rather by some other variable (for example, history). This type of reliability is most important for analyzing events and behavior data.

Consistency of measurement is determined by whether the set of items used to measure some phenomenon are highly related (associated with each other) and measuring the same concept. Schneider et al. (1978, pp. 2–50) explain:

> In attitude measurement it is frequently assumed that a fairly complex phenomenon is under investigation such as alienation and multiple items are required to operationalize the concept. Since each of the items is designed to measure the same concept (with slightly different aspects of the concept being dealt with by specific items), it is assumed that a reliable set of items will have a relatively high average inter-item correlation.

Statistics (Kuder–Richardson tests or Cronbach's alpha) are generally used to assess this type of reliability (Kuder and Richardson, 1967; Traub, 1994). *Three primary methods are used to demonstrate reliability:*

Test–retest
Multiple forms
Split-half techniques

All three assessments basically involve comparison of the instrument with itself to evaluate consistency.

Test–Retest

In the **test–retest method** of determining reliability, the same instrument is administered twice to the same population, and, if the results are the same, stability of measurement is assumed.

Test–retest method

A strong relationship between the two measures is assumed to indicate reliability. A reliability coefficient (correlation or alpha) of .80 is the most accepted indicator (Carmines and Zeller, 1979). Ideally, continued repeated measures of the same population with the same instrument would provide a means of assessing reliability. Such repeated measures are likely to be regarded as annoying to respondents if the purpose is not explained, and, if it were explained, the responses would most likely be invalid because of reactivity.

In measuring "fear of crime," for instance, a scale should yield the same measurement or score for individuals if applied at different times. If it does not, either an actual change may have taken place in the individual's attitude (for example, having been victimized recently) or the scale is not a good measuring instrument. Assuming no change in attitude, if the first administration of the scale indicates that an individual is very fearful and a subsequent administration indicates little fear, then the scale may be questioned as being unreliable.

The fundamental problem with this method of demonstrating reliability relates to our discussion in Chapter 3 of rival causal factors. Having already experienced the pretest, the subjects are no longer naive regarding the subject of measurement and therefore are liable to "testing effects" on second measurement. That is, the scores may differ in the posttest, not because the instrument is unreliable, but because the subjects were affected by pretesting.

Another way of attempting to resolve this reactivity problem is to wait longer before giving the second test. This, however, also presents problems, because it is more likely that an actual change in attitude will occur the longer the period between tests. A quasi-experimental model similar to those discussed in Chapter 3 can in part measure this. Randomly assigned, the experimental group could receive the pretest/posttest, and the control group only the posttest (Orenstein and Phillips, 1978, p. 272). Additionally, other rival causal factors such as history and maturation may also pose problems. For these reasons, researchers attempt to masquerade the nature of the retest by changing its appearance.

Multiple Forms

Multiple forms

Multiple forms involve the administration of alternate forms of the instrument to the same group. This actually is a disguised test–retest in which, hopefully, the subjects do not realize they are being retested. As in the test–retest, a strong relationship between the two administrations is indicative of reliability or stability. Despite the charade, the possibility remains that the subjects may be aware of the similarity of the pretest and posttest; thus, multiple forms could be subject to the same shortcomings as the test–retest approach. For this reason, the most popular and widely used technique in the social sciences for demonstrating reliability is the split-half technique.

Split-Half Technique

Split-half reliability

Thus far, the demonstration of reliability has involved temporal stability, in which two different administrations of basically the same instrument to the same group should correlate highly. **Split-half reliability** does not involve retesting and substitutes the assessment of internal consistency for temporal consistency; each half of a scale is analyzed as if it were a separate scale (Crano and Brewer, 1973, pp. 228–229). If a respondent were to receive the same score on even-numbered items as on odd-numbered items, then the scale would be assumed to be internally consistent or reliable.

The split-half technique administers only one measure to one group at one time. After the data are gathered, the instrument is randomly divided in half, and each half is treated as if it were a separate test or instrument. For example, the even-numbered items might be correlated with the odd items or the random halves compared; and if they are highly correlated, reliability would be supposed. The logic of the split-half approach is that, if an instrument is reliable, it should be consistent throughout. Such an approach removes the problem of testing effects or, for that matter, any other internal rival causal factor that would have been introduced with a posttest. Generally, a coefficient of reliability or equivalence, alpha (Cronbach, 1951), where high correlation is taken to indicate reliability, is used. A correlation of at least .80 is assumed to be indicative of internal consistency or reliability. A problem with both multiple forms and split-half techniques is the concern as to whether the two forms or halves really are equivalent.

For statistical calculations on reliability, see Cronbach (1970), or Guilford and Fruchter ED.

Arrestee Drug Abuse Monitoring (ADAM) Program

Drug Use Forecasting (DUF)

An excellent case illustration of the effectiveness of using urine tests to validate self-reported drug usage was provided by the **Drug Use Forecasting (DUF)**, a research program sponsored by the National Institute of Justice. This program asked volunteers from a population of arrestees in various cities to provide urine specimens that were then tested for drugs. Since 1987 arrestees in as many as twenty-three cities had first been asked questions regarding their drug usage; then they had been asked to submit to urine tests. The data were used only for research purposes, and anonymity was assured.

In 1998, National Institute of Justice (NIJ) began the process of replacing DUF with a new program, ADAM, Arrestee Drug Abuse Monitoring. In 2004, the George W. Bush administration discontinued the ADAM program, citing budgetary reasons.

Other Examples of Research Validation

In the development of a police career index (Bownas and Dunnette, 1975), Dunnette and associates employed a number of means of validating the final instrument. The intent was to develop a scale that was tested in both the field and simulations. The goal was a predictive scale for measuring job performance of police officers. In addition to completed tests and inventories, job ratings were collected and matched for several hundred officers in nine cities. On the basis of observational studies of actual police performance, a variety of simulations was developed. A number of police psychologists and officials reviewed and rated these simulations. A series of tests were administered that solicited personal and biographical information and opinion and self-description inventory to tap personality dimensions, as well as various cognitive performance tests. A group of senior police officers then discarded those items for which there was a low correlation between raters' scores and the instruments. The raters provided criterion or concurrent validation.

Utilizing triangulated methodology, Konecni (1979) compared the bail setting and sentencing decisions of eighteen San Diego judges in simulated cases with actual bail hearings, interviews, rating scale responses, observations of live hearings, and archival analysis of files pertaining to sentencing. While the simulations showed that the judges' decisions required people who had little reason to remain in the area while awaiting trial to post more bail than people with local ties, actual bail hearings showed that the local ties factor was insignificant and that judges relied heavily on attorneys' bail recommendations.

"Crime in Public Housing" (Fagan et al., 1998) has become a major area of interest to NIJ in recent years. Triangulated strategies for examining crime in public housing have included:

- Public housing authority records of crime-related complaints including reports by tenant patrols
- Police department records including National Incident-Based Recording System data
- Mortality and morbidity data for intentional injuries
- Annual tennant surveys can measure crime rates, residents' fear of crime, victimization rates of residents, and crime hot spots
- Observational studies of public housing
- Key informant strategies involving identifying and interviewing those with extensive knowledge of neighborhood life (Holzman, 1996)

In our earlier discussion of errors in surveys, we mentioned that an important source of invalidity may be introduced by coding, the process of assigning numbers to and scoring responses. To control for this, Dunnette and associates employed cross-validation. They randomly split the sample of respondents into two groups and then developed scoring keys separately for each. Each key was separately applied to the other subsample to estimate its validity. Additional scaling procedures such as item analysis and factor analysis were also employed.

Hood and Sparks (1971, pp. 30–31) discuss the use of validity checks on victim surveys in which research assistants determine whether a crime has been committed. The assistants agreed that about one quarter of all incidents reported to them by respondents were not crimes and excluded these along with doubtful cases. A sample of the retained victimizations was examined by a group of criminal lawyers and police officers who agreed that about two-thirds of the retained incidents recorded as crimes by the assistants were not crimes at all.

Issues of validity and reliability in criminal justice research are not limited to quantitative studies, as much of our discussion suggests, but are also applicable to more qualitative findings (Kirk and Miller, 1986). No area of criminology contains a literature as nonscientific as that of the study of organized crime. The subject has been much the province of sensationalistic tabloids, with much fiction confused for fact. In a great deal of the literature, statements of fact are made without supporting documentation. Albini (1971) found this to be the case for theories regarding the origin of the term *Mafia*. On the basis of an examination of historical archives, painstaking literature review, field visits, and interviews, he was able to dispute many theories that had been unquestioningly presented by others. Block (1978) indicates that much of the early history of the American Mafia is based on the testimony of informants Valachi and Reles (Maas, 1968; Turkus and Feder, 1951). Valachi's account of the Castellammarese wars in New York City claimed fifty to ninety gangland slayings, whereas later in Senate testimony he indicated only four or five victims. Block's (1978) search of newspapers of the period found only four possible gangland slayings during that time. Similar "myths" may have been accepted with respect to "La Cosa Nostra," "omerta," and other legends regarding the Mafia.

Brantingham and Brantingham (1984, p. 91) point out the numerous sources utilized by Shaw and McKay (1931) in their classic studies of delinquency in Chicago. They skillfully combined ecological analysis of group rates by mapped areas with in-depth case studies of individuals living in these areas. Some of the sources they utilized were criminal justice records of crime and delinquency distribution by area; personal memoirs of delinquents; interviews with parents, siblings, friends, and significant others; analysis of friendship patterns; and clinical analysis of physical, mental, and social health.

Summary

The question of error unreliability and invalidity is central to criminal justice research. Validity refers to the accuracy of findings, whereas reliability is concerned with consistency and predictability of research. In its assessment of the state of *Criminal Justice Research and Development*, the National Advisory Committee on Criminal Justice Standards and Goals partly explains why there has been a lack of validation studies in criminal justice. These include little professional self-esteem in replication, lack of complexity in technique, design faults in the original study, unfavorable research climate, interjurisdictional disputes, and lack of a research tradition that emphasizes such studies.

The principal measures of validity are face validity, content validity, construct validity, pragmatic validity (which includes concurrent and predictive validity), and convergent–discriminant validity (triangulation). Face validation involves simply the judgment that the instrument appears to be measuring that which it is intended to measure. Content validity is concerned with the examination of each item to assess whether the instrument is measuring what it is intended to measure. Construct (or concept) validity questions the tag or concept assigned to the scale. Pragmatic validity simply asks, "Does it work?" and comprises concurrent validity, which asks whether the scale predicts present events, and predictive validity, which asks whether it predicts future events. Triangulation is the use of multiple methods to measure the same phenomenon and is also referred to as convergent validity. Discriminant validation suggests that use of the same method to measure different things yields different findings. The use of different methods (triangulation) to measure the same thing should yield similar results (convergence). The validity of any one measure at one time is relatively inconsequential. Triangulation is the logical method to assessing validity.

Reliability is usually approached through test–retest, multiple forms, and split-half techniques. In test–retest, the instrument is administered at two different times to the same population, and the results are compared. The multiple forms technique is similar to the test–retest, except the retest is disguised by rearranging the items or hiding them as part of a larger questionnaire. Both of these techniques may be subject to testing effects; however, the split-half procedure involves one administration with random halves of the scale intercorrelated. If the correlation is sufficiently high, internal consistency of reliability is assumed.

The chapter concluded with illustrations of triangulated studies—and particularly the ADAM program.

KEY CONCEPTS

Validity	Predictive validity	Arrestee Drug Abuse
Reliability	Convergent–	Monitoring (ADAM)
Face validity	discriminant validation	program
Content validity	Triangulation	Drug Use Forecasting
Construct validity	Test–retest	(DUF)
Pragmatic validity	Multiple forms	
Concurrent validity	Split-half reliability	

REVIEW QUESTIONS

1. Why has there been a lack of validation studies in criminal justice? What is the importance of developing a tradition of such studies in the field?

2. Discuss the various ways of determining the validity of a particular measure. Of what importance is triangulation in resolving the issue of validity?

3. Discuss the three means of demonstrating reliability of measurement.

4. What is the "mark-recapture technique," and how might it raise problems in being employed to measure hidden human populations such as the addict population?

5. Using various examples from this chapter describe how researchers attempt to approach the issues of reliability and validity in their studies.

6. Discuss the methodology of the DUF program. How does this program benefit criminal justice research?

USEFUL WEB SITES

Research Validity *www.gseis.ucla.edu/courses/ed230a+z/internal.html*

All Psych Online: The Virtual Psychology Classroom *http://allpsych.com/researchmethods/variablesvalidityreliability.html*

Turning an Internship into a Research Opportunity *www.web.mit.edu/~ssilbey/www/pdf/intern_to_research.pdf*

Trustworthiness of Research *http://herkules.oulo.fi/isbn95142463/htm/xew.1.html~*

10

Scaling and Index Construction

Levels of Measurement

Variables may be measured on four levels:

Nominal   Interval
Ordinal   Ratio

Nominal variables

Nominal-level variables represent the simplest level of measurement. Objects are usually placed into mutually exclusive categories or types, and there is often no necessary quantitative or statistical meaning to numbers assigned to these categories, except as a convenience in distinguishing groups. Thus, any numbers assigned are merely qualitative descriptions, or labels, that enable us to keep track of differences. Demographic variables such as sex, race, religion, and city are examples of nominal variables. Values might be assigned, such as 1 to Protestant, 2 to Catholic, 3 to Jewish, and 4 to other. Three Protestants, however, do not equal one Jewish. The numbers merely assist in categorizing qualitative distinctions. Another example of this would involve writing down five telephone numbers of friends and calculating the "average" telephone number from these data, then calling it and waiting for an "average" friend to answer (Dowdall, Babbie and Halley, 1997, p. 185). Many variables that should take on higher scale value may be treated as nominal level, although information is lost as a result. In criminal justice, numbers could be arbitrarily assigned to different types of crimes in order to categorize them, for instance:

1. Homicide

2. Assault

3. Robbery

4. Burglary

Obviously, as in the previous example, the actual numbers assigned have no mathematical meaning. That is, a homicide (1) plus a robbery (3) does not equal a burglary (4), nor do four homicides equal one burglary. Other qualitative or nominal categories to which numbers are assigned are telephone numbers, social security numbers, room numbers, addresses, and officer badge numbers. Any reduction in the level of measurement of a variable from higher level to nominal measurement involves a loss of precision or detail. Similarly, any increase in the level of measurement to ordinal, interval, or ratio involves an increase in information, or precision, over the previous categories.

Table 10.1 ranks data on violent criminal victimization.

In a representation of the same data using only nominal-level information, the cities would be classified as either Eastern or Western, for example:

1. Eastern cities 8

2. Western cities 5

Another nominal means of assigning values to the data in Table 10.1 would be to consider scores above fifty-four as high, and assign them a value of 1, and scores of fifty-four or below as low, and assign them a value of 2.

For instance, weight, which could be measured in pounds and inches, could be reduced to simply heavy and light. Similarly, "sentence imposed," which could be measured in months, might be reduced to simply "long" and "short."

Table 10.1
VIOLENT CRIMINAL VICTIMIZATION RATES IN THIRTEEN SELECTED CITIES (PER 1,000 RESIDENTS 12 AND OLDER)

		Rank	Location
Detroit	68	1	Eastern
Denver	67	2	Western
Philadelphia	63	3	Eastern
Portland	59	4	Western
Baltimore	56	5.5	Eastern
Chicago	56	5.5	Eastern
Cleveland	54	7	Eastern
Los Angeles	53	8	Western
Atlanta	48	9	Eastern
Dallas	43	10	Western
Neward	42	11.5	Eastern
St. Louis	42	11.5	Western
New York	36	13	Eastern

Source: National Crime Panel Surveys. Law Enforcement Assistance Administration, 1974.

Ordinal variables

Ordinal-level variables contain all the properties of nominal variables, but they also enable the placement of objects into ranks, that is, highest to lowest. In Table 10.1, the city with the highest victim rate was assigned a rank of 1, the city with the second highest a rank of 2, and so forth to 13 for the lowest. For cities that were tied, the average of the ranks that would have been assigned is given to each of the tied values. Most attitudinal scales used in the social sciences and criminal justice are ordinal in nature. They enable us to rank respondents, but they must not be mistaken for real numbers. For example, a person whose attitudinal scale score is 50 is higher than a person who scored 30, which is again higher than one who scored 10. Thus, we know that each is higher than the next. We do not know by how much each is higher; the ranks are not comparable to meters or dollars. As another example, although we know that a student with a 3.6 quality point average in college is .6 higher than one with a 3.0, we would have no idea of the unit differences in points among students who ranked first, fifth, and tenth unless the actual averages were provided.

Interval-level variables contain all the elements of nominal and ordinal data and also assume equal distance between objects on a scale. They not only provide a ranking of objects but also reflect equal intervals or a standard unit between scale scores. Thus, the distance between scores 2 and 4 is exactly the same as the distance between 8 and 10. Using our victimization rate example from Table 10.1, the assignment of nominal-level measurement to the data merely resulted in mutually exclusive categories of east-west or high-low, whereas ordinal assignment ranked the cities from highest to lowest. Interval-level data, the actual rates, give us this same information plus the unit differences between each value. That is, we now know not only which city ranks higher or lower but also how much higher or lower. Interval-level measurement also contains an arbitrary zero point.

Ratio variables

Ratio-level variables not only assume the interval quality of data, but they also have a fixed meaningful zero point. Such data enable one to show how many times greater one value is than another. Some examples of ratio variables are variables such as age, weight, income, education, number of children, and frequency of crime commission. Although it is possible to have zero income or education, one would not have zero IQ or attitude toward crime. Each scale is more complex and takes on the properties of the preceding.

Upon waking in the morning, a typical American may "hit the scales" and discover that he or she has gained three pounds. While reading the morning newspaper one discovers that the gross domestic product has increased by only 2 percent, whereas the Dow Jones industrial average is up three points, the consumer price index is 1.2 percent for the previous month, and the FBI reports that the crime rate for the first six months is up 6 percent. In addition, the pollution index is 65 (which is in the fair range) and an earthquake in California registered 3.6 on the Richter scale. Without realizing it, most of us are quite familiar with the use of scales to measure degrees of change in factors affecting our lives.

Chapter 1 pointed out how meaningful concepts or abstractions of reality are created to provide insight and useful tags with which to manipulate and understand reality. Previously, variables were described as operationalized concepts, or concepts that vary or take on various values. Scales reflect levels of measurement or various degrees of quantitative value that a variable can take on. As we shall see in this chapter, each level of measurement has appropriate corresponding statistical measures.

Scaling Procedures

The purpose of measurement is to make connections between concepts and numbers. Mere observation, measurement, and assignment of numbers to responses are not the same as a proper measure. Scales can be viewed as calibrated instruments with which to interrogate concepts (Wright, 1980). Thus, there is a difference between scaling and scoring of test items. The level of measurement of a variable is very important in the utilization of various statistical procedures. Many statistical procedures, for instance, require interval variables and are inappropriate if used with nominal or ordinal variables.

Although many of the scaling procedures discussed in this chapter can be calculated by hand, the increased availability of inexpensive computer hardware and "canned" or prewritten computer programs makes these procedures easier to perform.

Scaling procedures involve attempts to increase the complexity of the level of measurement of variables from nominal to at least ordinal and hopefully interval/ratio. They build more complex, composite indicators of phenomena. A great many well-constructed scales already exist and should be consulted and analyzed before construction of a new scale. Established scales may be used as they are or modified to fit the special needs of a specific study. Such scales have an established track record.

Scaling

Various excellent handbooks that catalog scales exist. These not only classify scales by the concept to be measured but also report reliability, validity, previous studies that employed the scale where one could obtain the instrument, as well as usual sample items from the scale.[1] Strong consideration of previously developed scales is important because *replication*, the repetition of measures with different populations, enables establishment of a comparative and universal social science.

Although some writers attempt to make major distinctions between scales and indexes, in reality they are referred to quite interchangeably. One distinction is that a scale is generally concerned with only one attribute of a concept, whereas an index involves many dimensions or scales. With an index the researcher combines or averages the results for more than one phenomenon. It is this writer's preference to view the terms *scale* and *index* as synonyms.

Scales are useful for a number of reasons, but primarily because they avoid reliance on any single response alone as an indicator. For example, the response to any single item may be an error, may be misclassified or misinterpreted by subjects, or may not adequately tap the full dimension of the idea being measured (Orenstein and Phillips, 1978, pp. 258–259).

Arbitrary Scales

Arbitrary scales are developed by the researcher and are based primarily on face validity (the scale appears to be measuring what one intends to measure) and professional judgment. They are intended to measure relative degrees of a concept or provide a rough estimate. A simple way of developing arbitrary scales is to begin with ordinal or interval scales of phenomena that lend themselves readily to accepted measurement, for example, income, education, and attendance. Figure 10.1 presents a hypothetical example of the construction of a social class index using three subscales: income, education, and occupation.

Arbitrary scales

[1]Some examples of excellent reference handbooks for scales include the following: Delbert C. Miller, ed. *Handbook of Research Design and Social Measurement*, 5th ed. New York: Longman, 1991; Stanley Brodsky and O'Neal Smitherman, eds. *Handbook of Scales for Research in Crime and Delinquency.* New York: Plenum Press, 1983; and J.P. Robinson, P.R. Shaver, and L.S. Wrightsman, eds. *Measures of Personality and Social Psychological Attitudes*, San Diego: Academic Press, 1991.

Income (Annual)		Education		Occupation (Using U.S. Census Ratings)	
$40,000 and over = 5		College Graduate	= 5	Higher Professional, Managerial = 5	
$30,000–$39,999 = 4		Some College	= 4	Less Professional, Managerial,	
$20,000–$29,999 = 3		High School Graduate = 3		Technical and Sales	= 4
$10,000–$19,999 = 2		Some High School	= 2	Services	= 3
Under $10,000 = 1		Grade School or Less = 1		Skilled Labor	= 2
				Unskilled Labor	= 1

Figure 10.1
An Arbitrary Social Class Scale.

In reality, it would make far better sense to utilize an existing, well-accepted social class scale from one of the handbooks discussed previously than to construct a new scale.

It might be quite misleading for a researcher to use one of the three subscales alone as a measure of social class; however, use of an index that takes into account all three measures overcomes this. But how might an index be constructed using this arbitrary scale of social class? Suppose we have a respondent who earns $40,000, is a college graduate, and has a career in sales. Such a case would score 14 out of a possible 15 on our scale. One might arbitrarily decide that scores of 1–5 represent lower class, 6–10 middle class, and 11–15 upper class. Thus, according to our operationalization of social class, our respondent would be upper class.

Because the construction of arbitrary scales rests primarily on the judgment of the researcher, they are easily criticized. For this reason attitudinal scaling procedures have been developed that permit logical and methodological defenses for scale operationalization.

The Uniform Crime Report as an Arbitrary Scale

A lengthy exposition of the Uniform Crime Report (UCR) was presented in Chapter 4. Using the original UCR, a simple summation of the eight index offenses is made. The **UCR index** *offenses* are those crimes that are considered serious and that the police feel are fairly accurately reported and uniformly measured:

UCR index

> Homicide
> Larceny
> Forcible rape
> Car theft
> Robbery
> Burglary
> Aggravated assault
> Arson (not actually calculated in index due to unreliability of measurement)

Table 10.2
THE UCR CRIME INDEX*

Offense	Number
Murder and nonnegligent manslaughter	23,400
Forcible rape	102,560
Robbery	639,270
Aggravated assault	1,054,860
Burglary	3,073,900
Larceny-theft	7,945,700
Motor vehicle theft	1,635,900
Arson	—
Index total	14,475,600
Index rate	5,820.3 (per 100,000)

*Offenses may not add to index total because of rounding.
Source: U.S. Department of Justice, *FBI Uniform Crime Reports: Crime in the United States*, 1990. Washington, DC: U.S. Government Printing Office, August 11, 1991, p. 50.

Although arson is listed as part of the index, the unreliability of such data prevents it from being included in any calculations. As discussed in Chapter 4, the crime index is the total number of such offenses recorded by police per 100,000 population. Table 10.2 presents a typical UCR crime index summary.

In addition to all of the shortcomings presented in Chapter 4, a principal difficulty with the UCR as an index of crime in the United States is that it is an unweighted index. That is, each crime incident, whether it is homicide or auto theft, is added to the total index without any consideration of its relative seriousness. No monetary or differential psychological value is attached. A city with 50 burglaries per 100,000 and a city with 50 homicides per 100,000 would actually have the same UCR crime index. Similar problems exist with unweighted victimization rates. Later in this chapter we discuss attempts to develop crime seriousness scales to measure not only the quantity but also the severity of crime.

Attitude Scales

Three major types of attitude scales that have been developed in the social sciences are used in criminology and criminal justice:

Thurstone scales
Likert scales
Guttman scales

Thurstone Scales

Thurstone scales

Thurstone scales were the first to be developed (Thurstone and Chave, 1929). Thurstone had actually devised various techniques for developing scales, but all shared in common the *use of judges to select items*. Judges are individuals whose expertise is respected and who might be in a position to help in the determination of the most useful items.

The earliest method developed by Thurstone was the *method of paired comparisons*. A number of judges are presented with all possible pairs of items to be used in a scale. Items or questions are then rated by the judges as to which of each pair is more favorable to the issue in question. Such a procedure tends to be quite tedious and time consuming.

Equal appearing intervals

As a judgmental technique, Thurstone's method of **equal appearing intervals** is superior to the paired comparisons method in that it requires only one judgment per item. Each judge is required to sort the items into a predetermined number of categories so that the intervals between them are subjectively equal. Figure 10.2 illustrates the rating of three items by five different judges using an eleven-point scale in which 1 indicates that the item is a positive measure of the entity being measured, and 11 indicates a negative measure.

The ratings for item 1 by five judges were 9, 10, 10, 11, and 11; that is, the judges generally agreed that the item was a negative measure of the entity in question. On item 2 the judges were in basic agreement that the item was positive, whereas they disagreed on item 3. According to Thurstone's procedure, the third item would be eliminated because of the conflicting interpretations of the judges. Sometimes investigators assign weights to the items on the basis of the median scores of the values assigned by the judges. The logic of *weighting* assumes that responses to the first item carry a more negative meaning (a weight of 10) than those to item 2 (a weight of only 3). The final form of the scale is made up of those agreed-upon items that provide even intervals on the scale from high to low.

An interesting application that partly involved Thurstone methods was the development of police assessment centers (Dunnette and Motowidlo, 1976). As part of the procedure to develop a police career index that would permit police departments to predict likely successful candidates for both hiring and promotion, a group of psychologists and senior police officials reviewed a series of items, including simulations that had been constructed by

Figure 10.2
Method of Equal Appearing Intervals: Five Judges Assign an Eleven-Point Scale to Three Items.

Judge No.	Item 1	Item 2	Item 3
1	9	2	2
2	10	3	3
Median 3	10	3	9
4	11	3	10
5	11	4	11

the researcher. Those items deemed most promising and on which there was the greatest agreement were then pretested.

The following is a *summary of the Thurstone scaling procedure*:

- A large number of questions believed to be related to the concept under investigation are constructed.
- A number of judges are asked to assign weight to each item using a predetermined scale ranging from favorable to unfavorable.
- The median (midpoint) of the values assigned to each item is taken as its score or weight.
- Those items on which there was significant disagreement by the judges are eliminated.
- Selected items with weights spread at intervals along the scale are retained for the final scale, which can now be administered to respondents. (Miller, 1991, p. 88)

Likert Scales

Likert scales, the scales most commonly used in attitudinal research, are named for Rensis Likert who developed the procedure (Likert, 1932). Figure 10.3 illustrates a typical Likert scale. **Likert scales** consist of a simple summation of usually a five-point bipolar response ranging from strongly agree to strongly **Likert scales**

For each of the following questions circle the response that best represents your attitude:

	Strongly Agree	Agree	Don't Know	Disagree	Strongly Disagree
1. The best way to handle people is to tell them what they want to hear.	SA	(A)	DK	D	SD
2. When you ask someone to do something for you, it is best to give the real reasons for wanting it rather than giving reasons which might carry more weight.	SA	A	DK	(D)	SD
3. It is hard to get ahead without cutting corners here and there.	(SA)	A	DK	D	SD
4. Barnum was wrong when he said, "There's a sucker born every minute."	SA	A	DK	(D)	SD
5. It is wise to flatter important people.	SA	A	(DK)	D	SD
6. All in all, it is better to be humble and honest than important and dishonest.	SA	A	DK	(D)	SD

Note: Those circled represent hypothetical response.

Figure 10.3
A Likert Scale: Adaptation of the Machiavellianism Scale.
Source: Christie, R., and F.L. Geis. *Studies in Machiavellianism.* New York: Academic Press, 1970.

Figure 10.4
*Scoring for a Likert
Scale: the
Machiavellianism
Scale in Figure 10.3
(hypothetical
response).*

		SA	A	DK	D	SD
1.	"Handle People"	+5	(+4)	+3	+2	+1
2.	"Give Real Reasons"	+1	+2	+3	(+4)	+5
3.	"Cut Corners"	(+5)	+4	+3	+2	+1
4.	"Barnum"	+1	+2	+3	(+4)	+5
5.	"Flatter"	+5	+4	(+3)	+2	+1
6.	"Better To Be Honest"	+1	+2	+3	(+4)	+5

disagree. Figure 10.4 portrays the scoring key for Figure 10.3, the six Machiavellianism[2] items in which the more manipulative orientation is given the higher score or +5.

According to the scoring system in Figure 10.4, our hypothetical respondent scored 24 on a scale that ranged from 6 (low Machiavellianism) to 30 (high Machiavellianism). The low or high numbers are arbitrarily assigned by the researcher. Low scores could have been assigned to high orientations or vice versa, as long as the investigator remembers the assignment for later analysis. The even items, questions 2, 4, and 6, are examples of *reversal items*, in which the substance of the question is worded in a negative fashion relative to the orientation being measured; that is, strong agreement is assigned a low score or denotes low *Machiavellianism*. Such reversals are standard in Likert scales to avoid *response sets*—patterns of consistent responses in which the respondent reads only the first few items and, on the basis of these responses, merely circles the remaining responses in a similar pattern. Such response sets can be spotted by noting straight vertical patterns or widely inconsistent extreme responses that are highly unlikely. If response sets appear despite reversals, the analyst may decide to discard the case entirely because the subject did not act in good faith by providing his or her true feelings. Standardized examinations such as the Scholastic Aptitude Test (SAT) and Graduate Record Exam (GRE) discourage test takers from merely guessing the answers to questions as time runs out by deducting two points for incorrect items, while giving only one point for correct ones.

The Thurstone procedure for discarding weak questions was based on the disagreement by the judges on the scoring weight to be assigned. Likert procedures skip this step of using judges and accomplish the same thing by analyzing the responses after the fact. In the Likert method the respondents do the job that the judges do in the Thurstone procedure. Basically, item analysis asks whether both high and low scorers answered particular items the same way. If so, these items are considered nondiscriminating and therefore are eliminated from the scale. By nondiscriminating we mean that the responses to these questions add nothing to the final scale measurement because they do not distinguish between high and low scores. For example, if both high Machiavellians

[2]Machiavellianism takes its name from the sixteenth-century Italian philosopher Niccolo Machiavelli, whose classic work *The Prince* (1952) has often been described as a "handbook for dictators" in its espousal of the "end justifies the means" in obtaining power. Socially, Machiavellianism refers to a manipulative orientation toward others.

(scores over 20) and low Machiavellians (scores under 20) agreed that "There's a sucker born every minute," then perhaps that question is not measuring manipulative orientations and should be eliminated from the scale. It would be as if everyone got a question correct or incorrect on a competitive test; such items do nothing to predict who will do well or poorly and therefore should be eliminated. The final scale then would consist of only those items that appeared to have variability or distinguish between high and low scores.

In the process of developing a scale, researchers begin with a much larger number of items than they expect to employ in the final score. On the basis of elimination, the final scale is trimmed down to the most useful items. Table 10.3 illustrates a hypothetical item analysis.

Taking the first item in Table 10.3 we find that the highest scorers (those that fell into the top 25 percent of all respondents) scored 3.6, whereas the lowest scorers (bottom 25 percent) scored 3.2. Little difference was exhibited between high and low scorers and therefore this item is dropped from the final scale. Items 2 and 3 show large differences between high and low scorers and thus are discriminating items to be retained. Item 4 shows little ability to distinguish high from low scorers and is also eliminated.

A major shortcoming of Likert scaling is that on the basis of the total scale score it is impossible to predict the exact endorsement of each individual item. Suppose a person's Machiavellianism score from Figure 10.4 was 20. On the basis of this score, can we predict how the individual responded to item 4, "Barnum was very wrong when he said, 'There's a sucker born every minute'"? No, such a total score could be obtained with a person circling any of the response categories supplied.

The following is a summary of Likert scaling procedures:

- A large number of items are selected and about evenly expressed as either positive or negative statements regarding the subject of investigation.
- For each item, the respondent is asked to respond using usually a five-point scale (strongly agree, agree, don't know, disagree, and strongly disagree).

Table 10.3
HYPOTHETICAL ITEM ANALYSIS

Item	Average Score of Top Quartile	Average Score of Low Quartile
1	3.6	3.2
2	4.1	1.7
3	3.9	1.2
4	2.6	2.2

- The total score for each individual is the simple sum of all items, although the researcher should exercise caution in identifying and scoring appropriate reversals or items that were negative.
- Items that lack variability or fail to distinguish between high and low scores are eliminated from the final scale.
- Only those items retained in the final index are scored and used in the final analysis.

Handling Missing Data in Likert Scale Construction.
Even with the provision of "don't know" categories, some respondents may answer all but a few items in a scale. If a large number of respondents fail to answer a particular item, then that item should be eliminated from the scale. If the missing item is one of a series of measures of the same basic dimension, we could assign to that item the average score for the items answered. For example, if an individual answers nine of ten questions on the same subject and the nine scores average 2.5, then a score of 2.5 can be assumed for the missing response. Obviously, if too many nonresponses exist, it may be necessary to drop the respondent from analysis. Although there is no universal rule, it would seem reasonable that if more than three of ten responses are not ascertained, the individual's responses for the entire set of scale items should be dropped from the analysis. Another alternative to substituting the average score from the items answered is to assign an intermediate score to missing responses (Orenstein and Phillips, 1978, p. 268). For instance, if the scoring for the item ranges from 1 to 5, a 3 would be assigned. Although simpler than the other procedure, such assignment tends to reduce or inflate the total scores of high and low scorers.

Guttman Scales

Guttman scales were developed as one outcome of a research series conducted by social scientists during World War II (Guttman, 1944, 1950). Sometimes referred to as scalogram analysis, but more often referred to by the name of its developer, Louis Guttman, **Guttman scaling** insists that an attitudinal scale be based on **unidimensionality**; that is, it should measure one and only one dimension or concept. In our Machiavellianism example, it may appear that the items are measuring things other than Machiavellianism, for instance, cynicism, honesty, practical judgment. Guttman procedures provide a quantitative procedure by which to approach this issue.

Guttman scales

Unidimensionality

The major advantage of Guttman scaling over Likert scaling is that from the final scale score one should be able to predict the exact pattern of item endorsement. As in our previous example, a score of 20 on the Machiavellianism scale (Figure 10.3) would enable a fairly accurate prediction that a person scored, let us say, 2 on the "Barnum" question. Before going into the quantitative aspects of the Guttman procedure, let us first provide some examples and follow the logic of the procedure. Figure 10.5 presents two hypothetical examples.

Theft Scale	Fear of Crime Scale		
Have you ever taken:	Are you afraid:		
1. Things of little value? YES NO	In the city?	YES	NO
2. Things of moderate value? YES NO	Down the block?	YES	NO
3. Things of large value? YES NO	Outside own house?	YES	NO
	Inside own house?	YES	NO

Figure 10.5
Hypothetical Guttman Scales.

Source: The Theft Scale is from Hirshi and Selvin (1973, p. 64), and the Fear of Crime Scale was suggested by Baumer and Rosenbaum (1980).

In examining each of the scales in Figure 10.6, note that the items are progressively more difficult. Additionally, endorsement of the more difficult items almost presupposes that one would have affirmatively answered the previous items. Figure 10.7 presents a Guttman analysis of the possible response patterns for these scales.

There are eight possible combinations of responses to these items. Assume that these scales measure spelling or mathematical ability, and that anyone who can do the more difficult problems can do the less difficult ones and the opposite is seldom true. Which response patterns are unlikely? Patterns 3, 5, 6, and 7 are unlikely or are considered errors in the predictability of the scales. Because no scale can be completely accurate, Guttman suggests that a 90 percent coefficient of reproducibility is the minimum acceptable level of accuracy and, if achieved, is indicative of scalability. It is this quality, a cumulative nature of scoring, that Guttman attempted to build into his scaling procedure.

The *coefficient of reproducibility* is calculated in the following manner:

$$\text{reproducibility} = 1 - \frac{\text{numbers of errors}}{\text{numbers of responses}}$$

That is, on the basis of the scale score one should be able to predict the exact pattern of response, although as much as 10 percent of the time one

Mathematical Ability Scale	Spelling Ability Scale
1. Can you *add* and *subtract*?	1. Can you spell *CAT*?
YES NO	YES NO
2. Can you do *long division*?	2. Can you spell *CATTLE*?
YES NO	YES NO
3. Can you *solve equations* with one unknown?	3. Can you spell *CATASTROPHE*?
YES NO	YES NO

Figure 10.6
Hypothetical Guttman Scales.

Source: The Mathematical Ability Scale is from Cole (1972, p. 52).

		Question #1 (Add and Subtract) (Cat)	Question #2 (Long Division) (Cattle)	Question #3 (Simple Equation) (Catastrophe)
	1.	+	+	+
	2.	+	+	−
	3.	+	−	+
Response	4.	+	−	−
Patterns	5.	−	+	+
	6.	−	+	−
	7.	−	−	+
	8.	−	−	−

Figure 10.7
Possible Response Patterns in the Guttman Scales: +, Ability to Perform; −, Inability to Perform.

could be in error in doing so. The "Spelling Ability Scale" in Figure 10.7 ranges from 0 (no spelling ability) to 3 (very good spelling ability). Although a score of 2 could be obtained by means of response patterns 2, 3, and 5, only response pattern 2 (ability to spell "cat" and "cattle") is acceptable. Rarely would an individual be able to spell "cat" and "catastrophe" but not "cattle," as in response 3, or be able to spell the latter two without knowing how to spell "cat," as in response 5. Thus, if the scale is unidimensional, a score of 2 should enable you to predict with at least 90 percent accuracy that the individual endorsed items 1 and 2 but not 3. If greater than 10 percent error were introduced by anomalies with regard to item 2, "cattle," the scale would need to be reconstructed with "cattle" dropped in favor of a more workable substitute.

Although Guttman scaling has a distinct advantage over Likert scaling in that it provides the facility to predict a fairly precise pattern of response to each item, given the final scale score, its insistence on unidimensionality may be too rigid a demand. Many concepts, particularly abstract ones, may be multidimensional in nature and therefore not amenable to Guttman scaling.

A different series of complex traits may feed together to provide similar composite scores. For example, perhaps in a scale measuring counselor effectiveness it is discovered that people scoring above average on a hypothetical scale are most effective; however, such a score could be obtained by those rated excellent in knowledge but average in empathy, as well as those rated only average in knowledge but excellent in empathy. An insistence on unidimensionality in this instance would be inappropriate. Many important concepts are multidimensional. The insistence on Guttman scaling procedures may become a "fetish" (Hirschi and Selvin, 1973, p. 209) similar to the misuse of some statistical tests of significance.

The following is a *summary of Guttman scaling procedures*:

- Construct a large number of items that appear on face validity to measure the concept.
- Pretest the instrument by administering it to a sample of people.
- Any item with greater than 80 percent agreement or disagreement should be discarded from the analysis and final scale.

- Order respondents from highest score (most responding "yes" to each item) to lowest score (fewest "yes" responses).

- Also order items from left to right from most favorable to least favorable responses.

- After discarding those items that fail to discriminate between high and low scorers, calculate the coefficient of reproducibility where errors are defined as those responses that are out of the predictable pattern.

- If the coefficient of reproducibility equals 0.90 or higher, then scalability or unidimensionality is assumed.

- The respondent's final score is calculated by simply summing the number of favorable items. (Miller, 1991, p. 90)

Judy Andrews et al. (1991) used Guttman scaling procedures to construct an Adolescent Substance Use scale. The scale was constructed using the following progression:

1. Had never used substances
2. Had used alcohol
3. Had used cigarettes
4. Had used marijuana
5. Had used at least one hard drug during the previous six months

The coefficient of reproducibility for the scale was approximately 0.96, which exceeded the 0.90 limit for a Guttman scale.

Some examples of the use of Guttman scales in criminal justice research are found in Scott (1959), Arnold (1965), Nye and Short (1957), and Dentler and Monroe (1961). One of the earliest pieces of research in the social sciences that exhibited cumulative qualities was Bogardus' "Social Distance Scale" (1933). Each respondent was asked to indicate the closeness of relationship they were willing to accept with a variety of ethnic groups. The response categories were as follows:

1. Would exclude from my country
2. As visitors only to my country
3. To citizenship in my country
4. To employment in my occupation
5. To my street as neighbors
6. To my club as personal chums
7. To close kinship by marriage

With 7 indicating highest acceptance or least social distance and 1 indicating the converse, index scores could be devised to rate the relative acceptance of various groups. Similar criminal justice applications in which types of criminals are substituted for ethnic groups seem possible.

In their excellent review of delinquency research, Hirschi and Selvin (1973) indicate an element of Guttman scaling that may be overlooked by those analyzing self-report data. Guttman scaling of items such as Figure 10.5 is appropriate only if the period during which the acts could have taken place is relatively long. If the time span were short, it would be possible that an individual committed a more serious act and not less serious ones, during the specified period, thus making a Guttman scale inapplicable (see also Dentler and Monroe, 1961). In measuring delinquent acts it makes more sense to concentrate on more recent acts, rather than those that occur over an extended time period. "Suppose the boy with three delinquent acts committed all of them within the preceding year, while the boy with five delinquent acts committed none in that period. At the time of the study, which boy is more delinquent?" (Hirschi and Selvin, 1973, p. 65). A more valid measurement would be gained by restricting the time period and thus not using Guttman scaling because it makes sense to concentrate on more recent acts, rather than those that may have occurred at any time.

Other Scaling Procedures

The three types of attitude scales that we have discussed—Thurstone, Likert, and Guttman—are the key generic classifications of such scales; most others can be viewed as variations.

Q Sort

Q sort methodology

Q sort methodology is a newer variation of the Thurstone process; the respondents rather than the judges place a series of statements into previously predetermined categories (Stephenson, 1953). The individual's sorting is scored and summed into an index. Farrington (1973) had a group of English juveniles place thirty-eight cards on which various crimes were printed in two different piles—"have done it" and "have not done it." In investigating attractiveness and juvenile delinquency, Cavior and Howard (1973) had a group of college students sort pictures of delinquents and nondelinquents into five categories ranging from 1 (very attractive) to 5 (very unattractive).

Sherman et al.'s Scientific Methods Scale (SMS)

Scientific Methods Scale (SMS)

The Scientific Methods Scale (SMS) was developed as part of the evaluation of "What Works?" commissioned by the U.S. Congress and carried out by the University of Maryland's Department of Criminology and Criminal Justice in 1997 (Sherman et al., 1997). The Maryland Report as it became known was later updated (Sherman et al., 2002). The SMS is a five-point scale that evaluates the methodological rigor and type of research design of studies. The SMS scores were awarded and determined as follows:

1. A relationship exists between a crime prevention program and a measure of crime or crime risk factors.
2. A temporal sequence or time order exists between the program and the crime, or risk outcome or a comparison group is present without demonstrated comparability to the treatment group.

3. A comparison between two or more units of analysis, one with and one without the program, is present.

4. A comparison of multiple units with and without the program, controlling for other factors, or a nonequivalent comparison group has only minor differences evident.

5. Random assignment and analysis of comparable units to the program and comparison groups take place.

Programs with scores of "1" to "4" are considered "non-experiments," while those with a score of "5" were considered randomized controlled experiments (Lum and Yang, 2005).

Semantic Differential

The **semantic differential** usually consists of a seven- or nine-point bipolar rating scale in which individuals are asked to indicate their perception of a tag or description that is provided. Originally developed in the field of linguistics as a nondirective means of measuring the subjective meaning of words to respondents (Osgood et al., 1957; Snider and Osgood, 1969), it has been found to be an exceptionally versatile tool in attitudinal research. In particular, the semantic differential has been found to be useful in cross-cultural research and with a wide cross section of the population with broad ranges in education and vocabulary level. An illustration of the use of the semantic differential in research related to criminal justice would be an examination of labeling theory—seeing whether people are viewed as being what they do. That is, a person who has an alcohol problem is viewed as an alcoholic or one with a drug problem as a drug addict. Figure 10.8 illustrates a typical semantic differential scale.

Suppose our sample scale were to be used in this study: Subjects would be asked to respond to their interpretation of the term *heroin* using the scale, and then *heroin addicts* using a second page containing the same scale. Subjects asked to fill out a semantic differential scale typically say "What is it that I am to do?" or "I do not see where some of the things we are to rate are applicable to the subject." The monitor should merely reply: "Do the best you can."

Semantic differential

1.	painful	:___:___:___:___:___:___:	pleasurable
2.	orderly	:___:___:___:___:___:___:	disorderly
3.	trivial	:___:___:___:___:___:___:	important
4.	masculine	:___:___:___:___:___:___:	feminine
5.	popular	:___:___:___:___:___:___:	lonely
6.	poor	:___:___:___:___:___:___:	wealthy
7.	individualistic	:___:___:___:___:___:___:	conformist
8.	mature	:___:___:___:___:___:___:	childish
9.	right	:___:___:___:___:___:___:	wrong
10.	lonely	:___:___:___:___:___:___:	well liked

Figure 10.8
Semantic Differential Scale.

Each respondent checks off the point on the scale for each item that corresponds to their reaction to that concept. One obvious advantage of the semantic differential is that the researcher need not tediously prepare a large series of statements, but rather merely add the concept to be rated to a previously constructed scale as in Figure 10.8. Obviously, the bipolar descriptors must be altered so that they are appropriate for the evaluation of the concept under analysis.

In an interesting use of the semantic differential scale, Thielbar and Feldman (1978) had subjects rate different forms of deviant behavior and those who perform such activities on an eleven-point scale featuring twenty-four bipolar adjectives for each type, such as kind-cruel, good-bad, and honest-dishonest. Of the eleven types of behavior evaluated, rapists and child molesters were the most negatively regarded and welfare recipients and marijuana smokers the least negatively regarded.

In a Chicago study, Short and Strodtbeck (1965) asked black and white gangs to rate various forms of conduct by means of the semantic differential. They found that gang boys tended to rate such middle-class values as school, saving, and reading as high, as did nongang middle-class boys; however, these same gang boys tended to rate pimping, fighting, and similar behavior higher than did the nondelinquent nongang boys. Nevertheless, that nongang nondelinquent and gang boys gave the same ratings to middle-class values has important implications with respect to some leading subcultural theories of juvenile delinquency (Cloward and Ohlin, 1961; Cohen, 1955).

Other Variations

There are perhaps an infinite variety of scales depending on subject matter. In addition to consulting handbooks that review scales used in previous studies, researchers should examine useful literature that discusses scaling procedures (Edwards, 1957; Maranell, 1974; Oppenheim, 1966; Shaw and Wright, 1967; Summers, 1970; Torgerson, 1958).

Brodsky and Smitherman, in their *Handbook of Scales for Research in Crime and Delinquency* (1983), have performed a real service for researchers in criminology and criminal justice by collating hundreds of scales and indexes applicable to these fields. This handbook outlines the scales available to measure a particular concept, describes their development and scoring, and generally assesses their reliability (consistency/stability) and validity (accuracy). The scales are organized by topical area, and references to sources are provided. In some cases, actual scale items are included. The scales are also classified by target and purpose. The *research targets* of criminal justice scales are law enforcement/police, courts/the law, corrections, delinquency, offenders, crime/criminality, and general scales/citizens. *Scale purposes* include attitudes, behavior ratings, personality assessment, milieu ratings, prediction, and description. The following list is a sample of the scales described:

Niederhoffer Cynicism Scale
Police Job Stress Interview
Attitude Toward Law Scale

Competency Screening Test
Judicial Role Perception Scale
Attitude Toward Death Penalty
Prison Adjustment Index
Prisoner–Therapist Q Sort
Parole Adjustment Scale
Recidivism Prediction Scale
Prison Guard Job Perception
Delinquency Attitude Scale
Nye and Short Self-Reported Delinquency Scale
Compulsive Masculinity Scale
Rokeach Dogmatism Scale
Delinquency Proneness Scale
Teenage Slang Test
Differential Association Questionnaires
Sellin–Wolfgang Delinquency Index
Severity of Offense Scale
Criminally Insane Attitude Scale
Inmate Personality Survey
I-Level Classification
Perception of Addicts Scale
Attitude Toward Violence Scale
Legal Dangerousness Scale
Crime Seriousness Ratings
Authoritarianism Scale
F Scale (Fascism)
Alienation Scale

Instead of developing their own measurements, researchers should review available measures and, unless theirs are clearly superior, consider using or modifying an existing index. By utilizing an available measure, a researcher is also replicating findings, an important feature of maturing sciences.

Below is a list of useful handbooks of scales in the social sciences:

Stanley Brodsky and H. O'Neal Smitherman. *Handbook of Scales for Research in Crime and Delinquency.* New York: Plenum Press, 1983.

A.L. Comrey, E. Baker, and M. Glaser. *A Sourcebook for Mental Health Measures.* Los Angeles, CA: Human Interaction Research Institute, 1973.

B.A. Goldman and J.L. Saunders. *Directory of Unpublished Experimental Mental Measures.* New York: Behavioral Publications, 1974.

O.G. Johnson. *Test and Measurements in Child Development: Handbook II.* Vols. 1 and 2. San Francisco, CA: Josey Bass, 1976.

D.G. Lake, B. Miles, and R.B. Earle, Jr. *Measuring Human Behavior*. New York: Columbia University, 1973.

S.B. Lyerly. *Handbook of Psychiatric Rating Scales*. 2nd ed. Washington, DC: U.S. Government Printing Office, 1973.

Delbert C. Miller. *Handbook of Research Design and Social Measurement*. 4th ed. Thousand Oaks, CA: Sage, 1987.

J.L. Price. *Handbook of Organizational Measurement*. Lexington, MA: D.C. Heath, 1972.

J.P. Robinson and R. Shaver. *Measures of Social Psychological Attitudes*. Ann Arbor: Institute for Social Research, 1971.

M.E. Shaw and M. Wright. *Scales for the Measurement of Attitudes*. New York: McGraw-Hill, 1967.

A. Simon and E.G. Boyer. *Mirrors for Behavior III: An Anthology of Observation Instruments*. Wyncote, PA: Communication Materials Center, 1974.

Murray A. Straus. *Family Measurement Techniques: Abstracts of Published Instruments*, 1935–1965. Minneapolis, MN: University of Minnesota Press, 1969.

Murray Straus' measurement of domestic violence serves as an example of a popular scale. Straus, in 1975, and again in 1985, conducted some of the first national surveys of domestic violence in the United States. Using face-to-face interviews in 1975 and telephone surveys in 1985 Straus and associates developed a "conflict tactics scale" that consisted of the following items (Straus and Gelles, 1986):

TYPES OF VIOLENCE
   A. Minor
      1. Threw something
      2. Pushed/grabbed/shoved
      3. Slapped/spanked

   B. Severe
      4. Kicked/bit/hit with fist
      5. Hit, tried to hit with something
      6. Beat up
      7. Threatened with gun or knife
      8. Used gun or knife

The violence indexes were overall (1–8), severe (4–8), and very severe (4, 6, 8).

Crime Seriousness Scales

Previous criticism of the UCR crime index indicated that one of its major shortcomings is that it represents an unweighted index. No consideration is given to the type of crime; that is, a homicide and a petty theft have equal weight.

Crime seriousness scales attempt to assign weight to crimes in terms of their relative severity.

Crime seriousness scales

Sellin–Wolfgang Index

Despite early work by Thurstone (1929), the pioneering work in the area of crime seriousness ratings was performed by Sellin and Wolfgang (1966), who had a group of respondents (police officers, juvenile court judges, and college students) rate descriptions of criminal incidents on the basis of amount stolen, method of intimidation, and degree of harm inflicted. They actually employed two different types of measures: an eleven-point rating scale and a magnitude scale (to be discussed shortly). On the basis of a relatively complex methodology (see their book *The Measurement of Delinquency* for greater detail), they were able to develop a crime seriousness scale or weighting system for crime based on bodily injury, property theft, and damage. This **Sellin–Wolfgang index** tries to account for both the quality (seriousness) and the quantity of an act. For example, a robbery involving no injury but a loss of $5 because of verbal intimidation would receive a crime seriousness score of 3: no points for lack of injury, 1 point for economic loss of $5, and 2 points for verbal intimidation. These scores were arrived at on the basis of analysis of respondents' previous seriousness ratings of descriptions of various crimes. The following are some of the scores (weights) produced by the Sellin–Wolfgang index:

Sellin–Wolfgang index

Assault (death)	26
Forcible rape	11
Robbery (weapon)	5
Larceny ($5,000)	4
Auto theft (no damage)	2
Larceny ($5)	1
Assault (minor)	1

An extensive literature has since developed on crime seriousness measures and, although some cross-cultural and subcultural differences have been found (Akman et al., 1967; Hsu, 1973), various replications have demonstrated striking similarities (Rossi and Henry, 1980). Blumstein (1974) assigned similar seriousness weights to UCR data and came up with results similar to the Sellin–Wolfgang index, and the index was found useful in a Prosecutor's Management Information System (PROMIS) in which prosecutors set prosecution priorities on the basis of various factors including crime seriousness (Jacoby, 1975).

Types of Crime Seriousness Scales

There are two basic types of crime seriousness (severity) scales: simple rating scales and magnitude scales. Simple rating scales of crime seriousness ask respondents to rate crime usually on a scale ranging from 1 (not serious at all) to 9 (extremely serious). In surveys of residents of Baltimore, Maryland (Rossi et al., 1974; Rossi and Henry, 1980), and Macomb, Illinois (Cullen, Link, and Polanzi, 1982), respondents were asked to rate roughly 140 descriptions of crime using the nine-point scale. The average score for each crime is used as the measure of crime seriousness. Strong relative agreement is found among the Rossi and Cullen studies and similar studies. Following are some examples of scores (rounded) from Cullen, Link, and Polanzi (1982, pp. 88–90):

Planned killing for a fee	8.9
Forcible rape of a neighbor	8.4
Armed bank robbery	8.2
Child battering	8.0
Armed robbery ($200)	7.6
Loitering in public place	3.5

Such simple rating scales are ordinal (result in relative rankings) and are unable to take into account the magnitude of the differences between scale scores. For example, is a planned killing only about three times more serious than loitering? They cannot be used to weight crime seriousness, although they are useful in examining relative changes in public ratings (rankings of crime seriousness) over time. This problem becomes apparent when almost all of the 140 crimes rated were given scores above the theoretical midpoint of 5.

Magnitude scales measure public rankings of the degrees of relative seriousness of various crimes. They are an attempt to develop interval- or ratio-level scores that can be assigned to various criminal acts. Our description of the Sellin–Wolfgang index was such an example. Another is the following case of the *National Survey of Crime Severity*, which was designed by Wolfgang et al. (1985) and conducted in 1977 as a supplement to the National Crime Survey (NCS). As you may recall, the NCS surveys 60,000 households and thus is the *largest crime seriousness study ever conducted*. Similar to the methodology employed in the Sellin–Wolfgang index, respondents were

> Each given a description of a crime, "A person steals a bicycle parked on the street," and told that the seriousness of this crime was 10. They were then given a list of other crimes and told to compare them in seriousness to the bicycle theft. If a crime seemed to be twice as serious, they were to rate it at 20. If it were four times as serious, they were to rate it 50, and so on. Each person rated twenty-five crimes, but not everyone had the same twenty-five. Overall, 204 items, each of which was illegal in at least one state, were rated.
>
> Combining the ratings given by each of the 60,000 respondents, a single severity score was developed for each of the 284 items (crimes). (Klaus and Kalish, 1984, p. 2)

Table 10.4 reports some of the scores of the 204 events measured in the NCS crime seriousness study.

The present emphasis on "just desserts"—"let the punishment fit the crime"—suggests that research on crime seriousness scales and other attempts to quantify dangerousness and career criminals will continue.

Table 10.4
THE NATIONAL SURVEY OF CRIME SEVERITY: HOW PEOPLE RANK THE SEVERITY OF CRIME*

Severity Score	Offense
72.1	A person plants a bomb in a public building. (highest score)
52.8	A man forcibly rapes a woman. As a result of physical injury, she dies.
47.8	A parent beats his young child with his fists. As a result, the child dies.
33.8	A person runs a narcotics ring.
30.0	A man forcibly rapes a woman. Her physical injuries require hospitalization.
21.2	A person kidnaps a victim.
18.3	A man beats his wife with his fists. She requires hospitalization.
16.9	A legislator takes a bride of $10,000 from a company to vote for a law favoring the company.
14.6	A person, using force, robs a victim of $10. The victim is hurt and requires hospitalization.
9.0	A person, armed with a lead pipe, robs a victim of $1,000. No physical harm occurs.
6.2	An employee embezzles $1,000 from his/her employer.
3.1	A person breaks into a home and steals $100.
1.6	A person is a customer in a house of prostitution.
0.8	A person under 16 years old runs away from home.
0.8	A person is drunk in public.
0.5	A person takes part in a dice game.
0.2	A person under 16 years old plays hooky from school.

*This represents only a selection of 204 items rated.

Source: Wolfgang, Marvin E., et al. *The National Survey of Crime Severity*. Washington, DC: U.S. Department of Justice, 1985, pp. vi–x.

Prediction Scales

A rich tradition exists in the field of corrections of attempting to develop **prediction scales**, or experience tables, as they are sometimes called. Such scales attempt to assign scores that hopefully predict the likelihood of an

Prediction scales

individual committing crime or being a success or failure on probation or parole (Gottfredson and Ballard, 1966; Hood and Sparks, 1971, pp. 171–192; Simon, 1971, p. 1015). Some of the earliest work in this area was performed by the Gluecks (1960) and Mannheim and Wilkins (1955). The Gluecks attempted to develop a Social Prediction Table that would forecast the risk of a child becoming delinquent. An index was developed based on the scores assigned to such items as family togetherness, parental love, disciplinary policies, and supervision (Glueck and Glueck, 1950). Mannheim and Wilkins developed statistical prediction tables attempting to forecast parole success. These are often referred to as experience tables or base expectancy tables, because they are based on the experience of those who have already undergone treatment. Risk groups are usually developed on the basis of past probabilities of failure using items such as past record of offenses, seriousness of offenses, family conditions, age, and work record. Mannheim and Wilkins used techniques such as multiple regression to choose the most predictive variables and the relative weights to be assigned to each. Wilkins also assisted the California Department of Corrections in developing similar "base expectancy tables" (Hood and Sparks, 1971, p. 183). Ohlin (1951) developed parole prediction scales based on case records, personality assessments, and more traditional items.

In criminal justice, prediction scales may be employed to assess probation/parole risk, establish sentencing guidelines, predict "dangerousness," and establish a scoring system for targeting and incapacitating "career criminals."

Statistical predictions are based on the behavior patterns of an individual compared with others of similar background. This is common in insurance or actuarial predictions. *Clinical predictions*, on the other hand, are based on professional evaluation of individual behavior. Farrington and Tarling (1983) indicate that actuarial predictions of human behavior have been more successful than the individualized clinical element.

The Salient Factor Score

Salient Factor Score

The **Salient Factor Score** has been used by the U.S. Parole Commission since the early 1970s to objectively assess the likelihood of a prisoner's recidivism on parole. Six items are used to construct a ten-point scale, which ranges from 0 (poor risk) to 10 (very good risk) (Hoffman, 1985):

1. The offender's prior criminal convictions
2. The offender's prior criminal commitments for longer than thirty days
3. The offender's age at the time of the new offense
4. How long the offender was at liberty since the last commitment
5. Whether the prisoner was on probation, parole, or escape status at the time of the most recent offense
6. Whether the prisoner has a record of heroin dependence

The salient factor score is combined with the seriousness of the current offense in a grid to establish a guideline range for sentencing (see Table 10.5).

The example in Table 10.5 shows that an offender with a very low salient factor score may serve a sentence two or three times as long for the same

Table 10.5
SALIENT FACTOR SCORE GRID*

Offense Severity Category	Example	Salient Factor Score			
		Very Good (10–8)	Good (7–6)	Fair (5–4)	Poor (3–0)
1 Low	Minor theft	6–10	8–12	10–14	12–14
2 Low/moderate	Forgery/fraud (under $1,000)	8–12	12–16	16–20	20–25
3 Moderate	Motor vehicle theft	12–16	16–20	20–24	24–30
4 High	Robbery (no weapon)	16–20	10–16	26–32	32–38
5 Very high	Robbert (weapon)	24–36	36–48	48–60	60–72
6 Greatest	Willful homicide	(scores vary because of extreme variations in cases)			

*This is a compilation and abridgement for illustration purposes, as the salient factor scores undergo revision over time and may not reflect current sentencing guidelines. (All figures are months for a given sentencing guideline range.)

Source: Compilation of Peter Hoffman, "Predicting Criminality." *Crime File Series*, Washington, DC: National Institute of Justice, 1985; and Peter Hoffman, "Screening for Risk: A Revised Salient Factor Score." *Journal of Criminal Justice* 11 (1984): 539–547.

offense as an offender with a high score. Although problems exist with any prediction efforts (see Hoffman, 1984, 1985), the salient factor score has demonstrated clear differences in recidivism rates between categories, although perfect prediction within categories is perhaps impossible.

Greenwood's "Rand Seven-Factor Index"

Greenwood's **Rand Seven-Factor Index** was aimed at *selective incapacitation*, individualization of sentences on the basis of predictions that particular offenders are likely to commit serious crimes at a high rate if not incarcerated (Blumstein et al., 1986; Cohen, 1983a, p. 1). A self-report survey of inmates in which robbers and burglars admitted crime commission during the two years preceding incarceration yielded an index that came up with predictive results quite similar to those of the salient factor score (Greenwood and Abrahamse, 1982; Hoffman, 1985, p. 3). Seven variables were selected to form a simple additive scale from 0 (low risk) to 7 (high risk):

Rand Seven-Factor Index

1. Prior conviction for same charge
2. Incarcerated more than 50 percent of preceding two years
3. Convicted before age sixteen
4. Served time in state juvenile facility
5. Drug use in preceding two years
6. Drug use as a juvenile
7. Employed less than 50 percent of preceding two years

Although space prohibits a full detailing of such predictive efforts (see Cohen, 1983b), the forecasts of such scales are probabilistic, that is, not 100 percent accurate for each score. The Greenwood scale had a 45 percent rate of "true positives" (sometimes called "hits") or correctly identified that percentage of high-rate offenders; however, the "false-positive" ("misses" or inaccurate prediction) rate was 55 percent, which was similar to findings by Monahan (1981) who analyzed scales that attempt to predict potential violence or dangerousness. Kratcoski (1985) points out that in the use of such instruments to decide probation supervision, it should not be assumed that recidivism will be reduced at all supervision levels; instead, these instruments should be used to ensure efficiency and productive allocation of resources within supervision levels. Vito (1986) points out that in using different measures of the success of such efforts, multiple outcomes of success must be employed: "The goals of intensive supervision must be clearly specified and measured so that we avoid the premature crucifixion of intensive supervision upon the cross of recidivism" (p. 24).

Career Criminal Programs

The police have had much less experience in using prediction devices to target police resources on "repeat offenders" or "career criminals." The Repeat Offenders Project (ROP; pronounced "rope") of the Washington, DC, Metropolitan Police uses criminal informants and other sources of information on criminals to concentrate police efforts on those most active in crime (Martin and Sherman, 1985; Sherman, 1985). A similar program in Minneapolis combines formal and informal methods reviewing "nominations" (of criminals to target) from many sources and extensive information and established criteria in focusing on a small group of active criminals. Validation of the criteria employed in both programs is incomplete, but the evaluation of the ROP targets by the Police Foundation noted that all had criminal histories, all had been arrested the previous year, and, as a result of the program, all were five times more likely to be arrested than were those randomly assigned to a control group (Sherman, 1985). Officers assigned to the ROP program had a smaller number of arrests, but more "quality arrests" of more serious, active criminals with records. The Police Foundation study was not able to determine the impact of the program on reducing crime in the District of Columbia.

Prediction criteria employed by prosecutors (district attorneys) tend to be more formal than those used by the police. A system employed in Charlotte, North Carolina, assigns weight to such factors as alcohol or drug abuse, age, and length of criminal career to create a scale for deciding which cases are most likely to be successfully prosecuted (Sherman, 1985).

An important caution in the utilization of prediction tables is that the administrator should be careful that the group to be rated does not differ significantly in experience from the group on which the base expectancy table was calculated. It is important that the table be validated or tested on samples other than the original on whose experience it was developed (Simon, 1971; Wilkins, 1969).

Related to the prediction table tradition are numerous psychological studies that use personality inventories and scales to discover a distinctive criminal personality. Tennenbaum (1977), in an update of earlier reviews by Scheussler and Cressey (1950) and Waldo and Dinitz (1967), reviewed studies employing various personality scales that attempt to distinguish criminal from noncriminal personalities. Although 80 percent of the studies claimed to have found personality differences, they failed to identify the complex, multidimensional nature of these differences. The majority had greater variation within groups than between groups, and thus no significant differences can be claimed (Tennenbaum, 1977, p. 19).

Advantages of Scales

The development of scale measurement *enables more exact measurement of phenomena* from simple nominal to ordinal or interval level. Rather than vaguely suggesting that City A has a bigger problem than City B, one could indicate that, according to the 1980 victimization index for eight specific crimes, the rate of crime was 30.6 per 1,000 in City A and 21.2 per 1,000 in City B. Thus, more quantitatively precise measurement can be obtained by means of scales.

Scales lend themselves to replication and the longitudinal measurement of even small changes in the phenomena under investigation. For example, the index offense crime rate may increase from 30.6 to 30.8 per 1,000. The construction of scaled measurement *forces more rigorous thinking* in that the researcher is involved in a systematic approach to operationalization.

Disadvantages of Scales

A principal critique of the use of scales is a philosophical one and relates to an antiquantitative approach to research. Those who oppose the scaling tradition question whether it really measures what it is claimed to measure or *whether a person's true attitude or behavior can be measured on a five- or seven-point scale.* In the same light, there may be little relationship between a scaled measurement and the entity being measured. Some antiempiricists feel that rather than speak of errors in measurement we should speak of the *"error of measurement."* As with any measurement, scales are subject to problems of unreliability and invalidity.

Despite these and other criticisms, scaling is widely used in the social sciences and criminal justice and has been found useful in measuring a variety of concepts such as personality, occupational aptitude, authoritarianism, self-concept, cost of living, urbanization, industrialization, anomie, alienation, social class, crime, marital satisfaction, and job satisfaction.

These problems are not by any means exclusive to the development of scales in criminal justice. In the field of economics, the widely used consumer price index (CPI) has been under attack despite the fact that it is generally considered one of the best price measures in the world. This index represents the composite average increase in prices consumers pay for such items as shelter, food, utilities, clothing, furnishings, upkeep, transportation, health, and entertainment. With the double-digit inflation of the early 1980s being fired primarily by high housing costs, interest, and gasoline prices, critics charged that the CPI tended to exaggerate the inflation rate for those consumers whose spending pattern differed from the average pattern. That is, consumers who already owned their home or car in that given year may have been unaffected by as much as 40 percent of the rise in the inflation rate (Fritz, 1980, p. 86; Samuelson, 1974, pp. 34–35).

There is no mysterious, magical, mechanized process that will ensure adequate indicators for concepts. In this sense, scaling procedures and methodological wizardry are no substitute for creative, logical, and sensitive theoretical conceptualization.

Summary

Scaling is the process of attempting to develop composite measurement or ranked or unit measurement of phenomena. The *levels of measurement* are nominal, ordinal, interval, and ratio. *Nominal* measurement is the simple placement of objects into categories in which the actual numbers assigned have no mathematical meaning. *Ordinal* measurement entails the ability to assign ranks, higher to lower. *Interval* measurement assumes equal units or distances between the scores. *Ratio* measurement assumes, in addition to equal units, a meaningful zero point.

Arbitrary scales are constructed on the basis of the judgment of the researcher. The UCR is an arbitrary scale that, in the opinion of those who constructed it, reflects most serious crimes as well as those crimes for which police departments generally have the best records. A major limitation of the UCR is that it fails to take into account the relative seriousness of the crimes, which are simply summated into an index.

There are *three major types of attitude scales*: Thurstone, Likert, and Guttman. Other scaling procedures covered in this chapter are Q sort, semantic differential, factor analysis, and prediction scales. *Thurstone scales* make use of a series of judges to decide on appropriate scale items. A *Likert scale* is a simple summated scale of items usually containing a five-point response category ranging from "strongly agree" to "strongly disagree." Likert scales typically make use of reversal items to eliminate response sets. In addition, **item analysis** is employed to eliminate nondiscriminating items. *Guttman scales* insist on unidimensionality—that one and only one dimension be measured by a particular scale. The cumulative nature of such a scaling procedure ensures a reasonable (if proper reproducibility) ability to predict the exact pattern of responses on the basis of an individual's scale score.

Q sort methodology is a variation of the Thurstone procedure in which the respondents place statements written on cards into assigned scale categories. The *semantic differential scale*, originally developed in the field of linguistics, is a seven- or nine-point bipolar rating system in which respondents

Item analysis

are asked to indicate their perception of a concept or subject. *Factor analysis* is a procedure that identifies underlying dimensions among a series of scale items. Because many concepts are multidimensional, factor analysis not only is useful in identifying subscales but also assigns factor loadings or weights to items. Thus, the relative importance of each item is taken into account in calculating scale scores. The SMS is a five-point scale that measures the methodological rigor and type of research design.

 Crime seriousness scales attempt to measure the gravity, or seriousness, of crime by means of public ratings using either simple rating scales (e.g., a zero-to-nine scale) or magnitude ratings (e.g., the Sellin–Wolfgang index or National Survey of Crime Severity). *Prediction scales*, sometimes called experience or base expectancy scales, are constructed on the basis of past experience to predict future performance usually in probation and parole. The *Salient Factor Score* is used by the U.S. Parole Commission in assessing the likelihood of prisoner recidivism and in the determination of sentencing. The Rand Seven-Factor index and career criminal programs represent similar prediction efforts.

 The relative *advantages* of using scales is that they provide more composite and exact measurement. They lend themselves to longitudinal assessment and replication studies, and they force more rigorous thinking on the part of the investigator. Disadvantages, on the other hand, point to the artificiality of such measurement and the question as to whether people really think in scale patterns. Scaling is by no means a substitute for good theoretical and substantive knowledge of the subject under investigation.

KEY CONCEPTS

Nominal variables	Equal appearing intervals	Crime seriousness scales
Ordinal variables	Likert scales	Sellin–Wolfgang index
Internal variables	Guttman scales	Prediction scales
Ratio Variables	Unidimensionality	Salient factor score
Scaling	Q sort methodology	Rand seven-factor index
Arbitrary scales	Scientific methods	Advantages/
UCR index	scale(SMS)	disadvantages of scales
Thurstone scales	Semantic differential	Item analysis

REVIEW QUESTIONS

1. Discuss the three major types of attitude scales. What are the unique features of each?

2. In a recent journal, find an example of a study employing a scale. Describe the characteristics, scoring, reliability, and validity of this measure.

3. What are the two types of crime seriousness scales and of what utility are they in criminal justice research?

4. Discuss and give examples of the use of prediction scales in criminology and criminal justice.

USEFUL WEB SITES

Eric Clearinghouse on Assessment and Evaluation *www.ericae.net*

Scales (Social Sciences) *http://pse.cs.vt.edu/SoSci/converted/Measurement/*

Identifying and Locating Mental Measurements *www.lib.auburn.edu/socsi/docs/measurements.htm*

Internet Resource Links for Research Methods *http://www.apsu.edu/oconnort/*

Guidelines for Developing Likert-Scale Items *http://isis.fastmail.usf.edu/ugrads/mmc4420/guidelines%20for%20writing%20likert%20items.htm*

Reliability and Item Analysis *www.statsoft.com/textbook/streliab.html*

Scales and Standard Measures *www2.chass.ncsu.edu/garson/pa765/standard.htm*

11

Policy Analysis and Evaluation Research

In the introductory chapter, we addressed the criticism that much criminological and criminal justice research is either common sense or impractical. This chapter focuses on the latter concern: "So what; of what practical use are these research findings?" We will apply what we have learned to the tasks of policy analysis and evaluation research—the cutting edge of government-sponsored criminal justice research today.

Policy Analysis

Policy analysis

Policy analysis is the "study of whatever governments choose to do or not to do," "the description and explanation of the causes and consequences of government behavior" (Dye, 1995, pp. 3–4). Jones (1977, p. 4) views policy analysis as the study of proposals (specified means for achieving goals), programs (authorized means for achieving goals), decisions (specified actions taken to implement programs), and effects (the measurable impacts of programs). Policy analysis is an applied subfield of economics, political science, public administration, sociology, law, and statistics. It involves the identification and description of social problems, the development of public policies that may alleviate these problems, and determination of whether these policies work (Dye, 1995, p. 17). Although there are many models, perspectives, and approaches to policy analysis, the policy process could be viewed as a series of political activities consisting of the following:

Identifying problems	Demands are expressed for government action.
Formulating policy proposals	Agenda is set for public discussion. Development of program proposals to resolve problem.
Legitimating policies	Selecting a proposal. Building political support for it. Enacting it as a law.
Implementing policies	Organizing bureaucracies. Providing payments or services. Levying taxes.
Evaluating policies	Studying programs. Reporting "outputs" of government programs. Evaluating "impacts" of programs on target and nontarget groups in society. Suggesting changes and adjustments (Dye, 1995, p. 21).

Thus the policy process involves identification, formulation, legitimation, implementation, and evaluation.

Evaluation Research

Evaluation research is the last stage of the policy process; questions such as the following are asked:

- Do the programs work?
- Do they produce the desired result?
- Do they provide enough benefits to justify their costs?
- Are there better ways to attack these problems?
- Should the programs be maintained, improved, or eliminated?

Evaluation research is an applied branch of social science that is intended to supply scientifically valid information with which to guide public policy. Historically, research in the social sciences had its origins in the physical sciences and was oriented toward development of theories and utilization of the experimental model to test those theories. Its concern was much more akin to pure or basic research discussed in Chapter 1—the acquiring and testing of new knowledge.   Evaluation research

Evaluation research as a type of applied research has different roots as well as intentions. It evolved from the world of technology rather than science and emphasizes mission or goal accomplishment and product/service delivery rather than theory formation. Evaluation research aims to provide feedback to policy makers in concrete, measurable terms. Although such an approach has existed informally since early times, the introduction of computer technology in the 1950s and its successful application to "defense systems" and "space systems" have led to the application of evaluation research to "social systems" such as the "criminal justice system." Much of this thinking grew out of the "Planning, Programming, Budgeting Systems" (PPBS) approach originally employed by the U.S. Department of Defense in the 1960s, a method of policy evaluation widely adopted by other government agencies. PPBS attempts to specify (by clearly defining program objectives) and quantify (by developing measures of accomplishments) the output of a government program and to analyze the relative costs and benefits of the program (see Rossi and Freeman, 1993).

As billions of dollars were poured into social programs in the 1960s, the following questions were increasingly asked: Do the programs work or make a difference? Are they cost-effective? Are they the most efficient method of providing services? With fewer funds available at the turn of the century the same questions are still relevant: How can the best use be made of limited resources to accomplish maximum program benefits?

Other than its very practical bent and some relatively esoteric techniques such as cost-benefit analysis, many of the methodological procedures employed in evaluation research have already been covered earlier in this text in Chapters 1–10. Thus, rather than viewing it as a different type of research, readers can confidently assume that they can master the essentials of evaluation research on the basis of knowledge of many of the issues we have already described. Quite simply, *evaluation research can be defined as measurement of the effects of a program in terms of its specific goals, outcomes, or particular program criteria.* Weiss (1972, p. 4) states that the purpose of evaluation research is "to measure the effects of a program against the goals it set out to accomplish as a means of contributing to subsequent decision making about the program and improving future programming." It is essential to this purpose that the research methodology we have discussed be used to measure program outcomes in terms of specifically identified criteria in order to accomplish an applied or practical research objective—better programs. Similar to a scientific experiment, the research methodology is applied to evaluate social action programs to accomplish more efficient programs (Schwarz, 1980).

The National Advisory Committee on Criminal Justice Standards and Goals feels very strongly about the importance of evaluation research:

> A high quality evaluation is expensive and time-consuming. Indeed, it may be many times more expensive than the operational program it is designed to test. Viewed in the context of that single program, such an expenditure may appear absurd. But in the context of advancement of knowledge, this type of concentration of funds is more likely to be fruitful than the same expenditure on a large number of inadequate evaluations would be. Progress does not depend on every program being evaluated; in fact, with limited resources for evaluation, it may be retarded by such a practice. (National Advisory Committee, 1976, p. 52)

Some workers involved in administering applied or action programs in criminal justice may have either little understanding of evaluation, past exposure to poor evaluations, or perhaps little regard for the necessity of evaluation as they are already committed to a particular programmatic strategy. The logic of the National Advisory Committee statement would argue that a few expensive, well-designed evaluations are in the long run more cost-effective in revising or eliminating unnecessary treatments or procedures. The last point—elimination—is perhaps at the crux of the resistance to evaluations. Similar to early applications of social, scientific, and managerial studies in industry, many of those to be studied obviously have an understandably vested interest in maintaining a favorable image of the current procedures, practices, and staffing of their organizations.

Policy Experiments

Policy experiments

A close link between experimental methods and the assessment of public policy programs has increased dramatically since 1970 (Fagan, 1990, p. 108). **Policy experiments** are applied field experiments that address themselves to immediate practical policy questions. The National Research Council's Committee on Research on Law Enforcement and the Administration of Justice summarized the following steps in designing policy experiments (Garner and Visher, 1988, pp. 7–8):

1. Choose an interesting problem—a policy question that people really care about or an existing procedure that clearly needs improvement.
2. Do some creative thinking to solve legal and ethical issues that may arise.

3. Rigorously maintain the random assignment of persons, cases, or other units into treatment and control groups throughout the experiment.

4. Choose a design and methods of investigation that are appropriate both to the questions to be answered and the available data.

5. Adopt a team approach between researchers and practitioners, and keep working in close cooperation.

6. Put as much into your experiment as you want to get out of it.

7. Use an experiment to inform policy, not to make policy.

8. Understand and confront the political risks an experiment may involve.

9. Insofar as possible, see that the experiment is replicated in a variety of settings before encouraging widespread adoption of experimentally successful treatments.

Before exploring evaluation research more thoroughly, let us first provide an example of a policy analysis program that utilizes evaluation research.

Policy Analysis: The Case of the National Institute of Justice Research Program

Although policy analysis and evaluation research in criminology and criminal justice are not restricted solely to government-funded research of primarily government-funded projects, and the National Institute of Justice (NIJ) is not the only agency sponsoring criminal justice research, NIJ does utilize the largest, most ambitious policy-oriented program of its type and has been heralded by the National Academy of Sciences as a pioneer and model for other programs. For this reason we explore the philosophy, aims, and research program plan of the NIJ.

NIJ Mission Statement

The NIJ is a research branch of the U.S. Department of Justice. The institute's mission is to develop knowledge about crime, its causes, and control. Priority is given to policy-relevant research that can yield approaches and information that state and local agencies can use in preventing and reducing crime. The decisions made by criminal justice practitioners and policy makers affect millions of citizens, and crime affects almost all our public institutions and the private sector as well. Targeting resources, assuring their effective allocation, and developing new means of cooperation between the public and private sector are some of the emerging issues in law enforcement and criminal justice that research can help illuminate.

Carrying out the mandate assigned by Congress in the Justice Assistance Act of 1984, the NIJ aims to:

- Sponsor research and development to improve and strengthen the nation's system of justice with a balanced program of basic and applied research.
- Evaluate the effectiveness of criminal justice and law enforcement programs and identify those that merit application elsewhere.
- Support technological advances applicable to criminal justice.

■ Test and demonstrate new and improved approaches to strengthen the justice system.

■ Disseminate information from research, development, demonstrations, and evaluations (NIJ, 1994, p. 1).

In establishing its research agenda, the institute is guided by the priorities of the Attorney General and the needs of the criminal justice field. The institute actively solicits the views of police, courts, and corrections practitioners as well as the private sector to identify the most critical problems and to plan research that can help resolve them. Recent priorities include the following:

■ Reducing violent crime

■ Reducing drug and alcohol-related crime

■ Reducing the consequences of crime

■ Improving the effectiveness of crime prevention programs

■ Improving law enforcement and the criminal justice system

■ Developing new technology for law enforcement and the criminal justice system

Studies that involve the use of randomized experimental designs are encouraged, as are multiple strategies for data collection and well-controlled, quasi-experimental designs and equivalent comparison group designs. Qualitative studies, including ethnographic data collection, are also encouraged (NIJ, 1994, p. 2).

NIJ Research Priorities

Some recent research priorities of NIJ (NIJ, 2004) include the following:

Violence and other criminal behavior

Sex offenders/offenses

Crime and delinquency prevention

Child abuse and neglect

Juvenile delinquency

Policing practices, organization, and administration

Terrorism or counterterrorism

Drugs, drugs and crime/alcohol, and drug testing

Drug treatment

White-collar crime/cybercrime

Transnational crime and organized crime

Justice systems

Courts, prosecution, and defense

Corrections

Offender programs and treatment

Crime mapping and spatial analysis

Other thematic areas

A Systems Model of Evaluation Research

Although a variety of terms and competing models of evaluation research exist, the "systems model" is presented here to acquaint the reader with a general evaluation approach. A *model* is a simplified schema that outlines the essential points of a theory. A **systems model** assumes that all parts of an organism, organization, or program are interrelated and could be represented in basic computer language as a system of inputs into an existing system, processing of these inputs, and subsequent outputs (or outcomes). Figure 11.1 presents a systems model for evaluating programs in the criminal justice system.

    The project components to be evaluated in this model are inputs, activities, results, outcomes, and feedback (Schneider, 1978, pp. 3,23–3,31):

Systems model

Inputs	Resources, guidelines, rules, and operating procedures provided for a program, for example, funds for personnel, equipment, operating costs, and authorization to introduce new policies (often an experimental treatment)
Activities	What is done in the project with these inputs (resources), for example, services provided, staffing patterns, and use of materials and human and physical resources (called "process" in many models)

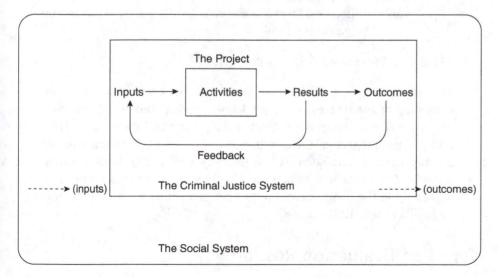

Figure 11.1

A Systems Model of Evaluation Research: System and Project Components.

Source: Schneider, Anne L., et al. *Handbook of Resources for Criminal Justice Evaluators.* Washington, DC: U.S. Department of Justice, 1978, pp. 3–24.

Results	*Specific* consequences of the project activities or the specific objectives of the program, for example, amount of services provided, work completed, production accomplished, or cases closed or cleared (called "output" or "products" in many models)
Outcomes	Accomplishment of broader-range societal goals; these are general consequences of the specific accomplishments (outputs/results) of the program, for example, better justice, health, safety, and education
Feedback	Recycling of results/outcomes into the operation as additional (or modified) inputs; profits may induce a corporation to reinvest in a particularly profitable line, just as losses may lead it to eliminate a less profitable line (also called "feedback loop")

Inputs and process represent specific organizational/program *efforts* and outputs represent specific organizational/program *results*. Outcomes represent impacts on general, external societal activities. Note this *very* simple illustration:

Input	Grant of $100,000 for a foot patrol program
Process	Two officers assigned to foot patrol in Precinct A for one year
Results	Fifty percent increase in arrests in Precinct A
Outcome	Crime rate declines 10 percent and fear of crime declines 40 percent
Feedback	Allocate $1,000,000 and twenty officers to expanded foot patrol program

Figure 11.1 is summarized as follows:

In this scheme, a criminal justice project is conceived of as a system consisting of *inputs* (resources, guidelines, and operating procedures); *activities* (those things the project and its personnel do); *results* (the initial consequences of the activities); and *outcomes* (the long-range, socially relevant consequence of the project). The system should contain a *feedback* loop through which the results and outcomes of a project impact upon the operation of the project and act as additional inputs. (Schneider et al., 1978, pp. 3–8)

Types of Evaluation Research

With the evolution and growth of evaluation research as a field has come a whole lexicon of descriptive tags. Franklin and Thrasher (1976), for instance, mention a variety of research approaches as they relate to evaluation: continuous-versus-one-shot evaluations, "hip pocket"-versus-formal evaluations, policy research, applied research, decision-oriented research, social audits, action research, operations research, discipline-related research, basic research, frontline evaluations, utilization reviews, and continuous monitoring and quality control. Unfortunately, many of these terms are used interchangeably by various writers, and there is no consistent agreement on their meaning in the field. Even the terms *policy analysis* and *evaluation research* are often used as synonyms.

Evaluation research is different from other types of applied research in that the data are used to make a decision(s) regarding a specific program, rather than simply to represent findings of theoretical interest. Although numerous types have been identified, there are *two general types of evaluation research*: process evaluation and impact evaluation. In most instances, it is the latter term by which "evaluation research" is most often described in references. **Process evaluation** establishes causal relationships between results (such as an increase in arrests) and project inputs and activities (see Figure 11.2).

Process evaluation

Impact evaluation establishes causal relationships between outcomes (such as crime reduction) and inputs, activities, and results of programs.

Impact evaluation

Evaluation research is often confused with two related information-gathering activities: assessment and monitoring. **Assessment** (sometimes called needs assessment) is the enumeration of some activity or resource, for instance, the need for a particular service in some target area. "It is a method of finding service delivery gaps and substantiating unmet needs in a community and is used to establish priorities for addressing problems" (Office of Juvenile Justice, 1978, p. 2). **Monitoring** is assessment of whether the plans for a project have in fact been realized: Are the activities related to the inputs? Monitoring is similar to an audit, an assessment of program accountability: Is the program doing what it is supposed to be doing (Waller et al., 1975)? A certain portion of the operating budget of an organization might be set aside to fund such a monitoring task.

Assessment

Monitoring

Evaluation research need not be restricted to solely an analysis of output; it can involve any systematic assessment of various aspects of program review (Suchman, 1967). Effort, efficiency, operation, effectiveness of performance,

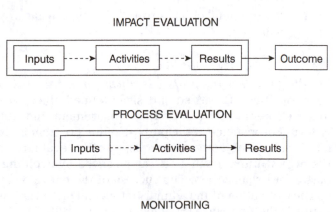

IMPACT EVALUATION

Inputs ----→ Activities ----→ Results → Outcome

PROCESS EVALUATION

Inputs ----→ Activities → Results

MONITORING

Inputs → Activities

Figure 11.2
Types of Evaluation.
Source: Schneider, Anne L., et al. *Handbook of Resources for Criminal Justice Evaluators.* Washington, DC: U.S. Department of Justice, 1978, pp. 3–33.

adequacy of performance, and the like can all be subject to evaluation (Office of Juvenile Justice, 1978, p. 3). *Before an evaluation is undertaken*, it is important that it be decided whether an evaluation can and should be done. According to the Office of Juvenile Justice and Delinquency Prevention (1978, p. 508), *three crucial questions must be answered*:

Will the findings be used?

Is the project evaluable?

Who can do this work?

Will the Findings Be Used?

Evaluation research has an applied quality to it that *requires the active support and cooperation of the agency or program to be evaluated.* Levine, Musheno, and Palumbo (1980, p. 551) put the matter succinctly: "The program administrator's desire to reaffirm his or her position with favorable program evaluations may conflict with the social scientist's desire to acquire an objective appraisal of a program's impact. The end result may be either a research design with low scientific credibility and tainted results, or a credible study that never receives a public hearing because the administrator does not like the results" (Levine, Musheno, and Palumbo, 1980, p. 551). Unless a sincere need for the research has been expressed by the agency administrators and the effort is viewed as something other than a public relations plume, evaluation research may become nothing more than a sham. In discussing problems with contract research in which the researcher is paid by the researchee, Punch (1986, p. 73) says "Having paid the piper they want copyright on the tune." This reflects concern that academic reliance on commercial funds may damage academic freedom. Grinyer (1999) suggests that researchers should think through potential questions before agreeing to contract research. These include the following:

■   What happens if the client does not like the research findings?

■   What ethical issues are raised by the client becoming the subject of the research?

■   If the client objects to the findings, what are the implications for publication?

Is the Project Evaluable?

In asking *whether the project is capable of being evaluated*, the researcher is concerned with the existing design, defined objectives, and other programmatic elements that enable the measurement and assessment of specified criteria. For instance, if the purpose of the program is simply defined as "to do good" and no objectives, records, or other evaluable materials are kept by the organization, much grief can be saved by avoiding an evaluation of this particular organization. The success of the entire evaluation process hinges on the motivation of the administrators and organization in calling for an evaluation in the first place (Schulberg and Baker, 1977).

It should be possible to locate specific organizational objectives that are measurable. "The key assumptions of the program must be stated in a form

which can be tested objectively. That is, not only must the outcome be definable, but also the process used to achieve it must be specifiable" (Office of Juvenile Justice, 1978, p. 7). If proper data for evaluation and clear outcomes or criteria of organizational "success" are absent, then a proper evaluation cannot be undertaken. Rutman (1977) refers to this process as "formative research," a reconnaissance operation to determine program evaluability. Wholey (1977) suggests the following steps in **evaluability assessment**   Evaluability assessment
(assessing whether the program is evaluable):

1. Bounding the problem or program or determining what the objectives of the program are and where it fits in the service picture
2. Collecting program information that defines its activities, objectives, and assumptions
3. Modeling of the program and the interrelationships of program activities
4. Analyzing plans or determining whether the model and activities are measurable
5. Presenting to management (intended user) or reporting results of evaluation assessment and determination of the next steps to be taken

Rabow (1964, p. 69), in speaking specifically to corrections research, suggests that before any results are attributed to a particular treatment, the evaluation should address important questions, as outlined in the three stages of Rabow's research model.

Stage I is concerned with the population of offenders from which treatment and control groups will be selected.

1. How is the population of offenders from which groups will be selected defined with respect to age, record of offenses, geographical location, or any social or personality characteristics thought to be important?
2. How is selection carried out in order to eliminate bias—by random means or some matching process?
3. When and by whom is selection carried out? What are the mechanics?
4. What steps are taken to demonstrate the lack of bias in selection?

Stage II is concerned with the treatment process and the need to understand what is involved in it.

1. What is the theory of causation upon which treatment is proceeding?
2. What is the intervention strategy utilized in the treatment by which the causation variables will be modified?
3. Can a logical relationship between causation variables and intervention strategy be demonstrated?
4. Can it be demonstrated that the treater is fulfilling role requirements specified by the intervention strategy?
5. Assuming that treatment role requirements are being fulfilled, can it be demonstrated that variables cited in the theory of causation are being modified?
6. How shall any change in the variables be measured?

Stage III involves actual comparisons of groups subsequent to treatment.

1. What are the goals of treatment; that is, how shall success be defined in terms of recidivism, attitudinal change, new social relationships, and personality modification?
2. How is the measurement of these characteristics carried out?
3. Over what period of time are comparisons to continue?
4. How is the cooperation of subjects outlined?

Who Can Do This Work?

In asking *"Who can do this work?"* one must decide on internal or external evaluators. If the evaluation is to be "in-house," that is, to be conducted by the internal staff of the agency to be evaluated, then adequate time and workforce must be allocated to permit a careful and hopefully objective evaluation. Outside evaluators may lend greater objectivity to the evaluation task but, as we will discuss later, require orientation to, and cooperation of, the agency to address the relevant objectives and goals from a policy perspective.

Steps in Evaluation Research

The actual *steps in evaluation research* do not differ significantly from the basic steps in the research process that were identified in Chapter 1:

- Problem formulation
- Design of instruments
- Research design (evaluation model)
- Data collection
- Data analysis
- Findings and conclusions
- Utilization

Only in the last step does evaluation research differ significantly from other research processes. There are, of course, a variety of ways of slicing a pie; but most alternative listings of steps one way or another includes the key elements we have identified above. For instance, Albright et al. (1973), in *Criminal Justice Research: Evaluation in Criminal Justice Programs: Guidelines and Examples*, an evaluator's manual prepared on behalf of the National Institute of Law Enforcement and Criminal Justice (now NIJ), focus primarily on the data collection and analysis stages. They outline five essential

Steps in evaluation planning **steps in evaluation planning** (Albright et al., 1973, p. 5):

- Quantify the objectives and goals
- Determine a quantifiable objective/goal relationship
- Develop evaluation measures
- Develop data needs considering requirements, constraints, and reporting
- Determine methods of analysis

These steps would be assumed or included in the design of instruments, research design, data collection, and data analysis stages that we have discussed throughout this text.

Problem Formulation

Just as in the other types of research we have discussed, evaluation researchers are also often in a hurry to get on with the task without thoroughly grounding the evaluation in the major theoretical issues in the field. Glaser (1974) feels that evaluation research in criminal justice would be more useful were it to differentiate offenses and offenders utilizing causal theory. Without this theoretical grounding, familiarization with past and current literature, and valid operationalization of concepts, many evaluation studies can easily deteriorate into glorious exercises in social accounting.

Glaser (1973) comments on how much of what is regarded as in-house evaluations in correctional agencies has been co-opted and is little more than head counting or the production of tables for annual reports.

The problem formulation stage, to reiterate a point that has been emphasized throughout this text, is the most crucial stage of research.

Design of Instruments

On the basis of problem formulation, review of the relevant literature, and program reconnaissance, a most important element in evaluation research is the identification and operationalization of key components of the program to be analyzed. The National Advisory Committee on Criminal Justice Standards and Goals (1976, p. 113) suggests that professional associations be commissioned to establish standardized definitions based on the following:

> A major problem in research on criminal justice organizations is the absence of standardized definitions for such basic terms as dangerousness, recidivism, discretion, disparity, equity, proportionality, uniformity, individualization, commitment sentence, probation, parole and length of follow-up. The confusion over definitions has not only impeded communication among researchers and, more importantly, between researchers and practitioners, but also has hindered comparisons and replications of research studies. R&D-funding agencies, such as the National Institute of Law Enforcement and Criminal Justice and the National Institute of Mental Health, should be sensitive to the way in which the terminology is used in the research studies being supported. Where appropriate, the use of common definitions can facilitate the direct comparison of research findings and, hence, the aggregation of research knowledge. For example, the development of standardized definitions has already occurred in the use of some identically worded questions in victimization surveys.

The greater use of replication of instruments employed by others can contribute to more confidence in the reality and validity of evaluation methodologies, as well as to more useful cross-site comparisons.

Research Design

Ideally, researchers would prefer control over treatment and a classic experimental design, with random assignment of cases to experimental and control groups. Seldom does the evaluation researcher enjoy such a luxury in analyzing ongoing programs. Despite arguments to the contrary (see Boruch, 1976), in many instances, it is very difficult to find organizations that would be willing to undergo experimentation, particularly if it involves the denial of certain treatments (control group) to some clients. Cook, Cook, and Mark (1977) describe some *problems related to the attempt to use randomized designs in field evaluations*:

1. The program planners and staff may resist randomization as a means of allocating treatments, arguing for assignment based on need or merit.
2. The design may not be correctly carried out, resulting in nonequivalent experimental and control groups.
3. The design may break down as some people refuse to participate or drop out of different treatment groups (experimental mortality).
4. Some feel that randomized designs create focused inequity because some groups receive treatment others desire and thus can cause reactions that could be confused with treatments.

Strasser and Deniston (1978) distinguish between preplanned and postplanned evaluations. Although the former may interfere with ongoing program functioning, the latter is less costly, involves less interference in the organization, and is less threatening to the personnel being evaluated. As per our discussion, much of the bemoaning concerning the inadequacy of research design in evaluation methodology in criminal justice has arisen because of an overcommitment to experimental designs and a deficient appreciation of the utility of post hoc controls by means of multivariate statistical techniques (see, for instance, Cain, 1975; Posavec and Carey, 1992).

Logan (1980, p. 36) agrees with this point when he states:

It may be that more rapid progress can be made in the evaluation of preventive or correctional programs if research designs are based on statistical rather than experimental model. It was noted, above, that one major difficulty in evaluation research is in procuring adequate control groups. Modern statistical techniques can provide a means of resolving this problem by substituting statistical for experimental methods of control.

Data Collection

One principal shortcoming of much evaluation research has been its overreliance on questionnaires as the primary means of *data gathering*. The use of a triangulated strategy of data collection employing multiple methodologies would assure greater confidence in the validity of findings (see, for instance, Fry, 1973). Where possible, agencies' records as outcome measures should be cross-checked against other data sources. Many of the issues discussed previously in this text are, of course, also appropriate to evaluation research. All of the sources of error, particularly in data collection, must be continually checked, to ensure that the findings are true findings and not the result of measurement error. Schwarz (1980, p. 14) presents the issue succinctly:

> In practice, the cup seldom reaches the lip intact. Designs must be compromised. There are mishaps in the field. Expecting both valid results and an impeccable process is overly optimistic. The most that can be expected is that the findings will be valid despite compromise and mishaps. Flaws cannot be avoided.

Although program supporters will jump on methodological or procedural problems in any evaluation that comes to a "negative" conclusion, Schwarz echoes a theme that has been emphasized throughout this text: There is no such thing as research without error. The only way to avoid error is to do no research at all.

MacKenzie and McCarthy (1990, p. 8) indicate that criminal justice researchers should not ignore secondary analysis; nor should they be afraid to reanalyze data previously collected by someone else. Two particularly important sources for such data are the National Archive of Criminal Justice Data (formerly the Criminal Justice Archive and Information Network [CJAIN]) and the National Center for Juvenile Justice (NCJJ). National Archive of Criminal Justice Data databases include many classic and well-known criminal justice studies, as well as data from recent NIJ-sponsored studies. NCJJ archives data on juvenile justice system transactions in about half of the states.

Data Analysis

The choice of appropriate statistical analysis must be based on whether the data meet the assumptions necessary for each technique to be employed. An important additional consideration is pointed out by Glaser (1976, p. 771):

> Some research reports from correctional agencies are not suppressed, but might as well be, for few officials—or even researchers—can understand them. Most notable among such reports are those which describe the use of various types of multiple correlation or multiple association statistical analysis of case data in administrative records to find guides for correctional operations. These reports are submitted to correctional officials who do not understand the statistical terminology and who feel no urgency to learn to understand it since the researchers share with the operations officials the impression that this statistical analysis has little or no practical value at present. Thus these researchers operate in a separate world, inadequately

linked either with the university social system which seems to be their reference group, or with the leaders of the correctional system, which they are presumed to serve.

What might be excellent choices of statistical analysis for professional or academic purposes may not be appropriate in form for presentation to a lay audience. Recall in the first chapter of this text the point that, unlike the chemist or physicist, the criminologists must compete with "commonsensical" views and explanations and, unfortunately, must often pitch their evidence toward the lowest common denominator. How, then, can the evaluation researcher in criminal justice resolve this dilemma of treating data with the most appropriate and rigorous statistical methodology they require, however esoteric, yet attempting to communicate these findings so that even politicians would understand? A useful practice is to perform the evaluation and write a report geared for a professional audience and then issue a *report for laypeople*, in which the crucial findings are simplified, summarized, and understood by nonresearch professionals. In writing such reports the researcher may take license in generalizing findings, but it is exactly this succinct presentation that is usually viewed as most useful by the consumer. Instead of the results of stepwise multiple regressions and intercorrelation matrices, the critical relationships or statistically significant findings could be presented in simple bivariate tables, which are more easily understood by more people. An interesting exercise is boiling down the entire evaluation report to a two-page summary, the type that might be released as a press report. Although, of course, such a brief document does not do justice to the complexity of the analysis, anyone desiring the details can consult the full report.

Utilization

Previous points, particularly with respect to data analysis, have a direct bearing on the *utilization of evaluation findings*.

In discussing the "politicization of evaluation research," Maida and Faucett (1978) point out the increasing political nature of evaluations as they are increasingly used to decide the future of programs. Adams describes the dilemma of the agency administrator who is to be evaluated:

> Part of the administrator's concern about evaluative research comes from the dilemma that research creates for him. The evaluation process casts him in contradictory roles. On the one hand, he is the key person in the agency, and the success of its various operations, including evaluation, depends on his knowledge and involvement. On the other hand, evaluation carries the potentiality of discrediting an administratively sponsored program or of undermining a position the administrator has taken. (Adams, 1975, p. 19)

Factors that limit the utilization of evaluation research findings in criminal justice are much the same obstacles that prevent effective evaluation research.

Wellford (2010, p. 21) feels that criminologists should stop complaining about their lack of influence on policy and practice. He suggests that we need to:

> Identify and celebrate the contributions criminological research has and continues to make to crime policy and practice. Hot spots policing, problem-oriented policing, sentencing guidelines, correctional management and programming, parole release, and crime prevention through environmental design, are just a few of the current policies and practices that have largely been determined by the research, theories, and methods of criminological research. Our basic measure of crime, the National Crime Victimization Survey, and our basic measure of law enforcement agencies, LEMAS, were created by and have been largely advanced by criminologists. The Blueprints effort and the Campbell Coalition have identified empirically sound programs for crime prevention and control. These examples and many more should be used to demonstrate our profound impact.

What Works in Criminal Justice?

If we ran GE, GM, or GTE the way we sometimes run our criminal justice systems, they would all be out of business. Ford would still be making Edsels. A revolution has taken place in criminal justice at the dawn of the twenty-first century. Let us find out what works in criminal justice, what is promising, and what does not work. About thirty years ago, Robert Martinson (1974) rocked the correctional community after reviewing over a 100 programs and concluding that "nothing works." It turns out that Martinson was wrong; some programs do work, but how do we know?

In 1996, the United States Congress required the Attorney General to provide a "comprehensive evaluation of the effectiveness" of over $3 billion annually in Department of Justice grants to assist state and local law enforcement and communities in preventing crime. Congress required that the research for the evaluation be "independent in nature" and "employ rigorous and scientifically recognized standards and methodologies." The Assistant Attorney General for the Office of Justice Programs asked the NIJ to commission an "independent review" of over 500 program impact evaluations.

The congressionally mandated evaluation examined hundreds of different strategies used in communities, families, schools, labor markets, places, and police and criminal justice settings (Sherman et al., 1997). It found that very few operational crime prevention programs have been evaluated using scientifically recognized standards and methodologies, including repeated tests under similar and different social settings. Based on a review of more than 500 prevention program evaluations meeting minimum scientific standards, the report (ibid.) concluded that there is minimally adequate evidence to establish a provisional list of what works, what does not, and what is promising. Exhibit 11.1 lists each of these.

EXHIBIT 11.1 ▶

Preventing Crime: What Works, What Doesn't, What's Promising

What Works?

- **For infants**: Frequent home visits by nurses and other professionals.
- **For preschoolers**: Classes with weekly home visits by preschool teachers.
- **For delinquent and at-risk preadolescents**: Family therapy and parent training.
- **For schools**:

  Organizational development for innovation.

  Communication and reinforcement of clear, consistent norms.

  Teaching of social competency skills.

  Coaching of high-risk youth in "thinking skills."
- **For older male ex-offenders**: Vocational training.
- **For rental housing with drug dealing**: Nuisance abatement action on landlords.
- **For high-crime hot spots**: Extra police patrols.
- **For high-risk repeat offenders**: Monitoring by specialized police units.

  Incarceration.
- **For domestic abusers who are employed** On-scene arrests.
- **For convicted offenders**: Rehabilitation programs with risk-focused treatments.
- **For drug-using offenders in prison**: Therapeutic community treatment programs.

What Doesn't Work

- Gun "buyback" programs.
- Community mobilization against crime in high-crime poverty areas.
- Police counseling visits to homes of couples days after domestic violence incidents.
- Counseling and peer counseling of students in schools.
- Drug Abuse Resistance (DARE).
- Drug prevention classes focused on fear and other emotional appeals, including self-esteem.
- School-based leisure-time enrichment programs.

- Summer jobs or subsidized work programs for at-risk youth.
- Short-term, nonresidential training programs for at-risk youth.
- Diversion from court to job training as a condition of case dismissal.
- Neighborhood watch programs organized with police.
- Arrests of juveniles for minor offenses.
- Arrests of unemployed suspects for domestic assault.
- Increased arrests or raids on drug market locations.
- Storefront police offices.
- Police newsletters with local crime in-formation.
- Correctional boot camps using traditional military basic training.
- "Scared Straight" programs whereby minor juvenile offenders visit adult prisons.
- Shock probation, shock parole, and split sentences adding jail time to probation or parole.
- Home detention with electronic monitoring.
- Intensive supervision on parole or probation (ISP).
- Rehabilitation programs using vague, unstructured counseling.
- Residential programs for juvenile offenders using challenging experiences in rural settings.

What's Promising?

- Proactive drunk driving arrests with breath testing (may reduce accident deaths).
- Community policing with meetings to set priorities (may reduce perceptions of crime).
- Police showing greater respect to arrested offenders (may reduce repeat offending).
- Police field interrogations of suspicious persons (may reduce street crime).
- Mailing arrest warrants to domestic violence suspects who leave the scene before police arrive.
- Higher numbers of police officers in cities (may reduce crime generally).

- Gang monitoring by community workers and probation and police officers.
- Community-based mentoring by Big Brothers/Big Sisters of America (may prevent drug abuse).
- Community-based afterschool recreation programs (may reduce local juvenile crime).
- Battered women's shelters (may help some women reduce repeat domestic violence).
- "Schools within schools" that group students into smaller units (may prevent crime).
- Training or coaching in "thinking" skills for high-risk youth (may prevent crime).
- Building school capacity through organizational development (may prevent substance abuse).
- Improved classroom management and instructional techniques (may reduce alcohol use).
- Job Corps residential training programs for at-risk youth (may reduce felonies).
- Prison-based vocational educational programs for adult inmates (in federal prisons).
- Moving urban public-housing residents to suburban homes (may reduce risk factors for crime).
- Enterprise zones (may reduce area unemployment, a risk factor for crime).

- Two clerks in already-robbed convenience stores (may reduce robbery).
- Redesigned layout of retail stores (may reduce shoplifting).
- Improved training and management of bar and tavern staff (may reduce violence, DUI).
- Metal detectors (may reduce skyjacking, weapon carrying in schools).
- Street closures, barricades, and rerouting (may reduce violence, burglary).
- "Target hardening" (may reduce vandalism of parking meters and crime involving phones).
- "Problem-solving" analysis unique to the crime situation at each location.
- Proactive arrests for carrying concealed weapons (may reduce gun crime).
- Drug courts (may reduce repeat offending).
- Drug treatment in jails followed by urine testing in the community.
- Intensive supervision and aftercare of juvenile offenders (both minor and serious).
- Fines for criminal acts.

Source: Lawrence W. Sherman, et al. *Preventing Crime: What Works, What Doesn't, What's Promising.* Washington, DC: Office of Justice Programs, 1997, NCJ 165366.

The clearinghouse for these evaluations had been contracted to the University of Maryland by the NIJ. The reports were intended to be updated regularly (www.preventingcrime.org). A major development has since taken place in attempting to identify "evidence-based" criminal justice interventions (Sherman et al., 2002). These are ones that have been demonstrated to work through replicable, controlled experiments. A strong movement has taken place domestically and internationally to identify "best practice" programs and exemplary programs that might serve as models in crime prevention. Similar lists of what works have been compiled for juvenile justice programs (Waller and Welsh, 1998) and for international programs (International Center for the Prevention of Crime in Montreal). The list of what works will grow more quickly if the nation invests more resources in scientific evaluations to hold all crime prevention programs accountable for their results.

Clear (2010, xvii) indicates that we are at the beginning of a new, empirically based era in crime and justice policy—evidence-based crime policy. None of these evaluations or placements as "working" or "not working" is final. Constant replication and reevaluation is required; but a persistent, independent, scientific program of evaluation will go a long way in replacing what we think works or what does not with what does work. Perhaps the field of rehabilitation has overreacted to the previously discussed Martinson report that concluded that "nothing works" in rehabilitation. Marlowe (2006) discusses the danger to researchers who conclude that a program does not work of risking being branded with the "Scarlet M" (for Martinson). The message to researchers is that if they question the value of rehabilitation, they risk their professional reputations.

The Campbell Collaboration (C2)

The Campbell Collaboration is an international research organization founded in 2000 and dedicated to preparing, maintaining, and publicizing systematic reviews of research on the effects of social and educational programs and interventions. Modeled after the successful Cochrane Collaboration in health care, the C2 program is named in honor of Donald Campbell, an innovator in research and experimental designs. In examining "what works," the systematic reviews use scientific and explicit methods to identify, screen, and analyze evaluation studies. The purpose of these reviews is to assist decision makers to better understand the existing research and better inform their decisions using evidence-based research. A number of Web sites have been created in a number of fields by organizations to address evidence-based research. These include the Blueprints program (Center for the Study and Prevention of Violence), child trends (programs to enhance child development), the Cochrane collaboration (health care), helping America's youth, programs for justice-involved persons with mental illness, medical clinical practice, juvenile delinquency prevention, addiction, strengthening families, alcohol abuse, as well as other sites (U.S. Department of HEW, 2008).

The nature of a C2 analysis can be illustrated by Brandon Welsh and David Farrington (2002), who did a meta-analysis of the *Crime Prevention Effects of Closed Circuit Television* (CCTV). An outline or summary of their procedure is instructive. They reviewed forty-six relevant studies from both the United States and Britain on the effectiveness of CCTV according to strict methodological criteria. CCTV had to be the main intervention and the outcome measure was crime. There had to be measures of crime levels both before and after the intervention, and there had to be a comparable control area. Twenty-two of the forty-six studies met these criteria and were included. They concluded that the best evidence suggested that the CCTV reduced crime to a small degree and was most effective with vehicle crime in car parks but had least impact in public transportation and in the center city. The poorly controlled (excluded) studies produced more desirable results than the better controlled (included) studies (ibid.).

Another example of a comprehensive effort to evaluate successful program implementation has been the Blueprints for Violence Prevention program at the University of Colorado (OJJDP, 2004). Figure 11.3 describes the Blueprint Initiative as well as the model and promising programs.

ABOUT THE BLUEPRINTS INITIATIVE

Blueprints for Violence Prevention began at the Center for the Study and Prevention of Violence (CSPV) as an initiative of the state of Colorado, with funding from the Colorado Division of Criminal Justice, the Centers for Disease Control and Prevention, and the Pennsylvania Commission on Crime and Delinquency. The project was originally conceived as an effort to identify model violence-prevention programs and implement them within Colorado. Soon after the creation of Blueprints, the Office of Juvenile Justice and Delinquency Prevention (OJJDP) became an active supporter of the project and provided funding to CSPV to sponsor program replications in sites across the United States. As a result, Blueprints evolved into a large-scale prevention initiative.

The Blueprints for Violence Prevention initiative has two overarching goals:

- Identify effective, research-based programs.
- Replicate these effective programs through a national dissemination project sponsored by OJJDP designed to
  - Provide training and technical assistance (through the program designers) to transfer the requisite knowledge and skills to implement these programs to sites nationwide.
  - Monitor the implementation process to troubleshoot problems, provide feedback to sites, and ensure that programs are implemented with fidelity to their original intent and design.
  - Gather and disseminate information regarding factors that enhance the quality and fidelity of implementation.

IDENTIFYING EFFECTIVE PROGRAMS

Identifying effective programs has been at the forefront of the national agenda on violence prevention for the last decade. Federal funding agencies have increasingly emphasized the need to implement programs that have been demonstrated effective. The focus on research-based practices has stimulated communities to search for the best practices and to determine what types of programs would be most effective and appropriate for their local problems and population.

In recent years, various governmental agencies, and some private organizations, have produced lists of programs that demonstrate at least some evidence of positive effects on violence / aggression, delinquency, substance abuse, and their related risk and protective factors. Taken as a whole, this work has resulted in a large repertoire of research-based programs from which the practitioner community may choose. Although these lists provide a valuable resource for communities, they can be confusing. Some lists are narrow in focus—for example, limiting their descriptions to drug abuse, family strengthening, or school-based programs only. In addition, and perhaps more importantly, the criteria for program inclusion vary tremendously, with some agencies adopting a more rigorous set of criteria than others. In fact, one must be diligent when examining the lists to ensure that at least a minimal scientific standard has been applied; for example, programs should demonstrate effectiveness using a research design that includes a comparison (i.e., control) group. Anything less rigorous than this approach cannot provide sufficient evidence to justify disseminating and implementing programs on a wide scale.

Figure 11.3

Successful Program Implementation: Lessons from Blueprints

Source: Sharon Mihalic et al. "Blueprints for Violence Prevention." *OJJDP Juvenile Justice Bulletin*, July 2001; Janine Muller and Sharon Mihalic. "Blueprints: A Violence Prevention Initiative." *OJJDP Fact Sheet*, #110, June 1999; and Sharon Mihalic et al., "Blueprints for Violence Prevention Report." Office of Juvenile Justice and Delinquency Prevention, NCJ204274, July 2004.

The Blueprints initiative likely uses the most rigorous set of criteria in the field:

- Demonstration of significant deterrent effects on problem behavior (violence, aggression, delinquency, and / or substance abuse) using a strong research design (experimental or quasi-experimental with matched control group).
- Sustained effects at least one year beyond the intervention.
- Replication in at least one other site with demonstrated effects.

This high standard is necessary if programs are to be widely disseminated because conducting an outcome evaluation during every implementation effort will be costly, time consuming, and not always possible. Therefore, it is important that programs demonstrate effectiveness, based on a rigorous evaluation, before their widespread dissemination. Programs meeting all three of the criteria are classified as "model" programs, whereas programs meeting at least the first criterion but not all three are considered "promising." To date, Blueprints has identified eleven model programs and twenty-one promising programs.

THE BLUEPRINTS PROGRAMS

The Blueprints for Violence Prevention initiative has identified the following model and promising programs.

MODEL PROGRAMS

Big Brothers Big Sisters of America (BBBSA)
Bullying Prevention Program
Functional Family Therapy (FFT)
Incredible Years: Parent, Teacher, and Child Training Series
Life Skills Training (LST)
Midwestern Prevention Project
Multidimensional Treatment Foster Care (MTFC)
Multisystemic Therapy (MST)
Nurse-Family Partnership
Project Towards No Drug Abuse (Project TND)
Promoting Alternative Thinking Strategies (PATHS)

PROMISING PROGRAMS

Athletes Training and Learning to Avoid Steroids (ATLAS)
Brief Strategic Family Therapy (BSFT)
CASASTART
Fast Track
Good Behavior Game
Guiding Good Choices
High/Scope Perry Preschool
Houston Child Development Center
I Can Problem Solve
Intensive Protective Supervision
Linking the Interests of Families and Teachers
Preventive Intervention
Preventive Treatment Program

Figure 11.3
Continued

Project Northland
Promoting Action Through Holistic Education (PATHE)
School Transitional Environment Program (STEP)
Seattle Social Development Project
Strengthening Families Program: Parents and Children 10–14
Student Training Through Urban Strategies (STATUS)
Syracuse Family Development Program
Yale Child Welfare Project

Descriptions of these programs are available on the Blueprints Web site www.colorado.edu/cspv/blueprints/index.html.

Figure 11.3
Continued

Obstacles to Evaluation Research

In its first annual review volume of criminal justice evaluation, the National Criminal Justice Reference Service (NCJRS, 1979) surveyed most of the authors whose works appeared in the volume, members of the editorial board of the volume, as well as a companion volume, *Crime and Justice: An Annual Review of Research* (Morris and Tonry, 1979). In the order of perceived importance, the following dangerous pitfalls were identified by this group of evaluation experts (NCJRS, 1979, p. 370):

- Poorly done evaluation design and methodology
- Unsound and/or poorly done data analysis
- Unethical evaluations
- Naive and unprepared evaluation staff
- Poor relationships between evaluation and program staff
- Co-optation of evaluation staff and/or design
- Poor quality data
- Poorly done literature reviews of subject area
- Focusing on the method not the process

Geller (1997, p. 4) describes impediments to police departments becoming learning organizations:

- Skepticism about research as ivory tower and impractical.
- Resistance to cooperating with outside researchers because too often they have failed to provide feedback soon enough to assist practitioners.
- Distrust of evaluation research because of the blisters that linger from the last time the department was burned by a poorly conducted study.
- Skepticism that research findings developed in another jurisdiction have any application at home.
- The myth that encouraging critical thinking among the rank and file will undermine necessary paramilitary discipline.

- The belief that thinking inhibits doing.
- An indoctrination process in most police departments that inhibits employees from contributing meaningfully to organizational appraisal.
- A police department that denigrates rank-and-file thinking about the organization's basic business establishes a culture likely to ridicule or demean those who would take time from routine activities (random preventive patrol, etc.), which police have taught themselves, politicians, and the public, and constitute real and tough police work.
- Reluctance to have cherished views challenged.
- Difficulty in engaging in organizational self-criticism while continuing to work with those whose current efforts are criticized.
- Insufficient time for employees to reflect on their work and a lack of time, authority, resources, and skills for them to conduct research.
- Fear of change.

Researchers and Host Agencies

The National Advisory Committee (1976, p. 133) suggests the following guidelines with respect to relationships between those performing evaluation research and the *host agencies*:

R&D funding agencies that support studies of criminal justice organizations should be sure that researchers who conduct such studies are sensitive to the needs of the organizations that are part of the study. Such sensitivity will increase the likelihood of completing the project to the satisfaction of the funding agency, the organization that is part of the study (host agency), and the research team.

1. Before the research begins, clear agreements should be reached between the researcher and the host agency on such issues as the purpose of the research, duration of effort, data to be collected, plans for protecting confidentiality of sensitive information, resources required of the host agency, extent to which the host agency may be identified by name in publications, form and timing of public disclosure of the results of the study, and any other topic of mutual concern.

2. Funding agencies should assist researchers in establishing favorable relationships with host agencies by:

   a. Assuring that the research design does not necessarily interfere with the host agency's normal operations.

    b. Arranging for host agencies to receive timely feedback on research progress or results.

    c. Considering the reimbursement of expense incurred by the host agency in cooperating with the research project.

3. Existing educational programs for researchers could be broadened to include relevant courses, on-site projects conducted in cooperation with an operating agency, internships, and exchange programs to make researchers more cognizant of procedures that may improve their relations with criminal justice organizations. These programs should stress the necessity of developing a viable partnership with the host agency during the planning, conduct, and follow-up of a research study.

Summary

Policy analysis is the study of government behavior. It includes proposals, programs, decisions, and effects. The policy process involves identification, formulation, legitimation, implementation, and evaluation. *Policy experiments* are applied field experiments with immediate practical policy implications. *Evaluation research* is an applied branch of social science that evaluates policies and programs to determine whether and how well they work. The NIJ's research program emphasizes policy-oriented programs and attempts to link researchers with practitioners. A *systems model* of evaluation research consists of inputs, activities, results, outcomes, and feedback.

    Before an evaluation is undertaken, three crucial questions must be answered: Will the findings be used? Is the project evaluable? Who can do this work? Formative research, or an evaluability assessment, addresses these questions before an evaluation is agreed to be undertaken.

    The *steps in evaluation research* are problem formulation, design of instruments, research design (evaluation model), data collection, data analysis, findings and conclusions, and utilization. *Some obstacles or pitfalls in evaluation research are* poor evaluation design and methodology, poor data analysis, unethical evaluations, naive or unprepared evaluation staff, poor relationships between evaluation and program staff, co-optation of evaluation staff and/or design, poor-quality data, poor literature reviews, and focus on method rather than process. Much evaluation research exemplifies some of these problems, particularly the politics of evaluation.

    Of particular importance in effective evaluation is the need for effective relationships between the researcher and the host agency (site to be evaluated). The National Advisory Committee on Criminal Justice Standards and Goals (1976) suggests clear agreements beforehand, assistance from funding agencies in bringing the two parties to suitable agreements, and training programs to acquaint researchers with agency problems and needs.

KEY CONCEPTS

Policy analysis	Impact evaluation	Steps in evaluation
Evaluation research	Assessment	planning
Policy experiments	Monitoring	Obstacles to evaluation
Systems model	Evaluability assessment	research
Process evaluation		

REVIEW QUESTIONS

1. How does evaluation research fit into the general scheme of policy analysis? Using the NIJ program, what role can research have in public policy debates in criminal justice?

2. Describe the "systems model" of evaluation research. In what way can such a model inform public policy in criminal justice?

3. Evaluation research seldom takes place as planned. Using the discussions in the chapter, elaborate on obstacles to evaluation research in criminal justice.

USEFUL WEB SITES

American Evaluation Association *www.eval.org*

Guide for Writing a Funding Proposal *www.learnerassociates.net/ proposal*

Writing Your Thesis or Dissertation *www.learnerassociates.net/dissthes/*

Successful Program Implementation: Lessons from Blueprints *www. ncjrs.org/pdffiles1/ojjdp/204273.pdf*

Resources for Methods in Evaluation *http://gsociology.icaap.org/ methods/*

Juvenile Justice Evaluation Needs *www.jrsa.org/pubs/reports/jj_ needs_assessment.htm*

Juvenile Justice Evaluation Center Online *www.jrsa.org/jjec/*

Blueprints: Successful Program Implementation *www.ojp.usdoj.gov*

Bureau of Justice Assistance Center for Program Evaluation *http://ojp. usdoj.gov/BJA/evaulation/*

Basic Guide to Program Evaluation *www.mapnp.org/library/evaluatn/ fnl_eval.htm*

References

Chapter 1 Introduction to Criminal Justice Research Methods: Theory and Method

Adler, Freda. *Nations Not Obsessed by Crime*. Littleton, CO: Fred B. Rothman, 1983.

Bayley, David H. "Comment: Perspectives on Criminal Justice Research." *Journal of Criminal Justice* 6 (1978): 287–298.

Black, Thomas. *Evaluating Social Science Research*. Thousand Oaks, CA: Sage, 1993.

Blankenship, Michael B., and Stephen E. Brown. "Paradigm or Perspective?: A Note to the Discourse Community." *Journal of Crime and Justice* 16 (1993): 167–175.

Blumer, Herbert. *Symbolic Interactionism: Perspective and Method*. Englewood Cliffs, NJ: Prentice-Hall, 1969.

Blumstein, Alfred, and Joan Petersilia. "NIJ and Its Research Program." In *25 Years of Criminal Justice Research*, 1–42. Washington, DC: National Institute of Justice, December 1994.

Bohm, Robert, and Jeffrey Walker. *Demystifying Crime and Justice*. Los Angeles, CA: Roxbury, 2006.

Brown, Stephen E., and John H. Curtis. *Fundamentals of Criminal Justice Research*. Cincinnati, OH: Anderson, 1987.

Chesney-Lind, Meda. "Girls' Crime and Woman's Place: Toward a Feminist Model of Female Delinquency." *Crime and Delinquency* 35 (1989): 5–30.

Clinard, Marshall B. *Cities with Little Crime: The Case of Switzerland*. Cambridge: Cambridge University Press, 1978.

Clinard, Marshall B., and Peter C. Yeager. *Illegal Corporate Behavior*. Washington, DC: Law Enforcement Assistance Administration, 1979.

Comte, Auguste. *System of Positive Policy*. London: Longmans, Green, 1877.

Denzin, Norman. "An Interpretation of Recent Feminist Theory: Review-Essay." *Sociology and Social Research* 68 (1984): 712–718.

———. *The Research Act: A Theoretical Introduction to Sociological Methods*. Englewood Cliffs, NJ: Prentice-Hall, 1989.

Dorworth, Vicky, and Marie Henry. "Optical Illusions: The Visual Representation of Blacks and Women in Introductory Criminal Justice Textbooks." *Journal of Criminal Justice Education* 3 (Fall 1992): 251–260.

Durkheim, Emile. *Suicide: A Study in Sociology*. Translated by John A. Spaulding and George Simpson. New York: Free Press, 1951.

Eichler, Magrit. *Nonsexist Research Methods: A Practical Guide*. Boston, MA: Allen and Unwin, 1988.

Evans, Bergen. *The Natural History of Nonsense*. New York: Anchor Paperbacks, 1958.

Friedman, Herman P. Roundtable Discussion: "Classification," National Workshop on Research Methodology and Criminal Justice Program Evaluation. Baltimore, MD, March 1980.

Garfinkel, Harold. *Studies in Ethnomethodology*. Englewood Cliffs, NJ: Prentice-Hall, 1967.

Gottlieb, Steven, Sheldon Arenberg, and Raj Singh. *Crime Analysis: From First Report to Final Arrest*. Montclair, CA: Alpha Publishing Company, 1994.

Hagan, Frank E. "Comparative Professionalization in an Occupational Arena: The Case of Rehabilitation." Ph.D. dissertation, Case Western Reserve University, 1975.

———. "The Global Fallacy and Theoretical Range in Criminological Theory." *Journal of Justice Issues* 2 (Winter 1987): 19–31.

———. *Introduction to Criminology: Theories, Methods and Criminal Behavior*. 6th ed. Thousand Oaks, CA: Sage, 2008.

Harcourt, Bernard E. *Illusion of Order: The False Promise of Broken Windows Policing*. Cambridge, MA: Harvard University Press, 2001.

Hills, Stuart L. *Corporate Violence: Injury and Death for Profit*. Totowa, NJ: Rowman and Littlefield, 1987.

Hirschi, Travis, and Hanan Selvin. *Principles of Survey Analysis*. New York: Free Press, 1973.

Hirschi, Travis, and Rodney Stark. "Hellfire and Delinquency." *Social Problems* 17 (Fall 1969): 202–213.

Kappeler, Victor E., and Gary W. Potter. *The Mythology of Crime and Justice*. 4th ed. Prospect Heights, IL: Waveland Press, 2005.

Karmen, Andrew. *New York Murder Mystery: The True Story behind the Crime Crash of the 1990s*. New York: New York University Press, 2001.

Kelling, George A. "Police and Communities: The Quiet Revolution." *Perspectives in Policing*. Washington, DC: National Institute of Justice, June 1998.

———, and James Q. Wilson. *Broken Windows and Police Discretion*. Washington, DC: U.S. Department of Justice, October 1999, NCJ 178259.

Kraska, Peter. "Criminal Justice Theory: Toward Legitimacy and Infrastructure." *Justice Quarterly* 23 (June 2006): 167–185.

Kuhn, Thomas. *The Structure of Scientific Revolutions*. 2nd ed. Chicago, IL: University of Chicago Press, 1970.

Light, Stephen C, and Theresa K. Newman. "Awareness and Use of Social Science Research Among Executive and Administrative Staff Members of State Correctional Agencies." *Justice Quarterly* 9 (June 1992): 299–324.

MacKenzie, Doris L. "Using the U.S. Land-Grant University System as a Model to Attack This Nation's Crime Problem." *The Criminologist* 23 (March/April 1998): 1–4.

Mann, Coramae R. *Unequal Justice: A Question of Color*. Bloomington, IN: Indiana University Press, 1993.

Martinson, Robert. "What Works?—Questions and Answers about Prison Reform." *The Public Interest* 35 (Spring 1974): 22–54.

———. "Martinson Attacks His Own Earlier Work." *Criminal Justice Newsletter* 9 (December 1978): 4.

McCaghy, Charles. *Deviant Behavior*. 5th ed. New York: Macmillan, 1999.

McDermott, M. Joan. "The Personal Is Empirical: Feminism, Research Methods, and Criminal Justice Education." *Journal of Criminal Justice Education* 3 (Fall 1992): 237–249.

Miller, D. W. "Poking Holes in the Theory of Broken Windows." *Chronicle of Higher Education*, February 9, 2001: B5.

Morris, Norval. "Insanity Defense." *Crime File*. Washington, DC: National Institute of Justice, 1987.

National Institute of Justice. *Building Knowledge About Crime and Justice: Research Prospectus, 1998*. Washington, DC: National Institute of Justice, November, 1997.

———. *Solicitation for Crime and Justice Research*. Washington, DC: Office of Justice Programs, February 2004.

———. *Funding Opportunities, Fiscal Year 2006. www. ojp.usdoj.gov/nij/funding/expired/fund2006exp.htm*, 2006.

———. *Funding Opportunities for Fiscal Year 2009*, Washington, DC: Office of Justice Programs, 2008.

———. *Program Plan, 2009*. Washington, DC: National Institute of Justice, 2010.

National Science Foundation. (NSF). *NSF Report*. Washington, DC: Government Printing Office, April 1988.

Pepinsky, Harold E., and Paul Jesilow. *Myths That Cause Crime*. 2nd ed. Cabin John, MD: Seven Locks Press, 1985.

Prewitt, Kenneth, and David L. Sills. "Federal Funding for the Social Sciences: Threats and Responses." *Footnotes* (American Sociological Association) (December 1981): 4–8.

Reinharz, Shulamit. *Feminist Methods in Social Research*. New York: Oxford University Press, 1992.

Renzetti, Claire M. "On the Margins of the Malestream (Or, They Still Don't Get It, Do They?): Feminist Analyses in Criminal Justice Education." *Journal of Criminal Justice Education* 4 (Fall 1993): 219–234.

Russell, Katheryn K. "Development of a Black Criminology and the Role of the Black

Criminologist." *Justice Quarterly* 9 (December 1992): 667–683.

Sampson, Robert, and John Laub. "Seductions of Method: Rejoinder to Nagin and Tremblay's." 2005.

Sherman, Larry W., et al. *Preventing Crime: What Works, What Doesn't, What's Promising.* Reports to the United States Congress, Washington, DC: National Institute of Justice, 1997.

Sontheimer, Henry, and Lynne Goodstein. "An Evaluation of Juvenile Intensive Aftercare Probation: Aftercare Versus System Response Effects." *Justice Quarterly* 10 (June 1993): 197–227.

Stanko, Elizabeth. *Everyday Violence: How Women and Men Experience Sexual and Physical Dangers.* London: Pandora, 1990.

Sutherland, Edwin H. "White Collar Criminality." *American Sociological Review* 5 (February 1940): 1–12.

Taylor, Ralph B. *Breaking Away from Broken Windows.* Boulder, CO: Westview Press, 2001.

Tontodonato, Pamela, and Frank E. Hagan, eds. *The Language of Research in Criminal Justice: A Reader.* Boston, MA: Allyn and Bacon, 1998.

Turner, Jonathan H. *The Structure of Sociological Theory.* 6th ed. Homewood, IL: Dorsey, 1997.

U.S. Department of Justice. *Myths and Realities About Crime.* Washington, DC: Law Enforcement Assistance Administration, National Criminal Justice Information and Statistics Service, 1978.

Visher, Christy A. "Understanding the Roots of Crime: The Project on Human Development in Chicago Neighborhoods." *National Institute of Justice Journal.* (November 1994): 9–15.

Walker, Samuel. *Sense and Nonsense About Crime and Drugs: A Policy Guide.* 6th ed. Monterey, CA: Wadsworth, 2005.

Weber, Max. *The Methodology of Social Sciences.* Translated by Edward A. Shils and Henry A. Finch. New York: Free Press, 1949.

Wilkins, Leslie T. "The Concept of Cause in Criminology." In *Classes, Conflict and Control: Studies in Criminal Justice Management,* edited by J. Munro. Cincinnati, OH: Anderson, 1976.

———. "The Unique Individual." In *Crime in Society,* edited by Leonard D. Savitz and Norman Johnston, 233–238. New York: Wiley, 1978.

Willis, Cecil. "Criminal Justice Theory: A Case of Trained Incapacity." *Journal of Criminal Justice* 11, no. 5 (1983): 447–458.

Wilson, James Q., and George L. Kelling. "Broken Windows: The Police and Neighborhood Safety." *Atlantic Monthly,* March 1982, 27–38.

Worrall, John L. "In Defense of the 'Quantoids': More on the Reason for the Quantitative Emphasis in Criminal Justice Education and Research." *Journal of Criminal Justice Education* 11 (Fall 2000): 353–362.

Wright, Kevin N. *The Great American Crime Myth.* Westport, CT: Greenwood Press, 1985.

Chapter 2 Ethics in Criminal Justice Research

Adamitis, James A., and Bahram Haghighi. "Ethical Issues Confronting Criminal Justice Researchers in the United States." *The Criminologist* 13 (July 1989): 235–242.

Alfred, Randall. "The Church of Satan." In *The New Religious Consciousness,* edited by Charles Glock and Robert Bollah. Berkeley, CA: University of California Press, 1976.

Altman, Laurence K. "Revisionist History Sees Pasteur as Liar Who Stole Rival's Ideas." *New York Times,* May 16 1995, B5, B8.

American Sociological Association. *Code of Ethics.* Washington, DC: American Sociological Association, 1984.

Armstrong, Gary. "Like That Desmond Morris." In *Interpreting the Field: Accounts of Ethnography,* edited by Dick Hobbs and Tim May, 2–43. Oxford: Clarendon, 1993.

Associated Press. "Kid Drug Experiments Investigated." *ABCNews.com,* April 14, 1998.

Associated Press. "Orphans Granted Settlement for 'Monster Study.'" *Erie Times-News,* August 18, 2007, 8A.

Atkinson, Rowland, and John Flint. "Accessing Hidden and Hard-to-Reach Populations: Snowball Research Strategies." *Social Research Strategies* 33 (Summer 2001): 1–4.

Bailey, Kenneth. *Methods of Social Research.* 3rd ed. New York: Free Press, 1987.

Barnes, John A. "Some Ethical Problems in Modern Fieldwork." In *Qualitative Methodology,* edited by William J. Filstead, 235–251. Chicago, IL: Markham, 1970.

Basinger, Julianne. "Research at What Cost?" *Chronicle of Higher Education,* July 27, 2001, A12–17.

Berg, Bruce L. *Qualitative Research Methods for the Social Sciences.* 6th ed. Boston, MA: Allyn and Bacon, 2007.

Bourgois, Philippe. "In Search of Horatio Alger: Culture and Ideology in the Crack Economy." *Contemporary Drug Problems* 16 (1989): 619–649.

Brandt, Allan. M. "Racism, Research and the Tuskegee Syphilis Study." *Hastings Center Report* 7 (1978): 15–21.

Branson, Roy. "Prison Research: National Commission Says 'No,' Unless. . . ." *Hastings Center Report* 7 (February 1977): 17–21.

Broad, William, and Nicholas Wade. *Betrayers of the Truth: Fraud and Deceit in the Halls of Science.* New York: Simon and Schuster, 1983.

Carey, Benedict. "Psychologists Clash on Aiding Interrogations." *New York Times,* August 16, 2008, A1.

Chambers, Eve. "Fieldwork and the Law: New Contexts for Ethical Decision Making." *Social Problems* 27 (February 1980): 330–341.

Code of Federal Regulations, Title 45, A. Department of Health, Education, and Welfare, General Administration, Part 46, Protection of Human Subjects, in *Federal Register* 40 (March 13, 1975): 11854–11858.

Cook, Fred J. *Maverick Ethics: Fifty Years of Investigative Reporting.* New York: G.P. Putnam's Sons, 1984.

Cousins, Norman. "How the U.S. Used Its Citizens as Guinea Pigs." *Saturday Review,* November 10, 1979, 10.

Craig, Gary, Anne Corden, and Patricia Thornton. "Safety in Social Research." Social Policy Research Unit, University of York, 20 (Summer 2000).

Dahmann, Judith, and Joseph Sasfy. *Criminal Justice Information Policy: Research Access to Criminal Justice Data.* Washington, DC: Bureau of Justice Statistics, 1982.

Denzin, Norman K. *The Research Act: A Theoretical Introduction to Sociological Methods.* 3rd ed. New York: McGraw-Hill, 1989.

Department of Health, Education, and Welfare. *Institutional Guide to DHEW Policy on Protection of Human Subjects.* Washington, DC: U.S. Government Printing Office, 1971.

Desruisseaux, Paul. "Canadian Professors Decry Power of Companies in Campus Research." *Chronicle of Higher Education,* November 12, 1999, A59–A61.

"Diet drug company accused of funding favorable journal articles" (Associated Press). *Erie Times-News,* May 18, 1999, 3A.

Douglas, Jack D. "Major Tactics of Investigative Research." In *Focus: Unexplored Deviance,* edited by Charles H. Swanson, 206–221. Guilford, CT: Dushkin, 1978.

———. "Living Morality versus Bureaucratic Fiat." In *Deviance and Decency,* edited by Carl B. Klockars and Finbarr O'Connor, 13–33. Beverly Hills, CA: Sage, 1979.

"Embedded Anthropologists." *Chronicle of Higher Education,* October 19, 2007, B4.

Ephron, Dan, and Sylvia Spring. "A Gun in One Hand, A Pen in the Other." *Newsweek* (April 28, 2008): 34–35.

Erikson, Kai T. "A Comment on Disguised Observation in Sociology." In *Focus: Unexplored Deviance,* edited by Charles H. Swanson, 240–244. Guilford, CT: Dushkin, 1978.

———. "Letter to the General Membership of the American Sociological Association on Behalf of Mario Brajuha's Legal Defense." 1984.

"Ethical Aspects of Experimentation with Human Subjects." *Daedalus* (Spring 1969).

Federal Register. "Department of Health and Human Services Guidelines" (January 26, 1981): 389–392.

Ferrell, Jeff, and Mark S. Hamm, eds. *Ethnography at the Edge: Crime, Deviance, and Field Research*. Boston, MA: Northeastern University Press, 1998.

Fichter, Joseph H., and William L. Kolb. "Ethical Limitations on Sociological Reporting." *American Sociological Review* 18 (1953): 455–550.

Fletcher, Ronald. *Science, Ideology and the Media: The Cyril Burt Affair*. New Brunswick, NJ: Transaction Publishers, 1991.

Fluehr-Lobban, Carolyn. "How Anthropology Should Respond to an Ethical Crisis." *Chronicle of Higher Education*, October 6, 2000, B24.

Foster, Andrea L. "Professor's Fake Survey Prompts Columbia's Business School to Revise Ethics Rule." *Chronicle of Higher Education*, September 21, 2001, A14.

"Fraud in Research." *Society* 31 (March/April 1994), series of articles, 5–63.

Fund to Protect Scholars from Defamation. "*Solicitation Letter*." Box 263, Augusta, MI, April 22, 1980.

Galliher, John F. "The Protection of Human Subjects: A Reexamination of the Professional Code of Ethics." *American Sociologist* 9 (August 1973): 93–100.

———. "Social Scientists' Ethical Responsibilities to Superordinates: Looking Upward Meekly." *Social Problems* 27 (February 1980): 298–308.

Gans, Herbert. *The Urban Villagers*. New York: Free Press, 1962.

Glenn, David. "Blood Feud: A controversy over South American DNA samples held in North American laboratories ripples through anthropology." *The Chronicle of Higher Education,* March 3, 2006, A14.

Goldstein, Evan. "Enlisting Social Scientists." *Chronicle of Higher Education*, July 4, 2008, B4, B5.

Glenn, David. "Security and Paperwork Keep Prison Research on the Outside." *Chronicle of Higher Education,* March 28, 2008, A12.

Guterman, Lila. "Scientists may have Put Their Names on Papers Written by Drug Companies." *Chronicle of Higher Education*, April 25, 2008, A12.

Hagan, Frank E. *Goals in New Town Planning: The Case of Columbia, Maryland*. Master's thesis, University of Maryland, 1968.

———. *Comparative Professionalization in an Occupational Arena: The Case of Rehabilitation*. Ph.D. dissertation, Case Western Reserve University, 1975.

———. *Introduction to Criminology: Theories, Methods and Criminal Behavior*. 6th ed. Thousand Oaks, CA: Sage, 2006.

Hearnshaw, Leslie S. *Cyril Burt, Psychologist*. Ithaca, NY: Cornell University Press, 1979.

Henslin, James M. "Studying Deviance in Four Settings: Research Experiences with Cabbies, Suicides, Drug Users and Abortionees." In *Research on Deviance*, edited by Jack D. Douglas, 35–70. New York: Random House, 1972.

HEW. *The Belmont Report: Ethical Principles and Guidelines for the Protection of Human Subjects Research*. Washington, DC: U.S. Government Printing Office, 1978.

Hornblum, Allen. *Acres of Skin: Human Experiments at Holmesburg Prison: A True Story of Abuse and Exploitation in the Name of Science*. New York: Routledge, 1998.

Horowitz, Irving L. "The Life and Death of Project Camelot." *Transaction* 3 (1965): 3–7, 44–47.

Humphreys, Laud. *Tearoom Trade*. Chicago, IL: Aldine, 1970.

———. "Some Considerations on the Methods, Dangers, and Ethics of Crack House Research." In *Women and Crack Cocaine*, edited by James A. Inciardi, Dorothy Lockwood, and Anne Pottieger, 147–157. New York: Macmillan, 1993.

Irwin, John. "Participant-Observation of Criminals." In *Research on Deviance*, edited by Jack D. Douglas, 17–138. New York: Random House, 1972.

James, Jennifer. "On the Block: Urban Research Perspectives." *Urban Anthropology* 1 (1972): 125–140.

Jones, James H. *Bad Blood: The Tuskegee Syphilis Experiment*. New York: Free Press, 1982.

Joynson, Robert B. *The Burt Affair.* London: Routledge, 1989.

Katz, Jay. *Experimentation with Human Subjects.* New York: Russell Sage Foundation, 1972.

Kiely, Kathy. "Measure to Shield Reporters' Secret Sources likely to Pass." *USAToday*, October 15, 2007, 12A.

Kinney, David. "Book Describes Experiments on Inmates." *Erie Morning News*, June 1, 1998, 7A.

Klockars, Carl B. "Field Ethics for the Life History." In *Street Ethnography*, edited by Robert S. Weppner, 201–226. Vol. 1, Beverly Hills, CA: Sage, 1977.

LaFollette, Marcel C. *Stealing into Print: Fraud, Plagiarism, and Misconduct in Scientific Publishing.* Berkeley, CA: University of California Press, 1992.

Law Enforcement Assistance Administration. *Confidentiality of Research and Statistical Data.* Washington, DC: National Criminal Justice Information and Statistics Service, 1979.

Lawrence, Jill. "Feds Used Human Subjects in Radiation Exposure Experiments." *Erie Times-News*, October 25, 1988, 1A, 12A.

Lee, Raymond. *Doing Research on Sensitive Topics.* Newbury Park, CA: Sage, 1993.

"Lessons Turn Orphans into Outcasts" (Associated Press). *Erie Times-News*, May 11, 2001, 1A.

Long, Karen. "AIDS Research Abroad Raises Ethical Concerns." *Cleveland Plain Dealer*, May 20, 1998, A–1.

Longmire, Dennis R. "Ethical Dilemmas in the Research Setting." *Criminology* 21 (August 1983): 333–348.

Maldonado, Lionel. "Ofshe Wins Case Against Synanon." *Footnotes* (American Sociological Association), 15 (April 1987): 3.

Marks, John. *The Search for the Manchurian Candidate: The CIA and Mind Control.* New York: Times Books, 1979.

Marshall, Eliot. "Anthropologists Debate Tasaday Hoax Evidence." *Science* 246 (1989): 1113–1114.

Milgram, Stanley. *Obedience to Authority: An Experimental View.* New York: Harper, 1974.

Miller, J. Mitchell, and Richard Tewksbury. *Extreme Methods: Innovative Approaches to Social Science Research.* Boston, MA: Allyn and Bacon, 2001.

Mitford, Jessica. *Kind and Unusual Punishment.* New York: Random House, 1973.

Monaghan, Peter. "A Journal Article Is Expunged and Its Authors Cry Foul." *Chronicle of Higher Education*, December 8, 2000, A14–A18.

National Advisory Committee on Criminal Justice Standards and Goals. *Criminal Justice Research and Development*, Report of the Task Force on Criminal Justice Research and Development, Washington, DC: Law Enforcement Assistance Administration, December 1976.

National Commission for the Protection of Human Subjects of Biomedical and Behavioral Research. *The Belmont Report: Ethical Principles and Guidelines for the Protection of Human Subjects of Research*, DHEW OS 78–0012, Washington, DC: U.S. Government Printing Office, 1978a.

National Institute of Justice. "Data Confidentiality and Human Subjects Protection." Research Program Plan: Fiscal Years 1995–96, Washington, DC: National Institute of Justice, 1994.

Neuman, William L. *Social Research Methods: Qualitative and Quantitative Methods.* Boston, MA: Allyn and Bacon, 1991.

O'Connor, Finnbar W. "The Ethical Demands of the Belmont Report." In *Deviance and Decency* edited by Carl B. Klockars and Finnbar W. O'Connor, 225–258. Beverly Hills, CA: Sage, 1979.

"On Being a Scientist: Responsible Conduct in Research." National Academy Press Website, *www.nap.edu/readingroom/books/obas/contents/misconduct.html*, 1998.

Payton, Melissa. *Evaluating Online Resources with Research Navigator: Criminal Justice*, 23–27. Upper Saddle River, NJ: Pearson/Prentice Hall, 2004. *www.researchnavigator.com*.

Polsky, Ned. *Hustlers, Beats and Others.* Chicago, IL: Aldine, 1967.

Punch, Maurice. *The Politics and Ethics of Fieldwork.* Beverly Hills, CA: Sage, 1986.

Rabow, Jerome. "Research and Rehabilitation: The Conflict of Scientific and Treatment Roles in Corrections." In *Criminal Justice Research:*

Approaches, Problems, and Policy, edited by Susette M. Talarico, 237–254. Cincinnati, OH: Anderson, 1980.

Rampell, Catherine. "Journals may Soon use Anti-Plagiarism Software on their Authors." *Chronicle of Higher Education*, April 25, 2008, A17.

"Regulations on the Protection of Human Subjects." *Federal Register*, Book 2, Section 8366 (January 26, 1981).

Reiman, Jeffrey H. "Research Subjects, Political Subjects, and Human Subjects." In *Deviance and Decency*, edited by Carl B. Klockars and Finbarr O'Connor, 35–61. Beverly Hills, CA: Sage, 1979.

Reynolds, Paul D. *Ethical Dilemmas and Social Science Research*. San Francisco, CA: Jossey-Bass, 1979.

———. *Ethics and Social Science Research*. Englewood Cliffs, NJ: Prentice-Hall, 1982.

Roth, Julius A. "Comments on 'Secret Observation.'" *Social Problems* 9 (1962): 283–284.

Saul, Stephanie. "Merc wrote Drug Studies for Doctors." *New York Times*, April 16, 2008, C1, C6.

Scarce, Rik. *Eco-Warriors: Understanding the Radical Environmental Movement*. Chicago, IL: Noble Press, 1990.

———. "Scholarly Ethics and Courtroom Antics: Where Researchers Stand in the Eyes of the Law." In *Extreme Methods: Innovative Approaches to Social Science Research*, edited by J. Mitchell Miller and Richard Tewksbury, 258–272. Boston, MA: Allyn and Bacon, 2001.

———. *Contempt of Court: A Scholar's Battle for Free Speech*. New York: Alta Mira Press, 2005a.

———. "A Law to Protect Scholars." *Chronicle of Higher Education*, August 12, 2005b, B24.

Scheflin, Alan W., and Edward M. Opton, Jr. *The Mind Manipulators*. New York: Paddington Press, 1978.

Shamoo, Adil E. "Deregulating Low-Risk Research." *Chronicle of Higher Education*, August 3, 2007, B16.

Sieber, Joan E. *Summary of Human Subjects Protection Issues Related to Large Sample Surveys*. Washington, DC: Bureau of Justice Statistics, June 2001, NCJ 187692.

Simon, David R., and Stanley D. Eitzen. *Elite Deviance*. 6th ed. Boston, MA: Allyn and Bacon, 1996.

Situ, Yingi, and David Emmons. *Environmental Crime*. Thousand Oaks, CA: Sage, 1999.

Soloway, Irving, and James Walters. "Workin' the Corner: The Ethics and Legality of Ethnographic Fieldwork among Active Heroin Addicts." In *Street Ethnography*, edited by Robert S. Weppner, 159–178. Vol. 1, Beverly Hills, CA: Sage, 1977.

Spencer, Frank. *Piltdown: A Scientific Forgery*. New York: Oxford University Press, 1990.

Talarico, Susette M., ed. *Criminal Justice Research: Approaches, Problems and Policy*. Cincinnati, OH: Anderson, 1980.

Thaler, Ruth E. "Fieldnotes Case Resolved; Scholars' Rights Supported." *Footnotes* (American Sociological Association) 13 (May 1985): 1.

Thorne, Barrie. "You Still Takin' Notes? Fieldwork and Problems of Informed Consent." *Social Problems* 27 (February 1980): 284–297.

Tierney, Patrick. *Darkness in El Dorado: How Scientists and Journalists Devastated the Amazon*. New York: W.W. Norton, 2001.

Titus, Sandra, James Wells, and Lawrence Rhoades. "Repairing Research Integrity." *Nature* 453 (June 19, 2008): 980–982.

Trend, M.G. "Applied Social Research and the Government: Notes on the Limits of Confidentiality." *Social Problems* 27 (February 1980): 342–349.

Wade, Nicholas. "IQ and Heredity: Suspicion of Fraud Beclouds Classic Experiment." *Science* 194 (1976): 916–919.

Wax, Murray L. "Paradoxes of "Consent" to the Practice of Fieldwork." *Social Problems* 27 (February 1980): 272–283.

Weiner, Joseph S. *The Piltdown Forgery*. London: Oxford Press, 1955.

Weiss, Rick. "Scary Days for Human Guinea Pigs." *Washington Post National Weekly Edition*, August 10, 1998, 6–7.

Wells, Matt. "BBC Halts 'Prison Experiment.'" *Guardian*, January 24, 2002, *www.guardian.co.uk_news/story/0.3604.638243.00.html*

Weppner, Robert S. "Street Ethnography: Problems and Prospects." In *Street Ethnography*, edited by Robert S. Weppner, 21–51. Beverly Hills, CA: Sage, 1977.

Wexler, Sandra. "Ethical Obligations and Social Research." In *Measurement Issues in Criminology*, edited by Kimberly L. Kempf, 78–107. New York: Springer-Verlag, 1990.

"When Reporters Can't Shield Sources, the Public Loses Out." *USAToday*, October 16, 2007, 12A.

Whyte, William F. *Streetcorner Society*. Chicago, IL: University of Chicago Press, 1955.

Wilkins, Leslie T. "The Concept of Cause in Criminology." In *Classes, Conflict and Control: Studies in Criminal Justice Management*, edited by J. Munro, Cincinnati, OH: Anderson. 1976.

Wilson, Robin. "When Should a Scholar's Notes Be Confidential?" *Chronicle of Higher Education*, May 16, 2003, A10–A12.

Witt, Howard. "CIA Sued for Attempts at Brainwashing." *Erie Daily Times*, October 3, 1988, 2A.

Wolfgang, Marvin E. "Confidentiality in Criminological Research and Other Ethical Issues." *Journal of Criminal Law and Criminology* 72 (1981): 75–86.

———. "Ethics in Research." In *Ethics, Public Policy and Criminal Justice*, edited by Frederick Elliston and Norman Bowie, 391–418, Cambridge, MA: Oelgeschlager, Gunn and Hain, 1982.

Wolfgang, Marvin E., Figlio, R.M., and Sellin. *Delinquency in a Birth Cohort*. Chicago, IL: University of Chicago Press, 1972.

Yablonsky, Lewis. *The Hippie Trip*. New York: Pegasus, 1968a.

———. "On Crime, Violence, LSD and Legal Immunity for Social Scientists." *Criminologica* 3 (May 1968b): 148–149.

Zimbardo, Philip G. "Pathology of Imprisonment." *Society* 9 (1972): 4–6.

———. "On the Ethics of Intervention in Human Psychological Research: With Special Reference to the Stanford Prison Study." *Cognition* 22 (March 1973): 243–246.

———, et al. "The Psychology of Imprisonment: Privation, Power and Pathology." In *Doing Unto Others*, edited by Zick Rubin. Englewood Cliffs, NJ: Prentice-Hall, 1974.

———. *The Lucifer Effect: Understanding How Good People Turn Evil*. New York: Random House, 2007a.

———. "Revisiting the Stanford Prison Experiment: A Lesson in the Power of Persuasion." *Chronicle of Review (Chronicle of Higher Education)*, March 30, 2007b, B6, B7.

Chapter 3 Research Design: The Experimental Model and Its Variations

"Albuquerque Study Confirms KC Findings." *Criminal Justice Newsletter* 10 (September 10, 1979): 4–5.

Binder, Arnold, and James Meeker. "Experiments as Reforms." *Journal of Criminal Justice* 16 (1988): 347–358.

———. "Arrest as a Method to Control Spousal Abuse." In *Domestic Violence: The Changing Criminal Justice Response*, edited by Eve S. Buzawa and Carl G. Buzawa. Dover, Maine: Auburn House, 1991.

Blakeslee, Sandra. "Placebos Prove So Powerful Even Experts Are Surprised." *New York Times*, October 13, 1998, D1.

Brown, Barry S., et al. "Released Offenders' Perceptions of Community and Institution." *Corrective Psychiatry and Journal of Social Therapy* 16, nos. 1–4 (1970): 1–9.

Browning, Katharine, and David Huizinga. "Highlights of Findings from the Denver Youth Survey." *OJJDP Fact Sheet*, #106, April 1999.

Buzawa, Eve S., and Carl G. Buzawa, eds. *Domestic Violence: The Changing Criminal Justice Response*. Dover, Maine: Auburn House, 1991.

Campbell, Donald T. "Reforms as Experiments." In *Readings in Evaluation Research*. 2nd ed., edited by Francis G. Caro. New York: Russell Sage, 1977.

———, and H. Laurence Ross. "The Connecticut Crackdown on Speeding: Time Series Data in Quasi-Experimental Analysis." In *Criminal Justice Research*, edited by Susette M. Talarico, 70–88. Cincinnati, OH: Anderson, 1980.

————, and Julian C. Stanley. *Experimental and Quasi-Experimental Designs for Research.* Chicago, IL: Rand McNally, 1963.

Chaiken, Jan M. "What's Known about Deterrent Effects of Police Activities." Santa Monica, CA: Rand Corp., paper presented at the Joint National Meeting of the Operations Research Society of America and the Institute of Management Sciences, Miami, November 3, 1976.

"Community Policing in the 1990s." *National Institute of Justice Journal*, August (1992): 2–8.

Cook, Thomas D., and Donald T. Campbell. *Quasi-Experimentation: Design and Analysis Issues for Field Settings.* Chicago, IL: Rand McNally, 1979.

Cooper, William H. "Ubiquitous Halo." *Psychological Bulletin* 90 (September 1981): 218–244.

Cressey, Donald R. *Other People's Money: A Study in the Social Psychology of Embezzlement.* Belmont, CA: Wadsworth, 1957.

Cresswell, John W. *Research Design: Qualitative and Quantitative Approaches.* Thousand Oaks, CA: Sage, 1994.

Davis, Edward M., and Lyle Knowles. "A Critique of the Report: An Evaluation of the Kansas City Preventive Patrol Experiment." *The Police Chief* 42 (June 1975): 31–32.

Denzin, Norman K. *The Research Act.* 3rd ed. New York: McGraw-Hill, 1989.

Dunford, Franklyn W., David Huizinga, and Delbert S. Elliott. *The Omaha Domestic Violence Police Experiment.* Final Report, Washington, DC: National Institute of Justice, 1989.

————. "The Role of Arrest in Domestic Assault: The Omaha Police Experiment." *Criminology* 28 (1990): 183–206.

Empey, Lamar T., and Maynard L. Erickson. *The Provo Experiment: Evaluating Community Control of Delinquency.* Lexington, MA: Heath, 1972.

Empey, Lamar T., and Steven G. Lubeck. *The Silverlake Experiment: Testing Delinquency Theory and Community Intervention.* Chicago, IL: Aldine, 1971.

Erez, Edna. "Randomized Experiments in Correctional Context: Legal, Ethical and Practical Concerns." *Journal of Criminal Justice* 14 (1986): 389–400.

Esbensen, Finn, and Scott Menard. "Is Longitudinal Research Worth the Price?" *The Criminologist* 15, no. 2 (March–April 1990): 1, 3–5.

Fagan, Jeffrey A. "Natural Experiments in Criminal Justice." In *Measurement Issues in Criminology*, edited by Kimberly Kempf, 108–137. New York: Springer-Verlag, 1990.

Farrington, David P. "Effectiveness of Sentencing." *Justice of the Peace* 142 (February 1978): 68–71.

————. "Longitudinal Research on Crime and Delinquency." In *Crime and Justice: An Annual Review of Research*, edited by Norval Morris and Michael Tonry, 289–348. Vol. 1, Chicago, IL: University of Chicago Press, 1979.

————. "Randomized Experiments in Crime and Justice." In *Crime and Justice: An Annual Review of Research*, edited by Michael Tonry and Norval Morris, 257–308. Vol. 4. Chicago, IL: University of Chicago Press, 1983.

Feinberg, S. B., B. Singer, and J. M. Tanur. "Large Scale Social Experimentation in the United States." In *A Celebration of Statistics*, edited by A. C. Atkinson and S. B. Feinberg. New York: Springer-Verlag, 1985.

Field, Hubert S. "Simulated Jury Trials: Students Versus 'Real' People as Jurors." *Journal of Social Psychology* 104 (April 1978): 287–293.

Finckenauer, James O. *Scared Straight! and the Panacea Phenomenon.* Englewood Cliffs, NJ: Prentice-Hall, 1982.

Garwood, David W. "Edsel Murphy's Law: Anything That Can Go Wrong Will Go Wrong." *The Loop: A Newsletter for Evaluators* 8 (December 1978): 17–22.

Gelles, Richard J. "Etiology of Violence: Overcoming Fallacious Reasoning in Understanding Family Violence and Child Abuse." Manuscript available through National Criminal Justice Reference Service, 1977.

Glaser, Daniel. "Correctional Research: An Elusive Paradise." In *Probation, Parole and Community Corrections*, 2nd ed., edited by Robert M. Carter and Leslie T. Wilkins, 765–777. New York: Wiley, 1976.

Glueck, Sheldon, and Eleanor Glueck. *Later Criminal Careers.* New York: The Commonwealth Fund, 1937.

———. *Juvenile Delinquents Grown Up.* New York: The Commonwealth Fund, 1940.

Gordon, Andrew C., et al. "Critique by Four Illinois Researchers Questions Validity of UDIS Evaluation." *Criminal Justice Newsletter* 9 (1978): 1–6.

Hackler, James C. "Dangers of Political Naivete and Excessive Complexity in Evaluating Delinquency Prevention Programs." *Evaluation and Program Planning* 1 (1978): 278–283.

Heussenstamm, Frances K. "Bumper Stickers and the Cops." *Transaction* 8 (1971): 32–33.

"Hidden Cameras Project, Seattle, Washington." *Exemplary Projects: A Program of the National Institute of Law Enforcement and Criminal Justice.* Washington, DC: National Institute of Justice, August 1978.

Hirschi, Travis, and Hanan C. Selvin. "False Criteria of Causality in Delinquency." *Social Problems* 13 (Winter 1966): 254–268.

Hood, Roger, and Richard Sparks. *Key Issues in Criminology.* New York: McGraw-Hill, 1971.

Isaac, Stephen, and William B. Michael. *Handbook in Research and Evaluation.* 2nd ed. San Diego, CA: EdITS Publishers, 1981.

Kaptchuk, Ted, David Eisenberg, and Anthony Komaroff. "Pondering the Placebo Effect." *Newsweek,* December 3, 2002, 71–72.

Kelling, George L. "Foot Patrol." In *Crime File.* Washington, DC: National Institute of Justice, 1985.

———, et al. *The Kansas City Preventive Patrol Experiment: A Summary Report and a Technical Report.* Washington, DC: The Police Foundation, 1974.

Kelling, George L., and Tony Pate. "Response to the Davis-Knowles Critique of the Kansas City Preventive Patrol Experiment." *The Police Chief* 42 (June 1975): 33–34.

Larson, Richard C. "What Happened to Patrol Operations in Kansas City? A Review of the Kansas City Preventive Patrol Experiment." *Journal of Criminal Justice* 3 (Winter 1975): 267–297.

Loranger, Armand W., Curtis T. Prout, and Mary A. White. "The Placebo Effect in Psychiatric Drug Research." *Journal of the American Medical Association* 176 (1961): 920–926.

Luskin, Mary L. "Building a Theory of Case Processing Time." *Judicature* 62 (September 1978): 115–127.

Mackenzie, Doris L., and James W. Shaw. "The Impact of Shock Incarceration on Technical Violations and New Criminal Activities." *Justice Quarterly* 10 (September 1993): 462–488.

Mackenzie, Doris L., and Claire Souryal. *Multisite Evaluation of Shock Incarceration,* Rockville, MD: National Criminal Justice Reference Service, NCJ #150062, 1994.

Mastrofski, Stephen D. "What Does Community Policing Mean for Daily Police Work?" *National Institute of Justice Journal* 225 (August 1992): 23–27.

McCord, William, and Joan McCord. *Origins of Crime: A New Evaluation of the Cambridge Somerville Youth Study.* New York: Columbia University Press, 1959.

Menard, Scott. *Longitudinal Research.* Newbury Park, CA: Sage, 1991.

Monahan, John, and Laurens Walker. *Social Science in Law: Cases and Materials.* 2nd ed. Westbury, NY: The Foundation Press, 1990.

Morris, Norval, and Michael Tonry. *Between Prison and Probation: Intermediate Punishments in a Rational Sentencing System.* New York: Oxford University Press, 1990.

Oakley, Ann. "Experimentation and Social Interventions: A Forgotten, but Important History." *British Medical Journal* (October 31, 1998): 1239.

Orne, Martin T. "Demand Characteristics and the Concept of Quasi-controls." In *Artifacts in Behavior Research,* edited by Robert Rosenthal and Ralph L. Rosnow, 147–177. New York: Academic Press, 1969.

Ostrom, Elinor, Roger B. Parks, and Gordon Whitaker. "Do We Really Want to Consolidate Urban Police Forces? A Reappraisal of Some Old Assertions."

Public Administration Review (September/October 1973): 423–432.

Pate, Tony, et al. "A Response to 'What Happened to Patrol Operations in Kansas City.'" *Journal of Criminal Justice* 3 (Winter 1975): 299–320.

Petersilia, Joan, and Sue Turner. *Intensive Supervision for High-Risk Probationers*. Santa Monica, CA: Rand Corporation, 1990.

Petrosino, Anthony, Carolyn Turpin-Petrosino, and James O. Finckenauer. "Well-Meaning Programs Can Have Harmful Effects! Lessons from Experiments of Programs Such as Scared Straight." *Crime and Delinquency* 46 (2000): 354–379.

Pierce, Glenn, and William Bowers. *The Impact of the Bartley-Fox Gun Law on Crime in Massachusetts*. Boston, MA: Northeastern University Center for Applied Social Research, 1979.

Police Foundation. *Domestic Violence and the Police: Studies in Detroit and Kansas City*. Washington, DC: The Police Foundation, 1977.

———. *Newark Foot Patrol Experiment*. Washington, DC: The Police Foundation, 1981.

Ray, Maria. "Four Thousand Partners in Violence: A Trend Analysis." In *The Abusive Partner: An Analysis of Domestic Battering*, edited by Maria Ray. New York: Van Nostrand Reinhold, 1982.

Reid, Sue T. *Crime and Criminology*. 11th ed. New York: Holt, Rinehart and Winston, 2005.

Roethlisberger, Fritz. J., and William J. Dixon. *Management and the Worker*. Cambridge, MA: Harvard University Press, 1939.

Rosenberg, Milton J. "The Conditions and Consequences of Evaluation Apprehension." In *Artifacts in Behavioral Research*, edited by Robert Rosenthal and Ralph L. Rosnow, 280–348. New York: Academic Press, 1969.

Rosenthal, Robert. *Experimenter Effects in Behavioral Research*. New York: Century, 1966.

"Scared Straight Found Ineffective Again." *Criminal Justice Newsletter* 10 (1979): 7.

Schneider, Anne L., and L. A. Wilson. "Introduction to Interrupted Time Series Designs." In *Handbook of Resources for Criminal Justice Evaluators*, edited by

Anne L. Schneider, et al., 2–66. Washington, DC: National Institute of Law Enforcement and Criminal Justice, 1978.

Schneider, Anne L., et al., eds. *Handbook of Resources for Criminal Justice Evaluators*. Washington, DC: National Institute of Law Enforcement and Criminal Justice, 1978.

Schneider, Victoria, and John Smykla. "War and Capital Punishment." *Journal of Criminal Justice* 18 (1990): 253–260.

Sherman, Larry. "Neighborhood Safety." In *Crime File*. Rockville, MD: National Institute of Justice, 1985.

Sherman, Larry, and Richard A. Berk. *The Minneapolis Domestic Violence Experiment*. Washington, DC: The Police Foundation, 1984a.

———. "The Specific Deterrent Effects of Arrest for Domestic Assault." *American Sociological Review* 49 (1984b): 261–272.

Sherman, Larry, James W. Shaw, and Dennis P. Rogan. *The Kansas City Gun Experiment*. Washington, DC: National Institute of Justice Research in Brief, 1995.

Smykla, John, et al. "Effects of Prison Facility on the Regional Economy." *Journal of Criminal Justice* 12 (1984): 521–539.

Solomon, Richard L. "Extension of Control Group Design." *Psychological Bulletin* 46 (1949): 137–150.

Steffensmeier, Darrell J., and Robert M. Terry. "The Experimental Study of Human Behavior." In *Examining Deviance Experimentally*, 38–49. Port Washington, NY: Alfred 1975.

Sykes, Gary W. "Saturated Enforcement: The Efficacy of Deterrence and Drunk Driving." *Journal of Criminal Justice* 12 (1984): 185–197.

Thomas, William. I., and Dorothy Swaine. *The Child in America*. New York: Knopf, 1928.

Thorndike, Edward L. "A Constant Error in Psychological Ratings." *Journal of Applied Psychology* 4 (1920): 25–29.

Tracy, Paul E., Marvin E. Wolfgang, and Robert M. Figlio. *Delinquency in Two Birth Cohorts: Executive Summary*. Philadelphia, PA: Center for Studies in Criminology and Criminal Law, The Wharton School, University of Pennsylvania, 1985.

Travis, Jeremy. "Researchers Evaluate Eight Shock Incarceration Programs." National Institute of Justice Update, October 1994.

Trojanowicz, Robert C., and Dennis W. Banas. *Perceptions of Safety: A Comparison of Foot Patrol versus Motor Patrol Officers*. East Lansing, MI: National Neighborhood Foot Patrol Center, School of Criminal Justice, Michigan State University, 1985.

Visher, Christy A. "Understanding the Roots of Crime: The Project on Human Development in Chicago Neighborhoods." *National Institute of Justice Journal* (November 1994): 9–15.

Weubben, Paul L., Bruce C. Straits, and Gary F. Shulman, eds. *The Experiment as a Social Occasion*. Berkeley, CA: Glendessary Press, 1974.

Widom, Cathy S. "The Cycle of Violence." *National Institute of Justice Research in Brief*, October 1992.

———. "Victims of Childhood Sexual Abuse—Later Criminal Consequences." *National Institute of Justice Research in Brief*, March 1995.

Wilkins, Leslie T. "The Concept of Cause in Criminology." In *Classes, Conflict and Control: Studies in Criminal Justice Management*, edited by J. Munro. Cincinnati, OH: Anderson, 1976.

Wilson, James Q., and George L. Kelling. "Broken Windows: The Police and Neighborhood Safety." *The Atlantic*, March 1982, 27–38.

Witkin, Herman A., et al. "XYY and Criminality." In *Crime in Society*, edited by Leonard D. Savitz and Norman Johnston, 275–291. New York: Wiley, 1978.

Wolfgang, Marvin, et al. *Delinquency in a Birth Cohort*. Chicago, IL: University of Chicago Press, 1972.

Wycoff, Mary A., and Wesley K. Skogan. "Community Policing in Madison: Quality from the Inside Out—An Evaluation of Implementation and Impact." In *Update on NIJ-Sponsored Research: Six New Reports*. National Institute of Justice Research in Brief, April 1994, 4–5.

Wycoff, Mary A., Wesley Skogan, Anthony Pate, and Lawrence W. Sherman. *Personal Contact Patrol: The Houston Field Test*. Washington, DC: The Police Foundation, 1985a.

———. *Police Community Stations: The Houston Field Test*. Washington, DC: The Police Foundation, 1985b.

Zimring, Franklin E. "Firearms and Federal Law." *Journal of Legal Studies* 4 (January 1975): 133–198.

Chapter 4 The Uniform Crime Reports and Sampling

Alex, Nicholas. *Black in Blue: A Study of the Negro Policeman*. New York: Appleton, Century Crofts, 1969.

Associated Press. "Missing Police Reports Skew Crime Statistics." *Erie Times-News*, March 3, 2004, 12A.

Babbie, Earl R. *The Practice of Social Research*. 6th ed. Belmont, CA: Wadsworth, 1992.

Bachman, Ronet, and Raymond Paternoster. *Statistical Methods for Criminology and Criminal Justice*. New York: McGraw-Hill, 1997.

BBC "Government Crime Research Slammed." *BBC News*, April 16, 2008, *www.news.bbc.co.uk/2/hi/uk_news/7322324.stm*

Biernacki, Patrick, and Dan Waldorf. "Snowball Sampling: Problems and Techniques of Chain Referral Sampling." *Sociological Methods and Research* 10 (1981): 141–163.

Bouchard, Thomas J., Jr. "Field Research Methods: Interviewing, Questionnaires, Participant Observation, Systematic Observation, Unobtrusive Measures." In *Handbook of Industrial and Organizational Psychology*, edited by Marvin D. Dunnette. Chicago, IL: Rand McNally, 1976.

Bowser, Benjamin P., and Joan E. Sieber. "AIDS Prevention Research." In *Researching Sensitive Topics*, edited by C. M. Renzetti and R. M. Lee, 160–176. Newbury Park, CA: Sage, 1993.

Criminal Victimization Surveys in Milwaukee. National Crime Survey Report No. SD-NCS-C-12, Washington, DC: National Criminal Justice Information and Statistics Service, July 1977.

Dance, Phyll. "Befriending Friends: Methodological and Ethnographic Aspects of a Study of a Canberra Group of Illicit Drug Users." *International Journal of Drug Policy* 2, no. 4 (1991): 34–36.

Dodenhoff, Peter C. "LEN Salutes Its 1989 People of the Year, the UCR Redesign Team." *Law Enforcement News* 15, no. 307 (1990): 1, 10–11.

Douglas, John E., and Alan E. Burgess. "Crime Profiling: A Viable Investigative Tool Against Violent Crime." *FBI Law Enforcement Bulletin*, December 1986, 9–13.

Douglas, John E., et al. *Crime Classification Manual*. New York: Lexington Books, 1992.

Fagan, Jeffrey. "The Social Organization of Drug Use and Drug Dealing Among Urban Gangs." *Criminology* 27 (November 1989): 633–669.

Federal Bureau of Investigation. *Crime in the United States, 2004: The Uniform Crime Reports*. Washington, DC: U.S. Government Printing Office, September, 2005.

Filstead, William J., ed. *Qualitative Methodology*. Chicago, IL: Markham, 1971.

Fitzpatrick, Kevin M., Mark E. LaGory, and Ferris J. Ritchey. "Criminal Victimization among the Homeless." *Justice Quarterly* 10 (September 1993): 353–368.

Garofalo, James. *Public Opinion about Crime: The Attitudes of Victims and Nonvictims in Selected Cities*. Washington, DC: U.S. Department of Justice, 1977.

Glaser, Daniel. *Crime in Our Changing Society*. New York: Holt, 1978.

Goldkamp, John S., and Michael R. Gottfredson. *Final Report of the Judicial Guidelines for Bail: The Philadelphia Experiment Project*. Washington, DC: National Institute of Justice, 1984.

Goodman, Leo A. "Snowball Sampling." *Annals of Mathematical Statistics* 32 (March 1969): 148–170.

Goodstein, Lynne I. et al. "Defining Determinancy: Components of the Sentencing Process: Ensuring Equity and Release Certainty." *Justice Quarterly* 1 (1984): 47–74.

Greenberg, David, and Nancy J. Larkin. "Age-Cohort Analysis of Arrest Rates." *Journal of Quantitative Criminology* 1 (1985): 227–240.

Greenberg, Stephanie J., Jay. R. Williams, and William M. Rohe. *Safe and Secure Neighborhoods: Physical Characteristics and Informal Territorial Control in High and Low Crime Neighborhoods*. Washington, DC: National Institute of Justice, 1982.

Hazelwood, Robert R., and Janet Warren. "The Serial Rapist: His Characteristics and Victim." *FBI Law Enforcement Bulletin* 60 (1989): 10–17.

Heberlein, Thomas A., and Robert Baumgartner. "Factors Affecting Response Rates to Mailed Questionnaires: A Quantitative Analysis of the Published Literature." *American Sociological Review* 43 (August 1978): 447–462.

Holmes, Ronald M. *Profiling Violent Crimes: An Investigative Tool*. Newbury Park, CA: Sage, 1989.

Holmes, Ronald M., and Stephen T. Holmes. *Profiling Violent Crimes: An Investigative Tool*. 2nd ed. Thousand Oaks, CA: Sage Publications, 1996.

Jackson, Patrick D. "Assessing the Validity of Official Data on Arson." *Criminology* 26 (February 1988): 181–195.

Jacob, Herbert. *The Frustration of Policy Response to Crime in American Cities*, Boston, MA: Little, Brown, 1984.

Japha, Tony. *The Nation's Toughest Drug Law: Evaluating the New York Experience*. Washington, DC: National Institute of Justice, 1978.

Karmen, Andrew. *New York Murder Mystery: The True Story Behind the Crime Crash of the Nineties*. New York: New York University Press, 1999.

Kish, Leslie. *Survey Sampling*. New York: Wiley, 1965.

Krueger, R. *"Focus Group Interviewing on the Telephone."* http://www.tc.umn.edu/~rKrueger/focus_tfg.html, 1994.

Krueger, Richard A. *Analyzing and Reporting Focus Group Results*. Thousand Oaks, CA: Sage, 1997.

Levitt, Steven, and John Donohue. "Legalized Abortion and Crime." *Chicago Tribune*, August 8, 1999, A1.

Loftin, Colin. *Data Resources of the National Institute of Justice*. Washington, DC: U.S. Department of Justice, May 1987.

Merton, Robert K., Marjorie Fiske, and Patricia L. Kendall. *The Focused Interview*. New York: Free Press, 1956.

Miethe, Terance D., and Richard McCorkle. *Crime Profiles: The Anatomy of Dangerous Persons, Places, and Situations*. Los Angeles, CA: Roxbury, 1998.

Moore, Harvey A. "Applied Sociology and Corporate Legal Practice." 1998, *www.trialpractice.com/noframes/research.htm*

Morgan, David L. *Successful Focus Groups.* Thousand Oaks, CA: Sage, 1993.

Nurco, David N., et al. "Crime as a Source of Income for Narcotics Addicts." *Journal of Substance Abuse Treatment* 2 (1985): 113–115.

O'Keefe, Garrett J., et al. *Taking a Bite Out of Crime: The Impact of a Mass Media Crime Prevention Campaign,* Unpublished Report, University of Denver, Center for Mass Communications Research and Policy, 1984.

Pate, Anthony, et al. *Final Report of the Effects of Police Fear Reduction Strategies: A Summary of Findings from Houston and Newark.* Washington, DC: The Police Foundation, 1986.

Poggio, Eugene C., et al. *Blueprint for the Future of the Uniform Crime Reporting Program: Final Report of the UCR Study.* Washington, DC: U.S. Department of Justice, May 1985.

Polsky, Ned. *Hustlers, Beats and Others.* Chicago, IL: Aldine, 1967.

President's Commission on Law Enforcement and the Administration of Justice. *The Challenge of Crime in a Free Society.* Washington, DC: U.S. Government Printing Office, 1967.

Rantala, Ramona R. "Effects of NIBRS on Crime Statistics." *Bureau of Justice Statistics Special Report,* July 2000, NCJ 178890.

Reaves, Brian A. "Using NIBRS Data to Analyze Violent Crime." Bureau of Justice Statistics Technical Report, October 1993.

Rhodes, Robert P. *The Insoluble Problem of Crime.* New York: Wiley, 1977.

Rosenthal, Robert. *Experimenter Effects in Research.* New York: Appleton, 1966.

Rovetch, Emily L., Eugene C. Poggio, and Henry H. Rossman. *A Listing and Classification of Identified Issues Regarding the Uniform Crime Reporting Program of the FBI.* Cambridge, MA: Abt Associates, Inc., 1984.

Sack, Kevin. "Research Guided Jury Selection in Bombing Trial," *New York Times,* May 3, 2001: A12.

Savitz, Leonard D. "Official Police Statistics and Their Limitations." In *Crime in Society,* edited by Leonard D. Savitz and Norman Johnston, 69–81. New York: Wiley, 1978.

Sheley, Joseph F., and James D. Wright. "Gun Acquisition and Possession in Selected Juvenile Samples." Research in Brief, National Institute of Justice, Office of Juvenile Justice and Delinquency Prevention, December 1993.

Schuerman, Leo A., and Solomon Kobrin. "Community Careers in Crime." In *Communities and Crime,* edited by Albert Reiss and Michael Tonry. Crime and Justice series Vol. 8, Chicago, IL: University of Chicago Press, 1986.

Sherman, Lawrence W. "Needed: Better Ways to Count Crooks." *Wall Street Journal,* December 3, 1998, A22.

Sigler, Robert T., and Donna Haygood. "The Criminalization of Forced Marital Intercourse." In *Deviance and the Family,* edited by Frank E. Hagan and Marvin B. Sussman. New York: Haworth Press, 1988.

Sigler, Robert T., and Ida M. Johnson. "Public Perceptions of the Need for Criminalization of Sexual Harassment." *Journal of Criminal Justice* 14 (1986): 229–237.

Singer, Eleanor, et al. "The Effects of Incentives on Response Rates in Face-to-Face and Telephone Surveys." *Journal of Official Statistics* 15 (1999): 217–230.

Solomey, Joseph. *The Glory Boys: Notes on the Police Underground.* Senior Thesis, Mercyhurst College, 1979.

Sparks, Richard F. *Massachusetts Statewide Criminal Justice Guidelines Evaluation, 1979; Sentencing Data.* Washington, DC: National Institute of Justice, 1982.

Toy, Calvin. "A Short History of Asian Gangs in San Francisco." *Justice Quarterly* 9 (December 1992): 647–665.

Stamp, Josiah. *Some Economic Factors in Modern Life.* London: P.S. King and Sons, Ltd., 1929.

Stewart, David W., and Prem. N. Shamdasani. *Focus Groups: Theory and Practice.* Newbury Park, CA: Sage, 1990.

"Thousands of Rape Claims Dismissed or Hidden by Philadelphia Police During the Last Twenty Years" (Associated Press). *Erie Times-News,* October 18, 1999, 1A.

Toborg, Mary. *Pretrial Release: A National Evaluation of Practices and Outcomes.* Washington, DC: National Institute of Justice, 1981.

van Dijk, Jan, and Kristina Kangaspunta. "Piecing Together the Cross-National Crime Puzzle." *National Institute of Justice Journal* (January 2000).

Webb, Eugene, et al. *Unobtrusive Measures: Nonreactive Research in the Social Sciences.* Chicago, IL: Rand McNally, 1966.

———. *Nonreactive Measures in the Social Sciences.* 2nd ed. Boston, MA: Houghton Mifflin, 1981.

Weber, Max. *The Methodology of Social Sciences.* Translated by Edward A. Shils and Henry A. Finch. New York: Free Press, 1949.

Wilbanks, William. "Professor Disputes Crime Rate Rankings." *Miami News,* January 30, 1986, 1H.

Wilson, James Q., and Kelling, George L. "The Police and Neighborhood Safety: Broken Windows." *Atlantic Monthly* 249 (March 1982): 29–38.

Witkin, Gordon. "Did the FBI Ignore the 'Tafoya Profile'?" *U.S. News and World Report,* 17 November 1997, 24.

Witkin, Gordon. "The Crime Bust: What's Behind the Dramatic Drug Bust?" *U.S. News and World Report,* May 25, 1998, 28–37.

Chapter 5 Survey Research: Questionnaires

American Statistical Association. "Report on the ASA Conference on Surveys of Human Populations." *The American Statistician* 28 (February 1974): 30–34.

Bachman, Jerald G. *Monitoring the Future.* Ann Arbor, MI: University of Michigan, Institute for Social Research, 1978.

Bachman, Jerald G., Patrick M. O'Malley, and Jerome Johnston. *Youth in Transition.* 4th ed. Ann Arbor, MI: University of Michigan, Institute for Social Research, 1978.

Barton, Allen J. "Asking the Embarrassing Question." *Public Opinion Quarterly* 22 (1958): 67–68.

Baruch, Jahuda. "Response Rates in Academic Studies—A Comparative Analysis." *Human Relations* 52 (April 1999): 421–438.

Bersoff, David M., and Donald M. Bersoff. "Ethical Issues in the Collection of Self-Report Data." In *The Science of Self-Report,* edited by A.A. Stone, et al., 9–24. Mahwah, NJ: Lawrence Erlbaum Associates, 2000.

Brehm, John. *The Phantom Respondent: Opinion Surveys and Political Representation.* Ann Arbor, MI: University of Michigan Press, 1993.

Cantor, David, and Lynch, James P. "Self-Report Surveys as Measures of Crime and ED: Please note addition Criminal Victimization. In *Measurement and Analysis of Crime and Justice,* edited by David Duffee, et. al., 85–138. Washington, DC: US Department of Justice. NCJ 182411, 2000.

Chilton, Roland. "Twenty-Five Years After the Crime Commission Report: Is the Field Still Data Starved?" *The Criminologist* 18 (September/October 1993): 1, 6–8.

Church, Allan H. "Estimating the Effects of Incentives on Mail Survey Response Rates: A Meta-Analysis." *Public Opinion Quarterly* 57 (1993): 62–79.

Clark, John P., and Larry L. Tifft. "Polygraph and Interview Validation of Self-Reported Deviant Behavior." *American Sociological Review* 31 (August 1966): 516–523.

Coleman, James S. *The Adolescent Society.* Glencoe, IL: The Free Press, 1961.

Criminal Victimization Surveys in Milwaukee. National Crime Survey Report No. SD-NCS-C-12, Washington, DC: National Criminal Justice Information and Statistics Service, July 1977.

Dentler, Robert A., and Lawrence J. Monroe. "Social Correlates of Early Adolescent Theft." *American Sociological Review* 26 (October 1961): 733–743.

Deutscher, Irwin. "Words and Deeds: Social Science and Social Policy." *Social Problems* 13 (Winter 1966): 235–265.

Dillman, Don A. "Increasing Mail Questionnaire Response in Large Samples of the General Public." *Public Opinion Quarterly* 36 (Summer 1972): 254–257.

———. *Mail and Telephone Data Collection Methods.* New York: Wiley-Interscience, 1976.

———. *Mail and Telephone Surveys: The Total Design Method.* New York: John Wiley and Sons, 1978.

———. *Mail and Internet Surveys: The Total Design Method.* New York: John Wiley and Sons, 2000.

Dillman, Don A., and James H. Frey. "The Contributions of Personalization to Mail Questionnaire Response as an Element of a Previously Tested Method." *Journal of Applied Psychology* 59 (1974): 297–301.

Empey, Lamar T., and Maynard L. Erickson. "Hidden Delinquency and Social Status." *Social Forces* 44 (1966): 546–554.

Erez, Edna, and Pamela Tontodonato. "Victim Participation in Sentencing and Satisfaction with Justice." *Justice Quarterly* 9 (September 1992): 393–415.

Erickson, Maynard L., and LaMar T. Empey. "Court Records, Undetected Delinquency and Decision-Making." *Journal of Criminal Law, Criminology and Police Science* 54 (1963): 456–469.

Farrington, David P. "Self-Reports of Deviant Behavior: Predictive and Stable?" *Journal of Criminal Law and Criminology* 64 (1973): 99–110.

Frankel, Mark S., and Sanyin Siang. *Ethical and Legal Aspects of Human Subjects Research on the Internet: A Report of a Workshop.* Washington, DC: American Association for the Advancement of Science, June 10–11, 1999. *www.aaas.org/spp/dspp/strl/projects/intres/main.htm*

Gertz, Marc G., and Susette M. Talarico. "Problems of Reliability and Validity in Criminal Justice Research." In *Criminal Justice Research: Approaches, Problems and Policy,* edited by Susette M. Talarico, 166–176. Cincinnati, OH: Anderson, 1980.

Gold, Martin. "Undetected Delinquent Behavior." *Journal of Research in Crime and Delinquency* 3 (January 1966): 27–46.

Gold, Martin, and David J. Reimer. *Changing Patterns of Delinquent Behavior Among Americans 13 to 17 Years Old—1972.* Report Number 1 of the National Survey of Youth, 1971, Ann Arbor, MI: University of Michigan, Institute for Social Research, 1974.

Glaser, Daniel. *Crime in Our Changing Society.* New York: Holt, 1978.

Greenwood, Peter W., and Allan Abrahamse. *Selective Incapacitation.* Santa Monica, CA: Rand Corp., August, 1982

Hagan, Frank E. *Comparative Professionalization in an Occupational Arena: The Case of Rehabilitation.* Ph.D. dissertation, Case Western Reserve University, 1975.

———, Marie R. Haug, and Marvin B. Sussman. *Comparative Profiles of the Rehabilitation Counseling Graduate: 1965 and 1972.* 2nd series. Working Paper No. 5. Cleveland: Case Western Reserve University, Institute on the Family and the Bureaucratic Society, 1975.

Hamilton, Henry, and John O. Smykla. "Guidelines for Police Undercover Work: New Questions About Accreditation and the Emphasis of Procedure Over Authorization." *Justice Quarterly* 11 (March 1994): 135–151.

Hamilton, James. "The Ethics of Conducting Social Science Research on the Internet." *Chronicle of Higher Education,* December 5, 1999, B6–B7.

Hamm, Mark S. "Legislator Ideology and Capital Punishment: The Special Case for Indiana Juveniles." *Justice Quarterly* 6 (June 1989): 219–232.

Hardt, Robert H., and Sandra P. Hardt. "On Determining the Quality of the Delinquency Self-Report Method." *Journal of Research in Crime and Delinquency* 14 (July 1977): 247–261.

Heberlein, Thomas A., and Robert Baumgartner. "Factors Affecting Response Rates to Mailed Questionnaires." *American Sociological Review* 43 (August 1978): 447–462.

Hirschi, Travis. *Causes of Delinquency.* Berkeley, CA: University of California, 1969.

Hood, Roger, and Richard Sparks. *Key Issues in Criminology.* New York: McGraw-Hill, 1971.

Huizinga, David, and Delbert S. Elliott. *Self-Reported Measures of Delinquency and Crime: Methodological Issues and Comparative Findings.* Boulder, CO: Behavioral Research Institute, 1984.

Inciardi, James A. "Heroin Use and Street Crimes." *Crime and Delinquency* 25 (July 1979): 335–346.

Jackson, Patrick G. "Sources of Data." In *Measurement Issues in Criminology*, edited by Kimberly L. Kempf, 21–50. New York: Springer-Verlag, 1990.

Jacob, Herbert. *The Frustration of Policy: Response to Crime in American Cities.* Boston, MA: Little, Brown, 1984.

Junger-Tas, Josine, and Ineke H. Marshall. *The Self-Report Methodology in Crime Research.* Washington, DC: Bureau of Justice Statistics, 1999, NCJ 178734.

Kivitis, J. "Online Interviewing and the Research Relationship." In Virtual Methods: Issues in Research on the Internet, edited by C. Hine, New York: Oxford University Press, 2005.

Krauss, Michael. "Research and the Web: Eyeballs or Smiles?" *Marketing News* 32 (December 7, 1998): 18–23.

Kulik, James A., et al. "Disclosure of Delinquent Behavior Under Conditions of Anonymity and Nonanonymity." *Journal of Counseling and Clinical Psychology* 32, no. 5 (1968): 506–509.

LaPiere, Richard T. "Attitudes vs. Actions." *Social Forces* 13 (March 1934): 230–237.

Levine, James P. "The Potential for Overreporting in Criminal Victimization Surveys." *Criminology* 14 (November 1976): 307–330.

McCandless, Boyd R., et al. "Perceived Opportunity, Delinquency, Race and Body Build Among Delinquent Youth." *Journal of Consulting and Clinical Psychology* 38, no. 2 (1972): 281–287.

McCullough, Dick. "Market Research on the Web: Guidelines for Success." *Communication World* 15 (October–November 1998): 29–36.

Miller, Delbert C. *Handbook of Research Design and Social Measurement.* 5th ed. New York: McKay, 1991.

Morin, Richard. "A Pollster's Worst Nightmare: Declining Response Rates." *The Washington Post National Weekly Edition*, July 5–11, 1993, 37.

———. "Will Traditional Polls Go the Way of the Dinosaur?" *Washington Post National Weekly Edition*, May 15, 2000, 34.

Narins, Pamela. "Guidelines for Creating Better Questionnaires." *Keywords: Tips and News for Statistical Software Users* (Published by SPSS) 58 (1995): 8–9.

Nesbary, Dale K. *Survey Research and the World Wide Web.* Boston, MA: Allyn & Bacon, 2000.

Nettler, Gwynn. *Explaining Crime.* 2nd ed. New York: McGraw-Hill, 1978.

Nye, F. Ivan, and James F. Short, Jr. "Scaling Delinquent Behavior." *American Sociological Review* 22 (1957): 326–331.

O'Donnell, John A., et al. *Young Men and Drugs: A Nationwide Survey.* Rockville, MD: National Institute on Drug Abuse, 1976.

Osgood, D. Wayne, et al. "Time Trends and Age Trends in Arrests and Self-Reported Illegal Behavior." *Criminology* 27 (August 1989): 389–417.

Panel for the Evaluation of Crime Surveys. *Surveying Crime.* Washington, DC: National Academy of Sciences, 1976.

Petersilia, Joan, Peter W. Greenwood, and Marvin Lavin. *Criminal Careers of Habitual Felons.* Santa Monica, CA: Rand Corp., 1977.

Porterfield, Austin L. *Youth in Trouble.* Austin, TX: Leo Polishman Foundation, 1946.

Question Wording. *American Association for Public Opinion Research*, January 1, 2009, p. 4.

Radwin, David. "High Response Rates Don't Ensure Survey Accuracy," *The Chronicle Review*, October 9, 2009, B8–B10.

Sack, Kevin. "Research-Guided Jury Selection in Bombing Trial." *New York Times*, May 3, 2001, A12.

Schaefer, David R., and Don A. Dillman. "Development of a Standard E-Mail Methodology: Results of an

Experiment." *Public Opinion Quarterly* 62: 378–397, 1998.

Schonlai, Matthias, Ronald D. Fricker, and Marc N. Elliott. *Conducting Research Surveys via E-mail and the Web.* Santa Monica, CA: Rand Corporation, 2002.

Schuman, Howard, and Stanley Presser. *Questions and Answers in Attitude Surveys: Experiments on Question Form, Wording and Context.* Orlando, FL: Academic Press, 1981.

———. *Questions and Answers in Attitude Survey.* Thousand Oaks, CA: Sage Publishers, Inc., 1996.

Sigler, Robert T., and Ida M. Johnson. "Public Perceptions of the Need for Criminalization of Sexual Harrassment." *Journal of Criminal Justice* 14 (1986): 229–237.

Short, James F., and Fred L. Strodtbeck. *Group Process and Gang Delinquency.* Chicago, IL: University of Chicago Press, 1965.

Singer, Eleanor, et al. "The Effect of Incentives on Response Rates in Face-to-Face and Telephone Surveys." *Journal of Official Statistics* 15 (1999): 217–230.

Sudman, Seymour, and Norman M. Bradburn. *Asking Questions: A Practical Guide to Questionnaire Design.* San Francisco, CA: Jossey-Bass, 1982.

SurveyMonkey.com. 2008, *www.surveymonkey.com/Home_FeaturesDesign.aspx*

Tittle, Charles W., and Wayne J. Villemez. "Social Class and Criminality." *Social Forces* 56 (December 1977): 474–502.

Voss, Harwin L. "Ethnic Differentials in Delinquency in Honolulu." *Journal of Criminal Law, Criminology and Police Science* 54 (September 1963): 322–327.

Wallerstein, James S., and Clement J. Wyle. "Our Law-abiding Law Breakers." *Probation* 35 (April 1947): 107–118.

Ziegler, Stephen J. "Increasing Response Rates in Mail Surveys Without Increasing Error: A Research Note." *Criminal Justice Policy Review* 17 (March 2006): 22–31.

Chapter 6 Survey Research: Interviews and Telephone Surveys

Albini, Joseph L. *The American Mafia: Genesis of a Legend.* New York: Appleton, 1971.

Bachman, Ronet, and Bruce M. Taylor. "The Measurement of Family Violence and Rape by the Redesigned National Crime Victimization Survey." *Justice Quarterly* 11 (September 1994): 499–512.

Berg, Bruce L. *Qualitative Research Methods for the Social Sciences.* 4th ed. Boston, MA: Allyn and Bacon, 2001.

Biderman, Albert. *Time Distortions of Victimization Data and Mnemonic Effects.* Washington, DC: Bureau of Social Research, 1970.

Black, Donald J. "The Production of Crime Rates." *American Sociological Review* 35 (August 1970): 733–748.

Britton, Dana. *At Work in the Iron Cage: The Prison as Gendered Organization.* New York: New York University Press, 2003.

Buffalo Police Department. *Workable Solutions to the Problem of Street Prostitution in Buffalo, New York,* 2001.

Bureau of Justice Statistics. *National Crime Victimization Survey, 2006.* Washington, DC: Bureau of Justice Statistics, 2007.

———. *Redesign of the National Crime Survey.* Washington, DC: Bureau of Justice Statistics, February 1989.

———. "Domestic Violence: Violence Between Intimates." *Bureau of Justice Statistics Selected Findings* (November 1994a): p. 10.

Burnham, David. "New York Is Found Safest of 13 Cities in Crime Study." *New York Times,* April 15, 1974, 1, 51.

Cantor, David, and James P. Lynch. "Self-Report Surveys as Measures of Crime and Criminal Victimization." In *Measurement and Analysis of Crime and Justice,* edited by David Duffee, et al., 85–138. Washington, DC: U.S. Department of Justice, NCJ 182411, 2000.

Chula Vista Police Department. *The Chula Vista Residential Burglary Reduction Project.* 2001. *www.popcenter.org/Library/Goldstein/2001/2001.pdf*

Clinard, Marshall B. "Comparative Crime Victimization Surveys: Some Problems and Results." *International Journal of Criminology and Penology* 6 (1978).

Converse, Jean M., and Howard Schuman. *Conversations at Random: Survey Research as Interviewers See It.* New York: Wiley, 1974.

Cressey, Donald. *Other People's Money.* New York: The Free Press, 1953.

Crittenden, Kathleen S., and Richard J. Hill. "Coding Reliability and Validity of Interview Data." *American Sociological Review* 36 (December 1971): 1073–1080.

Cromwell, Paul, James Olson, and D'Aunn Avery. *Breaking and Entering: An Ethnographic Analysis of Burglary.* Newbury Park, CA: Sage, 1991.

Decker, Scott. *Using Offender Interviews to Improve Police Problem-Solving.* Problem Oriented Guides for Police Problem Solving, Tools Series No. 3. U.S. Department of Justice, COPS Community—Oriented Policing Services, April 12, 2005.

"Do Cell Phones Affect Survey Research?" *American Association for Public Opinion Research,* 2009, *http://www.aapor.org/Content/NavigationMenu/PollampSurveyFAQs/DoCellPhonesAffectSurveyResearch?default.htm*

Douglas, Jack. *Investigative Social Research.* Beverly Hills, CA: Sage, 1976.

Eigenberg, Helen M. "The National Crime Survey and Rape: The Case of the Missing Question." *Justice Quarterly* 7 (December 1990): 655–671.

Finch, J. "The Vignette Technique in Survey Research," *Sociology* 21 (1987): 105–114.

Firestone, Thomas "Mafia Memoirs: What They Tell Us About Organized Crime." *Journal of Contemporary Criminal Justice* 9 (September 1993): 197–220.

Fox, James A., and Paul E. Tracy. *Randomized Response: A Method for Sensitive Surveys.* Newbury Park, CA: Sage, 1986.

Frey, James H. *Survey Research by Telephone.* 2nd ed. Newbury Park, CA: Sage, 1989.

Glaser, Daniel. *Crime in Our Changing Society.* New York: Holt, 1978.

Glasser, Gerald J., and Dale D. Metzger. "Random-Digit Dialing as a Method of Telephone Sampling." *Journal of Marketing Research* 9 (February 1972): 59–64.

Glenn, D. "Security and Paperwork Keep Prison Research on the Outside." *Chronicle Of Higher Education,* March 28, 2008, A13–A14.

Groves, Robert M., and Robert L. Kahn. *Surveys by Telephone: A National Comparison with Personal Interviews.* New York: Academic Press, 1979.

Groves, Robert M., et al. *Telephone Survey Methodology.* New York: John Wiley and Sons, 1988.

Guerts, Michael D., Roman R. Andrus, and James Reinmuth. "Researching Shoplifting and Other Deviant Customer Behavior Using the Randomized Response Research Design." *Journal of Retailing* 51 (Winter 1976): 43–47.

Hagan, Frank E. *Introduction to Criminology: Theory, Methods and Criminal Behavior.* 6th ed. Thousand Oaks, CA: Sage, 2008.

———. *Crime Types and Criminals.* Thousand Oaks, CA: Sage, 2009.

Hoinville, Gerald, Roger Jowell, et al. *Survey Research Practice.* London: Heinemann, 1978.

Hurworth, Rosalind. "Telephone Focus Groups." *Social Research Update* 44 (Winter 2004).

Jensen, Gary F., and Maryaltani Karpos. "Managing Rape: Exploratory Research on the Behavior of Rape Statistics." *Criminology* 31 (August 1993): 363–385.

Kivitis, J. "Online Interviewing and the Research Relationship." In *Virtual Methods: Issues in Research on the Internet,* edited by C. Hine. New York: Oxford University Press, 2005.

Krueger, Richard A. *Focus Group Interviewing on the Telephone* 2002, *http://www.tc.umn.edu/~rkrueger/focus_tfg.html*

Klockars, Carl B. "A Theory of Contemporary Criminological Ethics." In *Ethics, Public Policy and Criminal Justice,* edited by Frederick Elliston and Norman Bowie, 419–458. Cambridge, MA: Oelgeschlager, Gunn and Hain, 1982.

Lancashire Constabulary. *Operation Curb: Multi-Agency Problem-Solving Approach to Street Prostitution in Preston.* 2003, *www.popcenter.org/Library/Goldstein/2003/03-56%20(F).pdf*

Laub, John H. *Criminology in the Making: An Oral History.* Boston, MA: Northeastern University Press, 1983.

Lavrakis, Paul J. "Citizen Self-Help and Neighborhood Crime Prevention." *American Violence and Public Policy.* New Haven, CT: Yale University Press, 1984.

———. *Telephone Survey Methods: Sampling, Selection and Supervision.* 2nd ed. Beverly Hills, CA: Sage, 1993.

Levine, James P. "The Potentials for Crime Over-Reporting in Criminal Victimization Surveys." *Criminology* 4 (November 1976): 307–330.

Liu, P. T., and L. P. Chow. "A New Discrete Quantitative Randomized Response Model." *Journal of the American Statistical Association* 71 (1976): 72–73.

Loftin, Colin. *Data Resources of the National Institute of Justice.* Washington, DC: U.S. Department of Justice, May 1987.

McDermott, M. Joan. "The Personal Is Empirical: Feminism, Research Methods and Criminal Justice Education." *Journal of Criminal Justice Education* 3 (Fall 1992): 237–249.

Menard, Scott. "Short-Term Trends in Crime and Delinquency: A Comparison of UCR, NCS and Self-Report Data." *Justice Quarterly* 4 (September 1987): 455–474.

Merton, Robert K., Marjorie Fiske, and Patricia L. Kendall. *The Focused Interview.* New York: Free Press, 1956.

Monette, Duane R., Thomas J. Sullivan, and Cornell R. DeJong. *Applied Social Research: Tools for the Human Services.* Fort Worth, TX: Harcourt, Brace, 1994.

Morin, Richard. "From Confusing Questions, Confusing Answers." *Washington Post National Weekly Edition,* July 18–24, 1994a, p. 37.

———. "Ask and You Might Deceive." *Washington Post National Weekly Edition,* December 6–12, 1994b, p. 37.

———. "When the Method Becomes the Message." *Washington Post National Weekly Edition,* December 19–25, 1994c, p. 33.

National Advisory Committee on Criminal Justice Standards and Goals. *Criminal Justice Research and Development.* Report of the Task Force, Washington, DC: Law Enforcement Assistance Administration, 1976.

"National Crime Victimization Survey Redesign." *Bureau of Justice Statistics Fact Sheet,* October 30, 1994.

Nettler, Gwynn. *Explaining Crime.* 2nd ed. New York: McGraw-Hill, 1978.

Neuman, W. Lawrence. *Social Research Methods: Qualitative and Quantitative Approaches.* 3rd ed. Boston, MA: Allyn and Bacon, 1993.

Panel for the Evaluation of Crime Surveys. *Surveying Crime.* Washington, DC: National Academy of Sciences, 1976.

Reiss, Albert J. Jr., *Studies in Crime and Law Enforcement in Major Metropolitan Areas.* Field Surveys III, President's Commission on Law Enforcement and the Administration of Justice, Washington, DC: U.S. Government Printing Office, 1967.

Rengert, George, and John Wasilchick. *Suburban Burglary: A Tale of Two Suburbs.* Springfield, IL: Charles C. Thomas, 2000.

Sanders, William B. "Pumps and Pauses: Strategic Use of Conversational Structure in Interrogations." In *The Sociologist as Detective,* edited by William B. Sanders, 273–281. New York: Praeger, 1976.

Schonlai, Matthias, Ronald D. Fricker, and Marc N. Elliott. *Conducting Research Surveys via E-mail and the Web.* Santa Monica, CA: Rand Corporation, 2002.

Singer, Simon I. "Comment on Alleged Overreporting." *Criminology* 16 (May 1978): 99–103.

Skogan, Wesley G. *Victimization Surveys and Criminal Justice Planning.* Monograph. Washington, DC: National Institute of Law Enforcement and Criminal Justice, July 1978.

Skogan, Wesley G., and Michael G. Maxfield. *Coping with Crime: Individual and Neighborhood Reactions.* Beverly Hills, CA: Sage, 1981.

Smykla, John O. "The Human Impact of Capital Punishment: Interviews with Families of Persons on Death Row." *Journal of Criminal Justice* 15 (1987): 53–68.

Sparks, Richard F., Haxel G. Genn, and David J. Dodd. *Surveying Victims: A Study of the*

Measurement of Criminal Victimization, Perceptions of Crime and Attitudes to Criminal Justice. New York: Wiley, 1977.

Stanko, Elizabeth. Everyday Violence: How Men and Women Experience Sexual and Physical Danger. London: Pandora, 1990.

Sudman, Seymour. Applied Sampling. New York: Academic Press, 1976.

————. "Eliciting Sensitive Information by Telephone Survey." Paper presented at the National Workshop on Research Methods and Criminal Justice Evaluation, Baltimore, MD, March 17–19, 1980.

Survey Monkey.com. 2008, www.surveymonkey.com/Home_FeaturesDesign.aspx

Survey Research Center. Interviewer's Manual. Ann Arbor, MI: University of Michigan, 1969.

Sussman, Marvin B., and Marie R. Haug. "Human and Mechanical Error: An Unknown Quantity in Research." American Behavioral Scientist 2 (November 1967): 55–56.

Sutherland, Edwin H. The Professional Thief. Chicago, IL: University of Chicago Press, 1937 (reissued 1956).

Taylor, Bruce M. "New Directions for the National Crime Survey." Bureau of Justice Statistics Technical Report. Washington, DC: Bureau of Justice Statistics, March 1989.

Thomas, William I., and Dorothy Swaine. The Child in America. New York: Knopf, 1928.

Tjaden, Patricia, and Nancy Thoennes. "Stalking in America: Findings from the National Violence Against Women Survey." Research in Brief (National Institute of Justice and Centers for Disease Control and Prevention), April 1998.

Tourangeau, Roger, and Tom W. Smith. "Asking Sensitive Questions: The Impact of Data Collection, Mode of Question Format, and Question Context." Public Opinion Quarterly 80 (1996): 275–304.

Tracy, Paul E., and James A. Fox. "The Validity of Randomized Response for Sensitive Measurement." American Sociological Review 46 (April 1981): 187–200.

Tuchfarber, Alfred J., and William R. Klecka. Random Digit Dialing—Lowering the Cost of Victimization Surveys. Washington, DC: Police Foundation, 1976.

————, et al. "Reducing the Cost of Victim Surveys." In Sample Surveys of the Victims of Crime. Edited by Wesley G. Skogan. Cambridge, MA: Ballinger, 1976.

Trulson, Chad, James Marquart, and Janet Mullings. "Breaking In: Gaining Entry to Prisons and Other Hard-to-Access Criminal Justice Organizations." Journal of Criminal Justice Education 15 (Fall 2004): 451–478.

U.S. Bureau of Census. "Victim Recall Pretest (Washington, DC: Household Surveys of Victims of Crime)." Washington, DC: Bureau of Census, Demographic Surveys Division, mimeograph, 1970.

Vasu, Michael, and G. David Garson. "Computer-Assisted Survey Research and Continuous Audience Response Technology for the Political and Social Sciences." Social Science Computer Review 8 (1990): 535–557.

Warner, Stanley L. "Randomized Responses: A Survey Technique for Eliminating Evasive Answer Bias." Journal of the American Statistical Association 60 (1965): 63–69.

Whitaker, Catherine J. "The Redesigned National Crime Survey: Selected New Data." Bureau of Justice Statistics Special Report. Washington, DC: Bureau of Justice Statistics, January, 1989.

Wright, Richard, and Scott Decker. Burglars on the Job: Streetlife Culture and Residential Break-ins. Boston, MA: Northeastern University Press, 1994.

Wright, Richard and Scott Decker. Armed Robbers in Action: Stickups and Streetlife Culture. Boston, MA: Northeastern University Press, 1997.

Chapter 7 Participant Observation and Case Studies

Abadinsky, Howard. The Criminal Elite: Professional and Organized Crime. Westport, CT: Greenwood Press, 1983.

————. The Mafia in America: An Oral History. 3rd ed. New York: Praeger, 1993.

Adler, Patricia A., and Peter Adler. Wheeling and Dealing: An Ethnography of Upper Level Drug Dealing and

Smuggling Community. New York: Columbia University Press, 1985.

———. "Researching Dealers and Smugglers." In *Constructions of Deviance*, edited by Patricia A. Adler and Peter Adler, 116–131. Belmont, CA: Wadsworth, 2000.

Agar, Michael H. *Ripping and Running: A Formal Ethnography of Urban Heroin Addicts*. New York: Seminar Press, 1973.

———. "Ethnography in the Streets and in the Joint: A Comparison." In *Street Ethnography*, edited by Robert S. Weppner, 143–156. Vol. 1, Beverly Hills, CA: Sage, 1977.

Aho, Jim. *The Politics of Righteousness: Idaho Christian Patriotism*. Seattle, WA: University of Washington Press, 1990.

———. *This Thing of Darkness: The Sociology of the Enemy*. Seattle, WA: University of Washington Press, 1994.

———. "Hate Groups." Presentation at the Social Science Division Speakers' Series, Mercyhurst College, Erie, PA, April 1996.

Albini, Joseph. "The Guardian Angels: Vigilantes or Protectors of the Community?" Paper presented at the Academy of Criminal Justice Sciences Meetings, Orlando, FL, March 1986.

Allen, John. *Assault with a Deadly Weapon: The Autobiography of a Street Criminal*, edited by Diane H. Kelly and Philip Heymann. New York: Pantheon, 1977.

Anderson, Annelise G. *The Business of Organized Crime*. Stanford, CA: Hoover Institution Press, 1979.

Becker, Howard S. *Outsiders: Studies in the Sociology of Deviance*. New York: Free Press, 1963.

———. "Practitioners of Vice and Crime." In *Sociological Methods: A Sourcebook*, edited by Norman K. Denzin, 85–101. New York: McGraw-Hill, 1978a.

———. "The Relevance of Life Histories." In *Sociological Methods: A Sourcebook*, edited by Norman K. Denzin, 289–295. New York: McGraw-Hill, 1978b.

Bennett, James. *Oral History and Delinquency: The Rhetoric of Criminology*. Chicago, IL: University of Chicago Press, 1981.

Berg, Bruce L. *Qualitative Research Methods for the Social Sciences*. 6th ed. Boston, MA: Allyn and Bacon, 2007.

Bernard, H. Russell. *Research Methods in Anthropology*. Thousand Oaks, CA: Sage, 1994.

Bertaux, Daniel, ed. *Biography and Society: The Life History Approach in the Social Sciences*. Beverly Hills, CA: Sage, 1981.

Bigus, Odis E. "The Milkman and His Customer: A Cultivated Relationship." In *Interaction in Everyday Life*, edited by John Lofland, 85–119. Beverly Hills, CA: Sage, 1978.

Blok, Anton. *The Mafia of a Sicilian Village: 1860–1960*. New York: Harper and Row, 1975.

Britton, Dana. *At Work in the Iron Cage: The Prison as Gendered Organization*. New York: New York University Press, 2003.

Bryan, James H. "Apprenticeships in Prostitution." *Social Problems* 12 (Winter 1965): 287–297.

Campbell, Donald T., and Julian C. Stanley. *Experimental and Quasi-experimental Designs for Research*. Chicago, IL: Rand McNally, 1963.

Caputo, Gail. *Out in the Storm; Drug Addicted Women Living as Shoplifters and Sex Workers*. New York: NYU Press, 2008.

Carey, James T. "Problems of Access and Risk in Observing Drug Scenes." In *Research on Deviance*, edited by Jack D. Douglas, 71–92. New York: Random, 1972.

Carroll, Leo. *Hacks, Blacks and Cons*. Toronto, ON: Lexington Books, 1974.

Caudill, William A. *The Psychiatric Hospital as a Small Society*. Cambridge, MA: Harvard University Press, 1958.

Cavan, Sheri. *Liquor License*. Chicago, IL: Aldine, 1966.

Chambliss, William J. *The Box Man: A Professional Thief's Journal, by Harry King*. New York: Harper and Row, 1975.

Clemmer, Donald. *The Prison Community*. New York: Holt, Rinehart and Winston, 1940.

Corti, Louise. "Using Diaries in Social Research." *Social Research Update* (March 1993).

Cressey, Donald R. *Other People's Money.* New York: Free Press, 1953.

Cromwell, Paul, ed. *In Their Own Words: Field Research on Crime and Criminals—An Anthology.* Los Angeles, CA: Roxbury Press, 1996.

Cromwell, Paul F., James N. Olson, and D'Aunn W. Avary. *Breaking and Entering: An Ethnographic Analysis of Burglary.* Newbury Park, CA: Sage, 1991.

Davis, Fred. "The Cabdriver and His Fare: Facets of a Fleeting Relationship." *American Journal of Sociology* 65 (September 1959): 158–165.

Deming, W. Edwards. "On Errors in Surveys." *American Sociological Review* 9 (August 1944): 359–369.

Denfield, Duane, ed. *Streetwise Criminology.* Cambridge, MA: Schenkman, 1974.

Dennis, Deborah L. "Word Crunching: An Annotated Bibliography on Computers and Qualitative Data Analysis." *Qualitative Sociology* 7 (1984): 148–156.

Denzin, Norman K., and Yvonna S. Lincoln, eds. *Handbook of Qualitative Research.* Thousand Oaks, CA: Sage, 1993.

Deutscher, Irwin. "Words and Deeds: Social Science and Social Policy." *Social Problems* 13 (1966): 233–254.

Douglas, Jack D. *Research on Deviance.* New York: Random, 1972.

———. *Investigative Social Research.* Beverly Hills, CA: Sage, 1976.

Emmison, Michael, and Philip Smith. *Researching the Visual.* Thousand Oaks, CA: Sage, 2000.

Ferrell, Jeff. "Criminological Verstehen." In *Ethnography at the Edge: Crime, Deviance, and Field Research*, edited by Jeff Ferrell and Mark S. Hamm, 20–42. Boston, MA: Northeastern University Press, 1998.

Ferrell, Jeff, and Mark S. Hamm, eds. *Ethnography at the Edge: Crime, Deviance, and Field Research.* Boston, MA: Northeastern University Press, 1998.

Festinger, Leon, Henry Riecken, and Stanley Schachter. *When Prophecy Fails.* New York: Harper, 1956.

Fielding, Nigel G., and Raymond M. Lee. *Using Computers in Qualitative Research.* Newbury Park, CA: Sage, 1991.

Firestone, T. "Mafia Memoirs: What They Tell Us About Organized Crime." *Journal of Contemporary Criminal Justice* 9 (1993): 197–220.

Fox, Renee C. "Bill Whyte: In Essence a Participant Observer." *Footnotes* (American Sociological Association) (August 1980): 2.

Fujisaka, Sam, and John Grayzel. "Partnership Research: A Case of Divergent Ethnographic Styles in Prison Fieldwork." *Human Organization* 37 (1978): 172–179.

Gans, Herbert J. "The Participant Observer as a Human Being: Observations on the Personal Aspects of Field Work." In *Institutions and the Person: Essays Presented to Everett C. Hughes*, edited by Howard S. Becker, Blanche Greer, David Riesman, and Robert S. Weiss, 300–317. Chicago, IL: Aldine, 1968.

Gardiner, John, and David J. Olson. *Wincanton: The Politics of Corruption.* President's Commission on Law Enforcement and Administration of Justice Task Force Reports: Organized Crime, Appendix B, Washington, DC: U.S. Government Printing Office, 1968.

Garfinkel, Harold, ed. *Studies in Ethnomethodology.* Englewood Cliffs, NJ: Prentice-Hall, 1967.

Gittings, James A. *Life Without Living: People of the Inner City.* Philadelphia, PA: Westminster Press, 1966.

Glaser, Barney G., and Anselm Strauss. *The Discovery of Grounded Theory.* Chicago, IL: Aldine, 1967.

Glenn, David. "All the City's a Stage." *Chronicle of Higher Education,* January 18, 2008a, B16, B18.

Glenn, David. "Peacekeeper and Scholar is Killed in War Zone." *Chronicle of Higher Education,* July 4, 2008b, A1, A6, A9.

Goffman, Erving. *Asylums.* Garden City, NY: Doubleday, 1961.

Gold, Raymond L. "Roles in Sociological Field Observations." *Social Forces* 36 (March 1958): 217–223.

Goldstein, E. "Enlisting Social Scientists." *Chronicle of Higher Education.* July 4, 2008, B4–B5.

Goldstein, Paul J., et al. "Ethnographic Field Stations." In *From Collection and Interpretation of Data from Hidden Populations,* edited by Elizabeth Y. Lambert.

Washington, DC: National Criminal Justice Reference Service, 1990.

Grazian, David. *On the Make: The Hustle of Urban Nightlife.* Chicago, IL: University of Chicago Press, 2008.

Greek, Cecil. "Visual Criminology" (Unpublished Manuscript), 2005, *www.criminology.fsu.edu/faculty/greek/visualCriminology.pdf*

Hagan, Frank E. "The Rural Elderly in Erie County, Pennsylvania," a survey report prepared on behalf of the Appalachian Regional Commission and the Greater Erie Community Action Commission, Erie, Pennsylvania, 1972.

———. "Single Subject Designs: A Strategy for Quantitative Case Studies." Paper presented at the Academy of Criminal Justice Sciences Meetings, Washington, DC, March 1989.

Hagedorn, John M. "Homeboys, Dope Fiends, Legits and New Jacks." *Criminology* 32 (May 1994): 197–219.

Haley, Alex. *Roots.* Garden City, NY: Doubleday, 1976.

Hamm, Mark S. *American Skinheads: The Criminology and Control of Hate Crime.* Westport, CT: Praeger, 1993.

Holzman, Harold R., and Sharon Pines. "Buying Sex: The Phenomenology of Being a John." Paper presented at the American Society of Criminology Meetings, Philadelphia, PA, November 1979.

Hopper, Columbus B. "The Changing Role of Women in Motorcycle Gangs: From Partner to Sexual Property." Paper presented at the American Society of Criminology Meetings, San Francisco, CA, November 1991.

Humphreys, Laud. *Tearoom Trade: Impersonal Sex in Public Places.* Chicago, IL: Aldine, 1970.

Hurwitz, Jacob I. "The Idiographic Evaluation Model in Crime Control." *Journal of Offender Counseling Services and Rehabilitation* 8 (Summer 1984): 41–48.

Hurworth, Rosalind. "Photo-interviewing for Research." *Social Research Update* 40 (Spring 2003).

Ianni, Francis A., and Elizabeth Ianni. *A Family Business: Kinship and Social Control in Organized Crime.* New York: Russell Sage, 1972.

Irwin, John. "Participant-Observation of Criminals." In *Research on Deviance*, edited by Jack D. Douglas, 17–138. New York: Random House, 1972.

Irwin, John. *The Jail.* Berkeley, CA: University of California Press, 1985.

Jackson, Bruce, ed. *In the Life: Versions of the Criminal Experience.* New York: Mentor Book, 1972.

Jacobs, James B. *Stateville: A Penitentiary in Mass Society.* Chicago, IL: University of Chicago Press, 1977.

Jankowski, Martin S. *Islands in the Streets: Gangs and American Urban Society.* Berkeley, CA: University of California Press, 1991.

Johnson, Jeffrey C. *Selecting Ethnographic Informants.* Newbury Park, CA: Sage, 1990.

Kazdin, Alan E. *Single-Case Research Designs.* New York: Oxford University Press, 1982.

Keiser, R. Lincoln. *The Vice Lords: Warriors of the Streets.* New York: Holt, 1969.

King, Harry, and William J. Chambliss. *Harry King: A Professional Thief's Journal.* New York: Wiley, 1984.

Kirkham, George. *Signal Zero.* New York: J.B. Lippincott, 1976.

Klein, J. F., and A. Montague. *Check Forgers.* Lexington, MA: Lexington Books, 1977.

Klockars, Carl P. *The Professional Fence.* New York: Free Press, 1974.

———. "Field Ethics for the Life History." In *Street Ethnography*, edited by Robert S. Weppner, 201–226. Vol. 1, Beverly Hills, CA: Sage, 1977.

Kobrin, Solomon. "The Use of Life History Documents for the Development of Delinquency Theory." In *The Jack-Roller at Seventy: A Fifty-Year Follow-up*, edited by Jon D. Snodgrass, 153–165. Lexington, MA: D.C. Heath, 1982.

LaPiere, Richard. "Attitudes vs. Actions." *Social Forces* 13 (March 1934): 230–237.

Laub, John H. *Criminology in the Making: An Oral History.* Boston, MA: Northeastern University Press, 1983.

———. "Talking About Crime: Oral History in Criminology and Criminal Justice." *Oral History Review* 12 (1984): 29–42.

Lee, Nancy H. *The Search for an Abortionist.* Chicago, IL: University of Chicago Press, 1969.

Letkemann, Peter. *Crime as Work*. Englewood Cliffs, NJ: Prentice-Hall, 1973.

Levine, James P. "The Potential for Overreporting in Criminal Victimization Surveys." *Criminology* 14 (November 1976): 307–330.

Liebow, Elliot. *Tally's Corner*. Boston, MA: Little, Brown, 1967.

Lozano, Wendy G., and Tanice G. Foltz. "Into the Darkness: An Ethnographic Study of Witchcraft and Death." In *Extreme Methods: Innovative Approaches to Social Science Research*, edited by J. Mitchell Miller and Richard Tewksbury, 155–167. Boston, MA: Allyn & Bacon, 2001.

Maas, Peter. *The Valachi Papers*. New York: Bantam Books, 1968.

Malinowski, Bronislaw. *Argonauts of the Western Pacific*. New York: Dutton, 1922.

———. *Crime and Custom in Savage Society*. London: Routledge and Kegan Paul, 1926.

———. *A Diary in the Strict Sense of the Word*. New York: Harcourt, 1967.

Manning, Peter K. "Observing the Police: Deviants, Respectables, and the Law." In *Research on Deviance*, edited by Jack D. Douglas, 213–268. New York: Random, 1972.

Manning, Peter K., and John Van Maanen, eds. *Policing: A View from the Streets*. Santa Monica, CA: Goodyear, 1979.

Marquart, James W. "Doing Research in Prison: The Strengths and Weaknesses of Full Participation as a Guard." *Justice Quarterly* 3 (March 1986): 15–32.

Mattley, Christine. "(Dis) Courtesy Stigma: Fieldwork among Phone Fantasy Workers." In *Ethnography at the Edge: Crime, Deviance, and Field Research*, edited by Jeff Ferrell and Mark S. Hamm, 146–158. Boston, MA: Northeastern University Press, 1998.

McKinney, John C. *Constructive Typology and Social Theory*. New York: Appleton, 1966.

McLuhan, Marshall. *The Medium Is the Message*. New York: Touchstone Press, 1989.

Miller, Eleanor. *Street Woman*. Philadelphia, PA: Temple University Press, 1986.

Miller, J. Mitchell, and Richard Tewksbury, eds. *Extreme Methods: Innovative Approaches to Social Science Research*. Boston, MA: Allyn and Bacon, 2001.

Mills, James. *The Underground Empire: Where Crime and Government Embrace*. Garden City, NY: Doubleday, 1986.

Monette, Duane R., Thomas J. Sullivan, and Cornell R. DeJong. *Applied Social Research: Tool for the Human Services*. 3rd ed. New York: Holt, Rinehart and Winston, 1994.

Myers, James. "Nonmainstream Body Modification: Genital Piercing, Branding, Burning, and Cutting." In *Extreme Methods: Innovative Approaches to Social Science Research*, edited by J. Mitchell Miller and Richard Tewksbury, 183–205. Boston, MA: Allyn and Bacon, 2001.

National Advisory Committee on Criminal Justice Standards and Goals. Criminal Justice Research and Development. Report of the Task Force on Criminal Justice Research and Development. Washington, DC: Law Enforcement Assistance Administration, December 1976.

Orenstein, Alan, and William R. F. Phillips. *Understanding Social Research: An Introduction*. Boston, MA: Allyn, 1978.

Orne, Martin T. "On the Social Psychology of the Psychological Experiment: With Particular Reference to Demand Characteristics." In *The Experiment as a Social Occasion*, edited by Paul L. Wubben, Bruce C. Straits, and Gary I. Schulman, 139–152. Berkeley, CA: Glendessary Press, 1974.

Phillips, Derek L. *Knowledge from What? Theories and Methods in Social Research*. Chicago, IL: Rand McNally, 1971.

Plate, Tom. *Crime Pays: An Inside Look at Burglars, Car Thieves, Loan Sharks, Hit Men, Fences and Other Professionals in Crime*. New York: Ballantine, 1975.

Plimpton, George. *Paper Lion* (1981 Edition). New York: Holtzman Press, 1965.

———. *The Open Net*. New York: Norton, 1985.

Polsky, Ned. *Hustlers, Beats and Others*. Chicago, IL: Aldine, 1967, especially pp. 117–149.

Quarles, Chester L. *Terrorism: Avoidance and Survival.* Boston, MA: Butterworth Heinemann, 1991.

———. "Christian Identity: A Common Threat of Far-Right Activism." Paper presented at the Academy of Criminal Justice Sciences Meetings, March 1997.

Reichel, Philip L. "Regulating the Criminal Justice Snooper." *Journal of Criminal Justice* 13 (1985): 75–84.

Reiss, Albert J., Jr. *The Police and the Public.* New Haven, CT: Yale University Press, 1971.

Rettig, Richard P., Manuel J. Torres, and Gerald R. Garrett. *Manny: A Criminal-Addict's Story.* Boston, MA: Houghton Mifflin, 1977.

Robinson, Elizabeth, Denise E. Bronson, and Betty J. Blythe. "An Analysis of the Implementation of Single-Case Evaluation by Practitioners." *Social Service Review* 62 (June 1988): 285–301.

Ronai, Carol, and Carolyn Ellis. "Turn-Ons for Money: Interactional Strategies of the Table Dancer." In *Extreme Methods: Innovative Approaches to Social Science Research*, edited by J. Mitchell Miller and Richard Tewksbury, 168–182. Boston, MA: Allyn & Bacon, 2001.

Rose, Gillian. *Visual Methodologies.* Thousand Oaks, CA: Sage, 2001.

Rosenhan, David L. "On Being Sane in Insane Places." *Science* 19 (1973): 250–258.

Sanders, William B. *Detective Work.* New York: Free Press, 1977, especially pp. 190–207.

Schneider, Alison. "CUNY Scholar Is Accused of Using Grant to Buy Heroin for Research Subjects." *Chronicle of Higher Education*, November 12, 1999, A18.

Shaw, Clifford R. *The Jack-Roller.* Chicago, IL: University of Chicago Press, 1930.

———. *The Natural History of a Delinquent Career.* Chicago, IL: University of Chicago Press, 1931.

Shaw, Clifford R., Henry D. McKay, and James F. McDonald. *Brothers in Crime.* Chicago, IL: University of Chicago Press, 1938.

Sherizen, Sanford. "Videotaping as a Method of Dialogue: A New Teaching and Research Method in Criminal Justice." *Journal of Criminal Justice* 4 (Spring 1976): 63–68.

Shils, Edward A. "The Calling of Sociology." In *Theories of Society*, edited by Talcott Parsons et al., 1405–1448. New York: Free Press, 1961.

Skipper, James K. "Stripteasers: A Six Year History of Public Reaction to a Study." In *Sociological Footprints*, edited by L. Cargan and J. Ballantine. Boston, MA: Houghton Mifflin, 1979.

Skolnick, Jerome H. *Justice Without Trial: Law Enforcement in Democratic Society.* New York: Wiley, 1966.

Smykla, John Ortiz. "Placing Uruguayan Corrections in Context, 1973–1984: A Note on the Visiting Criminologist's Role." *Journal of Criminal Justice* 17 (1989): 25–37.

Snodgrass, Jon. *The Jack-Roller at Seventy: A Fifty-Year Follow-Up.* Lexington, MA: D.C. Heath, 1982.

Soloway, Irvine, and James Walters. "Workin' the Corner: The Ethics and Legality of Ethnographic Fieldwork among Active Heroin Addicts." In *Street Ethnography*, edited by Robert S. Weppner, 159–178. Beverly Hills, CA: Sage, 1977.

Spradley, James P. *You Owe Yourself a Drunk: An Ethnography of Urban Nomads.* Boston, MA: Little, Brown, 1970.

Steffens, Lincoln. *The Shame of the Cities.* New York: McClure, Phillips, 1904.

Steffensmeier, Darrell J. *The Fence: In the Shadow of Two Worlds.* Totowa, NJ: Rowman and Littlefield, 1986.

Steffensmeier, Darrell, and Jeffrey Ulmer. *Confessions of a Dying Thief.* Somerset, NJ: Transaction Publishing, 2006.

Stein, Martha L. *Lovers, Friends, Slaves. . . . The Nine Male Sexual Types.* Berkeley, CA: Berkeley Publishing Corp., 1974.

Sullivan, Mercer. *Getting Paid: Youth Crime and Work in the Inner City.* Ithaca, NY: Cornell University Press, 1989.

Sussman, Marvin B., and Marie R. Haug. "Human and Mechanical Error: An Unknown Quantity in Research." *American Behavioral Scientist* 11 (November 1967): 55–56.

Sutherland, Edwin H. *The Professional Thief.* Chicago, IL: University of Chicago Press, 1937.

Sutherland, Edwin H., and Donald Cressey. *Principles of Criminology.* 10th ed. Chicago, IL: Lippincott, 1978.

Sykes, Gresham. *The Society of Captives.* Princeton, NJ: Princeton University Press, 1958.

Talese, Gay. *Honor Thy Father.* Greenwich, CT: Fawcett, 1971.

———. *Thy Neighbor's Wife.* Greenwich, CT: Fawcett, 1979.

Tawney, J. W., and D. L. Gast. *Single Subject Research in Special Education.* Columbus, OH: Charles C. Merrill, 1984.

Taylor, Laurie. *In the Underworld.* Oxford, England: Blackwell, 1984.

Teresa, Vincent, with Thomas C. Renner. *My Life in the Mafia.* New York: Doubleday, 1973.

Terkel, Louis (Studs). *Hard Times: An Oral History of the Great Depression.* New York: Avon, 1970.

———. *Working.* New York: Pantheon, 1974.

———. *American Dreams: Lost and Found.* New York: Pantheon, 1980.

———. *The Good War: An Oral History of World War II.* New York: Pantheon, 1984.

Tesch, Renata. *Qualitative Research: Analysis Types and Software Tools.* New York: The Falmer Press, 1990.

———. "Introduction." *Qualitative Sociology* 14, no. 3 (1991): 225–243.

Trulson, Chad, James Marquart, and Janet Mullings. "Breaking In: Gaining Entry to Prisons and Other Hard-to-Access Criminal Justice Organizations." *Journal of Criminal Justice Education* 15 (Fall 2004): 451–478.

Tewksbury, Richard, and Gagne, P. "Assumed and Presumed Identities: Problems of Self Presentation in Field Research." In *Research Methods: A Qualitative Reader*, edited by J.M. Miller and R. Tewksbury, 51–73. Upper Saddle River, NJ: Pearson Prentice Hall, 2006.

Thompson, Hunter. *Hell's Angels.* New York: Ballantine Books, 1967.

Thrasher, Frederick M. *The Gang: The Study of 1313 Gangs in Chicago.* Chicago, IL: University of Chicago Press, 1927.

Toby, Jackson. "Going Native in Criminology" (Letter to the Editor). *The Criminologist* 11 (May–June 1986): 2.

Travis, Lawrence F., III. "The Case Study in Criminal Justice Research: Applications to Policy Analysis." *Criminal Justice Review* 8 (Fall 1983): 46–51.

Trice, Harrison M. "The 'Outsider' Role in Field Study." In *Qualitative Methodology*, edited by William J. Filstead, 77–82. Chicago, IL: Markham, 1970.

Walker, Andrew L., and Charles W. Lidz. "Methodological Notes on the Employment of Indigenous Observers." In *Street Ethnography*, edited by Robert S. Weppner, 103–124. Beverly Hills, CA: Sage, 1977.

Webb, Eugene, Donald T. Campbell, Richard D. Schwartz, and Lee Sechrest. *Unobtrusive Measures: Nonreactive Research in the Social Sciences.* Chicago, IL: Rand McNally, 1966.

Weber, Max. *The Methodology of Social Sciences.* Translated by Edward A. Shils and Henry A. Finch. New York: Free Press, 1949.

Weinberg, Martin. "Sexual Modesty: Social Meanings and the Nudist Camp." In *Sociology and Everyday Life*, edited by Marcello Truzzi. Englewood Cliffs, NJ: Prentice-Hall, 1968.

Weinberg, Martin S., and Colin J. Williams. "Fieldwork Among Deviants: Social Relations with Subjects and Others." In *Research on Deviance*, edited by Jack D. Douglas, 165–186. New York: Random, 1972.

Whyte, William Foote. *Street Corner Society.* Chicago, IL: University of Chicago Press, 1943.

———. "Report of the President: Whyte Reviews Term; Emphasizes Field Work." *Footnotes* (American Sociological Association) (October 1981): 6.

Wright, Richard, and Trevor Bennett. "Exploring the Offender's Perspective: Observing and Interviewing Criminals." In *Measurement Issues in Criminology*, edited by Kimberly Kempf, 138–151. New York: Springer-Verlag, 1990.

Wright, Richard T., and Scott H. Decker. *Burglars on the Job: Streetlife and Residential Break-Ins.* Boston, MA: Northeastern University Press, 1994.

———. *Armed Robbers in Action: Stickups and Street Culture.* Boston, MA: Northeastern University Press, 1997.

Yablonsky, Lewis. *The Violent Gang.* Baltimore, MD: Penguin, 1962.

———. *Synanon: The Tunnel Back.* Baltimore, MD: Penguin, 1965a.

———. "Experiences with the Criminal Community." In *Applied Sociology*, edited by Alvin W. Gouldner and S. M. Miller. New York: Free Press, 1965b.

Yin, Robert K. *Case Study Research: Design and Methods.* 2nd ed. Beverly Hills, CA: Sage, 1994.

Chapter 8 Unobtrusive Measures, Secondary Analysis, and the Uses of Official Statistics

Albini, Joseph. *The American Mafia: Genesis of a Legend.* New York: Appleton, 1971.

American Society of Criminology and Academy of Criminal Justice Sciences. *Oral History Project.* 3 vols. Belmont, CA: Thomson, Wadsworth, 2004. Videotapes.

Anderson, Annelise G. *The Business of Organized Crime: A Cosa Nostra Family.* Stanford, CA: Stanford University Press, 1979.

Archer, Dane, and Rosemary Gartner. *Violence and Crime in Cross-National Perspective.* New Haven, CT: Yale University Press, 1984.

Asch, Solomon E. "Effects of Group Pressure upon the Modification and Distortion of Judgment." In *Groups, Leadership and Men*, edited by Harold Guetzkow. Pittsburgh, PA: Carnegie Press, 1951.

Bailey, William C. "Murder, Capital Punishment, and Television: Execution Publicity and Homicide Rates." *American Sociological Review* 55 (October 1990): 628–633.

Banton, Michael. *The Policeman in the Community.* New York: Basic, 1964.

Becker, Howard S. "Practitioners of Vice and Crime." In *Sociological Methods: A Sourcebook*, edited by Norman K. Denzin, 143–156. Beverly Hills, CA: Sage, 1970.

Bennett, Richard R., and James P. Lynch. "Does a Difference Make a Difference? Comparing Cross-National Crime Indicators." *Criminology* 28 (February 1990): 153–181.

Berelson, Bernard. *Content Analysis in Communication Research.* New York: Free Press, 1952.

Berg, Bruce. *Qualitative Research Methods for the Social Sciences.* 6th ed. Boston, MA: Allyn and Bacon, 2007.

Bielby, William T., and Richard A. Berk. "Source of Error in Survey Data Used in Criminal Justice Evaluations: An Analysis of Survey Respondents' Reports of 'Fear of Crime.'" Paper presented at the National Workshop on Research Methodology and Criminal Justice Program Evaluation, Baltimore, MD, March 17–19, 1980.

Black, Donald J. "Police Encounters and Social Organization: An Observational Study." Ph.D. dissertation, University of Michigan, 1968.

———. "Production of Crime Rates." *American Sociological Review* 35 (1970): 733–748.

Block, Alan A. *East Side-West Side: Organizing Crime in New York.* Swansea, United Kingdom: Christopher Davis, 1979.

Bonanno, Joseph, with Sergio Lalli. *A Man of Honor: The Autobiography of Joseph Bonanno.* New York: Simon and Schuster, 1983.

Bouchard, Thomas, Jr. "Unobtrusive Methods: An Inventory of Uses." *Sociological Methods and Research* 4 (February 1976): 267–300.

Buckner, H. Taylor. "The Police: The Culture of a Social Control Agency." Ph.D. dissertation, University of California, 1967.

Bureau of Justice Statistics. "Criminal Cases in Five States, 1983–1986." *Bureau of Justice Statistics Special Report.* Washington, DC: Bureau of Justice Statistics, September 1989.

Burnham, Kenneth P. "Mark-Recapture Techniques for Estimating Animal Populations: What Has Been Done in Ecology." Paper presented at the National Workshop on Research Methodology and Criminal Justice Program Evaluation, Baltimore, MD, March 1980.

Cameron, Mary O. *The Booster and the Snitch: Department Store Shoplifting.* Glencoe, IL: Free Press, 1964.

Caudill, William C., et al. "Social Structure and Interaction Processes on a Psychiatric Ward." *American Journal of Orthopsychiatry* 22 (1952): 314–334.

Cavoir, Norman, and L. Ramona Howard. "Facial Attractiveness and Juvenile Delinquency among Black and White Offenders." *Journal of Abnormal Child Psychology* 1 (1973): 202–213.

Chappell, Duncan, and Marilyn Walsh. "No Questions Asked: A Consideration of the Crime of Criminal Receiving." *Crime and Delinquency* (1974): 157–168.

Chermak, Steven M. "Body Count News: How Crime Is Presented in the News Media." *Justice Quarterly* 11 (December 1994): 561–582.

Clarke, James W. *American Assassins: The Darker Side of Politics.* Princeton, NJ: Princeton University Press, 1982.

Clinard, Marshall B. *The Black Market: A Study of White Collar Crime.* New York: Holt, 1952.

Clinard, Marshall B., and Richard Quinney. *Criminal Behavior Systems.* 2nd ed. New York: Holt, 1973.

Clinard, Marshall B., and Peter C. Yeager. *Illegal Corporate Behavior.* Washington, DC: U.S. Government Printing Office, 1979.

———. *Corporate Crime.* New York: Macmillan, 1980.

Colasanto, Diane, and Joseph Sanders. "Methodological Issues in Simulated Jury Research." Paper presented at the Annual Meeting of the Law and Society Association, May 1978.

Courtright, Kevin E. "An Overview of the Use and Potential Advantages of the Diary Method." Paper presented at the Academy of Criminal Justice Sciences Meetings, Boston, MA, March 1995.

Cox, Edward R., Robert C. Fellmeth, and John E. Schulz. *Nader's Raiders: Report on the Federal Trade Commission.* New York: Grove Press, 1969.

Crow, Matthew S., Richard M. Hough, Sr., Jason Moseley, John Ortiz Smykla, and Kimberly Tatum. "Drunk and Alone in the K-Mart Parking Lot: The Pedagogy of Simulations and Contemporary Attitudes Toward Drinking and Driving." *Journal of Criminal Justice Education* 19 (November 2008): 417–431.

Davies, Margaret G. *The Enforcement of English Apprenticeship: A Study in Applied Mercantilism, 1563–1642.* Cambridge, MA: Harvard University Press, 1956.

Davis, F. James. "Crime News in Colorado Newspapers." *American Journal of Sociology* 57 (1952): 325–330.

Demaree, Robert G. "Estimating the Size of Drug User Populations." Paper presented at the National Workshop on Research Methodology and Criminal Justice Program Evaluation, Baltimore, MD, March 17–19, 1980.

Denzin, Norman K. *The Research Act.* 3rd ed. Englewood Cliffs, NJ: Prentice-Hall, 1989.

Douglas, Jack D. "Observing Deviance." In *Research on Deviance*, edited by Jack D. Douglas, 3–34. New York: Random, 1972.

Durkheim, Emile. *Suicide: A Study in Sociology.* Translated by John A. Spaulding and George Simpson. New York: Free Press, 1951.

Earls, Felton J., and Christy A. Visher. "Project on Human Development in Chicago Neighborhoods: A Research Update." *National Institute of Justice Research in Brief*, February 1997.

Erickson, Kai T. *The Wayward Puritans.* New York: Wiley, 1966.

Erickson, Maynard L., and Jack P. Gibbs. "Further Findings on the Deterrence Question and Strategies for Future Research." *Journal of Criminal Justice* 4 (Fall 1976): 175–189.

Esposito, John C., and Larry J. Silverman. *Vanishing Air: Ralph Nader's Study Group Report on Air Pollution.* New York: Grossman, 1970.

Farrington, David P., and Barry J. Knight. "Two Nonreactive Field Experiments on Stealing from a 'Lost' Letter." *British Journal of Social and Clinical Psychology* 18 (1979): 277–284.

Feldman, Roy E. "Response to Compatriot and Foreigner Who Seeks Assistance." *Journal of Personality and Social Psychology* 10 (1968): 202–214.

Formby, William A., and John O. Smykla. "Citizen Awareness in Crime Prevention: Do They Really Get Involved?" *Journal of Police Science and Administration* 9 (1981): 398–403.

———. "Attitudes and Perceptions Towards Drinking and Driving: A Simulation of Citizen Awareness." *Journal of Police Science and Administration* 12 (1984): 379–384.

Glaser, Daniel, and Max S. Zeigler. "The Use of the Death Penalty v. the Outrage at Murder." *Crime and Delinquency* (October 1974): 333–338.

Glass, Gene V. "Primary, Secondary, and Meta-Analysis of Research." *Educational Researcher* 5 (1976): 3–8.

Glueck, Sheldon, and Eleanor Glueck. *Unraveling Juvenile Delinquency.* New York: The Commonwealth Fund, 1950.

———. *Delinquents and Nondelinquents in Perspective.* Cambridge, MA: Harvard University Press, 1968.

Gosch, Martin A., and Richard Hammer. *The Last Legacy of Lucky Luciano.* New York: Dell, 1974.

Gottschalk, Louis, Clyde Kluckhohn, and Robert Angell. *The Use of Personal Documents in History, Anthropology and Sociology.* New York: Social Science Research Council, 1945.

Graff, Harvey J. "Crime and Punishment in the Nineteenth Century: A New Look at the Criminal." *Journal of Interdisciplinary History* 7 (1977): 477–491.

———. "Systematic Criminal Justice History: Some Suggestions: A Reply." *Journal of Interdisciplinary History* 9 (Winter 1979): 465–472.

Green, Bert F., and Judith A. Hall. "Quantitative Methods for Literature Reviews." *Annual Review of Psychology* 35 (1984): 37–53.

Green, Mark J., et al., eds. *The Monopoly Makers: Ralph Nader's Study Group Report on Regulation and Competition.* New York: Grossman, 1973.

Guetzkow, Harold, ed. *Simulation in Social Science.* Englewood Cliffs, NJ: Prentice-Hall, 1962.

Hagan, Frank E. *Introduction to Criminology.* 2nd ed. Chicago: Nelson Hall, 1990.

Hagan, Frank E. "Comparative Professionalization in an Occupational Arena: The Case of Rehabilitation." Ph.D. dissertation, Case Western Reserve University, 1975.

———. "Comparative Attitudinal Professionalism in Nine Occupations: Some Empirical Findings." Paper presented at the Pennsylvania Sociological Society Meetings, Bloomsburg, PA, October 1976.

———. "The Organized Crime Continuum: A Further Specification of a New Conceptual Model." *Criminal Justice Review* 8 (Fall 1983): 52–57.

———. *Introduction to Criminology: Theories, Methods and Criminal Behavior.* 5th ed. Chicago, IL: Wadsworth, 2002.

———. "'Organized Crime' and 'organized crime': Indeterminate Problems of Definition." *Trends in Organized Crime* 9 (Summer, 2006): 127–137.

Haney, C. "Play's the Thing: Methodological Notes on Social Simulations." In *The Research Experience*, edited by Patricia Golden. Itasca, IL: F.E. Peacock, 1976.

Haney, Craig, Curtis Banks, and Philip Zimbardo. "Interpersonal Dynamics in a Simulated Prison." *International Journal of Criminology and Penology* 1 (1973): 69–97.

Heussenstamm, Frances K. "Bumper Stickers and the Cops." *Trans-Action* 8 (1971): 32–33.

Holsti, Ole. *Content Analysis for the Social Sciences and Humanities.* Reading, MA: Addison-Wesley, 1969.

Howson, Gerald. *Thief-Taker General: The Rise and Fall of Jonathan Wild.* London: Hutchinson, 1970.

Huang, W. S. Wilson, and Charles F. Wellford. "Assessing Indicators of Crime Among International Crime Data Series." *Criminal Justice Policy Review* 3 (March 1989): 28–48.

Humphreys, Laud. *Tearoom Trade: Impersonal Sex in Public Places.* Chicago, IL: Aldine, 1970.

Hyman, Herbert. *Secondary Analysis of Sample Surveys: Principles, Procedures and Potentialities.* New York: Wiley, 1972.

Ianni, Francis A., and Elizabeth Ianni. *A Family Business: Kinship and Social Control in Organized Crime.* New York: Russell Sage, 1972.

Inciardi, James A., Alan A. Block, and Lyle A. Hallowell. *Historical Approaches to Crime: Research Strategies and Issues.* Beverly Hills, CA: Sage, 1977.

Jacob, Herbert, et al. "The Study of Governmental Responses to Crime." Paper presented at the National Workshop on Research Methodology and Criminal Justice Evaluation. Baltimore, MD, March 17–19, 1980.

Joseph, Lori, and Marcy E. Mullins. "Testing Honesty Throughout the World." *USA Today*, May 1, 2001, A1.

Kalish, Carol B. "The Beginning of Wisdom." Paper presented at the International Society of Criminology Meetings, Hamburg, Germany, September 1989.

Kenadjian, Berdj. "Estimating the Amount of Unreported Income." Paper presented at the National Workshop on Research Methodology and Criminal Justice Program Evaluation, Baltimore, MD, March 1980.

Klofas, John, and Charles Cutshall. "Unobtrusive Research Methods in Criminal Justice: Using Graffiti in the Reconstruction of Institutional Cultures." *Journal of Research in Crime and Delinquency* 22 (1985): 355–373.

Knox, Robert E., and Timothy J. McTiernan. "Lost Letters and Social Responsibility in Dublin." *Social Studies* 2 (1973): 511–518.

Landy, David, and Elliot Aronson. "The Influence of the Character of the Criminal and His Victim on the Decisions of Simulated Jurors." *Journal of Experimental Social Psychology* 5 (1969): 141–152.

Laub, John H., Robert J. Sampson, and Kenna Kiger. "Assessing the Potential of Secondary Data Analysis: A New Look at the Gluecks' *Unraveling Juvenile Delinquency Data*." In *Measurement Issues in Criminology*, edited by Kimberly Kempf, 241–257. New York: SpringerVerlag, 1990.

Lieber, Arnold L., and Carolyn R. Sherin. "Homicides and the Lunar Cycles: Toward a Theory of Lunar Influence on Human Emotional Disturbance." *American Journal of Psychiatry* 129 (July 1972): 101–106.

Loeber, Rolf, and Magda Stouthamer-Loeber. "Family Factors as Correlates and Predictors of Juvenile Conduct Problems and Delinquency." In *Crime and Justice: An Annual Review of Research*, edited by Michael Tonry and Norval Morris, 334–355. Vol. 7, Chicago, IL: University of Chicago Press, 1986.

Lupscha, Peter A. "Networks vs. Networking: An Analysis of Organized Criminal Groups." Paper presented at the American Society of Criminology Meetings, Toronto, ON, Canada, November 1982.

Lutzker, M., and E. Ferrall. *Criminal Justice Research in Libraries: Strategies and Resources*. New York: Greenwood Press, 1986.

Maas, Peter. *The Valachi Papers*. New York: Bantam Books, 1968.

Mandel, Jerry. "Hashish, Assassins, and the Love of God." *Issues in Criminology* 2 (1966): 149–156.

Mann, Coramae R. "Getting Even? Women Who Kill in Domestic Encounters." *Justice Quarterly* 5 (March 1988): 33–51.

Manning, Peter. "Observing the Police." In *The Ambivalent Force*, edited by Arthur Niederhoffer and Abraham Blumberg. Hinsdale, IL: Dryden Press, 1976.

Mastrofski, Stephen, Roger B. Parks, and Robert E. Worden. "Community Policing in Action: Lessons from an Observational Study." *National Institute of Justice Research Preview*, June 1998.

Mastrofski, Stephen D., et al. *Systematic Observation of Police: Applying Field Research Methods to Policy Issues*. Washington, DC: Office of Justice Programs, 1998.

McDonald, William F., and James A. Cramer. *Plea Bargaining*. Lexington, MA: D.C. Heath, 1980.

Messner, Steven F. "Economic Discrimination and Societal Homicide Rates: Further Evidence on the Cost of Inequality." *American Sociological Review* 54 (August 1989): 597–611.

Miles, Matthew B., and A. Michael Huberman. *Qualitative Data Analysis*. 2nd ed. Thousand Oaks, CA: Sage, 1994.

Milgram, Stanley. "The Lost-Letter Technique." *Psychology Today* 3 (1969): 30–33, 60–68.

———. *Obedience to Authority: An Experimental View*. New York: Harper, 1974.

Miller, Herbert S., William F. McDonald, and James A. Cramer. *Plea Bargaining in the United States.* Washington, DC: National Institute of Justice, 1980.

Miller, Walter. *Violence by Youth Gangs and Youth Groups as a Crime Problem in Major American Cities.* Washington, DC: Law Enforcement Assistance Administration, 1975.

Mockridge, N. *The Scrawl of the Wild: What People Write on Walls and Why.* Cleveland, OH: World Publishing Co., 1968.

Monkkonen, E. "Systematic Criminal Justice History: Some Suggestions." *Journal of Interdisciplinary History* 9 (Winter 1979): 451–464.

———. *Crime and Justice in American History* (A 16-volume series). Westport, CT: Meckler, 1990.

National Advisory Committee on Criminal Justice Standards and Goals. *Criminal Justice Research and Development.* Report of the Task Force on Criminal Justice Research and Development, Washington, DC: Law Enforcement Assistance Administration, December 1976.

"Not So Quietly Flows the Don: The Mafia Memoirs of Joe Bonanno Are Seized by the Law." *Time*, June 11, 1979, 24.

Olson, Sheldon. *Ideas and Data: The Process and Practice of Social Research.* Homewood, IL: Dorsey Press, 1976.

Page, Joseph, and Mary Win O'Brien. *Bitter Wages: Ralph Nader's Study Group Report on Disease and Injury on the Job.* New York: Grossman, 1973.

Payne, Brian K., and Randy R. Gainey. "Is Good-Time Appropriate for Offenders on Electronic Monitoring? Attitudes of Electronic Monitoring Directors." *Journal of Criminal Justice* 28 (2000): 497–506.

Pearson, Edmund, ed. *The Autobiography of a Criminal: Henry Tufts.* New York: Duffield, 1930 (originally published 1807).

Peterson, Marilyn. *Applications in Criminal Analysis: A Sourcebook.* Westport, CT: Greenwood Press, 1994.

Phillips, David P. "Motor Vehicle Fatalities Increase Just after Publicized Suicide Stories." *Science* 196 (1977): 1464–1465.

———. "Airplane Accident Fatalities Increase Just after Newspaper Stories about Murder and Suicide." *Science* 201 (1978): 748–750.

Pileggi, Nicholas. *Wiseguy: Life in a Mafia Family.* New York: Simon and Schuster, 1985.

Plummer, Ken. *Documents of Life.* London: Allen and Unwin, 1983.

Pool, Ithiel de Sola, ed. *Trends in Content Analysis.* Urbana, IL: University of Illinois Press, 1959.

Pratt, Travis C., and Francis T. Cullen. "Empirical Status of Gottfredson and Hirschi's General Theory of Crime: A Meta-Analysis." *Criminology* 38 (August 2000): 931–964.

Reinharz, Shulamit. *Feminist Methods in Social Research.* New York: Oxford University Press, 1992.

Reiss, Albert J., Jr. "Stuff and Nonsense About Social Surveys and Observation." In *Institutions and the Person*, edited by Howard S. Becker, 351–367. Chicago, IL: Aldine, 1968.

Riis, R. W. "The Repair Man Will Gyp You If You Don't Watch Out." *The Reader's Digest* 39 (1941a): 1–6.

———. "The Radio Repair Man Will Gyp You If You Don't Watch Out." *The Reader's Digest* 39 (1941b): 6–10.

———. "The Watch Repair Man Will Gyp You If You Don't Watch Out." *The Reader's Digest* 39 (1941c): 10–12.

Rosenhan, David. L. "On Being Sane in Insane Places." *Science* 179, no. 19 (1973): 250–258.

Rosenthal, Robert. *Experimenter Effects in Behavior al Research*, enlarged ed. New York: Wiley, 1976.

———. "How Often Are Our Numbers Wrong?" *American Psychologist* 33 (November 1978): 1005–1007.

Roth, Julius A. "Comments on 'Secret Observation.'" *Social Problems* 9 (1962): 283–284.

Sampson, Robert J., and John H. Laub. *Crime in the Making: Pathways and Turning Points through Life.* Cambridge, MA: Harvard University Press, 1992.

———. "Life-Course Desisters? Trajectories of Crime Among Delinquent Boys Followed to Age 70." *Criminology* 41 (August 2003): 555–592.

Sanders, Todd R. "Virtual Law II, VR in the Courtroom." 1998 *www.vremag.com/vr/features/ virtuallaw/virtuallawII/html.*

Sanders, William B., ed. *The Sociologist as Detective.* 2nd ed. New York: Praeger 1976.

Sawyer, H. G. "The Meaning of Numbers." Speech before the American Association of Advertising Agencies, cited in Eugene Webb et al., *Unobtrusive Measures.* Chicago, IL: Rand McNally, 1961.

Scheff, Thomas J. *Being Mentally Ill.* Chicago, IL: Aldine, 1966.

Schwartz, Richard D., and Jerome H. Skolnick. "Two Studies of Legal Stigma." *Social Problems* 10 (1962): 133–142.

Sechrest, Lee, ed. *Unobtrusive Measurement Today.* San Francisco, CA: Jossey-Bass, 1980.

Sechrest, Lee, and A. Kenneth Olson. "Graffiti in Four Types of Institutions of Higher Education." *Journal of Social Research* 7 (1971): 62–71.

Shakur, Sanyika. *Monster: The Autobiography of an L.A. Gang Member.* New York: Atlantic Monthly Press, 1993.

"Sharp Blows at the High Bench." *Time,* March 10, 1980, 48–49.

Sherick, L. G. *How to Use the Freedom of Information Act (FOIA).* New York: Arco, 1980.

Sherif, Muzafer, and Carolyn Sherif. *Groups in Harmony and Tension.* New York: Octagon, 1966.

Simon, Julian L. *Basic Research Methods in Social Science.* 3rd ed. New York: Random, 1989.

Singer, Max. "The Vitality of Mythical Numbers." *The Public Interest* 23 (Spring 1971): 3–9.

Smith, Mary L., and Gene Glass. "Meta-analysis of Psychotherapy Outcome Studies." *American Psychologist* 32 (September 1977): 752–777.

Steffensmeier, Darrell, and Renee H. Steffensmeier. "Who Reports Shoplifters? Research Continuities and Further Developments." *International Journal of Criminology and Penology* 5 (1976): 79–95.

Steffensmeier, Darrell J., and Robert M. Terry. "Deviance and Respectability: An Observational Study of Reactions to Shoplifting." *Social Forces* 5 (1973): 417–426.

Stein, Martha L. *Lovers, Friends, Slave . . . : The Nine Male Sexual Types.* Berkeley, CA: Berkeley Publishing Corp., 1974.

Stewart, David W. *Secondary Research: Information Sources and Methods.* Beverly Hills, CA: Sage, 1984.

Stewart, John E. "Defendant's Attractiveness as a Factor in the Outcome of Criminal Trials: An Observational Study." Paper presented at the Southeastern Psychological Association Meetings, New Orleans, LA, 1979.

Stewart, John E., and Daniel A. Cannon. "Effects of Perpetrator Status and Bystander Commitment on Response to a Simulated Crime." *Journal of Police Science and Administration* 5 (1977): 318–323.

Stricker, L. J. "The True Deceiver." *Psychological Bulletin* 68 (1967): 13–20.

Sutherland, Edwin H. *White Collar Crime.* New York: Dryden, 1949.

Taylor, C. Barr, Leslie Fried, and Justin Kenardy. "The Use of a Real-Time Computer Diary for Data Acquisition and Processing." *Behavior Research and Therapy* 28, no. 1 (1990): 93–97.

Teresa, Vincent, with Thomas C. Renner. *My Life in the Mafia.* Greenwich, CT: Fawcett, 1973.

Thomas, William I., and Florian Znaniecki. *The Polish Peasant in Europe and America.* Boston, MA: Badger, 1918.

Tittle, Charles R., Wayne Villemez, and Douglas A. Smith. "The Myth of Social Class and Criminality: An Empirical Assessment of the Empirical Evidence." *American Sociological Review* 43 (1978): 643–656.

Tracy, Paul E., and James A. Fox. "A Field Experiment on Insurance Fraud in Auto Body Repair." *Criminology* 27 (August 1989): 598–603.

Tracy, Paul E., Marvin E. Wolfgang, and Robert M. Figlio. *Delinquency in Two Birth Cohorts: Executive Summary.* Philadelphia, PA: Center for Studies in Criminology and Criminal Law, The Wharton School, University of Pennsylvania, 1985.

Truzzi, Marcello. "Sherlock Holmes: Applied Social Psychologist." In *The Sociologist as Detective,* 2nd ed., edited by William B. Sanders, 50–86. New York: Praeger, 1976.

Tucker, Lyle, et al. "The Effects of Temptation and Information about a Stranger on Helping." *Personality and Social Psychology Bulletin* 3 (1977): 416–420.

Turner, James S. *The Chemical Feast: Ralph Nader's Study Group Report on the Food and Drug Administration.* New York: Grossman, 1970.

Uchida, Craig D., Laure Brooks, and Christopher S. Koper. "Danger to Police During Domestic Encounters: Assaults on Baltimore County Police, 1984–86." *Criminal Justice Policy Review* 2 (December 1987): 357–371.

Vaughn, Ted R. "Governmental Intervention in Social Research: Political and Ethical Dimensions in the Wichita Jury Recordings." In *Ethics, Politics and Social Research*, edited by Gideon Sjoberg. Cambridge, MA: Schenkman, 1967.

Volz, Joseph, and Peter J. Bridge, eds. *The Mafia Talks.* Greenwich, CT: Fawcett, 1969.

Von Hoffman, Nicholas. "Sociological Snoopers." *Washington Post*, January 30, 1970.

Wallis, W. Allen, and Harry V. Roberts. *The Nature of Statistics.* Rev. ed. New York: Free Press, 1966.

Wanat, John, and Karen Burke. "Estimating Juvenile Recidivism by Cross-level Inference." Paper presented at the National Workshop on Research Methodology and Criminal Justice Program Evaluation, Baltimore, MD, March 1980.

Webb, Eugene, Donald T. Campbell, Richard D. Schwartz, and Lee Sechrest. *Unobtrusive Measures: Nonreactive Research in the Social Sciences.* Chicago, IL: Rand McNally, 1966.

Webb, Eugene J., et al. *Nonreactive Measures in the Social Sciences.* 2nd ed. Boston, MA: Houghton Mifflin, 1981.

Weber, Robert P. *Basic Content Analysis.* Newbury Park, CA: Sage, 1990.

Welch, Michael, Melissa Fenwick, and Meredith Roberts. "Primary Definitions of Crime and Moral Panic: A Content Analysis of Experts' Quotes in Feature Newspaper Articles on Crime." *Journal of Research on Crime and Delinquency* 34 (April 1997): 474–495.

Wells, Gary L., and Amy L. Bradford. "Good, You Identified the Suspect: Feedback to Eyewitnesses Distorts Their Reports of the Witnessing Experience." *Journal of Applied Psychology* 8, no. 3 (May 1998): 1–14.

Wells, L. Edward. "The Utility of Meta-Analysis in Criminal Justice Research." Paper presented at the Academy of Criminal Justice Sciences Meetings, Nashville, TN, March 1991.

Wells, L. Edward, and Joseph H. Rankin. "Families and Delinquency: A Meta-Analysis of the Impact of Broken Homes." *Social Problems* 38 (February 1991): 71–93.

Wessel, David. "Racial Bias Against Black Job Seekers Remains Pervasive, Broad Study Finds." *Wall Street Journal*, May 15, 1991, A9.

Wheeler, Stanton, ed. *On File: Records and Dossiers in American Life.* New York: Russell Sage, 1970.

Whitehead, John T., and Steven P. Lab. "A Meta-Analysis of Juvenile Correctional Treatment." *Journal of Research in Crime and Delinquency* 26 (1989): 276–295.

Wolf, George, and Joseph DiMona. *Frank Costello: Prime Minister of the Underworld.* New York: Bantam Books, 1975.

Wolfgang, Marvin E., Robert M. Figlio, and Terence P. Thornberry. *Evaluating Criminology.* New York: Elsevier/North-Holland, 1978.

Wolfgang, Marvin E., Robert Figlio, and Thorsten Sellin. *Delinquency in a Birth Cohort.* Chicago, IL: University of Chicago Press, 1972.

Woodward, Bob, and Scott Armstrong. *The Brethren: Inside the Supreme Court.* New York: Simon and Schuster, 1979.

Wynter, Leon E. "Testing for Discrimination Gains Wider Acceptance." *Wall Street Journal*, July 1, 1998, B1.

Zimmerman, Don H., and Candace West. "Sex Roles, Interruptions, and Silences in Conversations." In *Language and Sex: Differences and Dominance*, edited by Barry Thorne and Nancy Henley. Rowley, MA: Newbury House, 1975.

Zimmerman, Don H., and D. Lawrence Wieder. "The Diary: Diary Interview Method." In *Social Science Methods: A New Introduction*, edited by Robert Smith. New York: Free Press, 1974.

Chapter 9 Validity, Reliability, and Triangulated Strategies

Albini, Joseph L. *The American Mafia: Genesis of a Legend*. New York: Appleton, 1971.

Bailey, William C. "Correctional Outcome: An Evaluation of 100 Reports." In *Crime and Justice*, Vol. III, edited by Leon Radzinowicz and Marvin E. Wolfgang. New York: Basic, 1971.

Block, Alan A. "The History and Study of Organized Crime." *Urban Life* 6 (January 1978): 455–474.

Bownas, D. A., and Marvin D. Dunnette. *The Development of the Police Career Index*. Minneapolis, MN: Personal Decisions, Inc., 1975.

Brantingham, Paul, and Patricia Brantingham. *Patterns in Crime*. New York: Macmillan, 1984.

Brewer, John, and Albert Hunter. *Introducing Multimethod Research*. Belmont, CA: Wadsworth, 1983.

Campbell, Donald T., and Donald W. Fiske. "Convergent and Discriminant Validation by the Multitrait-Multimethod Matrix." *Psychological Bulletin* 56 (1959): 81–105.

Carmines, Edward G., and Richard A. Zeller. *Reliability and Validity Assessment*. Newbury Park, CA: Sage, 1979.

Clarke, James W. *American Assassins: The Darker Side of Politics*. Princeton, NJ: Princeton University Press, 1982.

Collins, James J., and Marianne Zawitz. "Federal Drug Data for National Policy." *Drugs and Crime Data*. A Report from the Drugs and Crime Data Center and Clearinghouse, Washington, DC: Bureau of Justice Statistics, April 1990.

Crano, William D., and Marilynn B. Brewer. *Principles of Research in Social Psychology*. New York: McGraw-Hill, 1973.

Cronbach, Lee. *Essentials of Psychological Testing*. 3rd ed. New York: Harper and Row, 1970.

Cronbach, Lee, and Paul E. Meehl. "Construct Validity in Psychological Tests." *Psychological Bulletin* 52 (1955): 281–302.

Cronbach, Lee J. "Coefficient Alpha and the Internal Structure of Tests." *Psychometrika* 16 (1951): 297–334.

Earls, Felton H., and Christy A. Visher. "Project on Human Development in Chicago Neighborhoods: A Research Update." *National Institute of Justice Research in Brief*, February 1997.

Fagan, Jeffrey, et al. "Crime in Public Housing: Clarifying Research Issues." *National Institute of Justice Journal* (March 1998): 2–9.

Fishman, Janet. E. *Measuring Police Corruption*. Monograph No. 10, New York: John Jay College of Criminal Justice, 1978.

Guilford, J. R., and B. Fruchter. *Fundamental Statistics in Education and Psychology*. New York: McGraw-Hill, 1978.

Hardt, Robert H., and Sandra P. Hardt. "On Determining the Quality of the Delinquency Self-report Method." *Journal of Research in Crime and Delinquency* 14 (July 1977): 247–261.

Holzman, Harold. "Criminological Research on Public Housing: Toward a Better Understanding of People, Places, and Spaces." *Crime and Delinquency* 42, no. 3 (1996): 361–378.

Hood, Roger, and Richard Sparks. *Key Issues in Criminology*. New York: McGraw-Hill, 1971.

House, Ernest R. *Evaluating with Validity*. Beverly Hills, CA: Sage, 1980.

Kerstetter, Wayne A., and Anne M. Heinz. "Pretrial Settlement Conference: Evaluation of a Reform in Plea Bargaining." *Law and Society Review* 13 (1979): 349–366.

Kirk, Jerome, and Marc L. Miller. *Reliability and Validity in Qualitative Research*. Beverly Hills, CA: Sage, 1986.

Koniecni, V. J. "External Validity of Research in Legal Psychology." *Law and Human Behavior* 3, no. 1, 2 (1979): 39–70.

Kuder, G. Frederic, and Marion W. Richardson. "The Theory of the Estimation of Test Reliability." In *Principles of Educational and Psychological*

Measurement: A Book of Selected Readings, edited by William A. Mehrens and Robert L. Ebel. New York: Rand McNally, 1967.

Lupscha, Peter A. "Networks vs. Networking: An Analysis of Organized Criminal Groups." Paper presented at the American Society of Criminology Meetings, Toronto, ON, Canada, November 1982.

Maas, Peter. *The Valachi Papers*. New York: Putnam, 1968.

Maltz, Michael D., and Richard McCleary. "The Mathematics of Behavioral Change: Recidivism and Construct Validity." *Evaluation Quarterly* 1 (August 1977): 421–438.

Martinson, Robert. "What Works? Questions and Answers about Prison Reform." *The Public Interest* 35 (Spring 1974): 22–54.

Mash, Eric J., and David A. Wolfe. "Methodological Issues in Research on Physical Child Abuse." *Criminal Justice and Behavior* 18 (March 1991): 8–29.

Miller, Herbert S., William F. McDonald, and James A. Cramer. *Plea Bargaining in the United States*. Washington, DC: National Institute of Justice, 1980.

National Advisory Committee on Criminal Justice Standards and Goals. *Criminal Justice Research and Development*. Report of the Task Force on Criminal Justice Research and Development, Washington, DC: Law Enforcement Assistance Administration, December 1976.

Orenstein, Alan, and William R. F. Phillips. *Understanding Social Research*. Boston, MA: Allyn and Bacon, 1978.

Reed, R. S. "Three Approaches to the Study of Jury Trials: Observation, Interview and Experimentation." Ph.D. dissertation, Florida State University, 1976.

Reppucci, N. Dickson, and W. Glenn Clingempeel. "Methodological Issues in Research with Correctional Populations." *Journal of Consulting and Clinical Psychology* 46 (August 1978): 727–746.

Schlesinger, Stephen E. "Prediction of Dangerousness in Juveniles: A Replication." *Crime and Delinquency* 24 (January 1978): 40–48.

Schneider, Anne L., et al. *Handbook of Resources for Criminal Justice Evaluation*. Washington, DC: National Institute of Law Enforcement and Criminal Justice, 1978.

Selltiz, Clair, et al. *Research Methods in Social Relations*. New York: Holt, 1959.

Shaw, Clifford D., and Henry D. McKay. *Social Factors in Juvenile Delinquency*. National Commission on Law Observance and Enforcement, Report on the Causes of Crime, Vol. 2, Washington, DC: U.S. Government Printing Office, 1931.

Shusman, Elizabeth J., and Robin E. Inwald. "A Longitudinal Validation Study of Correctional Officer Job Performance as Predicted by the IPI and MMPI." *Journal of Criminal Justice* 19, no. 2 (1991): 12–180.

Thorndike, Robert L., and Elizabeth P. Hagen. *Measurement and Evaluation in Psychology and Education*. New York: Wiley, 1977.

Traub, Ross E. *Reliability for the Social Sciences: Theory and Applications*. Thousand Oaks, CA: Sage, 1994.

Turkus, Burton B., and Sid Feder. *Murder, Inc.: The Story of the Syndicate*. New York: Farrar, Straus, and Young, 1951.

Walters, Glenn D., and Thomas W. White. "Heredity and Crime: Bad Genes or Bad Research." *Criminology* 27 (August 1989): 455–485.

Webb, Eugene J., et al. *Unobtrusive Measures: Nonreactive Research in the Social Sciences*. Chicago: Rand McNally, 1966.

Chapter 10 Scaling and Index Construction

Akman, Dogan D., et al. "The Measurement of Delinquency in Canada." *Journal of Criminal Law, Criminology and Police Science* 58 (1967): 241–243.

Andrews, Judy A., et al. "The Construction, Validation and Use of a Guttman Scale of Adolescent Substance Use: An Investigation of Family Relationships." *Journal of Drug Issues* 21 (March 1991): 557–572.

Arnold, William R. "Continuities in Research: Scaling Delinquent Behavior." *Social Problems* 13 (Summer 1965): 59–66.

Baumer, Terry, and Dennis Rosenbaum. "Measuring Fear of Crime." Paper presented at the National Workshop on Research Methodology and Criminal Justice Program Evaluation, Baltimore, MD, March 1980.

Blumstein, Alfred. "Seriousness Weights in an Index of Crime." *American Sociological Review* 39 (December 1974): 854–864.

Blumstein, Alfred, et al., eds. *Criminal Careers and "Career Criminals."* Vol. 2. Washington, DC: National Academy of Sciences, 1986.

Bogardus, Emory S. "A Social Distance Scale." *Sociology and Social Research* 17 (January 1933): 265–271.

Brodsky, Stanley, and O'Neal Smitherman, eds. *Handbook of Scales for Research in Crime and Delinquency.* New York: Plenum Press, 1983.

Cavior, Norman, and L. Ramona Howard. "Facial Attractiveness and Juvenile Delinquency among Black and White Offenders." *Journal of Abnormal Child Psychology* 1 (1973): 202–213.

Christie, Richard, and Florence L. Geis, eds. *Studies in Machiavellianism.* New York: Academic Press, 1970.

Cloward, Richard A., and Lloyd E. Ohlin. *Delinquency and Opportunity: A Theory of Delinquent Gangs.* London: Routledge and Kegan Paul, 1961.

Cohen, Albert K. *Delinquent Boys: The Culture of the Gang.* Glencoe, IL: Free Press, 1955.

Cohen, Jacqueline. "Incapacitation as a Strategy for Crime Control: Possibilities and Pitfalls." In *Crime and Justice: An Annual Review*, Vol. 5, edited by Michael Tonry and Norval Morris. Chicago, IL: University of Chicago Press, 1983a.

———. "Incapacitating Criminals: Recent Research Findings." *NIJ Research in Brief.* Washington, DC: National Institute of Justice, December 1983b.

Cole, Stephen. *The Sociological Method.* Chicago, IL: Markham, 1972.

Cullen, Francis T., Bruce G. Link, and Craig W. Polanzi. "The Seriousness of Crime Revisited." *Criminology* 20 (May 1982): 83–102.

Dentler, Robert A., and Lawrence J. Monroe. "Social Correlates of Early Adolescent Theft." *American Sociological Review* 26 (October 1961): 733–743.

Dowdall, George W., Earl Babbie, and Fred Halley. *Adventures in Criminal Justice Research: Data Analysis Using SPSS for Windows.* Thousand Oaks, CA: Sage Publications, 1997.

Dunnette, Marvin D., and Stephan Motowidlo. *Police Selection and Career Assessment.* Washington, DC: National Institute of Law Enforcement and Criminal Justice, November 1976.

Edwards, Allen. *Techniques of Attitude Scale Construction.* New York: Appleton, 1957.

Farrington, David P. "Self-Reports of Deviant Behavior: Predictive and Stable?" *Journal of Criminal Law and Criminology* 64 (1973): 99–110.

Farrington, David, and Roger Tarling. *Criminological Prediction.* London: Home Office Research and Planning Unit, 1983.

Fritz, Sara. "Is Consumer Price Index 'Loaded'?" *U.S. News and World Report*, February 4, 1980, 86.

Glueck, Sheldon, and Eleanor Glueck. *Unraveling Juvenile Delinquency.* New York: The Commonwealth Fund, 1950.

———. *Predicting Delinquency & Crime.* Cambridge, MA: Harvard University Press, 1960.

Gottfredson, Don M., and Kelley M. Ballard. "Differences in Parole Decisions Associated with Decision Makers." *Journal of Research in Crime and Delinquency* 3 (1966): 112–119.

Greenwood, Peter W., and Allan Abrahamse. *Selective Incapacitation.* Santa Monica, CA: Rand Corp., August 1982.

Guttman, Louis L. "A Basis for Scaling Qualitative Data." *American Sociological Review* 9 (April 1944): 139–150.

———. "The Basis for Scalogram Analysis." In *Studies in Social Psychology in World War II, Vol. 4, Measuring and Prediction*, edited by Samuel A. Stouffer et al., Princeton, NJ: Princeton University Press, 1950.

Hirschi, Travis, and Hanaan C. Selvin. *Principles of Survey Analysis.* New York: Free Press, 1973.

Hoffman, Peter. "Screening for Risk: A Revised Salient Factor Score." *Journal of Criminal Justice* 11 (1984): 539–547.

———. "Predicting Criminality." *Crime File Series.* Washington, DC: National Institute of Justice, 1985.

Hood, Roger, and Richard Sparks. *Key Issues in Criminology.* New York: McGraw-Hill, 1971.

Hsu, Marlene. "Cultural and Sexual Differences on the Judgment of Criminal Offenses: A Replication Study of the Measurement of Delinquency." *Journal of Criminal Law and Criminology* 64 (September 1973): 348–353.

Jacoby, Joan E. "Case Evaluation: Quantifying Prosecutorial Policy." *Judicature* 58 (1975): 486–493.

Klaus, Patsy, and Carol B. Kalish. "The Severity of Crime." *Bureau of Justice Statistics Bulletin.* Washington, DC: U.S. Department of Justice, January 1984.

Kratcoski, Peter C. "The Functions of Classification Models in Probation and Parole Control or Treatment-Rehabilitation?" *Federal Probation* 49, no. 4 (1985): 49–56.

Likert, Rensis. "A Technique for the Measurement of Attitudes." *Archives of Psychology* 140 (1932).

Lum, C., and Yang, S.M. "Why Do Evaluation Researchers in Crime and Justice Choose Non-experimental Methods." *Journal of Experimental Criminology* 1 (2005): 191–213

Machiavelli, Niccoló. *The Prince.* New York: New American Library, 1952.

Mannheim, Hermann, and Leslie T. Wilkins. *Prediction Methods in Relation to Borstal Training.* London: Her Majesty's Stationery Office, 1955.

Maranell, Gary M., ed. *Scaling: A Sourcebook for Behavioral Scientists.* Chicago, IL: Aldine, 1974.

Martin, Susan, and Larry Sherman. *The Washington Repeat Offender Project.* Washington, DC: The Police Foundation, 1985.

Miller, Delbert C., ed. *Handbook of Research Design and Social Measurement.* 5th ed. New York: Longman, 1991.

Monahan, John. *Predicting Violent Behavior: An Assessment of Clinical Techniques.* Beverly Hills, CA: Sage, 1981.

Nye, F. Ivan, and James F. Short, Jr. "Scaling Delinquent Behavior." *American Sociological Review* 22 (June 1957): 326–331.

Ohlin, Lloyd E. *Selection for Parole.* New York: Russell Sage, 1951.

Oppenheim, A.N. *Questionnaire Design and Attitude Measurement.* New York: Basic, 1966.

Orenstein, Alan, and William R. F. Phillips. *Understanding Social Research.* Boston, MA: Allyn and Bacon, 1978.

Osgood, Charles, et al. *The Measurement of Meaning.* Urbana, IL: University of Illinois Press, 1957.

Robinson, John P., Phillip R. Shaver, and Lawrence S. Wrightsman, eds. *Measures of Personality and Social Psychological Attitudes.* San Diego, CA: Academic Press, 1991.

Rossi, Peter H., and J. Patrick Henry. "Seriousness as a Measure for All Purposes?" In *Handbook of Criminal Justice Evaluation,* edited by M. Klein and K. Teilmann, 489–505. Beverly Hills, CA: Sage, 1980.

Rossi, Peter H., et al. "The Seriousness of Crimes: Normative Structure and Individual Differences." *American Sociological Review* 39 (April 1974): 224–237.

Samuelson, R. "Riding the Monthly Escalator: The Consumer Price Index." *New York Times Magazine,* December 8, 1974, 34–35.

Scheussler, Karl B., and Donald B. Cressey. "Personality Characteristics of Criminals." *American Journal of Sociology* (1950): 476–484.

Scott, John F. "Two Dimensions of Delinquent Behavior." *American Sociological Review* 24 (April 1959): 240–243.

Sellin, Thorsten, and Marvin E. Wolfgang. *The Measurement of Delinquency.* New York: Wiley, 1966.

Shaw, Marvin E., and Jack M. Wright. *Scales for the Measurement of Attitudes.* New York: McGraw-Hill, 1967.

Sherman, Larry. "Repeat Offenders." *Crime File.* Rockville, MD: National Institute of Justice, 1985.

Sherman, Lawrence W., et al. *Preventing Crime: What Works, What Doesn't, What's Promising.* Washington, DC: Office of Justice Programs, 1997, NCJ 165366.

Sherman, Lawrence W., et al., eds. *Evidence-Based Crime Prevention*. London: Routledge, 2002.

Short, James F., Jr., and Fred L. Strodtbeck. *Group Process and Gang Delinquency*. Chicago, IL: University of Chicago Press, 1965.

Simon, Frances H. *Prediction Methods in Criminology*. Home Office Research Studies, No. 7, London: Her Majesty's Stationery Office, 1971.

Snider, James G., and Charles E. Osgood, eds. *Semantic Differential Technique*. Chicago, IL: Aldine, 1969.

Stephenson, W. *The Study of Behavior: Q-Technique and Its Methodology*. Chicago, IL: University of Chicago Press, 1953.

Straus, Murray A., and Richard J. Gelles. "Societal Change and Change in Family Violence from 1975 to 1985 As Revealed in Two National Surveys." *Journal of Marriage and the Family* 48 (1986): 466–479.

Summers, Gene F., ed. *Attitude Measurement*. Chicago, IL: Rand McNally, 1970.

Tennenbaum, David J. "Research Studies of Personality and Criminality: A Summary and Implications of the Literature." *Journal of Criminal Justice* 5 (Spring 1977): 1–19.

Thielbar, Gerald W., and Saul D. Feldman. "Images of Deviants and Their Behavior: Stereotypes and Social Context." In *Deciphering Deviance*, edited by Saul D. Feldman, 265–281. Boston, MA: Little, Brown, 1978.

Thurstone, Louis L., and Ernest J. Chave. *The Measurement of Attitudes*. Chicago, IL: University of Chicago Press, 1929.

Torgerson, Warren. *Theory and Methods of Scaling*. New York: Wiley, 1958.

Vito, Gennaro F. "Felony Probation and Recidivism: Replication and Response." *Federal Probation* 50, no. 4 (1986): 17–25.

Waldo, Gordon P., and Simon Dinitz. "Personality Attributes of Criminals: An Analysis of Research Studies, 1950–1965." *Journal of Research in Crime and Delinquency* 4 (1967): 185–202.

Wilkins, Leslie T. *The Evaluation of Penal Measures*. New York: Random, 1969.

Wolfgang, Marvin E., et al. *The National Survey of Crime Severity*. Washington, DC: U.S. Department of Justice, 1985.

Wright, Benjamin D. "The Objective Construction of Scales." Paper presented at the National Workshop on Research Methodology and Criminal Justice Program Evaluation, Baltimore, MD, March 1980.

Chapter 11 Policy Analysis and Evaluation Research

Adams, Stuart. *Evaluative Research in Corrections: A Practical Guide*. Washington, DC: National Institute of Law Enforcement and Criminal Justice, 1975.

Albright, Ellen, et al. *Criminal Justice Research: Evaluation in Criminal Justice Programs: Guidelines and Examples*. Washington, DC: National Institute of Law Enforcement and Criminal Justice, June 1973.

Boruch, Robert F. "On Common Contentions about Randomized Field Experiments." In *Evaluation Studies Review Annual*, edited by Gene V. Glass, 158–194. Vol. 1, Beverly Hills, CA: Sage, 1976.

Cain, Glen G. "Regression and Selection Models to Improve Non-Experimental Comparisons." In *Evaluation and Experiment*, edited by Carl A. Bennet and Arthur A. Lumsdaine, 297–317. New York: Academic Press, 1975.

Clear, Todd R. Introduction, in Natasha Frost, Joshua D. Freilich and Todd R. Clear, editors. *Contemporary Issues in Criminal Justice Policy: Policy Perspectives for the American Society of Criminology Conference*, Belmont, CA: Wadsworth, 2009: xvii.

Cook, Thomas D., F. L. Cook, and M. M. Mark. "Randomized and Quasi-Experimental Designs in Evaluation Research: An Introduction." In *Evaluation Research Methods: A Basic Guide*, edited by Leonard Rutman. Beverly Hills, CA: Sage, 1977.

Dye, Thomas R. *Understanding Public Policy*. 8th ed. Englewood Cliffs, NJ: Prentice-Hall, 1995.

Fagan, Jeffrey A. "Natural Experiments in Criminal Justice." In *Measurement Issues in Criminology*, edited by Kimberly Kempf, 108–137. New York: Springer-Verlag, 1990.

Finckenauer, James. *Scared Straight! and the Panacea Phenomenon.* Englewood Cliffs, NJ: Prentice-Hall, 1982.

Franklin, Jack L., and Jean H. Thrasher. *Introduction to Program Evaluation.* New York: Wiley, 1976.

Fry, Lincoln J. "Participant Observation and Program Evaluation." *Journal of Health and Social Behavior* 14 (September 1973): 274–278.

Garner, Joel, and Christy A. Visher. "Policy Experiments Come of Age." *National Institute of Justice Reports.* September/October, 1988, 2–8.

Geller, William A. "Suppose We Were Really Serious About Police Departments Becoming 'Learning Organizations.'" *National Institute of Justice Journal* (December 1997): 2–7.

Glaser, Daniel. *Routinizing Evaluation: Getting Feedback on Effectiveness of Crime and Delinquency Programs.* Rockville, MD: Center for Studies of Crime and Delinquency, 1973.

———. "Remedies for the Key Deficiency in Criminal Justice Evaluation Research." *Journal of Research in Crime and Delinquency* 11 (July 1974): 144–154.

———. "Correctional Research: An Elusive Paradise." In *Probation, Parole and Community Corrections*, 2nd ed. edited by Robert M. Carter and Leslie T. Wilkins, 765–777. New York: Wiley, 1976.

Grinyer, Anne. "Anticipating the Problems of Contract Research." *Social Research Update* (Winter 1999): 27.

Jones, Charles O. *An Introduction to the Study of Public Policy.* Boston, MA: Duxbury, 1977.

Levine, James P., Michael C. Musheno, and Dennis J. Palumbo. *Criminal Justice: A Public Policy Approach.* New York: Harcourt, 1980.

Logan, Charles H. "Evaluation Research in Crime and Delinquency: A Reappraisal." In *Criminal Justice Research: Approaches, Problems and Policy*, edited by Susette M. Talarico, 29–44. Cincinnati, OH: Anderson, 1980.

MacKenzie, Doris L., and Belinda McCarthy. *How to Prepare a Competitive Grant Proposal: A Guide for University Faculty Members Pursuing Criminal Justice*

Research Grants. Highland Heights, KY: Academy of Criminal Justice Sciences, 1990.

Maida, Peter R., and Jeanne E. Faucett, eds. *Crime and Delinquency Prevention Reader.* 2nd ed. College Park, MD: University of Maryland, 1978.

Marlowe, Douglas. "When 'What Works' Never Did: Dodging the 'Scarlet M' in Correctional Rehabilitation." *Criminology and Public Policy* 5 (2006): 339–346.

Martinson, Robert. "What Works?—Questions and Answers about Prison Reform." *The Public Interest* 35 (Spring 1974): 22–54.

Morris, Norval, and Michael Tonry, eds. *Crime and Justice: An Annual Review of Research*, Vol. 1. Chicago, IL: University of Chicago Press, 1979.

National Advisory Committee on Criminal Justice Standards and Goals. *Criminal Justice Research and Development: Report of the Task Force on Criminal Justice Research and Development.* Washington, DC: Law Enforcement Assistance Administration, 1976.

National Criminal Justice Reference Service. *How Well Does It Work? Review of Criminal Justice Evaluation, 1978.* Washington, DC: National Institute of Law Enforcement and Criminal Justice, June 1979.

National Institute of Justice. *NIJ Research Plan, 1995–1996*, Washington, DC: National Institute of Justice, 1994.

———. *2001 Solicitation for Investigator-Initiated Research* Washington, DC: Office of Justice Programs, September, 2000.

National Institute of Justice, *NIJ Research Plan 2005*, Washington, DC: National Institute of Justice, 2004.

Office of Juvenile Justice and Delinquency Prevention. *Evaluation Issues.* Washington, DC: U.S. Department of Justice, June 1978.

———. "Successful Program Implementation: Lessons from Blueprints." *Juvenile Justice Bulletin*, July 2004.

Posavec, Emil J., and Raymond Carey. *Program Evaluation: Methods and Case Studies.* 4th ed. Englewood Cliffs, NJ: Prentice-Hall, 1992.

Punch, Maurice. *The Politics and Ethics of Fieldwork.* Beverly Hills, CA: Sage, 1986.

Rabow, Jerome. "Research and Rehabilitation: The Conflict of Scientific and Treatment Roles in Corrections." *The Journal of Research in Crime and Delinquency* 1 (January 1964): 67–79.

Rossi, Peter H., and Howard E. Freeman. *Evaluation: A Systematic Approach.* 5th ed. Newbury Park, CA: Sage, 1993.

Rutman, Leonard. "Formative Research and Program Evaluability." In *Evaluation Research Methods: A Basic Guide,* edited by Leonard Rutman. Beverly Hills, CA: Sage, 1977.

Schneider, Anne L., et al. *Handbook of Resources for Criminal Justice Evaluators.* Washington, DC: U.S. Department of Justice, 1978.

Schulberg, Herbert C., and Frank Baker. "Program Evaluation Models and the Implementation of Research Findings." *American Journal of Public Health* 58 (1977): 1248–1255.

Schwarz, Paul A. "Program Devaluation: Can the Experiment Reform?" Paper presented at the National Workshop on Research Methodology and Criminal Justice Program Evaluation, Baltimore, MD, March 1980.

Sherman, Lawrence W., et al. *Preventing Crime: What Works, What Doesn't, What's Promising.* Washington, DC: Office of Justice Programs, 1997, NCJ 165366.
———. eds. *Evidence-Based Crime Prevention.* London: Routledge, 2002.

Strasser, Stephen, and O. Lynn. Deniston. "Pre- and Post-Planned Evaluation: Which Is Preferable?" *Evaluation and Program Planning* 1, no. 3 (1978): 195–202.

Suchman, Edward A. *Evaluative Research: Principles and Practice in Public Service and Social Action Programs.* New York: Russell Sage, 1967.

Waller, Irvin, and Brandon Welsh. "Reducing Crime in Harnessing International Best Practice." *NIJ Journal* (October 1998): 26–32.

Waller, John D., et al. *Monitoring for Criminal Justice Planning Agencies.* Washington, DC: National Institute of Law Enforcement and Criminal Justice, March 1975.

Weiss, Carol H. *Evaluation Research: Methods for Assessing Program Effectiveness.* Englewood Cliffs, NJ: Prentice-Hall, 1972.

Wellford, Charles F. "Criminologists Should Stop Whining About their Impact on Policy and Practice," in Natasha Frost, Joshua D. Freilich, and Todd R. Clear, editors, *Contemporary Issues in Criminal Justice Policy: Policy Proposals for the American Society of Criminology Conference.* Belmont, CA: Wadsworth, 2009: 20-24.

Welsh, Brandon C., and David P. Farrington. *Crime Prevention Effects of Closed Circuit Television: A Systematic Review.* London: Home Office Research Study #252, 2002.

Wholey, Joseph S. "Evaluability Assessment." In *Evaluation Research Methods: A Basic Guide,* edited by Leonard Rutman. Beverly Hills, CA: Sage, 1977.

U.S. Department of HEW. *A Pocket Guide to Evidence-Based Practices on the Web.* Substance Abuse and Mental Health Services, August 2008.

Glossary

ADAM   Arrestee Drug Abuse Monitoring Program; the successor to DUF (Drug Use Forecasting), which interviewed and tests booked arrestees in order to document drug use.

arbitrary scales   Scales developed by the researcher based primarily on face validity and personal judgment.

bounding (in victim surveys)   The initial interview in a panel serves as a boundary or means of establishing exactly when events have taken place.

branching procedure   Interview technique used to narrow down sensitive responses such as income into less threatening categories or ranges.

CAPI   Computer-assisted programmed interviewing in which portable laptop computers are used in field interviews.

CART   Continuous audience response technology in which respondents register their reaction to various stimuli on a continuous basis using a handheld keypad.

case study (life history)   In-depth investigation of a single case (individual, group, or community).

CATI   Computer-assisted telephone interviewing.

codebook   Guidebook for numerically classifying each question to be coded.

coding   Assignment of numbers to responses.

compensatory equalization of treatment   Desirable services (treatment) in the experimental group cause complaints and demands that the control group be supplied with this same treatment.

concepts   Abstract or symbolic tags placed on reality.

confederates   Research assistants who pose as subjects in a study.

confidentiality   Requirement that any information obtained in research be treated as confidential and not be revealed in any manner that would identify or harm subjects.

construct validity   Accuracy of the scale or measurement in tapping the correct concept or construct.

content analysis   Systematic classification and analysis of data such as the content of mass media.

content validity   Accuracy of individual items in a scale in measuring the concept being measured.

convergent–discriminant validity   Different measures of the same concept should yield similar results (convergence), whereas the same measure of different concepts should yield different results (discrimination).

crime analysis   Systematic, analytic processes aimed at providing practical information related to crime patterns.

crime dip   The decline in recorded crime in the 1980s believed to be caused primarily by demographic change.

crime index   Part I Uniform Crime Report offenses divided by population, then multiplied by 100,000. Later succeeded by the violent crime index and the property crime index.

crime rate   Number of crimes divided by population, per 100,000 population.

crime seriousness scales   Procedures that assign weight or severity rating to various crimes.

criminal profiling   An attempt to construct typical characteristics of certain types of criminals.

"dark figure" of crime   Crime that is unmeasured by official statistics or that has not come to the notice of police.

debriefing   After completion of a study (particularly one involving deception), reassurance of subjects and explanation of the purposes of the research.

demand characteristics   Overagreeableness on the part of those surveyed; respondents give the researcher the response they believe is demanded (expected).

diffusion of treatment   The control group learns about and imitates the experimental group.

disguised observation   Informed consent of subjects is not sought, and researchers pretend to be part of the study group.

double-blind experiment   Neither the subjects nor administrators in an experiment know which group is receiving the treatment.

Drug Use Forecasting (DUF)   NIJ research program that asks volunteer arrestees to provide urine specimens to test for drug usage.

dummy tables   Blank tables that are constructed prior to gathering data to suggest the type of data needed in the analysis.

ecological fallacy   Error of assuming that relationships proven true of groups are true of individuals.

elaboration   Examination of a relationship on introduction of a third variable.

experimental mortality   Loss of subjects over the course of time.

explanation   In elaboration, the relationship observed in the original bivariate table weakens or disappears in the partial tables.

external validity   Accuracy in the ability to generalize or infer findings from a study to a larger population.

face validity   Accuracy of the instrument in measuring (on face value) that which is intended.

field experiment   Experiment conducted in a natural (field) setting.

focus groups   Purposively selected groups brought together in order to measure their reaction to some stimuli (for example, a commercial).

GIS   *Geographic Information Systems*; the analytic mapping of crime incidents, arrests, and complaints expressing the extent and type of crime problem with respect to location.

Guttman scales   Scaling procedure that insists on unidimensionality (measures only one dimension) and that on the basis of the total score one should be able to predict the pattern of response on each item.

halo effect   Observer bias; observers follow an initial tendency to rate certain objects or subjects in a biased manner.

Hawthorne effect   (named for an experiment at the Hawthorne plant of Western Electric Company). Subjects behave atypically if aware of being studied.

historicism   View of all social events as a distinct chronicle of unique happenings.

history   Specific events other than the treatment that during the course of a study may be responsible for producing the results.

hot spots   The use of GIS computer software to identify clusters (hot spots) of crime.

hypotheses   Specific statements or predictions regarding the relationship between two variables.

impact evaluation   Examination of relationship between outcome and input, activities and results of a program.

informed consent   Agreement of subjects to participate in research after they have been briefed.

institutional review boards (IRBS)   College/university research committees that oversee and ensure ethical research standards.

instrumentation   Changes in the measuring instrument during the course of a study that invalidate comparisons.

internal validity   Accuracy within the study itself.

interpretation   In elaboration, the partial table relationships weaken or disappear, and the control variable is an intervening one (occurs between X and Y).

interval variable(level measurement)   Measurement in which equal distance (or intervals) between objects on a scale is assumed.

interviewer effect   Biases introduced by the interviewer.

item analysis   Procedure employed in Likert scaling in which questions (items) that do not discriminate (distinguish) high and low scores are eliminated from the scale.

known-group validation (reverse record checks)   Involves validation of reported behavior by studying groups whose behavior is already known.

lie scales (truth scales)   Series of questions that measure truthfulness of respondents in answering a survey.

Likert scales   Simple summated attitude scale consisting of a five-point bipolar response scheme for each item ranging from strongly agree to strongly disagree.

local history   Special case of "history" in which an event happens to the experimental or the control group, but not both.

maturation   Biological or psychological changes in the respondents during the course of a study that are not due to the treatment variable.

meta-analysis (the analysis of analysis)   Statistical analysis of data from many different studies dealing with the same research question in order to determine general findings.

methodological narcissism   Fanatical adherence to a preferred method at the expense of substance; view that there is one and only one way of doing research, that is, by employing the one, best method.

methodology (methods)   Collection of accurate facts or data; attempt to address the issue of "what is."

mnemonics   Simple memorizing devices that are particularly useful in field studies.

monitoring   Similar to auditing; assessment of whether a program is doing what it is supposed to be doing in terms of process or program activities.

multiple-form reliability   Administration of alternate forms of an instrument to the same group should produce similar results, thus demonstrating consistency (reliability) of measurement.

multiple-treatment interference   Outcome produced by combinations of treatments; it may be difficult to isolate the specific combination(s) responsible.

national crime victimization survey (NCS)   Victim surveys conducted by the Census Bureau on behalf of the Bureau of Justice Statistics. The survey consists of a rotating crime panel of 60,000 households.

National Incident-Based Reporting System (NIBRS)   The unit-record reporting system used in the redesigned UCR in which each local law enforcement agency reports on each individual arrest.

nominal variable (level measurement)   Measurement that places responses in mutually exclusive categories and has no mathematical meaning.

nonreactivity   Research conducted in such a manner that subject reactivity, or awareness of being studied, is eliminated.

normal distribution (curve)   Bell-shaped curve that describes a variety of phenomena, for example, a large sample of a population will be normally distributed and resemble a normal curve.

objectivity   Basic canon of research; approach to subject matter from an unbiased, ethically neutral or value-free perspective.

operationalization   Definition of concepts on the basis of how they are measured; "I measured it by ____."

ordinal variable   (level measurement) Placement of objects into ranks, for example, first, second, and third.

paradigm   A model or schema that provides a perspective from which to view reality.

participant observation   Temporary participation in group activity by researchers for the purpose of observing the group.

physical trace analysis   Type of unobtrusive measurement that involves the analysis of deposits, accretion of matter, and other indirect substances produced by previous human interaction.

placebo effect("sugar pill effect")   Tendency of control groups to react to believed treatment in a positive manner.

policy analysis   Study of the causes and consequences of government behavior (what governments do or do not do).

post hoc error   Incorrect assumption that because one variable precedes another in time, it is the cause of the outcome.

pragmatic validity   Accuracy of the measuring instrument in predicting current status (concurrent validity) or future status (predictive validity).

prediction scales   Attempts to forecast crime commission or success or failure on probation/parole.

pretest(pilot study)   Exploratory test of an instrument on subjects who are similar to the group to be studied.

primary sources   Raw data, unaccompanied by analysis or interpretation.

probability sample   Sample chosen by an equal probability of selection method.

probing   Follow-up question(s) that focuses, expands, or clarifies the response given.

problem formulation   Selection, identification, and specification of the research topic to be investigated.

process evaluation   Establishment of relationships between results and project inputs and activities.

pseudonyms   Aliases used in research reports to protect the identity of respondents.

Q sort   (question sort)An attitudinal scale procedure in which the respondents sort questions (on cards) into predetermined categories.

random digit dialing   Sampling procedure employed in telephone surveys in which random numbers are used to obtain unlisted numbers.

randomized response technique   Means of coping with resistance to sensitive questions by using indeterminate questions, ones in which the actual question answered is known only to the respondent.

reactivity   Atypical or artificial behavior produced by respondent's awareness of being studied.

reciprocity   A system of mutual obligation between subjects and researchers; because the subject's cooperation assisted the researcher, the researcher owes the subject professional regard.

reliability Consistency and/or stability of a measuring instrument.

replication Repetition of experiments or studies utilizing the same methodology.

research, applied Research concerned with solving or addressing immediate policy problems.

research, pure Acquisition of knowledge for science's sake; acquisition of knowledge that contributes to the scientific development of a discipline.

research, qualitative Research for the purpose of developing "sensitizing concepts" and verstehen (understanding) rather than quantitative measurement.

research, quantitative Operationalization and numerical measurement of variables.

researchese Language of research.

reverse record check Validation of reported behavior on the basis of studying a group whose behavior is already known.

rival causal factors Variables other than X, the independent variable that may be responsible for the outcome, for example, history, maturation, selection bias.

salient factor score Sentencing/parole prediction scheme used by the U.S. Parole Commission to predict recidivism.

sampling frame Complete list of the universe or population under investigation.

scales(scaling) Attempts to increase the complexity of the level of measurement of variables from nominal to at least ordinal and hopefully interval/ratio level.

scientism View that, if one cannot quantitatively measure a phenomenon, it is not worth studying.

screening questions Preliminary questions employed to determine appropriate respondents for the main portion of a survey. For example, in victim surveys they are used to locate victims, who are then asked the incident questions.

secondary analysis Reanalysis of data that were gathered for other purposes.

secondary sources Sources that analyze, synthesize, and evaluate information.

selection bias Involves choosing nonequivalent groups for comparison.

selection–maturation interaction Combination of errors introduced by selection bias plus the differential maturation of groups.

self-report surveys Surveys in which subjects are asked to admit to the commission of various delinquent and/or criminal acts.

semantic differential Attitude scaling procedure that consists of usually a seven- or nine-point bipolar rating scale; respondents are asked to indicate their perception of the tag or description provided.

Sellin–Wolfgang Index Procedure for assigning crime seriousness weights.

shield laws Laws that protect researchers from being forced to reveal sources in a court of law.

simulation Situation or game that attempts to mimic key features of reality.

single-subject designs Quantitative case studies that involve longitudinal measurement of a dependent variable on a single subject or case.

SPSS *Statistical Package for the Social Sciences*; canned or prewritten computer programs for statistical analysis in the social sciences.

spuriousness A false relationship that can be explained away by other variables.

statement analysis A form of applied content analysis in which investigators examine words and independent case facts to detect deception.

statistical regression   Tendency of groups that have been selected for study on the basis of extreme high or low scores to regress (fall back) toward the mean (average) on second testing.

suppression   In elaboration, when despite no relationship in the original bivariate table, a relationship occurs in the partial tables.

systems model   Model in which all parts of an organism, organization, or program are interrelated and consist of a series of inputs and outputs.

telescoping   Tendency of respondents to move forward and report as having occurred events that actually occurred before the reference period.

testing effects   Pretest effects or bias that is introduced as a result of having been pretested. Testing effects may also invalidate the ability to generalize to larger populations.

test–retest reliability   Ability of the same instrument, when administered twice to the same population, to produce the same results, thus demonstrating the stability (reliability) of the measure.

theory   Plausible explanation of reality (why and how do things occur).

Thurstone scales   Attitude scales that rely on ratings by judges of scale items.

time-series design   Measurement of a single variable at successive points in time.

triangulation   Use of multiple measures of the same concept.

Unidimensionality   Requirement of the Guttman scales that the items measure only one dimension (or concept); this is assumed if 90 percent reproducibility is achieved.

Uniform Crime Report (UCR)   Annual FBI publication of official statistics of crimes recorded by police.

unobtrusive measures (nonreactive methods)   Ways of studying groups so that they remain unaware of being studied, thus eliminating reactivity.

validity   Accuracy of measurement; does the instrument in fact measure that which it purports to measure?

variable, dependent   Outcome variable (Y), or the subject of study.

variable, independent   Predictor variable (X); precedes in time and causes change in the dependent variable.

variables   Concepts that can vary or take on different numerical values; operationalized concepts.

variables list   A list of variables being measured keyed to the question number in the questionnaire that is designed to measure each variable.

verification   Confirmation of the accuracy of findings; attainment of greater certitude in conclusions through additional observations.

Verstehen   Weber's notion that the purpose of research is to gain a qualitative "understanding" of phenomena from the perspective of the subjects.

Author Index

Subject Index